Word Parts Dictionary

*Standard and Reverse Listings of
Prefixes, Suffixes, Roots and
Combining Forms*

Second Edition

MICHAEL J. SHEEHAN

McFarland & Company, Inc., Publishers
Jefferson, North Carolina, and London

LIBRARY OF CONGRESS CATALOGUING-IN-PUBLICATION DATA

Sheehan, Michael, 1939–
   Word parts dictionary : standard and reverse listings of prefixes,
suffixes, roots, and combining forms / Michael Sheehan.— 2nd ed.
      p.   cm.

   ISBN 978-0-7864-3564-7
   library binding : 50# alkaline paper ∞

   1. English language — Suffixes and prefixes— Dictionaries.
   2. English language — Reverse indexes.   I. Title.
PE1175.S45   2008
423'.1— dc22   2008000041

British Library cataloguing data are available

Manufactured in the United States of America

*McFarland & Company, Inc., Publishers
   Box 611, Jefferson, North Carolina 28640
   www.mcfarlandpub.com*

To Dona Sheehan,
salubrious wife and gift

Table of Contents

Preface

The Second Edition

Aside from catering to those who wish to expand their vocabulary, the purpose of this dictionary is to provide word parts in convenient form to those who may be interested in deciphering or inventing words bearing an established and embedded meaning. This includes students, academicians, inventors, advertising agencies, authors, readers, librarians, scientists, scholars, word buffs, historians, avid amateurs, cruciverbalists, and anyone else with a vested interest in words, professional or personal.

Because comprehensiveness was a goal, some of the examples included as illustrations are no longer current. Along with contemporary usages, you will occasionally find words that are obsolescent, obsolete, rare, antiquated, and archaic. You may even find a hapax legomenon or two. This provides a trip through the history of the English language, a guide to word parts that once were—and still could be—vital and expressive, and it places at your fingertips the snap-together tools to create words yet to be. It also provides a glimpse of the immense inventive possibilities provided to English by Greek and Latin borrowings.

Part I, the Dictionary, benefits from many additions to the first edition, the most noticeable of which will be the freshly embedded etymologies. In addition, examples have been doubled. In Part II, the Finder, well over 1,000 new terms have been added. In Part III, Categories, three entirely new categories have been added (*Eating*, *Experts*, and *Measurement Science*), and the others have been expanded when possible. So, while the second edition builds on the strengths of the first, it contains significant improvements.—M.J.S. (*verbmall.blogspot.com*)

The First Edition

This dictionary is based on word parts—those prefixes, suffixes, combining forms and roots that show up repeatedly to form words—and is meant

1

to be used in conjunction with a standard dictionary and a thesaurus. It can help to retrieve words only dimly remembered, or it can lead to specific new words which otherwise might never have been discovered. And since a single recurrent letter combination often unlocks the partial meaning of dozens of words, it can act as an efficient way to expand one's general vocabulary.

The *Word Parts Dictionary* is divided into three sections.

Part I, the standard Dictionary, allows a reader to find the meaning of word parts conveniently arranged in alphabetical order, together with an example. For instance, Part I would reveal that the word part -nov- can mean either "new" (novelty) or "nine" (novenary), so the user would then become alert to context clues. This section is particularly useful to the person who has set out to expand his or her vocabulary. It is also a convenient place to consult to find actual examples after using Section II. Generally, one example is provided for each meaning.

Part II, the Finder, allows a user to start with a meaning or concept and then find the word parts which express that meaning. It is a reverse dictionary. For instance, one would learn that the meaning "color" is carried by the word parts **chromato-**, **-chrome**, **chromo-**, **-chroous**, **-pigm-**, **-tinct-**, and **-ting-**. Armed with that information, a user could then consult his or her memory or turn to the appropriate pages of a standard dictionary to find a variety of words which a thesaurus would not have contained. The alternative to finding such word parts is endless paging through an unabridged dictionary.

Part III, Categories, is also a reverse dictionary, but this time with the word parts arranged in clusters of meaning. For example, Part III would enable a reader to find, in one convenient listing, word parts that express many specific colors. Each color would also appear in Part II, of course, but in an isolated, alphabetical fashion.

This dictionary focuses on four kinds of word parts.

Prefixes (*pre*): A prefix is a syllable, group of syllables, or word united with or joined to the beginning of another word to alter its meaning or create a new word. For example, **re-** is a prefix in the word "redevelop." The hyphen at the end of the prefix indicates that it usually starts a word.

Suffixes (*suf*): A suffix is a syllable, group of syllables, or word added at the end of a word or word base to change its meaning, give it grammatical form, or form a new word. For example, **-ette** is a suffix in the word "kitchenette." The hyphen at the start of the suffix indicates that it normally ends a word.

Combining forms (*comb*): A combining form is a word form that occurs only in compounds, or in compounds and derivatives, and that can combine with other such forms or with prefixes and suffixes to form a word. For example, **cryo-** is one of the combining forms in the word "cryogenic," and **-genic** is the other one. The hyphens indicate that **cryo-** usually starts the word in which it appears and that **-genic** usually ends the word in which it appears.

Bases (*base*): A base is a stem or a root, a generally short letter combination that conveys a recurrent meaning all by itself without being involved in a compound word. Prefixes and suffixes may be added to it. For example, -dict- is a base in the word "predictable." The two hyphens indicate that it may appear at any location in a word: front, back, or middle. Thus, we have "dictation," "contradict," and "predictable."

PART I
Dictionary

(Prefixes, bases, combining forms,
and suffixes, with examples)

A

a-¹ *see* ad-

a-², ab-, abs- [L. *ab-*, away from] *pre* from; off; away; down (avert, abduct, abscond)

a-³, an- [Gr. *a-* without] *pre* not; without (anoxia, anandrous)

-a⁴ [L. suf -*a*] 1. *suf* singular feminine ending (Roberta); 2. plural ending (data, phenomena)

abdomino- [L. *abdomen*, belly] *comb* abdomen (abdominocentesis, abdominoscopy)

abiet- [L. *abies*, silver fir] *base* fir (abietic, abietite)

-able [L.–*abilis*, capable of] 1. *suf* able to (durable); 2. capable of being (drinkable); 3. worthy of being; (lovable); 4. having qualities of (comfortable); 5. tending to (peaceable)

ablut- [L. *ab-* + *luere*, to wash] *base* bathe; wash away (ablution, ablutionary)

-ably [L. suf -*abilem*] *suf* adverb form of -able (affably, unspeakably). *See* -ible

ac-¹ *see* ad-

-ac² [Gr.–*akos*, pertaining to] *suf* of; pertaining to (cardiac, celiac). *See* -ic

acantho- [Gr. *akanthos*, thorn] *comb* spiny; thorny (acanthocyte, acanthophorous)

acar-, acari-, acarin-, acaro- [Gr. *akari*, mite] *comb* mite; tick (acarine, acariasis, acarinosis, acarophobia)

accipit- [L. *accipiter*, bird of prey] |*base* falcon; hawk (accipitral, accipitrine)

-acea [L. -*acea*, pl. neut.] *suf* plural for names of animal classes or orders (Cetacea, Crustacea)

-aceae [L. -*aceae*, pl. fe.] *suf* plural for names of plant families or orders (Liliaceae, Rosaceae)

-acean, -aceous [L.–*aceus*, nom. masc. sing.] *suf* of the nature of; like; characterized by; belonging to (crustacean, crustaceous)

acer-¹ [L. *acerbus*, harsh] *base* sharp; needle-like (acerose, acrid)

acer-² [L. *acer*, maple] *base* maple (acerate, aceric)

acerb- [L. *acerbus*, harsh] *base* harsh; bitter (acerbic, exacerbate)

acerv- [L. *acervare*, to heap up] *base* heap (acervate, acervose)

acest- [Gr. *akestos*, healed] *base* healing (acesodyne, acestoma)

acet-, aceto-, acetyl- [L. *acere*, to be sour] *comb* acetic; acetyl; vinegar (acetamid, acetometer, acetylcholine)

acetabul- [L. *acetabulum*, cup-shaped vessel] *base* saucer (acetabular fractures, acetabuliform)

acetar- [L. *acetaria*, salad plants] *base* salad (acetarious, acetary)

acheron- [Gr. *akheron*, river of the Lower World] *base* hell; underworld (Acherontia, acherontical)

achlu- [Gr. *akhluo*, to grow dark] *base* darkness (achluophobia)

aci- [L. *acicula*, small needle] *base* needle (acicular, aciculate)

acid- [L. *acidus*, sharply sour] *comb* sour (acidify, acidosis)

acinaci- [L. *acinus*, berry growing in a cluster] *comb* scimitar (acinacifolious, acinaciform)

acini- [L. *acinus*, berry growing in a cluster] *comb* grape (acinarious, aciniform)

-acious [L.–*acius*, abounding in] *suf* characterized by; full of (audacious, mendacious)

acipenser- [Gr. *akkipesios*, sturgeon] *base* sturgeon (acipenserine, acipenseroid)

-acity [L. suf.–*acitas*] *suf* quality of (tenacity, vivacity)

acou-, acoust- [Gr. *akouein*, to hear]

comb hearing; sound (acouesthesia, acoustical)

acrid- [L. *acridium*, grasshopper] *base* grasshopper (acridian, acridid)

acro- [Gr. *akhros*, furthest, highest, pointed] **1.** *comb* pointed (acrocephaly); **2.** highest (acrospire); **3.** extremity (acroataxia)

acromio- [Gr. *akromion*, point of the shoulder blade] *comb* upper arm; shoulder (acromion, acromioclavicular)

actino- [Gr. *aktis*, ray] **1.** *comb* [zoology] possession of tentacles (actinomorphic); **2.** [physics/chemistry] presence of actinic rays (actinometry); **3.** light ray (actinotherapy)

acu-, acul- [L. *aculeatus*, prickly] *comb* sharp (acumen, aculeate)

aculei- [L. *aculeatus*, prickly] *base* spine (aculeiform, aculeolate)

acuti- [L. *acutus*, sharp] *comb* sharp-pointed (acutifoliate, acutilobate)

-acy [L.–*acia*, state of] *suf* quality; position; condition (democracy, primacy)

acyro- [*a*-, lacking + *kuros*, authority] *comb* incorrect use of words (acyrological, acyrology)

ad-[1] [L. *ad*-, toward] **1.** *pre* motion toward (advance); **2.** addition to (admit); **3.** nearness to (adjoin) NOTE: ad- can change to: a- (ascribe); ab- (abbreviate); ac- (acclaim); af- (affirm); ag- (aggrade); al- (allege); an- (announce); ap- (approve); ar- (arrive); as- (assent); at- (attrition)

-ad[2] [Gr. n. suffix] *suf* of or relating to; used to form names of **1.** collective numerals (monad); **2.** some poems (Iliad); **3.** some plants (cycad)

-ad[3] [L. *ad*-, toward] *suf* [anatomy] toward; in the direction of (dextrad, dorsad)

-ade [L. suf.–*atus*] **1.** *suf* the act of (blockade); **2.** product of (pomade);

3. participant (brigade); **4.** drink made from (lemonade)

adelph- [Gr. *adelphos*, brother] *base* brother (adelphous, Philadelphia)

aden-, adeni-, adeno- [Gr. *aden*, gland] *comb* gland or glands (adenalgia, adeniform, adenography)

adip-, adipo- [L. *adeps*, fat] *comb* fat (adipose, adipocellular)

adjut-, adjuv- [L. *adjutare*, assist] *base* help (adjutant, adjuvant)

adren-, adreno- [L. *ad*-, to + *renes*, kidney] *comb* adrenal gland (adrenalitis, adrenotoxin)

adul- [L. *adulari*, to fawn upon] *base* flattery (adulation, adulatory)

adular- [NL. *Adula*, a mountain group in the Grison Alps] *base* blue (adularia, adularescent)

adunc- [L. *adunctus*, hooked] *base* hooked; bent inward (aduncate, aduncous)

-ae [L. nom. pl. -*ae*] *suf* plural ending (antennae, minutiae)

aed- [Gr. *aedes*, unpleasant] *base* yellow fever mosquito (Aedes)

-aede- [Gr. *aidoia*, private parts] *base* genitals (aedeagus). *Also* **aedoe-** (aedoeomania)

aedi- [L. *aedes*, edifice] *base* temple; shrine; habitat (aedicule, aedile). *See* **edi-**

aegag- [Gr. *aigagros*, wild goat] *base* wild goat (aegagropila, aegogrus) *Also* **egag-**

aegr- [L. *aegrotare*, to be sick] *base* illness (aegritude, aegrotat)

aei- [Gr. *aei*, ever] *base* always; ever; continued (aeipathy)

aeluro- *see* **ailuro-**

-aemia [Gr. *aima*, blood] *comb* blood condition (acetonaemia, hyperaemia). *See* **-emia**

-aen(io)- [L. *aeneus*, brazen] *base* brass (aeneous, aeniolithic)

aequor- [L. *aequor*, level, as a calm, smooth sea] *base* sea; ocean (Aequoria, aequorial) aer-, aeri-, aero- [Gr. *aer*, air] *comb* air; gas (aerate, aeriferous, aerobatics)

aerug- [L. *aerugo*, rust of copper] *base* green-blue; verdegris (aeruginous, aerugo)

aerumn- [L. *aerumna*, toil] *base* toil; trouble (aerumnous)

aescul- [L. *aesculus*, Italian oak] *base* horse chestnut (aesculetin, aesculin). *Also*, **escul-**

aestiv- [L. *aestivus*, of summer] *base* summer (aestival, aestivate) *Also*, **estiv-**

aestu- [L. *aestuare*, to boil] *base* boil up (aestuation, exaestuating). *Also* **estu-** (estuosity)

aet- [Gr. *aetos*, eagle] *base* eagle (Aëtian, aetites)

aetheo- [Gr. *a-*, not + *ethos*, custom] *base* unusual (aetheogam, aetheogamous)

aetio- [Gr. *aitia*, cause] *base* cause (aetiologue, aetiology). *See* **etio-**

aev- [L. *aevum*, age] *base* time; age (aeviternal, mediaeval)

af- *see* **ad-**

afflat- [L. *af-*, to + *flare*, blow] *base* breathe on; inspiration (afflate, afflatus)

Afro- [L. *Afer*, African] *comb* African (Afro-American, Afroasiatic)

ag- *see* **ad-**

agalma- [Gr. *agalma*, work of art] *base* image; statue (agalmatolite, stylagalmatic)

agap- [Gr. *agape*, love] *base* love (agape, agapetae)

agar- [Gr. *Agaria*, town in Sarmatia] *base* mushroom (agariciform, agaricoid)

agath- [Gr. agathos, good] *base* good (agathism, agathopoietic)

agati- [Gr. *akhates*, agate < River Achates in Sicily] *comb* agate (agatiferous, agatiform)

-age [L. suff.–*aticum*] 1. *suf* act; condition; result of (marriage); 2. amount; number of (acreage); 3. cost of (postage); 4. place of (steerage); 5. collection of (peerage); 6. home of (hermitage); 7. to act (forage)

agglut- [L. *ad-*, to + *glutinare*, to glue] *base* stick to (agglutination, agglutinogen)

agito- [L. *agitare*, < *agere*, to drive] *comb* excited; restless (agitomania, agitophasia)

agmat- [Gr. *agmat*, fragment] *base* fracture; break (agmatology, catagmatic)

agn- [L. *agnus*, lamb] *base* lamb (agnel, agnification)

-agnosia [Gr. *a-*, without + *gnosis*, knowledge] *comb* loss of knowledge (prosopoagnosia, simultanagnosia)

-agogue [Gr. *agein*, to drive] 1. *comb* leading; directing (pedagogue); 2. inciting (demagogue); *adj.* -agogic (hemagogic)

agon- [Gr. *agein*, to drive] *base* contest; struggle (antagonist, protagonist)

agora- [Gr. *agora*, marketplace] *comb* open space (agoranome, agoraphobic)

-agra [Gr. *agra*, a seizing] *comb* sudden pain; seizure (coxagra, pellagra)

agrest- [L. *agrestis*, rural < *ager*, field] *base* rural; field (agrestic, agrestian)

agri- [L. *ager*, field] *comb* field; earth; soil (agriculture, agribusiness)

agrio- [Gr. *agrios*, savage] *base* wild; savage (agriologist, agriology)

agro- [Gr. *agros*, field] *comb* field; earth; soil (agrobacterium, agronomy)

agrost- [Gr. *agrostis*, grass] *base* grass (agrostography, agrostology)

-agrypn- [Gr. *agrein*, hunt + *hupnos*, sleep] *base* sleeplessness (agrypnocoma, agrypnode)

-aholic [Eng. compression of *alcoholic*] *comb* person addicted to or obsessed with ___ (chocaholic, workaholic)

aichm- [Gr. *aichme*, point of a spear]

base needle (aichmomania, aichmophobia)

aichur- [Gr. *aichme*, point of a spear] *base* pointed (aichurophobia)

ailuro- [Gr. *ailouros*, cat] *comb* cat (ailurophile, ailurophobia). *Also* **aeluro-** (aeluromania)

-aire [adaptation of Fr. *millionaire*] *suf* person characterized by or occupied with (billionaire, legionnaire)

aischro- [Gr. *aischros*, distasteful] *base* smut; obscenity (aischrolatria, aischrologia)

al-¹ *see* **ad-**

al-² [Arabic *al*, the] *comb* the (alchemy, algebra)

-al³ [L.–*alis*, adj. suf.] 1. *suf* belonging to; like; of (theatrical); 2. nouns from adj. (perennial); 3. act or process of (acquittal); 4. [chemistry] having aldehydes (chloral)

ala- [L. *ala*, wing] *base* wing (alar, alation)

alacr- [L. *alacer*, lively] *base* promptness (alacrify, alacrity)

alaud- [L. *alauda*, lark] *base* skylark (Alaudidae, alaudine)

-alb- [L. *albus*, white] *base* white (albino, album)

alcelaph- [Gr. *alke*, elk + *elaphos*, deer] *base* antelope (alcelaphine, Alcelaphinae)

alcid- [L. *alca*, auk] *base* auk (Alcidae, alcidine)

alea- [L. *alea*, game of chance] *base* dice; chance (aleatoric, aleatory)

alectoro-, alectryo- [Gr. *alektrion*, cock] *comb* cock; rooster (alectoromachy, alectryomancy)

-ales [L. pl. suf.] *suf* ending for scientific Latin names of plant orders (Agavales, Liliales)

aleth- [Gr. *alethes*, truth] *base* truth (alethic, alethiology)

aletud- [L. *aletudo*, grossness] *base* fatness (aletude, aletudinous)

aleuro- [Gr. *aleuron*, meal] *base* flour (aleuromancy, aleurone)

alex-, alexi-, alexo- [Gr. *alexein*, ward off] *comb* to ward off; keep away (alexiteric, alexipyretic, alexocyte)

alg- [L. *algere*, to be cold] *base* cold (algid, algidity)

alge-, algesi-, -algia, algo-, -algy [Gr. *algos*, pain] *comb* pain (algetic, algesiometer, neuralgia, algophobia, coxalgy)

ali-¹ [L. *ala*, wing] *comb* wing (aliferous, aliform)

-ali-² [L. *alius*, other] *base* another; other (alien, alienation)

-alim- [L. *alere*, to nourish] *base* nourishment; food (alimentary, alimentation)

-aliph- [Gr. *alephein*, to anoint with oil] *base* unguent; fat (aliphatic)

-alis [L. suf.–*alis*] *suf* ending for scientific Latin names (Australis, borealis)

-allac-, -allag- [Gr. *allasein*, to exchange] *base* exchange; mutually binding (synallactic, synallagmatic)

allant(o)- [Gr. *allas*, sausage] 1. *comb* membrane: fetal (allanto-chorion); 2. sausage-shaped (allantoid)

-allaxis- [Gr. *allaxis*, to exchange] *base* exchange (morphallaxis, trophallaxis)

allelo- [Gr. *allos*, other] *comb* of one another; reciprocal (allelomorph, allelopathy)

alli- [L. *alium*, garlic] *base* garlic (alliaceous, Allium)

allo- [Gr. *allos*, other] *comb* variation; reversal; departure from normal (allonym, allopathy)

allotrio- [Gr. *allotrios*, strange] *comb* abnormal, unnatural (allotriolith, allotriophagy)

-ally [ON suf.–*liga*, bind] *suf* to form certain adverbs (abdominally, terrifically)

alog(o)- [Gr. *a-*, not + *logos*, reason] *base* unreasonable (alogism, alogotrophy)

alopec- [Gr. *alopekia*, fox mange] *base* fox (alopecoid); baldness (alopecia)

alphito- [Gr. *alphiton*, barley] *base* barley (alphitomancy, alphitomorphous)

alter- [L. *alter*, other] *comb* another; other (alter, alternate)

alti-, alto- [L. *altus*, high] *comb* high (altimeter, altocumulus)

alumino- [L. *alumen*, alum] *comb* aluminum (aluminosilicate, aluminothermic)

alut- [L. *aluta*, soft leather] *base* leather (alutaceous, alutation)

alv- [L. *alvus*, belly] *base* belly (alviducous, alvine)

alve- [L. *alveus*, basket, beehive] *base* beehive (alveary, alveated)

alveolo- [L. *alveus*, a cavity] **1.** *comb* connected with alveolus (alveolodental); **2.** small cavity; socket (alveolopalatal)

alyt- [Gr. *alutes*, police officer] *base* police officer (alytarch)

-am- [L. *amare*, to love] *base* love; friendship (amity, amorous)

amar- [L. *amarus*, bitter] *base* sour (amaretto, amarine)

amaranth- [Gr. *a-*, not + *marainein*, to wither] *base* purple (amaranthine, amaranthoid)

amath- [Gr. *amathos*, sand] *base* dust (amathigerous, amathophobia)

amaur- [Gr. *amaros*, dark] *base* dim; dark (amaurosis, amaurotic)

amaxo- [Gr. *amaxis*, little wagon] *base* automobile (amaxomania, amaxophobia)

ambag- [L. *ambi*, around + *agere*, to drive] *base* oblique; indirect (ambagious, ambagatory)

ambi-, ambo- [L. *ambi*, around] *comb* both; around (ambience, amboceptor). *See* **amphi-**

ambig- [L. *ambi*, around + *agere*, to drive] *base* uncertain (ambiguity, unambiguous)

ambly- [L. *amblus*, dim, dulled] *comb* dullness; dimness (amblyopia, Amblystoma)

ambul- [L. *ambulare*, to walk] *comb* walk (ambulatory, somnambulate)

amebi-, amebo- [Gr. *amoibe*, change] *comb* ameba (amebicide, amebocyte)

amelo- [short form of *enamel* < Fr. *enamayller*] *comb* enamel (ameloblast, amelogenesis)

amensi- [L. *a-*, not + *mens*, mind] *base* amnesia (amensiphobia)

ament-¹ [L. *a-*, not + *mens*, mind] *base* insanity; feeble-mindedness (amentia, amenty)

ament-² [L. *amentum*, strap] *base* catkin (amentaceous, amentiferous)

ametro- [Gr. *ametros*, irregular] *comb* irregular, imperfect (ametrometer, ametropia)

amic-¹ [L. *amicus*, friend] *base* friend (amicable, amicableness)

-amic² [ML *am(monia)*, ammonia + *-ic*] *suf* amide related (allocinnamic, lactamic acid)

amita- [L. *amita*, paternal aunt] *base* aunt (amitate, amitation)

ammino- [am(monia) + -ine] *comb* containing ammines (ammino-chloride)

ammo- [Gr. *ammos*, sand] *comb* sand (ammochryse, ammodromous)

ammonio-, ammono- [ML. *ammonia*, from *sal ammoniac* < Gr. *Ammon*, Egyptian deity] *comb* containing ammonia (ammonioferric, ammonotelic)

amn- [L. *amnis*, river] *base* river (amnicoline, amnicolist)

amnes- [Gr. *a-*, not + *mnesthai*, to remember] *base* forgotten (amnesia, paramnesia)

amnio- [Gr. *amnion*, membrane around the fetus] *comb* amniotic sac; membrane: fetal (amniocentesis, amnioscopy)

amorpho- [Gr. *a-*, without + *morphe*, shape] *comb* shapeless; irregularly shaped (amorphous, amorphogranular)

-ampel- [Gr. *ampelos*, vine] *base* vine (ampelography, ampelopsis)

amphi-, ampho- [Gr. *amphi*, on both sides] *comb* on both sides; surrounding (amphibology, amphoteric). *See* ambi-

-ampl- [L. *amplus*, spacious] *base* large (amplification, amplifier)

ampull- [Gr. dimin. of *amphoreus*, jar with two handles] *base* bottle (ampulla, ampullaceous)

amycho- [Gr. *amussein*, lacerate] *base* scratch; irritate (amychophobia, amyctic)

amygdalo- [Gr. *amugdale*, almond] *comb* almond-shaped (amygdalotomy, amygdalophenin)

amyl-, amylo- [Gr. *amulon*, starch] *comb* of starch (amylamine, amylometer)

an-¹ [variant of Gr. *a*-, not] *pre* not; lacking (anacanthous, anarchy)

an-² *see* ad-

-an³ [L. suf.–*anus*] 1. *suf* belonging to; of; characteristic of (diocesan); 2. born in; living in (American); 3. believing in; following (Mohammedan)

ana-¹ [Gr. *ana*, up] *pre* up; upon; back; again; anew; throughout (anabolism, anaphylaxis)

-ana² [L. suf. -*ana*] *suf* plural: collective (Americana, Victoriana)

anacard- [Gr. *ana*, resembling + *kardia*, heart] *base* cashew (anacardiaceous, anacardic)

anaps- [Gr. *an*-, upwards + *apsis*, arch] *base* turtle (anapsid, anapsida)

anat- [L. *anas*, duck] *base* duck (anatiferous, anatine)

anathem- [Gr. *anathema*, an accursed thing] *base* curse (anathema, anathematize)

-ance [L. suf.–*antia*] 1. *suf* the act of (utterance); 2. quality or state of being (vigilance); 3. a thing that __ (conveyance); 4. a thing that is __ (dissonance); *n.* -ancy (constancy, vacancy)

ancip- [Gr. *anceps*, two-headed] *base* doubtful; two-edged (ancipital, ancipitous)

ancis- [Gr. *ankistron*, hook] *base* hook-shaped (ancistroid)

-ancon- [Gr. *ankon*, elbow] *base* elbow (anconad, anconitis)

ancyr- [Gr. *ankura*, anchor] *base* anchor (Ancyrene, ancyroid)

ancylo- [Gr. *ankulos*, crooked] *comb* bent; crooked; stiff (ancylomele, ancylostomiasis). *Also* ankylo- (ankyloglossia)

ancylostom- [Gr. *ankulos*, crooked + *stoma*, mouth] *base* hookworm (Ancylostoma)

andro-, -andry [Gr. *andros*, man] *comb* man; male (androgenous, polyandry)

-androus [Gr. -*androus*, having men] 1. *comb* man; male (polyandrous); 2. *BOT*: having stamens (diandrous)

-ane [Gr.–*ene*, fem. adj. suf.] *suf* a saturated hydrocarbon (hexane, methane)

anemo- [Gr. *anemos*, wind] *comb* wind (anemometer, anemophilous)

anet- [Gr. *anetos*, relaxed] *base* soothing (anetic, anetodermia)

aneth- [Gr. *anethon*, anise or dill] *base* dill (anethated, anethene)

angin- [Gr. *ankhone*, strangling] *base* strangulation; heart attack (angina, angina pectoris)

angio- [Gr. *angos*, vessel] *comb* vessel; case; pot (angiocarp, angioma)

Anglo- [L. *Angli*, the English people] *comb* English (Anglo-Irish, Anglomania)

angui- [L. *angere*, throttle or choke] *base* snake (anguiform, anguine)

anguill- [Gr. *enchelos*, eel] *base* eel (anguilliform, anguillous)

angul- [L. *angulus*, angle] *base* angle (angularity, angulation)

angusti- [L. *angustus*, constricted] *comb* narrow (angustation, angustifoliate) anhydro- [Gr. *an-*, without + *hudor*, water] *comb* anhydride (anhydroglucose, anhydrous)

-anim- [L. *anima*, soul] *base* spirit; life (animation, animatronics)

aniso- [Gr. *an-*, not + *isos*, equal] *comb* unequal; dissimilar (anisogamy, anisometropia)

ankylo- [Gr. *ankulos*, crooked] *comb* bent; crooked; stiff (ankylosaur, ankylosis). *Also* ancylo-

-ann-, -enn- [L. *annus*, year] *base* year; (annual, biennial); yearly (anniversary)

annul- [L. *annulus*, ring] *comb* ring (annular, annulation)

ano-¹ [Gr. *ano*, upward] *pre* upward; above (Anostoma, anotropia)

ano-² [L. *anus*, ring] *comb* anal; ring-shaped (anoplasty, anorectal)

anom-, anomo- [Gr. *an-*, not + *homos*, same] *comb* unusual; irregular; abnormal (anomalous, anomocarpous)

anomalo- [Gr. *an-*, not + *homalos*, even] *comb* irregular; uneven (anomalogonatous, anomalous)

anophel- [Gr. *an-*, without + *ophelos*, advantage] *base* mosquito (Anopheles, anopheline)

ansa- [L. *ansa*, handle] *base* handle (ansated, ansation)

anser- [L. *anser*, goose] *base* goose (anserine, anserous)

-ant [L. suf–*ant*] 1. *suf* performing an act (defiant); 2. person who performs (accountant); 3. impersonal physical agent (lubricant)

ante- [L. *ante*, before] *pre* before in time, order, or position (antecedent, antedate)

antero- [L. *anterus*, preceding] *comb* anterior; front (anterolateral, anteroparietal)

-anthema [Gr. *antheein*, to blossom] *comb* rash; eruption (enanthema, exanthema)

-antherous [Gr. *anthos*, flower] *comb* flowering; having anthers (anantherous, isantherous)

antho- [Gr. *anthos*, flower] *comb* of flowers (anthocarpous, anthomania)

-anthous [Gr. *anthos*, flower] *comb* having flowers of a specified kind or number (ananthous, monanthous)

anthraco- [Gr. *anthrak*, charcoal] *comb* coal; carbuncle (anthracomancy, anthracometer)

anthropo- [Gr. *anthropos*, human being] *comb* human (anthropology, anthropophagus)

anti- [Gr. *anti*, opposite] 1. *pre* against; hostile (antilabor); 2. operating against (antiballistic); 3. preventing, curing, neutralizing (antitoxin); 4. opposite; reverse (antiperistalsis); 5. rivaling (antipope)

antio- [Gr. *anti*, opposite to] *comb* set against (antiodont, antiopelmous)

-antiq- [L. *antiquus*, old] *base* old; ancient (antiquarian, antiquated)

antl- [Gr. *antlion*, bucket] *base* bucket (antlia, antliate)

antro- [Gr. antron, cave] *comb* nearly closed cavity; antrum (antral, antrozous)

anu- [L. *anus*, ring] *base* circular; ring-shaped (annulus, anus)

anur-¹ [Gr. *an-*, no + *oura*, tail] *base* tailless (anura, anurous)

anur-² [Gr. *an-* no + *ouron*, urine] *base* absence of urine (anuresis, anuria)

-anus [L. adj. suf.–*anus*] *suf* scientific word ending (Platanus, Raphanus)

aorto- [Gr. *aeirein*, to lift] *comb* aorta (aortoclasia, aortography)

ap- *see* ad-

apat- [Gr. *apate*, deceit] *base* illusion, deceit (apatite, Apatornis)

apeir- [Gr. *a-*, without + *peras*, an end] *base* infinite; endless (apeirogon, Apeiron)

apert- [L. *apertus*, open] *base* open (apertometer, aperture)

aphan- [Gr. *aphanes*, unmanifest] *base*

invisible, obscure (aphanite, aphanozygous)

aphe-, -aphia [Gr. *haphe,* touch] *comb* sense of touch (aphephobia, dysaphia)

aphn- [Gr. *aphneios,* wealthy] *base* rich, wealthy (aphnologist)

aphr- [Gr. *aphros,* foam] *base* foam (aphrite, Aphrodite)

aphrodisio- [Gr. *aphrodisiakos,* vene- real < Aphrodite] *base* sexual (aphrodisiac, aphrodisian)

api- [L. *apis,* bee] *comb* bee (apiary, apiculture)

-apical, apico- [L. *apex,* summit] *comb* apex; tip (periapical, apicotomy)

apio- [Gr. *apion,* pear] *base* pear (api- ocrinite, apioid)

apo- [Gr. *apo,* off] *pre* off; from; away from; separation (apoblast, apoco- pate)

apocris- [Gr. *apokrisis,* answer] *base* to give or receive answers (apocrisiary)

apodemi- [Gr. *apodemia,* journey] *base* journey (apodemialgia)

apolaust- [Gr. *apolaustos,* enjoyable] *base* enjoyment; self-indulgence (ap- olaustic, apolausticism)

aporet- [Gr. *aporos,* doubtful] *base* doubt (aporia, aporetic)

apostem- [Gr. *apostema,* distance, ab- scess] *base* abscess (apostemation, apostematous)

appell- [L. *appellare,* to address or ac- cost] *base* call to; name (appellation, appellative)

appet- [L. *appetere,* to strive after] *base* craving (appetite, appetizer)

apricat- [L. *apricus,* open to the sun] *base* sunbathing (apricate, aprica- tion)

-aps-, -apt-[1] [Gr. *hapsis,* to fasten] *base* joining (synapse, synaptic)

-apsia [Gr. *hapsis,* to fasten] *comb* touch (parapsia)

apt-[2] [L. *aptus,* fastened] *base* ability (apt, aptitude)

aqua-, aque-, aqui- [L. *aqua,* water]

comb water; (aquatic, aqueduct, aquiculture)

aquil- [L. *aquila,* eagle] *base* eagle (aquilated, aquiline)

ar-[1] *see* **ad-**

-ar[2] [L. suf.*–aris*] 1. *suf* pertaining to (angular); 2. one who __ (burglar); 3. connected with __ (collar)

arach- [Gr. *arakis,* leguminous plant] *base* peanut; ground nut (arachidic, Arachis)

arachn-, arachno- [Gr. *arachen,* spi- der] *comb* spider; cobweb (arachne- phobia, arachnodactylia)

araio- [Gr. *araios,* thin] *comb* thin, light (araiocardia)

-araneo- [L. *aranea,* spider] *base* spi- der (araneal, araneology)

arat- [L. *aratus,* plow] *base* farming; tillage (aration, aratory)

-arbor- [L. *arbor,* tree] *base* tree (arbo- raceous, arboretum)

arcan- [L. *arcanus,* secret < *arca,* chest] *base* secret (arcana, arcane)

arch-[1] [Gr. *arkos,* chief] *pre* main; chief; principal (archbishop, archri- val)

-arch[2] [Gr. *archein,* to be first] *comb* ruler (matriarch, patriarch)

archaeo-, archeo- [Gr. *arkhaios,* an- cient] *comb* ancient; original (ar- chaeology, Archeozoic)

archi- [Gr. *archi,* first] *pre* [biology] primitive (archiplasm, archistome)

-archy [Gr. *archein,* to be first] *comb* rule; government (monarchy, oli- garchy)

arci- [L. *arcus,* bow] *base* arch; bow (arciform; arcigerous)

arct- [Gr. *arktia,* moth] *base* moth (arctian)

arcto- [Gr. *arktos,* bear] *comb* bear (arctic, cynarctomachy)

arctoid- [Gr. *arktos,* bear] *base* rac- coon; weasel (Arctoidea, arctoidean)

ard-[1]**, ars-** [L. *ardere,* to burn] *base* burn (ardor, arson)

-ard[2]**, -art** [O.F. n. suf.*–ard*] *suf* one

who is or does too much (drunkard, braggart)

ard-³, ardu- [L. *arduus*, hard or steep] *base* erect; steep; laborious (arduity, arduous,)

arde- [Gr. *erodios*, heron] *base* heron (ardeid, ardeine)

ardu- [L. *arduus*, steep, difficult] *base* difficult (arduously, ardurous)

aren- [L. *arena*, sand] *comb* sand (arenaceous, arenicolous)

arenaceo- [L. *arena*, sand + suf. -*aceus*] *comb* sandy (arenaceo-argillaceous, arenaceocalcareous)

arene- [L. *aranea*, spider] *base* spider (areneiform)

areo-¹ [Gr. *Ares*, planet Mars] *comb* Mars (areocentric, areology)

areo-² [Gr. *araios*, thin; not dense] *base* thin; rare (areometer, areostyle)

areto- [Gr. *arete*, virtue] *comb* virtue (aretologist, aretology)

arg- [Gr. *argos*, idle] *base* idle, unused (argamblyopia)

argent-, argenti-, argento- [L. *argentum*, silver] *comb* silver (argentite, argentiferous, argento-cuprous)

argillaceo- [Gr. *argillos*, white clay] *comb* clay (arenaceo-argillaceous)

argillo- [Gr. *argillos*, white clay] *comb* clay (argillo-calcareous, argilloarenaceous)

argyro- [Gr. *argyros*, silver] *comb* silver (Argyropelecus, argyrophyllus)

-aria [L. pl. n, suf.-*aria*] *suf* [botany/zoology] used to form names of groups and names of genera (Alternaria, Planaria)

-arian [L. comp. suf.] *suf* age; sect; occupation; social belief (humanitarian, Unitarian)

arid- [L. *aridus*, dry] *base* dry (aridity, aridness)

ariet- [L. *aries*, ram] *base* ram (arietiform, arietine)

-arious [L. adj. suf.] *suf* relating to; connected with (gregarious, vicarious)

-aris [L. suf.–*aris*] *suf* scientific word ending (Muscularis, Polaris)

aristo- [Gr. *aristos*, best] *comb* best (aristocracy, aristotype)

arithm- [Gr. *arithmos*, number] *base* number (arithmancy, arithmetic)

-arium [L. neut. suf.] *suf* location; receptacle (aquarium, solarium)

armo- [L. *armus*, shoulder] *base* shoulder (armomancy)

arrheno- [Gr. *arreno*, male] *comb* male (arrhenotokous, arrhenotoky)

arseno- [Old Iranian *zarna*, golden] *comb* having arsenic (arsenolite, arsenopyrite)

arterio- [Gr. *arteria*, artery] *comb* artery (arteriosclerosis, arteriovenous)

arthr-, arthro- [Gr. *arthron*, joint] *comb* connected with a joint (arthrectomy, arthrodynia)

arthropod- [Gr. *arthro*, joint + *pod*, foot] *base* millipede (arthropodal, arthropodan)

arti- [L. *ars*, art + *factum*, something made] *comb* workmanship (artifact, artifice)

-articul- [L. *articulus*, small joint] *base* joint (articulated, multiarticular)

artio- [Gr. *artios*, even] *comb* even number (artiad, Artiodactyla)

artiodactyl- [Gr. *artios*, even + *daktulos*, finger or toe] *base* cloven-footed (artiodactyl, artiodactylous)

arto- [Gr. *artos*, bread] *comb* bread (artocarpous, artophagous)

arundi- [L. *harundo*, a reed] *base* reed (arundiferous, arundinaceous)

arvicol- [L. *arvum*, field + *colere*, dwell] *base* meadow mouse (arvicoline, arvicolous)

-ary [L. suf.–*arius*] **1.** *suf* relating to; like (legendary); **2.** thing/person connected to __ (military)

as-¹ *see* **ad-**

as-², asin- [L. *asinus*, ass] *base* jackass (asinine, asininity)

ascari- [Gr. *askaris*, intestinal worm]

comb intestinal worm (ascariasis, Ascaridae)

ascid- [Gr. *askidion*, little leather bag] *base* molluscs with leathery tunic (ascidian, Ascidium)

asco- [Gr. *askos*, bag] *comb* [botany] sac (ascocarp, ascophore)

-ase [suf. from *diastase* < Gr. *diastasis*, separation] *suf* names of enzymes (amylase, angiotensinase)

-asis *see* –iasis

-asm [Gr. suf.*–asmos*] *suf* result of an action (enthusiasm, orgasm)

asmato- [Gr. *asma*, song] *comb* song (asmatographer, asmatography)

aspala- [Gr. *aspalaks*, mole] *base* mole (aspalasoma)

asper- [L. *asper*, rough] *comb* rough (asperation, asperity)

aspido- [Gr. *aspid*, shield] *base* shield (aspidomancy, Aspidogaster)

assid- [L. *assiduous*, sitting down to] *base* unceasing (assiduity, assiduous)

-ast [Gr. suf.*–astes*] *suf* one who is __ (chiliast, enthusiast)

astac- [Gr. *astakos*, lobster or crawfish] *base* lobster (astacian, astacite)

aster-[1] [Gr. *aster*, star] *comb* star (asteraceous, asteria)

-aster[2] [L. suf.*–aster*] *suf* diminution; inferiority; worthlessness; slight resemblance (parasitaster, poetaster) *contemptuous diminutive*

asteroid- [Gr. *aster,* star + *eidos*, form] *base* starlike; starfish (asteroidal, asteroidean)

asthen-, astheno- [Gr. *asthenes*, without strength] *comb* weakness (asthenopia, asthenobiosis). *See* -esthenia

astigm- [Gr. *a-*, not + *stigma*, point] *base* structural eye defect (astigmatic, astigmatism)

astra- [Gr. *astrapaios*, of lightning] *comb* lightning (Astrapaeus, astraphobia)

astragalo- [Gr. *astragalos*, a bone] *comb* anklebone; dice; (astragalonavicular, astragalomancy)

astro- [Gr. *aster*, star] *comb* star; celestial activity (astrologer, astronomy)

asty- [Gr. *astu*, city] *base* city (astyclinic)

at- *see* **ad-**

-ata [L. suf.*–ata*] *suf* result of; plural ending (Articulata, stomata)

atax-, ataxi-, -ataxia, ataxio-, ataxo- [Gr. *a-*, without + *taktos*, order] *comb* confusion; disorder (ataxaphasia, ataxiamnesic, psychataxia, ataxiophemia, ataxophobia)

-ate[1] [L. suf.*–atus*] *v.* **1.** *suf* to become (maturate); **2.** cause to become (invalidate); **3.** form or produce (salivate); **4.** provide or treat with (refrigerate); **5.** put in the form of; form by means of (delineate); **6.** to arrange for (orchestrate); **7.** to combine; infuse; treat with (chlorinate)

-ate[2] [L. suf.*–atus*] *adj.* **1.** *suf* characteristic of (collegiate); **2.** having; filled with (passionate); **3.** [biology] having or characterized by (caudate)

-ate[3] [L. suf.*–atus*] *n.* **1.***suf* office; function; agent; official (directorate); **2.** person or thing that is the object of an action (legate); **3.** [chemistry] a salt made from an acid ending in -ic (nitrate)

ate-[4] [Gr. *Até*, goddess of mischief] *base* ruinous; reckless impulse (atemania, atephobia)

atelia-, atelo- [Gr. *a-*, without + *telos, completion*] *comb* incomplete; undeveloped (myelatelia, atelocardia)

ather- [Gr. *atherine*, smelt] *base* smelt (atherine, atherinid)

athero- [Gr. *athere*, porridge] *comb* deposit: soft materials (atherogenic, atheromatous)

-athlon, -athon [extraction from Gr. village *Marathon*] *suf* event; contest (pentathlon, walkathon)

-atic [L. suf.*–aticus*] *suf* of the kind of (chromatic, dramatic)

-atile [L. suf. *-atilis*] *suf* possibility; quality (versatile, volatile)

-ation [L. suf. *-atio*] 1. *suf* the act of (alteration); 2. condition of being (gratification); 3. the result of (compilation)

-ative [L. suf.*–ativus*] *suf* relating to; tending to (correlative, demonstrative)

atlanto- [Gr. god *Atlas*] *comb* [anatomy] pertaining to the atlas, top vertebra (atlantoaxial, atlanto-occipital)

atlo- [Gr. god *Atlas*] *comb* of the neck (atlo-axoid, atloid)

atmo- [Gr. *atmos*, vapor] *comb* steam; vapor; air (atmologist, atmosphere)

-ator [L. suf *-tor*] *suf* doer; agent; actor (adjudicator, educator)

-atory [L. suf *-orius*] *suf* of the nature of; pertaining to; produced by (accusatory, celebratory)

atrament- [L. *atramentum*, black ink < *ater*, black] *base* ink, inky (atramental, atramentarious)

-atresia [Gr. *a-*, not + *tretos*, perforated] *comb* imperforate; lacking an opening (colpatresia, proctatresia)

atreto- [Gr. *a-*, not + *tretos*, perforated] *comb* imperforate; lacking an opening (atretocyst, atretorrhinia)

atrio- [L. *atrium*, central hall] *comb* cavity, esp. a chamber of the heart (atriopore, atrioventricular)

atro- [L. *ater*, black] *comb* black (atroceruleus, atrorubent)

-atrophia, atrophic [Gr. *a-*, without + *trephein*, to nourish] 1. *comb* malnutrition (metatrophia); 2. progressive decline (neuratrophia, myotrophic)

atto- [Old Norse *attjan*, eighteen] *pre* one-quintillionth —10^{18} (attogram, attotesla)

atychi- [Gr. *atucheo*, to fail] *base* failure (atychimania, atychiphobia)

auant- [Gr. *auantikos*, wasted] *base* wasting away (auantic)

-auchen- [Gr. *auchen*, neck] *base* neck (Auchenia, maerauchenia)

audac- [L. *audax*, bold] *base* boldness (audacity)

audi-, audio- [L. *audire*, to hear] *comb* hearing (auditorium, audiology)

-aug- [L. *augere*, to increase] *base* grow; increase (augment, augmentation)

augur- [perh. L *augere*, to promote] *base* soothsaying; divination (augurous, augury)

aulo- [Gr. *aulos*, a tube] *comb* pipe; reed (auletic, aulophyte)

auranti- [L. *aurantium*, an orange] *base* orange (aurantiaceous, Aurantieæ)

aur(i)-[1] [L. *aurus*, ear] *comb* ear (auricle, auriform)

aur(i)-[2]**, auro-** [L. *aurum*, gold] *comb* gold (auriferous, aurous)

auricalc- [Gr. *aurichalkon*, yellow copper ore] *base* copper; gold-colored (auricalceous, aurichalcite)

auriculo- [L. *auricula*, outer ear] *comb* outer ear; lobe (auriculo-temporal, auriculoventricular)

aurig- [L. *auriga*, chariot] *base* coach or carriage (aurigal, aurigation)

-auror- [L. *aurora*, dawn] *base* dawn (auroral, aurorean)

aurora- [L. *aurora*, dawn] *comb* radiant emissions in both hemispheres (aurora australis, aurora borealis)

austro- [L. *auster*, south wind] 1. *comb* wind: south (austromancy); 2. eastern (Austro-Hungarian)

auto- [Gr. *autos*, self] *comb* self; self-moving (autobiography, autoclastic)

autumn- [L. *autumnus*, autumn] *base* fall (autumnal, autumnity)

auxano-, auxeto-, auxo- [Gr. *auxesis*, increase] *comb* increase; growth (auxanogram, auxetophone, auxochrome)

auxil- [L. *auxilium*, help] *base* help; assistance (auxiliary, auxiliate)

avar- [L. *avaritia*, covetousness] *base* greed (avarice, avaricious)

aven- [L. *avena*, oats] *base* oats (avenaceous, avenage)

avern- [L. *Lake Avernus*, considered

the entrance to hell] *base* hellish (avernal, Avernian)

avia-, avio- [L. *avis*, bird] 1. *comb* bird (aviary); 2. flight (avionics, aviator)

avid- [L. *avidus*, greedy] *base* eager (avidly, avidity)

avion- [Fr. *avion*, aviator] *base* of flying (avionic, avionics)

avit- [L. *avitus*, grandfather] *base* grandfather (avital, avitic)

-avunc- [L. *avunculus*, uncle] *base* uncle (avuncular, avunculate)

axi-, axio-¹, axo-, axono- [L. *axis*, pole of the earth] *comb* related to an axis (axial, axiomesial, axometer, Axonophora)

-axill- [L. *axilla*, armpit] *base* armpit (axillar, periaxillary)

axin- [Gr. *axine*, ax] *base* ax (axinite, axinomancy)

axio-² [Gr. *axios*, worth] *comb* values (axiology, axiopisty)

azo- [Gr. *a-*, not + *ksoein*, to live] *comb* [chemistry] nitrogen (azobenzene, azotobacter)

-azur- [Persian *lajward*, lapis lazuli] *base* sky-blue (azureous, azurite)

B

baccato- [L. *bacca*, berry] *comb* bearing berries (baccate, baccato-tuberculous)

bacci- [L. *bacca*, berry] *comb* berry (bacciform, baccivorous)

bacill-, bacilli-, bacillo- [L. *bacillum*, rod or staff] *comb* rod-shaped bacillus (bacillemia, bacilliform, bacillotherapy)

back- [Dan. *bag*, back] 1. *comb* of the back (backache); 2. behind (backfield); 3. prior (backdate); 4. opposing (backlash)

-bacter, bacteri-, bacterio- [Gr. *bakterion*, little stick] *comb* of bacteria (aerobacter, bactericide, bacteriology)

bacul- [L. *bacul*, rod] *base* rod, stave (baculine, baculometry)

balaen- [L. *balaena*, whale] *base* whale (Balaenidae, balaenoid)

balani-, balano- [Gr. *balanos*, acorn] *comb* acorn; gland (balaniferous, balanitis)

balatro- [L. *balatro*, jester] *base* buffoon (balatronic, balatrophobia)

balaust- [Gr. *balaustion*, flower of the wild pomegranate] *base* pomegranate (balaustine, Balaustion)

balbut- [L. *balbus*, stammering] *base* stutter; stammer (balbutiate, balbutient)

ballist- [Gr. *ballein*, to throw] *base* projectile (ballistic, ballistics)

balneo- [L. *balnaeum*, warm bath] *comb* baths; bathing (balneary, balneology)

bambus- [L. *bambusa*, bamboo] *base* bamboo (bambusaceous, bambusicoline)

banaus- [Gr. *banausikos*, of mechanics] *base* mechanical (banausian, banausic)

bapt- [Gr. *baptein*, to dip] *base* dip (baptize, baptosaurus)

-bar [Gr. *baros*, weight] *comb* atmospheric pressure; weight (decibar, isobar)

barb- [L. *barba*, beard] *comb* beard; tufted (barbate, barbellate)

barbar- [Gr. *barbaros*, foreign] *base* barbarian (barbarian, barbarocracy)

bari-, baro- [Gr. *baros*, weight] *comb* atmospheric pressure; weight (baritone, barometer)

bary- [Gr. *baros*, weight] *comb* heavy; difficult (barycentric, baryphonia)

bas- [L. *basium*, kiss] *base* kiss (basial, basiator)

Basco- [Fr. *Basque*, Basque] *comb* Basque (Bascologist, Bascology)

basi-, baso- [Gr. *basis*, base] *comb* [biology] the base; at or near base (basidigitale, basocellular)

-basia [Gr. *basis*, step] *comb* [medicine] ability to walk (abasia, dysbasia)

basiat- [L. *basium*, kiss] *base* kiss (basiate, basiation)

basidio- [L. *basidium*, base] *comb* base (basidiomycetes, basidium)

basil- [Gr. *basileus*, king] *base* king; royal (basilic, basilica)

bassar- [Gr. *bassaris*, fox] *base* fox (Bassaricyon, Bassarididae)

-bat- [Gr. *bainein*, go] *base* walk; go; pass (diabatic, katabatic)

bathmo- [Gr. *bathmos*, threshold] *comb* excitability, responsiveness (bathmotropic, bathmotropism)

batho-, bathy- [Gr. *bathos*, depth] *comb* depth; deep (bathometer, bathysphere)

bato-¹ [Gr. *batos*, passable] *comb* height (batomania, batophobia)

bato-² [Gr. *batos*, bramble-bush] *comb* brambles (batologist, batology)

batracho- [Gr. *batraxos*, frog] *comb* frog; toad (batrachoid, batrachophagous)

batto- [Gr. *battos*, stammerer] *comb* repetition (battologize, battology)

bdell- [Gr. *bdella*, leech] *base* leech (bdellatomy, bdellometer)

be- [L.–*bi* in *ambi*, both] **1.** *pre* around (beset); **2.** completely (besmear); **3.** away (bereave); **4.** about (bemoan); **5.** make (besot); **6.** furnish with (befriend); **7.** cover(ed) with; (becloud)

beati- [L. *beatus*, happy] *base* happy; blessed (beatific, beatitude)

-bell- [L. *bellum*, war] *base* war (bellicose, belligerence)

-belo- [Gr. *belos*, arrow] *base* arrow (beloid, belomancy)

-belon- [Gr. *belone*, needle] *base* needle; pin; sharp object (belonite, belonoid)

bene- [L. *bene*, well] *pre* good; well (benefactor, beneficence)

benzo- [It. *benzoinzo*, frankincense] *comb* [chemistry] benzine; (benzophenone, benzopyrene)

beryl- [Gr. *berrulos*, beryl] *base* green (beryline, berylloid)

betul- [L. *betulla*, birch] *base* birch (Betula, betulaceous)

bi- [L. *bi*, two] **1.** *pre* having two (biangular); **2.** on both sides; in two ways (bilingual); **3.** every two (biweekly); **4.** using two (bilabial); **5.** involving two (bipartisan); **6.** [botany/zoology] twice; doubly; in pairs (bipinnate); **7.** [chemistry] having twice as many atoms or chemical equivalents for a definite weight of the other constituent of the compound (sodium bicarbonate); **8.** organic compounds having a combination of two radicals of the same composition (biphenyl)

bib- [L. *bibere*, to drink] *base* drink (bibulous, imbibe)

biblio- [Gr. *biblion*, book] **1.** *comb* of books (bibliography); **2.** of the Bible (bibliomancy)

bili- [L. *bilis*, bile] *comb* gall; bile (biliary, biligenic)

-bility [L. suf–*bilitas*] *suf* power to do or be (credibility, responsibility)

bin- [L. *bini*, two by two] *pre* two (binary, binaural)

bio- [Gr. *bios*, life] *comb* living; life (biograph, biology)

-biosis, -biotic [Gr. *bios*, life] *comb* way of living (parabiosis, symbiosis, aerobiotic)

-bis- [L. *bis*, twice] *pre* two; twice (biscroma, bisferious)

blaes- [L. *blaesus*, lisping or stammering] *base* stammering (blaesitas, blaesiloquent) *Also* **bles-**

bland- [L. *blandus*, flattering] *base* flattery (blandiloquence, blandishment)

-blast, -blastic, blasto-, -blasty [Gr. *blastos*, germ or sprout] *comb* forma-

tive; germinal; embryonic; developing (mesoblast, osteoblastic, blastoderm)

blatt-[1] [L. *blatta*, cockroach] *base*
cockroach (Blatta, blattiform)

blatt-[2] [L. *blatta*, purple silk] *base* purple (blattean)

-ble *see* **-able**

blenn-, blenno- [Gr. *blennos*, mucus]
comb mucus; slime (blennadenitis,
blennostasis)

-blep- [Gr. *blepso*, I see] *base* sight
(ablepsia, ablepsy)

blepharo- [Gr. *blepharon*, eyelid] *comb*
eyelid (blepharospasm, blepharotomy)

blesi- [L. *blaesus*, lisping or stammer-
ing] *base* stammering (blesiloquent)

-bly *see* **-ably**

-bole [Gr. *ballein*, to throw] *comb*
thrown down/out/in/together/be-
yond (amphibole, hyperbole)

bolet- [Gr. *boletes*, type of mushroom]
base fungus; mushroom (boletic, bo-
letus)

-bolic, bolo-[1], **-boly** [Gr. *ballein*, to
throw] *comb* thrown down/out/in/
together/beyond (catabolic, bolometer, epiboly)

bolo-[2] [Gr. *bole*, throw, glance, ray]
base ray; radiant energy (bolometer,
bolometric)

-bomb- **1.** [L. *bombus*, bumblebee]
base bee (bombilation); **2.** [L. *bom-
byx*, silkworm] silk; silkworm
(bombic, bombycinous) **3.** [L. *bom-
bare*, to buzz] buzzing or droning
sound (bombilate, bombilation)

bon- [L. *bonus*, good] *base* good (bona
fide, bonanza)

borbor- [Gr. *borborugmos*, bowel rum-
bling] *base* **1.** intestinal rumbling
(borborygmus) **2.** filthy talk (bor-
borology)

borea- [Gr. *boreas*, north wind] *base*
north (boreal, borean)

boro- [Pers. *burah*, borax] *comb*
[chemistry] boron (boroflouride,
borosilicate)

-bosc-[1] [OHG *busc*, a thicket] *base*
mass of growing trees or shrubs
(boscage, bosky)

-bosc-[2] [Gr. *boskein*, to feed] *base* to
feed (Boscades, hippoboscid)

-boss- [Gr. *bossen*, strike or beat] *base*
protuberant part (bosselated, em-
boss]

bostrych- [Gr. *bostruchos*, curl or
lock of hair] *base* coiled or curled
(bostrychite, bostryx)

botano- [Gr. *botane*, herb or plant]
comb plant (botanical, botanomancy)

botaur- [L. *bos*, ox + *taurus*, bull] *base*
bittern (Botaurinae, botaurus)

-bothr- [Gr. *bothros*, pit or trench]
base pitted; grooved (bothrenchyma,
Bothrophera)

botry(o)- [Gr. *botrus*, grape cluster]
comb grapes; clustered like grapes
(botryose, botyroidal)

-botul- [L. *botulus*, sausage] *base*
sausage (botuliform, botulism)

bou-, bu- [Gr. *bous*, ox] *comb* ox; cow
(boustrophedon, bulemia)

-bound **1.** [OE *bindan*, place under
bond] *comb* constrained (snow-
bound); **2.** [ON *bua*, to get ready]
going toward (homebound, west-
bound)

-bov- [L. gen. case *bovis*, ox] *base* cow
(boviculture, bovine)

brachi-, brachio- [L. *brachium*, arm]
comb arm; upper arm (brachialgia,
brachiopod)

brachisto- [Gr. *braxis*, short] *comb*
short (brachistocephaly, brachis-
tochrone)

brachy- [Gr. *braxis*, short] *comb* short
(brachycardia, brachycerous)

bract- [L. *bractea*, gold-leaf veneer]
base thin plate; leaf (bracteate,
bracteiform)

brady- [Gr. *bradys*, slow] *comb* slow;
delayed (bradyarthria, bradyphasia)

-branchia, branchio- [Gr. *branchia*,
gills] *comb* gills (pulmobranchia,
branchiopod)

brassic- [L. *brassica*, cabbage] *base* broccoli; cabbage (Brassica, brassicacious)

brepho- [Gr. *brephos*, babe] *comb* baby (brepholatry, brephotrophic)

brevi- [L. *brevis*, short] *comb* brief; little; short (brevifoliate, breviloquence)

broch- [L. *brochatus*, having projecting teeth] *base* having tusks (Brochata, brochate)

brom-, bromo- [Gr. *broma*, food] *comb* stench (bromidrosis, bromopnea)

bromato- [Gr. *broma*, food] *comb* food (bromatography, bromatology)

bromel- [L. *Bromelia*,< Swed. botanist Olaf Bromel] *base* pineapple (Bromelia, bromeliaceous)

bromo- [Gr. *bromos*, stench] *comb* [chemistry] bromine (bromoderma, bromogelatin)

bronch-, bronchi-, bronchio-, broncho- [Gr. *bronchos*, windpipe] *comb* the windpipe (bronchadenitis, bronchiectasis, bronchiogenic, bronchoscope)

bronto- [Gr. *bronte*, thunder]
1. *comb* thunder (brontograph);
2. [paleontology] hugeness (brontosaurus)

-brotic [Gr. *brotikos*, inclined to eat] *comb* corrosive; inclined to eat (diabrotic, scolecobrotic)

bruch- [Gr. *brouchos*, wingless locust] *base* beetle (bruchid, Bruchidae)

brum- [L. *bruma*, winter] *base* winter; foggy (brumal, brumous)

brun- [F. *brun*, dimin. of brown] *base* dark brown (brunette, brunneous)

brux- [Gr. *brukein*, to gnash] *base* grind (bruxism, bruxomania)

bryo- [Gr. *bruon*, moss] *comb* moss (bryology, bryophyte)

bu- *see* bou-

bubal- [Gr. *boubalos*, antelope, buffalo] *base* antelope; buffalo (bubaline, Bubalus)

bubo- [Gr. *boubon*, groin] *base* groin (bubonic, bubonocele)

buccin- [L. *bucina*, trumpet < Gr. .cow's horn] *base* trumpet (buccinal, buccinatory)

bucco- [L. *bucca*, cheek] *comb* cheek (buccal, buccolabial)

bucerat-, bucorac- [Gr. *bous*, ox + *keras*, horn] *base* hornbill (Buceratinae, Bucoracinae)

bufo- [L. *bufo*, toad] *comb* toad (bufoniform, bufotoxin)

bulbi-, bulbo- [L. *bulbus*, bulb] *comb* bulb; bulbous (bulbiform, bulbospinal)

-bulia [Gr. *boule*, will] *comb* will; (abulia, dysbulia)

bullat- [L. *bulla*, bubble] *base* bubble; blister (bullate, bullescence)

buno- [Gr. *bonnos*, hill or mound] *base* elevated (bunodont, bunotherian)

-burg, -burgh [OE *burg*, town] *comb* city; town; village (Vicksburg, Pittsburgh)

-burger [Ger. city *Hamburg*] *comb* sandwich made on a roll or bun (cheeseburger, mooseburger)

burs-, burso- [L. *bursa*, pouch] *comb* pouch; purse; sac (bursar, bursopathy)

buteo- [L. *buteo*, buzzard-hawk] *comb* hawk; buzzard (Buteoninae, buteonine)

butyro- [L. *buturum*, butter] *comb* butter (butyraceous, butyrometer)

bux- [L. *buxeus*, box tree] *base* boxtree (buxeous, buxiferous)

by- [L.–*bi*< *ambi*, both] 1. *pre* near; close by (bystander); 2. side (bystreet); 3. secondary (by-product)

-byon- [Gr. *buein*, to stuff] *base* plug; stuff (rhinobyon)

-byss-[1] [Gr. *bussos*, depth] *base* depth (hypabyssal, hyperbyssal)

-byss-[2] [Gr. *bussos*, flax-like] *base* flax (byssaceous, byssinosis)

C

caball- [Gr. *kabales*, pack horse] *base* horse (caballaria, caballine)

caca- [Gr. *kakke*, excrement] *base* excrement (cacagogue, cacatory)

-cace [Gr. *kake*, bad, flawed] *base* disease, deformity (chilocace, stomacace)

cachex- [Gr. *kachexia*, disease] *base* ill health (cachectic, cachexia)

cachin- [L. *cacinnare*, to laugh immoderately] *base* laugh (cachinnate, cachinnation)

caco- [Gr. *kakos*, bad] *comb* bad; poor; harsh (caconym, cacophony). *Also* kako- (kakistocracy)

cacumin- [L. *cacumina*, summit] *base* tip (cacuminal, cacuminate)

cad- [L. *cadere*, to fall] *base* fall (cadence, cadenza)

cadav- [L. *cadaver*, corpse] *base* corpse (cadaveric, cadaverous)

-cade [*suf* from *cavalcade*] *comb* procession; parade (aquacade, motorcade)

caduc- [L. *caducus*, fleeting] *base* transitory; perishable (caducicorn, caducous)

caec- [L. *caecus*, blind] 1. *base* blind (caecilian); 2. intestinal pouch (caeciform)

caed- *see* -cide

cael- [L. *caelestis*, celestial] *base* heavens (caelestial, caelometer). Also cel- (celestial) *see* celest-

caeno-[1], ceno-, coeno- [Gr. *koinos*, common] *comb* in common (caenobite, cenobite, coenobium)

caeno-[2] [Gr. *kainos*, recent] *comb* new (caenogenesis, Caenozoic). *Also* caino- (cainophobia)

caes- [L. *caesius*, bluish-gray] *base* blue; gray; green (caesiellus, caesious)

-caine [taken from *cocaine*, coca + -ine] *comb* synthetic alkaloid in anesthetic drugs (lidocaine, novocaine)

cal-, cale- [L. *calere*, to be warm] *base* heat (decalescence, caleficient)

calam- [L. *calamus*, reed] *base* reed (calamarious, calamiform)

calar-, calat- [L. *calare*, to proclaim solemnly] *base* inserted (intercalary, intercalated)

calathi- [Gr. *kalathos*, basket] *comb* cup; basket (calathiform, calathus)

calcaneo- [L. *calx*, heel] *comb* heelbone (calcaneo-fibular, calcaneum)

calcareo- [L. *calcarius*, pert. to lime] *comb* of lime (calcareosulfurous, calcariferous)

-calce- [L. *calceus*, shoe] *base* shoe (discalceate, discalced)

calci- [L. *calx/calc-*, lime] *comb* calcium; lime (calcification, calcify)

calcitr- [L. *calcitrare*, to kick] *base* kick (calcitrant, recalcitrant)

-calcul- [L. *calculus*, pebble] *base* count; pebble (calculary, calculator)

-cali- [Gr. *kalia*, hut] *base* nest; hut (caliological, caliology)

calic- [L. *calix/calic-*, cup] *base* like a cup (calicula, calicular) *Also* calyc-

calig- [L. *caligo*, gloom, mist] *base* fog; mist (caliginous, caligo)

callain- [Gr. *kallais*, turquoise] *base* turquoise (callainite)

calli- [Gr. *kalos*, beautiful] *comb* beautiful (calligraphy, callipygous)

callithri- [Gr. *kalos*, beautiful + *trix*, hair] *base* marmoset (callithricid, callithrix)

callo- [Gr. *kalos*, beautiful] *base* beautiful (callomania, callotechnics)

calo-, calori- [L. *calor*, heat] *comb* heat (caloreceptor, calorimeter)

calumn- [L. *calumnia*, slander] *base* slander (calumniate, calumniator) calv- [L. *calva*, scalp without hair] *base* bald (calvarium, Calvary)

calyc- [Gr. *kaluk-*, cup-shaped] *base* cup-shaped (calycanthemy, calyciferous)

calypto- [Gr. *kaluptos*, covered] *comb* hidden; covered (calyptoblastic, calyptomerous)

calyptri- [Gr. *kaluptra*, veil] *base* hood (calyptriform, calyptrimorphous)

camar- *see* camer-

-camb- [L. *cambire*, to exchange] *base* change; exchange (cambistry, excambition)

cambar- [L. *camarus*, sea-crab] *base* crayfish variety (cambarine, cambaroid)

cameli- [Gr. *kamelos*, camel] *base* camel (camelid, cameline)

camer- [Gr. *kamara*, vault] *base* vault (Camarasaurus, camerastoma)

-camp-¹ [L. *campus*, field] *base* field (campaign, campestral)

-camp-² [Gr. *kampe*, caterpillar] *base* caterpillar (campodeiform, campophagine)

campan- [L. *campana*, bell] *base* bell (campaniform, campanology)

campho- [Arab. *kafur*, bitter aromatic] *comb* camphor (camphogen, campholide)

-campsis, campto- [Gr. *kamptos*, bent] *comb* bent (phallocampsis, camptomelia)

campylo- [Gr. *kampilos*, bent or curved] *comb* crooked; bent (campylospermous, campylotropal)

can-¹ [L. *canis*, dog] *base* dog (canid, canine)

can-² [L. *canus*, hoary] *base* gray (canescence, canescent)

canal- [L. *canalis*, channel, groove] *base* groove (canaliculated, canalirostrate)

cancell- [L. *cancellatus*, latticed] *base* barrier; latticed (cancellate, cancellous)

cancr- [L. *cancer*, crab] *base* crab (cancriform, cancrine)

cand- [L. *candidus*, bright] *base* white (candescent, candidate)

cann- [L. *canna*, reed] *base* reed (cannula, cannoid)

cantho- [Gr. *kanthos*, corner of the eye] *comb* eye: corner of (canthectomy, canthoplasty)

-cap- [L. *capere*, seize] *base* take; hold; receive (captivate, recapture). *Also* cep/cip (receptacle, recipient)

capel- [Gr. *kapelos*, shopkeeper] *base* shopkeeper (capelocracy)

capilli- [L. *capillus*, hair] *comb* hair (capillaceous, capilliform)

-capit- [L. *caput*, head] *base* head (capillary, decapitate)

-capnia, capno- [Gr. *kapnos*, smoke] *comb* smoke; vapor; carbon dioxide (acapnia, capnomancy)

capri- [L. *caper/capr-*, goat] *base* goat (Capricorn, capriform)

capsuli-, capsulo- [L. *capsa*, chest] *comb* capsule (capsuliform, capsulolenticular)

carbo- [L. *carbo*, coal] *comb* [chemistry] carbon (carbohydrate, carboniferous)

carbol- [L. *carbo*, coal] *base* of phenol (carboloc, carbolize)

carbon- [L. *carbonem*, charcoal] *base* charcoal (carbonaceous, carbonify)

carcer- [L. *carcer*, prison] *base* jail (carceral, incarcerate)

carcharin- [Gr. *karxaros*, jagged] *base* shark (carcharinid, carcharoid)

carcin(o)- [Gr. *karkinos*, crab, cancer] *comb* cancer; crab (carcinogenesis, carcinophagous)

cardi-, -cardia, cardio-, -cardium [Gr. *kardia*, heart] *comb* heart (cardiagra, tachycardia, cardiology, myocardium)

cardo- [Gr. *kardos*, thistle] *comb* thistle (cardophagous)

carico- [L. *carex/caric-*, sedge] *base* sedge (caricography, caricologist)

carid- [Gr. *karis*, shrimp or prawn] *base* shrimp, prawn (caridean, caridomorphic)

-carin- [L. *carina*, keel] *base* keel; ridge (carinate, carinula)

cario- [L. *caries*, decay] *comb* tooth disease; caries (cariogenic, carious)

carni- [L. *caro*, flesh] *comb* flesh (carnality, carnivore)

carnoso- [L. *caro*, flesh] *comb* fleshy (carnoso-fibrous, carnoso-tuberose)

carot- [Gr. *karos*, stupor] *base* stupefying; soporific (carotic, carotid)

-carp, -carpic, carpo-[1]**, -carpous** [Gr. *karpos*, fruit] *comb* fruit; seeds (endocarp, endocarpic, carpophore, monocarpous)

carpho- [Gr. *karphos*, straw] *comb* straw; dry (carpholite, carphology)

carpo-[2] [Gr. *karpos*, wrist] *comb* wrist; (carpocerite, carpoptosis)

cartilag- [L. *cartilago*, gristle] *base* cartilage (cartilage, cartilaginous)

carto- [L. *carta*, a card] *comb* map; card; piece of paper (cartographer, cartomancy). *Also* **charto-** (chartometer)

caryo- [Gr. *karuon*, nut] *comb* nucleus (cartophyllus, caryopsis). *Also* **karyo-** (karyokinesis)

cas- [L. *casus*, fall] *base* fall (cascade, grammatical case)

case- [L. *caseus*, cheese] *base* cheese (caseation, casefied)

cassidi- [L. *cassis*, helmet] *base* helmet (cassidiform, cassidula)

cassiter- [Gr. *kassiteros*, tin] *base* tin (cassiterite, cassiterotantalite)

-cast [ON *casta*, to throw, scatter] *comb* transmit (broadcast, telecast)

castan- [L. *castanea*, chestnut] *base* brown; chestnut (castaneous, castanet)

castella- [L. *castellum*, castle] *base* fortification (castellar, incastellate)

castig- [L. *castigare*, correct] *base* chasten; reprove (castigate, castigatory)

castor- [L. *castor*, beaver] *base* beaver (castoreum, castorine)

castr- [L. *castra*, camp] *base* camp (castrametation, castrensian)

casuar- [L. *casuarius*, cassowary] *base* cassowary (Casuariidae, casuary)

cata-, cath- [Gr. *kata*, down] *pre* down; through; against; completely (catabolism, cathartic). *Also* **kata-** (katabatic)

catagelo- [Gr. *katagelos*, mockery] *base* ridicule (catagelomania, catagelophobia). *Also* **katagelo-**

cataglott- [Gr. *kataglottisma*, lascivious kiss] *base* tongue-kissing (cataglottism, cataglottistic)

catagm- [Gr. *kata*, intensive + *agnunai*, break in pieces] *base* fracture (catagmatic, catagmatical)

cattall- [Gr. *katallaktikos*, having to do with exchange] *base* money exchange (catallactically, catallactics)

catech- [Gr. *katechein*, to instruct] *base* oral instruction, esp. Q & A (catechetics, catechism)

caten- [L. *catena*, chain] *base* chain (catenary, concatenation)

cathar- [Gr. *katharos*, clean, pure] *base* clean; purge; purify (catharize, catharsis)

cathart- [Gr. *katharein*, to cleanse] *base* buzzard (Cathartes, cathartine)

-cathex- [Gr. *kathexis*, retention] *base* retention (acathexis, hypercathexis)

cathis- [Gr. *cathizein*, to sit] *base* sit; seat (cathisma, cathismata)

catoptro- [Gr. *katoptron*, mirror] *comb* mirror (catoptrics, catoptromantic)

caudo- [L. *cauda*, tail] *comb* tail (caudo-femoral, caudotibial)

cauli-, caulo- [L. *caulis*, a stalk] *comb* stem; stalk (caulicolous, caulocarpic)

caum- [Gr. *kauma*, heat] *base* heat (caumatic, caumesthesia)

caupon- [L. *caupo*, huckster] *base* huckster; innkeeper (cauponate, cauponation)

-caust- [Gr. *kaustos*, capable of burning] *base* burn (caustic, holocaust)

caut- [L. *cautela*, caution] *base* heed; carefulness (cautelous, precautionary)

cauter- [Gr. *kauter*, branding iron] *comb* caustic; burning (cauterize, cautery)

cava-, -cave, cavi-, cavo- [L. *cavus*, hollow] *base* hollow (cavate, concave, cavernicolous, cavicorn)

caval- [L. *caballus*, horse] *base* horse (cavalier, cavalry)

-ce *suf* multiplicative suffix (thrice, twice)

cebo- [L. *cebus*, monkey] *comb* monkey (Cebidae, cebocephalic)

cecid- [Gr. *kekis*, gallnut] *base* gall: tumorous plant tissue (Cecidomyia, cecidomyian)

cec- [L. *cecus*, blind] *base* blindness (cecity, cecutiency)

ceco- [L. *cecus*, blind] *comb* intestinal pouch; cecum; (cecostomy). *Also* caec- (caeciform)

-ced-, -cess- [L. *cedere*, yield] *base* move; go; give way (concede, procession). *See* -cid-

cedr- [L. *cedrus*, cedar] *base* cedar (cedrine, cedron)

-cele [Gr. *kele*, tumor] *comb* tumor; swelling (adenocele, cystocele); hernia; (bubonocele, perineocele)

-celer- [L. *celer*, swift] *base* speed (accelerate, celerity)

celest- [L. *coelum*, heaven] *base* heavens (celestial, celestify)

celido- [Gr. *kelis*, a spot] *comb* spot; surface marking (celidography)

celio- [Gr. *koilia*, belly] *comb* abdomen; (celiomyositis, celiotomy)

celli- [L. *cella*, cell] *comb* cell (celliferous, celliform)

cello- [L. *cella*, chamber] *comb* cellulose (cellobiose, cellophane)

celluli-, cellulo- [L. *cellula*, little cell] *comb* cell; cell wall (celluliferous, cellulo-fibrous)

celo-¹ [Gr. *koilos*, hollow] 1. *comb* celom (celomate); 2. hernia (celotomy); 3. abdomen (celoscope). *Also* coelo- (coeloscope)

-celo-² [Gr. *kelos*, dry, burnt] *base* dry; burnt (celosia)

celsi- [L. *celsus*, lofty] *base* dignity; eminence; lofty position (celsitude, celsity)

Celto- [Gr. *keltos*, Western people] *comb* Celt; Celtic (Celto-Germanic, Celtomania)

cen- [L. *cena*, dinner] *base* meal (cenation, cenatory)

-cene [Gr. *kainos*, new] *comb* geological epoch (Eocene, Miocene)

ceno-¹ [Gr. *kainos*, new] *comb* new; recent (cenogenesis, Cenozoic). *Also* caeno-, caino-, kaino- (Caenozoic, Cainozoic, Kainozoic)

ceno-² [Gr. *koinos*, common] *comb* in common; common (cenobite, cenogonous). *Also* coeno- (coenobite)

ceno-³ [Gr. *kenos*, empty] *comb* empty (cenotaph, cenotaphic). *Also* keno- (kenosis)

cenoto- [Gr. *kainos*, new] *comb* new (cenotomania, cenotophobia) *Also* cainoto-, kainoto- (cainotophobia, kainotophobia)

-centered [Gr. *kentron*, center of a circle] *comb* focused on (child-centered, market-centered).

-centesis [Gr. *kentesis*, pricking] *comb* puncture (amniocentesis, pericardiocentesis)

centi- [L. *centum*, hundred] 1. *comb* hundred-fold (centipede); 2. hundredth part (centigram)

centri-, centro- [Gr. *kentron*, center of a circle] *comb* center (centripetal, centrobaric)

-centric [Gr. *kentron*, center of a circle] 1. *comb* having __ center (polycentric); 2. focused around __ (ethno-centric)

-cep-¹ [L. *capere*, take] *base* take (accept, receptor). *See* -cap-

-cep-[2] [L. *cepa*, onion] *base* onion;
bulb (cepaceous, cepivorous)

cephal-, -cephalic, cephalo-, -cephalous, -cephaly [Gr. *kephale*,
head] *comb* head; skull (cephalitis,
dolichocephalic, cephalopod,
brachycephalous, dolichocephaly)

cephalopod- [Gr. *kephale*, head +
pous, foot] *base* squid (Cephalapoda,
cephalopodal)

-ceptor [L. *capere*, to take] *comb* taker;
receiver (chemoceptor, neuroreceptor)

cera- [L. *cera*, wax] *base* wax (ceraceous, cerein)

ceramo- [Gr. *keramos*, potters' clay]
comb ceramic (ceramodontia)

ceras- [L. *cerasus*, cherry] *base* cherry
(cerasin, cerasinous)

cerato- [Gr. *keras*, horn] *comb* horn;
hornlike (ceratocele, ceratophyllous).
Also kerato- (keratoglobus)

cerator- [Gr. *keras*, horn + *hris*, snout]
base rhino (ceratorhine, Ceratorhina)

cerauno- [Gr. *keraunos*, thunderbolt]
comb thunder (ceraunic, ceraunoscope).
Also kerauno- (keraunoscope)

-cerca, -cercal, cerco- [Gr. *kerkos*, tail
of a beast] *comb* having a __ tail
(Schistocerca, heterocercal, Cercopithecus)

cerebri-, cerebro- [L. *cerebra*, brain]
comb brain (cerebritis, cerebrospinal)

ceri-, cero- [L. *cera*, wax] *comb* wax
(ceriferous, ceromancy)

-cern- [L. *cernere*, perceive] *base* to sift
(discern, excernent)

cerr- [L. *cerrus*, oak] *base* evergreen
oak (cerrial, cerris)

cerul- [L. *caerulus*, dark blue] *base*
blue (cerulean, cerulescent)

cerumini- [L. *cera*, wax] *comb* waxlike secretion (ceruminiferous, ceruminous)

cerus- [L. *cerussa*, white lead] *base*
white (ceruse, cerussal)

-cerv- [L. *cervus*, deer] *base* deer; elk;
moose (cervicide, cervine)

cervico- [L. *cervix*, neck] *comb* cervical; of the neck (cervicodorsal, cervicispinal)

cervis- [L. *cervesia*, beer] *base* beer
(cervisial, cervisomania)

cespit- [L. *caespes*, turf or sod] *base*
growing in dense tufts or clumps
(cespitose, cespitulose) *Also* cespitoso- *comb* (cespitoso-arboriform,
cespitoso-ramose)

-cess-, -ced- [L. *cedere*, yield] *base*
move; go; give way (procession, concede)

cest- [Gr. *kestos*, girdle] *base* tapeworm
(cestoid, Cestoidea)

-cet- [Gr. *ketos*, whale] *base* whale
(cetaceous, cetology)

-chaem- [Gr. *khamai*, on the ground]
base low (chaemacephalic). *Also*
-cham-

chaeti-, chaeto-, -chaeta [L. *chaeta*,
bristle] *comb* hair; bristle; seta
(chaetiferous, chaetophorous,
Spirochaeta)

chalast- [Gr. *khalastikos*, laxative] *base*
laxative; relaxant (chalastic)

chalax- [Gr. *khalaxes*, hailstone] *base*
hailstone (chalaxa, chalaxite)

chalco- [Gr. *khalkos*, copper] *comb*
copper; brass (chalcocite, chalcography)

chalic- [Gr. *khalik*, gravel] *base* particles, gravel (Chalicomys, chalicosis)

chalyb- [Gr. *khalups*, steel] *base* steel
(chalybean, chalybeous). *See* iron

chamae- [Gr. *khamai*, on the ground]
comb low-growing; dwarflike
(chamaecephaly, chamaedorea)

chao- [Gr. *khaos*, chaos] 1. *base* abyss
(chaology, chaotic); 2. atmosphere
(chaomancy)

charadr- [Gr. *kharadra*, cleft, ravine]
base sandpiper, snipe, plover, woodcock (charadrine, charadrioid)

charit- [L. *caritas*, love] *base* love (charitably, charity)

charto- [L. *charta*, paper] *comb* paper; map (chartomancy, chartometer) *Also* **carto-**

chasmo- [Gr. *khasma*, gulf, yawning hollow] *comb* fissure (chasmogamy, chasmophobia)

cheilo- [Gr. *kheilos*, lip] *base* lip (Cheilanthes, cheiloplasty). *See* **chilo-**

cheima- [Gr. *kheima*, frost, winter] *comb* cold (cheimaphilic, cheimaphobia)

cheir(o)- [Gr. *kheir*, hand] *comb* hand (Cheiranthus, macrocheiria). *See* **chiro-**

-chela, cheli- [Gr. *kele*, claw] *comb* claw (isochela, cheliferous)

chelid- [Gr. *khelidon*, swallow] *base* a swallow (chelidonian)

-chelo(n)-, chelys [Gr. *khelus*, turtle] *base* turtle (chelonian, Lepidochelys)

chemo- [L. *chimia*, alchemy] *comb* chemicals; (chemosmosis, chemotherapy)

cheno- [Gr. *khen*, goose] *base* goose (chenomorphic, chenopod)

chero-¹ [Gr. *khara*, joy, delight] *comb* happy (cheromania, cherophobia)

chero-² [Gr. *khoiros*, young pig] *base* hyrax (cherogril)

cherso- [Gr. *khersos*, dry land] *base* dry (chersonese, Chersydrus)

-chezia [Gr. *khezein*, to defecate] *comb* defecation condition (dyschezia, hematochezia)

chias-, chiasto- [Gr. *khiazein*, marked with crossed lines] *comb* paired; diagonal (chiasmus. chiastic, chiastolite)

chicor- [Gr. *kikhoreia*, succory, endive] *base* chicory (chicoried, chicory)

chili- [Gr. *khilioi*, thousand] *comb* one thousand (chiliasm, chiliastic)

chilo- [Gr. *kheilos*, lip] *comb* lip (chilognathous, chiloplasty)

chilopod- [Gr. *kheilos*, lip + *pous*, foot] *base* centipede (chilopodal, chilopodifirm)

chim- [Gr. *khimaira*, fabled monster] *base* unreal; fantastic (chimera, chimerical)

Chino- [Sanskrit *cinah*, Chinese people] *comb* Chinese (Chino-Japanese, Chino-Tibetan). *See* **Sino-**

-chion- [Gr. *khion*, snow] *base* snow (Chionis, chionodoxa). *See* **-chium**

chiro- [Gr. *kheir*, hand] *comb* hand (chirognomy, chiromancy). *Also* **cheiro-**

chirur- [Gr. *khirourgos*, doing by hand] *base* surgeon (chirurgery, chirurgic)

-chium [Gr. *khion*, snow] *base* snow (hedychium, sisyrinchium) *see* **-chion-**

chlamyd- [Gr. *khlamus,* mantle] *comb* cloak; sheath (chlamydeous, chlamydospore)

chloro- [Gr. *khloros*, greenish-yellow] 1. *comb* green (chlorophyll); 2. . having chlorine; (chloroform)

choano- [Gr. *khoane*, funnel] *comb* funnel (choanocyte, choanoid)

chol-, chole-,cholo- [Gr. *khole*, bile] *comb* bile; gall; anger (cholagogue, cholecyst, chololith)

chondr-, chondrio-, chondro- [Gr. *khondros*, cartilage, grain] *comb* cartilage ;(chondrify, chondriosome, chondroblast)

chord-, -chorda [Gr. *khorde*, string of a musical instrument] *comb* cord; sinew (chorditis, Protochorda). *Also* **cord-** (cordotomy)

-chorea, choreo- [Gr. *khorea*, dance] *comb* involuntary movement; spasm; dance (labiochorea, choreophrasia)

chori- [Gr. *khoris*, asunder] *comb* apart; separate (choripetalous, choryphyllus)

chorio- [Gr. *khorion*, membrance] *comb* membrane; skin (choriocapilaris, choriocele)

choristo- [Gr. *khoristos*, separate]

comb apart; separate (choristophyllus, choristopodous)

choro- [Gr. *khoros*, place, country] *comb* region; land (chorology, chorometry)

choroid- [Gr. *khorion*, membrane + *eidos*, form] *comb* membrane; skinlike (choroideremia, choroiditis)

chrem-, chremat- [Gr. *khremata*, money, wealth] *base* wealth; money (chrematistic, chrematistics)

chreo- [Gr. *khreios*, useful] *comb* useful (chreotechnical, chreotechnics)

chresis- [Gr. *khresthai*, to use] *base* used for doing (catachresis, catachrestical)

chresmo- [Gr. *khresmo*, oracle] *comb* oracle (chresmomancy, chresmological)

chresto- [Gr. *khrestos*, worthy, useful] *base* useful (chrestomathic, chrestomathy)

Christo- [Gr. *khristos*, the anointed one] *comb* Christ (Christocentric, Christomaniac)

chromato- [Gr. *khromat*, color] *comb* color; chromatin (chromatogenous, chromatopathic)

-chrome, -chromy [Gr. *khromat*, color] 1. *comb* color (lithochromy, monochrome); 2. chromium (ferrochrome)

chromo- [Gr. *khromat*, color] *comb* color (chromogenic, chromosome)

chrono-, -chronous [Gr. *khronos*, time] *comb* time (chronography, chronometer, isochronous)

-chroous [Gr, *khroia*, color] *comb* colored (allochroous, xanthocroous)

chrys(o)- [Gr. *khrusos*, gold] *comb* yellow; golden (chrysoberyl, chrysocarpous)

chyl-, chyli-, chylo-, -chylia [Gr. *khulos*, juice, moisture] *comb* connected with chyle; digestive fluid; gastric juice (chylaqueous, chyliferous, chylocyst, achylia)

chthono- [Gr. *khthonos*, earth] *comb* earth (chthonic, chthonography)

chymo- [Gr. *khymos*, juice] *comb* partially digested food (chymification, chymotrypsin)

-chys-, -chyt- [Gr. *khein*, to pour] *base* to pour (synchysis, synchytic)

-cib- [L. *cibus*, food] *base* food (cibarian, cibarious)

cica- [L. *cicatrix*, scar] *base* scar (cicatricose, cicatrix)

cichlo- [Gr. *cikhla*, bird like a thrush; also a sea fish] *base* thrush (cichlomorphous); fish (Cichla)

cichor- [Gr. *cikhorion*, chicory] *base* chicory (cichoraceous, Cichorium)

ciconi- [L. *ciconia*, stork] *comb* stork (ciconian, ciconiiform)

cicur- [L. *cicurare*, to tame] *base* tame (cicurate, cicuration)

-cid- [L. *cadere*, to fall] *base* fall (deciduous, incident) *see* -ced-, -cess-

-cidal, -cide, -cidious, -cidism [L. *caedere*, to kill] *comb* killing (homicidal, patricide, parricidious, suicidism)

cilii-, cilio- [L. *cilium*, eyelid] *comb* cilia; hairlike process (ciliiferous, cilioretinal)

cimic- [L. *cimex/cimic-*, bug] *base* bug (cimicoid, Cimicifuga)

cimol- [Gr. *Kimolos*, name of an island] *base* chalk; light earth (cimolian, cimolite)

-cinc- [L. *cingere*, to gird, encircle] *base* ring; girdle (cincture, precinct)

cinchon- [Sp. town *Chinchon*] *base* quinine (cinchonism, cinchotannic)

cincinn- [L. *cincinnus*, curl] *base* curl (cincinnal, Cincinnurus)

cine- [Gr. *kinein*, to move] *comb* movement; movie (cinematography, cinenchyma). *Also* **kine-** (kinescope)

ciner- [L. *cinis*, ashes] *base* ashes (cineraceous, incinerate)

-cing- [L. *cingere*, to gird] *base* ring; girdle (cingulated, circumcingle)

cinque- [Fr. *cinq*, five] *base* five (cinque, cinquefoil)

-cion [L.–*tio*, state or condition of being] *suf* variation of -tion (coercion, suspicion)

ciono- [Gr. *khion*, pillar, uvula] *base* uvula (cionitis, cionotomy)

-cip- [L. *capere*, to take] *base* take (anticipate, recipient). *See* -cap-

circin- [L. *circinare*, to make round] *base* round (circinal, circinate)

circul- [L. *circularis*, circular] *base* circle (circulate, circulatory)

circum- [L. *circum*, around, about] *suf* around; about; surrounding (circumscribe, circumstances)

cirrh- [Gr. *kirros*, tawny] *base* yellow appearance (cirrhosis, cirrhotic)

cirri-, cirro- [L. *cirrus*, curl or tuft] *comb* curl; ringlet; tendril (cirrrigerous, cirrocumulus)

cirso- [Gr. *kirsos*, enlargement of a vein] *comb* enlarged vein (cirsoid, cirsotomy)

cis-[1] [L. *cis*, on this side] *suf* on this side of; near (cisalpine, cisatlantic). *See* citra-

-cis[2], -cise- [L. *caedere*, to cut] *base* cut; cut off (incision, precise)

ciss- [Gr. *kissos*, ivy] *base* ivy (cissoid, cissoidal)

-cisto- [L. *cista*, box, chest] *base* chest; container (cistern, cistophorous)

-cit- [L. *citare*, to stimulate] *base* arouse (incite, recitation)

citra- [L. *citer*, hither] *comb* on this side of; near (citracaucasian, citramontane). *See* cis-

citro- [L. *citrus*, citron tree] *comb* citric; lemon-colored (citrometer, citrine)

civ- [L. *civis*, city] *base* citizen (civic, civilization)

clado-, -cladous [Gr. *klados*, branch] *comb* branch (cladogenous, cladophyll, acanthocladous)

-claim, clam- [L. *clamare*, to call out] *comb* say; speak; tell (exclaim, exclamation)

clar- [L. *clarus*, clear] *base* clear (clarified, clarity)

-clasia, -clasis, -clastic [Gr. *klastos*, broken] *comb* break; fracture; fragment (osteoclasia, onychoclasis, aclastic)

-clasm, clasmato- [Gr. *klasma*, fragment] *comb* fragment (clasmatocyte, cataclasm)

clathr- [Gr. *klethron*, lattice] *base* lattice; bars (clathrate, clathroid)

claud- [L. *claudus*, lame] *base* lame (claudicant, claudication)

claustro- [L. *claustrum*, closed place] *comb* closed; shut (claustral, claustrophobia)

-clav- [L. *clavus*, nail] *base* nail (clavus, inclavate)

clavato- [L. *clavatus*, club-shaped] *comb* studded; club-shaped (clavato-elongate, clavato-turbinate)

clavi-[1] [L. *clavis*, key] *comb* key; collarbone (clavichord, clavicle)

clavi-[2] [L. *clava*, knotty branch or club] *base* club (clavicorn, claviform)

-cle [L. suf–*culus*] 1. *suf* diminutive spelling (particle); 2. place; means (receptacle)

cleido- *see* clido-

-cleisis [Gr. *enkleiein*, to shut up] *comb* closure (colpocleisis, iredencleisis)

cleisto- [Gr. *kleistos*, closed] *comb* shut; closed (cleistocarp, cleistogamic)

clem-[1] [Gr. *klemat*, vine] *base* vine (clematine, clematis)

clem-[2] [L. *clemens*, mild] *base* mercy; leniency (clemency, clement)

clepto- [Gr. *kleptein*, steal] *comb* robber (clepsamnia, cleptobiosis). *See* klepto-

clerico- [L. *clericus*, clergyman] *comb* clerical and __ (clerico-liberal, clerico-political)

clero- [Gr. *kleros*, lot, share] *comb* chance; lot (cleromancy, cleronomy)

clethr- [Gr. *klethra*, alder] *base* alder (clethra, Clethraceae)

clido- [Gr. *kleidos*, key] 1. *comb* key (clidomancy); 2. clavicle (clidomastoid). *Also* **cleido-** (cleidomancy)

climac- [Gr. *klimakter*, step of a staircase or ladder; critical period of life] *base* stairs; ladder rungs (climacophobia, climacteric)

clin- [Gr. *kline*, bed] *base* bed (clinical, clinoid)

-clinal, -clinate, -cline, -clinic, clino-, -clinous [Gr. *klinein*, to bend or slope] *comb* sloped; bent; directed toward; inclined (anticlinal, proclinate, incline, matroclinic, clinodiagonal, patroclinous)

-clisis [Gr. *klinein*, to lean] *comb* proneness; bending (enclisis, pathoclisis)

clisto- [Gr. *kleistos*, able to close] *comb* closed; closeable (clistocarp, clistogamous)

-clit- [Gr. *klinein*, to lean] *base* bend; inflect; lean (enclitic, heteroclital)

-clithr- [Gr. *kleithria*, keyhole, chink] 1. *base* closed; shut (clithral); 2. keyhole (clithridiate)

-cliv- [L. *clivus*, rising ground] *base* slope (acclivity, proclivity)

cloac- [L. *cloaca*, common sewer] *base* sewer; bowel cavity (cloacal, intracloacal)

-clonic, -clonus [Gr. *klonos*, confused motion or turmoil] *comb* spasm; twitching (synclonic, myoclonus)

-clud-, -clus- [L. *claudere*, to shut] *base* closed; shut (exclude, reclusive)

clupe- [L. *clupea*, small river fish] *base* herring (clupeiform, clupeoid)

clype- [L. *clypeus*, shield] *comb* like a shield (clypeate, clypeiform)

-clysis [Gr. *kluzein*, to wash out] *comb* irrigation (peritoneoclysis, venoclysis)

clysm-, clyst- [Gr. *kluzein*, to wash out] *base* enema (clysmic, clysterize)

-cnem- [Gr. *kneme*, lower part of the leg] *base* leg; tibia (cnemial, gastrocnemius)

cnido- [Gr. *knide*, nettle] *comb* nettle; stinging organ (cnidoblast, cnidophore)

co-¹ [L. pref. *com-*, with] 1. *suf* together; with (co-operation); 2. joint (co-owner); 3. equally (coextensive); 4. complement of (cosine). NOTE: co- can change to: **col-** (colleague); **com-** (commingle); **con-** (convulse); **cor-** (correlate)

-co² [abbrev. < *company*] *suf* trade names (Amoco, Pepsico)

cobalti-, cobalto- [Ger. *kobalt*, demon of the mines] *comb* cobalt (cobalticyanide, cobalto-cyanide)

-coccal, -coccic, cocco-, -coccoid, -coccus [Gr. *kokkos*, berry, kernel] *comb* of or like a bacterium; bacteria names; berry-like; grainlike (staphylococcal, staphylococcic, coccobacillus, staphylococcoid, staphylococcus)

cocci-, -coccus [Gr. *kokkos*, berry, kernel] *comb* berry-shaped (coccigerous, streptococcus)

coccy-, coccygo- [Gr. *kokkyx*, coccyx] *comb* coccyx (coccyalgia, coccygodynia)

cochin- [L. *coccinus*, scarlet < Gr. *kokkos*, berry] *base* crimson dyestuff (cochineal, cochinillifera)

cochle(a)- [Gr. *kochlias*, snail] *base* snail (cochleate, cochleiform)

cochlear(i)- [L. *cochlear*, spoon] *base* spoon (cochlear, cochleariform)

cochlio- [Gr. *kochlias*, snail] *comb* spiral; twisted (cochliocarpous, cochliodontoid)

-coct- [L. *coquere*, to cook] *base* cook; boil (coctible, decoction)

codico- [L. *codex/codic-*, manuscript] *base* manuscript (codicologically, codicologist)

-codonic [Gr. *kodon*, bell] *comb* bell-shaped (adelocodonic, phanerocodonic)

-coele [Gr. *koilos*, hollow] *comb* cavity; chamber (blastocoele, hydrocoele)

coeli- [L. *coelum*, heaven] *comb* heaven; sky (celestial, coelicolist)

coelo-, -coelous [Gr. *koilos*, hollow] *comb* hollow (coelodont, procoelous)

coen- [L. *cena*, principal meal] *base* meal (cenacle, coenaculous)

coeno- [Gr. *koinos*, common] *comb* in common (coenobite). *Also* **ceno-** (cenobite)

cogit- [L. *cogitare*, to think] *base* know; think (cogitation)

-cogn-¹ [L. *cogitare*, to think] *base* know (recognize, cognition)

-cogn-² [L. *gnatus, natus*, born] *base* allied by blood (cognate, cognation)

coimet- [Gr. *koimeterion*, burial ground] *base* cemetery (coimetrophobia). *Also* **coemet-**

coit- [L. *coire*, come together] *base* intercourse; coming together (coition, coitus)

col-¹ *see* **co-**

col-² [L. *colum*, strainer or sieve] *base* strain; filter (colander, colation)

colaco- [Gr. *kolak*, parasite] *base* parasite (colacobiosis, colacobiotic)

colar-, colat- [L. *colare*, to strain] *base* strain (colarin, percolated)

-cole, -colent [L. *colere*, to inhabit] *comb* [botany] inhabit; habitat (arboricole, accolent). *See* **-colous**

coleo- [Gr. *koleos*, sheath] *comb* sheath; scabbard (coleorhiza, coleophyllous)

coleopter- [L. *coleopterum*, beetle] *base* beetle (coleopteran, coleopterous)

coli-¹, colo- [Gr. *kolon*, intestine] *comb* colon (coliform, coloenteritis)

coli-² [L. *colum*, strainer or sieve] *comb* sieve (coliform)

coll-¹ [L. *collum*, neck] *base* neck; collar (decollate, colliform)

coll-² [Gr. *kolla*, glue] *base* glue (collenchyma, collencyte)

coll-³ [L. *collis*, hill] *base* hill (colliculate, colliculus)

-colleto- [Gr. *kolla*, glue] *base* one who glues or fastens (colletic, colletocystophore)

collodio- [Gr. *kollodes*, like glue] *comb* collodion (collodio-chloride, collodiotype)

collut- [L. *col*, together + *colluere*, wash] *base* mouthwash (collution, collutorium)

colo- [Gr. *kolos*, docked, defective] *base* curtailed; mutilated (Colobus, colocephalous)

-colous [L. *colere*, to inhabit] *comb* growing in; living among (arenicolous). *See* **-cole**

colp(o)- [Gr. *kolpos*, womb] *comb* vagina (colpocele, colpoplasty)

colubri- [L. *coluber*, serpent] *comb* snake (colubriform, colubrine)

columb- [L. *columba*, dove] *base* dove; pigeon (columbaceous, columbarium)

columelli- [L. *columella*, little column] *comb* small column (columellar, columelliform)

column- [L. *columna*, column] *base* pillar (columnar, columniferous)

coly- [Gr. *koluein*, to hinder] *comb* inhibitory (colyone, colytic) *Also* **koly-**

-com- [Gr. *komeo*, to attend to] *base* treatment (gerocomic, gerocomy)

-coma, comi-, como- [Gr. *kome*, hair] *comb* having hair or a hairlike structure (Abrocoma, comiferous, comophorous)

combur- [L *comburere*, burn up, consume] *base* burn (comburence, comburent)

comest- [L. *com-*, intensifier + *edere*, to eat] *base* edible (comestible, comestibles)

comico- [Gr. *komikos*, pert. to revelry] *comb* humorous (comico-cynical, comicography)

comit- [L. *comis*, courteous, friendly] *base* affable; courteous (comitive, comity)

comminat- [L. *com-*, intensifier + *mi-*

nari, to threaten] *base* menace, threaten (commination, comminatory)

conat- [L. *conari*, attempt, undertake] *base* attempt; desire to (conation, conative)

concavo- [L. *concavus*, hollow] *comb* concave (cancavo-concave, concavo-convex)

concess- [L. *concedere*, to grant] *base* grant; yield (concession, concessory)

conchi- [L. *concha*, shell] *comb* shell (conchiferous, conchiform)

concinn- [L. *concinnus*, fitly put together] *base* adjusted; suitable; harmonious (concinnation, inconcinnity)

-cond- [L. *condere*, put together] *base* put together (condite, incondite)

condyl- [Gr. *kondulos*, knuckle, knob] *comb* knob; protuberance (condylar, condyloid)

conger- [L. *congerere*, bring together] *base* pile (congeriate, congeries)

congru- [L. *congruere*, agree] *base* come together (congruency, incongruent)

coni-[1], -conia, conio- [Gr. *konis*, dust] *comb* dust; granules (coniosis, fibroconia, coniofibrosis). *Also* konio- (koniosis)

coni-[2], cono- Gr. *konos*, cone] *comb* cone (coniferous, conodont)

conico- [Gr. *konos*, cone] *comb* conical (conico-cylindrical, conicoid)

conist- [Gr. *konis*, dust, ashes] *base* dust (conistery)

conjugato- [L. *con-*, together + *jugum*, yoke] *comb* coupled; paired (conjugative, conjugato-palmate)

connict- [L. *con-*, with + *nictare*, to wink] *base* blink (connictation. connictatory)

conniv- [L. *con-*, with + *nivere*, to wink] *base* blink (connivance, connive)

connochaet- [Gr. *konnos*, beard + *khaite*, mane] *base* gnu (connochaetes)

conoido- [Gr. *konoeides*, cone-shaped]

comb nearly conical (conoidical, conoido-hemispherical)

conop- [Gr. *konops*, gnat] *base* gnat (Conopidae, Conops)

consil- [L. *con-*, together + *salire*, to leap] *base* in accord; agreeing (consilience, consilient)

contig- [L. *contingere*, to touch] *base* adjacent (contiguity, contiguous)

contin- [L. *continere*, hold together] *base* unceasing (continuation, continuous)

contorto- [L. *con-*, together + *torquere*, to twist] *comb* twisted (contorto-foliaceous, contortuplicate)

contra-, contro- [L. *contra*, against] *pre* against; contrary; opposite (contraband, contradiction, controversy)

contre- [Fr. *contre*, against] *pre* opposite (contrecoup, contretemps)

contum- [L. *contumax*, stubborn] *base* insolence; stubborness (contumacious, contumely)

convexo- [L. *convexus*, arched] *comb* rounded; convex (convexo-concave, convexo-convex)

-cop- [Gr. *koptein*, to beat] *base* beat; strike (apocope, syncope)

coph- [Gr. *kophos*, deaf] *base* deaf (cophosis, Cophyla)

copi- [L. *copia*, plenty] *base* abundance (copious, copiousness)

copro- [Gr. *kopros*, dung] *comb* excrement; filth (coprolite); obscenity (coprology)

coraci-, coraco- [Gr. *korax*, raven] 1. *comb* coracoid bone; beaklike (coraco-acromial); 2. crow; raven (coraciiform, coracomorphic)

coralli- [Gr. *kouralion*, coral] *comb* coral (coralligenous, corallidomous)

corb- [L. *corbus*, basket] *base* basket (corbiculate, corbula)

cord- [Gr. *korde*, string of a musical instrument] *comb* cord; sinew (cordillera, cordotomy) *Also* chord (chorditis)

cordato- [Gr. *kardia*, heart] *comb*

heart-shaped (cordate-oblong, cordato-ovate)

cordi- [Gr. *kardia*, heart] *comb* heart (cordiality, cordiform)

core-¹, coreo-, -coria, coro- [Gr. *kore*, the pupil] *comb* pupil of the eye (corelysis, coreoplasty, isocoria, coroplastic). *Also* -koria (leukokoria)

core-² [Gr. *koris*, bedbug] *base* bug (Coreoidea, coreopsis)

-cori- [L. *corium*, leather] *base* leather (coriacious, coriuym)

cormo- [Gr. *kormos*, tree trunk] *comb* trunk; stem (cormophyte, cormophyly)

-corn, corni- [L. *cornu*, horn] *comb* horn (unicorn, corniform)

corneo- [L. *corneus*, horny] 1. *comb* with a horny admixture (corneo-silicious); 2. cornea of eye (corneoiritis)

cornic- [L. *corniculum*, little horn] *base* little tentacles; antennae (cornicular, corniculate)

cornu- [L. *cornu*, horn] *base* horn (cornupete, cornucopia)

coro- [Gr. *koros*, satiety] comb satiety (acoria)

corolli- [L. *corolla*, little crown] *comb* crown; flower garland (corolliflorous, corolliform)

coron- [Gr. *korone*, crow] *base* crow's beak (coronoid)

coroni-, corono- [L. *corona*, crown] *comb* crown (coroniform, coronofacial)

-corp- [L. *corpus*, body] *base* body; bulk (corporal, incorporate)

corrig- [L. *corrigere*, to correct] *base* correction (corrigent, incorrigible)

corrugato- [L. *cor*, together + *rugare*, to wrinkle] *comb* wrinkled (corrugated, corrugato-striate)

corrusc- [L. *coruscare*, to flash] *base* flash; gleam (coruscate, coruscation)

cortici-, cortico- [L. *cortex/cortic-*, bark, rind] *comb* bark; cortex (corticiform, corticotropin)

corv- [L. *corvus*, raven] *base* crow; magpie, raven (corviform, corvine)

corybant- [Gr. *Korybas*, priest of Cymbele in Phrygia] *base* frenzied (corybantic, corybantism)

coryd- [Gr. *korudos*, lark] *base* lark (Corydalis, Corydonix)

corymbi- [Gr. *korumbos*, head or cluster] *comb* cluster (corymbiferous, corymbulose)

coryn- [Gr. *korune*, club] *base* rod; club (coryniform, corynoid)

-coryph- [Gr. *koruphe*, highest point] *base* top; summit (corypheus, coryphodon)

corys- [Gr. *korus*, helmet] *base* helmet (corysterium, coryza)

coscino- [Gr. *koskinon*, sieve] *comb* sieve (coscinomancy, Cosinoptera)

-cosm, cosmo- [Gr. *kosmos*, universe] *comb* world; universe (macrocosm, cosmotheism)

costi-, costo- [L. *costa*, a rib] *comb* rib (costiform, costotome)

coturn- [L. *coturnix*, quail] *base* quail (Coturniculus, coturnine)

cotyle-, cotyli-, cotylo- [L. *cotula*, vessel or hollow] *comb* cup-shaped; hollow; hipjoint socket (cotyledonary, cotyliform, cotylosacral)

counter- [L. *contra*, against] 1. *comb* opposite; contrary to (counterclockwise); 2. in retaliation (counterplot); 3. complementary to (counterpart)

coupho- [Gr. *kouphos*, tender] *comb* frail; fragile; tender (coupholite). *Also* koupho- (koupholite)

coxo- [L. *coxa*, hip] *comb* hip (coxodynia, coxofemoral)

-cracy [Gr. *kratos*, strength, rule] *comb* form of government (democracy, theocracy)

-craft [Swed. *kraft*, strength] *comb* work; skill; art; practice of (filmcraft, woodcraft)

cranio- [L. *cranium*, skull] *comb* skull (cranioclasm, craniofacial)

-cranter- [Gr. *kranteres*, wisdom teeth] *base* wisdom teeth (diacranteric, syncranterian)

crapul- [L. *crapula*, drunkenness] *base* excessive drinking (crapulence, crapulent)

-crasia 1. *comb* mixture (spermacrasia); 2. loss of control (coprocrasia). *Also* **-crasy** (idiocrasy)

crasp- [Gr. *kraspedon*, edge or border] *base* bordered (Craspedacusta, craspedote)

-crass- [L. *crassus*, dense, solid] *base* thickened; condensed (crassiped, incrassated)

crastin- [L. *cras*, tomorrow] *base* delay (crastination, procrastinate)

-crat [Gr. *kratos*, strength, rule] *comb* participant in government (democrat, theocrat)

-crataeg- [Gr. *krataigos*, flowering thorn] *base* hawthorn (crataegin, Crataegus)

crater- [Gr. *krater*, vessel] *base* bowl (cratera, crateriform)

crateri- [Gr. *krater*, crater of a volcano] *base* crater (crateral, crateriform)

cratic- [L. *cratis*, hurdle] *base* lattice (craticle, craticulated)

-crease [L. *crescere*, to grow] *comb* grow (increase, decrease)

crebr- [L. *creber*, frequent] *base* frequent (crebrity, crebrous)

crebri- [L. *creber*, closely placed] *comb* ridged (crebricostate, crebrisulcate)

-cred- [L. *credere*, to believe] *base* belief; trust (credulity, incredible)

-crem- [L. *cremare*, to burn] *base* burn (crematorium, incremable)

cremno- [Gr. *kremnos*, overhanging cliff] *base* precipice (cremnomania, cremnophobia)

cremo- [Gr. *kreman*, to hang] *comb* hanging (cremaster, cremocarp)

cren-¹, crenato-, crenulato- [Late L. *crenatus*, notched] *comb* notched; scalloped (crenellation, crenatoserrate, crenulato-dentate)

cren-² [Gr. *krene*, a spring] *base* fountain; spring (apocrenic, crenic)

creo- [Gr. *kreas*, flesh] *comb* flesh (creophagous, creosote) *Also* **kreo-** (kreophagy)

-crep- [Gr. *krepis*, boot, base] *base* shoe (crepidarian, hippocrepian)

-crepit- [L. *crepare*, to crackle] *base* crack; creak; crackle (crepitation, decrepit)

-crepus- [L. *creper*, dusky] *base* twilight (crepuscular, crepusculous)

-cresc- [L. *crescere*, increase] *base* grow; build up (crescitive, decrease)

crescenti- [L. *crescens*, increasing] *base* crescent (crescentiform, crescentoid)

cretaceo- [L. *creta*, chalk] *comb* [geology] chalk formation (cretaceo-oolitic, cretaceo-tertiary)

crev- [L. *crepare*, to crack] *base* crack; rift (crevasse, crevice)

cribri- [L. *cribrum*, sieve] *comb* sieve (cribriform, cribrose)

cricet- [It. *criceto*, hamster] *base* gerbil; hamster (cricetine, Cricetodon)

crico- [Gr. *krikos*, ring] *comb* ring; circle (crico-arytenoid, cricothyroid)

-crin- [Gr. *krinon*, lily] *base* cupshaped; calyx (crinoidal, crinoidean)

crini- [L. *crinis*, hair] *comb* hair (criniferous, crinite)

crino-, -crine [Gr. *krinein*, to separate] *comb* secretion (crinogenic, endocrine)

crio- [Gr. *krios*, a ram] *comb* a ram (criocephalous, criocerate)

-crisp- [L. *crispus*, curled] *base* curl; wrinkle (crispate, incrispated)

crist- [L. *crista*, crest] *base* crested (cristate, cristiform)

crit-¹ [Gr. *krites*, a judge] *base* judge; decide (critical, criticism). *Also* krit- (kritarchy)

-crit² [Gr. *kritein*, to separate] *comb* separate (hematocrit, microhematocrit)

criterio- [Gr. *kriterion*, test, standard] *base* criterion (citeriology, criterion)

crith- [Gr. *krithe*, barley] *comb* barley (crithology, crithomancy)

critico- [Gr. *krites*, judge] *comb* critical and (critico-historical, critico-theological)

croce- [L. *crocus*, saffron] *base* saffron (croceal, croceous)

crocodil- [Gr. *krokodeilos*, lizard, crocodile] *base* crocodile (crocodilian, crocodility)

cromny- [Gr. *krommuon*, onion] *base* onion (cromnyomancy, cromnyophobia)

cross- [< *across*, transverse] *comb* transverse; contrary (cross-reference, crossroads)

crosso- [Gr. *krossoi*, fringe or border] *comb* fringed; tasseled (Crossopterygian, Crossorhinus)

-crot- [Gr. *krotos*, striking, clapping] *base* beat; strike (anacrotic, catacrotic)

crotal- [Gr. *krotalon*, a rattle] *base* rattlesnake (crotaliform, crotaline)

crotaph- [Gr. *krotaphos*, the temple] *base* the temple (crotaphion)

crouno- [Gr. *krounos*, spring] *comb* spring water (crounotherapy)

cruci- [L. *crux*, cross] *comb* cross (crucial, cruciferous)

-cruent- [L. *cruentus*, bloody] *base* bloody (cruentate, incruent)

cruor- [L. *cruor*, blood] *base* blood (chlorocruorin, cruorin)

-crur- [L. *crus*, the leg] *base* leg (bicrural, crural)

crymo-, cryo- [Gr. *krumos*, cold] *comb* cold; freezing (crymophilic, cryogenics)

crypto- [Gr. *kruptos*, secret, hidden] *comb* secret; hidden; covered (cryptodirous, cryptogram)

crystallo- [Gr. *krustallos*, clear ice] *comb* crystal (crystallogenic, crystalloid)

cteino- [Gr. *kteinein*, to kill] *comb* destructive (cteinophyte)

cteno- [Gr. *kteis*, comb] *comb* comb (ctenobranch, ctenoid)

ctet- [Gr. *ktetos*, that may be acquired] *base* acquired characteristics (ctetology, ctetologist)

-cub- [L. *cubare*, to lie down] *base* lie; recline (cubicle, incubator)

cubi-, cubo- [Gr. *kubos*, a die or cube] *comb* cube; dice (cubicontravariant, cubo-octahedron)

cubil- [L. *cubile*, nest] *base* nest (cubilose)

cubito- [L. *cubitum*, elbow] *comb* [anatomy] ulna and __ (cubito-carpal, cubitidigital)

cucul- [L. *cuculus*, cuckoo] *comb* cuckoo; roadrunner (cuculiform, cuculine)

cuculli- [L. *cucullus*, cap, hood] *comb* hood; cowl (cucculate, cuculliform)

cucumi- [L. *cucumis*, cucumber] *comb* cucumber (cucumiform, Cucumis)

cucurbit- [L. *curcurbita*, gourd] *base* gourd (cucurbital, cucurbitine)

-cula, -cule, [L. *culus*, dim. suf] *suf* diminutive (Auricula, molecule)

culici- [L. *culex*, gnat or flea] *base* gnat; mosquito (culiciform, culicifuge)

culin- [L. *culina*, kitchen] *base* kitchen (culinarian, culinary)

culmi- [L. *culmus*, stalk] *comb* plant stem; straw (culmicolou, culmiferous)

culmin- [L. *culmen*, summit] *base* peak; top (culminant, culmination)

culp- [L. *culpare*, to blame] *base* fault; blame (culpable, exculpate)

cult- [L. *cultus*, worship, cultivation] *base* worship (cultish, cultism)

cultel- [L. *culter*, knife] *base* knife (cultellary, cultellation)

cultri- [L. *culter*, knife] *comb* knife (cultrirostral, cultrivorous)

-culture [L. *cultus*, attended to] *comb* tillage; raising (agriculture, viniculture)

-culum, -culus [L. *ulus*, dim. suf] *suf* diminutive (curriculum, fasciculus)

cuma- [Gr. *kuma*, wave] *base* wave; surf (cumaceous, cumaphytism)

-cumb- [L. *cumbere*, to lie down] *base* lie; recline (incumbent, recumbent)

cumulo- [L. *cumulare*, to heap up] *comb* heaplike; cumulus and __ (cumulonimbus, cumulostratus)

cunct- [L. *cunctari*, to delay] *base* delay; tardy action (cunctation, cunctator)

cunei-, cuneo- [L. *cuneus*, wedge] *comb* wedge (cuneiform, cuneoscaphoid)

cunic- [L. *cuniculus*, rabbit] *base* hare; rabbit (cuniculate, cuniculous)

cunicul- [L. *cuniculum*, underground passage; warren] *base* underground (cunicular, cuniculate)

cup- [L. *cupere*, to desire] *base* desire (concupiscence, cupidity)

cupreo-, cupri-, cupro-, cuproso- [L. *cuprium*, copper] *comb* copper; (cupreo-violaceous, cupriferous, cupromagnesite, cuproso-ferric)

cupress- [Gr. *kuparissos*, cypress] *base* cypress (cupressineous, Cupressus)

cupuli- [L. *cupa*, cup] *comb* cup (cupuliferous, cupuliform)

cur- [L. *cura*, health, attention] *base* health; healing (curate, curative)

curculion- [L. *curculio*, weevil] *base* weevil (Curculio, curculionid)

-cur(r)-, -curs- [L. *currere*, to run] *base* run; go (recurrent, cursory)

curt- [L. *curtus*, docked mutilated] *base* short; abbreviated (curtail, curtate)

curvi- [L. *curvare*, make crooked] *comb* curved; bent (curvicaudate, curvilinear)

cusp- [L. *cuspis*, point, spear] *base* point (cuspated, cuspid)

cuss- [L. *quatere*, strike forcibly] *base* strike; shake (concussion, percussion)

custod- [L. *custos*, guardian] *base* watchman (custodial, custodianship)

cutaneo- [L. *cutaneus*, of the skin] *comb* skin (cutaneo-osseous, cutaneo-skeletal)

cuti- [L. *cutis*, skin] *comb* skin (cuticle, cutisector)

-cy [L. suf–*cia*] 1. *suf* quality; fact of being; state; condition (democracy); 2. position; rank; (captaincy)

-cyam- [Gr. *kuamos*, bean] *base* bean (cyamoid, hyoscyamine)

cyano- [Gr. *kuanois*, dark blue] 1. *comb* dark blue (cyanosis); 2. cyanide (cyanohydrin)

cyathi-, cyatho- [Gr. *kuathos*, cup] *comb* cuplike (cyathiform, cyatholith)

cyber- [Gr. *kubernan*, to steer] *comb* relating to computers (cyberphobia, cyberspace)

cyclo- [Gr. *kuklos*, circle] *comb* wheel; circle; cycle (cyclograph, cyclometer)

cyclorraph- [Gr. *kuklos*, circle + *raphe*, a seam] *base* fly (Cyclorhapha, cyclorhaphous)

cyclostom- [Gr. *kuklos*, circle + *stoma*, mouth] *base* eel (cyclostomate, cyclostomatous)

cyem- [*kuema*, embryo] *base* embryo (cyema, cyemology)

cyesi-, -cyesis [*kuesis*, conception] *comb* pregnancy (cyesiognosis, polycyesis)

cygn- [Gr. *kuknos*, swan] *base* swan (cygneous, cygnine). *Also* cycn- (cycnean)

cylico- [Gr. *kulix*, cup] *base* bowl (cylicomancy, cylicotomy). *Also* kylixo-

cylindro- [Gr. *kulindros*, cylinder, roller] *comb* cylinder (cylindroconical, cylindro-ogival)

cyma-, cymato-, cymo- [Gr. *kuma*, wave] *comb* wave; billow (cymagraph, cymatolite, cymoscope) *Also* kymo- (kymograph)

cymbi-, cymbo- [Gr. *kumbe*, boat; bowl] *comb* boat; bowl (cymbiform, cymbocephalic)

cyn-, cyno- [Gr. *kuon*, dog] *comb* dog (cynanthropy, cynophobia). *Also* kyno-

cyo- [Gr. *kuos*, fetus] *comb* fetus (cyogenic, cyophoria)

cyper- [Late L. *cyperus*, sedge] *base* sedge (cyperaceous, cyperologist)

cyphell- [Gr. *kuphella*, hollow of the ear] *base* cuplike (cyphella, cyphellaeform)

cypho- [Gr. *kuphoma*, hump] *comb* humped; bent; crooked (cyphonism, cyphosis). *Also* kypho- (kyphosis)

cypriani- [Gr. *kuprios*, pert. to Cyprus, famous for worshipping Venus] *base* lewd; harlot (Cyprian, cyprianite)

cyprid- [Gr. *kuprios*, pert. to Cyprus] *base* sexual (Cypridacea, cypridophobia)

cyprin- [Gr. *kuprinos*, carp] *base* carp; goldfish; minnow (cyprinid, cypriniform)

cypsel- [L. *cypselus*, a swift] *base* swift (cypseliform, cypseline)

cyrio- [Gr. *kurios*, authorized, proper] *base* regular; proper (cyriologic, cyriological)

cyrto- [Gr. *kurtos*, curved, arched] *comb* curved; arched (cyrtoceratitic, cyrtometer)

cyst-, -cyst, cysti-, -cystis, cysto- [Gr. *kustis*, bladder, bag] *comb* like a bladder; pouch; sac; cyst (cystalgia, statocyst, cystiform, macrocystis, cystocarp)

-cyte, cyto- [Gr. *kutos*, hollow, cavity] *comb* cell (lymphocyte, cytology) *Also* cytio- (cytioderm) and cytulo- (cytulococcus)

-cythemia [Gr. *kutos*, hollow + *aima*, blood] *comb* blood cell condition (macrocythemia, leukocythemia)

D

dacn- [Gr. *daknein*, bite, sting] *base* bite; kill (dacnidine, Tridacna) *Also* daco- (Dakosaurus)

dacry(o)- [Gr. *dakruein*, weep] *comb* a tear (dacryocystitis, dacryops)

dactyl-, dactylo-, -dactylous, -dactyly [Gr. *dactulos*, finger, date] *comb* finger; toe (dactyliology, dactylology, tridactylous, brachydactyly)

dactylio- [Gr. *dactulios*, finger ring] *comb* finger ring (dactylioglyphic, dactyliomancy)

daedal- [Gr. *Daidalos*, builder of the Crete labyrinth] *base* cunning; skillful (daedalenchyma, logodaedaly)

daemono- *see* demono-

Dano- [L. *Danicus*, Danish] *comb* Danish and __ (Dano-Irish, Dano-Norwegian)

dapat- [L. *dapaticus*, sumptuous] *base* sumptuous; costly (dapatical)

daphn- [Gr. *daphne*, laurel] *base* laurel (daphniaceous, daphnomancy)

dasy- [Gr. *dasus*, think, dense, hairy]

comb hairy or wooly; thick or dense (Dasyprocta, dasyphyllous)

dasypod- [Gr. *dasus*, hairy or rough + *pous*, foot] *base* armadillo (Dasypodid, dasypodine)

dasyproct- [Gr. *dasus*, hairy + *proctos*, buttocks] *base* agouti (Dasyprocta, dasyproctid)

dativo- [L. *dativus*, of or belonging to] *comb* dative (dativo-gerundial, dativo-locative)

de- [L. *de-*, away from, down from, out of, etc.] 1. *pre* away from; off (detrain); 2. down; (decline); 3. entirely (defunct); 4. undo; reverse (defrost)

debil- [L. *debilis*, weak] *base* weakness (debilitate, debility)

dec(a)- [Gr. *deka*, ten] *comb* ten; (decagon, decalogue) *Also* deka-

decalco- [Fr. *decalquer*, counter-trace] *comb* tattoo (decalcomania, decalcophobia)

decem- [L. *decem*, ten] *base* ten (decemcostate, decemfid)

deci- [L. *decimus*, tenth] *comb* one-tenth (decimate, decimeter)

decid- [L. *de-*, down + *cadere*, to fall] falling (decidual, deciduous)

-decker [M. Du. *dec*, roof, covering] *comb* having __ decks or in layers (double-decker, three-decker)

declin- [L. *de*, down + *clinare*, bend] *base* bending, sloping (declination, declinometer)

decliv- [L. *de*, down + *clinare*, slope] *base* sloping downward (declivate, declivity)

decoct- [L. *de*, down + *coquere*, cook] *base* boiled (decoctible, decoction)

decrep- [L. *decrepitus*, very old] *base* broken down (decrepit, decrepitude)

decresc- [L. *decrescere*, decrease] *base* wane; lessen (decrescendo, decrescent)

decub- [L. *de*, down + *cubare*, to lie] *base* lying down (decubation, decubital)

decuss- [L. *decussare*, to cross] *base* divided crosswise; x-shaped (decussate, decussative)

defalc- [L. *defalcare*, cut off, take away] *base* default one's accounts (defalcate, defalcation)

degen- [L. *degeneratus*, ignoble] *base* decline; lose quality (degenerate, degenerative)

deglut- [L. *deglutinare*, swallow down] *base* swallowing (deglutition, deglutitory)

dehydro- [Gr. *de-*, privative + *hudor*, water] *comb* dehydrogenated (dehydro-chlorinate, dehydrogenizer)

de(i)- [L. *deus*, a god] *base* God (deistic, deification)

deict-, -deictic [Gr. *deiktikos*. serving to show] *base, comb* demonstrating (deictically, epideictic)

deipno- [Gr, *deipnon*, dinner] *comb* dinner (deipnophobia, Deipnosophist)

deka- [Gr. *deka*, ten] *comb* ten (dekadrachm, dekaliter) *Also* deca-

delect- [L. *delectare*, to delight] *base* please (delectable, delectation)

delet- [L. *delere*, blot out] *base* expunge, erase (delete, deletory)

deleter- [Gr. *deleisthai*, damage, spoil] *base* noxious, injurious (deleterious, deleteriously)

delinq- [L. *delinquere*, to fail] *base* fault (delinquency, delinquent)

deliqu- [L. *deliquescere*, to melt away] *base* melt, become liquid (deliquescence, deliquescent)

delo- [Gr. *delos*, evident] *comb* well-defined, limited (delomorphic, delomorphous)

delphin- [Gr. *delphis*, dolphin] *base* porpoise; dolphin (delphine, delphinoid)

delto- [Gr. *delta*, triangular Greek letter D] *comb* triangular (deltohedron, deltoidal)

-dema [Gr. *oidema*, swelling] *base* swelling (lymphedema, scleredema)

dement- [L. *de-*, out of + *mentis*, mind] *base* insane (dementate, dementia)

demi- [L. *dimidius*, half] 1. *pre* half (demivolt); 2. less than usual (demigod)

-demia [Gr. *demos*, tallow] *comb* fatty degeneration (hypertriglyceridemia, myodemia)

demo- [Gr. *demos*, the people] *comb* people (demographics, democracy)

demono- [Gr. *daimon*, god of lower rank] *comb* demon (demonocracy, demonology)

dendri-, dendro-, -dendron [Gr. *dendron*, tree] *comb* tree; treelike (dendriform, dendrology, rhododendron)

dentato- [L. *dentis*, tooth] *comb* toothed; dentate and __ (dentato-serrate, dentate-sinuate)

denti-, dento-, -dentate [L. *dentis*, tooth] *comb* tooth (dentiform, dentosurgical, multidentate). *Also* dont- (pedodontics)

deoxy- [Gr. *de-*, privative + *oxus*,

sharp, acid] *comb* oxygen removed (deoxygenize, deoxyhemoglobin)

depil- [L. *de-* away + *pilus*, hair) *base* deprive of hair (depilation, depilatory)

deprav- [L. *depravare*, corrupt] *base* perverted, corrupt (deprave, depravity)

deris- [L. *deridere*, laugh at] *base* mockery; scorn (derision, derisory)

derm-, -derm, derma, -derma, dermato-, -dermatous, -dermis, dermo- [Gr. *derma*, skin] *comb* skin; covering (dermabrasion, endoderm, dermatherm, scleroderma, dermatology, xerodermatous, epidermis, dermoneural)

dero- [Gr. *dere*, the neck] *base* animal neck (derotrematous, derotreme)

des- [OF *des-*, away from] *pre* missing; deprived of (desoxalic, desoxydation). *See* **dis-**

desicc- [L. *de-*, intensifier + *siccus*, dry] *base* dry (desiccate, desiccation)

desid- [L. *desiderare*, to desire] *base* wish; desire (desideration, desiderative)

-desis [Gr. *desis*, binding] *comb* binding (iridodesis, syndesis)

desit- [L. *desinere*, to cease] *base* final; conclusive (desition, desitive)

desmo- [Gr. *desmos*, band] *comb* bond; band; ligament (desmogen, desmognathous)

desmodont- [Gr. *desmos*, band + *odont-*, tooth] *base* bat (Desmodontes, desmodontid)

detrit- [L. *detritus*, rubbing away] *base* matter produced by wearing away (detrition, detrivorous)

deuter(o)-, deuto- [Gr. *deuteros*, second] *comb* second; secondary (deuterogamy, deutoplasm)

dexio- [Gr. *dexios*, on the right hand] *comb* on the right side (dexiocardia, dexiotropic)

dextr(o)- [Gr. *dexios*, on the right hand] 1. *comb* on the right side (dex-

trocardia); 2. [chemistry] clockwise (dextrorotatory)

di-[1] [Gr. *dis*, twice] 1. *pre* twice; double (dichroism); 2. having two (diacid)

di-[2] [L. privative] *pre* away; apart (diverse, divest). *See* **dis-**

dia- [Gr. *dia*, through] 1. *pre* through; across (diagonal); 2. apart; between (diaphony)

-diabol- [L. *diabolus*, devil] *base* devil (diabolic, diabolism)

dialy- [Gr. *dialuein*, to separate] *comb* separate; distinct (dialysepalous)

diaped- [Gr. *dia*, through + *pedan*, to leap] *base* migration (diapedesis, diapedetic)

diaphano- [Gr, *diaphanes*, transparent] *comb* transparent (diaphaneity, diaphanometer)

diaphor- [Gr. *diaphorein*, persire] *base* perspiration (diaphoresis, diaphoretic)

-diastasis [Gr. *dia*, apart + *stasis*, placing] *comb* displacement (adenodiastasis, myelodiastasis)

dicac- [L. *dicax*, witty talk] *base* satirical (dicacious, dicacity)

dicaeo- [Gr. *dikaiologia*, plea in defense] *base* jurisdiction (dicaeologist, dicaeology)

dicho- [Gr. *dikha*, apart] *comb* in two; split; separately (dichogamy, dichotomy)

dichro- [Gr. *dikhcroos*, two-colored] *comb* two-colored (dichromatic, dichromatism)

diclid- [Gr. *diklides*, valves] *base* valves (dicliditis, diclidotomy)

-dict- [L. *dictum*, a thing said] *base* say; speak; tell (contradiction, dictation)

dictyo- [Gr. *diktuon*, net] *comb* net (Dictyocysta, dictyogen)

did- [L. *didus*, dodo] *base* dodo (Dididae, didine)

didact- [Gr. *didaktikos*, apt at teaching] *base* teach (didactic, didacticism)

didelph- [Gr. *di-*, two + *delphus*, womb] *base* opossum (didelphian, didelphine)

didym-, didymo- [Gr. *didumos*, twin] *comb* twofold; relating to the testis (didymous; didymalgia)

dif- [L. *dis-*, apart] *pre* away; apart (differ, differentiate). *See* **dis-**

digitato- [L. *digitus*, finger] *comb* having fingerlike divisions (digitato-palmate, digitato-pinnate)

digiti- [L. *digitus*, finger] *comb* finger; toe (digitigrade, digitinerved)

digito- [NL. *digitalis*, digitalis] *comb* digitalis; foxglove (digitoleic acid, digitoxin)

dihydro- [Gr. *di-*, two + *hudor*, water] *comb* having two atoms of hydrogen in combination (dihydrobromide, dihydrostreptomycin)

dike- [Gr. *dike*, justice] *comb* justice (dikemania, dikephobia)

dilat- [L. *dilitare*, dilate] *base* expansion (dilitator, dilation)

diluv- [L. *diluvio*, deluge] *base* flood (antediluvian, diluvial)

(di)mid- [L. *dimidium*, half] *base* half (dimidiation, dimidiate)

(di)min- [L. *diminuere*, break into small pieces] *base* lessen (diminish, diminution)

dino-[1] [Gr. *deinos*, terrible] *comb* terrible; mighty; huge (dinosaur, Dinotherium)

dino-[2] [Gr. *dinos*, whirling] *comb* whirling (Dinoflagellata, dinoflagellate)

diomed- [Gr. *Diomedes*, hero at the siege of Troy] *base* albatross (Diomedia, Diomedeinae)

dior- [Gr. *dia*, through + *horizein*, to draw a boundary] *base* distinction; definition (diorism, dioristic)

dioscorea- [Gr. *Dioscorides*, famous botanist] *base* yam (Dioscorea, dioscoreaceous)

diphy- [Gr. *diphues*, of double form] *comb* double; bipartite (diphycercal, diphyodont)

diplo- [Gr. *diploos*, double] *comb* two; double; twin (diploblastic, diplocephaly)

diplopod- [Gr. *diploos*, double + *pous*, foot] *base* millipede (Diplopoda, diplopodal)

dipso- [Gr. *dipsa*, thirst] *comb* thirst (dipsomania, dipsosis)

diptero- [Gr. *dipteros*, two-winged] *comb* having two wings (dipterology, dipterous)

dis- 1. *pre* away; apart (dismiss); 2. deprive of (disbar); 3. cause to be the opposite of (disable); 4. fail; refuse to (disallow); 5. not (dishonest); 6. lack of (disunion) NOTE: dis- can change to **di-** (divest) or **dif-** (differ). *See* **des-**

dirig- [L. *dirigere*, to direct] *base* able to be steered (dirigent, dirigible)

discip- [L. *discipulus*, learner] *base* follower; learner (disciple, discipline)

disco- [Gr. *diskos*, disk] *comb* disk-shaped (discocarp, discophile)

discophor- [Gr. *diskos*, disk + *pherein*, to bear] *base* jellyfish; leech (discophoran, discophorous)

-disso- [Gr. *dissos*, double] *base* double (dissoconch, dissogony)

disto- [<*distant*, modeled on *centro-*] *comb* remote; farther away (distobuccal, distolabial)

diures- [Gr. *diourein*, urinate] *base* pert. to urine (diuresis, diuretic)

diurn- [L. *diurnus*, daily] *base* day (diurnal, diurnation)

diuturn- [L. *diuturnus*, of long duration] *base* lasting; long duration (diuturnal, diuturnity)

divergenti-, divergi- [L. *di-*, apart + *vergere*, incline] *comb* divergent (divergentiflorous, divergivenate)

diversi- [L. *diversus*, diverse] *comb* various (diversiflorous, diversiform)

doc- [L. *docere*, teach] *base* teach (docent, indoctrinate)

docim- [Gr. *dokimastes*, assayer, examiner] *base* testing, assaying (docimastic, docimology)

dodeca- [Gr. *dodeka*, twelve] *comb* twelve (dodecagon, dodecapetalous)

dogmato- [Gr. *dogmatikos*, dogma] *comb* pertaining to dogma (dogmatology, dogmatopoeic)

dolabri- [L. *dolabra*, hatchet or ax] *comb* ax; cleaver (Dolabrifera, dolabriform)

dolero- [Gr. *dolos*, deceit] *comb* deceptive (dolerite, dolerophanite)

dolicho- [Gr. *dolikhos*, long] *comb* long; narrow (dolichocephalic, dolichodirous)

dolio- [L. *dolium*, very large jar] *base* barrel (dolioform, Doliolum)

-dolor- [L. *dolor*, grief or pain] *base* pain; sorrow (doloriferous, dolorific)

-dom-¹ [L. *domus*, house, household] *base* house; dwelling (domestic, domestication)

-dom² [OE *dom*, position, condition] 1. *suf* rank of; position of; domain of (kingdom); 2. state of being (wisdom); 3. total of all who are (officialdom)

-don- [L. *donare*, to give] *base* give (condone, donation). *Also* **-dor-** gift (Dorothy)

-dont [Gr. *odont*, tooth] *comb* tooth (orthodontist, pedodontics). *Also* **dent-** (dentifrice)

dora- [Gr. *dora*, hide or skin] *base* fur; hide (doramania, doraphobia)

-dorm- [L. *dormire*, sleep] *base* sleep (dormant, dormitive)

dorsi-, dorso- [L. *dorsum*, the back] *comb* the back (dorsibranch, dorsoventral)

dory- [Gr. *doru*, spear] *base* spear (Doryanthes, doryphore)

dosio- [Gr. *dosis*, giving] *base* dose (dosimetric, dosiology)

dot- [L. *dotare*, to endow] *base* dowry; endowment (dotal, dotation)

double- [L. *duplus*, double] *comb* in combination (double-barreled, double-breasted)

draco-, draconi- [Gr. *drakon*, serpent, dragon] *base* dragon (dracocephalum, draconiform)

drapeto- [Gr. *drapetes*, runaway slave] *comb* flee; fugitive (drapetomania, drapetophobia)

drepani- [Gr. *drepane*, sickle] *comb* sickle (drepaniform, drepanium)

-drome, dromo-, -dromous [Gr. *dromas*, running] *comb* running; moving; race course (hippodrome, dromomania, catadromous)

droso- [Gr. *drosos*, dew, juice] *comb* dew (drosometer, drosophore)

drosophyl- [Gr. *drosos*, juice + *philos*, loving] *base* fruitfly (Drosophila, Drosophylidae)

dryo- [Gr. *drus*, tree] *base* tree (Dryopithecus, dryopithecine)

du- [Gr. *duo*, two] *pre* two (dual, duplicate)

dub- [L. *dubius*, doubtful] *base* doubtful (dubiety, indubitably)

-duc(e), -duct- [L. *ducere*, to lead] *base* lead (induce, conductor)

ducen- [L. *ducenarius*, two hundred] *base* two hundred (ducenarious, ducenary)

ductil- [L. *ductilis*, capable of being extended] *base* capable of being led or drawn (ductile, ductilimeter)

-dulc- [L. *dulcis*, sweet] *base* sweet (dulcet, dulcify)

dulo- [Gr. *doulos*, slave] *comb* slave (dulia, dulocracy). *Also* **doulo-** (doulocracy)

duo- [Gr. *duo*, two] *comb* two; double (duodrama, duologue)

duodec-, duodecim-, duoden- [Gr. *dodeka*, twelve] *base* twelve (duodecuple, duodecimfid, duodenary)

duodeviginti- [L. *duodeviginti*, eighteen] *base* eighteen (duodevigintiangular)

duplicato- [L. *duplicatus*, doubled] *comb* doubly (duplicato-dentate, duplicato-pinnate)

duplici- [L. *duplicatus*, doubled] *comb* duplex (duplicidentate, duplicipennate)

dur-, duro- [L. *durus*, hard, lasting] *base* hard; lasting (endurance, durometer)

dy-, dyo- [Gr. *duo*, two] *base* two (dyad, diarchy, Dyophysite)

dyna-, dynamo-, -dyne [Gr. *dunamis*, power] *comb* power; strength; energy (dynamic, dynamogeny, heterodyne)

-dynia [Gr. *odune*, pain] *comb* pain (gastrodynia, inguinodynia)

dys- [Gr. *dus*, bad, unlucky] *pre* hard; ill; bad; difficult (dysentery, dyslexia)

-dyte- [Gr. *duein*, to dive or go into] *base* to enter; dive (ammodyte, troglodyte)

E

e- *see* **ex-**

-ea [L. suf. *-ea*] *suf* noun ending (amenorrhea, cornea)

-eae [L. suf. *-eae*] *suf* plant tribes: plural ending (Fabineae, Gramineae)

-ean [L. suf. *-ean*] *suf* belonging to; like (Aeschylean, European)

ebon- [Gr. *ebenos*, ebony tree] *base* black (ebonize, ebony)

ebriet- [L. *ebrietas*, drunkenness] *base* drunkenness (ebriecation, ebriety)

ebullio- [L. *ebullire*, to bubble out] *base* boiling (ebulliometer, ebullioscope)

ebur- [L. *ebur*, ivory] *base* ivory (eburnation, eburneous)

ec- *see* **ex-**

ecclesiastico- [Gr. *ekklesia*, church] *comb* of the church or clergy (ecclesiastico-conservative, ecclesiastico-military)

eccrino- [Gr. *ekkrinein*, to secrete] *base* secretion (eccrinologist, eccrinology)

-echia [Gr. *ekhein*, to hold] *comb* have; retain (anterior synechia, posterior synechia)

echidno- [Gr. *ekhidna*, adder, viper] *comb* viper (echidnine, echidnotoxin)

echin- [L. *echinus*, prickly, hedgehog] *base* hedgehog; sea urchin; bristly (echinate, echiniform)

echinato-, echino- [L. *echinatus*, prickly] *comb* prickly; spiny (echinato-dentate, echinococcus)

echinoderm- [Gr. *ekhinos*, sea-urchin + *dermos*, skin] *base* hedgehog, sea-urchin (echinoderm, echinodermatous)

echinulato-, echinuli- [Gr. *ekhinos*, sea-urchin, prickly] *comb* prickly; spiny (echinulato-striate, echinuliform)

echo- [Gr. *ekhos*, sound] *comb* repeated sound (echolalia, echometry)

eco- [Gr. *oikos*, house] *comb* environment (ecologist, ecosystem)

-ecoia [Gr. *ekhouein*, to hear] *comb* hearing condition (dysecoia, oxyecoia)

ecphia- [Gr. *ekphuos*, appendix] *comb* appendix (ecphyadectomy, ecphyaditis)

-ectasia, -ectasis [Gr. *ektasia*, extension] *comb* dilation; expansion (colpectasia, anectasis)

ect(o)- [Gr. *ektos*, outside] *comb* outside; external (ectocardia, ectoderm)

-ectomy [Gr. *ektome*, cutting out] *comb* surgical operation; excision; cutting (appendectomy, bursectomy)

ectro- [Gr. *ektro*, to damage] *comb* congenital absence of a part (ectrodactyly, ectromelia)

ed-[1] [L. *edere*, to eat] *base* eat (edacious, edible)

-ed[2] [OE suf. *-ede*] *suf* having; provided with; characterized by (pileated, softhearted)

edaph- [Gr. *edaphos*, bottom] *base* floor; ground (edaphic, edaphodont)

-edema [Gr. *oidema*, swelling, tumor] *comb* swelling (myoedema, scleredema)

-edent- [L. *edentatus*, toothless] 1. *base* lacking teeth (edentulous); 2. order of New World mammals which includes armadillos, sloths, anteaters (edentate)

edi- [L. *aedificare*, to build] *base* building (edicule, edifice). *Also* aedi-

-ee [AF -*e*, p.p.] 1. *suf* recipient (appointee); 2. person (employee); 3. thing (goatee)

-een [Irish dim. -*in*] *suf* diminutive (buckeen, colleen)

-eer [L. suf. -*arius*] 1. *suf* person who does (engineer); 2. person who writes (sonneteer)

ef- *see* ex-

efficac- [L. *efficax/efficac*-, efficacious] *base* effective; competent (efficacious, efficacy)

egagro- [Gr. *aigogros*, wild goat] *base* wild goat (egagrophobia, egagropile)

ego- [L. *ego*, I] *comb* self (egomania, egotism)

egress- [L. *egressus*, a going out] *base* depart; leave (egress, egressive)

egro- [Corrupt form of *necro*-, dead] *comb* dead (egromancy, egromantic) *see* necro-

Egypto- [Gr. *aiguptos*, Egypt] *comb* Egyptian and __ (Egypto-Arabic, Egypto-Syrian)

eico- [Gr. *eikosi*, twenty] *comb* twenty (eicosanoic, eicosapentaenoic) *see* ico-

eid-, eido- [Gr. *eidos*, form] *comb* shape; form; that which is seen (eidetic, eidoclast)

eiren- [Gr. *eirene*, peace] *base* peace (eirenarchy, eirenical). *Also* iren-

eis- [Gr. *eis*, into] *pre* into (eisegesis, eisegetical)

eisoptro- [Gr. *eis*, into + *optos*, visible] *comb* mirror (eisoptromania, eisoptrophobia)

-eity [L. suf. -*tatem*] *suf* noun of quality or condition (contemporaneity, spontaneity)

eka- [Skt. *eka*, one] *comb* one (ekaholmium, ekaselenium)

ekist- [Gr. *oikos*, dwelling] *comb* settlement; house (ekistician, ekistics)

-el [L. suf. -*alis*] *suf* diminutive (satchel, tunnel)

elao-, elaeo- [Gr. *elaia*, olive tree] *comb* oil (elaolite, elaeometer) *see* eleo-

elaph- [Gr. *elaphos*, deer] *base* deer; stag (elaphine, Elaphmyces)

-elasmo- [Gr. *elasma*, metal plate] *base* metal plate (elasmognathous, elasmosaurus)

elasto- [Gr. *elastikos*, that which drives] *comb* rubber or plastic; stretchable (elastomer, elastometry)

elat- [L. *elatus*, lift up] *base* joy (elated, elation)

electro- [L. *electrum*, amber] *comb* electrical (electrobiology, electromagnetic)

eleo- [Gr. *elaia*, olive tree] *comb* oil (eleoma, eleoplast) *see* oleo-

elephant- [Gr. *elephas*, elephant, ivory] *base* elephant (elephantiasis, elephantine)

eleuthero- [Gr. *eleutheros*, free] *comb* freedom (eleutheromania, eleutheropetalous)

-ella [L. dim. -*ella*] 1. *suf* diminutive (umbrella); 2. bacteria genus (salmonella)

elytri- [Gr. *elutron*, a cover] *comb* wing case (elytriform, elytrine)

elytr(o)- [Gr. *elutron*, sheath] *comb* [medicine] vagina (elytrocele, elytropolypus)

em- [Gr. *en*, into; intensifier] 1. *pre* in (embed); 2. cause to be (empower); 3. to place (emplacement); 4. to restrict (embrace)

embado- [Gr. *embadon*, by land] *base* land (embadometrist, embadometry)

emberiz- [Gr. *ammer*, a bunting] *base* bunting (Emberiza, emberizine)

embol-, emboli-, embolo- [Gr. *embolus*, thrown in] *comb* plug; obstruction; patch; stopper (embolism, emboliform, embololalia)

embryo- [Gr. *embruos*, growing in] *comb* fetus (embryogeny, embryology)

-eme [Gr. suf. *-ema*] *suf* [linguistics] significant contrastive unit (archiphoneme, phoneme)

-emesis, -emetic, emeto- [Gr. *emesis*, vomiting] *comb* vomiting (hematemesis, antiemetic, emetophobia)

-emia [Gr. *haima*, blood] *comb* blood condition; blood disease; (anemia, leukemia). *Also* -aemia (hyperaemia)

emmen- [Gr. *emmenos*, monthly] *comb* monthly; menstrual (emmeniopathy, emmenology)

emmetrop- [Gr. *emmetros*, proportional, in measure] *base* eyes normal as to refraction (emmetrope, emmetropia)

empor- [Gr. *emperos*, merchant, traveler] *base* trade; merchant; merchandise (emporetic, emporium)

-empt- [L. *emptus*, bought] *base* buy; take (emptional, exempt)

emul- [L. *aemulus*, envious] *base* jealous; rivalrous (emulate, emulation)

emunct- [L. *emungere*, blow the nose] *base* nose blowing; excretory (emunction, emunctory)

emydo- [Gr. *emus*, tortoise] *comb* tortoise (emydian, emydosaurian)

en-[1] [Gr. *en-*, into] **1.** *pre* in; within (energy); **2.** to place (entomb); **3.** to cause to be in (enshrine); **4.** to restrict (encircle) NOTE: **en-** becomes **em-** before B and P: (embed). *See* **eis-**

-en[2] [OE suf. *-nian*] **1.** *suf* plural form (oxen); **2.** cause to be (weaken); **3.** cause to have (strengthen); **4.** made

of (wooden); **5.** female (vixen); **6.** diminutive (kitten)

enalio- [Gr. *enalios*, of the sea] *base* of the sea (enaliosaur, enaliosaurian)

enantio- [Gr. *enantios*, opposite] *comb* opposite; (enantioblastous, enantiopathic)

-enarthra- [Gr. *enarthrosis*, a kind of jointing] *base* jointed; ball-and-socket joint (enarthrodial, enarthrosis)

-ence [L. suf. *-entia*] *suf* action; state; quality (excellence). *See* **-ance**

encephalo- [Gr. *enkephalos*, in the head] *comb* brain (encephalalgia, encephalocele)

enchely- [Gr. *enkelus*, eel] *base* eel, conger (Enchelycephali, enchelycephalous)

enchor- [Gr. *en*, in + *khora*, country] *base* native, indigenous (enchorial, enchoristic)

-enchyma [Gr. *enkhein*, infuse] *comb* infusion; wavy (enchymatous, protenchyma; colpenchyma)

encom- [Gr. *enkhomion*, laudatory ode] *base* praise (encomiastic, encomium)

-ency [ME suf. *-ence*] *suf* act; fact; quality; degree; state; result (complacency, emergency)

endeca- [Gr. *hendeka*, eleven] *comb* eleven (endecagon, endecaphyllous). *Also* **hendeca-** (hendecasyllabic)

endo- [Gr. *endou*, within] *comb* inside; within (endocardium, endogamous)

-ene [Gr. suf. *-ene*] *suf* hydrocarbons (benzene, ethylene)

enerv- [L. *enervus*, without nerves or sinews] *base* weakness (enervated, enervose)

engraul- [Gr. *engraulis*, small fish] *base* anchovy (Engraulid, Engraulis)

engus- [Gr. *engus*, near at hand] *base* near (engyscope, engysseismologist)

enigmato- [Gr. *ainigma*, riddle] *comb* obscure; enigmatic (enigmatography, enigmatology)

enisso- [Gr. *enisso*, to attack] *comb* reproach; criticism (enissomania, enissophobia)

-enn- [L. *annus*, year] *base* year (biennial, centennial). *Also* **-ann-** (annual)

-enne [Fr. fem. ending] *suf* feminine ending (comedienne, Parisienne)

ennea- [Gr. *ennea*, nine] *comb* nine (enneahedron, enneander)

enneacent- [Gr. *ennea*, nine + L. *centum*, one hundred] *base* nine hundred (enneacentenary)

enneaconta- [Gr. *enneaconta*, ninety] *base* ninety (enneacontahedral)

enneakaideca- [Gr, *ennea*, nine + *deka*, ten] *comb* nineteen (enneakaidecagon, enneakaidecahedron)

-ennial [L. *annus*, year] *comb* years (biennial, novennial)

-enoic [Gr. suf. *-ene* + *-ic*] *suf* unsaturated acid (eicosatrienoic, polyenoic)

enoptro- [Gr. *enoptron*, a mirror] *comb* mirror (enoptromancy)

enosi- [Gr. *enosi*, quaking] *base* terror (enosiomania, enosiophobia)

ensi- [L. *ensis*, sword] *comb* sword-shaped (ensiferous, ensiform)

-ensis [L. suf. *-iensis*] *suf* scientific derivatives of place names (canariensis, carolinensis)

-ent [L. pp. suf. *-entis*] **1.** *suf* having the quality of (insistent); **2.** person who (superintendent); **3.** material agent (emolient). *See* **-ant**

enter- [L. *inter*, between] *pre* between; among; mutually (enterclose, entertain). *Usually* **inter-**

entero- [Gr. *enteron*, intestine] *comb* intestines (enterectomy, enteropathy)

ento- [Gr. *entos*, within] *comb* within; inner (entoglossal, entophyte)

entomo- [Gr. *entomon*, insect] *comb* insect (entomogenous, entomology)

entostho- [Gr. *entosthe*, from within] *comb* from within (entosthoblast)

entre- [Fr. *entre*, within] *base* in; undertaking (entrepeneur, entrepot)

eo- [Gr. *eos*, dawn] *pre* early time period; dawn (eohippus, eolithic)

eoso- [Gr. *eos*, dawn] *comb* dawn (eosomania, eosophobia)

-eous [L. suf. *-osus*] *suf* having the nature of; like (beauteous, gaseous)

epana- [Gr. *epi*, upon + *ana*, again] *comb* repetition (epanastrophe, epanodos)

-epeiro- [Gr. *epeiros*, continent] *base* mainland; continent (epeirogenic, epeirogeny)

epheb- [Gr. *ephebos*, youth] *base* adolescent (ephebic, ephebolic)

ephem- [Gr. *ephemeros*, lasting for a day] *base* lasting for a day (ephemeral, ephemeris)

ephipp- [Gr. *ephippios*, saddle-cloth] *base* saddle-like (Ephippiorhynchus, ephippium)

epi- [Gr. *epi*, on or upon] *pre* on; upon; up to; over; on the outside; among; beside; following (epicardium). NOTE: **epi-** can change to **ep-** (epaxial)

epiced- [L. *epicideum*, funeral song] *base* pertaining to funeral rites (epicedial, epicedian)

epige- [Gr. *epi*, on + *gea*, earth, ground] *base* living near the ground (epigene, epigeous)

episcop- [L. *episcopus*, bishop] *base* bishop (episcopate, episcopicide)

episio- [Gr. *episeion*, pubes] *comb* vulva (episiorrhagia, episiotomy)

epistem- [Gr. *episteme*, knowledge] *base* knowledge (epistemological, epistemology)

eponym- [Gr. *eponumos*, giving one's name to] *base* eponym (eponymic, eponymous)

equ- [L. *equus*, horse] *base* horse (equestrian, equine)

equi- [L. *aequus*, equal] *comb* equal; (equidistant, equidiurnal)

equiset- [L. *equus*, horse + *seta*, a bristle] *base* horsetail (equisetiform, Equisetum)

-er [L. suf. -arius] 1. suf person who (farmer) ; 2. person living in (New Yorker); 3. thing or action (double-header); 4. repeatedly (flicker); 5. comparative degree (cooler)

-erel [ME diminutive -erel] suf pejorative (doggerel, pickerel)

eremo- [Gr. eremos, desert] 1. comb alone; solitary (eremophobia); 2. of/in a desert (eremophyte)

-erethis- [Gr. erethein, to excite] base irritate, stimulate (erethism, erethistic)

-ergasia [Gr. ergon, work] comb interfunctioning of mind and body; work; activity (exergasia, hypoergasia) Also ergasio- (ergasiophobia)

ergato- [Gr. ergates, worker] comb worker (ergotocracy, ergatotelic)

ergo-, -ergic, -ergy [Gr. ergon, work] comb work; activity; result (ergonomics, neurergic, allergy)

eric- [L. erica, heath] base heath (ericaceous, ericetal)

erinac- [L. erinaceus, hedgehog] base hedgehog (erinaceid, erinaceous)

erio- [Gr. erion, wool] base wool; fiber (Eriogaster, eriometer)

eris- [Gr. eristikos, given to strife] base controversy; strife (eristic, eristical)

-ern [L. suf. -aneus] suf direction names (southern, western)

eroso- [L. erosus, incised] comb incised; indentated (erosodentate, eroso-denticulate)

erotis-, erotet- [Gr. erotan, ask] base question (erotesis, erotetic)

eroto- [Gr. erotikos, pert. to love] comb sexual desire (erotomania, erotomaniac)

err- [L. errare, to wander] base wander (errant, erratic)

eruci- [L. eruca, caterpillar] base caterpillar (eruciform, erucivorous)

eruct- [L. eructare, to belch] base belching (eructate, eructation)

-ery [ME suf. -erie] 1. suf a place to (brewery); 2. a place for (nunnery);

3. practice/act of (robbery); 4. product/goods of (pottery); 5. collection of (crockery); 6. condition/state of (slavery)

erysi- [Gr. erusipelas, red skin] comb red; inflamed (erysipelas, erysipeloid)

erythro- [Gr. eruthros, red] comb red; erythrocyte (erythema, erythrocarpous)

es- see ex-

-es [Suf. variation of -s] suf plural ending (dishes)

-esce [L. suf. -escere, in process] v. suf incomplete action (effervesce, incandesce)

-escence [L. suf. -escere, in process] n. suf something becoming (convalescence, excrescence)

-escent [L. suf. -escere, in process] adj. suf starting to be; becoming (adolescent, obsolescent)

eschar- [Gr. eskhara, scar, scab] base scarring; caustic (Escharipora, escharotic)

eschato- [Gr. eskhaton, the end] base last (eschatologist, eschatology)

escul- [L. esculentus, good to eat] base food (esculency, esculent)

-ese [L. suf. -ensis] 1. suf of a country (Portuguese); 2. of a language (Chinese); 3. in the style of (journalese)

-esis [Gr. suf. -esis, nouns of process] suf condition; process; action (anoesis, enuresis)

-esmus [Gr. n. suf. -ismos] comb spasm; contraction (tenesmic, tenesmus). Also -ismus (vaginismus)

eso- [Gr. eso, within] comb inner; within (esoderm, esotropia)

esoc- [L. esox/esoc-, pike] base pike, the fish (esocifor, esocoid)

esophag- [Gr. oisophagos, gullet] base gullet (esophageal, esophagus). Also oesophag- (oesophagalgia)

-esque [L. suf. -iscus] 1. suf in the style of (Romanesque); 2. like (picturesque)

-ess [Gr. suf. *-issa*] *suf* female who (actress, princess)

esse- [L. *esse*, to be] *base* being; existence (essence, essential)

-est [Gr. suf. *-istos*] *suf* superlative degree (coolest, tallest)

-esthesia, esthesio- [Gr. *aesthesis*, feeling] *comb* sensation; perception (myesthesia, esthesiogenic)

estu- [L. *aestuare*, to boil] *base* 1. boil (estuant); 2. tide (estuary). *Also* aestu-

esur- [L. *esurire*, be hungry] *base* hunger; appetite (esurient, esurine)

-et [Fr. suf. *-et*] *suf* diminutive (pullet, rivulet)

-eth [OE suf. *-the*] *suf* ordinal numbers (twentieth, fiftieth)

ethico- [Gr. *ethikos*, moral] *comb* ethical and (ethico-political, ethico-religious)

ethmo- [Gr. *ethmos*, strainer] *comb* sieve; ethmoid bone (ethmomaxillary, ethmo-turbinal)

ethno- [Gr. *ethnos*, people, nation] *comb* race; people; culture; nation (ethnocentric, ethnology)

etho- [Gr. *ethon*, being accustomed] *comb* character; behavior (ethology, ethopoietic)

-etic [Gr. suf. *-etikos*] *suf* adjective ending (kinetic, pathetic)

etio- [Gr. *aitia*, cause or reason + *logia*, discourse] *comb* cause; origin (etiologist, etiology) *Also* aetio- (aetiology)

-ette [OF suf. *-et*] 1. *suf* diminutive (dinette); 2. female (suffragette); 3. substitute (leatherette)

-etum [L. suf. *-etum*] *suf* a grove of the plant specified (arboretum, pinetum)

etym- [Gr. *etumon*, the true, literal, historical sense of a word] *base* root or primitive meaning (etymologist, etymology)

eu- [Gr. *eu-*, good] *pre* good; well (eulogy, euphony)

eulog- [Gr. *eulogia*, praise, blessing] *base* laudatory speech (eulogize, eulogy)

-eum [Gr. suf. *-aios*] *suf* scientific name ending (ileum, peritoneum)

-eur [L. suf. *-or*] *suf* one who (hauteur, voyeur)

euro- [Gr. *Euros,* east or east-southeast wind] *comb* east (euroboreal, Eurus)

Euro- [Gr. *Europe,* Europe] *comb* European (Eurodollars, Europocentric)

Europaeo-, Europeo- [Gr. *Europe,* Europe] *comb* European (Europaeo-Siberian, Europeo-Asiatic)

eury- [Gr. *eurus,* broad] *comb* [science] broad; wide (eurycephalic, eurystomatous)

-eus [L. suf. *-eus*] *suf* scientific name ending (aculeus, nucleus)

eusuch- [Gr. *eu*, good + *soukhos*, crocodile] *base* alligator, crocodile (Eusuchia, eusuchian)

eutax- [Gr. *eutakhs*, good order] *base* good or right order (eutaxiology, eutaxy)

even- [OE *efen*, even] *comb* smooth; consistent (even-handed, even-tempered)

ever- [OE *aefre*, ever] *comb* always (ever-abiding, everlasting)

ex- [L. *ex*, out of, away from] 1. *pre* from; out (expel); 2. beyond (excess); 3. away from; out of (expatriate); 4. thoroughly (exterminate); 5. upward (exalt); 6. not having (exanimate); 7. former (ex-husband). NOTE: ex- can change to: e- (eject); ec- (eccentric); ef- (efferent); es- (escape)

exa- *comb* quintillion (exahertz, exameter)

exanim- [L. *exanimare*, deprive of life] *base* without life (exanimate, exanimation)

excern- [L. *excernere*, to excrete] *base* evacuate, discharge (excernant)

excito- [L. *excitare*, excite] *comb* [anatomy] stimulating (excitomotor, excito-nutrient) excub- [L. *excubatio*, keeping watch] *base* watchman (excubation, excubitorium)

-exia *see* -orexia

exig- [L. *exigere*, to exact] **1.** *base* demanding (exigency); **2.** scanty (exiguous)

exo- [Gr. *exo*, outside] *pre* without; outside; outer part (exocardia, exogamous)

exousia- [Gr. *exousia*, authority] *comb* authority (exousiastic)

exped- [L. *expedire*, dispatch] *base* promptness, speed (expeditious, expeditory)

explanato- [L. *explanatus*, flattened, spread out] *comb* spread out in a plane or flat surface (explanate, explanato-foliaceous)

expurg- [L. *expurgare*, purge] *base* remove, purge (expurgate, expurge)

extero- [L. *externus*, external + *-ceptor*, receive] *comb* outside (exteroceptive, exteroceptor)

extra-, extro- [L. *extra-*, beyond, outside] *pre* outside; beyond; more than; besides (extraordinary, extrovert)

exuv- [L. *exuere*, cast off, molt] *base* shed, molt, cast off (exuvial, exuviate)

-ey [variant of *-y*] *suf* characterized by; inclined to (clayey, gooey)

F

-faba-, -fabi- [L. *faba*, bean] *base* bean (fabaceous, fabiform)

-fabr- [L. *fabricari*, make, construct] *base* make; construct (fabrication, fabricator)

fabul- [L. *fabula*, fable] *base* tale (fabulist, fabulous)

-fac-, -fec-, -fic- [L. *facere*, to do] *base* make; do (factory, efficient, fictitious)

-facient [L. *facere*, to do] *comb* causing to become; making; (calefacient, liquefacient)

facil- [L. *facilis*, easy] *base* easy (facile, facilitate)

facin- [L. *facinorosus*, atrocious, wicked] *base* wicked; vile (facinorous, facinorously)

facio- [L. *facies*, face] *comb* face (facioplasty, facioplegia)

-faga- [L. *fagus*, beech] *base* beech (fagaceous, Fagus)

fagopyr- [L. *fagopyrum*, buckwheat] *base* buckwheat (fagopyrism)

-falc- [L. *falx/falc-*, sickle] *base* sickle; hooked (falcate, falciform)

falco-, falconi- [L. *falco*, falcon < its hooked, sickle-like claws] *base* falcon; kestrel; hawk (falconine, falconry)

fam- [L. *fames*, hunger] *base* hunger (famelic, famished]

fan- [Gr. *phanos*, torch, lantern] *base* lighthouse; beacon (fanal)

farct- [L. *farcere*, to stuff] *base* to stuff; obstruct (infarct, infarction)

farin- [L. *farina*, meal, grain] *base* flour (farinaceous, farinose)

farr-, farrag- [L. *far*, spelt] *base* mixed feed grains; spelt (confarreation, farraginous)

fasciculato- [L. *fasciculus*, small bundle] *comb* arranged in a bundle (fasciculato-glomerate, fasciculato-ramose)

fascio- [L. *fascia*, bundle or band] *comb* fibrous tissue; fascia; bundle (fasciation, fasciotomy)

fascin- [L. *fascinnum*, witchcraft] *base* bewitched (fascinate, fascinous)

fastid- [L. *fastidium*, loathing] *base* disgust (fastidious, fastidiousness)

fastig- [L. *fastigatus*, sloping] *base* gabled; pointed; tapered (fastigate, fastigiated)

fati- [L. *fatum*, fate] *base* prophet (fatidic, fatiferous)

fatisc- [L. *fatiscere*, open in chinks] *base* cleft (fatiscence, fatiscent)

fatu- [L. *fatuus*, foolish] *base* foolish (fatuitous, fatuous)

fauc- [L. *faux/fauc-*, throat] *base* throat (faucal, fauces)

faust- [L. *faustus*, favored] *base* fortune; chance (faustitude, faustity)

fav- [L. *faveolus*, honeycomb-like cell] *base* honeycomb (faveolate, faviform)

favill- [L. *favilla*, embers] *base* ashes (favillous)

favon- [L. *Favonius*, west wind] *base* west wind (favonian, favonious)

favoso- [L. *favus*, honeycomb] *comb* honeycombed (favose, favoso-dehiscent)

febri- [L. *febris*, fever] *comb* fever (febrifacient, febrifuge)

-fec-[1] [L. *facere*, to do] *base* make; do (effective). *See* **fac-**

-fec-[2] [L. *feces*, dregs] *base* filth; dregs (feculence, feculent)

fedi- [L. *federe*, to league together] *base* compact; covenant (federation, fedifragous)

fel- [L. *felis*, cat] *base* cat (Felidae, feline)

felic- [L. *felix*, happy] *base* happy (felicify, felicitation)

femin- [L. *femina*, woman] *base* woman (feminine, feminization)

femto- [ON *fimmtan*, fifteen] *pre* one-quadrillionth (femtometer, femtovolt)

fener- [L. *fenus/fener-*, proceeds, profit] *base* lending on interest (fenerate, feneration)

fenest- [L. *fenestra*, window] *base* window (fenestral, defenestration)

-fer [L. *ferre*, to carry] *comb* one that bears; one that produces (aquifer, conifer)

-fer- [L. *fera*, wild animal] *base* wild animal (feral, ferine)

ferment- [L. *fermentum*, leaven, yeast] *base* yeast (fermentable, fermentareous)

feroc- [L. *ferox/feroc-*, fiece, savage] *base* bold; fierce (ferocious, ferocity)

-ferous [L. *ferre*, to carry] *comb* bearing; producing; yielding (coniferous, pestiferous)

ferri-, ferro- [L. *ferrum*, iron] *comb* containing ferric iron (ferricyanide, ferromagnetism)

ferrug- [L. *ferrum*, iron] *base* iron-rust color (ferruginous, ferrugo)

ferul- [L. *ferula*, rod, whip] *base* rod; stalk (ferulaceous, ferule)

ferv- [L. *fervere*, boil, glow] *base* boil; glow (fervency, fervidity)

fescinn- [L. *Fescennia*, city in Tuscany] *base* obscene, scurrilous (fescinnine, Fescinnines)

-fest [L. *festum*, holiday] *comb* assembly or celebration (chilifest, songfest)

festin- [L. *festinatio*, haste] *base* haste; speed (festinate, festination)

festuc- [L. *festuca*, stalk, straw] *base* stalk; straw (Festuca, festucine)

fetid- [L. *fetidus*, stinking] *base* stink (fetid, fetidness)

fibri-/fibro- [L. *fibra*, fiber] *comb* fiber (fibriform, fibrocystic)

fibrilloso- [L. *fibrilla*, fibril] *comb* fibril-shaped (fibrilloso-squamulous, fibrilloso-striate)

fibrino- [L. *fibra*, fiber] *comb* fibrin (fibrinogen, fibrinoplastic)

fibroso- [L. *fibra*, fiber] *comb* fibrous (fibroso-calcareus, fibroso-cartilaginous)

-fic [L. *facere*, to make] *comb* making; creating (beatific, scientific). *See* **fac-**

-fication [L. suf. *-ficatio*] *comb* a making; a creating; a causing (amplification, calcification)

fici- [L. *ficus*, fig] *base* fig (ficiform, ficoid)

fict- [L. *facere*, to make] *base* made up (fiction, fictitious)

-fid-[1] [L. *fides*, trust] *base* faith; belief (confide, fidelity)

-fid-[2] [L. *findere*, to split] *comb* cleft; segment (multifid, pennatifid)

figur- [L. *figure*, figure] *base* form; shape (disfiguration, figurative)

fil-[1]**, fili-, filo-** [L. *filum*, thread] *comb* threadlike (filament, filigrain, filoplume)

fil-[2] [L. *filius/filia*, son/daughter] *base* child (affiliation, filial)

filamento- [L. *fila*, thread] *comb* threadlike (filamento-caudal, filamento-cribrate)

filari- [NL *filaris*, thread] *base* slender worm (filarial, filariform)

filic- [L. *filix/filic-*, fern] *base* fern (filiciform, filicology)

fim-, fimi- [L. *fimus*, dung] *comb* dung (fimetic, fimicolous)

fimbr- [L. *fimbria*, fringe] *comb* fringe; border (fimbrial, fimbricate)

fimbriato- [L. *fimbriatus*, fringed] *comb* fringed with hairs (fimbriato-ciliate, fimbriato-lacinate)

fimbrilli- [L. *fimbrilla*, small fringe] *comb* small fringe (fimbrillate, fimbrilliferous)

-fin- [L. *finis*, end] *base* end; limit (finite, infinity)

Finno- [Fin. *Suomennmaa*, swampy region] *comb* Finnish; (Finno-Ugrian, Finno-Ugric)

fissi- [L. *fissus*, cleft] *comb* [anatomy] cleft (fissicostate, fissidactyl)

fissuri- [L. *fissura*, cleft] *comb* fissure (fissuriform)

fistul- [L. *fistula*, pipe, reed] *base* reed; pipe; tube (fistuliform, fistulous)

flabelli- [L. *flabellum*, fan] *comb* fanlike (flabellifoliate, flabelliform)

flacc- [L. *flaccus*, flabby] *base* drooping; weak (flaccid, flaccidity)

-flagel- [L. *flagellare*, scourge] *base* whip; lash (flagellate, flagelliferous)

flagit- [L. *flagitare*, urge with violence] *base* vicious; wicked (flagitious, flagitiousness)

-flat- [L. *flatus*, blowing, snorting] *base* windy; gassy (flatulence, flatulent)

flavido- [L. *flavus*, yellow] *comb* yellowish (flavido-alba, flavido-cinerascent)

-flavin [L. *flavus*, yellow] *comb* natural derivatives of flavin (lactoflavin, riboflavin)

flavo- [L. *flavus*, yellow] 1. *comb* yellow (flavopurpurin); 2. flavin (flavoprotein)

fleb- [L. *flebilis*, tearful] *base* weeping; doleful (flebile)

-flect-, -flex-, flexi- [L. *flectere*, bend] *base* bend (inflection, flexible, flexicostate)

-flet- [L. *fletus*, tears] *base* weep; cry (fletiferous)

flexuoso- [L. *flectere*, bend] *comb* winding; bending; undulating (flexuoso-clavate, flexuoso-convex)

-flocc- [L. *floccus*, lock of wool] *base* wool; tuft (floccose, flocculent)

flori-, -florous [L. *flos*, flower] *comb* flower; having flowers (floriferous, multiflorous)

-flu- [L. *fluere*, flow] *base* flowing (fluent, fluid)

flucti- [L. *fluctus*, wave] *comb* undulation; wave (fluctifragous, fluctisonant)

flum- [L. *flumen*, river] *base* river (flume, fluminal)

fluo-, fluor-, fluoro- [L. *fluere*, flow] *comb* fluorine; fluorescent (fluophosphate, fluorhydric, fluoroscope)

-fluv- [L. *fluere*, flow] *base* flowing (effluvia, fluviatile)

fluvio- [L. *fluvius*, river] *comb* [geology] river; stream (fluvio-marine, fluvio-terrestrial)

fod- [L. *fodere*, dig up] *base* dig; burrow (exfodiation, fodient)

-fold [AS multiplicative suf. *-feald*] 1. *suf* having parts (twofold); 2. larger; more (hundredfold)

foliato- [L. *foliatus*, leafy] *comb* leaflike (foliato-explanate, foliato-ramose)

folii-, folio-, -folious [L. *folium*, leaf]
comb leaf (foliiferous, foliolar, unifo-
lious)

follic- [L. *folliculus*, small bag] *base*
tube; small bag (follicle, follicular)

fomen- [L. *fomentum*, warm lotion]
base heat up; incite (foment, fomen-
tation)

-foot(er) [OE *fot*, foot] *comb* so many
feet long (six-footer, twelve-footer)

for- [Dan. pref. *for-*] 1. *pre* away; apart;
off (forgo); 2. very much (forlorn)

foramin- [L. *foramina*, hole] *base* hole
(foramiferous, foraminate)

forbi- [Gr. *phorbe*, fodder, forage] *base*
grasshopper (forbivorous)

-forc-, -fort- [L. *fortis*, strong] *base*
strength (enforcement, fortification)

fore- [AS *fore*, before] 1. *pre* before
(forecast); 2. front part of (forehead)

-forfic- [L. *forfex/forfic-*, scissors] *base*
scissors; deeply notched (forficate,
forficulate)

forficul- [L. *forficula*, earwig] *base* earwig (forficulate, forficulid)

-foris- [L. *foris*, outside] *base* outside
(forisfamiliate, forisfamiliation)

-form [L. *forma*, shape] 1. *suf* shaped
like (oviform); 2. having __forms
(uniform)

-formic- [L. *formica*, ant] *base* ant
(formicary, formication)

formo- [L. *formica*, ant] *comb* [chem-
istry] formic acid (formobenzoate,
formo-benzoic)

-fornic- [L. *fornix*, arch] *base* arch;
vault (fornication, forniciform)

fortuit- [L. *fortuitus*, accidental] *base*
happening by chance (fortuitous,
fortuity)

foss- [L. *fossilis*, dug out] *base* dig (fossil, fossorial)

fov- [L. *fovea*, pit] *base* pitted; pock-
marked (foveate, foveolet)

-fract- [L. *fractus*, broken] *base* break
(fraction, fracture). *Also* -frag- and -
frang-

fracto- [L. *fractus*, broken] *comb*

ragged mass of cloud (fracto-nim-
bus, fracto-stratus)

-frag- [L. *frangere*, to break] *base* break
(fragile, fragmented). *Also* -fract-
and -frang-

fraga- [L. *fraga*, strawberry] *base*
strawberry (Fragaria, fragarol)

frambes- [L. *frambesia*, raspberry]
base raspberry-like (frambesia,
frambesioma)

Franco- [L. comb. form *Franci-*, the
Franks] *comb* French (Franco-Amer-
ican, Franco-Canadian)

-frang- [L. *frangere*, to break] *base*
break (frangible, irrefrangible). *Also*
-fract- and -frag-

frat- [L. *frater*, brother] *base* brother
(fraternity, fratricide)

-frax- [L. *fraxinus*, ash tree] *base* ash
tree (fraxetin, fraxin)

-frem- [L. *fremere*, roar, growl] *base*
roar; murmur, thrill (fremescent,
fremitus)

frend- [L. *frendere*, to gnash the teeth]
base grind; gnash (frendent, fren-
dently)

frenet- [OF *frenetique*, frenzied] *base*
frenzied (frenetic, frenetical)

freno- [L. *fraena*, bridle] *comb* re-
straining (frenosecretory, frenotomy)

-frig- [L. *frigor*, cold] *base* cold (frigid-
ity, frigorific)

-fringill- [L. *fringilla*, small bird] *base*
finch (fringillaceous, fringilliform)

from- [Fr. *fromage*, cheese] *base* cheese
(fromologist, fromology)

-frond- [L. *frondere*, to put forth leaves]
base leaf (frondent, frondivorous)

fronto- [L. *frons*, the brow] 1. *comb*
frontal bone (fronto-parietal); 2. meteorological front (frontogenesis)

fructi-, fructo- [L. *fructus*, fruit] *comb*
fruit; fructose (fructiferous, fructo-
suria)

frug-¹ [L. *frux*, fruit] *base* fruit; fructose (frugiferous, frugivorous)

frug-² [L. *fruges*, fruits of the earth]
base sparing; thrifty (frugal, frugality)

-frument- [L. *frumentum*, grain, corn] *base* grain; cereal; corn (frumentaceous, frumentarious)

frust- [L. *frustum*, piece] *base* fragment; piece (frustulent, frustulose)

fruticuloso- [L. *fruticulus*, small shrub] *comb* shrub-like (fruticuloso-hylocomiosum, fruticuloso-ramose)

-fuc- [L. *fucus*, seaweed] *base* seaweed (fucoid, fucivorous)

-fuge, fugal [L. *fugere*, flee] *comb* driving out; driving away (febrifuge, vermifugal)

-ful [OE *full*, full] **1.** *suf* full of (painful); **2.** having qualities of (masterful); **3.** having ability to (forgetful); **4.** amount that fills (handful)

fulic- [L. *fulica*, coot] *base* coot (fulicarian, fulicinae)

-fulg- [L. *fulgur*, flashing] *base* bright; flashing (fulgurant, fulguration)

-fulig- [L. *fuligo*, soot] *base* black; sooty (fuliginated, fuliginous)

fuligul- [L. *fulica*, coot] *base* sea duck (Fuligulinae, fuliguline)

-fulmin- [L. *fulminare*, hurl lightning] *base* lightning; thunder (fulminant, fulmination)

-fulv- [L. *fulvus*, flame-colored] *base* tawny; yellow-brown (fulvescent, fulvous)

-fum- [L. *fumus*, smoke] *base* smoke (fumid, fumigate)

-fun- [L. *funis*, rope] *base* rope (funambulation, funambulist)

-fund- [L. *fundamentum*, bottom] *base* bottom; base (fundament, fundamental)

-fundi- [L. *funda*, sling] *base* sling (fundiform, fundiform ligament)

funest- [L. *funestus*, deadly] *base* fatal; deadly; disastrous (funest, funestous)

fungi- [L. *fungus*, mushroom] *comb* fungus (fungicide, fungivorous)

funi- [L. *funis*, rope or cord] *comb* cord; rope; fiber (funiculus, funiform)

fur-[1] [L. *furia*, anger] *base* angry (furious, furor)

fur-[2] [Gr. *phor*, thief] *base* stealing (furacious, furacity)

-furc- [L. *furca*, fork] *base* forked (bifurcation, furcular)

-furfur- [L. *furfur*, bran] *base* bran; dandruff (furfuraceous, furfural)

furt- [Gr. *phor*, thief] *base* theft; stealth (furtive, furtively)

furunc- [L. *furunculus*, a boil] *base* having boils (furuncle, furunculosis)

-fus- [L. *fundere*, to pour] *base* flow; pour; melt (infusion, transfusion)

fusco- [L. *fuscus*, dark] *comb* dark brown; dusky; gloomy (fusco-ferruginous, fusco-piceous)

fusi-, fuso- [L. *fusus*, spindle] *comb* spindle; rod (fusiform, fusobacterium)

-fustig- [L. *fustigare*, beat with a cudgel] *base* beat; cudgel (fustigate, fustigation)

futil- [L. *futilis*, untrustworthy] *base* useless (futile, futility)

-fy [L. suf. *-ficare*] **1.** *suf* make; cause to be (deify); **2.** cause to have; imbue with (dignify); **3.** become (putrefy)

G

-gaea/-gea [Gr. *Gaea*, goddess of Earth] *comb* earth (Paleogaea, Pangea)

galact(o)- [Gr. *galakt*, milk] *comb* milk; milky (galactagogue, galactocele)

-gale[1] [Gr. *gale*, weasel, ferret] *base* weasel (phascogale, potamogale)

-gale-[2] [Gr. *galeos*, shark] *base* shark (galeidan, galeod)

-gale-³ [Gr. *gale*, cat] *base* cat (galeanthropy, galeophobia)

-galea- [L. *galea*, helmet] *base* helmet (galeate, galeated)

galero- [Gr. *galeros*, cheerful] *comb* cheerful (galeropia, galeropsia)

-gallinac-, -gallinag- [L. *gallina*, hen] *base* poultry: chicken, grouse, partridge, pheasant, quail, turkey, woodcock (gallinaceous, gallinaginous)

Gallo- [L. *Gallus*, a Gaul] *comb* French; Gallic (Gallomania, Gallophobia)

galvano- [It.<. *Luigi Galvani*] *comb* galvanic; electricity (galvanocaustic, galvanometer)

gambog- [ML gambogium, < *Camboja*, Cambodia] *base* brilliant yellow (gambogian, gambogic)

gameto- [Gr. *gamein*, to marry] *comb* gamete; union (gametophore, gametophyte)

-gammar- [Gr. *kammaros*, lobster] *base* sea crab; lobster (gammarid, gammarolite)

gamo- [Gr. *gamos*, marriage] **1.** *comb* sexually united (gamogenesis); **2.** joined (gamosepalous)

-gamous, -gamy [Gr. *gamos*, marriage] *comb* marrying; uniting sexually (polygamous, polygamy)

ganglio- [Gr. *ganglion*, tumor] *comb* nerve cells; swelling; ganglion (ganglioform, ganglioplexus)

-gano- [Gr. *ganos*, brightness] *base* bright; shiny (ganocephalus, ganoidal)

garrul- [L. *garrulus*, chattering] *base* chatter; magpie, jay (garrulous, garruline)

gaso- [word invented by Flemish chemist Van Helmont < Gr. *chaos*] *comb* gas (gasohol, gasometer)

gastero-, -gastria, gastro- [Gr. *gaster*, stomach] *comb* stomach (gasteropod, microgastria, gastroenteritis)

gastropod- [Gr. *gaster*, stomach + *pod*, foot] *base* snail (gasteropodous, gastropodal)

-gate [< Watergate scandal] *comb* [journalism] concealed scandal (Enrongate, Irangate)

gato- [ML *gattus* < L. *cattus*, cat] *comb* cat (gatomania, gatophobia)

gaud- [L. *gaudium*, gladness, joy] *base* joy (gaudiloquence, gaudy)

gavi- [L. *gavia*, sea-mew] *base* gull (Gaviae, gavialid)

gavial- [Hindi *ghariyal*, crocodile] *base* crocodile (Gavialidae, gavialoid)

-gea- [Gr. *ge*, earth] *base* earth (epigeal, Pangea)

gecco- [NL. *geccon*, gecko] *base* gecko or wall lizard (gecconoid, geccotoid)

geisso- [Gr. *geisson*, cornice] *comb* cornice (Geissorhiza, geissospermine)

geitono- [Gr. *geiton*, neighbor] *base* neighbor (geitonogamy, geitonophobia)

-gel-¹ [L. *gelum*, frost, cold] *base* ice; frost; freeze (gelidity, regelation)

-gel-² [Gr. *gelan*, to laugh] *base* laughter (Gelasimus, gelastic)

gelatino- [L. *gelatus*, frozen] *comb* gelatin (gelatino-albuminous, gelatino-chlorid)

-gemelli- [L. *gemellus*, twin] *base* twins (Gemellaria, gemelliparous)

-gemin- [L. *geminus*, born at the same time] *base* double (gemination, geminiflorous)

gemm-¹ [L *gemma*, swelling, bud] *base* leaf buds (gemmaceous, gemmate)

gemm-² [L. *gemmarius*, pert. to gems] *base* jewel (gemmary, gemmiferous)

-gen [L. *genus*, produced] **1.** *comb* something that produces; origin (oxygen); **2.** something produced (endogen). *Also* -genic (endogenic); -genous (endogenous); -geny (endogeny)

-genesis [Gr. *genesis*, origin, source] *comb* origination; creation; formation; evolution (abiogenesis, parthenogenesis)

-geneth- [Gr. *genethle*, race, stock, family] *base* birthday (genethliacon, genethlialogy)

-genetic [Gr. *genesis*, origin, source] *comb* origin (phylogenetic)

-genia, genio-, geny-¹ [Gr. *geneion*, chin, beard] *comb* jaw; cheek; chin (microgenia, genioplasty, genyplasty)

genic-, genu- [L. *genu*, knee] *base* knee (geniculate, genuflect)

genito- [L. *genitus*, begotten] *comb* genital (genitocrural, genitourinary)

geno- [Gr. *genos*, sex, kind] *comb* race; genetic makeup (genoblast, genotype)

-geny² [Gr. *genos*, sex, kind] *comb* product of (cosmogeny, phylogeny)

geo- [Gr. *geo*, earth, land, country] *comb* earth (geocentric, geophagy)

gephyr- [Gr. *gephura*, bridge] *base* bridge (gephyrocercal, gephyrophobia)

ger-¹ [L. *gerere*, carry on, perform] *base* hold; manage (gerenda, gerent)

ger-² [Gr. *geras*, old age] *base* old age (gerontological, geriatric)

gerasco- [Gr. *geras*, old age] *comb* aging (gerascophobia)

Germano- [L. *Germanus*, German] *comb* German (Germanophile, Germanophobe)

gero-, geronto- [Gr. *geras*, old age] *comb* old; elderly (gerodontics, gerontology)

-gerous [L. *gerere*, carry, perform] *comb* producing; bearing; carrying (cerigerous, dentigerous)

gestat- [L. *gestare*, to bear or carry] *base* carrying; pregnancy (circumgestation, gestation)

gestic- [L. *gestus*, gesture] *base* to make gestures (gesticulate, gesticulatory)

-geton- [Gr. *geiton*, neighbor] *base* neighbor (Potamogeton illinoensis, Potamogeton pectinatus)

geum-, geumat- [Gr. *geusis*, sense of taste] *base* taste (geumaphobia, geumatophobia)

-geusia [Gr. *geusis*, sense of taste] *comb* taste (ageusia, parageusia)

gibboso- [L. *gibberosus*, hunched] *base* rounded; humped; convex; protuberant (gobboso-glomerate, gibboso-lobate)

giga- [Gr. *gigas*, giant] *pre* billion (gigabyte, gigacycle)

giganto- [Gr. *gigas*, giant] *comb* gigantic; large (gigantology, gigantomachia)

gilv- [L. *gilvus*, pale yellow] *base* yellow (gilvous)

gingivo- [L. *gingivoe*, the gums] *comb* gums (gingivoglossitis, gingivostomatitis)

-gingly- [Gr. *ginglumos*, hinge joint] *base* hinge (ginglyform, ginglymoid)

glabello- [L. *glaber*, smooth] *comb* space between the eyebrows (glabellous, glabello-occipital)

-glabr- [L. *glaber*, smooth] *base* smooth; bald (glabrate, glabrous)

glacio- [L. *glacies*, ice] *comb* glacier; ice (glacio-aqueous, glaciologist)

gladi- [L. *gladius*, sword] *comb* sword (gladiator, gladiolus)

gland- [L. *glans*, acorn] *base* 1. acorn (glandiferous); 2. yellow-brown (glandaceous)

glare- [L. *glarea*, gravel] *base* gravel; sand (glareose, glareous)

glauco- [Gr. *glaukos*, bluish-green, gray] *comb* bluish-green; gray; silvery; opaque (glaucoma, glaucopyrite)

-glea [Gr. *gloia*, glue] *comb* glue; cement (mesoglea) *Also* -gloia, -gloea

-gleb- [L. *glebosus*, full of clods] *base* clod; lump; dirt (glebulose, glebous)

gleno- [Gr. *glene*, socket] *comb* shallow joint-socket (gleno-humeral, glenovertebral)

-glia, glio- [Gr. *glia*, glue] *comb* glue; gluelike (neuroglia, glioblastoma)

glico- *see* gluco-

-glir- [L. *glis*, dormouse] *base* dormouse (gliriform, glirine)

globi-, globo- [L. *globus*, ball] *comb* round; ball-shaped; spherical (globiferous, globospherite)

glom- [L. *glomus*, ball, round heap] *base* cluster; ball (conglomeration, glomerulus)

gloio- [Gr. *gloia*, glue] *comb* glue (gloiocarp, Gloiopeltis)

glosso- [Gr. *glossa*, tongue] 1. *comb* of the tongue (glossoplegia); 2. the tongue plus (glossopharyngeal); 3. of words; of language (glossology). *Also* -glossia (macroglossia)

-glot, glotto- [Gr. *glotta*, tongue] *comb* language, communication in; languages, knowledge of (polyglot, glottogony)

gluco- [Gr. *glukus*, sweet] *comb* glycerin; glycerol; glycogen; sugar; (glucokinase)

glut- [L. *gluteus*, buttocks] *base* rump (gluteofemoral, gluteus maximus)

-glutin- [L. *agglutinare*, to fasten with glue] *base* glue (agglutinate, glutinize)

glutt- [L. *gluttire*, devour] *base* eat; gulp (glutton, gluttony)

glycero-, glyco- [Gr. *glukus*, sweet] *comb* glycerin; glycerol; glycogen; sugar (glycerolysis, glycogenesis)

glycyr- [Gr. *glukus*, sweet + *hrizha*, root] *base* licorice (glycyrize, Glycyrrhiza)

-glyph [Gr. *gluphein*, carve] *comb* carve; engrave; notch (diglyph, hieroglyph)

-glypha [Gr. *gluphein*, to carve] *comb* [zoology] snakes with grooved fangs (Opisthoglypha, proteroglypha)

glypto- [Gr. *gluphein*, to carve] *comb* carved; engraved (glyptodont, glyptograph)

gnatho-, -gnathous [Gr. *gnathos*, jaw] *comb* [zoology] jaw (gnathodynamics, prognathous)

-gnomy, -gnosia, -gnosis, -gnostic [Gr. *gnosis*, knowledge] *comb* judging; determining; knowledge (physiognomy, dysgnosia, diagnosis, diagnostic)

gnoto- [Gr. *gnotos*, known] *comb* known (gnotobiology, gnotobiote)

gog-, -gogue *see* -agogue

-gomph- [Gr. *gomphos*, bolt, fastening] *base* bolt; socket; nail (gomphiasis, gomphosis)

-gon, -gonal [Gr. *gonia*, angle] *comb* figure with __ angles (pentagon, polygonal)

gonado- [Gr. *gone*, generation, seed] *comb* gonad; sex gland (gonadopathy, gonaduct)

-gone, -gonium, gono-, -gony [Gr. *gone*, generation, seed] *comb* reproduction; generation; origin; formation (myelogone, sporogonium, gonothecal, cosmogony)

gonido- [Gr. *gone*, generation, seed] *comb* reproductive (gonidogenous, gonidophore)

gonio- [Gr. *gonia*, angle] *comb* angle (goniognathous, goniometry)

-gracil- [L. *gracilis*, slender] *base* slender; lean (gracilescent, gracility)

gracul- [L. *graculus*, jackdaw] *base* jackdaw, grackle (Graculinae, graculine)

grad- [L. *gradus*, step] *base* walk; move; go (gradation)

-grade [L. *gradus*, step] *comb* a specified manner of walking or moving (plantigrade, tardigrade) *see* -gress-

Graeco- [L. *Graecus*, Greek] *comb* Greek (Graecomania). *Also* Greco- (Grecophile)

-grall- [L. *grallae*, stilts] *base* wading bird (grallae, gralline)

grallator- [L. *grallator*, one who walks on stilts] *base* stork; heron (grallatorial, grallatory)

-gram [Gr. *gramma*, what is written] 1. *comb* written or drawn (telegram); [LL. *gramma*, a small weight]

2. grams: x number of (kilograms);
3. gram: fraction of (centigram)

-gramen-, -gramin- [L. *gramen*, grass]
base grass (gramenite, graminiferous)

grand- [L. *grandis*, having high dignity
or rank] *comb* of the generation older
than or younger than (grandfather,
granddaughter)

grandi- [L. *grandis*, large] *base* great;
large (grandiloquent, grandiosity)

grandin- [L. *grandinus*, full of hail]
base hail (grandination, grandinous)

grani- [L. *granum*, grain] *comb* grain;
corn (graniferous, granivorous)

graniti- [It. *granito*, grained] *comb*
granite; (graniticoline, granitiform)

grano- [L. *granum*, grain] 1. *comb*
granite: like/of (granolithic); 2. granular (granophyre)

granulo- [L. *granulus*, granular] *comb*
granular (granulo-adipose, granduloma)

grao- [Gr. *graus*, old woman] *comb* old
woman (graocracy)

-graph [Gr. *graphein*, write] 1. *comb*
that which writes/draws/describes
(telegraph); 2. that which is written/
drawn (autograph). *Also* **-grapher**
(stenographer); **-graphic** (telegraphic); **grapho-** (graphology);
-graphy (autobiography)

grapto- [Gr. *graptos*, marked, written]
comb writing (graptolitic, graptomancy)

grat- [L. *gratus*, pleasing] *base* thankful
(grateful, gratitude)

-graticul- [L. dim,. of *cratis*, wickerwork] *base* gridiron (graticulation,
graticule)

-grav- [L. *gravis*, heavy] *base* weight;
heavy; serious (gravigrade, gravimeter)

-gravid- [L. *gravidus*, pregnant] *base*
pregnant (gravidity, multigravida)

Greco- [L. *Graecus*, Greek] *comb*
Greek; (Greco-Roman). *Also*
Graeco- (Graecophile)

-greg- [L. *grex/greg-*, flock] *base* herd;
flock (congregation, gregarious)

grem- [It. *gremio*, lap, bosom] *base*
bosom; lap (gremial, gremiale)

-gress- [L. *gressor*, walker] *base* walk;
move; go (aggressive). *See* **-grad-**

-gris- [ML *griseus*, gray] *base* gray (grisaille, griseous)

grossul- [NL *grossula*, gooseberry]
base gooseberry (grossulaceous,
grossular)

-grui- [NL *grus*, crane] *base* crane
(gruiform, Gruiformes)

-grum- [L. *grumus*, a little heap] *base*
clot (grumous, grumousness)

gryll- [L. *grillus*, grasshopper, cricket]
base cricket; grasshopper (Gryllotalpa, Gryllus)

gubern- [L. *gubernacula*, helm, rudder] *base* ruler; guide (gubernation,
gubernatorial)

gul(os)- [L. *gula*, throat] *base* gluttony; voracity (gullet, gulosity)

gurg- [L. *gurges*, whirlpool] *base* gush,
swirl (gurgitation, gurgle)

-gust- [L. *gustare*, taste] *base* taste; eat
(gustation, gustatory)

gutti- [L. *gutta*, a drop] *base* drop;
gum-yielding (guttiferous, guttulate)

gutturo- [L. *guttur*, the throat] *comb*
throat (gutturo-labial, gutturonasal)

gymno- [Gr. *gumnos*, naked] *comb*
naked; stripped; bare (gymnoblastic,
gymnocarpous)

gyn-, gyno- [Gr. *gune*, female] 1. *comb*
woman; female (gynarchy); 2. ovary;
pistil (gynophore). *Also* **-gynia**
(polygynia), **-gynic** (androgynic),
-gynist (philogynist), **-gynous**
(polygynous), and **-gyny** (monogyny)

gynandro- [Gr. *gune*, female + *aner*,
male] *comb* of uncertain sex (gynandrosporous, gynandromorphism)

gyne-, gyneco-, gyneo- [Gr. *gune*, female] *comb* woman; female (gynephobia, gynecocracy, gyneolatry) gypo- [Gr. *gups*, vulture] *base* vulture (Gypogeranus, Gypohierax)

-gypso- [Gr. *gupsos*, chalk, gypsum] *base* chalk (gypsiferous, gypsophila)

gyro- [Gr. *guros*, circle] 1. *comb* gyrating (gyroscope); 2. spiral (gyroidal); 3. gyroscope (gyrocompass)

gyroso- [Gr. *guros*, circle] *comb* marked with wavy lines (gyroso-labyrinthiform, gyroso-rugose)

H

haben- [L. *habena*, thong, strap, strip] *base* resembling a thong (habena, habennula)

habil- [L. *habilis*, suitable, fit] 1. *base* ability; equipped (rehabilitate); 2. clothing (habiliments)

-habro- [Gr. *habros*, graceful, delicate] *base* graceful; delicate (habroneme, habroreme)

-hadro- [Gr. *hadros*, stout, bulky] *base* thick (hadrosaur, Hadrosaurus)

haema- *see* hema-

hagi-, hagio- [Gr. *hagios*, holy] *comb* saintly; holy (hagiheroical, hagiology)

halcyon- [Gr. *alkon*, kingfisher] *base* kingfisher (halcyoneum, halcyonine)

-hale [L. *halare*, to breathe] *base* breath; vapor (exhale, inhalation)

-halec- [NL *halec*, herring] *base* herring (halecoid, halecomorphic)

hali- [Gr. *hals*, the sea] *base* sea (halichondroid, Halicore)

-halieut- [Gr. *halieuein*, to fish] *base* fishing (halieutical, halieutics)

-halit- [L. *halare*, to breathe] *base* breath; vapor (halitosis, halitous)

halluc- [ML *hallux* < *hallus*, thumb + *hallex*, big toe] *base* toe (hallucal, hallucar)

halo- [Gr. *hals*, sea] 1. *comb* of the sea (halosaurian); 2. of salt (halophyte); 3. of halogen (halogenous)

-ham-/hamat- [L. *hamus*, hook] *base* hook (hamated, hamulate)

hama- [Gr. *hama*, together with] *comb* together with; at the same time; united (hamadryad, hamarchy)

-hamart- [Gr. *hamartia*, error, sin] 1. *base* sin (hamartiology); 2. corporal defect (hamartoma)

hand- [AS *hentan*, hand] *comb* hand: of/with/by/for (handbell, handcuff)

-hapal- [Gr. *hapalos*, soft to the touch] *base* soft (Hapalidae, hapalote)

haph- [Gr. *hapalos*, soft to the touch] *base* touch (haphalgesia)

haplo- [Gr. *haplous*, single] *comb* one-fold; single (haplodont, haplography)

hapt-, hapto-¹ [Gr. *haptesthai*, to touch] *comb* touch; sensation (haptics, haptotaxis)

-hapto-² [Gr. *haptein*, to fasten] *base* fasten; combine (haptophore, haptotropism)

harengi- [NL *harengus*, herring] *comb* herring (harrengiform)

hariol- [L. *hariolatio*, foretelling] *base* divination (hariolate, hariolation). *Also see* "Divination" in Part III

harmat- [Gr. *harma*, war chariot] *base* car; chariot (harmatian)

harpact- [Gr. *harpaktikos*, rapacious] *base* crustacean (harpacticid, harpacticoid)

harpag- [Gr. *harpage*, hook, rake] *base* hook or grapple (harpagon, Harpagus)

harpax- [Gr. *harpactor*, robber] *base* robber (Harpactor, harpaxophobia)

harusp- [L. *haruspex*, soothsayer] *base* divination by entrails (haruspication, haruspicy)

-hastato-, hasti- [L. *hasta*, spear] *comb* spear (hastato-lanceolate; hastiform)

-haur-, -haust- [L. *haurire*, to draw

water] *base* draw (forth); drain; suck (exhauriate, haustellum)

-headed [AS *heafala*, head] **1.** *comb* having a __ head (clearheaded); **2.** having __ heads (two-headed)

heauto- [Gr. *heautou*, of himself] *comb* of oneself (heautomorphism, heautophony)

hebdom- [Gr. *hebdomas*, week] *base* week; seven days (hebdomadal, hebdomadary)

hebe- [Gr. *hebe*, pubescent] *comb* pubescent (hebegynous, hebepetalous)

-hebet- [L. *hebes*, blunt, sluggish] *base* dull; blunt (hebetude, hebetudinous)

Hebraico- [Gr. *Hebraios*, Hebrew] *comb* Hebrew (Hebraico-Germanic, Hebraico-Hibernian)

hecato-, hecto- [Gr. *hecato*, one hundred] *comb* one hundred (hecatophyllous, hectoliter). *Also* **hekto-** (hektograph)

hecatonicosa- [Gr. *hecato*, 100 + *icosa*, 20] *comb* one hundred twenty (hecatonicosachoron)

-heder- [L. *hedera*, ivy] *base* ivy (hederaceous, hederal)

-hedon- [Gr. *hedone*, delight] *base* pleasure (anhedonia, hedonist)

-hedral, -hedron [Gr. *hedron*, -sided] *comb* geometric figure with x number of surfaces (hexahedral, hexahedron)

hedro- [Gr. *hedra*, anus] *comb* anus (hedratresia, hedrocele)

-hedy- [Gr. *hedus*, sweet] *base* sweet, pleasant (hedychium, hedyphane)

hegemon- [Gr. *hegemon*, leader, guide] *base* leader; chief (hegemonic, hegemony)

-hekisto- [Gr. *hekistos*, least, worst] *base* smallest (hekistotherm, hekisthothermic)

helco- [Gr. *helkos*, ulcer] *comb* festering wound; ulcer (helcology, helcoplasty)

helici-, helico- [Gr. *heliks*, spiral] *comb* spiral-shaped (heliciform, helicopter)

helio- [Gr. *helios*, sun] *comb* sun; bright; radiant (heliocentric, heliocomete)

helminth(o)- [Gr. *helminth*, worm] *comb* [botany] worm; (helminthiasis, helminthogogue)

helo-¹ [Gr. *helos*, a nail] *comb* nail; spike (heloderma, helodont)

helo-² [Gr. *helos*, a marsh] *comb* marsh, bog (helobious, Helophilous)

helv- [L. *helvus*, yellow] *base* yellow (helvenac, helvolous)

Helvet- [L. *Helveticus*, the Swiss] *base* Swiss (Helvetian, Helvetic)

hema-, hemato-, hemo- [Gr. *haima*, blood] *comb* blood; (hemachrome, hematogenic, hemophilia). *Also* **haem-** (haemachrome)

hemangio- [Gr. *haima*, blood + *angaio*, vessel] *comb* blood vessels (hemangioblastoma, hemangiosarcoma)

hemer- [Gr. *hemera*, day] *base* day (hemeralopia, monohemerous)

hemi- [L. *hemi*, half] *pre* half (hemicardia, hemicylindrical)

hemispherico- [F. *hemispherique*, hemispherical] *comb* hemispheric (hemispherico-conical, hemispherico-conoid)

hendeca- [Gr. *hendeka*, eleven] *comb* eleven (hendecagon, hendecahedron)

-heno- [Gr. *eis/ev-*, one] *base* one (henotheism, henotic)

heort- [Gr. *heorte*, feast, festival] *base* feast day; festival (heortologist, heortology)

hepatic-, hepato- [Gr. *hepatikos*, of the liver] *comb* liver (hepaticostomy, hepatogastric)

hepta- [Gr. *hepta*, seven] *comb* seven (heptagon, heptasepalous)

heptakaideca- [Gr. *hepta*, seven + *kai*, and + *deka*, ten] *comb* seventeen (heptakaidecagon, heptakaidecahedron)

-herbi- [L. *herba*, grass] *base* plant (herbiferous, (herbivorous)

-herco- [Gr. *herkos*, fence, barrier] *base* wall; barrier (hercogamous, hercogamy)

heredo- [L. *hereditas*, heirship] *comb* heredity (heredofamilial, heredomacular degeneration)

heresio- [Gr. *hairesis*, sect] *base* heresy (heresiologist, heresiography)

heri- [L. *herus*, master] *base* master (hericide, herile)

-hermen- [Gr. *hermeneutes*, interpreter] *base* interpretation (hermeneutical, hermeneutics)

hernio- [L. *hernia*, hernia] *comb* hernia (herniated, herniotomy)

herpeti-, herpeto- [Gr. *herpeton*, reptile, snake] *comb* reptile (herpetiform, herpetology)

-hesper- [L. *Hesperus*, evening star] *base* west, evening (hesperanopia, Hesperian)

-hesperid- [Gr. *Hesperides*, nymphs who guarded the golden apples] *base* fleshy fruit with a leathery rind — orange, lemon, etc. (hesperidin, hesperidium)

-hesson- [Gr. *hesson*, less] *base* less; inferior (hessonite)

-hestern- [L. *hesternus*, of yesterday] *base* yesterday (hestern, hesternal)

hestho- [Gr. *hesthes*. clothing] *base* clothing; dress (hesthogenous)

hesy- [Gr. *hesu*, quiet] *base* still; quiet (Hesychasm, hesychastic)

hetaero- [Gr. *hetaira*, female companion] *base* companion; courtesan (hetaerism, hetaerocrasy)

hetero- [Gr. *heteros*, other, different] *comb* other; another; different (heteradenic, heterosexual)

hetto- [Gr. *hetton*, less] *comb* slight, less (hettocyrtosis)

-heur- [Gr. *heuretikos*, inventive] *base* discover; invent (heuretic, heuristic)

hexa- [Gr. *heks*, six] *comb* six (hexad, hexameter)

hexaconta- [Gr. *heksenta*, sixty] *comb* sixty (hexacontagon, hexacontahedron)

hexacosi- [Gr. *heksacosia*, 600] *comb* six hundred (hexacosichora, hexacosichoron)

hexadeca-, hexakaideca- [Gr. *heks*, six + *deka*, ten] *comb* sixteen (hexadecachoron, hexakaidecahedron)

hexakis- [Gr. *heksakis*, six times] *comb* six times (hexakisoctahedron, hexakistetrahedron)

hexametro- [Gr. *heks*, six + *metron*, measure] *comb* hexameter (hexametrographer, hexametromania)

-hexi- [Gr. *hekhein*, be in a given state] *base* habit; behavior (hexiological, hexiology)

hibern- [L. *hibernus*, of winter] *base* winter (hibernal, hibernation)

Hiberno- [L. *Hibernia*, Ireland] *comb* Irish (Hiberno-Celtic, Hibernology)

-hidro- [Gr. *hidrosis*, sweat] *base* sweat; (anhidrosis, hidrotic)

hiem- [L. *hiems*, winter] *base* winter (hiemal, hiemation)

hieraco- [Gr. *hieraks*, hawk, falcon] *comb* hawk (hieracosophic, hieracosphinx)

hiero- [Gr. *hiero*, sacred] *comb* holy; consecrated; sacred (hierocracy, hierophobia)

hilasm- [Gr. *hilasmos*, means of appeasing] *base* propitiatory (hilasm, hilasmic)

-himant- [Gr. *himas*, thong] *base* strap; thong (Himanthalia, Himantopus)

hind- [Goth. *hinduma*, posterior] *comb* rear; following (hindbrain, hindmost)

hippo-, -hippus [Gr. *hippos*, horse] *comb* horse (hippocrepian, eohippus)

hippocamp- [Gr. *hippokampos*, mythical sea monster with a horse's body and a fish's tail] *base* seahorse (hippocampine, hippocampus)

hippocrepi- [Gr. *hippos*, horse + *krepis*, shoe, boot] *base* horseshoe (hippocrepian, hippocrepiform)

hippogloss- [Gr. *hippos*, horse + *glossa*, tongue] *base* halibut, flounder (Hippoglossinae, hippoglossoid)

-hircin- [L. *hircus*, goat] *base* goat (hircine, hircinous)

-hirmo- [Gr. *hermos*, connection, series] *base* series; connection (hirmologion)

hirsuto- [L. *hirsutus*, shaggy] *comb* having hair of a certain color or type (hirsuto-castaneous, hirsuto-rufus)

-hirudin- [NL *hirudo*, leech] *base* leech (hirudiniculture, hirudinid)

-hirund- [L. *hirundo*, swallow] *base* swallow; martin (hirundine, Hirundo)

Hispano- [L. *Hispanicus*, Spanish] *comb* Spanish (Hispano-American, Hispano-Italian)

-hispid- [L. *hispidus*, rough, shaggy] *base* shaggy; hairy (hispidating, hispidulous)

histio-, histo- [Gr. *histos*, web, tissue] *comb* tissue (histiocytoma, histology)

historico- [Gr. *historikos*, of history] *comb* historical (historico-geographical, historico-tropological)

-histrion- [L. *histrio*, stage player] *base* stage-player (histrionically, histrionics)

-hodiern- [L. *hodiernus*, of this day] *base* today (hodiern, hodiernal)

hodo- [Gr. *hodos*, way] *comb* way; road (hodograph, hodometer). *See* **odo-**

-holco- [Gr. *holkos*, furrow, track] *base* furrow (holcodont, Holcus)

holo- [Gr. *holos*, entire] *comb* complete; entire; whole; (holarthritis, holograph)

hom- [L. *homo*, human] *base* humankind (homicide, hominid)

homalo-, homolo- [Gr. *homalos*, even] *comb* even; regular; level; ordinary (homalographic, homologous)

-homar- [ML. *Homarus*, lobster] *base* lobster (Homaridae, homarine)

homeo- [Gr. *homoios*, like] *comb* similar; like (homeomorphism, homeoplastic)

homichlo- [Gr. *homikhle*, fog] *base* cloud; fog; dimness (homichlomania, homichlophobia)

homil- [Gr. *homilia*, instruction, lecture] *base* sermon (homiletics, homily)

homin- [L. *homo*, human] *base* humankind (hominiform, hominivorous)

homo- [Gr. *homos*, same] *comb* same; equal (homocarpous, homochromous)

homoeo-, homoio- [Gr. *hoimoios*, like] *comb* similar; like (homoeodont, homoiothermal)

homolo- [Gr. *homologos*, agreeing] *comb* corresponding; assenting (homologous, homolographic). *See* **homalo-**

-hood [Dan. *-hed*, quality, condition] 1. *suf* quality; character; state; condition (childhood); 2. whole group of __ (brotherhood)

hoplo- [Gr. *hoplon*, large shield] *comb* weapon; armor (Hoplocephalus, hoplophorous)

-horde- [L. *hordeum*, barley] *base* barley (hordeaceous, Hordeum)

horizo- [Gr. *horizon*, horizon] *comb* horizon (horizocardia)

horm- [Gr. *hormaein*, to urge on] *base* urge; impel (hormetic, hormetically)

hormo- [Gr. *hormos*, cord, chain, necklace] *base* chainlike (hormogonium, hormogonous)

horo- [L. *hora*, hour, season] *comb* hour; time; season (horology, horoscope)

-hort- [L. *hortari*, encourage] *base* urge; encourage (exhortation, hortatory)

-horti- [L. *hortus*, garden] *base* garden (horticulture, horticulturist)

hosp- [L. *hospes*, host] *base* host (hospitable, hospitality)

-hum- [L. *humus*, ground] *base* ground (exhumation, posthumous)

humano- [L. *humanus*, human] *comb*
human and (humano-solar, hu-
mano-taurine)

-humect- [L. *humectus*, moist] *base*
moist; wet (humectant, humecta-
tion)

humero- [L. *humerus*, shoulder] *comb*
shoulder; upper arm (humero-
cubital, humeroradial)

hyalo- [Gr. *hualos*, glass] *comb*
[chemistry] transparent; glassy (hya-
line, hyalophane)

-hybo- [Gr. *hubos*, humpbacked] *base*
hump (hybodont, Hybodontes)

-hydno- [Gr. *hudnon*, truffle] *base*
truffle (hydnocarpous, Hydnum)

hydraulico- [Gr. *hudraulos*, water
pipe] *comb* hydraulic (hydraulico-
pneumatical, hydraulicostatics)

-hydric [Gr. *hudor*, water] *comb* the
presence of x number of hydroxyl
radicals or replaceable hydrogen
atoms (chlorohydric, monohydric)

hydro- [Gr. *hudor*, water] 1. *comb*
water (hydrometer); 2. [chemistry]
hydrogen (hydrocyanic)

hydroxy- [*hydro* + *oxy*gen] *comb* hydroxyl group (hydroxy-benzene, hy-
droxyurea)

hyeto- [Gr. *huetos*, rain] *comb* rain;
rainfall (hyetal, hyetograph)

hygeio-, hygien- [Gr. *hugeia*, health]
comb health; hygiene (hygeiolatry,
hygienist)

hygro- [Gr. *hugros*, wet] *comb* wet;
moisture (hygrology, hygrometer)

hylac- [Gr. *hulaktein*, to bark] *base*
barking (hylactic, hylactism)

hylaeo- [Gr. *hulaios*, of wood or forest]
comb forest (hylaeosaurus)

hyle-, hylo- [Gr. *hule*, wood] 1. *comb*
wood (hylephobia, hylophagous); 2.
matter (hylozoism)

hylobat- [Gr. *hulobates*, one who
haunts the woods] *base* gibbon (Hy-
lobates, hylobatine)

hymeno- [Gr. *Humen*, god of mar-
riage] *comb* membrane (hymeneal,
hymenogeny)

hyo- [shape of Gr. letter *upsilon*] *comb*
hyoid bone (hyoglossal, hyoideal)

hyos- [Gr. *hus*, hog] *base* hog
(hyoscyamine, Hyoscyamus)

hypegia- [Gr. *hupenguos*, liable to be
called to account] *base* responsibility
(hypegiaphobia)

hypengy- [Gr. *hupenguos*, liable to be
called to account] *base* responsibility
(hypengiomania, hypengyophobia)

hyper- [Gr. *huper*, over, above] 1. *pre*
over; above; excessive (hypercriti-
cal); 2. [chemistry] maximum (hy-
peroxide)

-hypho- [Gr. *huphe*, web, weaving]
base web, tissue (hyphodrome, hy-
phomycetes)

hypno- [Gr. *hupnos*, sleep] *comb* sleep;
hypnotism (hypnophobia, hypnotic)

hypo- [Gr. *hupo*, under] 1. *pre* under;
below (hypodermic); 2. less than
(hypotaxis); 3. [chemistry] having a
lower state of oxidation (hypophos-
phorous)

hypocrater- [Gr. *hupo*, under + *krater*,
mixing vessel] *base* tray (hypocrateriform, hypocraterimorphous)

hypsi-, hypso- [Gr. *hupsi*, on high]
comb high; height (hypsicephalic,
hypsodont)

hyraci-, hyraco- [Gr. *huraks*, shrew-
mouse] *comb* hyrax: rabbit-like
quadruped (hyraciform, hyracodont)

hystero-[1] [Gr. *hustera*, uterus] 1. *comb*
uterus; womb (hysterodynia); 2. hysteria (hysteroepilepsy)

hystero-[2] [Gr. *husteros*, later] *comb*
later; inferior (hysteresis, hystero-ge-
netic)

-hystric- [L. *hystrix*, porcupine] *base*
porcupine, hedgehog (hystriciasis,
histricine)

I

-i [L. pl. suf. -i] *suf* plural ending (alumni, foci)

-ia [L. nom. suf. -ia] 1. *suf* country names (India); 2. disease names (pneumonia); 3. festival names (Lupercalia); 4. Gk/Lat. words (militia); 5. plurals > Gk/Lat. (genitalia); 6. [biology] class names (Reptilia); 7. [botany] some generic plant names (zinnia); 8. [chemistry] alkaloid names (strychnia)

-ial [L. suf. -ialis] *suf* of; pertaining to (imperial, magisterial)

-ian [L. suf. -ianus] *suf* 1. relating to (Bostonian) 2. relating to, resembling (academician)

-iana *see* -ana

ianth- [Gr. ianthus, violet-colored] *base* violet (Ianthina, ianthine)

-iasis [Gr. suf. -iasis] 1. *comb* process; condition; 2. morbid condition (hypochondriasis, psoriasis)

-iatrics, -iatrist, iatro-, -iatry [Gr. iatrikos, of physicians] *comb* medical treatment (pediatrics, podiatrist, iatrophysical, psychiatry)

Ibero- [Gr. Iberia, Spain] *comb* Spanish (Iberian, Ibero-French)

-ibility, -ible, -ibly [L. suf] *suf* capable of (sensibility, sensible, visibly)

-ic [L. suf. -icus] 1. *suf* having to do with; of (volcanic); 2. like; having the nature of; characteristic of (angelic); 3. produced by; caused by (symphonic); 4. made up of; containing; consisting of; (dactylic); 5. [chemistry] higher valence than is indicated by the suffix -ous (nitric); 6. nouns from adjectives; (magic)

-ical, -ically [L. suf. -ic + -al] *suf* adjective/adverb forms parallel to -ic (angelical, magically)

-ice[1] [< L. suf. -itius] *suf* condition; state; quality of; action (malice, service)

-ice[2] *suf* feminine ending (mediatrice)

-ichno [Gr. ikhnos, track] *comb* [paleontology] track; trace; posture; position (ichnolite, ichnology)

ichor- [Gr. ikhor, juice] *comb* serous fluid (ichorremia, ichorose)

ichthyo- [Gr. ikhthus, fish] *comb* fish; fishlike (ichthyologist, ichthyophagous)

-ician [OF suf. -icien] *suf* practitioner; specialist (beautician, logician)

-icity [Fr. suf. -icite] *suf* nouns formed from -ic adjectives (authenticity, publicity)

icono- [Gr. eikon, image] *comb* figure; likeness; image (iconograph, iconostasis)

icosa-, icosi- [Gr. eikosi, twenty] *comb* [mathematics/botany] twenty (icosahedron, icositetrahedron: 24)

-ics [Gr. suf. -ikos] 1. *suf* art; science (mathematics); 2. activities; practice; properties; system (statistics)

icter-[1], ictero- [Gr. ikteros, jaundice] *comb* yellow; jaundice (icteric, icteroanemia)

icter-[2] [Gr. ikteros, bird that supposedly cured jaundice] *base* blackbird; bobolink; meadowlark; oriole (Icteridae, icterine)

-id[1] [NL. suf. -ides] 1. *suf* belonging to; connected with (Aeneid); 2. animal group name (arachnid); 3. meteor names (Perseid)

-id[2] [L. suf. -idus] *suf* filled with (morbid, vivid)

-ida [L. suf. -ida] *suf* [zoology] order/class names (Annelida, Acarida)

-idae [Gr. suf. -idai] *suf* [zoology] family names (Felidae, Laniadae)

-idan [L. suf. -id + -an] *suf* [zoology] of or pertaining to (arachnidan, araneidan)

-ide [< oxide] *suf* [chemistry] compound names (cyanide, chloride)

ideo- [Gr. *idea*, idea] *comb* idea; creation (ideograph, ideology)

-ides [Gr. suf. *-ides*] *suf* [science] name endings (cantharides)

-idine [L. suf. *-id* + *-ine*] *suf* chemical compound related to another (pyridine, toluidine)

idio- [Gr. *idios*, one's own] *comb* one's own; distinct; personal (idiocrasy, idiomorphic)

-idion [Gr. dim. suf. *-idion*] *suf* diminutive (enchiridion, pyramidion)

-idium [< Gr. dim. suf. *-idion*] *suf* [science] diminutive (aecidium, phyllidium)

idolo- [Gr. *eidolon*, idol] *comb* idol (idoloclast, idolomancy)

idon- [L. *idoneus*, fit] *base* suitable (idoneal, idoneus)

-ie [ME dim. suf. *-ie*] *suf* diminutive (doggie, sweetie)

-ier [ME suf. *-ier*] *suf* person concerned with (courier, glazier)

-iferous *see* -ferous

-ific *see* -fic

-ification *see* -fication

-iformes [L. sci. order suf. *-iformes*] *suf* [zoology] names: having the form of (Passeriformes, Pelicaniformes)

-ify *see* -fy

igneo- [L. *igneus*, of fire] *comb* fire (igneo-aqueous, igneo-metamorphic)

igni- [L. *ignis*, fire] *base* fire (igniferous, ignipuncture)

il- *see* in-

-il, -ile [L. suf. *-ilis*] *suf* like; having to do with; suitable for (civil, docile)

ilast- [Gr. *ilasseai*, to appease] *base* propitiatory, conciliatory (ilastic, ilastical)

ileo-, ilio- [NL *ilium*, ilium] 1. *comb* of the ileum (ileostomy); 2. ileac plus (iliosacral)

-ilia [L. suf. *-ilius*] *suf* able to be __ (juvenilia, memorabilia)

ilic- [L. *ilex/ilic-*, holm oak, holly] *base* holly (ilicate, ilicic)

-ility [L. suf. *-ilitas*] *suf* quality; condition (sensibility)

-illa [L. dim. suf. *-illus*] *suf* diminutive (banderilla, cedilla)

-illo [L. dim. suf. *-illus*] *suf* diminutive (cigarillo, lapillo)

illyngo- [Gr. *illingos*, spinning around] *base* vertigo (illyngomania, illyngophobia)

im- *see* in-

-im [Heb. plu. suf. *-im*] *suf* Hebrew plural ending (cherubim, seraphim)

imbri- [L. *imber/imbr-*, shower] *base* rain; rain tile (imbriferous, imbricated)

imbricato- [L. *imbricatus*, covered with gutter tiles] *comb* composed of parts which overlap like tiles (imbrication, imbricato-granulous)

immuno- [L. *immunis*, exempt from public service or charges] *comb* resistant to disease; immune (immunochemistry, immunotherapy)

immut- [L. *im-*, privative + *mutabilis*, changeable] *base* unalterable (immutability, immutable)

impari- [L. *impar*, unequal] *comb* odd-numbered; unpaired (imparipinnate, imparisyllabic)

imped- [L. *impedire*, to hinder] *base* snare; delay (impedance, impediment)

imper- [L. *imperare*, to command] *base* power; authority (imperative, imperial)

impet- [L. *impetus*, a rushing upon] *base* rush; assault (impetuosity, impetus)

in-[1] [L. *in*, into; *in*, not] 1. *pre* within; inside; into; toward (inbreed); 2. intensifier (instigate); 3. not; without (insane). NOTE: **in-** can change to: **il-** (illuminate); **im-** (impossible); **ir-** (irrigate)

-in[2] [L. suf. *-inus*] *suf* [chemistry] names of neutral substances (albumin, insulin)

-ina [L. fem. suf. *-ina*] 1. *suf* feminine

ending (ballerina); 2. characterized by (sonatina); 3. [biology] name endings (Nemertina)

-inae [L. pl. suf. -inae] suf names of subfamilies of animals (Caninae, Felinae)

inan- [L. inanis, void] base empty; foolish (inane, inanity)

inaug- [L. inaugurare, to consecrate after checking omens] base start, install (inaugural, inaugurate)

incess- [L. in, privative + cessare, to cease] base unceasing (incessable, incessant)

incip- [L. in, on + capere, to take] base take in hand; begin (incipience, incipient)

incisi-, inciso- [L. incisio, a cutting into] comb cut into (incisiform, inciso-lobate)

increp- [L. in, on + crepare, make a noise] base scold; rebuke (increpation, increpatory)

incudo- [L. incus, anvil] comb small bone of the ear (incudo-malleal, incudo-stapidial)

-indag- [L. indagare, to search] base trace; search; investigate (indagation, indigative)

indi-, indo-¹ [Gr. indikon, indigo] comb indigo; metallic violet-purple (indirubin, indophenol)

-indigen- [LL indigenus, native] base native (indigenous, indigenously)

Indo-² [Gr. Indo, Indian] comb India (Indo-Chinese, Indo-Malayan)

inducto- [L. in, into + ducere, to lead] comb electrical induction (inductometer, inductoscope)

-ine [L. suf. -inus] 1. suf of; like; pertaining to; characterized by (canine); 2. feminine ending (heroine); 3. abstract noun ending (discipline); 4. commercial names (Vaseline); 5. [chemistry] names of: halogens (iodine); alkaloid/nitrogen bases (morphine); hydrides (stibine); 6. of the nature of (crystalline)

inebr- [L. in, into + ebriare, to make drunk] base drunk (inebriant, inebriated)

inequi- [L. in, privative + aequus, even] comb unequal (inequidistant, inequilobate)

infern- [L. infernus, underground] base underworld; hell (infernal, inferno)

infero- [L. inferus, low] comb underneath; low; below (inferolateral, inferoposterior)

infra- [L. infra, below] pre below; beneath (infrabuccal, infrastructure)

infundib- [L. infundibulum, funnel] base funnel (infundibulate, infundibuliform)

-ing [OE suf. -ing] 1. suf belonging to; descended from (atheling); 2. present participle (shifting sand); 3. act of; process (talking); 4. produced by (painting); 5. material for (roofing)

ingen- [L. ingenium, natural capacity, gifted] base versatile; clever (ingenious, ingenuity)

ingress- [L. ingressus, a going into] base enter (ingress, ingressive)

inguino- [L. inguinalis, of the groin] comb inguinal; groin (inguino-femoral, inguino-scrotal)

-ini [NL. suf. -ini] suf [zoology] group names (Acanthurini, Salmonini)

inimic- [L. inimicus, enemy] base hostile (inimical, inimicitous)

iniq- [L. iniquitas, injustice] base bad; uneven (iniquitous, iniquity)

init- [L. initium, beginning] base begin; enter (initialize, initiate)

innato- [L. innatus, inborn] comb inborn; natural (innato-erumpent, innato-sessile)

ino- [Gr. iz/inos, fiber] comb fiber; fibrous growth (inocarpin, inolith)

inquis- see -quire

insecti-, insecto- [L. insectum, insect] comb bug (insecticide, insectology)

insul- [L. insula, island] base island (insularity, insulation)

integri-/integro- [L. *integer*, whole] *comb* whole (integripallial, integropalliate)

inter- [L. *inter*, between] 1. *comb* between; among (interchange); 2. mutual; reciprocal; with each other; (interact)

interno-, intero- [L. *internus*, inner] *comb* internal; inside; within (internomedial, interoceptive)

intestini, intestino- [L. *intestinum*, intestine] *comb* intestine (intestiniform, intestino-vesical)

intra- [L. *intra*, within] *comb* within; inside (intracellular, intramural)

intro- [L. *intro*, within] *comb* into; within; inward (introgression, introvert)

inund- [L. *inundatus*, inumdated] *base* flood; overflow (inundate, inundation)

inutil- [L. *inutilis*, useless] *base* useless (inutile, inutility)

-invid- [L. *invidia*, envy] *base* envy; resentment (invidious, invidiously)

involucr- [L. *involvere*, wrap or roll up] *base* wrapped (involucral, involucriform)

-involver- [L. *involvere*, wrap or roll up] *base* wrapping; covering (involveriform)

iodi-, iodo- [Gr. *iodes*, like a violet] *comb* iodine (iodiform, iodoform)

-ion [L. suf. *-ion-*] 1. *suf* act; process (solution); 2. state; condition (ambition)

iono-, ionto- [Gr. *ion*, something that goes] *comb* ion (ionophore, iontophoresis)

-ior [ME suf. *-eor*] 1. *suf* one who __ (warrior); 2. comparative form (inferior)

-ious [L. suf. *-ius*] *suf* characterized by; having (ambitious, contentious)

ipse- [L. *ipse*, self] *base* self (ipseity, ipsilateral)

ir- see **in-**

-ira-, -irasc- [L. *ira*, anger] *base* hatred; anger (irate, irascible)

-iren- [Gr. *eirene*, peace] *base* peace (irenic, irenics)

irid-, iris- [Gr. *iris*, rainbow] *base* rainbow (iridial, iridescence, irisopsia)

iridico-, iridio- [Gr. *iris*, *irid-* rainbow] *comb* iridium (iridico-potassic, iridio-cyanide)

irido- [NL *iris*, *irid-*, iris] *comb* iris (iridectomy, iridomotor)

isch-, ischur- [Gr. *ischein*, to hold] *comb* restriction; deficiency (ischemia, ischuretic)

ischi-, ischio- [Gr. *ischiadikos*, of the hips] *comb* hip; ischium (ischialgia, ischiocapsular)

-ise [var. of *-ize* < L. *-itius*] *suf* quality; condition; function (franchise, merchandise)

-ish [OE suf. *-isc*] 1. *suf* national connection (Irish); 2. characteristic of; like (devilish); 3. tending to (bookish); 4. somewhat; rather (whitish); 5. approximately (thirty-ish)

-isk [Gr. suf. *-iskos*] *suf* diminutive (asterisk, obelisk)

-ism [Gr. suf. *-ismos*] 1. *suf* act; result of; practice (terrorism); 2. condition of being (barbarism); 3. qualities characteristic of; conduct characteristic of; (patriotism); 4. doctrine; theory; principle of (socialism); 5. devotion to (nationalism); 6. instance of; example of; peculiarity of (Gallicism); 7. abnormal condition caused by __ (alcoholism)

-ismus [L. suf. *-ismus*] *suf* spasm; contraction (strabismus, vaginismus). See **-esmus**

iso- [Gr. *iso*, equal] *comb* equality; identity; similarity (isochronal, isodactylous)

isoptero- [Gr. *iso*, equal + *pteron*, wing] *base* termite; white ant (Isoptera, isopterous)

-ist [Gr. suf. *-istes*] *suf* practitioner; believer; person skilled in (lobbyist, theorist)

isthm- [Gr. *isthmos*, narrow passage]

base narrow passage; neck of land (isthmian, isthmiate)

-istic, -istical [suf. *-ist* + *-ic* + *-al*] *suf* tending towards; acting like (communistic, egotistical)

istiophor- [Gr. *istiov*, sail + *phoros*, bearing] *base* marlin; sailfish (Istiophoridae, istiophorid)

Italo- [L. *Italia*, Italy] *comb* Italy (Italo-Byzantine, Italophile)

-ite [Gr. suf. *-ites*] 1. *suf* native; inhabitant; citizen of (Brooklynite); 2. adherent; believer (Benthamite); 3. manufactured product (dynamite); 4. fossil (coprolite); 5. bodily organ part (somite); 6. salt or ester of an acid ending in **-ous** (nitrite); 7. mineral or rock (anthracite)

itea- [Gr. *itea*, willow] *comb* willow tree (Itea, iteatic)

-iter- [L. *iterare*, to repeat] *base* repeat (iteration, reiterate)

ithy- [Gr. *ithus*, straight] *comb* erect; straight (ithyphallian, ithyphallic)

-itic [Gr. suf. *-ites* + *-ic*] *suf* relating to; of (dendritic, syphilitic)

-itiner- [L. *itinerari*, go on a journey] *base* journey (itinerant, itinerary)

-ition *see* **-ation**

-itious [L. suf. *-icius*] *suf* having the nature of; characterized by (ambitious, fictitious)

-itis [Gr. suf. *-itis*, now used to mean affliction] *suf* inflammation; disease (appendicitis, bronchitis)

-itive *see* **-ative**

-itol [suf. *-ite* + *ol*] *suf* Used to form the names of polyhydric alcohols other than di- or trihydric alcohols (dulcitol, mannitol)

-ity [L. suf. *-itas*] *suf* state; character; condition (nobility, stability)

-ium [L. suf. *-ium*] *suf* noun ending (delirium, opprobrium)

-ive [L. suf. *-ivus*] 1. *suf* related to; belonging to; (negative); 2. tending to (creative)

-ivus [L. suf. *-ivus*] *suf* [science] name endings (ampliativus, exfoliativus)

-ixo- [Gr. *iksos*, birdlime] *base* mistletoe; sticky or clammy like birdlime (ixia, ixolite)

ixobrych- [Gr. *iksos*, birdlime + *brukso*, eat greedily] *base* bittern (ixobrychus)

ixod- [Gr. *iksos*, birdlime + *eidos*, form] *base* tick (Ixodes, ixodicide)

-ization [suf. *-ize* + *-ation*] *suf* used to form noun from **-ize** verb (acclimatization, realization)

-ize [Gr. suf. *-izein*] 1. *suf* cause to be or become; resemble; make (sterilize); 2. become like (crystallize); 3. subject to; treat with; combine with; (oxidize); 4. engage in; act (theorize)

J

-jact-, -jacula-, -ject- [L. *jactare*, to throw, agitate, brag] *base* hurl; throw (jactation, ejaculation, inject)

jaun- [OF *jaunisse*, yellowness] *base* yellow (jaundice, jaundiced)

jecor- [L. *jecur*, liver] *base* liver (jecorary, jecorin)

-jejuno- [L. *jejunus*, fasting, barren] *comb* of the jejunum (jejunocolostomy, jejunoduodenal)

-jent- [L. *jentaculum*, breakfast] *base* breakfast (jentacular, jenticulation)

-joco(s)-, -jocu(l)- [L. *jocare*, to jest] *base* joke; jest (jocosity, jocularity)

journ- [L. *diurnalis*, daily] *comb* day; daily (journalism, journalistic)

juba- [L. *juba*, mane] *base* mane (juba, jubate)

-jubil- [L. *jubilare*, shout for joy] *base* joy; elation (jubilation, jubilee)

jud- [L. *judicare,* to judge] *base* wisdom; law; justice (judiciously, judgment)

Judaeo-, Judeo- [Gr. *Ioudaia,* Judea] *comb* Jewish (Judaeophobia, Judeo-Christian)

Judaico- [Gr. *Ioudaia,* Judea] *comb* Judaic (Judaico-Christian, Judaico-Moslem)

juglan- [L. *juglan,* walnut] *base* walnut (Juglandaceae, juglandaceous)

jugo-, jugulo- [L. *jugum,* yoke] *comb* neck; throat; yoke (jugo-maxillary, jugulocephalic)

-juli- [L. *iulus,* catkin] *base* catkin (julaceous, juliferous)

jument- [L. *jumentum,* beast of burden] *base* beast of burden; having a strong animal odor (jumentarious, jumentous)

jun- [L. *juvenis,* young] *base* young (junior, juniorship)

-junc- [L. *juncus,* a rush] *base* a rush (Junaceae, juncaceous)

junct- [L. *jungere,* to join] *comb* join (conjunction, juncture)

jur-, juris- [L. *jurare,* to swear] *comb* law (juridical, jurisprudence)

juscul- [L. *jusculum,* broth] *base* broth (Muraena jusculum)

-juss- [L. *jubere,* to command] *base* command (fidejussionary, jussive)

-jut-, -juv- [L. *adjuvare,* to aid] *base* aid; help (adjutant, adjuvant)

juven- [L. *juvenis,* youth] *comb* young; immature (juvenescent, juvenile)

juxta- [L. *juxta,* near] *comb* near; beside; close by (juxtapose, juxtaposition)

K

kaki-, kako- [Gr. *kakos,* bad] *comb* bad; evil (kakistocracy, kakogenesis). *Also* caco- (cacophony)

kakorrhaph- [Gr. *kakos,* bad + *rhaphe,* seam] *base* failure (kakorrhaphiophobia)

-kal- [Gr. *kalos,* beautiful] *base* beautiful (kaleidoscope, kallynteria)

kal(i)- [Ar. *qali,* potash] *comb* potassium (kaligenous, kaliopenia)

karyo- [Gr. *karuon,* nut] *comb* [biology] nucleus (karyokinesis, karyolysis). *Also* caryo- (caryopsis)

kata- *see* cata-

katheno- [Gr. *kata,* according to + *eis/eiv-,* one] *comb* each; every; one by one (kathenotheism, kathenotheistic)

kathis- [Gr. *kathizein,* to seat] *base* sit; seat (kathisophobia, kathismata)

kelo- [Gr. *kelis,* scar] *comb* scar (keloid, kelotomy)

kelyph- [Gr. *keluphos,* sheath] *base* shell; pod (kelyphite, kelyphitic)

keno- [Gr. *kainos,* empty] *comb* empty (kenosis, kenotic)

kephalo- [Gr. *kephale,* head] *comb* head (kephalometer, kephalotomy). *Also* cephalo- (cephalopod)

kera-, kerato- [Gr. *keras,* horn] 1. *comb* horn; hornlike; horny tissue; (keracele, keratogenous); 2. cornea (keratotomy). *Also* cerato- (ceratosaur)

keraulo- [Gr. *keras,* a horn + *aulos,* a pipe, flute] *comb* hornblower; organ stop name (keraulophon)

kerauno- [Gr. *kerauno,* thunder] *comb* thunder (keraunograph, keraunophobia). *Also* cerauno- (ceraunoscope)

keri-, kero- [Gr. *keros,* wax] *base* wax (keritherapy, kerosene)

kery- [Gr. *kerugma,* proclamation]

base proclamation; preaching (kerygma, kerygmatic)

keto- [Ger. *keton* < acetone] *comb* ketone; organic chemical compound (ketoacidosis, ketogenesis)

kibdelo- [Gr. *kibdelos,* spurious] *base* adulterated; spurious (kibdelophane, kibdelo-sporangium)

kil-, kill- [Gael. *ceall,* church] *comb* cell; church; burying place (Kilpatrick, Kilkenny)

kilo- [Gr. *khilioi,* thousand] *comb* thousand (kilogram, kilometer)

-kin [Du. dim. suf. *-ken*] *suf* diminutive (catkin, lambkin)

kinesi-, -kinesia, -kinesis, kineso- [Gr. *kinesis,* movement] *comb* movement; muscular activity (kinesiology, hyperkinesia, telekinesis, kinesodic)

-kinetic, kineto- [Gr. *kinein,* to move] *comb* motion (hyperkinetic, kinetograph). *See* **cine-**

-kinin [Gr. *kinein,* set in motion] *suf* hormone names (bradykinin, cytokinin)

kino- [Gr. *kinein,* set in motion] *base* movement; muscular activity (kinocilium, kinoplasmic)

kio- [Gr. *kion,* column] *comb* uvula (kiotome, kiotomy)

klepto- [Gr. *kleptein,* steal] *comb* steal (kleptomania, kleptomaniac). *Also* **clepto-** (cleptobiosis)

klino- [Gr. *klinein,* to slope] *comb* sloped; bent (klinocephalic, klinometer). *Also* **clino-** (clinograph)

klope- [Gr. *klope,* theft] *comb* steal (klopemania, klopephobia)

kniss- [Gr. *knisa,* savor and steam of burnt sacrifice] *base* incense (knissomancy, knissophobia)

koilo- [Gr. *koilos,* hollow] *comb* hollow (koilon, koilonychia)

koin- [Gr. *koinonia,* fellowship] *base* common (koine, koinonia). *See* **ceno-**[2]

koll(o)- [Gr. *kolla,* glue] *comb* glue (kolloxylin). *Also* **coll-** (colloblast, colloidal)

kolpo- [Gr. *kolpos,* womb, vagina] *comb* vagina (kolpalgia, kolpocele). *Also* **colpo-** (colpocele, colposcope)

koly- [Gr. *kolouo,* curtail, abridge] *comb* inhibit; restrain (kolypeptic, kolytic)

-kompo- [Gr. *kompos,* boast] *base* boasting (kompological, kompology)

koni(o)- [Gr. *konia,* dust] *comb* dust (konimeter). *Also* **conio-** (conidium, coniomycetes)

kopo- [Gr. *kopos,* fatigue] *base* exhaustion (kopophobia). *Also* **copo-** (copiopia, copodyskinesia)

kopro- [Gr. *kopros,* dung] *comb* filth; excrement (koprophilia). *See* **copro-**

-koria [Gr. *kore,* pupil] *comb* pupil of the eye (leukokoria). *Also* **-coria** (anisocoria)

koupho- [Gr. *kouphos,* light in weight] *base* light, fragile (koupholite). *Also* **coupho-** (coupholite)

krauro- [Gr. *krauros,* dry] *comb* dry (kraurosis)

kreo- [Gr. *kreas,* flesh] *comb* flesh (kreophagous). *Also* **creo-** (creophagists)

-krio [Gr. *krio,* ram] *base* ram (krioboly). *Also* **crio-** (criocephalous, criophoric)

krymo-, kryo- *See* **crymo-**

kryo- [Gr. *kruos,* frost] *comb* frost; cold (kryometer). *Also* **cryo-** (cryobiologist, cryogen)

kuttaro- [Gr. *kuttaros,* cavity] *comb* cavity (kuttarosome)

kyano- *see* **cyano-**

kylixo- [Gr. *kuliks,* cup, vase] *base* bowl (kylixes, kylixomancy)

kyma-, kymo- [Gr. *kuma,* wave] *comb* wave; (kymatism, kymograph). *Also* **cymo-** (cymophane)

kyno- [Gr. *kuon,* dog] *comb* dog (kynophagous). *Also* **cyno-** (cynocephalic, cynosure)

kypho- [Gr. *kuphosis,* hump] *comb*

hump (kyphoscoliosis, kyphosis).
Also **cypho-** (cyphonism)

-kyrio- [Gr. *kurios*, having authority]
base authorized; proper (kyriolexy).
Also **cyrio-** (cyriologic, cyriological)

kyto- [Gr. *kutos*, hollow] *comb* cell
(kytometry). *Usually* **cyto-** (cyto-
blast, cytopathic)

L

-lab- [L. *labare*, to totter] *base* totter;
shake; weaken (labefaction, labefy)

-labe [Gr., *lab*, to seize] *base* instrument (astrolabe, litholabe)

labar- [Gr. *labaron*, standard] *base*
banner; standard (labarum)

-labido- [Gr. *labis, labid-*, forceps] *base*
forceps (labidometer, Labidura)

labio- [L. *labium*, lip] *comb* lips, labia
(labiodental, labipalpus)

-labor- [L. *labor*, toil] *base* work (labo-
ratory, laboriousness)

labro- [Gr. *labros*, fierce, greedy] *base*
greedy, furious (Labridae,
Labrosaurus)

labrynthi-, labryntho- [Gr.
laburinthos, labyrinth] *comb*
labyrinth-like (labrynthiform,
labrynthodont)

lac- [L. *lac*, milk] *base* milk; milky-
white (lactation; lacteous)

-lacco- [Gr. *lakkos*, pit] *base* reservoir
(laccolite, laccolithic)

-lacer- [L. *laceratos*, torn] *base* mangle
(lacerable, laceration)

lacert- [L. *lacerta*, lizard] *base* lizard
(lacertiform, lacertilian)

-lachan- [Gr. *lachanon*, vegetable] *base*
vegetable (lachanopolist, lachanopoll)

-lacin- [L. *lacinia*, a flap] *base* fringed;
jagged (laciniform, laciniolate)

lacrim-, lacrimo- [L. *lacrima*, tear]
comb tears; crying (lachrimation, lac-
rimonasal). *Also* **lachrym-** (lachry-
mose)

lacti-, lacto- [L. *lac*, milk] 1. *comb* milk
(lactiflorous); 2.[chemistry] lactic
acid (lactophosphate)

lactuc- [L. *lactuca*, lettuce] *base* lettuce
(lactucarium, lactucic)

-lacun- [L. *lacuna*, ditch, pit] *base* cavity; hole (lacunary, lacunose)

-lacus- [L. *lacus*, lake] *base* lake; pool
(lacustral, lacustrine)

ladron- [L. *latro*, robber] *base* steal
(ladrone, ladronism)

laeo-, laevo- [Gr. *laios*, left] 1. *comb* on
the left (laeotropic); 2. counterclockwise (laevorotation). *Also* **levo-** (levogyrate)

-lagen- [Gr. *lagunos*, flask] *base* flask
(lageniform, Lagenorhynchus)

-lagnia [Gr. *lagneia*, lust] *comb* desire;
coition; fetish (algolagnia, klepto-
lagnia)

lago- [Gr. *lagos*, hare] *comb* [zoology]
hare (lagopodus, lagotic)

-lalia [Gr. *lalein*, talk, chatter] *comb*
speech disorder (coprolalia,
echolalia)

lalo- [Gr. *lalein*, talk, chatter] *comb*
babbling; speech defect (lalopathy,
lalophobia)

lamb- [L. *lambere*, lick] *base* lick (lam-
bent, lambitive)

lamelli- [L. *lamella*, plate] *comb* plate;
layer; scales (lamellibranch, lamelliform)

lamini-, lamino- [L. *lamina*, thin
plate] 1. *comb* plate; layer (laminifer-
ous); 2. blade of the tongue
(laminoalveolar)

-lampad- [Gr. *lampadias*, torch-
bearer] *base* torch; lamp (lampadite,
lampadomancy)

lampro- [Gr. *lampros*, bright] *comb*

clear; distinct (lamprophony, lamprophyre)

lampyr- [Gr. *lampuris,* glow-worm] *base* firefly (lampyrid, lampyrine)

-lana- [Gr. *lenos,* wool] *base* wool (lanary, lanate). *See* **lani-**

lanci- [L. *lancea,* lance] *base* lance (lanceolated, lanciform)

-land [Goth. *land,* land, country]
1. *comb* a kind of land (highland);
2. territory or country (England);
3. place with a specified character (cloudland)

lani- [Gr. *lenos,* wool] *base* wool; (laniferous, lanigerous). *See* **lana-**

-lania- [L. *laniare,* tear, lacerate] *base* to tear; butcher (laniary, Lanius)

laniar- [L. *laniarium,* pert. to a butcher] *base* canine tooth (laniariform, laniarious)

lanug- [L. *lanugo,* down, wooly substance] *base* hair; down (lanuginous, lanugo)

laparo- [Gr. *lapara,* the flank, loins] *comb* abdominal wall; flank; loins (laparocele, laparotomy)

-lapid- [L. *lapis,* stone] *base* stone; gem (lapidary, lapidification)

laps- [L. *lapsus,* falling] *base* slip away; error; fall (collapse, elapsed)

lar- [Gr. *laros,* ravenous sea bird] *base* gull (Laridae, larine)

-largi- [L. *largus,* abundant] *base* abundant; copious (largifluous, largiloquent)

larix- [L. *larix,* larch] *base* larch (larix, larixinic)

larvi- [L. *larva,* ghost, mask] *comb* larva (larviform, larvigerous) ;

laryngo- [Gr. *larunks,* throat, gullet] *comb* windpipe; larynx (laryngoscope, laryngotracheal)

-lass- [L. *lassus,* faint, weary] *base* weary (lassate, lassitude)

latax- [Gr. *lataks,* water quadruped] *base* otter (Latax)

latebr- [L. *latebra,* hiding place] *base* lurking hole (latebricole, latebrous)

later-[1] [L. *later,* brick] *base* brick (lateritious, laterite)

-later[2] [Gr. *latreia,* worship] *comb* one who worships (artolater, gastrolater). *See* **-latry**

lateri-, latero- [L. *later-,* side] *comb* on the side (laterigrade, laterodeviation)

lathro- [Gr. *lathraios,* hidden] *base* hidden; beetle (lathrobiiform, Lathrobiiformes)

lati- [L. *latus,* broad] *comb* wide; broad (latidentate, latipennate)

latib- [L. *latibulus,* lurking place] *base* hiding place (latibulate, latibulize)

latici- [L. *latex/latic-,* liquid] *comb* latex (laticiferous)

-latra- [L. *latrare,* to bark] *base* barking (latrant, latration)

latro- [L. *latrinatio,* highway robbery] *base* robber (latrocination, latronage)

latrodect- [Gr. *latris,* robber + *dexomai,* of a hunter waiting for game] *base* black widow spider (Latrodectus)

-latry [Gr. *latreia,* worship] *comb* excessive devotion; worship of; (bardolotry, idolatry). *See* **-later**

-laud- [L. *laudare,* to praise] *base* praise (applaud, laudatory)

lauri-, lauro- [L. *laurus,* laurel] *base* laurel (lauriferous, laurine, lauromitrile)

-lav- [L. *lavare,* to wash] *base* wash (lavage, lavatory)

-lax- [L. *laxare,* to loosen] *base* loose, open (laxative, relaxation)

lazul- [Pers. *lazhward,* blue color] *base* blue (lazuline, lazulite)

-le [OE suf. *-le*] *suf* 1. small (icicle);
2. person who does (beadle); 3. something used for doing (girdle);
4. frequent (wriggle)

lecano- [Gr. *lekos,* dish, pot] *comb* basin; pan; dish (lecanomancy, lecanorine)

lechrio- [Gr. *lechrios,* slanting] *comb* slanting (lechriodont, lechriopyla)

lecith-, lecitho- [Gr. *lekithos,* yolk] *comb* egg yolk (lecithin, lecithoprotein)

-leco- [Gr. *lekos*, dish or plate] *base* dish (lecotropal)

-lect- [L. *lectio*, reading] *base* read (lectionary, lecture)

-leg-[1] [L. *legere*, to read] *base* read (legenda, legendary)

leg-[2] [L. *lex, leg-*, law] *base* law (legality, legislation)

-legia [L. *legere*, to read] *comb* reading (bradylegia, tachylegia)

leio- [Gr. *leios*, smooth] *comb* smooth (leiomyoma, Leiophyllum). *Also* lio-

-lemma[1] [Gr. *lemma*, thing taken for granted] *comb* assumption; proposition (dilemma, pentalemma)

-lemma[2] [Gr. *lemma*, rind or husk] *comb* rind; peel; husk (neurilemma, sarcolemma)

-lemnisc- [L. *lemniscus*, ribbon] *base* ribbon (lemniscate, lemniscus)

lemur- [L. *lemures*, ghost, specter] *base* tarsier (Lemuridae, lemuroid)

-len- [L. *lenis*, soft] *base* gentle; mild; soothing (lenient, lenity)

-lenocin- [L. *leno*, pander] *base* allure; entice (lenocinant, lenocinium)

lent-[1] [L. *lentus*, slow] *base* slow (lentitude, lentitudinous)

lent-[2] [L. *lens/lent-*, lens] *base* lens (lenticular, lentiform)

-lent[3] [L. suf. *-lentus*] *suf* full of (pestilent, turbulent)

lentig- [L. *lentigo*, lentil-shaped spot] *base* freckle (lentiginose, lentigo)

-leo- [L. *leo*, lion] *base* lion (Leonides, leonine)

lepido- [Gr. *lepis*, a scale] *comb* [botany/zoology] scaly; (lepidocrocite, lepidodendron)

lepidopter- [Gr. *lepis*, scale + *pteron*, wing] *base* butterfly (lepidopterist, lepidopterology)

-lepor- [L. *lepus/lepor-*, hare] *base* hare (leporiform, leporine)

lepra-, lepro- [Gr. *lepra*, leprosy] *comb* leprosy (lepraphobia, leprologist)

-lepsia, -lepsis, -lepsy, lepti-, -leptic [Gr. *lambanein*, to take] *comb* fit; attack; seizure (Epilepsia, catalepsis, catalepsy, epileptiform, narcoleptic)

lepti-, lepto- [Gr. *leptos*, thin, slender] *comb* narrow; thin; fine; frail (leptiform, leptocephaly)

-less [AS *leas*, free] *suf* without; lacking; incapable of being (lawless, thankless)

lesto- [Gr. *lestes*, robber] *comb* thief; robber (lestobiosis, Lestodon)

-let [Fr. dim. suf. *-let*] 1. *suf* small (hamlet); 2. band (anklet)

leth-[1] [Gr. *lethe*, oblivion] *base* forgetfulness; drugged state (lethargy, lethonomania)

leth-[2] [L. *lethalis*, mortal, deadly] *base* deadly (lethal, lethiferous)

leuco-, leuko- [Gr. *leukos*, white] *comb* colorless; white (leucocyte, leukemia)

-levi- [L. *levitas*, lightness] *base* airy; light (levitate, levitation)

-levig- [L. *levigare*, make smooth] *base* smooth; polished (levigated, levigation)

levo- [L. *laevus*, left] 1. *comb* on the left (levogyrate); 2. counterclockwise (levorotatory). *Also* laevo- (laevorotation)

levul- [L. *laevus*, left + *-ule* + *-ose*] *base* sugar (levulinic, levulose)

-lexia, -lexis, -lexy [Gr. *leksis*, speaking] *comb* speech, reading (dyslexia, catalexis, kyriolexy)

lexico- [Gr. *leksikon*, lexicon] *comb* word; vocabulary (lexicographer, lexicology)

-libano- [Gr. *libanos*, frankincense tree] *base* incense (libanomancy, libanotophorousy)

libell- [L. *libellus*, little book] *base* dragonfly (libelluline, libelluloid)

-liber- [L. *liber*, free] *base* free (liberation, liberty)

libid- [L. *libido*, desire] *base* desirous; lustful (libidinous, libinidously)

-libr- [L. *liber*, written material < tree bark] *base* book (librarian, library)

-libra- [L. *libra*, pound] *base* balance; scale (libration, libratory)

libri- [L. *liber*, inner bark] *base* bark; book (libriform, libricide)

licheno- [Gr. *leiken*, tree moss] *comb* lichen; skin disease (lichenologist; licheno-lupoid)

lien(o)- [L. *lien*, spleen] *comb* spleen (lieno-gastric, lienomalacia)

-liga- [L. *ligare*, to bind] *base* tie; bind (ligament, ligature)

ligamenti-, ligamento- [L. *ligamentum*, a tie or band] *comb* having ligaments (ligamentiferous, ligamentomuscular)

ligni-, ligno- [L. *lignum*, wood] *comb* wood (lignivorous, lignoceric)

liguli- [L. dim. *ligula*, little tongue] *comb* tonguelike; strap (liguliflorate, liguliform)

ligur- [L. *lingere*, to lick] *base* lick (ligurate, ligurrition)

ligyr- [Gr. *ligaino*, cry aloud] *base* noise (ligyrophobia)

-like [AS *gelic*, like] **1.** *suf* characteristic of; suitable for (warlike); **2.** in the manner of (bird-like)

lilaps- [Gr. *lailaps*, hurricane, tempest] *base* tornado; hurricane (lilapsomania, lilapsophobia)

lili- [L. *lilium*, lily] *base* lily (liliaceous, liliform)

-lim- [L. *limus*, mud] *base* mud (limicoline, limicolous)

-limac- [L. *limax/limac-*, snail] *base* snail; slug (limaceous, Limacina)

limbat- [L. *limbatus*, edged] *base* bordered, margined (limbate, limbation)

limen- [Gr. *limen*, harbor, haven] *base* harbor (limenarch, Limenitis)

-limin- [L. *limen*, threshold] *base* threshold (eliminate, liminal)

limno- [Gr. *limen*, pool, lake, marsh] *comb* lake; pond; marsh (limnology, limnophagous)

limo-¹ [L. *limus*, mud] *comb* clayey and (limo-cretaceous, limosity)

limo-² [Gr. *limos*, hunger] *comb* fasting; famine (limotherapy)

lin-, linon- [Gr. *linon*, cord, fishing line] *base* string, web (linitis, linonophobia)

linar- [L. *linum*, flax] *base* flax (Linaria, linigerous)

lineo- [L. *linea*, line] *comb* line (lineolate, lineo-polar)

-ling¹ [ME suf. *-ling*] *suf* person or thing belonging to or concerned with (underling, worldling)

-ling² [Goth. suf. *-liggs*] *suf* diminutive (duckling, stripling)

-ling³ [ME suf. *-ling*] *suf* direction; extent; condition (darkling, groveling)

ling-⁴ [L. *lingere*, to lick] *base* lick (lingible)

lingui-, linguli-, linguo- [L. *lingua*, tongue] *comb* language; tongue (bilingual, lingulate, linguopalatal)

lipar- [Gr. *liparos*, oily] *base* grease; fat (Liparia, liparocele)

lipo-¹ [Gr. *lipos*, fat, lard] *comb* fatty (lipogenous, liposuction)

lipo-² [Gr. *lipein*, to leave] *comb* lacking; without (lipocephalous, lipostomosis)

lipsano- [Gr. *lipares*, earnest in praying] *comb* relics (lipsanographer, lipsanotheca)

-liqu- [L. *liquare*, to melt] *base* melt; make liquid; dissolve (liquefaction, liquescent)

lirell- [dim. of *lira*, furrow] *base* narrow and furrowed (lirellate, lirelliform)

-lirio- [Gr. *leirion*, lily] *base* lily (liriodendrin, Liriodendron)

-liss(o)- [Gr. *lissos*, smooth, bare] *base* smooth (lissoflagellate, lissotrichous)

-litan- [Gr. *litaneia*, an entreating] *base* prayer; entreaty (litaneutical, litany)

-lite [Gr. *lithos*, stone] *suf* names of minerals; stone (aciculate, chrysolite)

-lith [Gr. *lithos*, stone] *comb* stone (acrolith, monolith)

-lithic [Gr. *lithos*, stone] *comb* stone-using stage (Eolithic, neolithic)

litho- [Gr. *lithos*, stone] *comb* stone; rock; calculus (lithoglyph, lithosphere)

litig- [L. *litigare*, carry on a suit] *base* quarrel; lawsuit (litigation, litigious)

-littor- [L. *litus/litor-*, shore] *base* shore (littoral, Littorina)

-litu- [L. *lituus*, trumpet] *base* clarion, trumpet (lituate, lituiform)

livid- [L. *lividus*, black and blue] *base* black and blue (lividity, lividness)

lixiv- [L. *lixivius*, lye] *base* lye; alkaline (lixivation, lixiviate)

lobi-, lobo- [Gr. *lobos*, lobe] *comb* lobe (lobigerous, lobiole)

lobulato- [dim. of Gr. *lobos*, lobe] *comb* having small lobes (lobulato-crenate, lobulato-glomerate)

lochio- [Gr. *lochios*, of childbirth] *comb* childbirth (lochiometritis, lochioperitonitis)

loco- [L. *locus*, place] 1. *comb* from place to place (locomotive); 2. a particular place (locodescriptive)

-locu- [L. *locutus*, spoken] *base* word; speech; discourse (elocution, interlocutor). *Also* -loqu- (eloquence)

locul- [L. *loculus*, compartment] *base* box, cell (loculament, loculicidal)

locust- [L. *locusta*, locust] *base* cricket; locust; grasshopper (locustarian)

lodic- [L. *lodex/lodic-*, coverlet] *base* blanket; rug; scale (lodicula, lodicule)

logad- [Gr. *logades*, conjunctivae] *base* conjunctivitis (logadectomy, logaditis)

-logia [Gr. *logos*, word] *comb* speech (bradylogia, paromologia)

-logic, -logical [Gr. *logike*, reasoning] *comb* of a science (geologic, biological)

-logist [Gr. *logike*, reasoning] *comb* one versed in __ (biologist, philologist)

logo- [Gr. *logos*, word] *comb* word; speech; discourse (logographic, logorrhea)

-logue [Gr. *logos*, word] *comb* kind of speaking or writing (dialogue, monologue)

-logy [Gr. *logos*, word] 1. *comb* kind of speaking (eulogy); 2. science; doctrine; theory/study of (geology, theology)

-loimo- [Gr. *loimos*, plague] *base* pestilence (loimography, loimology). *Also* lœmo- (lœmology)

loligo- [L. *loligo*, cuttlefish] *base* squid (loligopsid, Loligopsis)

lom- [Gr. *loma*, hem or fringe] *base* fringed (lomarioid, lomatine)

-lonch- [Gr. *lonkhe*, spear head] *base* spearhead (lonchidite, Lonchitis)

longi- [L. *longus*, long] *comb* long (longicorn, longipennate)

lophio-, lopho- [Gr. *lophos*, crest] *comb* [zoology/anatomy] crest; ridge (lophiodont, lophocercal)

-loqu- [L. *loquere*, to speak] *base* talk; speech (eloquence, grandiloquent). *See* locu-

-lor- [L. *lorum*, thong or strap] *base* thong; strap (Loranthus, lorate)

lordo- [Gr. *lordosis*, bend back] *comb* hump (lordoscoliosis, lordosis)

-lorica- [L. *lorica*, corselet] *base* covering; hard shell (illoricated, loricate)

loxo- [Gr. *loksos*, slanting] *comb* [medicine/zoology] slanting; oblique (loxodromics, loxotomy)

-lubric- [L. *lubricare*, make smooth] *base* smooth; slippery (lubrication, lubricity)

luc-, luci [L. *lux/luc-*, light] *comb* light; clear; dawn (lucidity, lucifugal, antelucan)

lucern- [L. *lucerna*, lamp] *base* lamp (lucernal, Lucernaria)

-lucr(i)- [L. *lucrum*, gain] *base* profit; gain (lucriferous, lucrific)

-luct-[1] [L. *luctus*, sorrow] *base* sorrow (luctisonant, luctual)

luct-[2] [L. *luctatio*, wrestle, struggle] *base* wrestle (luctation, luctatory)

lucubr- [ML *lucubrum*, faint light]

base work; nocturnal study (lucubration, lucubratory)

-lude [L. *ludus*, play, diversion] *comb* a play; to play with (interlude, prelude)

ludif- [L. *ludificare*, make sport of] *base* hoax; deception (ludification, ludificatory)

-luetic [L. *lues*, plague] *comb* syphilis (luetic, paraluetic)

-lum- [L. *lumen*, light] *base* light (illumination, luminosity). *See* **-luc-**

lumbo- [L. *lumbus*, loin] *comb* loin; lumbar (lumbodorsal, lumbosacral)

-lumbric- [L. *lumbricus*, intestinal worm] *base* worm (lumbricide, lumbriciform)

luni- [L. *luna*, moon] *comb* moon; (lunistitial, lunitidal)

lunu- [L. *lunula*, little moon] *comb* crescent; moon-shaped (lunulated, lunulet)

-lup- [L. *lupinus*, of a wolf] *base* wolf; (lupine, Lupinus)

lupan- [L. *lupanar*, brothel] *base* brothel (lupanar, lupanary)

lur- [L. *luridus*, pale yellow, wan] *base* yellow-brown (lurid, luridly)

lurido- [L. *luridus*, pale yellow, wan] *comb* yellow (lurido-cinerascent, lurido-whitish)

-lusc- [L. *luscus*, one-eyed] *base* one-eyed (eluscate, Luscinia)

lustr- [L. *lustrum*, purificatory sacrifice] *base* shining; splendor (illustrious, lustral)

lut- [L. *lutum*, mud] *base* mud (lutarious, lutulent)

luteo- [L. *luteus*, golden-yellow] *comb* yellow; (luteo-cobaltic, luteo-fulvous)

lutjan- [NL *lutjanus*, snapper] *base* snapper (lutjanid, Lutjanidae)

lutr- [L. *lutra*, otter] *base* otter (Lutridae, lutrine)

-ly [OE suf. *-lice*] 1. *suf* characteristic of; suitable to (earthly); 2. happening every __ (hourly); 3. in a specified

way (harshly); 4. in some direction (outwardly); 5. in some order (thirdly)

lyc-, lyco- [Gr. *lukos*, wolf] *comb* wolf (lycanthropy, lycomania)

-lych- [Gr. *lukhnos*, lamp] *base* lamp (lychnapsia, lychnic)

lyg- [Gr. *lugaios*, gloomy] *base* dark; murky (lygaeid, Lygaeus)

lygod- [Gr. *lugos*, willow twig] *base* fern (Lygodiaceae, Lygodium)

lymphaden(o)- [NL *lympha*, lymph + Gr. *aden*, gland] *comb* lymph nodes (lymphadenoma, lymphadenopathy)

lymphangio- [NL *lympha*, lymph + Gr. *angeion*, vessel] *comb* lymphatic vessels (lymphangioplasty, lymphangitis)

lymphato- [NL *lymphaticus*, of the lymph] *comb* lymphatic (lymphatolysis)

lympho- [NL *lympha*, lymph] *comb* of the lymph; (lymphocyte, lymphosarcoma)

lync- [Gr. *lunks*, lynx] *base* lynx (lyncean, Lynceus)

lyo- [Gr. *luein*, dissolve] *comb* dissolution (lyomerous, lyophilic)

lype- [Gr. *lupe*, grief, distress] *comb* sadness; grief (lypemania, Lyperanthus)

lyri- [L. *lyra*, lyre] *base* lyre (lyriferous, lyriform)

lyrico- [Gr. *lurikos*, sung with a lyre] *comb* lyric (lyrico-dramatic, lyrico-epic)

lysi-, -lysis, lyso-, -lyte, -lytic, -lyze [Gr. *lusis*, a setting free] *comb* freeing; relieving; breaking up; dissolving; destroying (lysimeter, lysogen, electrolysis, gazolyte, paralytic, paralyze)

-lysso- [Gr. *lussa*, canine madness] *base* rabies (lyssic, lyssophobia)

-lyte [Gr. *lutos*, loosed] *comb* decomposed substance; dissolved (electrolyte, hydrolyte)

lyxo- [< xylose, 1st syllable reversed, Gr. *ksulon*, wood] *base* artificial sugar (lyxoflavin, lyxose)

M

-ma [Gr. *suf. -ma*] *suf* result of action (dogma, enigma)

macar- [Gr. *makar*, blessed, happy] *base* happy; blessed (macarism, macarize)

macell- [Gr. *makellos*, market] *base* meat market (macellarious)

macer- [L. *maceratus*, softened] *base* soften, soak (macerate, maceration)

-machaero- [Gr. *makhaira*, sword] *base* sword (machaerodont, Machaeropterus)

macho-, -machy [Gr. *makhe*, fight] *comb* struggle; contest; battle; fight (machopolyp, hieromachy)

maci- [L. *macere*, be lean] *base* thin; lean (macilence, macilent)

macro- [Gr. *makros*, long] *comb* long; large (macrobiotics, macrocosm)

macropod- [Gr. *makropous*, long-footed] *base* kangaroo (macropodal, macropodine)

macrur- [L. *macrurus*, long-tailed] *base* shrimp (macruran, macrural)

mact- [L. *mactare*, to sacrifice] *base* immolation; sacrifice (mactation, mactator)

-macul- [L. *macula*, spot, stain] *base* spot; stain (immaculate, maculation)

mad- [L. *madere*, to be wet] *base* wet; moist (madefacient, madefaction)

madar- [Gr. *madaros*, bold] *base* hair loss (madarosis)

mageir- [Gr. *mageiros*, cook] *base* cook (mageiric, mageiricophobia). *Also* magir- (magiric, magirology)

-magist- [L. *magister*, chief, director] *base* master; head; authority (magisterial, magistrate)

magneto- [Gr. *magnes*, Magnesia, Thessaly] *comb* magnetic force (magneto-electric, magnetometer)

magni- [L. *magnus*, great, large] *comb* great; large (magniloquent, magnitude)

mago- [Gr. *magos*, magical] *comb* magic (mago-chemical, magomany)

maha- [Sanskrit *maha*, great] *base* mastery; control (maharanee, mahatma)

maieusio- [Gr. *maieusis*, childbirth] *base* childbirth (maieusiomania, maieusiophobia)

maieut- [Gr. *maieutikos*, of midwifery] *base* bringing forth; midwifery (maieutic, maieutical)

-maj- [L. *major*, greater] *base* great; large (majoration, majority)

mal-[1] [L. *malus*, bad] *comb* bad; wrong; ill (maladroit, malcontent)

mal-[2] [L. *mala*, cheek] *base* cheek (malar)

-malacia, malaco- [Gr. *malakos*, soft] 1. *comb* soft (gastromalacia); 2. mollusks (malacology)

-malax- [L. *malaxare*, soften] *base* soften, knead (malaxate, malaxation)

Malayo- [Portuguese *malayo*, Malay land] *comb* Malay (Malayo-Indonesian, Malayo-Polynesian)

male- [L. *malus*, bad] *comb* evil (malediction, malefaction)

-mali- [L. *malum*, apple] *base* apple (malicorium, maliform)

malleo- [L. *malleus*, hammer] *comb* hammer (malleo-incudal, malleoramate)

-mallo- [Gr. *mallos*, lock of wool] *base* wool (mallophagan, mallophagous)

malneiro- [L. *malus*, bad + Gr. *neiros*, dream] *comb* nightmare (malneirophobia, malneirophrenia)

mammilli- [L. dim. of *mamma*, breast, nipple] *comb* nipple (mammilated, mammilliform)

mammato- [L. *mammatus*, having breasts] *comb* rounded clouds (mammato-cumulus)

mammi-, mammo- [L. *mamma*,

breast] *comb* breasts (mammiferous, mammogram)

-man [Sanskrit *manu*, man < Manu, mythical father of the human race] *comb* human; male (anchorman, woodsman)

-mancy, -mantic [Gr. *manteia*, divination] *comb* divination (necromancy, necromantic)

-mand- [L. *mandare*, to entrust] *base* command; oblige (mandate, mandatory)

mandibulo- [L. *mandibulum*, jaw] *comb* jaw (mandibuliform, mandibulo-maxillary)

manduc- [L. *manducare*, to chew] *comb* chew; eat (manducation, manducatory)

mangan-, mangani-, mangano-, manganoso- [L. *manganium*, manganese] *comb* manganese (manganbrucite, manganicyanide, manganosiderite, manganoso-manganic)

mani-, manu- [L. *manus*, hand] *comb* hand; (manipulate, manuscript)

-mania [L. *mania*, madness] 1. *comb* mental disorder (kleptomania); 2. excessive craving (bibliomania)

mano- [Gr. *manos*, rare] *comb* thin; rare (manometer, manometric)

mansue- [L. *mansuetus*, tame] *base* tame; mild (mansuete, mansuetude)

manubr- [L. *manubrium*, handle, hilt] *base* handle (manubrial, manubriated)

marasm- [Gr. *marasmos*, withering, wasting away] *base* wasting, withering (marasmic, marasmus)

-marc- [L. *marcescere*, wither, shrivel] *base* faded; withered (marcescent, marcescible)

mare- [L. *mare*, sea] *comb* sea (mareogram, mareography)

marg- [L. *margo*, border] *base* border; verge (marginal, marginate)

margarit- [Gr. *margarites*, pearl] *base* pearl (margaritaceous, margaritiferous)

-margy [Gr. *margos*, raging mad] *base* raging mad (gastrimargy, gastromargy)

mari- [L. *mare*, sea] *comb* sea (mariculture, marigraph)

marit- [L. *maritus*, of marriage] *base* spouse; marriage (marital)

-marm- [L. *marmor*, marble] *base* marble (marmoration, marmoreal)

-marsup- [L. *marsupium*, pouch] *base* pouch (marsupial, marsupiated)

-mas [mass < L. *missa*, dismissal] *comb* feast day (Christmas, Martinmas)

maschal- [Gr. *maskhale*, armpit] *base* armpit (maschaladenitis, maschaliatry)

masculo- [L. *masculus*, masculine] *comb* male (masculonuclear, masculo-nucleus)

masso- [Gr. *massein*, to knead] *comb* massage (massotherapist, massotherapy)

-mastia, masto- [Gr. *mastos*, breast] *comb* [medicine/zoology] breast: of or like (macromastia, mastodynia)

mastic- [L. *masticare*, chew] *base* chew (mastication, masticatory)

mastigo- [Gr. *mastiks*, whip] *comb* whiplike; scourge bearing (mastigophore, mastigopod)

masto- [Gr. *mastos*, breast] *comb* breast (mastodont, mastodynia)

mastoido- [Gr. *mastoeides*, like the breast] *comb* mastoid (mastoideum, mastoido-humeral)

-mateo- [Gr. *mataios*, vain, foolish] *base* unprofitable; useless; vain (mataeology, mateotechny)

mater-, matri-, matro- [L. *mater*, mother] *comb* mother (maternity, matriarchy, matroclinous)

matertera- [L. *matertera*, maternal aunt] *base* aunt on mother's side (materteral)

-math- [Gr. *manthanein*, to learn] *comb* learn (opsimath, polymath)

matur- [L. *maturare*, to make ripe] *base* ripe (maturation, maturity)

-matut- [L. *matutinum*, morning] *base* morning (matutinal, matutine)

maxi- [L. *maximus*, largest] *comb* very large; very long (maxibudget, maxicoat)

maxillo- [L. *maxilla*, jaw] *comb* of the maxilla; jaw (maxilliform, maxillopalatine)

mazo-[1] [L. *maza*, placenta] *comb* placenta (mazolysis, mazolytic)

mazo-[2] [Gr. *maksos*, breast] *comb* breast (mazologist, mazoplazia)

-meal [OE *mael*, appointed time] *comb* measure (heapmeal, piecemeal)

meato- [L. *meatus*, a passage] *comb* passage; channel (meatometer, meatoscopy)

mechanico- [Gr. *mechanikos*, pert. to machines] *comb* partly mechanical (mechanico-acoustic, mechanico-chemical)

mechano- [Gr. *mechane*, machine] *comb* machines (mechanochemical, mechanotherapy)

-meco- [Gr. *mekos*, length] *base* length (mecodont, mecometer)

-mecon- [Gr. *mekon*, poppy] *base* poppy; opium (meconic, meconidine)

-med- [Gr. *medos*, bladder] 1. *base s.* bladder (medorrhea); 2. *pl.* genitals (medorthophobia)

medi-, medio- [L. *medius*, middle] *comb* middle (medicommisure, mediodorsal)

mediastino- [L. *mediastinus*, medial] *comb* membranous partition (mediastino-pericardial, mediastinoscopy)

medico- [L. *medicus*, physician] *comb* medical; of healing (medicochirurgical, medico-legal)

medo- [Gr. *medos*, penis] *comb* penis (medorrhea, medorrhinum)

medull- [L. *medullosus*, full of marrow] *base* marrow, pith (medullary, medullose)

medus- [L. *medusa*, jellyfish] *base* jellyfish (Medusidae, medusiform)

mega- [Gr. *megas*, large, great] 1. *comb* large; powerful (megaphone); 2. a million of (megacycle)

megachiropter- [Gr. *megas*, large + *cheir*, hand + *pteron*, wing] *base* fruit- bat (megacheiropteran, megachiropterous)

megalo-, -megaly [Gr. *megas/megal-*, large] 1. *comb* large; powerful (megalomania); 2. abnormal enlargement (megalocardia, hepatomegaly)

meio- [Gr. *meion*, less] *comb* less (meiosis). *Also* mio- (miogeosyncline, Miolithic)

meizo- [Gr. *meizon*, greater] *comb* greater (meizoseismal, meizoseismic)

melan-, melano- [Gr. *melas/melan-*, black] *comb* black; very dark (melanosis, melanocomous)

-mele [Gr. *melos*, limb] *comb* limb; extremity (phocomele)

meleagr- [L. *meleagris*, turkey] *base* turkey (Meleagridinae, meleagrine)

melet- [Gr. *meletan*, to study, meditate] *base* meditation (meletetics)

-melia-[1] [Gr. *melos*, limb] *comb* limb; extremity (macromelia)

-melia-[2] [Gr. *melia*, a type of ash tree] *base* ash tree (meliaceous, melial)

melin- [L. *meles/melin-*, badger] 1. *base* badger (meline); 2. tawny (meline)

-melior- [L. *melior*, better] *base* make better; improve (ameliorate, meliorism)

melisso- [Gr. *melissa*, bee] *base* bee (Melissa, melissean)

melitto- [Gr. *melitta*, bee] *base* bee (melittology, melliturgy)

mell(i)- [Gr. *meli*, honey] *comb* honey; sweet (mellifluous, mellivorous)

melo-[1] [Gr. *melos/melod-*, melody] *comb* song; music (melodious, melomania)

melo-[2] [Gr. *mela*, cheeks < *melon*, apple] *comb* cheek; (meloplastic, meloplasty)

melo-[3] [Gr. *melos*, limb] *comb* limb;

extremity (melorheostosis, melorheostoses)

membrani/o- [L. *membrana*, skin] *comb* membrane plus (membraniform, membranocartilaginous)

mendac- [L. *mendax/mendac-*, lying, false] *base* falsehood (mendacious, mendacity)

mendic- [L. *mendicare*, to beg] *base* beggar; poor (mendicant, mendication)

-menia [Gr. *men*, month] *comb* [medicine] pertaining to the menses (catamenia, paramenia)

meningo- [Gr. *menig/mening-*, membrane] *comb* [medicine/anatomy] related to the meninges (meningocele, meningococcus)

-menisc- [Gr. *meniskos*, dim. of moon] *base* crescent-shaped (meniscoid, meniscus)

meno-¹ [Gr. *men*, month] 1. *comb* [medicine] pertaining to the menses (menopause); 2. month (menology)

meno-² [Gr. *menein*, to remain] *comb* persisting (menobranchus, menorhynchus)

mens- [L. *mensis*, month] *base* month; menses (mensual; menstrual)

-ment¹ [L. suf. *-mentum*, result of an act] 1. *suf* result; product (pavement); 2. instrument; means (adornment); 3. process of doing (measurement); 4. state of being acted on (disappointment)

ment-² [L. *mens/ment-*, mind] *base* mind; thought (mental, mentation)

menth- [L. *mentha*, mint] *base* mint (menthaceous, menthol)

mento- [L. *mentum*, chin] *comb* chin (mentohyoid, mentoplasty)

-mentul- [L. *mentula*, penis] *base* penis (mentula, mentulate)

mephit- [L. *mephitis*, pestilential exhalation] *base* skunk (mephitic, Mephitinae)

-mer, -meran [Gr. *meros*, part] *comb* part; unit (isomer, heteromeran). *Also* **-mere** (blastomere). *See* **mero-¹**

-merc- [L. *mercari*, trade or buy] *base* goods (mercantile, mercantilism)

-merd- [L. *merda*, dung] *base* dung (immerd, merdivorous)

-mere [Gr. *meros*, part] *comb* part; unit (blastomere). *See* **-mer** and **mero-¹**

meretric- [L. *meretrix/meretric-*, prostitute] *base* harlot (meretricious, meretriciousness)

-merge, -merse [L. *mergere*, dive, dip] *comb* plunge; dip (submerge, immerse)

merid- [L. *meridies*, midday] *base* noon (antemeridian, postmeridian)

merinth- [Gr. *merinthos*, cord, line, string] *base* bind (merinthophobia)

mersiti- [Gr. *meristos*, divided] *comb* divided (meristematic, meristiform)

merluc- [L. *merlucus*, haddock] *base* hake (merlucine, merlucoid)

mero-¹, **meri-, -meris, -merous, -mery** [Gr. *meros*, part] *comb* part; unit; partial; having __ parts; (meroblast, merihedric, Piptomeris, heteromerous, gonomery)

mero-² [Gr. *meros*, thigh] *comb* thigh (merocele, merocerite)

merul- [L. *merula*, blackbird] *base* blackbird (Merula, meruline)

mesati- [Gr. *mesatos*, midmost] *comb* medium (mesaticephaly, mesatipelvic)

mesmer- [< *Franz Mesmer*, German physician] *base* hypnotism (mesmerism, mesmeromania)

meso- [Gr. *mesos*, middle] 1. *comb* in the middle (mesocarp); 2. [anatomy] a mesentery (mesogastrium)

meta-¹ [Gr. *meta*, beside] 1. *pre* changed (metamorphosis); 2. after (metaphysics); 3. behind; in back (metathorax); 4. beyond; higher (metapsychosis)

meta-² [Gr. *meta*, beside] [chemistry] 1. *pre* polymer of (metaldehyde); 2. derivative of (metaprotein); 3. acid containing less water combined with the anhydride than other acids of the same non-metallic element (metaphosphoric); 4. characterized by substitutes in the 1,3 position in the benzene ring (metacoumarate)

metacarpo- [Gr. *meta*, beyond + *karpos*, wrist] *comb* metacarpus plus (metacarpophalangeal, metacarpotrapezial)

metalli-, metallo- [Gr. *metallon*, mine] *comb* metal (metalliferous, metallochrome)

metatarso- [Gr. *meta*, beyond + *tarsos*, tarsus] *comb* metatarsus plus (metatarsodigital, metatarso-phalangeal)

metax- [Gr. *metaksa*, silk] *base* silk (metaxin, metaxite)

-meter [Gr. *metron*, measure] 1. *comb* device for measuring (barometer); 2. so many meters (kilometer); 3. fraction of a meter (centimeter); 4. having __ metrical feet (pentameter)

metho- [Gr. *methu*, mead] *comb* methyl; mead (methoxyl; methomania)

methoxy- [Gr. *methu*, mead + *okhus*, sharp] *comb* methoxy group (methoxycaffeine, methoxychlor)

methyl- [Gr. *methu*, mead] *comb* methyl group (methyl-benzene, methyldopa)

methys- [Gr. *methusis*, drunkenness] *base* drunk; intoxicated (methysis, methystic)

metopo- [Gr. *metopon*, forehead] *comb* forehead (metoposcopical, metoposcopy)

metr- [Gr. *metron*, poetic meter] *base* poem (metrical, metrician)

metra-, metro-[1] [Gr. *metra*, womb] *comb* uterus (metratonia, metrorrhagia)

-metric, -metrics, metro-[2]**, -metry** [Gr. *metrikos*, rel. to measurement] *comb* measure (geometric, econometrics, metrology, chronometry)

-metrio- [Gr. *metrios*, moderate] *base* moderate (metriocephalic)

mezzo- [Ital. *mezzo*, middle] *comb* middle; half (mezzo-rilievo, mezzotint)

micro- [Gr. *mikros*, small] 1. *comb* little; small (microbarograph); 2. abnormally small (microcephalic); 3. enlarging what is small; (microscope); 4. relation to microscopes (microchemistry); 5. one millionth part of (microgram)

microchiropter- [Gr. *mikros*, small + *kheir*, hand + *pteron*, wing] *base* insectivorous bat (microchiropteran)

-mict- [L. *mingere*, urinate] *base* urine (micturate, micturient). *See* -**ming**-

mid- [Old English *midd*, central] *comb* middle part (midbrain, midseason)

-milit- [L. *militare*, serve as a soldier] *base* soldier (militancy, military)

milli- [L. *millia*, thousand] 1. *comb* one thousandth part of (millimeter); 2. one thousand (millifold)

milv- [L. *milvus*, the kite] *base* kite — the bird (Milvinae, milvine)

-mim- [Gr. *mimeisthai*, imitate] 1. *base* imitate (mimetic); 2. mockingbird (mimine)

min- [L. *minari*, threaten] *base* threat (minacious, minatory)

-ming- [L. *mingere*, to discharge urine] *base* urine (mingent, retromingent). *See* -**mict**-

mini- [L. *minimus*, least] *comb* smaller; shorter; lesser than usual (miniskirt, minimart)

mio- [Gr. *meion*, less] *comb* less; diminished (miosis, miotaxy). *Also* **meio-** (meiosis)

-mir- [L. *mirari*, to wonder] *base* wonder (admiration, mirabilia)

mis- [Gothic *missa*, wrong, bad] *pre* wrong; bad (miscalculate, misrule)

-misc- [L. *miscere*, mix] *base* mixed (immiscible, miscellaneous)

miso- [Gr. *misos*, hatred] *comb* hated; hating (misogamy, misogyny)

-miss-, -mit-[1] [L. *mittere*, send] *base* send (dismiss, remit)

mit-[2], mito- [Gr. *mitos*, thread] *comb* thread (mitosis, mitochondria)

miti-[1] [L. *mitis*, mild] *base* mild; soothing (mitigate, mitigatory)

miti-[2] [Dutch *mit*, woodworm] *base* mite (miticidal, miticide)

mitri- [L. *mitri*, miter, turban] *base* miter (Mitrephorus, mitriform)

mixo- [Gr. *mikso*, mixed] *comb* mixed (mixogamous, mixogamy)

mixti- [L. *mixtus*, mixed] *comb* mixed (mixtiform, mixtilineal)

-mnem-, -mnesia, -mnesis [Gr. *mnasthai*, remember] *base* memory (mnemonics, amnesia, anamnesis)

-mo [< duodeci*mo*, in twelve] *suf* printing books: a suffix to the number designating one of the equal parts into which a sheet is divided, the size of a page varying with the size of the sheet folded (12mo, twelvemo)

-mob- [L. *mobilis*, moveable] *base* move (immobility, mobile)

-mobile [< auto*mobile*] *comb* special type of vehicle (Batmobile, bookmobile)

-mochl- [Gr. *mokhlikos*, lever] *base* lever (hypomochlion, mochlic)

modul- [L. *modulari*, regulate] *base* regulate (modulate, modulatory)

mogi- [Gr. *mogis*, hardly] *comb* with difficulty (mogigraphia, mogilalia)

mol-, molin- [L. *molere*, grind] *base* grind (molar, molariform, molinologist)

-molend- [L. *molendinum*, mill-house] *base* mill (molendarious, molendinary)

-moll- [L. *mollis*, soft] *base* soft; (emollient, mollify)

mollusc- [L. *molluscum*, mollusk] *base* mollusk (molluscan, molluscous)

molybdo- [Gr. *molubdos*, lead] *comb* lead (molybdeniferous, molybdocolic)

molys- [Gr. *molunsis*, staining] *base* dirt (molysite, molysmophobia)

-mon- [L. *monere*, warn] *base* warn; (admonish, monitorial)

monach- [L. *monachus*, monk] *base* monk (monachal, monachism)

-monil- [L. *monile*, necklace] *base* necklace (monilated, moniliform)

mono- [Gr. *monos*, alone, single] 1. *comb* single; alone; one (monoclinal); 2. containing one atom (monochloride); 3. one molecule thick (monolayer)

monotrem- [Gr. *monos*, single + *trema*, hole] *base* platypus (monotremal, Monotremata)

-monstr- [L. *monstrare*, to show] *base* show; (demonstrate, monstrance)

mont- [L. *montanus*, mountain] *base* mountain (montagnard, montane)

-mony [L. suf. *-monia*] *suf* resulting state (patrimony, queremony)

-mor-[1] [L. *mos/mor-*, manner, custom] *base* usage; custom (morality, mores)

-mor-[2] [L. *morum*, blackberry, mulberry] *base* mulberry (moriform, morula)

-mora- [L. *mora*, delay] *base* delay (moration, remorate)

-morb- [L. *morbus*, disease] *base* sickly; diseased (morbidity, morbiferous)

morbilli- [L. dim. of *morbus*] *base* measles (morbilliform, morbillous)

-mord- [L. *mordax/mordac-*, biting] *base* sharp; biting; acrid (mordacity, mordant)

mori- [L. *morum*, mulberry] *base* mulberry (moric acid, moriform)

-moriger- [L. *morigerari*, comply with] *base* obedient; submissive (morigeration, morigerous)

-morilli- [Fr. *morille*, morel] *base* fungus; morel (morilliform)

moro- [Gr. *moros*, foolish] *base* foolish (morology, moronic)

moros- [L. *morosus*, sullen, peevish] *base* surly (morose, morosity)

-morph, -morphic, -morphism, morpho-, -morphosis, -morphous [Gr.

morphe, shape] *comb* having a specified form (pseudomorph, anthropomorphic, monomorphism, morphology, cytomorphosis, isomorphous)

mort-, morti- [L. *mor/mort-*, death] *comb* death (immortality, mortify)

-mosch- [Gr. *moschos*, musk] *base* musk (moschiferous, moschine)

-most [Old English *mest*, most] *suf* superlatives (foremost, hindmost)

motil- [L. *motilis*, motile] *base* capable of motion (motile, motility)

-motive [Fr. *motif*, that causes motion] *comb* moving (automotive, locomotive)

moto- [L. *motor*, mover] *comb* motor (motocross, moto-sensitive)

-mouthed [Old English *muth*, mouth] *comb* having a __ mouth; having __ mouths (foul-mouthed, large-mouthed)

mov- [L. *movere*, move] *base* move (movable, remove)

muci-, muco- [L. *mucus*, mucus] *comb* snot; mucous membrane (muciparous, mucoprotein)

mucid- [L. *mucidus*, moldy] *base* musty (mucidness, mucidous)

mucoso- [L. *mucosus*, slimy] *comb* partly mucous (mucoso-granular, mucoso-saccharine)

-mucro- [L. *mucro*, sharp point] *base* sharp tip or point (mucroniferous, mucronulate)

-mug- [L. *mugire*, bellow] *base* bellow (mugient, remugient)

mugil- [L. *mugil*, mullet] *base* mullet (mugiliform, mugiloid)

mulie(b)r- [L. *mulier*, woman] *base* woman (muliebrity, mulierose)

mult(i)- [L. *multus*, many] **1.** *comb* having many (multicolored); **2.** more than two (multilateral); **3.** many times (multimillionaire)

mummi- [Hindi *mum*, embalming wax] *base* mummy (mummiform, mummify)

mun- [L. *munus*, a present] *base* gift (munificent, remunerate)

-mund-¹ [L. *mundus*, world] *base* world (mundane, mundivagant)

-mund-² [L. *mundare*, cleanse] *base* cleanse (mundation)

-mur-¹ [L. *mus/mur-*, mouse] *base* mouse (murine)

-mur-² [L. *murus*, wall] *base* wall (immured, mural)

-mur-³ [Fr. *mure*, mulberry] *base* mulberry (muriform)

muraen- [L. *murena*, eel] *base* moray (muraenid, muraenoid)

-muri- [L. *muria*, brine] *base* brine (muriacite, muriatic)

-muric- [L. *murex/muric-*, pointed rock, spire] *base* pointed; sharp (muricated, muricatohispid)

musa- [Arabic *muze*, banana] *base* banana (Musaceae, musaceous)

-musc-¹ [L. *musca*, fly] *base* fly (Musca, musciform)

-musc-² [L. *muscus*, moss] *base* moss (emuscation, muscicole)

muscar- [L. *muscarium*, fly brush] *base* brush (muscariform, muscatorium)

muscicap- [L. *musca*, fly + *capere*, take] *base* flycatching bird; thrush (Muscicapidae, muscicapine)

musculo- [L. *musculus*, muscle] *comb* muscle (musculocutaneous, musculophrenic)

musico- [Gr. *mousike*, melodic art] *comb* music (musicodramatic, musicophobia)

muso- [Gr. *mousa*, muse] *base* poem (musomania, musophobia)

muss- [L. *mussitare*, murmur] *base* mutter; murmur (mussitate, mussitation)

-mustel- [L. *mustella*, weasel] **1.** *base* weasel; badger; skunk; polecat; ermine; marten; mink; wolverine; ferret (musteline); **2.** tawny (musteline)

-mut- [L. *mutare*, change] *base* change (immutable, mutability)

-mutil- [L. *mutilare*, mutilate] *base* maim (mutilate, mutilation)

-mutu- [L. *mutuus*, interchanged] *base* reciprocal (mutual, mutuality)

-mycete, myceto- [Gr. *mukes/muket-*, fungus] *comb* fungus of a specified group (schizomycete, mycetoma)

-mycin [< *myc*(o) + *-in*] *comb* derivative of a specified substance from bacteria or fungi; antibiotic (neomycin, streptomycin)

myco- [Gr. *mukes*, fungus] *comb* mushroom; fungus (mycobiont, mycology)

mycter- [Gr. *mukter*, snout] *comb* sneer; scoff; nose (Mycteria, mycterism)

mycto- [Gr. *mukter*, nostril] *comb* lanternfish (myctophid, myctophiform)

myda- [Gr. *mudan*, to be damp] *base* putrid (mydatoxin, mydin)

-myelia, myelo- [Gr. *muelos*, marrow] *comb* spinal cord; marrow (micromyelia, myelogenic)

myia- [Gr. *muia*, fly] *base* fly (myiasis, Myodioctes)

mylo- [Gr. *mule*, millstone, molar] *base* molar (mylodont, myloglossus)

myo-¹ [Gr. *mus*, muscle] *comb* [medicine/anatomy] muscle (myocardium, myodynamia)

myo-² [Gr. *mus*, mouse] *base* mouse (myomancy, myomorph)

myop- [Gr. *muopia*, short-sighted] *base* short-sightedness (myopia, myopic)

myox- [Gr. *muoksos*, dormouse] *base* dormouse (myoxine, Myoxus)

myria- [Gr. *murios*, numberless] 1. *comb* numerous; many (myriapod);

2. ten thousand (myriameter). *Also* myrio- (myriophyllus)

myringo- [L. *myringa*, membrana tympani] *base* tympanic (myringitis, myringoplasty)

myrist- [Gr. *muristikos*, fragrant (nut)] *base* nutmeg (myristic, myristicivorous)

myrmeco-, myrmic- [Gr. *murmek-*, ant] *comb* ant (myrmecology, myrmicine)

myrmecophag- [Gr. *murmek-*, ant + *phagein*, eat] *base* anteater (myrmecophagine, mymecophagous)

myrio- [Gr. *moira*, fate] *base* dirge, lament (myriologist, myriologue)

myro- [Gr. *muron*, unguent] *comb* ointment; perfume (myronic, myropolist)

-myrti- [Gr. *murtos*, myrtle] *base* myrtle (myrtaceous, myrtiform)

myso- [Gr. *musos*, uncleanness] *comb* dirt (mysophobia, mysomania). *Also* miso- (misophobia)

mystico- [Gr. *mustikos*, secret] *comb* partly mystical (mystico-allegoric, mystico-religious)

mythico- [Gr. *muthos*, myth] *comb* partly mythical (mythico-magical, mythico-romantic)

mytho- [Gr. *muthos*, myth] *comb* myth; story (mythoclast, mythological)

-mytil- [Gr. *mutilos*, sea-mussel] *base* mussel (mytilaceous, mytiliform)

-myxia, myxo- [Gr. *muksa*, nostril, mucus] *comb* slime; mucus (hypomyxia, myxomycete)

-myz- [Gr. *muzein*, suck] *base* suck (myzont, myzostoma)

N

-nacar- [Pg. *nacar*, mother-of-pearl] *base* orange-red, scarlet (nacarat, nacarine)

naev- [L. *naevus*, mole] *base* blemish, birthmark (naevoid, naevous)

nano- [L. *nanus*, dwarf] 1. *comb*

dwarfism; (nanocephalous); 2. one-billionth (nanosecond). *Also* **nanno-** (nannofossil)

-nao- [Gr. *naos*, temple] *base* temple (naological, naology)

-napi- [L. *napus*, turnip] *base* turnip (napifolious, napiform)

narco- [Gr. *narkoun*, benumb] *comb* numbness; stupor (narcolepsy, narcomatous)

-nari- [L. *naris*, nostril] *base* nostrils (naricorn, nariform)

narr- [L. *narrare*, report] *base* relate; tell (narrative, narrator)

nasc- [L. *nasci*, be born] *base* born (nascent, nascently)

nasi-, naso- [L. *nasus*, nose] *comb* nose; nasal (nasicornous, nasolabial)

-nastic, -nasty [Gr. *nastos*, pressed close] *comb* plant growth: unequal by some specified means or in a specified direction (hyponastic, hyponasty)

-nata- [L. *natare*, swim] *base* swim; (natation, natatorium)

-natal- [L. *natalis*, pert. to birth] *base* birth (antenatal, neonatal)

-nati- [L. *nates*, buttocks] *base* buttocks (naticine, natiform)

-natremia [Gr. *natrion*, sodium] *comb* sodium; (hyponatremia, pseudohyponatremia)

-natured [L. *natura*, natural constitution] *comb* having a __ nature or temperament (good-natured, mean-natured)

naus- [Gr. *nausia*, ship] *base* sick; seasick (nausea, nauseous)

-naut-, -nav-, navic- [Gr. *nautikos*, pert. to ships] *base* ship; sea (nautical, navigate, naviculoid)

navig- [L. *navigare*, go by sea] *base* voyage (navigable, navigation)

ne- [Gr. *ne*, not] *pre* not (nescience, nescient)

-nebul- [L. *nebula*, cloud, vapor] *base* cloud; mist; vapor (nebuliferous, nebulous)

necro- [Gr. *nekros*, dead body] *comb* death; corpse; dead tissue (necrolatry, necrology)

necto- [Gr. *nektos*, swimming] *comb* swimming (nectosome, nectozooid)

necyo- [Gr. *nekus*, corpse] *comb* demon; damned spirit (necyomancer, necyomancy)

-neg- [L. *negare*, deny] *base* deny (negation, negativist)

-negot- [L. *negotium*, business] *base* business (negotiation, renegotiate)

-nema- [Gr. *nema*, thread] *base* thread (hyalonema, nemalite)

nemato- [Gr. *nema/nemat-*, thread] *comb* thread; threadlike (nematoblast, nematocyst)

nemor- [Gr. *nemos*, wooded pasture] *base* woods; forest (nemoral, nemorous)

neo- [Gr. *neos*, new, young] 1. *comb* new; recent; latest (neo-classic); 2. [geology] chronologically last part of a period (Neocene)

neosso- [Gr. *neossos*, young bird] *comb* young birds (neossology, neossoptile)

nephal- [Gr. *nephalios*, sober] *base* sober; abstinent (nephalism, nephalist)

nephelo-, nepho- [Gr. *nephele*, cloud] *comb* cloud ;(nephelometer, nephology)

nephro- [Gr. *nephros*, kidney] *comb* kidney (nephrologist, nephrotomy)

nepi- [Gr. *nepios*, infant] *base* infant (nepiology, nepionic)

-nepo- [L. *nepos*, nephew] *base* nephew (nepotic, nepotism)

-ner- [Gr. *Nereus*, sea-god] *base* liquid (aneroid, nereocystis)

-nerter- [Gr. *nerteroi*, the dead] *base* the dead (nerterologist, nerterology)

nerv-, nervi-, nervo- [L. *nervus*, sinew, fiber, nerve] *comb* nerve (nervosity, nervifolious, nervovital)

neso- [Gr. *nesos*, island] *comb* island (Nesomys, Nesotragus)

-ness [AS suf. -nes] suf condition; quality of (greatness, sweetness)

neuro- [Gr. neuron, nerve] comb nervous system; nerve (neurography, neuropath)

neutro- [L. neuter, neither] comb neutral (neutropenia, neutrophile)

nev-, nevo- [L. naevus, mole] base birthmark; mole (nevoid, nevus)

-nex- [L. nexus, a bond] base connect; bind (annex, nexus)

nic- [Gr. nike, victory] base victory (epinician, epinicion)

-nict- [L. nictitare, wink] base wink (nictation, nictitate)

nid-, nidi- [L. nidus, nest] base nest (nidal, nidification)

nidor- [L. nidor, vapor, aroma] base smell (nidorosity, nidorous)

nigri-, nigro- [L. niger, black] comb black (nigricauline, nigrofuscous)

nihili- [L. nihil, nothing] comb nothing (nihili-parturient, nihility)

-nik suf one who is associated with __ (beatnik, peacenik)

nimb- [L. nimbus, cloud] base cloud; rainstorm (nimbiferous, nimbification)

ning- [L. ninguis, snow] base snow (ninguid)

nipha- [Gr. nipha, snow] comb snow blindness (niphablepsia, niphotyphlosis)

nitid- [L. nitidus, shining, bright] base lustrous; bright (nitidiflorous, nitidity)

nitro- [L. nitrum, niter] 1. comb presence of nitrogen compounds (nitrocellulose); 2. the presence of the NO_2 radical (nitrobenzene); 3. niter (nitrobacteria)

-niv- [L. nix/niv-, snow] base snow (nival, niveous)

noci- [L. nocere, harm] comb hurt; pain; injury (nociceptor, nocivous)

nocti- [L. nox/noct-, night] comb night (noctiferous, noctilucent)

noctilion- [L. noctilio, family of bats] base bat (Noctilio, noctilionid)

noctui- [L. noctua, family of moths] base noctuid moth (noctuidous, noctuiform)

-nod- [L. nodus, knot] base knot, knob (nodulated, nodulose)

-noe- [Gr. noema, thought, perception] base thought; intellect (noematic, noetic)

-noia [Gr. nous, mind] comb thought (metanoia, paranoia)

-nom-, -nym- [L. nomen name + Gr. onoma, name] base name (nomenclature, synonymous)

nomato- see onomato-

-nomia [L. nomen, name] comb name (anomia, paranomia)

nomo- [Gr. nomos, law] comb law; custom (nomotropic, nomology)

-nomy [Gr. nomos, arranging] comb systematized knowledge of (agronomy, astronomy)

non-[1] [L. non, not] pre negative; not (nonconforming, nondescript)

non-[2], nona- [L. nonus, ninth] base nine, ninth (nonagon, nonan)

nonagen-, nonages- [L. nonaginta, ninety] base ninety (nonagenarian, nonagesimal)

-noo- [Gr. noos, mind] base mind (noögenism, nooscopic)

Normanno- [L. Normannus, Norman] comb Norman (Normanno-Gallican, Normanno-Saxonic)

normo- [L. normalis, right-angled] comb usual; normal (normoblastic, normotensive)

noso- [Gr. nosos, disease] comb disease (nosology, nosophobia)

nosocom- [Gr. nosokomeion, infirmary] base hospital (nosocomial, nosocomially)

nosto- [Gr. nostos, return] comb a return; nostalgia (nostology, nostomania)

nota-, noto-[1] [Gr. notos, the back] comb the back; dorsum (notancephalia, notochord)

-notho- [Gr. nothos, spurious] base

spurious; false (Notholaena, nothosaurus)

-noto-² [Gr. *notos*, the south] *comb* south (Notornis, notothere)

-nov-¹ [L. *novus*, new] *base* new (innovation, renovate)

-nov-² [L. *novem*, nine] *base* nine (November, novenary)

-noverc- [L. *noverca*, stepmother] *base* stepmother (novercal, novercant)

-nox- [L. *noxa*, injury] *base* harmful; (noxiousness, obnoxious)

-nub-, -nupt- [L. *nubere/nuptus*, wed] *base* marry (connubial, nuptial)

-nubi- [L. *nubes*, cloud] *base* cloud (nubiferous, nubigenous)

nuci- [L. *nux/nuci-*, nut] *comb* nut (nuciferous, nucifragous)

nuclei-, nucleo- [L. *nucleus*, kernel] *comb* nucleus: relation to; kernel (nucleiform, nucleoplasm)

nudi- [L. *nudus*, naked] *comb* naked; bare (nudibranchiate, nudiflorous)

-nuga- [L. *nugae*, trifles] *base* trifling (nugation, nugatory)

nulli- [L. *nullus*, not any] *comb* none (nullify, nulliparous)

-num- [L. *numerare*, to number] *base* count (enumerate, numerous)

-numisma- [Gr. *nomisma*, coin] *base* coin (numismatics, numismatist)

nummi- [L. *nummus*, coin] *comb* coin; disk (nummiform, nummulary)

nuncup- [L. *nuncupare*, call by name] *base* declare, name (nuncupate, nuncupatory)

nundin- [L. *nundinare*, trade] *base* market; commerce (nundinal, nundination)

-nupt- [L. *nubere/nuptus*, wed] *base* wed (nuptial, prenuptial)

nur(us)- [L. *nurus*, daughter-in-law] *base* daughter-in-law (nurine)

nuta- [L. *nutare*, to nod] *base* sway; nod (nutant, nutation)

-nutr- [L. *nutrire*, nourish] *base* nourish (malnutrition, nutriment)

-nychia *see* onycho-

nycta-, nycti-, nycto- [Gr. *nux/nuct-*, night] *comb* night (nyctalopia, nyctitropic, nyctophobia)

-nym- *see* -nom

nympho- [Gr. *numphe*, bride; nymph; pupa] 1. *comb* labia minora (nymphotomy); 2. nymphs (nympholepsy); 3. pupa of an insect (nymphiparous)

-nyxis [Gr. *nuksis*, pricking] *base* stabbing, pricking (keratonyxis, scleronyxis)

O

-o [It. suf *-o*] 1. *suf* informal abbreviation (ammo); 2. person associated with (politico)

oario- [Gr. *oarion*, little egg] *comb* ovary (oariocele, oariopathy). *See* ovario-

ob- [L. *ob-*, toward, upon, about, for] 1. *pre* to; toward; before (object); 2. opposed to; against (obnoxious); 3. upon; over (obfuscate); 4. completely; totally (objurgate). NOTE: ob- can change to: o- (omission); oc- (occur); of- (offer); op- (oppose)

obdur- [L. *obdurare*, harden] *base* stubborn, inflexible (obdurate, obdure)

obes- [L. *obesus*, fat] *base* fat; heavy (obese, obesity)

obit- [L. *obitus*, death] *base* death (obitual, obituary)

oblit- [L. *obliterare*, to erase] *base* erase (obliterate, obliteration)

obliv- [L. *oblivium*, forgetfulness] *base* forgotten; lost to memory (oblivious, oblivescence)

oblongo- [L. *oblongus*, rather long] *comb* with oblong extension (ob-longo-elliptic, oblong-ovate)

obscur- [L. *obscurus*, dark, shady] *base* dark (obscurant, obscurity)

obstin- [L. *obstinatus*, resolute] *base* stubborn (obstinacy, obstinately)

obturat- [L. *obturatus*, closed, stopped up] *base* shut, occlude (obturation, obturator)

obtusi- [L. *obtusus*, blunted, dull] *comb* obtuse; blunted (obtusifolious, obtusi-pennate)

-occid- [L. *occidens*, setting sun] *base* west; (occident, occidental)

occipito- [L. *occiput*, back of the head] *comb* occipital; skull (occipito-axial, occipito-parietal)

occlud-/occlus- [L. *occludere*, shut up or close] *base* close; obstruct (occlude, occlusion)

occult- [L. *occultus*, concealed] *base* hidden (occult, occultation)

ocelli- [L. *ocelus*, little eye] *comb* spot; eyelet (ocelliform, ocelliferous)

ochlo- [Gr. *okhlos*, crowd] *comb* crowd; mob (ochlocracy, ochlophobia)

ocho-¹ [Gr. *okhos*, carriage] *base* vehicle (ochophobia, ochomania)

ocho-² [Gr. *okhos*, anything that holds] *base* capacious; ample (ochopetalous)

ochreo- [L. *ochreus*, containing ochre] *comb* containing ochre; light brownish yellow (ochreo-ferrous, ochreo-testaceous)

ochro- [Gr. *okhros*, pale yellow] *comb* pale yellow (ochrocarpous, ochroleucous)

-ock [Ger. suf. forming diminutives] *suf* diminutive: small (hassock, hillock)

-ocracy [Gr. *kratos*, strength, authority] *comb* the rule of any class (plutocracy, tradeocracy)

octa-, octi-, octo- [Gr. *okto*, eight] *comb* eight (octagon, octipara, octobrachiate)

octakaideca- [Gr. *okto*, eight + *kai*, and + *deka*, ten] *comb* eighteen (octakaidecahedral, octakaidecahedron)

octan- [Gr. *okto*, eight] *base* eighth (octandrous, octant)

octocent- [L. *octo*, eight + *centenarius*, consisting of a hundred] *base* eight hundred (octocentennial, octocentenary)

octogen-, octoges- [L. *octogenarius*, eighty] *base* eighty (octogenarian, octogesimal)

oculi-, oculo- [L. *ocularius*, pert. to the eye] *comb* eye (oculiform, oculomotor)

ocy- *comb* [Gr. *okus*, swift] swift (ocydrome, ocypodan)

-ode¹ [Gr. *hodos*, way] *comb* way; path (cathode, electrode)

-ode² [Gr. *odes*, of the nature of] *suf* like (geode, phyllode)

odi- [L. *odium*, hatred] *base* hatred (odious, odium)

-odic [Gr. stem *-od*, smell] *comb* smell (cacodic, euodic)

odo- [Gr. *hodos*, way] *comb* road; journey (odometer). *See* **hodo-**

odoben- [Gr. *odous*, tooth + *baino*, walk, step] *base* walrus (odobenidae)

-odont, odonto- [Gr. stem *odont-*, tooth] *comb* tooth (macrodont, odontoblast)

odori-, odoro- [L. *odor*, smell] *comb* smell; scent (odoriferant, odoroscope)

-odus [Gr. *odous*, tooth] *comb* having teeth; names of genera (ceratodus, Machairodus)

-odynia, odyno- [Gr. *odune*, pain] *comb* pain in __ (osteodynia, odynophagia)

oeco- [Gr. *oikos*, house] *comb* environment (œcological, œcology). *See* **eco-**

oego- [Gr. *oigein*, to open] *base* open (œgopsid). *Also* **oigo-** (oigopsid)

oeno- [Gr. *oinos*, wine] *comb* wine (œnomania, œnophile). *Also* **eno-** (enophile)

oesophago- *see* esophag-

off-[1] [ME *of*, separation] *comb* away from (offbrand, offcolor)

-off[2] [< horse racing: *they're off and running*] *suf* a competition (bakeoff, cookoff)

ogdo- [Gr. *ogdoas*, eight in number] *comb* eight (ogdoad, ogdoastich)

-oid, -oidal [Gr. *eidos*, resemblance] *suf* shape; like; resembling (spheroid, trapezoidal)

-oidea [NL. sci. suf *-oidea*] *comb* names of zoological classes; names of entomological superfamilies; (Molluscoidea, Nautiloidea)

-oigo- [Gr. *oigein*, to open] *base* open (oigopsid, Oigopsidae)

oiko- [Gr. *oikos*, house] *comb* environment (oikofugic, oikoid). *See* eco-

oino- [Gr. *oinos*, wine] *comb* wine (oinological, oinomania). *See* œno-

-ol [Abbrev. of L. *oleum*, oil] *suf* [chemistry] 1. alcohol or phenol (menthol); 2. same as -ole (anethol)

-ola [L. suf. *-olus/-a/-um*, somewhat] *suf* diminutive (aureola, variola)

-ole[1] [Abbrev. of L. *oleum*, oil] *suf* [chemistry] 1. compound: closed-chain with five members (pyrrole); 2. names of certain aldehydes and ethers (anethole)

-ole[2] [L. suf. *-olus/-a/-um*, somewhat] *suf* diminutive (foveole, variole)

olea-, -oleic, oleo- [Ge. *elaia*, olive tree] *comb* oil; olein; oleic (oleaginous, palmitoleic, oleomargarine)

olecran- [Gr. *olekranon*, elbow] *base* elbow (olecranarthritis, olecranon)

-olent [L. *olere*, to smell] *base* giving out a smell (grateolent, redolent)

oler- [L. *olus/oler-*, pot-herb] *base* vegetables; pot-herbs (oleraceous, olericulture)

olfacto- [L. *olfacere*, to smell] *comb* smell (olfactometer, olfactory)

oligo- [Gr. *oligos*, little] *comb* few; deficiency of (oligoglottism, oligophrenia)

olit- [L. *holitor*, kitchen-gardener] *base* vegetables (olitory)

oliv-, olivaceo- [L. *oliva*, olive] *comb* dusky green (olivaceous, olivaceocinereous)

-ologist [Gr. *logos*, discourse] *comb* specialist (mixologist, proctologist)

-oma, -ome [Gr. suf. *-oma*, tumor] *suf* morbid growth; tumor; neoplasm; formation (sarcoma, phyllome)

omalo- *see* homalo-

ombro- [Gr. *ombros*, rain shower] *comb* rain; shower (ombrometer, ombrophilous)

ommat- [Gr. *omma/ommat-*, eye] *base* eye (ommatophore, ommatophorous)

omni- [L. *omnis*, all] *comb* all; everywhere (omniscient, omnivorous)

omo-[1] [Gr. *omos*, shoulder] *base* shoulder (omodynia, omohyoid)

omo-[2] [Gr. *omos*, raw] *base* raw (omophagia, omophagous)

omphalo- [Gr. *omphalos*, the navel] *comb* navel; umbilicus (omphalitis, omphalophlebitis)

-on [< *ion*] *suf* [chemistry] 1. elementary particle (gluon); 2. inert gas (neon)

oncho- [Gr. *onkos*, barb] *comb* barb, hook (onchocerciasis, onchocercosis)

onco- [Gr. *onkos*, mass] *comb* tumor (oncologist, oncotomy)

-one [Gr. fem. suf. *-one*] *suf* [chemistry] a ketone (acetone, nitrone)

oneiro- [Gr. *oneiros*, dream] *comb* dream (oneirocritic, oneirodynia)

-oner- [L. *onus/oner-*, burden] *base* burden (onerative, onerous)

-onic [Gr. fem. suf. *-one* + *-ic*, of the nature of] *suf* names of acids (galactonic, gluconic acid)

onio- [Gr. *onios*, for sale] *base* buy (oniomania, oniophobia)

-onisc- [Gr. *oniskos*, woodlouse] *base* woodlouse (Oniscidae, onisciform)

ono- [Gr. *onos*, ass] *base* donkey; beast of burden (onology, Onopordon)

-onocrot- [Gr. *onokrotalos*, pelican]
base pelican (onocrotal, onocrotalus)

onom-, onomato- [Gr. *onoma*, name]
comb name (onomastic, ono-
matopoeia)

onto- [Gr. *on/ont-*, being] *comb* being;
existence (ontogenesis, ontology)

onych-, -onychia, onycho- [Gr. *onuks*,
fingernail] *comb* claw; nail (ony-
chosis, leukonychia, onychophagy)

-onym, -onymy [Gr. *onoma*, name]
comb name (paranym, pseudonym,
synonymy)

oo- [Gr. *oon*, egg] *comb* egg; ovum
(oocystic, oogamous)

oophoro- [Gr. *oon*, egg + *pherein*, to
bear] *comb* ovary (oophorectomy,
oophoritis)

op- [Gr. *ops*, eye] *comb* eye (opalgia,
optics)

-opac- [L. *opacus*, shady] *base* shade;
dimness (opacate, opacity)

-oper-[1] [L. *opus/oper-*, work] *base*
work; labor (operate, operosity)

-oper-[2] [L. *operculare*, furnish with a
lid] *base* lid; cover (inoperculate, op-
erculum)

ophio- [Gr. *ophis*, serpent] *comb* snake
(ophiomancy, ophiolatry)

-ophidia, ophidio- [Gr. *ophis/ophid-*,
serpent] *comb* [medicine] venemous
snakes (Thanatophidia, ophidiophobia)

ophry- [Gr. *ophrys*, eyebrow] *base* eye-
brow (ophritis, ophryosis)

ophthalmo- [Gr. *ophthalmos*, eye]
comb eye (ophthalmodynia, ophthalmoscope)

-opia [Gr. *ops*, eye] *comb* eye defect;
vision (amblyopia, diplopia)

opio- [Gr. *opion*, opium] *comb* poppy
juice (opiomania, opiophagy)

-opiso- [Gr. *opiso*, behind, again]
base backwards (opisometer, opi-
sometry)

opistho- [Gr. *opisthen*, behind] *comb*
behind; dorsal (opisthodont,
opisthopterous)

opo- [Gr. *opos*, juice] *comb* juice
(opobalsam, opopanax)

oppositi- [L. *oppositus*, opposite] *comb*
opposite (oppositiflorous, oppositifo-
lious)

opsi-[1] [Gr. *opse*, late] *comb* late (op-
sigamy, opsimathy)

opsi-[2] [Gr. *opsis*, eye] *comb* sight; eye
(opsin, opsiometer)

-opsia [Gr. *opsia*, sight or vision] *comb*
sight; view (dysopsia, hemianopsia)

-opsis [Gr. *opsis*, sight] 1. *comb* see;
(synopsis); 2. likeness; resembling
(coreopsis, stereopsis)

opso-[1] [Gr. *opsis*, sight] *comb* eye (opsoclonus)

opso-[2] [Gr. *opsonein*, to prepare food]
cooked meat; relish; rich fare; provisions; sweets (opsomania, opsonium)

-opsy [Gr. *opsia*, sight] *comb* examination (autopsy, biopsy)

-opt-[1] [L. *optio*, choice] *base* wish;
choice (optional)

-opt-[2] [L. *optimus*, best] *base* best (op-
timism, optimum)

optico- [Gr. *optikos*, of seeing] *comb*
pertaining to sight (optico-ciliary,
optico-kinetic)

opto- [Gr. *optikos*, of seeing] *comb*
sight; eye (optometry, optostriate)

opul- [L *opulentia*, wealth] *base* riches
(opulence, opulent)

opus- [L. *opus*, work] *base* work (opus,
opuscular)

or-[1] [L. *os/or-*, mouth] *base* mouth
(oral, orifice)

-or[2] [Gr. suf. *-tor*, nouns of agent] *suf*
person or thing that (counselor, in-
ventor)

-or[3] [L. n. suf. *-or*] *suf* quality; condition (horror, odor)

orag- [F. *orage*, storm] *base* storm
(orage, oragious)

-orama [Gr. *orama*, that which is seen]
comb display; spectacle (georama,
panorama)

-orat- [L. *oratus*, spoken] *base* speak
(orator, oratorical)

orbiculato- [L. *orbiculus*, small disk] *comb* partly rounded (orbiculato-cordate, orbiculato-elliptical)

orbito- [L. *orbita*, orbit] *comb* orbit; circle (orbitonasal, orbitorostral)

-orches- [Gr. *orkestra*, part of the stage where the chorus danced] *base* dance (orchesography, orchestic)

orchido-[1] [L. *orchis*, orchid] *comb* orchid (Orchidacae, orchidology)

orchido-[2] [Gr. *orkhis*, testicle] *comb* testicle (orchidotomy)

orchio- [Gr. *orkhis*, testicle] *comb* testicle (orchialgia, orchiocele)

orect-, -orexia [Gr. *orektikos*, pert. to appetite] *comb* appetite (orectic, dysorexia)

organo- [Gr. *organon*, organ] *comb* organ; organic (organography, organoplasty)

-orial [L suf. *-or*, one who + *-ialis*, relating to] *suf* pertaining to an action (conspiratorial, memorial)

orient- [L. *oriens*, rising] *base* east; sunrise (orientalism, orienteering)

-orious [L suf. *-orius*] *suf* relating to; characterized by (censorious, meritorious)

orismo- [Gr. *horismos*, bounding, defining] *comb* definition; boundary (orismological, orismology)

-orium [L. *-orium*, place for] *suf* a place for __ (auditorium, exploratorium)

orneo-, orni-, ornitho-, orno- [Gr. *orneion*, bird] *comb* bird (orneoscopic, orniscopic, ornithology, ornomancy)

oro-[1] [L. *os/or-*, mouth] *comb* mouth; (oro-anal, orolingual)

oro-[2] [Gr. *oros*, mountain] *comb* mountain (orogenic, orology). *Also* oreo- (oreology)

orrho- [Gr. *oros*, serum, whey] *comb* serum (orrhocyst, orrhoid)

ortho- [Gr. *orthos*, straight] 1. *comb* straight; regular; upright (orthodontia); 2. right angle (orthorhombic);

3. proper; correct; standard (orthography); 4. [chemistry] that acid of a group containing the same non-metallic element that has the largest number of OH groups per atom of the nonmetal (orthophosphoric); 5. [medicine] correction of; deformities (orthopedics)

-ory [L. suf. *-orium*] 1. *suf* having the nature of (hortatory); 2. a place for __ (observatory)

ortyg- [Gr. *ortuks/ortug-*, quail] *base* quail (ortygan, Ortiginae)

orycto- [Gr. *oruktos*, dug out] *comb* dug up: fossil or mineral (oryctological, orictologist)

-oryzi- [Gr. *oruksa*, rice] *base* rice (oryzivorous, Orizopsis)

oscheo- [Gr. *oskheon*, scrotum] *comb* scrotum (oscheitis, oscheocele)

-oscill- [L. *oscillare*, to swing] *base* swing (oscillation, oscillatory)

oscin- [L. *oscen*, singing bird] *base* songbirds (oscine, Oscines)

-oscit- [L. *oscitare*, to gape, yawn] *base* yawn (oscitancy, oscitation)

oscul- [L. *osculari*, to kiss] *base* kiss (osculation, osculatory)

-ose[1] [Fr. suf. *-ose* < Gr. *-os*] 1. *suf* carbohydrate (cellulose); 2. protein hydrolysis: product of (proteose)

-ose[2] [L. suf. *-osus*] *suf* full of; containing; like (verbose). *See* -osity

-osis [Gr. suf. *-osis*] 1. *suf* state; condition; action (osmosis); 2. abnormal condition; diseased condition (neurosis, tuberculosis)

-osity [L. suf. *-ositas*] *suf* full of; containing; like (generosity, verbosity). *See* -ose[2]

-osmia [Gr. *osme*, odor] *comb* smell; odor (anosmia, parosmia)

osmio- [Gr. *osme*, odor] *comb* osmium (osmio-chloride, osmiophilic)

osmo-[1] [Gr. *osme*, odor] *comb* smell; odor (osmoceptor, osmodysphoria)

osmo-[2] [Gr. *osmos*, impulsion] *comb* osmosis; (osmogene, osmolarity)

osphresio- [Gr. *osphresis*, smelling] *comb* odor; sense of smell (osphresiology, osphresiophobia)

osphy-, osphyo- [Gr. *osphus*, the loin] *comb* loins (osphyalgia, osphyocele)

-ossi, osseo-, osteo- [Gr. *osteon*, bone] *comb* bone (ossification, osseomucin, osteoplasty)

ossifrag- [L. *ossifraga*, sea-eagle < *os*, bone + *frag-*, to break] *base* osprey (ossifrage, ossifragous)

osti- [L. *ostium*, gate] *base* gate; opening (ostiolate, ostiole)

-ostraca, ostraco- [Gr. *ostrakon*, a shell] *comb* shell (Leptostraca, ostracoderm)

ostre-, ostrei-, ostreo- [Gr. *ostreion*, oyster] *comb* oyster (ostreaceous, ostreiform, ostreophage)

ot-, oto- [Gr. *ous/ot-*, ear] *comb* ear (othemorrhagia, otopyosis)

-ota [Gr. suf. *-ote*] *suf* plural ending of taxonomic names (amniota, biota)

-ote [Gr. suf. *-otes*] *suf* singular ending of taxonomic names (amniote, eukaryote)

oti- [L. *otium*, leisure] *base* idleness; leisure (otiose, otiosity)

-otic [Gr. suf. *-otikos*] 1. *suf* affected with; of (sclerotic); 2. producing (narcotic)

oulo-¹ [Gr. *oulan*, gums] *comb* gums (oulitis, oulorrhagy)

oulo-² [Gr. *oulas*, wooly] *base* curly, wooly (oulopholite, oulotrichous). *Also* **ulo-**

ourano- [Gr. *ouranos*, sky] *comb* heavens (ouranography, ouranomancy). *See* **urano-**

ouro- [Gr. *ouron*, urine] *comb* urine (ouromancy, ouromelanin). *Also* **uro-**

-ous [L. suf. *-osus*, full of] 1. *suf* characterized by; having; full of (gener-

ous); 2. [chemistry] having a valence lower than in a compound whose name ends in -ic (sulfurous)

-ousia, -ousian [Gr. *ousia*, substance] *comb* essence; substance (homoousia, heteroousian)

out- [O.E. *ut*, out] 1. *comb* situated at; outside (outpatient); 2. going away; outward (outcast); 3. better; greater; more than (outsell)

ovario- [L. *ovum*, egg] *comb* ovary (ovariocentesis, ovariotomy). *See* **oario-**

ovato- [L. *ovum*, egg] *comb* egg-shaped (ovato-deltoid, ovato-oblong)

over- [O.E. *ofer*, over] 1. *comb* above; upper; superior; eminent (overbearing); 2. beyond normal; excessive (overrate); 3. passing across; passing beyond (overshoot); 4. moving lower (overwhelm)

ovi-¹ [L. *ovum*, egg] *comb* egg; ovum (oviduct, ovigenous)

ovi-² [L. *ovis*, sheep] *comb* sheep (ovibovine, ovicide)

ovo- [L. *ovum*, egg] *comb* ovum; ovally (ovococcus, ovolecithin)

oxa-, oxo- [< *oxygen*] *pre* [chemistry] presence of oxygen (oxazine, oxopolysaccharide)

oxy-¹ [Gr. *oksus*, sharp] *comb* sharp; pointed; acute; acid (oxycephalic, oxyphonia)

oxy-² [< *oxygen*] *comb* oxygen-containing (oxyacetylene, oxygenous)

oxyur- [Gr. *oksus*, sharp + *oura*, tail] *base* worm (oxyuricide, oxyurous)

ozo- [Gr. *ozein*, smell] *comb* smell (ozocerite, ozostomia)

ozono- [Gr. *ozein*, smell] *comb* ozone (ozonolysis, ozonometry)

ozostom- [Gr. *ozostomos*, having bad breath] *base* bad breath (ozostomatic, ozostomia)

P

pac- [L. *pax/pac-*, peace] *base* peace (pacific, pacifist)

pachno- [Gr. *pakhno*, hoarfrost, rime] *comb* frost (pachnolite)

pachy- [Gr. *pakhus*, thick] *comb* thick; large; massive (pachycardia, pachycephaly)

pachyderm- [Gr. *pakhus*, thick + *derma*, skin] *base* elephant; tapir (pachydermatous, pachydermoid)

paedo-¹ [Gr. *pedon*, soil] *comb* dirt; soil (paedogenic). *Usually* pedo- (pedocal)

paedo-² [Gr. *pais/paid-*, child] *comb* child; immature; doll (paedomorphic). *Usually* pedo- (pedophile)

-pagia [Gr. *pagos*, something fixed] *comb* conjoined twins (ectopagia, sternopagia)

pago- [Gr. *pagos*, frost] *comb* cold; frost (pagophagia, Pagophila)

pagur- [Gr. *pagouros*, crab] *base* hermit crab (pagurian, paguroid)

-pagus [Gr. *pagos*, something fixed] *comb* conjoined twins (diplopagus, thoracopagus)

-paizo- [Gr. *paizo*, play with] *base* loveplay (paizogonous, paizogony)

pala- [L. *pala*, shovel, spade] *base* spade-shaped (palaceous, palette-knife)

palato- [L. *palatum*, palate] *comb* palate; roof of mouth (palatoglossal, palatonasal)

palea- [L. *palea*, chaff] *base* chaff; chaff-like (paleaceous, paleaeform)

paleo- [Gr. *palaios*, ancient] 1. *comb* ancient; prehistoric (Paleozoic); 2. primitive (paleolithic); 3. paleontological (paleozoology). *Also* paeleo- (paeleozoic)

palest- [Gr. *palaistra*, wrestling] *base* wrestling (palestral, palestric)

-pali-, palil-, -palin- [Gr. *palin*, again] *base* over; again (paliphrasia, palilogy, palingenesis)

pallia-, pallio- [L. *pallium*, cloak, mantle] *comb* pallium; mantle (palliament, palliopedal)

pallidi- [L. *pallidus*, pale] *comb* pale (pallidiflorous, pallidiventrate)

pallio- [L. *pallium*, cloak] *comb* mantle, pallium (pallio-cardiac, palliovisceral)

pallo- [Gr. *pallein*, quiver, quake] *comb* vibrations (pallometric, pallometrical)

palma-, palmi- [L. *palma*, palm tree] *base* palm tree (palmaceous, palmacite, palmicolous)

palmati-, palmato- [L. *palmatus*, marked with the palm of the hand] *comb* like the palm of the hand (palmatifid, palmatopeltate)

-palp- [L. *palpare*, to stroke] *base* touch; feel (palpable, palpiform)

palpebra- [L. *palpebra*, eyelid] *base* eyelid (palpebral, palpebrate)

paludi-, palus- [L. *palus/palud-*, swamp, marsh] *base* marsh (paludicole, palustrine)

palumb- [L. *palumbis*, pigeon or dove] *base* pigeon (palumbine, palumbus)

palyn- [Gr. *pale*, fine meal or dust] *base* pollen (palynology, palynomorph)

-pampin- [L. *pampinus*, tendril] *base* vine; tendril (pampinary, pampiniform)

pan-¹ [Gr. *pas/pan-*, all] 1. *comb* all (pantheism); 2. common to all/every (Pan-American); 3. belief in a unified group (Pan-Slavism)

pan-² [L. *panis*, bread] *base* bread (panary, panivorous)

pancreato-, pancreo- [NL *pancreas*, pancreas] *comb* of the pancreas (pancreatotomy, pancreopathy)

pand- [L. *pandus*, arched, bowed, warped] *base* bending under a weight, esp. in architecture (pandation)

pandicul- [L. *pandiculari*, stretch oneself] *base* stretched out (pandiculated, pandiculation)

pandur- [L. *pandura*, musical instrument] *base* fiddle (pandurate, panduriform)

pann- [L. *pannus*, a cloth] *base* raglike, cloth-like (Pannaria, pannose)

-pannychy [Gr. *pannukios*, lasting all night] *comb* lasting all night (psychopannychistic, psychopannychy)

pant-, panto- [Gr. *pas/pant-*, all] *comb* all; every (pantalgia, pantograph)

-papaver- [L. *papaver*, poppy] *base* poppy (Papavereae, papaverous)

papil- [L. *papilio*, butterfly] *base* butterfly (papilionaceous, papilionine)

papilli-, papillo-, papilloso- [L. *papilla*, nipple, pimple] *comb* papillary; nipple-like (papilliform, papillomatosis, papilloso-asperate)

papp- [L. *pappus*, down, fuzz] *base* plant down (pappiferous, pappose)

papulo- [L. *papula*, pustule] *comb* papule; skin elevation (papulation, papuliferous)

papyro- [L. *papyrus*, paper] *comb* papyrus (papyral, papyrology)

par-¹ [L. *pars/part-*, portion] *base* fraction; portion (partition, tripartite)

par-² [L. *parus*, titmouse] *base* titmouse; chickadee (Parinae, parine)

para-¹ [L. *parare*, prepare] 1. *comb* protecting from (parapet); 2. using a parachute (paratroop)

para-² [Gr. *para*, beside] 1. *pre* beside; beyond (parallel); 2. [chemistry] an isomer, modification, polymer, derivative of a specified substance (paradichlorobenzene); 3. [medicine] secondary capacity; accessory capacity (paramedical); 4. [medicine] functionally disordered; abnormal (parafunctional); 5. [medicine] like; resembling (paracholera)

-para³ [L. *parus*, bearing] *comb* woman who has given birth; parturient (multipara, primipara)

paral- [Gr. *paralios*, by the sea] *base* seashore (paralian, paralic)

paralip- [Gr. *paraleipein*, omit] *base* neglect; omission (paralipomena, paralipsis)

paraphil- [Gr. *para*, beyond + *philia*, sexual interest] *base* unusual sexual practices (paraphilia, paraphiliac)

parasit- [Gr. *parasitos*, one who eats at another's table] *base* parasite (parasitical, parasiticide)

pard- [Gr. *pardos*, pard] *base* leopard (pardalotus, pardine)

paremio- [Gr. *paroimia*, proverb, maxim] *comb* proverb (paremiographer, paremiology)

pares- [Gr. *paresis*, relaxation] *base* paralysis (paresis, pareso-analgesia)

pari- [L. *par*, equal] *comb* equal (paridigitate, paripinnate)

-paria [L. *par*, equal] *comb* genera and order of trilobytes; cheeks (Hypoparia, Opisthoparia)

parieto- [L. *paries/pariet-*, wall] *comb* forming a cavity; parietal; wall (parietofrontal, parietomastoid)

pariso- [Gr. *parisos*, almost equal] *comb* evenly balanced; almost equal (parisology, parison)

paroem- [Gr. *paroimia*, proverb] *base* proverb (paroemiographer, paroemiology). *Also* **parem-** (paremiography)

-parous [L. *parus*, bearing, producing] *comb* producing; bearing; bringing forth (oviparous, viviparous)

pars- [L. *parsimonia*, frugality] *base* spare; save (parsimonious, parsimony)

partheno- [Gr. *parthenos*, virgin] *comb* virgin (parthenogenesis, parthenology)

parti- [L. *pars/part-*, part] *base* division; part (parti-colored, partition)

-partur- [L. *parturire*, bring forth] *base* giving birth (parturifacient, parturition)

parvi-, parvo- [L. *parvus*, little] *comb* small (parvifolious, parvoline)

pascu- [L. *pascuum*, pasture] *base* grazing (pascuant, pascuous)

pasi- [Gr. *pasi*, for all] *comb* all; universal; gestures to communicate (passigraphic, pasigraphy, pasimology). *See* pan-

-passeri- [L. *passer*, sparrow] *base* perching bird; sparrow (passeriform, passerine)

pate- [L. *patere*, lie open] *base* revelation (patefaction, patefy)

-pated [poss. L. *patena*, dish] *comb* head: type of (bald-pated, muddle-pated)

patell- [L. *patella*, pan] *base* kneecap (patellar, patelliform)

-pater- [L. *pater*, father] *base* father (paternalism, paternity)

-path, -pathic, patho-, -pathy [Gr. *pathos*, suffering, misery] *comb* suffering; disease; feeling (psychopath, telepathic, pathopoeia, antipathy)

patri- [L. *pater/patr*-, father] *comb* father (patriarch, patrimony)

patroc- [L. *patrocinium*, protection] *base* support; defend (patrocinate, patrociny)

patroio- [Gr. *patrios*, hereditary] *comb* ancestor (patroiomania, patroiophobia)

patru- [L. *patruus*, father's brother] *base* uncle (patruel, patruity)

patul- [L. *patulus*, lying open] *base* open; spread out (patulent, patulous)

pauc-, pauci- [L. *paucus*, few, little] *comb* few (paucity, pauciflorous)

paulo- [Gr. *paula*, pause] *comb* pause (paulocardia, paulo-post)

paup- [L. *pauper*, poor] *base* poor (pauper, pauperize)

-pavid- [L. *pavidus*, fearful] *base* fearful (impavidity, pavid)

-pavon- [L. *pavo*, peacock] **1.** *base* peacock (pavonian); **2.** peacock blue (pavonine)

pax- [L. *pax*, peace] *comb* peace (Pax Germanica, Pax Romana)

paxill- [L. *paxillus*, stake, peg] *base* pillarlike; stalklike (paxilla, paxillose)

-pecca- [L. *peccare*, to sin] *base* fault; sin; disease (impeccable, peccant)

pect- [L. *pectus/pector*-, breast bone] *base* breastbone (pectoral, pectoriloquial)

pectinato- [L. *pectinare*, to comb] *comb* like the teeth of a comb (pectinato-denticulate, pectinato-fimbricate)

pecul- [L. *peculari*, to embezzle] *base* embezzle (peculation, peculator)

-pecun- [L. *pecunia*, wealth] *base* money (impecunious, pecuniary)

ped-^{1}, -pede, pedi-, pedo-^{1} [L. *pes/ped*-, foot] *comb* foot (pedal, centipede, pedicure, pedopathy). *Also* pod- (tripod)

ped-^{2} [Gr. *pais/paid*-, child] *comb* child (pedagogy)

ped-^{3} [Gr. *pedon*, soil] *comb* dirt, soil (pedology, pedocal)

pedati- [L. *pedatus*, having feet] *comb* pedately; like a foot (pedatifid, pedatisect)

-pedia [Gr. *paideia*, instruction] *comb* teach (encyclopedia, pharmacopedia)

pedicul- [L. *pediculus*, louse] *base* lice (pediculosis, pediculous)

pedio- [Gr. *pedion*, a plain] *base* flat surface; plain (pedion, pedionomite)

pedipalp- [L. *pes/ped*-, foot + *palpus*, feeler] *base* scorpion (pedipalpate, pedipalpous)

pedo-^{2} [Gr. *paid*-, child] *comb* child (pedobaptism, pedodontia)

pedo-^{3} [Gr. *pedon*, dirt] *comb* dirt; soil (pedocal, pedosphere)

pegm- [Gr. *pegmat*-, fastened together] *base* framework; fastening (pegmatite, pegmatoid)

pego- [Gr. *pege*, spring, fountain] *base* spring; fountain (pegomancy)

peino- [Gr. *peina*, hunger] *comb* hunger (peinotherapy)

peir- [Gr. *peiran*, attempt] *base* try; experiment (peirameter, peirastic)

pejor- [L. *pejor*, worse] *base* worse (pejorative, pejority)

-pel- [L. *pellere*, drive] *base* push; drive (propel, repel). *Also* **-pul-** (propulsion)

pelad- [Fr. *peler*, strip of hair] *base* bald (peladic, pelade)

pelag- [Gr. *pelagos*, the sea] *base* sea (archipelago, pelagic)

pelarg- [Gr. *pelargos*, stork] *base* stork (pelargic, pelargomorph)

pelec- [Gr. *pelekus*, ax] *base* hatchet (pelecoid, pelecypod)

pelecan- [Gr. *pelekan*, pelican] *base* pelican (pelecanid, Pelecanus)

pelico- [Gr. *pelika*, pelvis] *comb* pelvis (pelicology, pelicometer)

pell-, pelli- [Gr. *pella*, skin, hide] *base* skin; hide (pellagra, pellibranchiate)

-pelm-, -pelmous [Gr. *pelma*, sole of the foot] *base* sole of the foot (antiopelmous, pelmatogram, desmopelmous)

pelo- [Gr. *pelos*, mud, mire] *comb* mud; clay (Pelodytes, pelophilous)

pelor- [Gr. *pelor*, monster] *base* monster (pelorization, pelorize)

pelt-, pelti-, pelto- [Gr. *pelte*, small shield] *comb* shield (peltate, peltiferous, peltogaster)

peltati-, peltato- [Gr. *pelte*, small shield] *comb* shield-shaped (peltatifid, peltatodigitate)

pelvi- [L. *pelvis*, pelvis] *comb* pelvis; pelvic; basin-shaped (pelvimeter, pelvisacrum)

pemphred- [Gr. *pemphredon*, kind of wasp] *base* wasp (Pempredon, Pemphredoninae)

-pend- [L. *pendere*, hang] 1. *base* hang (pendant); 2. pay; weigh (expend). *Also* **-pens-** (pension)

pendulin- [L. *pendulus*, hanging] *base* birds with hanging nests (penduline, Pendulinus)

pen(e)- [L. *pene*, almost] *comb* almost; nearly (penannular, peninsula)

-penia [Gr. *penia*, poverty, need] *comb* poverty; deficiency; tightening (kaliopenia, neutropenia)

pennati- [L. *pennatus*, furnished with wings] *comb* feather (pennatifid, pennatilobate)

penni- [L. *penna*, feather] *comb* feather; featherlike (penniferous, penniform)

-penny [OE *penig*] *comb* monetary unit (catch-penny, halfpenny)

peno- [Gr. *poine*, penalty] *base* punishment (penologist, penology)

penta- [Gr. *pente*, five] *comb* five (pentacapsular, pentamerous)

pentecost- [Gr. *pentekonta*, fifty] *base* fifty (Pentecost, pentecostal)

pentakaideca- [Gr. *pente*, five + *kai*, and + *deka*, ten] *comb* fifteen (pentakaidecahedral, pentakaidecahedron)

penteconta- [Gr. *pentekonte*, fifty] *comb* fifty (pentacontadrachn, pentecontaglossal)

penther- [Gr. *penthera*, mother-in-law] *base* mother-in-law (pentheraphobia)

penur- [L. *penuria*, scarcity] *base* poverty; lack (penurious, penury)

-peo- [Gr. *peos*, penis] *base* penis (peotillomania, peotomy)

pepo- [Gr. *pepon*, large ripe melon] *base* gourd, melon, pumpkin (peponida, peponium)

peps-, -pepsia, pept-, pepto- [Gr. *pepsis*, digestion] *comb* digest (pepsinogen, dyspepsia, peptic, peptogenic)

per- [L. *per*, through] 1. *pre* through; away (percolate); 2. completely; very (persuade); 3. [chemistry] containing a specified element or radical in its maximum or a relatively high valence (perchlorate)

percepto- [L. *percipere*, to perceive] *comb* perceived (percepto-diagnostic, percepto-motor)

perces- [L. *perca*, perch] *base* barracuda, mullet (Percesoses, Percesocine)

percesoc-, -perci-, -perco- [L. *perca*, perch] *base* barracuda; perch (percesocine, perciform, percomorph)

perd- [L. *perdere*, to lose] *base* destroy; lose (perdifoil, perdition)

-perdic- [L. *perdrix*, partridge, quail] *base* partridge (Perdicinae, perdicine)

perdri- [L. *perdrix*, partridge, quail] *base* partridge (perdricide, perdrigon)

peregrin- [L. *per*, through + *ager*, field] *base* travel; wander (peregrinate, peregrine)

perempt- [L. *perimere*, to destroy] base destructive; decisive (perempt, peremptory)

perenn- [L. *per*, through + *annus*, year] *base* lasting (perennial, perennibranch)

-pergamen- [L. *pergamina*, parchment] *base* parchment (pergameneous, pergamentaceous)

peri- [Gr. *peri*, around, about] 1. *pre* around; surrounding (periscope, periadenitis); 2. near (periblepsis, perigee)

pericardiaco-, pericardio- [Gr. *peri*, around + *kardia*, heart] *comb* relating to the sac surrounding the heart; pericardial (pericardiaco-phrenic, pericardiostomy)

pericul- [L. *periculum*, danger] *base* danger (periculant, periculous)

perineo- [Gr. *perineon*, perineum] *comb* perineum (perineocele, perineoplasty)

periosteo- [Gr. *peri*, around + *osteon*, bone] *comb* periosteum; bone membrane (periosteophyte, periosteotome)

perisso- [Gr. *perissos*, irregular, superfluous] *comb* uneven; strange; redundant (perissodactyl, perissology)

perister- [Gr. *peristera*, pigeon] *base* pigeon (peristeronic, peristeropod)

peritoneo- [Gr. *peri*, around + *teinein*, to stretch] *comb* peritonium; abdominal sac (peritoneoclysis, peritoneoscopy)

perm- [L. *permeare*, to pass through] *base* capable of being passed through (permeate, permeable)

perman- [L. *per*, through + *manere*, to remain] *base* lasting; remaining (permanency, permanent)

pero- [Gr. *peros*, maimed] *comb* maimed; malformed (perocephalus, perodactyly)

peroneo- [Gr. *perone*, brooch, pin, fibula] *comb* peroneal; fibula (peroneo-calcaneal, peroneotibial)

peroxy- [Gr. *per*, through + *oxy*, oxygen] *comb* peroxy group (peroxynitrate, peroxyborate)

perpet- [L. *perpetuus*, constant] *base* unceasing (perpetual, perpetuate)

pers- [L. *persea*, fruit-bearing tree] *base* avocado (Persea)

persic- [L. *persicum*, peach] *base* peach (persicaria, persicot)

-person [L. *persona*, actor's mask] *comb* person in a specialized activity (chairperson, spokesperson)

pertuss- [L. *per*, intensifier + *tussis*, cough] *base* pert. to a cough (pertussal, pertussis)

-pervic- [L. *pervicax*, obstinate] *base* stubborn (pervicacious, pervicacity)

pesso- [Gr. *pessis*, oval gaming stone] *comb* pebble (pessomancy)

-pessul- [L. *pessulus*, bolt of a door] *base* bolt (pessular, pessulus)

pesti- [L. *pestis*, plague] *comb* injurious plant or animal; pest; plague (pestiferous, pestilence)

-pet- [L. *petere*, to seek] *base* seek; ask; require (compete, petition)

peta- [Gr. *pente*, five] *comb* quadrillion (petabyte, petameter)

-petal [L. *petere*, to seek] *comb* moving toward; seeking (acropetal, centripetal)

petalo- [Gr. *petalon*, leaf] *base* leaf (petalocerous, petalomania)

petri-, petro- [Gr. *petra*, rock] *comb* rock; stone (petrifaction, petroglyph)

petro- [Gr. *petra*, rock + *elaion*, oil] *comb* petroleum (petrodollars, petropolitics)

petrosel- [L. *petroselinum*, parsley] *base* parsley (petroseline, petroselinum)

-peuce- [Gr. *peuke*, pine] *base* pine (Peucaea, peucedaneous)

-pexy [Gr. *peksis*, putting together] *comb* fixation: surgical (nephropexy, orchidopexy)

-phacell- [Gr. *phakellos*, bundle] *base* bundle (phacellate, phacellus)

phaco- [Gr. *phakos*, lentil; lens of the eye] *comb* lens; lentil-shaped (phacitis, phacolytic). *Also* **phako-** (phakocyst, phakoscope) *See* **-phakia**

-phaein, phaeo- [Gr. *phaios*, dusky] *comb* dusky; gray; muddy brown (haemophaein, phaeophyl). *Also* **pheo-** (pheochrome)

-phaeno- [Gr. *phainein*, to show] *base* showing (phaenocarpous, phaenogamous). *Also* **pheno-** (phenocryst, phenomenon)

-phage, phago-, -phagous, -phagy [Gr. *phagein*, to eat] **1.** *comb* eating; destroying; **2.** phagocyte (xylophage, phagocytosis, xylophagous, anthropophagy)

-phakia [Gr. *phakos*, lentil] *comb* lens (aphakia, microphakia). *See* **phaco-**

-phalacr- [Gr. *phalakros*, bald] *base* bald (phalacrocorax, phalacrophobia)

phalacrocorac- [L. *phalacrocorax*, cormorant] *base* cormorant (phalacrocoracidae, phalacrocoracine)

-phalaen- [Gr. *phalaina*, moth] *base* moth (phalaenoid, Phalaenopsis)

-phalang- [Gr. *phalanks*, bone of finger or toe] *base* **1.** finger or toe bone (phalangeal, phalanx) **2.** marsupial mammal (phalanger, Phalangeridae) **3.** tracheate spider (Phalangidea, phalangidean) **4.** a soldier belonging to a phalanx (phalangite)

phaler- [Gr. *phaleris*, coot] *base* coot (phaleridine, Phaleris)

phall(o)- [Gr. *phallus*, penis] *comb* penis (phallalgia, phallocampsis)

-phane, -phanic, -phany [Gr. *phanein*, to show] *comb* appearance; resemblance (allophane, urophanic, epiphany)

phanero- [Gr. *phaneros*, visible, evident] *comb* visible; manifest (phanerocodonic, phanerogam)

phantas- [Gr. *phantasma*, appearance, apparition] *base* illusion (phantasmagoria, phantasmal)

-phar- [Gr. *pharos*, lighthouse] *base* lighthouse (pharology, pharos)

pharmaco- [Gr. *pharmakon*, drug, medicine] *comb* drugs (pharmacomaniacal, pharmacotherapy)

pharyngo- [Gr. *pharanks*, throat] *comb* the pharynx (pharyngalgia, pharyngology)

phasc- [Gr. *phaskos*, tree moss] *base* moss (Phascaceae, Phascum)

phascolo- [Gr. *phaskolos*, leather bag] *comb* wombat (phascolome, Phascolomyidae)

-phaseol- [Gr. *phaselos*, kind of bean] *base* kidney bean (phaseolite, phaseologist)

-phasia, -phasic, -phasis, -phasy [Gr. *phasis*, speech or utterance] *comb* speech disorder (aphasia, dysphasic, emphasis, aphasy)

-phasian- [Gr. *phasianos*, pheasant] *base* pheasant (phasianine, phasianoid)

phasm- [Gr. *phasma*, apparition] *base* apparition; walking-stick insect (Phasmidae, phasmophobia)

phat-¹ [Gr. *phatos*, spoken] *base* speak (emphatic, phatic)

phat-² [Gr. *phatein*, tooth socket] *base* tooth socket (phatnoma, phatnorrhea)

phaulo- [Gr. *phaulos*, bad, worthless] *comb* worthless (phaulographic)

pheg- [Gr. *phegos*, oak] *base* beech (Phegopteris)

-phein- [Gr. *phaos*, gray, dusky] *base* dusky (hemophein, phyllophein). *See* phaeo-

phello- [Gr. *phellos*, cork] *comb* cork (phellogen, phelloplastic)

-phemia, -phemy [Gr. *pheme*, voice, speech] *comb* speech disorder (paraphemia, heterophemy)

phenac-, phenakist- [Gr. *phenaks*, imposter] *base* imposter (phenacite, phenakistoscope)

phenanthro- [Gr. *phaineo*, bring to light + *anthrak*, coal] *comb* [chemistry] (phenanthrene , phenanthroline)

pheng(o)- [Gr. *phengos*, light] *base* light; luster (phengite, phengophobia)

phenic- [Gr. *phoiniks*, purplish-red] *base* purple (phenicine, phenicopter)

pheno- [Gr. *phainein*, show] 1. *comb* appearance; (phenomenon); 2. phenyl group (phenomenology, phenoxide)

pheo- [Gr. *phaios*, dusky] *comb* dusky; gray (pheochrome, pheochromocytoma). *Also* phæo- (phæophile)

-pher [Gr. *phoros*, carrying] *comb* bearing; carrying (Christopher, chronopher)

philatel- [Gr. *philos*, love + *ateles*, prepaid, free of tax] *base* postage stamp (philatelic, philately)

-phile, -philic, -philism, philo-, -philous [Gr. *philos*, love] *comb* favorably disposed to; loving; liking (Anglophile, Francophilic, bibliophilism, philology, photophilous)

-philia, -philiac [Gr. *philia*, attraction] 1. *comb* tendency toward (hemophilia, hemophiliac); 2. abnormal attraction to (coprophilia, logophilia)

philomel- [Gr. *philomela*, nightingale] *base* nightingale (philomel, philomelian)

philosophico- [Gr. *philosophia*, love of knowledge and wisdom] *comb* philosophical and ... (philosophico-historic, philisophico-religious)

-phim- [Gr. *phimosis*, a muzzling] *base* narrow (phimosis, phimotic)

phlebo- [Gr. *phleps*, vein] *comb* vein (phlebography, phlebotomy)

phlegm- [Gr. *phlegma*, fire, phlegm] *base* phlegm (phlegmagogic, phlegmatic)

-phloem- [Gr. *phloios*, bark] *base* tree bark (epiphloem, metaphloem)

phlog-, phlogo- [Gr. *phlox*, a flame] *comb* inflammation (phlogistic, phlogogenous)

phloro- [Gr. *phloios*, bark] *comb* crystalline compound (phlorectin, phlorizin)

phlyct- [Gr. *phluktaina*, blister, pustule] *base* blister (phlyctenoid, phlyctenous)

-phobe, -phobia, -phobic, phobo- [Gr. *phobos*, fear] *comb* fear; hatred; dread (Francophobe, claustrophobia, ailurophobic, phobophobia)

phoco- [Gr. *phoke*, seal] *comb* seal: sea mammal (phocine, phocomelia)

phoecaen- [Gr. *phokaina*, porpoise] *base* porpoise (phocaenine, Phoecaenoides)

phœnicopt- [Gr. *phoiniks*, purple-red + *kerkos*, tail] *base* flamingo (Phoenicopteridae, phœnicopterous)

pholc- [Gr. *pholkos*, squint-eyed] *base* type of spider (Pholcidae, Pholcus)

pholid-, -pholis [Gr. *pholiz*, scale] *base* scales (pholidosis, pholidote, Conopholis)

-phone, phono-, -phony [Gr. *phone*, sound] *comb* sound; tone; speech; voice (megaphone, phonology, cacophony)

phonetico- [Gr. *phonetos*, to be spoken] *comb* phonetic and (phonetico-etymological, phonetico-grammatical)

-phor, -phora, -phore, -phorous [Gr, *pherein*, to bear] *comb* bearer; producer (phosphor, Cladophora, carpophore, gonophorous)

-phoresis [Gr. *phoresis*, being carried]

comb transmission (cataphoresis, diaphoresis)

phoro- [*phorein*, to bear] *comb* bearing (phoroplast, phorozoon)

phos- [Gr. *phos*, light] *base* light (phosphene, phosphor)

phospho-, phosphoro- [Gr. *phos*, light + *pherein*, to bear] *comb* phosphorus (phosphoprotein, phosphoroscope)

photo- [Gr. *phos*, light] 1. *comb* of light (photocampsis, photodynamics); 2. of photography (photographic, photomontage)

-phragma, phragmo- [Gr. *phragma*, fence, partition] *comb* barrier; wall; fence (diaphragma, phragmophorous)

phraseo- [Gr. *phrasis*, speech] *comb* phrase; verbal expression (phraseogram, phraseology)

-phrasia [Gr. *phrasis*, speech] *comb* speech defect (bradyphrasia, paraphrasia)

-phrastic [Gr. *phraksein*, to declare] *comb* word choice (holophrastic, periphrastic)

-phrat- [Gr. *phrater*, brother, clansman] *base* clan (phratric, phratry)

phreato- [Gr. *phrear*, artificial well] *base* well (phreatic, phreatophyte)

phreni-, phreno- [Gr. *phren*, diaphragm, mind, will] comb 1. mind (phrenology); 2. diaphragm (phrenic)

-phrenia [Gr. *phren*, diaphragm, mind, will] *comb* mental disorder (hebephrenia, schizophrenia)

-phrenic, phrenico-, phreno- [Gr. *phren*, diaphragm, mind, will] 1. *comb* diaphragm; midriff (gastrophrenic); 2. mental condition; mind (schizophrenic, phrenicotomy, phrenogastric)

phricto- [Gr. *phriktos*, producing a shudder] *comb* shudder (phrictopathic)

phrontis- [Gr. *phrontis*, thought, meditation] *base* thought, consideration (phrontisterion, phrontistery)

phryno- [Gr. *phrunos*, toad] *comb* toad (phrynoderma, Phrynosoma)

phthart- [Gr. *phthartos*, corruptible] *base* destructive; deadly (phthartic, Phthartolatrae)

phthino- [Gr. *phthinein*, waste away] *comb* wasting away; decay (phthinode, phthinoplasm)

-phthir- [Gr. *phtheir*, louse] *base* louse (phthiriasis, phthirophagous). *Also* **phthyr-**

phthisi-, phthisio-, -phthisis, -phthysis [Gr. *phthinein*, waste away] *comb* wasting away; decay; tuberculosis (phthisiology, phthisiogenesis, myelophthisis, panmyelophthysis)

-phthong [Gr. *phthongos*, voice, sound] *comb* voice; sound (aphthong, diphthong)

-phthor- [Gr. *phthora*, destruction] *base* corruption (blastophthoria, thelyphthoric)

-phyceae, -phyceous, phyco- [Gr. *phukos*, seaweed] *comb* seaweed (Rhodophyceae, Rhodophyceous, phycology)

-phygo- [Gr. *phugein*, shun, avoid] *base* shun; flee (apophyge, phygogalactic)

-phylactic, phylacto-, -phylax, -phylaxis [Gr. *phulakter*, guard] *comb* protection; defense; guard (prophylactic, phylactocarp, chartophylax, tachyphylaxis)

-phyletic [Gr. *phule*, tribe] *comb* origin (monophyletic, polyphyletic)

-phyll, phyllo-, -phyllous [Gr. *phullon*, leaf] *comb* leaf (sporophyll, phyllophagous, monophyllous)

phylo- [Gr. *phule*, tribe] *comb* tribe; race; phylum (phyloanalysis, phylogenesis)

phym-, -phyma [Gr. *phuma*, tumor] *comb* tumor; swelling; outgrowth; (phymatosis, osteophyma)

-phyr-, -phyre, -phyric [Gr. *phurein*, mix, mingle] *comb* 1. mix; mingle (haunophyr) 2. porphyritic rock (granophyre, orthophyric)

physa- [Gr. *phusa*, bellows, wind] *base* flatulence (physagogal, physagogue)

physali- [Gr. *phusa*, bellows, wind] *comb* bladder; bubble (physaliphore, physalite)

physc- [Gr. *phuske*, blister, sausage] *base* swelling; potbelly (physconic, physcony)

physeter- [Gr. *phuseter*, blowpipe, type of whale] *base* sperm whale (Physeteridae, physeterine)

physi-, physico-, physio- [Gr. *phusis*, nature] *comb* nature; natural; physical; bodily (physitheism, physico-chemical, physiography)

-physis [Gr. *phusis*, natural growth] *comb* growth (apophysis, prophysis)

physo- [Gr. *phusa*, breath, air bubble] 1. *comb* tendency to swell (physocele); 2. relating to air or gas (physometra); 3. bladder (physogastric)

-phyta, -phyte, phyti-, -phytic, phyto- [Gr. *phuton*, plant] *comb* plant; flora; vegetation (Bryophyta, microphyte, phytiform, holophytic, phytogenesis)

piac- [L. *piare*, to appease] *base* expiatory; wicked (piacular, piacularity)

-piceo- [L. *piceus*, pitch-black] *comb* black-tinged (piceo-ferruginous, piceo-testaceous)

-pici- [L. *picus*, woodpecker] *base* woodpecker (picarian, piciform)

pico- [Sp. *pico*, small quantity] *comb* one-trillionth (picoampere, picogram)

picro- [Gr. *pikros*, bitter] *comb* bitter (picroerythrin, picrtoxin)

-pict- [L. *pictura*, painting] *base* paint (depiction, pictorial)

-piesis [Gr. *piesis*, pressure] *comb* pressure (anisopiesis, hyperpiesis)

piezo- [Gr. *piezein*, press] *comb* pressure; strain (piezo-electricity, piezometer)

pigm- [L. *pigmentum*, paint] *base* paint; color (pigment, pigmentation)

-pign- [L. *pignus*, pledge] *base* pledge; pawn; mortgage (impignorate, pignoration)

-pigr- [L. *piger*, slow, sluggish] *base* slow; sluggish; slothful (impigrity, pigritude)

pil-, pili-, pilo- [L. *pilus*, hair] *comb* hair; (depilatory, piliform, piloerection)

-pile- [L. *pileus*, cap] *base* cap (pileated, pileolus)

piloso- [L. *pilosus*, hairy] *comb* hairy (piloso-fimbriate, piloso-hispid)

pilul- [L. *pilula*, pill, pellet] *base* pill (pilular, pilulous)

pimel-, pimelo- [Gr. *pimele*, fat] *comb* fat; fatty (pimelitis, pimelosis)

pin- [L. *pinus*, pine] *base* pine (pinaceous, pinaster)

-pinac- [Gr. *pinaks*, tablet] *base* tablet; slab (pinacocyte, pinacoid). *Also -*pinak- (pinakoid)

-pingu- [L. *pinguis*, fat] *base* fat (pinguescence, pinguid)

pinnati-, pinnato- [L. *pinnatus*, pinnate] *comb* like a feather; pinnately (pinnatifid, pinnato-pectinate)

pinni- [L. *pinna*, fin, flipper] *comb* fin; flipper (pinnigrade, pinniped)

pino- [Gr. *pinein*, to drink] *comb* drink (pinocytic, pinocytosis)

pio- [Gr. *pion*, fat] *comb* fat (Piophila, pioscope)

-piper- [L. *piper*, pepper] *base* pepper (piperaceous, piperic)

-piq- [Fr. *piquer*, prick, sting] *base* stinging; sharp (piquant, pique)

piri-, piro- [L. *pirum*, pear] *comb* pear (piriform, piroplasmosis). *See* **pyri-**

pisci- [L. *piscis*, fish] *comb* fish (piscicolous, piscivorous)

pisi- [L. *pisum*, pea] *comb* pea (pisidiid, pisiform)

pist-, pisti- [Gr. *pistis*, faith] *base* faith (pistology, pistiology)

pistac- [Gr. *pistake*, pistachio] *base* pistachio (pistachio-nut, pistacite)

pithec-, -pithecus [Gr. *pithekos*, ape]

comb primate; apelike (pithecoid, Australopithecus)

pithi- [Gr. *peithein*, to persuade] comb *persuasion* (pithiatism, pithiatric)

pitta- [Gr. *pitta*, pitch] *base* like pitch (pittacal, pittizite)

pituit- [L. *pituita*, mucus, phlegm] *base* phlegm (pituital, pituitous)

-pityr- [Gr. *pituron*, bran] *base* bran (pityriasis, pityroid)

-plac- [L. *placare*, to appease] *base* please; appease (implacable, placidity)

placenti- [L. *placenta*, cake] *comb* placenta (placentiferous, placentiform)

placo- [Gr. *plaks*, tablet, plate] *comb* flat plate (placodermal, placoid)

plag- [L. *plagiarius*, kidnapper > *plaga*, trap] *base* kidnap; seize (plagiarist, plagiarize)

plagio- [Gr. *plagios*, oblique] *comb* slanting; oblique (plagioclastic, plagiotropic)

-plakia [Gr. *plaks*, flat surface] *comb* [medicine] patch (erythroplakia, leukoplakia)

-plang- [L. *plangere*, to strike noisily] *base* strike; beat (plangency, plangent)

planari- [L. *planus*, flat] *comb* in one plane; flat (planariform, planarioid)

plani-, plano-[1] [L. *planus*, flat] *comb* level; plane; flat (planimeter, planoconcave)

-plania, plano-[2] [Gr. *planos*, wandering] *comb* wandering; moving (uroplania, planogamete)

-plant- [L. *planta*, sole of the foot] *base* sole of the foot (plantar, plantigrade)

-plasia, -plasis [Gr. *plasis*, molding, configuration] *comb* development; growth; change (hypoplasia, cataplasis)

-plasm, plasmato-, plasmo- [Gr. *plasma*, formed, imaged] *comb* fluid cell substances of an animal or vegetable (endoplasm, plasmatoparous, plasmolysis)

-plast, -plastic, plasto- [Gr. *plastos*, formed, molded] *comb* molded; formed (protoplast, protoplastic, plastotype)

-plasty [Gr. *plastos*, formed, molded] **1.** *comb* forming: act or means (genioplasty); **2.** plastic surgery: specific part of the body (thoracoplasty); **3.** plastic surgery: tissue from specified source (autoplasty); **4.** plastic surgery: for a specific purpose (kineplasty)

plat-[1] [Gr. *platis*, flat, wide] *base* flat (platen, platform)

plat-[2] [L. *plata*, silver, precious metal] *base* silver (plateresque, platinum)

platini-, platino- [L. *platinum*, platinum, silvery-white element] *comb* platinum (plantiniferous, platinocyanide)

platy- [Gr. *platis*, flat, wide] *comb* broad; flat (platycephaly, platypus)

-plaud-, -plaus- [L. *plaudere*, to clap, strike] *base* clap (plaudits, plausible)

plaustr- [L. *plaustrum*, wagon, cart] *base* cart; wagon (plaustral, plaustrary)

-pleb- [L. *plebs*, common people] *base* common people (plebiscite, plebeian)

pleco-, plecto- [Gr. *plekein*, twist, twine] *comb* twist; twine; plait (plecopteran, plectognath)

-plegia, -plegy [Gr. *plege*, stroke] *comb* paralysis (hemiplegy, paraplegia)

pleio- [Gr. *pleion*, more] *comb* more (pleiochasial, pleiomastia)

-pleisto- [Gr. *pleistos*, most] *comb* most (Pleistocene, pleistodox)

plemyr- [Gr. *plemura*, flood tide] *base* flood-tide (plemyrameter). *Also* **plemmir-** (plemmirrulate)

-plen-, -pler(o)-, -plet- [L. *plenus*, full] *base* fill; full (replenish, pleroma, complete)

pleo-, pleon-, plio- [Gr. *pleion*, more] *comb* more; increased (pleomorphic, pleonasm, Pliosaurus). *Also* **pleio-** (pleiomorphy)

pleonec-, pleonex- [Gr. *pleonektikos*, greedy] *base* greed; avarice (pleonectic, pleonexia)

plesio- [Gr. *plesios*, near] *comb* near (plesiomorphous, plesiosaurus)

pless(i)- [Gr. *plessein*, to strike] *comb* striking; percussion (plessimeter, plessor)

plethys- [Gr. *plethus*, fullness] *comb* increase; large number (plethysmograph, plethysmometry)

pleuro- [Gr. *pleura*, the side] 1. *comb* side: on or near (pleurodont); 2. pleura: of or near (pleurotomy); 3. pleural (pleuropneumonia)

-plex [L. *plex*, fold] *comb* network; folds; layers (contraplex, decemplex)

-plexia [Gr. *plessein*, to strike] *comb* stroke (apoplexia, parapoplexia)

plicato-, plici- [L. *plicare*, to fold] *comb* folded (plicato-lobate, pliciform)

plinthi- [Gr. *plinthos*, brick, tile] *comb* brick; squared stone (plinthiform, plinthlike)

plio- *See* **pleo-**

ploc- [Gr. *plokos*, woven, plaited] *base* weaver bird (Ploceidae, ploceiform)

-ploid [Gr. *eidos*, form] *comb* chromosones: of a specified multiple of (diploid, haploid)

plor- [L. *plorare*, to weep, lament] *base* cry (implore, ploration)

plum-, plumi- [L. *pluma*, feather] *comb* feather (plumage, plumiform)

plumb-, plumbo- [L. *plumbum*, lead] *comb* lead (plumbism, plumbocalcite)

pluri- [L. *plus/plur-*, more] *comb* several; many (pluriflorous, pluriparous)

pluto- [Gr. *ploutos*, wealthy] *comb* wealth (plutocracy, plutology)

pluvial- [L. *pluvia*, rain] *base* plover (pluvialiform, pluvialine)

pluvio- [L. *pluvia*, rain] *comb* rain (pluviograph, pluvious)

-pnea, pneo- [Gr. *pnein*, to breathe] *comb* breath; respiration (dyspnea, pneograph)

pneum-, pneumato- [Gr. *pneuma*, wind, breath, spirit] 1. *comb* air vapor (pneumatophore); 2. breathing (pneumatometer); 3. spirits (pneumatology)

pneumo-, pneumono- [Gr. *pneuma*, wind, breath, spirit] *comb* lungs; air; gas (pneumobacillus, pneumonophorous)

pneusio-, -pneustic [Gr. *pneusis*, breathing] *comb* breathing (metapneustic, pneusiobiognosis)

-pnig- [Gr. *pnigein*, to choke] *base* choke; suffocate (pnigalion, pnigophobia)

-pocul- [L. *poculum*, goblet, cup] *base* drink; cup (poculent, poculiform)

-pod, -poda, -pode, podo-, -podous [Gr. *pous/pod-*, foot] 1. *comb* foot (pleopod, Cephalopoda, pseudopode, podomere, cephalopodous); 2. having __ feet (tripod)

podic- [L. *podex/podic-*, rump] *base* 1. rump (podical) 2. grebe (Podicipedidae)

-podium [L. *podium*, raised platform] *comb* supporting part; footstalk; (mesopodium, monopodium)

poe- [Gr. *poa*, grass] *base* grass (poephagous, Poephila)

poecilo- [Gr. *poikilos*, various, many-colored] *comb* irregular; many-colored (poecilomere, poecilonymy). *Also* **poicilo-** (poicilothermous)

pogon-, pogono- [Gr. *pogon*, beard] *comb* beard (pogoniasis, pogonotrophy)

-poiesis, -poietic [Gr. *poiein*, to make] *comb* making; forming; producing (leukopoiesis, onomatopoietic)

poikilo- [Gr. *poikilos*, various, many-colored] *comb* irregular; varied (poikiloblast, poikiloderma)

poimen- [Gr. *poimen*, shepherd] *base* pastoral (poimenic, poimenics)

poine- [Gr. *poinao*, to avenge, punish]

base punishment (poinemania, poinephobia)

polari- [L. *polaris*, polar] *comb* polar (polari-guttulate, polarimetry)

-polem- [Gr. *polemos*, war] *base* war (polemicist, polemics)

polio- [Gr. *polios*, gray] *comb* gray; gray matter (poliomyelitis, polioviral)

-polis, polit- [Gr. *polis/polit-*, city] *comb* city (metropolis, politician)

politico- [Gr. *polis/polit-*, city] *comb* political (politico-commercial, politico-religious)

pollaki- [Gr. *pollakis*, many times] *comb* many times (pollakiuria, pollakanthous)

pollic- [L. *pollex/pollic-*, thumb, great toe] *base* thumb (pollicar, pollicate)

pollin(i)- [L. *polis/pollin-*, fine dust, flour] *comb* pollen (pollination, pollinosis)

poly- [Gr. *pollos/pollu-*, many] 1. *comb* more than one (polychromatic); 2. more than usual; excessive (polyphagia); 3. many kinds or parts (polymorphous)

polymorpho- [Gr. *pollos*, many + *morphe*, form] *comb* multiform (polymorphocellular, polymorphonucleated)

polyped- [Gr. *poly*, much + *pedein*, to jump] *base* tree toad (Polypedates, polypedatid)

pomerid- [L. *pomeridianus*, post meridian] *base* afternoon (pomeridian)

pomi-, pomo- [L. *pomum*, fruit, apple] *comb* fruit; apple (pomiform, pomology)

-pomp- [Gr. *pompe*, a sending, procession] 1. *base* release; sending away (hypnopompic); 2. conductor; guide (psychopomp)

-pon-, -pos- [L. *ponere*, to place] *base* to place (opponent, opposition)

-pond- [L. *pondus*, weight] *base* weight; (ponderous, preponderant)

ponero- [Gr. *poneros*, injurious] *comb* evil; wicked; useless (ponerine, ponerology)

pong- [Fr. *pongo*, orangutan] *base* gorilla; orangutan (pongid, pongo)

-ponic [Gr. *penesthai*, to labor] *base* cultivation (geoponic, hydroponic)

pono- [Gr. *ponos*, toil, distress, suffering] *comb* hard work; pain; fatigue (ponograph, ponophobia)

pont- [L. *pons/pont-*, bridge] *base* bridge (pontal, pontiff)

poplit- [L. *poples/poplit-*, back of the knee] *base* back of knee (popliteal, popliteus)

-popul- [L. *populus*, the people] *base* people (depopulate, population)

porc-, porcin- [L. *porcus*, hog] *base* pork (porcelain, porcine)

pori-, poro- [L. *porus*, pore] *comb* pore; channel (poriferous, porencephalia)

porno- [Gr. *porne*, prostitute] *comb* harlot (pornocracy, pornography)

poroso- [L. *porosus*, full of pores] *comb* filled with pores (poroso-punctate)

porphyro- [Gr. *porphura*, purple] *comb* purple (porphyritic, porphyrogenite)

porr(ac)- [L. *porrum*, leek] *base* leek; green (porraceous, porre)

-porrig- [L. *porrigo*, dandruff] *base* dandruff (porriginous, porrigo)

-port- [L. *portare*, to carry] *base* carry (import, portable)

porto- [L. *porta*, city gate, door] *comb* portal; entrance (portobilioarterial, portosystemic)

portulac- [L. *portulaca*, purslane] *base* purslane (portulaca, portulaceous)

-pos- *see* -pon-

posio- [Gr. *posis*, drinking] *base* drinking (aposia, posiomania)

poso- [Gr. *posos*, how much] *comb* dose (posological, posology)

post- [L. *post*, behind] 1. *pre* after in time; following; later (postgraduate); 2. after in space; behind (postaxial, postprandial)

postero- [L. *posterus*, later, next] *comb*

posterior; behind (postero-lateral, postero-mesial)

pot-, poto- [L. *potare*, to drink] *comb* drink (potable, potomania)

potamo- [Gr. *potamos*, river] *comb* river (potamography, potamologist)

-poten- [L. *potentia*, power] *base* power; ability (impotency, potential)

poticho- [Fr. *potiche*, kind of pot] *comb* porcelain (potichomania, potichomanist)

pov- [OF *poverte*, destitution] *base* poor (impoverished, poverty)

-pragia [Gr. *prassein*, to achieve] *comb* a quality of action (bradypragia)

-prand- [L. *prandium*, late breakfast, luncheon] *base* dinner (postprandial, preprandial)

-pras- [Gr. *prasaios*, leek-green] *base* leek-green (prase, prasine)

praso- [Gr. *prasaios*, leek-green] *comb* leek (prasolite, prasophagous)

-prat- [L. *pratum*, meadow] *base* meadow (pratal, Praticola)

-prav- [L. *pravus*, wicked, bad] *base* crooked; wrong; bad (depravity, impravable)

-praxia, -praxis [Gr. *praksis*, action] *comb* movement; action (hyperpraxia, parapraxis)

pre- [L. *prae*, before] **1.** *pre* before in time; earlier; prior to; (presuppose); **2.** before in place; anterior; in front of (preaxial); **3.** before in rank; superior; surpassing (preeminent); **4.** in preparation for (preschool). *Also* **prae-** (praenomen)

-preca- [L. *precari*, to pray] *base* entreat; pray (imprecation, precarious)

precip- [L. *praeceps/praecipit*, headlong] *base* steep; headlong (precipice, precipitant)

pred- [L. *praedare*, to plunder] *base* robbery (predation, predatory)

-prehend, -prehens- [L. *prendere*, to grasp, seize] *base* hold; seize (apprehend, apprehensive)

presby- [Gr. *presbus*, old] *comb* old age (presbyacusis, presbyopia)

presbyter- [Gr. *presbuteros*, elder] *comb* elder; priest (presbyteral, presbytery)

preter- [L. *praeter*, beyond, over] *pre* past; beyond; outside the bounds (preternatural, preternuptial)

pri-, prion- [Gr. *prion*, a saw] *base* a saw (priodont, prionodont)

prid- [L. *pridianus*, day before] *base* yesterday (pridian)

prim-, primi-, primo- [L. *primus*, first] *comb* first; original; early (primacy, primigravida, primogenitor)

primaver- [Sp. *primavera*, springtime] *base* spring (pasta primavera, primaveral)

princip- [L. *principalis*, chief, first] *base* chief; first; main (principal, principiate)

prion- [Gr. *prion*, a saw] *base* a saw (prionodont, Prionurus)

prior- [L. *prior*, earlier, previous] *base* superior, better (prioress, priority)

prisc- [L. *priscus*, primitive] *base* ancient; primitive (priscal, priscan)

-priv-¹ [L. *privatus*, individual, private] *base* private (privacy, privilege)

-priv-² [L. *privare*, rob, strip] *base* divest (deprivation, privation)

privign- [L. *privignus*, born of one only of a married pair] *base* stepchild (Amanita privigna, privignal)

pro-¹ [L. *pro*, forward, onward] **1.** *pre* moving forward; moving ahead of (proclivity); **2.** forth (produce); **3.** substituting for; acting for (pronoun); **4.** defending; supporting (prolabor)

pro-² [Gr. *pro*, before] *pre* before in place or time; (proestrus, prologue)

prob- [L. *probare*, to test] *base* good; upright (probe, probity)

-probosc- [Gr. *pro*, before + *boskein*, to feed] *base* long flexible snout (proboscidiform, proboscis)

procac- [L. *procax/procac-*, forward,

bold] *base* bully; insolent (procacious, procacity)

procell- [L. *procella*, storm, hurricane] *base* storm (Procellaria, procellous)

procer- [L. *procerus*, high, tall, long] *base* tall; long (proceritic, procerity)

procto- [Gr. *proktos*, anus] *comb* rectum (proctalgia, proctology)

procyon- [Gr. *prokuon*, the constellation known as *Canis Minor*] *base* raccoon (procyoniform, procyonine)

-prodit- [L. *proditio*, betrayal] *base* traitor (proditomania, proditorious)

profan- [L. *profanare*, to desecrate] *base* unholy, violated (profanation, profanity)

-profund- [L. *profundus*, deep] *base* deep (profundiplantar, profundity)

prognos- [Gr. *progignoskein*, to know beforehand] *base* foreknowledge; forecast (prognosis, prognostication)

prohib- [L. *prohibere*, to hold off, stop] *base* hold back; forbid (prohibit, prohibitory)

proli- [L. *proles*, offspring] *comb* productive, fruitful (prolicide, proliferation)

prono- [L. *pronus*, bent downward] *comb* bent downward (pronorgade, pronometer)

-proof [L. *probare*, to prove] **1.** *suf* impervious to (waterproof); **2.** protected against (weatherproof); **3.** as strong as (armorproof); **4.** resistive to; unaffected by (womanproof)

proprio- [L. *proprius*, one's one] *comb* one's own (proprioceptive, proprioceptor)

pros- [Gr. *pros*, to, toward] *comb* to; toward (prosenchyma, prosody)

proso- [Gr. *proso*, forward] *comb* forward; anterior (prosopulmonate, prosopyle)

prosop(o)- [Gr. *prosopon*, a face] *comb* face (prosopagnosia, prosopalgia)

prostato- [Gr. *prostates*, one who stands before] *comb* of the prostate (prostatectomy, prostatocystitis)

proteo- [Gr. *proteios*, primary] *comb* protein (proteoclastic, proteolysis)

protero- [Gr. *proteros*, fore] *comb* earlier; before; former; anterior (proteroglyph, proterogyny)

proterv- [L. *protervitas*, boldness] *base* stubborn; insolent (protervity, protervous)

proto- [Gr. *protos*, first] **1.** *comb* first in time; original (protocol); **2.** first in importance; principal; chief (protagonist); **3.** primitive (proto-Arabic); **4.** [chemistry] being that member of a series of compounds having the lowest proportion of the specified element or radical; being the parent form of a specified substance (protoactinium)

protother- [Gr. *proto*, first + *ther*, wild beast] *base* platypus (Prototheria, prototherian)

prox-, proximo- [L. *proximus*, nearest] *comb* near (proxemics, proximocephalic)

prozym- [Gr. *pro*, for + *zume*, leaven] *base* yeast (prozymite, prozymogen)

-pruin- [L. *pruina*, hoarfrost] *base* frost (pruinate, pruinose)

-prur- [L. *prurire*, to itch] *base* itch (prurient, pruritic)

-psalid- [Gr. *psalis*, shears] *base* shears; scissors (psalidodect)

psall- [Gr. *psallein*, to play on a stringed instrument] *base* lyre (psallenda, psalloid)

psamm(o)- [Gr. *psammos*, sand] *comb* sand (psammitic, psammophilous)

-psar- [Gr. *psar*, starling] **1.** *base* speckled (Psaronius); **2.** starling (psarolite)

-pselaph [Gr. *pselaphan*, feel about] *base* grope (pselaphognath, pselaphotheca)

psell- [Gr. *psellos*, stammering] *base* stuttering (psellism, psellismologist)

pseph(o)- [Gr. *psephos*, pebble] *comb* pebble; counter (psephology, psephomancy)

psett- [Gr. *psetta*, flatfish] *base* turbot (psettaceous, psettine) pseudo- [Gr. *pseudes*, false] **1.** *comb* fictitious; sham (pseudonym); **2.** counterfeit; spurious (pseudepigrapha); **3.** closely similar or deceptively similar; (pseudomorph); **4.** illusory (pseudacusis); **5.** [chemistry] an isomer or related form (pseudocholinesterase)

psil-, psilo- [Gr. *psilos*, naked, blank] *comb* bare; smooth; mere (psilanthropy, psilodermatous)

-psithur- [Gr. *psithurizein*, to whisper] *base* whisper (psithurism)

-psittac- [L. *psittacus*, parrot] *base* parrot; macaw; parakeet (psittacine, psittacoid)

psoma- [Gr. *psomos*, morsel] *comb* morsel (psomophagia, psomophagy)

psor- [Gr. *psora*, itch] *comb* itch (psoriasis, psoroid)

psycho- [Gr. *psuke*, spirit, mind] *comb* mind; mental processes (psychodectic, psychology)

psychro- [Gr. *psuchros*, cold, chill] *comb* cold (psychrometer, psychrophobia)

psyll-¹ [Gr. *psulla*, flea] *base* flea (Psylla, psylly)

psyll-² [Gr. *Psulloi*, African people famed as snake charmers] *base* snake charmer (psyllic)

ptarm- [Gr. *ptarmos*, sneezing] *base* sneeze (ptarmic, Ptarmica)

pteno- [Gr. *ptenos*, having feathers] *comb* feathered (ptenoglossate, Ptenopleura)

-pter, ptero-, -pterous [Gr. *pteron*, wing, plumage] *comb* wing; wing-shaped; feather; fin (hymenopter, pterodactyl, homopterous)

pterido- [Gr. *pteris/pterid-*, fern] *comb* fern (pteridology, pteromania)

ptern- [Gr. *pterna*, heel] *base* heel bone (pterna, pternalgia)

pterocl- [L. *pterocles* < Gr. *pteron*, wing] *base* sand grouse (pteroclid, pteroclomorphic)

pterono- [Gr. *pteron*, wing] *comb* wing; feather; fin (pteronomania, pteronophobia)

pterop- [Gr. *pteropous*, wing-footed] *base* fruit bat (pteropine, pteropodial)

pterophyll- [Gr. *ptero*, wing + *phullon*, leaf] *base* angelfish (pterophyllous, Pterophyllum scalare)

pterygo- [Gr. *pterugion*, little wing, fin] *comb* wing; wing-shaped; feather; fin (pterygoblast, pterygoid)

-pteryl- [Gr. *pteron*, wing, plumage] *base* feather (pterylography, pterylosis)

ptilo-, -ptile [Gr. *ptilon*, feather] *comb* wing; feathery (ptilogenesis, protoptile)

ptis- [Gr. *ptisane*, peeled barley] *base* barley, barley-water (ptisan, ptisanery)

ptocho- [Gr. *ptokhos*, beggar] *comb* poor; beggar (ptochocracy, ptochology)

-ptosia, -ptosis [Gr. *ptosis*, falling] *comb* falling; drooping (phrenoptosia, nephroptosis)

ptyal-, ptyalo- [Gr. *ptuein*, to spit] *comb* saliva (ptyalagogue, ptyalogenic)

-ptych- [Gr. *ptukhe*, a fold] *base* folded (ptychodont, Ptychzoön)

-ptysis [Gr. *ptuein*, to spit] *base* spitting (hemoptysis, ptysmagogue)

pubio-, pubo- [L. *pubis*, pubic bone] *comb* pubic (pubiotomy, pubofemoral)

-puden- [L. *pudens/pudent-*, bashful, modest] *base* shame; modesty (impudent, pudency)

-puer- [L. *puer*, child] *base like a* child (puerile, puerility)

puerper- [L. *puer*, child + *parere*, bring forth] *base* childbirth (puerperal, puerperous)

pugio- [L. *pugio*, dagger] *base* dagger (pugioniform, pugioniphobia)

pugil- [L. *pugil*, boxer] *base* attack; fight; fist (pugilism, pugilistic)

-pugn- [L. *pugnare*, to fight] *base* fight; oppose (impugn, oppugn)

-pul- [L. *pellere*, to drive] *base* push; drive (appulsion, propulsion). *Also -* pel- (repel)

pulchr- [L. *pulchritudo*, beauty] *base* beautiful (pulchritude, pulchritudinous)

-puli- [L. *pulex/pulic-*, flea] *base* flea (pulicose, pulicosity)

pull- [L. *pullus*, chicken] *base* chicken (pullet, pullulate)

pullastr- [L. *pullastra*, young hen] *base* pigeon (pullastriform, pullastrine)

pulmo-, pulmoni-, pulmono- [L. *pulmo*, lung] 1. *comb* lung (pulmonate); 2. pulmonary (pulmocutaneous, pulmonigrade, pulmonogastropod)

-puls- [L. *pulsus*, a push or blow] *base* beating; knocking (pulsation, pulse)

pulver- [L. *pulvis*, dust, powder] *base* dust; ash (pulverious, pulverize)

-pulvin- [L. *pulvinus*, bolster, pillow] *base* cushion (pulvilliform, pulvinate)

pum- [L. *pumex/pumic-*, pumice] base pumice (pumicate, pumiceous)

-pun-[1] [L. *punire*, to punish] *base* punish (impunity, punishable)

-pun-[2] [L. *puniceus*, red, purple] *base* purple (puniceous, punicin)

-punct-, pung- [L. *punctum*, dot] *base* point; sharp (punctiform, pungent)

punctato- [L. *punctatus*, pointed] *comb* with points or dots (punctatostriate, punctato-sulcate)

pupa- [L. *pupa*, girl, doll] *base* 1. pupa (puparial, pupation) 2. puppet (pupaphobia)

pupillo- [L. *pupilla*, pupil] *comb* pupil of the eye (pupillography, pupillometer)

-pur- [L. *pus/pur-*, pus] *base* pus (purulent, suppuration)

-purg- [L. *purgare*, to cleanse] *base* cleanse (purgation, purgative)

purpureo- [Gr. *porfureos*, purple] *comb* [chemistry] purple compounds (purpureo-cobalt, purpureo-cobaltic)

purulo- [L. *purulentus*, pus-filled] *comb* pus (purulo-fibrinous, purulogangrenous)

pusill- [L. *pusillus*, very little] *base* petty; very small (pusillanimity, pusillanimous)

pustulo- [L. *pustula*, blister] *comb* pimple (pustuliform, pustulocrustaceous)

-put- [L. *putare*, think, suppose] *base* think (putative, reputed)

putamin- [L. *putamen*, waste, husk] *base* husk (putamen, putaminous)

putea- [L. *puteus*, a well] *base* a well (puteal, puteanic)

putre-, putri- [L. *putris*, rotten] *comb* rotten (putrefaction, putriform)

py-, pyo- [Gr. *puon*, pus] *base* pus (pyedema, pyemic, pyolymph)

pycn(i)o- [Gr. *puknos*, thick, dense] *comb* thick; compact; dense (pycnidiospore, pycnometer). *Also* pykn(o)- (pyknemia, pyknic)

pyelo- [Gr. *puelos*, pelvis] *comb* pelvis; kidney (pyelocystitis, pyelonephritis)

-pygia, pygo- [Gr. *puge*, rump] *comb* rump; buttocks (pygopod , steatopygia)

pygm- [L. *pugnus*, fist] *base* fist (pygmachy, pygmy)

-pyle [Gr. *pule*, gate] *comb* gate; aperture (astropyle, micropyle)

-pyle-, pylo- [Gr. *pule*, gate] *base* gate; aperture (pylemphraxis, pylephlebitis, pylon, pylorus)

pyloro- [Gr. *pule*, gate + *ora*, keeper] *comb* pylorus: stomach opening (pylorodiosis, pylorospasm)

pyo- [Gr. *puon*, pus] 1. *comb* pus (pyogenic, pyonephrotic); 2. suppurative (pyococcus, pyosis)

pyren- [Gr. *puren*, fruit stone] *base* nucleated; drupaceous (pyrenemia, pyrenocarp)

pyreto-, -pyrexia [Gr. *purektikos*, feverish < *pur*, fire] *comb* fever (pyretogenesis, pyretology, eupyrexia, hyperpyrexia)

-pyrgo- [Gr. *purgos*, tower] *base* tower (pyrgocephalic, pyrgoidal)

-pyri- [L. *pirum*, pear] *base* pear (pyridion, pyriform). *Also* piro- (piroplasm)

pyrito- [Gr. *purites*, flint] *comb* pyrites (pyritohedral, pyritohedron)

pyro- [Gr. *pur*, fire] 1. *comb* fire; heat (pyromania); 2. [chemistry] a substance derived from the specified substance by or as if by the action of heat (pryrogallol); 3. [geology] formed by heat (pyroxenite)

pyrrho- [Gr. *purros*, reddish] *comb* reddish (pyrrhoarsenite, pyrrhocorax)

pyrrhul- [Gr. *purros*, reddish] *base* bullfinch; bunting (pyrrhula, pyrrhuline)

pyrrhulox- [Gr. *purros*, reddish] *base* cardinal (Pyrrhuloxia, pyrrhuloxine)

pytho- [Gr. *puthein*, to rot] *comb* corrupt; decomposed (pythogenic, pythogenesis)

pyx- [Gr. *puksis*, box] *comb* box (pyxidate, pyxis)

Q

quadr- [L. *quadra*, square] *base* four; fourfold; square (quadrable, quadrangle)

quadragen- [L. *quadraginta*, forty] *base* forty (quadragenarian, quadragene)

quadrages- [L. *quadragesima*, Lent, 40 days] *base* forty (Quadragesima, quadragesimal)

quadrati-, quadrato- [L. *quadratus*, square] *comb* four; fourfold (quadratiformis, quadratocubic)

quadri- [L. *quattuor*, four] *base* four; fourfold (quadriceps, quadrilateral)

quadricent- [L. *quattuor*, four + *centennis*, 100 years] *base* four hundred (quadricentennial)

quadru- [L. *quattuor*, four] *base* four; fourfold (quadrumanous, quadruped)

quaest- [L. *quarere*, seek, obtain] *base* gain; money-making (quaesta, quaestuary)

quali- [L. *qualis*, of what kind?] *base* characteristics; competence (qualitative, quality)

quanti- [L. *quantus*, how much] *comb* amount; extent (quantity, quantitative)

quart-, quarter-, quarti- [L. *quartus*, fourth] *base* one-fourth (quartile, quartering, quartisect)

quasi- [L. *quasi*, about, nearly] *comb* seemingly; as if; resembling (quasijudicial, quasi-periodic)

quass- [L. *quassare*, to shake] *base* shake; beat (conquassate, quassative)

quat-, quater-, quatr- [L. *quattuor*, four] *comb* four (quatrain, quaternion, quatrefoil)

quattuordec- [L. *quattuor*, four + *decem*, ten] *base* fourteen (quatuordecangle, quatuordecillion)

-quer-¹, querul- [L. *queri*, to complain] *base* complain (querimonious, querulous)

-quer-² [L. *quaere*, to ask] *base* question (query, querying)

querc-, querci- [L. *quercus*, oak] *comb* oak (quercine, quercivorous)

quid- [L. *quid*, what] *base* nature; essence (quiddative, quiddity)

quiesc- [L. *quiescere*, keep quiet, rest] *base* quiet (acquiesce, quiescent)

quin-¹ [L. *quinque*, five] *base* five; multiple of five (quinary, quinate)

quin-² [SA *kina*, Peruvian bark] *base* quinine (quinidamine, quinology)

quincent- [L. *quinque*, five + *centenar-*

ius, having 100] *base* five hundred (quincentenary, quincentennial)

quindec(em)- [L. *quinque*, five + *decem*, ten] *base* fifteen (quinde- cemvirate, quindecima)

quinquagen- [L. *quinquaginta*, fifty] *base* fifty (quinquagenarian, quin- quagenary)

quinquages- [L. *quinquaginta*, fifty] *base* fifty (Quinquagesima Sunday, quinquagesimal)

quinque- [L. *quinque*, five] *comb* five (quinquefoliant, quinquennial)

quint-[1], **quinti-** [L. *quinque*, five] *comb* five; multiple of five (quintuplets, quintilateral)

quint-[2] [L. *quintus*, fifth] *comb* one- fifth (quintan, quintile)

-quire, -quiry [L. *quaerere*, to seek] *comb* seek; search for (require, in- quiry)

-quis- [L. *quaerere*, to seek] *base* seek; search for (inquisition, requisition)

quot- [L. *quoties*, how many] *base* how many (quota, quotient)

quotid- [L. *quot*, as many as + *dies*, day] *base* daily (quotidian, quotidi- anly)

R

-racem- [L. *racemus*, cluster of grapes] *base* cluster (racemation, racemi- form)

rachi-, rachio- [Gr. *rakhis*, spine] *comb* relating to the spine (rachicen- tesis, rachiometer). *See* -rrhachia

-rad- [L. *radius*, ray] *base* ray; rod; spoke (irradiate, radial)

radiati-, radiato- [L. *radiatus*, radiate] *comb* ray-like (radiatiform, radiato- striate)

radici- [L. *radix/radic-*, root] *comb* root (radiciform, radicicolous)

radiculo- [L. *radiculus*, rootlet] *comb* radicle; rootlike part (radiculogan- glionitis, radiculose)

radio- [L. *radius*, ray] **1.** *comb* ray; raylike (radiolarian); **2.** by radio (radiotelegram); **3.** [anatomy] radius and (radiobicipital); **4.** [medicine] by radiant energy (radiotherapy); **5.** [physics] radioactive (radiotho- rium)

raduli- [L. *radula*, scraper, rasp] *base* sharp-pointed; rasp-like (radulifer- ous, raduliform)

rall- [L. *Rallus*, the rail — a bird] *base* the rail (ralliform, ralline)

rami- [L. *ramus*, branch] *comb* branch (ramification, ramiflorous)

ramoso- [L. *ramosus*, full of branches] *comb* branchy (ramoso-palmate, ramoso-subpinnate)

ramul- [L. *ramulus*, little branch] *base* twig (ramuliferous, ramulose)

rang(if)- [L. *rangifer*, reindeer] *base* reindeer, caribou (rangerine, rangiferine)

rani- [L. *rana*, frog] *comb* frog (rani- form, raniverous)

rap- [L. *rapere*, to seize] *base* snatch; seize (rapacious, rapture)

-raphan- [Gr. *raphanis*, radish] *base* radish (raphania, raphanus)

raphi(d)- [Gr. *raphis/raphid-* needle] *base* needle (raphidiferous, raphi- graph)

raptor- [L. *raptor*, robber] *base* falcon (Raptores, raptorial)

rasor- [L. *radere/rasus*, to scrape] *base* scratching, shaving (Rasores, rasorial)

rat- [L. *ratis*, raft] *base* emu; ostrich (Ratitae, ratite)

-rater [L. *reri/ratus*, to think, judge] *comb* specified rate or class (first- rater, second-rater)

-ratio- [L. *ratio*, reasoning] *base* reason- ing; thought (irrational, rationalize)

re- [L. *re-*, back, again] **1.** *pre* back (re- store); **2.** again; anew (retell)

recti- [L. *rectus*, straight] *comb* straight; right (rectirostral, rectitude)

recto- [L. *rectum*, rectum] *comb* rectal (rectogenital, rectoscope)

recurvi-, recurvo- [L. *recurvus*, bent back] *comb* bent back (recurvirostral, recurvo-ternate)

-red [OE *raeden*, condition] *suf* condition; state (hatred, kindred)

regi- [L. *rex/reg-*, king] *base* of a king (regible, regicide)

regin- [L. *regina*, queen] *base* queen (reginal, reginist)

regm- [Gr. *regmunai*, to break] *base* separation, splitting (regma, regmacarp)

rego- [Gr. *rhugos*, blanket, rug] *comb* covering (regolith, regolithic)

-regn- [L. *regnum*, kingdom] *base* royal; ruling (interregnum, regnant)

regul- [L. *regula*, rule] *base* standard pattern (irregular, regulations)

-rel [OF *-erel*, diminutive suffix] *suf* diminutive (kestrel, wastrel)

religio- [L. *religiosus*, religious] *comb* religion (religio-educational, relgio-mystical)

relinq- [L. *relinquere*, to leave] *base* leave; jilt; abandon (relinquish, unrelinquished)

reliq- [L. *reliquiae*, relics] *base* remains; relic (reliquarian, reliquary)

-reme, -remi- [L. *remus*, oar] *base* oar (trireme, remiform)

reni-, reno- [L. *renes*, kidneys] *comb* kidney (reniform, renovascular)

rep- [L. *rapere*, to snatch] *base* snatch; seize (subreption, surreptitious)

repando- [L. *repandus*, bent back] *comb* bent back (repando-dentate, repando-lobate)

-rept- [L. *repere*, to creep] *base* creep; crawl (reptation, reptatorial)

reptil- [LL. *reptilis*, reptile] *base* reptile (reptilian, reptilivorous)

repud- [L. *repudium*, rejection] *base* jilt; reject (repudiate, repudiatory)

resino- [L. *resina*, resin] *comb* resin (resino-extractive, resino-vitreous)

respirato- [L. *respirare*, to breathe out] *comb* respiratory (respirato-prehensory, respirato-pulmonary)

-resti- [L. *restis*, cord, rope] *base* cord; cordlike (restibrachial, restiform)

reti- [L. *rete*, net] *base* net (reticular, retiform)

reticulato-, reticulo- *comb* net; network (reticulato-venose, reticulo-ramose)

retino- [NL *retina*, retina] *comb* of the retina (retinogen, retinoschisis)

retro- [L. *retro*, back, behind, formerly] *comb* backward; back; behind (retroactive, retroflex)

rhabdo- [Gr. *rhabdos*, rod] *comb* rod; wand (rhabdocoele, rhabdomancer)

-rhachia *see* rachia- *and* -rrhachia

rhachio-, rhacio- [Gr. *rhachis*, spine] *comb* spine (rhachiomyelitis, rhaciotomy)

-rhag- [Gr. *rhagodes*, like grapes] *base* grape (rhagon, rhagose)

-rhage *see* -rrhage

-rhamn- [Gr. *rhamnos*, buckthorn] *base* buckthorn (rhamneous, rhamnose)

rhampho- [Gr. *rhamphos*, curved beak] *comb* beak (rhamphoid, rhamphotheca)

rhap- [Gr. *rhapis*, rod] *base* tapered, wand-like (Rhapidophyllum, Rhapis)

rhaphio- [Gr. *rhaphion*, needle] *comb* needle-like (Rhaphiodopsis, Rhaphiosaurus)

-rhaphy *see* -rrhaphy

-rhaps- [Gr. *rhaptein/rhaps-*, stitch or fasten together] *base* stitched; strung together (rhapsodomancy, rhapsody)

-rhea *see* -rrhea

rhegma- [Gr. *rhegma*, a break] *comb* fracture; break (rhegma, rhegmatogenous)

rhema- [Gr. *rhematikos*, belonging to a verb] *base* word; verb (epirrhema, rhematic)

rheo- [Gr. *rhein*, to flow] *comb* flow; current (rheoscope, rheostat)

rhesto- [Gr. *rhaio*, to destroy] *comb* broken down (rhestocythemia). *Also* rhaesto-

rhet- [Gr. *rhetor*, a speaker] *base* say; speak (rhetorical, rhetorician)

-rheum- [Gr. *rheuma*, a flow] *base* flow; stream (rheumatic, rheumatoid)

-rhexis *see* -rrhexis

rhigo- [Gr. *rhigos*, cold] *comb* cold; frost (rhigolene, rhigosis)

rhino- [Gr. *rhis/rhin-*, nose] *comb* nose (rhinencephalon, rhinology)

rhipi-, rhipido- [Gr. *rhipis/rhipid-*, fan] *comb* fan (rhipidate, rhipidoglossate)

rhizo- [Gr. *rhiza*, root] *comb* root (rhizomorph, rhizophagous). *See* -(r)rhiza

rhodo- [Gr. *rhodon*, rose] *comb* rose; rose-red (rhodochrome, rhodolite)

-rhoeica *see* -rrhoeica

rhombi-, rhombo- [Gr. *rhombos*, rhomb, lozenge] *comb* rhombus (rhombiform, rhombohedral)

-rhonch- [Gr. *rhonkhos*, snoring, snorting] *base* snoring (rhonchal, rhonchisonant)

-rhopal- [Gr. *rhopalikos*, like a club] *base* club; cudgel (rhopalocerous, Rhopalodon)

rhopheo- (Gr. *rhophein*, gulp down] *comb* aspirate (rhopheocytosis)

-rhopo- [Gr. *rhopos*, petty wares] *base* petty; restricted (rhopographer, rhopography)

rhyaco- [Gr. *rhuaks*, a stream) *comb* torrent, stream (rhyacolite, Rhyacophilus)

rhyncho- [Gr. *rhunkhos*, snout] *comb* snout; beak (rhynchophore, rhyncosaurian). *See* -rrhyncha

rhyparo-, rhypo- [Gr. *rhuparos*, foul, dirty] *comb* dirt; filth (rhyparographer, rhypophagy). *Also* rypo- (rypophagy)

rhyss- [Gr. *rhusos*, drawn up, wrinkled] *base* wrinkled (Rhyssa, Rhyssodidae)

rhyti- [Gr. *rhutis*, a wrinkle] *comb* wrinkle (rhytidectomy, rhytidoma)

ribes- [Pers. *ribaj*, gooseberry] *base* gooseberry (ribes, Ribesieae)

-ric [OE *rice*, realm, province] *comb* jurisdiction; realm (abbotric, bishopric)

ricinol- [L. *ricinus*, error for *cicinus*, castor oil] *comb* castor oil (ricinolamide, ricinolein)

-ridden [past participle of *ride*] *comb* obsessed or burdened with (guilt-ridden, priest-ridden)

-rig- [L. *rigare*, to water] *base* wet (irrigate, rigation)

rigesc- [L. *rigescere*, grow stiff or numb] *base* stiff; rigid (rigescence, rigescent)

-rim- [L. *rima*, crack, opening] *base* opening; crack (rimiform, rimose)

ringi- [L. *ringi*, to gape] *base* open-mouthed (ringent, Ringiculidae)

-rip- [L. *ripa*, river bank] *base* river; water (riparian, ripicolous)

-ris- [L. *ridere/ris-*, to laugh] *base* laugh (risibility, risible)

riv- [L. *rivus*, a stream, channel] *base* grooved; pert. to a stream (rivose; rivulose)

-rix- [L. *rixari*, to brawl] *base* quarrel (rixation, rixatrix)

rizi-, ryzi- [Gr. *oruksa*, rice] *base* rice (oryzivorous, riziform)

-robor-[1] [L. *roborare*, to strengthen] *base* strength (roborant, roboration)

-robor-[2] [L. *robur*, oak, hard wood] *base* oak (roborean, roboreous)

rod- [L. *rodere*, to gnaw] *base* eat away (corrode, erode)

roentgeno- [<Wilhelm Konrad Roentgen] *comb* X-rays (roentgenology, roentgenotherapy)

-rog- [L. *rogare*, to ask] *base* ask; question (interrogate, rogatory)

Romano- [L. *Romanus*, Roman] *comb* Roman and (Romano-Byzantine, Romano-Lombardic)

romantico- [Fr. *romant*, romance, novel] *comb* romantic (romantico-heroic, romantico-historical)

rond- [ME *ronde*, round] *base* circular (rondache, rondure)

-ror- [L. *ros/ror-*, dew] *base* dew (roriferous, rorifluent)

roseo- [L. *roseus*, rosy] *comb* [chemistry] reddish salts (roseo-cobaltic, roseochrome)

-rostell- [L. *rostellum*, little beak] *base* snout; radicle (rostellate, rostelliform)

rostrato-, rostri-, rostro- [L. *rostratus*, having a beak or hook] *comb* beak; (rostrato-nariform, rostriform, rostrocarinate)

rot-, roti-, roto- [L. *rota*, wheel] *comb* turn; wheel (rotation, rotiform, rotograph)

rotundi-, rotundo- [L. *rotundus*, round] *comb* round (rotundifoliate, rotundo-tetragonal)

-rrhachia [Gr. *rakhis*, spine] *comb* spine (glycorrhachia). *See* **rachio-**

-rrhage, -rrhagia [Gr. *regnunai*, burst forth] *comb* abnormal discharge; excessive flow (hemorrhage, menorrhagia)

-rrhaphy [Gr. *rhaptein*, to sew] *comb* suture (arteriorrhaphy, cystorrhaphy)

-rrhea [Gr. *rroia*, flux, flow] *comb* flow; discharge (diarrhea, logorrhea). *Also* **-rrhœa** (diarrhœa). *See* **rheo-**

-rrhexis [Gr. *rheksis*, a breaking] *comb* rupture; bursting (karyorrhexis, myorrhexis). *See* **rhegma-**

-rrhiza [Gr. *rhiza*, root] *comb* root (mycorrhiza, pseudomycorrhiza). *See* **rhizo-**

-rrhoeic, -rrhoeica [Gr. *rroia*, flux, flow] *comb* flow (seborhoeic, seborrhoeica)

-rrhyncha [Gr. *rhunkhos*, snout] *comb* snout; beak (auchenorrhyncha, oxyrryncha). *See* **rhyncho-**

-rub- [L. *rubedo*, redness] *base* red; (rubedity, rubescent)

rubig- [L. *rubiginosus*, rusty] *base* rust (rubiginose, rubiginous)

-ruct- [L. *ructare*, to belch] *base* belch; emit (eructation, eruction)

-rud- [L. *rudis*, imperfect] *base* rough; elementary (rudimentary, rudiments)

ruder- [L. *ruderare*, cover with rubbish] *base* stone fragments; rubble; rubbish (ruderal, ruderation)

rufi-, rufo- [L. *rufus*, red] *comb* red (ruficaudate, rufo-fulvous)

-rug- [L. *ruga*, wrinkle] *base* wrinkle; (erugate, rugose)

rumen- [L. *rumen*, throat, gullet] *base* ruminant stomach (rumenitis, rumenotomy)

runc- [L. *runcare*, to weed] *base* weed (aberuncate, runcation)

runcin- [L. *runcina*, plane] *base* sawtoothed (runcinate, Runcinidae)

runo- [L. *runa*, rune] *comb* rune (runographic, runology)

rupes-, rupic- [L. *rupes/rupic-*, rock] *base* rock (rupestrine, rupicolous)

rupicap- [L. *rupes*, rock + *capra*, goat] *base* chamois (Rupicapra, rupicaprine)

rupo-[1] [Gr. *rhuparos*, foul, dirty] *base* filth (rupophobia). *See* **rhypo-**

rupo-[2] [Gr. *rhupos*, sealing wax] *base* impressing a coin or medal on sealing wax (rupography, rupographical)

-rupt- [L. *ruptura*, a breaking] *base* burst; break (disruption, eruption)

rur- [L. *rus/rur-*, the country] *base* the country (rural, rurigenous)

Russo- [L. *Russus*, Russia] 1. *comb* Russia (Russophobe); 2. Russian and (Russo-Japanese)

rut- [L. *rutaceus*, of or belonging to rue] *base* rue (Rutaceae, rutaceous)

-rutil- [L. *rutilus*, red, yellowish-red] *base* shining; reddish (rutilant, rutilate)

-ry *See* **-ery**

rypo- [Gr. *rhuparos*, foul, dirty] *base* filth (rypophagy). *Also* **rupo-**

S

-s [OE -es, pl. suff.] suf plural ending (dogs, zebras)

sabell-, sabul- [L. sabulum, sand, gravel] base sand; grit (sabellan, sabulosity)

saburr- [L. saburra, sand] base sand (saburral, saburration)

-sacc- [L. saccus, bag] base pouch; bag; cyst (saccate, sacculation)

saccharo- [Gr. sakkhraron, sugar] 1. comb sugar (saccharometer); 2. saccharin and (saccharo-mucilaginous)

saccomy- [Gr. Saccomys, pocket-mouse] base rodent with cheek pouches (saccomyian, saccomyoid)

sacerdot- [L. sacerdos/sacerdot-, priest] base priest (sacerdotal, sacerdotalize)

saco- [Gr. sakos, shield] base shield-like; type of beetle (Sacodes, Sacoglossa)

-sacr- [L. sacrare, dedicate, consecrate] base holy; set apart (sacrament, sacrificial); sacro- [L. sacrum, the sacrum] comb sacral and (sacrospinal, sacrovertebral)

saen- [Gr. sainein, wag the tail] base annelids (Saenuridomorpha, Saenuris)

safran- [Fr. safran, saffron] base yellow; saffron (saffranin, saffranophile)

sagac- [L. sagax/sagac-, acute, perceptive] base intellectually discerning (sagacious, sagacity)

sagen- [Gr. sagene, large fishing net] base like a fishing net (Sagenaria, sagene)

sagin- [L. sagina, fattening] base fattening (saginate, sagination)

-sagitt- [L. sagitta, arrow, bolt] base like an arrow (sagittal, sagittate)

sagma- [Gr. sagma, pack-saddle] base like a saddle (Sagmarius, sagmatorhine)

-salebr- [L. salebrosus, rugged] base rough; uneven (salebrosity, salebrous)

-sali- [L. sal, salt] base salt (desalination, salinity)

-salic- [L. salix/salic-, a willow] base willow (salicaceous, salicetum)

salino- [L. salinus, of salt] comb salt and (salinometry, salinosulphureous)

salmoni- [L. salmo, salmon] base salmon (salmonic, salmoniform)

salpingo- [Gr. salpinks, trumpet] 1. comb of a fallopian tube (salpingocyesis, salpingotomy); 2. of a eustachian tube (salpingitis, salpingonasal)

sals- [L. salsus, salted] base salted (salsamentarious, salsuginous)

-salta- [L. saltare, dance, leap] base leap; dance (saltation, saltatory)

saltu- [L. saltuosus, wooded] base of woods (saltuary)

-salub- [L. salubris, healthful] base healthy (salubrious, salubrity)

saluti- [L. salutifer, health-bringing] comb remedial; medicinal (salutiferous, salutigerous)

-salv- [L. salvare, save] base save (salvage, salvation)

-san- [L. sanare, heal] base health; healing (sanatorium, unsanitary)

sanct-, sancti- [L. sanctus, holy] comb holy (sanctuary, sancticolist)

sangui-, sanguineo-, sanguino- [L. sanguis, blood] comb blood (sanguicolous, sanguineo-vascular, sanguino-purulent)

sanguisug- [L. sanguisuga, bloodsucker] base leech (sanguisugent, sanguisugous)

-sapien- [L. sapientia, wisdom] base wise (sapience, sapiently)

sapon-, saponi- [L. sapo, soap] comb soap (saponaceous, saponification)

sapor-, savor- [L. sapor, taste, flavor] base of taste (saporific, saporous, unsavory) sapro- [Gr. *sapros*, rotten] *comb* [biology] dead; putrefying; decaying (saprogenic, saprophagous)

-sarc-, sarco- [Gr. *sarks/sark-*, flesh] *comb* flesh; tissue (ectosarc, sarcology)

sarcin- [L. *sarcina*, a bundle] *base* bundle (sarcina, sarcinic)

-sarmass- [Gr. *sarks*, flesh + *masso*, knead] *base* erotic caressing, loveplay (sarmassation, sarmassophile)

sarment- [L. *sarmentum*, twigs, brushwood] *base* stem; runner (sarmentaceous, sarmentose)

saro- [Gr. *saron*, broom] *base* hairlike, brushlike (Sarothamnus, sarothrum)

sartor- [L. *sartor*, tailor] *base* tailor (sartorial, sartorius)

sat- [L. *satis*, sufficient] *base* full; replete (insatiable, satiety)

sativ- [L. *sativus*, sown or planted] *base* sown; planted (sative, sativous)

sator- [L. *sator*, sower] *base* sow (satorious)

satur- [L. *satur*, full] *base* full (saturate, saturation)

sauciat- [L. *sauciare*, to wound] *base* wound (sauciate, sauciation)

-saur, sauro-, -saurus [Gr. *sauros*, lizard] *comb* lizard (dinosaur, saurophagous, icthyosaurus)

sax-, saxi- [L. *saxus*, rock] *comb* rock; stone (saxatile, saxicoline)

scabi- [L. *scabere*, to scratch] *base* itch (scabiophobia, scabiosity)

scaev- [L. *scaevus*, left-handed] *base* left-sided; unlucky (scaevity, Scaevola)

-scal- [L. *scala*, ladder, flight of stairs] *base* climb; ladder (escalation, scalariform)

scaleno- [Gr. *skalenos*, uneven] comb scalene; unequal (scalenohedral, scalenohedron)

scalpelli- [L. *scalpellum*, surgical knife] *comb* scalpel (scalpelliform)

-scalpri- [L. *scalprum*, chisel] *base* chisel (scalpriform)

-scan- [L. *scandere*, to climb] *base* climb; scan (scansion, scansorial)

-scape [Du, *landschap*, lay of the land] *comb* view; scenery (cityscape, seascape)

scapho- [Gr. *skaphe*, tub, skiff] *comb* boat-shaped (scaphocephalic, scaphoid)

scapi- [L. *scapus*, stem or stalk] *comb* stalk; shaft (scapiform, scapigerous)

scapo- [Gr. *skapos*, rod] *comb* rodlike (scapolite, scapolitization)

scapuli-, scapulo- [L. *scapula*, shoulder] *comb* scapula and; shoulder blade (scapulimancy, scapuloclavicular)

scarab- [L. *scarabaeus*, beetle] *base* beetle (scarabaeid, scaraboid)

scato- [Gr. *skor/skat-*, dung] *comb* excrement; feces (scatology, scatophagous)

scatur- [L. *scatere*, to bubble up, gush] *base* spring of water (scaturient, scaturiginous)

-scel- [Gr. *skelos*, leg] *base* leg (isosceles, scelidosaur)

sceler- [L. *scelus/sceler-*, crime] *base* wicked (scelerous, scelestic)

-scelia [Gr. *skelos*, leg] *comb* [medicine] condition of the legs (macroscelia, microscelia)

sceno- [Gr. *skene*, stage, scene] *comb* scene (scenographer, scenography)

sceuo- [Gr. *skeuos*, a vessel] *base* vessel; utensil (sceuophorion, sceuophylax)

-schem- [Gr. *schema*, shape, figure] *base* appearance; form (schematic, schematism)

schismato-, schismo- [Gr. *schisma*, cleft, split] *comb* split (Schismatobranchia, schismopnea)

schisto- [Gr. *schistos*, easily cleft] *comb* split; cleft (schistocephalus, schistoprosopia)

schizo- [Gr. *schizein*, to cleave, split] *comb* split; cleavage; division (schizocarp, schizogenesis)

-schœno- [Gr. *schoinos*, rush] *base* rope (schœnobatic, schœnocaulon)

schol- [L. *schola*, school] *base* school (scholar, scholastic)

-sci- [L. *scire*, to know] *base* know (omniscient, scientific)

-scia- [Gr. *skia*, shade, shadow] *base* shadow (macroscian, sciamachy). *Also* scio- (sciomancy). *See* skia-

scilli-, scillo- [Gr. *skilla*, squill, sea-onion] *comb* squill-shaped; pointed (scillitoxin, scillocephalous, scillocephalus)

scinci-, scinco- [L. *scincus*, skink] *comb* skink; lizard (scinciform, scincoid)

-scintill- [L. *scintilla*, spark] *base* spark (scintilla, scintillation)

-scio-[1] [Gr. *skia*, shade] *base* shadow (sciomancy, sciomantic). *Also* -scia- (macroscian)

scio-[2] [L. *sciolus*, one who knows little] *comb* shallow knowledge (sciolism, sciolus)

scirrho- [Gr. *skirros*, hard] *comb* hard cancer (scirrhoma, scirrhosarca)

sciss- [L. *scindere*, cut or divide] *base* cut; divide (scissible, scission)

-sciur- [Gr. *skiouros*, squirrel < shade-tailed] *base* squirrel; marmot (sciurine, sciuromorphic)

sclero- [Gr. *skleros*, hard or harsh] 1. *comb* hard (sclerometer); 2. of the sclera (sclerotomy)

-scob- [L. *scobis*, sawdust, filings] *base* sawdust (scobiform, scobina)

scoleci-, scoleco- [Gr. *skoleks*, worm] *comb* worm (scoleciform, scolecobrotic)

scoli(o)- [Gr. *skolios*, bent, curved] *comb* bent; crooked (scoliosis, scoliotic)

scolo- [Gr. *skolops*, stake, thorn] *comb* pointed like a spike (scolophore, scolopsite)

scolopac- [L. *scolopax*, snipe] *base* snipe; woodcock (scolopaceous, scolopacine)

scolopendri- [L. *scolopendra*, milliped] *base* centipede (scolopendriform, scolopendrine)

scolyt- [Gr. *skoluptein*, crop, strip, peel] *base* bark-beetle (scolytoid, Scolytus)

scombr- [Gr. *skombros*, mackerel] *base* mackerel (scombrid, scombroid)

scomm- [Gr. *skomma*, jest, taunt, jeer] *base* mocking (scomm, scommatic)

scopa- [L. *scopa*, brush, broom] *base* twigs; broom; brush (scoparious, scopate). *Also* scopi-

-scope, -scopic, scopo-, -scopy [Gr. *skopein*, to see] *comb* sight; observation; examination (telescope, microscopic, scopophilia, bioscopy)

scopeli- [Gr. *skopelos*, high rock] *base* bony fish; Scopelidae (scopeliform, scopeloid)

scophthalm- [Gr. *skopein*, to look, watch + *ophthalmos*, eye] *base* turbot (scophthalmus)

scopi- [L. *scopa*, twigs, shoots, broom] *base* twig; broom (scopiferous, scopiform)

scopul- [Gr. *skopelos*, cliff, promontory] *base* crag; cliff (scopulosity, scopulous)

scopuli- [L. *scopulae*, little broom] *comb* brush-like (scopuliform, scopulipede)

scor- [Gr. *skor*, dung] *base* fecal matter (scoracratia, scoretemia)

-scorb- [ML. *scorbutus*, scurvy] *base* scurvy (scorbutic, scorbutigenic)

-scoria- [Gr. *skoria*, refuse, dross] *base* slag (scoriaceous, scoriform)

-scoro- [Gr. *skordon*, garlic] *base* garlic (scorodite, scoro-doprasum)

-scort- [L. *scortator*, fornicator] *base* fornication; harlot (scortation, scortatory)

Scoto- [Gr. *Skotoi*, people in the northern part of Britain] *comb* Scottish and (Scoto-Irish, Scoto-Welsh)

scoto- [Gr. *skotos*, gloom] *base* darkness; dimness (scotoma, scotophobia)

-scrib-, -script- [L. *scribere*, write] *base* write (scribacious, manuscript)

scrin- [L. *scrinium*, box, shrine] *base* chest; shrine (scrine, scrinium)

-scrobic- [L. *scrobis*, ditch, dike, trench] *base* furrowed; pitted (scrobiculate, scrobiculus)

-scrot- [L. *scrotum*, scrotum] *base* scrotum; testicular sac (scrotiform, scrotocele)

-scrut- [L. *scrutari*, search or examine] *base* examine; search (inscrutable, scrutinize)

-scut- [L. *scutum*, shield] *base* shield; scale (scutate, scutiform)

scutel- [L. *scutella*, salver, tray] *base* dish (scutelliform, scutelligerous)

scyllio- [Gr. *skulion*, dogfish] *comb* a type of shark (scylliodont, Scylliorhinus)

scyphi-, scypho- [Gr. *skuphos*, drinking cup] *comb* cup; [botany] cup-shaped part (scyphiform, scyphomancy)

Scytho- [Gr. *Skuthes*, a Scythian] *comb* Scythian and (Scytho-Aryan, Scytho-Greek)

scyto- [Gr. *skutos*, hide, skin] *comb* leathery skin (scytodepsic, scytodermatous)

se- [L. *se*, without, apart, away] *pre* away from (seclude, secret)

-seb-, sebo- [L. *sebum*, tallow, fat] *base* tallow; grease (sebaceous, seborrhea)

sebasto- [Gr. *sebastos*, reverend] *comb* of religion (sebastomania, sebastophobia)

-sec-, -sect- [L. *secare*, cut] *base* cut (secant, intersection)

-secul- [L. *saecularis*, of an age or period] *base* worldly; temporal (secularism, secularize)

secundi-, secundo- [L. *secundus*, following] *comb* second (secundipara, secundogeniture)

securi- [L. *securi*, ax or hatchet] *comb* ax; hatchet (securiferous, securiform)

-secut- [L. *sequor/secut-*, to seek] *base* follow (consecutive, persecute). *See* -seq-

-sed- [L. *sedere*, to sit] *base* sit (sedent, sedentary)

sedat- [L. *sedatus*, composed] *base* allay; calm (sedate, sedation)

sedecim- [L. *sedecim*, sixteen] *base* sixteen (sedecimal, sedecimarticulate)

segn- [L. *segnitia*, slowness] *base* sloth; sluggishness (segnitude, segnity)

seiro- [Gr. *seiron*, garment] *comb* type of algae (Seirospora, seirospore)

seismo- [Gr. *seismos*, earthquake] *comb* earthquake (seismograph, seismology)

sela- [Gr. *selas*, brightness] *comb* flash; lightning (selaphobia, Selaphorus)

selach- [Gr. *selachos*, sea-fish, shark] *base* shark (selachoid, selachology)

seleno- [Gr. *selene*, moon] *comb* moon (selenography, selenological)

self- [AS. *seolf*, self] *comb* oneself (self-denial, self-closing)

selli- [L. *sella*, saddle] *comb* saddle (selliform)

sema-, -seme, semeio-, semio- [Gr. *sema*, sign] *comb* sign; signal; symbol; token; symptom (semaphore, microseme, semeiology, semiotics)

semi- [L. *semi*, half] **1.** *pre* half (semidiameter); **2.** partly; imperfectly (semicivilized); **3.** twice per __ (semiannual)

semin- [L. *seminalis*, relating to seed] *base* seedbed; germinal (seminal, seminality)

semit- [L. *semita*, narrow way, path] *base* fasciole (semita, semital)

semno- [Gr. *semnos*, revered, sacred] *comb* honored; sacred (semnopithece, Semnopithecus)

semper- [L. *semper*, always] *base* always (sempervirent, sempervivum)

-sen- [L. *senilis*, of old age] *base* old (senility, seniority)

sena- [L. *seni*, six] *base* six (senarius, senary)

-sens-, -sent- [L. *sensus*, perception] *base* feel (sensitive, sentimental)

sensori- [L. *sensorium*, organ of sensation] *comb* pertaining to the senses or to sensations (sensoridigestive, sensorimotor)

-sepalous [Gr. *skepe*, covering] *comb* having a specific kind or number of sepals (antisepalous, trisepalous)

sep- [Gr. *sepsis*, decay] *base* putrid (sepedogenesis, sepsometer)

sepi-¹ [Gr. *sepios*, cuttlefish] *base* cuttlefish (sepia, sepiacean)

sepi-² [L. *saepes/sepes*, hedge or fence] *base* hedge, fence, separation (sepicolous, sepiment)

sept- [L. *septem*, seven] *base* seven (septan, September)

septem- [L. *septem*, seven] *comb* seven (septempartite, septemvirate)

septen- [L. *septentrio*, north] *base* north (septentrion, septentrionate)

septendecim- [Latin *septem*, seven + *decem*, ten] *base* seventeen (septendecimal)

septi-¹ [L. *septem*, seven] *comb* seven (septifolious, septilateral)

septi-², septico- [Gr. *septos*, made rotten + *aima*, blood] *comb* decomposed; vitiated (septicemia, septicopyaemia)

septim- [L. *septimus*, seventh] *base* seventh (septimal, septimole)

septingenti- [L. *septingenti*, seven hundred] *base* seven hundred (septingentenary)

septo-¹ [Gr. *septos*, made rotten] *comb* decomposed; vitiated (septogenic, septometer)

septo-² [L. *septum*, fence] *comb* dividing wall (septocephalic, septonasal)

septuagen- [L. *septuagenarius*, seventy] *base* seventy (septuagenarian, septuagenary)

septuages- [L. *septuagesima*, seventieth] *base* seventy (Septuagesima Sunday, septuagesimal)

septuagint- [L. *septuaginta*, seventy] *base* seventy (Septuagint, septuagintal)

sepul- [L. *sepulcrum*, burial place] *base* grave; tomb; burial (sepulcher, sepulchral)

-seq- [L. *sequor*, to follow] *base* follow (consequence, sequential). *See* -secut-

-ser- [L. *serare*, to join] *base* bar; bolt (reseration, seraglio)

serang- [Gr. *seranks*, cavern] *base* cave (serangitis)

Serbo- [Fr. *Serbe*, a Serbian] *comb* Serbia (Serbo-Croatian, Serbo-Italian)

seri-, sericeo-, serico- [Gr. *Ser*, the Seres, northern China] *comb* silk (serigraph, sericeo-tomentose, sericostoma)

serio- [L. *serius*, grave, earnest] *comb* partly serious (serio-comedic, serio-comic)

sero- [L. *serum*, serum] *comb* serum; (serology, seropurulent)

serot- [L. *serotinus*, late, backward] *base* late in occurrence or development (serotine, serotinous)

serpen- [L. *serpens/serpent-*, snake] *base* snake (serpentiform, serpentine)

serrati-, serrato- [L. *serra*, a saw] *comb* saw-toothed (serratirostral, serratocrennate)

serri- [L. *serra*, a saw] *comb* [entomology/zoology] a saw (serricorn, serrirostrate)

serv- [L. *servire*, to serve] *base* attendant; slave (servant, servitude)

-serve [L. *servare*, to keep or protect] *comb* keep; attend to (preserve, reservation)

sesqui- [L. *sesqui-*, more by one half] *comb* one and one half (sesquibasic, sesquicentennial)

sesquipedal- [L. *sesqui-*, one half more + *pes/ped*, foot] *base* long words < Horace: "words a foot and a half long" (sesquipedalian, sesquipedalophobia)

-sess- [L. *sedere/sess-*, to sit] *base* sit; perch (insessorial, sessile)

setaceo- [L. *seta*, bristle] *comb* bristles and (setaceo-rostrate)

seti- [L. *seta*, bristle] *base* bristle (setiferous, setiparous)

setul- [L. *setula*, little bristle] *base* little bristle (setuliform, setulose)

sexagen- [L. *sexageni*, sixty each] *base* sixty (sexagenary, sexagenarian)

sexages- [L. *sexagesimus*, sixtieth] *base* sixty (Sexagesima Sunday, sexagesimal)

sexcent- [L. *sex*, six + *centenarius*, of one hundred] *base* six hundred (sexcentenary)

sexi- [L. *sex*, six] *comb* six (sexipolar, sexisyllabic)

sext- [L. *sextanus*, sixth] *comb* sixth (sextan, sextant)

sexti- [L. *sextanus*, sixth] *comb* six (sextipartite, sextisection)

she- [OE *sio*, she] *comb* female (she-bear, she-wolf)

-ship [AS *scapan*, shape] 1. *suf* quality; condition; state of (friendship); 2. rank; office; status (kingship); 3. ability; skill (leadership); 4. collective: all individuals of a specified class (readership)

-siagon- [Gr. *siagon*, jawbone] *base* jawbone (siagon, siagonology)

sial-¹ [Gr. *sialon*, spittle] *base* saliva (sialogogic, sialorrhea)

sial-² [Gr. *sialis*, kind of bird] *base* 1. bluebird (Sialia) 2. neuropterous insect (Sialidae)

-sibil- [L. *sibilare*, to hiss, whistle] *base* hiss; whistle (sibilant, sibilation)

sica- [L. *sica*, dagger] *base* knife; dagger (sicarian, sicarius)

-sicc- [L. *siccare*, to dry] *base* dry (desiccate, siccate)

Siculo- [Gr. *Sikeloi*, Sicilians] *comb* Sicilian (Siculo-Arabian, Siculo-Punic)

-sid- [L. *sidere*, to sit] *base* inhere; sit in (insident, reside)

-sider(e) [L. *sidus/sider-*, star] *comb* star (hagiosidere, sidereal)

sidero-¹ [Gr. *sideros*, iron] *comb* iron (siderazote, siderolite)

sidero-² [L. *sidus/sider-*, star] *comb* star (siderostat, siderostatic)

siderodromo- [Gr. *sideros*, iron + *dromos*, running] *comb* railroad — invented word (siderodromomania, siderodromophobia)

-sigil- [L. *sigillum*, little mark or token] *base* seal; signet (sigillary, sigillation)

sigma- [Gr. *sigma*, the letter s] *comb* S-shaped (sigmaspiral, sigmation)

siliceo-, silici-, silico- [L. *silex/silic-*, flint] *comb* [chemistry] silica: containing or relating to (siliceo-calcareous, siliciferous, silico-alkaline)

silicul- [L. *silicula*, little husk or pod] *base* seed-vessel, pod (silicular, siliculose)

silig- [L. *siligo*, fine wheat] *base* winter wheat (siliginose, siliginous)

siliqu- [L. *siliqua*, husk or pod] *base* pod (siliquiferous, siliquiform)

sillo- [Gr. *silos*, satire] *comb* of satire (sillograph, sillographist)

silph- [Gr. *silphe*, beetle] *base* carrion-beetle; larva (silphid, silphology)

-silur- [Gr. *silouros*, river-fish] *base* catfish (silurid, siluroid)

Siluro- [Gr. *Silures*, the Silures, a people of ancient Britain] *comb* Silurian (Siluro-Cambrian, Siluro-Devonian)

silvi- [L. *silva*, forest] *comb* tree; forest (silvicolous, silviculture). *Also* sylvi-

sim- [L. *simia*, ape, monkey] *base* ape; chimp (simian, Simiidae)

-simil- [L. *similis*, like or akin] *base* like; resembling (dissimilarity, similitude). *Also* simul- (simulation, simulatory)

-simo- [Gr. *simos*, snub-nosed] *base* snub-nosed (Simenchelys, simosaurus)

-simul- [L. *simul*, together] *base* at the

same time (simultaneity, simultaneous)

sinap- [Gr. *sinapi*, mustard] *base* mustard (Sinapis, sinapism)

sindon- [Gr. *sindon*, muslin] *base* shroud (sindonologist, sindonology)

singult- [L. *singultus*, hiccup, throat rattle] *base* hiccup; sob (singultous, singultient)

sinistro- [L. *sinister*, left] *comb* left: of, at, using (sinistro-cerebral, sinistro-gyric)

sino- [L. *sinus*, curve, bend, bay] *comb* sinus (sino-auricular, sinorespiratory)

Sino- [Gr. *Sinai*, the Chinese] *comb* Chinese: people/language (sinology, Sino-Soviet)

-sinu- [L. *sinus*, a bend or fold] *base* bending; winding (insinuate, sinuous)

sinuato-, sinuoso- [L. *sinus*, a bend or fold] *comb* wavy; uneven (sinuato-dentate, simuoso-lobate)

-sion *see* **-ion**

siphoni-, siphono- [Gr. *siphon*, tube, pipe] *comb* tube; pipe; siphon (siphoniform, siphonostele)

sipuncul- [L. *sipunculus*, little tube or siphon] *base* spoonworm (sipunculacean, sipunculiform)

-sis [Gr. *-sis*, a *suf* in nouns of action] *suf* action; condition (analysis, stasis)

-siti- [L. *sitire*, to thirst] *base* thirst (insitiency, sitient)

-sitia, sitio-, sito- [Gr. *sitos*, food] *comb* food; eating; appetite (asitia, sitiophobia, sitology)

sitt- [Gr. *sitte*, a kind of woodpecker] *base* nuthatch (Sittinae, sittine)

situ- [L. *situare*, to place] *base* located; inherent (situate, situation)

-size, -sized [L. *assidere*, to sit down while assessing a tax] *comb* having a specified size (life-size, small-sized)

skeleto- [Gr. *skeleton*, skeleton] *comb* skeleton (skeletology, skeletotrophic)

skeuo- [Gr. *skeuos*, vessel, implement] *base* decorated vessel; utensil (skeuomorph, skeuomorphic)

skia- [Gr. *skia*, shadow] *comb* shadow (skiagraphy, skiascopy). *See* **scia-**

Slavo- [Gr. *Sklabos*, a Slav] *comb* Slav; (Slavo-Lithuanian, Slavophile)

smaragd- [Gr. *smaragdos*, light-green precious stone] *base* emerald (smaragdine, smaragdochalcite)

sobol- [L. *soboles*, sprout or shoot < *sub*, under + *olere*, to grow] *base* shoot or creeping underground stem (soboles, soboliferous)

socer- [L. *socer*, father-in-law] *base* father-in-law (soceraphobia)

socio- [L. *sociare*, to join or accompany] *comb* society; social (sociobiological, sociogeny)

sodio- [NL. *soda*, alkaline substance] *comb* sodium (sodio-hydric, sodio-platinic)

-soever [OE *swa*, so + *ever*, a generalized, indefinite appendage] *comb* any __ of those possible; (whatsoever, whosoever)

sol-¹ [L. *sol*, sun] *comb* sun (solar energy, solarium)

sol-² [L. *solum*, ground, floor, bottom] *base* of the ground (solary)

solen-, soleno- [Gr. *solen*, channel or pipe] *comb* [zoology] channel; pipe (solenoid, solenoglypha)

soli- [L. *solus*, alone] *comb* alone (solitary, solitude)

-solu-, -solv- [L. *solvere*, to dissolve] *base* melt; dissolve (soluble, solvent)

-soma [Gr. *soma*, body] *comb* [zoology] names of genera (Schistosoma, Trypanosoma)

somato-, -somatous [Gr. *soma/somat-*, of the body] *comb* body (somatogenic, somatology, macrosomatous)

-some¹ [Gr. *soma*, body] *comb* body; (acrosome, chromosome)

-some² [OE *-sum*, tending to be] *suf* like; tending to be (loathsome, tiresome)

-some[3] [OE -*sum*, numerical suffix] *suf* number: in a specified (threesome, foursome)

somn(i)- [L. *somnus*, sleep] *comb* sleep (somnambulant, somniferous)

son-, soni-, sono-, sonoro- [L. *sonus*, sound] *comb* sound (sonancy, soniferous, sonogram, sonoro-sibilant)

-sophy [Gr. *sophos*, wise] *comb* knowledge; thought (misosophy, philosophy)

-sopor- [L. *sopor*, sleep] *base* sleep (soporific, soporous)

-sor- [Gr. *soros*, a heap] *base* heap (sorosis, sorotrochous)

-sorb-[1] [Gr. *sorbere*, suck in, swallow up] *base* soak up (absorbent, sorbefacient)

-sorb-[2] [L. *sorbus*, service-tree] *base* mountain ash (sorbic, sorbite)

-sord- [L. *sordes*, filth, dregs] *base* dirt; filth (insordescent, sordid)

soredi- [Gr. *soros*, a heap] *comb* reproductive unit of lichens (soridiferous, sorediform)

soric- [L. *sorex/soric-*, shrew] *base* shrew (soricident, soricine)

-soror- [L. *soror*, sister] *base* sister (sororicide, sorority)

-sote [Gr. *sozein*, to save] *comb* preserver (creosote)

-soter- [Gr. *soter*, savior] *base* salvation (autosoteric, soteriology)

spad- [Gr. *spadiks*, nut-brown, palm-colored] *base* brown (spadiceous)

spadici- [NL *spadix/spadic-*, palm-like] *comb* succulent spike (spadicifloral, spadiciform)

spalac- [Gr. *spalaks/spalac-*, mole] *base* mole-rat (Spalacidae, spalacine)

spano- [Gr. *spanos*, scarce or rare] *comb* scarce (spanemia, spanopnea)

sparasso-, sparax- [Gr. *sparassein*, to tear] *comb* laceration; tearing (sparassodont, sparaxis)

sparg- [L. *spargere*, to sprinkle, strew] *base* sprinkle; scatter (spargefication, sparger)

spars- [L. *sparsus*, scattered, sprinkled] *base* thinly scattered (sparsile, sparsity)

spasmato-, spasmo- [Gr. *spasmos*, a spasm] *comb* spasm; contraction (spasmatomancy, spasmology, spasmolysis)

spathi- [Gr. *spathe*, a broad flat blade] *base* spatula; broad blade (spathiform, spathiopyrite, spatuliform)

spatilo- [Gr. *spatile*, excrement] *comb* excrement (spatilomancy)

spatul-, spatuli- [L. *spatula*, broad blade] *base* shoulder; spatula-shaped (spatulamancy, spatuliform)

-spec(t)-, -spic- [L. *spectare*, see, behold] *base* look; *see* (spectator, conspicuous)

-specific [L. *species*, kind + *ficus*, made] *comb* applied or limited to the particular item named (age-specific, culture-specific)

specio- [L. *species*, species] *comb* specific (speciographic, speciology)

spectr- [L. *spectrum*, apparition] *base* ghost (spectral, spectrality)

spectro- [NL *spectrum*, spectrum] 1. *comb* radiant energy as exhibited in a spectrum (spectrogram); 2. of/by a spectroscope (spectro-heliogram); 3. mirror (spectrophobia)

speleo-, spelunc- [Gr. *spelaion*, cave] *base* cave (speleologist, speluncar)

sper- [L. *sperare*, hope] *base* hope (sperable, sperate)

-sperg-, -spers- [L. *spargere*, to sprinkle] *base* sprinkle (insperge, inspersion)

-sperm, sperma-, -spermal, spermatio-, spermato, spermi-,-spermic, spermo-,

-spermous [Gr. *sperma*, seed] *comb* seed; germ; beginning (gymnosperm, spermaphore, gymnospermal, spermatiogenous, spermatocyte, spermiducal, endospermic, spermogonium, monospermous)

sphacel- [Gr. *sphakelos*, gangrene] *base* gangrene (sphacelate, sphaceloderma)

sphag- [Gr. *sphage*, throat] *base* throat (sphagitis, sphagiasmus)

-sphagn- [Gr. *sphagnos*, kind of moss] *base* moss (sphagnicolous, sphagnologist)

-sphair- [Gr. *sphaira*, ball] *base* tennis (sphaeristerium, sphairistic)

-sphal- [Gr. *sphaleros*, slippery, uncertain] *base* error (sphalerite, sphalma)

-sphec- [Gr. *spheks/sphek-*, wasp] *base* wasp; hornet (Sphecidae, sphecoid)

sphenisc- [Gr. *spheniskos*, little wedge] *base* penguin (spheniscan, speniscomorph)

spheno- [Gr. *sphen*, wedge] 1. *comb* wedge-shaped (sphenogram); 2. sphenoid bone (sphenoccipital)

-sphere, spherico-, sphero- [Gr. *sphaira*, ball, sphere] *comb* sphere (stratosphere, spherico-cylindrical, spherocyte). *Also* sphaero- (sphaeroblast)

-sphingo- [Gr, *sphingein*, to shut tight or close] *base* bound tightly (sphingometer, sphingomyelin)

-sphrag- [Gr. *sphragis*, signet or seal] *base* seal; signet (sphragistes, sphragistic)

sphygmo- [Gr. *sphugmos*, pulse] *comb* pulse (sphygmograph, sphygmology)

sphyr- [Gr. *sphura*, hammer, mallet] *base* hammer (sphyrelaton)

sphyraen- [Gr. *sphura*, hammer, mallet] *base* barracuda; hammer-fish (Sphyraena, sphyraenoid)

sphyrn- [Gr. *sphura*, hammer] *base* hammer-head shark (Sphyrna, sphyrnine)

spici- [L. *spica*, point or spike] *base* spiked (spiciferous, spiciform)

spicul-, spiculi-, spiculo- [L. *spiculum*, little point or spike] *comb* spiky; pointed (spicular, spiculiferous, spiculofibrous)

-spil- [Gr. *spilos*, spot] *base* spot; speck (Spilogale, spilosite)

spini-, spino-, spinoso-, spinuloso- [L. *spina*, thorn, backbone] *comb* spine (spini-acute, spinocerebellar, spinoso-dentate, spinuloso-serrate)

-spinthar- [Gr. *spinther*, spark] *base* spark (spinthariscope, spinthere)

spiri- [L. *spira*, coil or spire < Gr. *speira*] *comb* coil; spiral (spiriferous, spiriform)

spiro-¹ [L. *spirare*, to breathe] *comb* respiration; breath (spirograph, spirometer)

spiro-² [Gr. *speira*, coil or spire] *comb* spiral; coil (spirochete, Spyrogyra)

-spiss- [L. *spissus*, thick, compact] *base* thick; dense (inspissation, spissitude)

-splachn- [Gr. *splanchnon*, moss] *base* moss (splachnoid, Splachnum)

splanchno- [Gr. *splanchna*, viscera] *comb* viscera (splanchnic, splanchnology)

splenico-, splen(o)- [Gr. *splen*, spleen] *comb* spleen (splenico-phrenic, splenocele)

spodo- [Gr. *spodos*, ashes] *base* ashes (spodogenous, spodomancy)

spondylo- [Gr. *spondulos*, vertebra, joint] *comb* vertebra (spondylalgia, spondylitis)

spongi-, spongio-, spongo- [Gr. *spongos*, sponge] *comb* sponge-like (spongiculture, spongiocyte, spongolith)

spor- [Gr. *sperein*, to sow or scatter] *base* scatter (sporadic, sporadically)

-spore, spori-, sporo-, -sporous [Gr. *sporos*, seed] 1. *comb* spore; seed (teliospore, sporiferous, sporocarp); 2. specific number/kind of spores (monosporous)

-spum- [L. *spuma*, foam] *base* foam; froth (spumescence, spumiferous)

-spurc- [L. *spurcus*, foul, impure] *base* dirty; foul (conspurcation, spurcitious)

-squal- [L. *squalus*, shark] *base* shark (squaliform, squaloid) squamato-, squamo-, squamoso-, squaroso- [L. *squama*, scale] *comb* squama; scalelike (squamato-granulous, squamo-cellular, squamoso-dentated, squaroso-laciniate)

stabil- [L. *stabilire*, to make firm] *base* lasting; fixed (destabilize, stability)

-stact- [Gr. *staktos*, dropping, oozing out] *base* drop (stacte, stactometer)

-stagm- [Gr. *stagma*, a drop] *base* drop (stagma, stagmoid)

-stagn- [L. *stagnare*, to form a pool of standing water] *base* pool (stagnant, stagnicolous)

-stal- [Gr. *stalsis*, checking of a flow] *base* motion; contraction (antiperistalsis, peristalsis)

-stalac(ti)-, -stalag- [Gr. *stalaktos*, dropping] *base* dropping; dripping (stalactite, stalagmite)

stamini- [L *stamen*, thread, fiber] *comb* stamen (staminiferous, staminigerous)

-stann- [L. *stannum*, tin] *base* tin (stannic, stanniferous)

-stap- [L. *stapes*, stirrup] *base* stirrup; stapes (stapedectomy, stapediferous)

staphylo- [Gr. *staphule*, bunch of grapes] 1. *comb* uvula; grapelike (staphylorrhaphy); 2. staphylococcus (staphylodermatitis)

stasi-, -stasis, -stasia [Gr. *stasis*, a stoppage] *comb* standing still; balance; arrest; halt (stasimetry, phlebostasis, menostasia)

stasio- [Gr. *stasis*, party, faction] *comb* political party (stasiologist, stasiology)

-stat [Gr. *statos*, standing, fixed] *comb* scientific instrument (aerostat, thermostat)

stathmo- [Gr. *stathmos*, day's journey] *base* stage of development (stathmograph, stathmokinesis

stato- [Gr. *statos*, standing, fixed] *comb* stationary; stabilized (statoblast, statocyst)

stauro- [Gr. *stauros*, a cross] *comb* cross (stauraxonia, staurophobia)

-stead [OE *stede*, place] *comb* place (bedstead, homestead)

stearo-, steato- [Gr. *stear/steat-*, fat, tallow, suet] *comb* fatty substance (stearoglucose, steatopygia)

-stegano- [Gr. *steganos*, covered] *base* covered (steganography, steganopodous)

stegno- [Gr. *stegnos*, watertight, tightly covered] *comb* constricting; styptic (stegnotic, thecostegnosis)

stego- [Gr. *stegein*, to cover] *comb* covered; closed (stegocephalous, stegosaur)

-stell- [L. *stella*, star] *base* star (interstellar, stellate)

stellio- [L. *stellio*, newt] *base* lizard; newt (stellion, Stellionidae)

-stema- [Gr. *stema*, filament] *base* filament (stemapod, stemonozone)

stemma- [Gr. *stemma*, wreath, garland] *base* circular (stemma, stemmatous)

sten(o)- [Gr. *stenos*, narrow] *comb* small; thin; narrow; abbreviated (stenocardia, stenographer)

stentor- [Gr. *Stentor*, A Greek herald in the Trojan war with a trumpet-like voice —*Homer*] *base* having a powerful voice (stentorian, stentorophonic)

step- [OE *steop*, affinity arising from remarriage] *comb* relationship not by blood (stepchild, stepfather)

-ster [AS -*estre*, *suf* designating occupation] 1. *suf* person who is/does/creates __ (spinster); 2. person associated with __ (gangster)

sterco- [L. *stercus*, dung] *comb* dung; feces (stercoraceous, stercoricolous)

stereo- [Gr. *stereos*, solid, hard, stiff] *comb* three-dimensional; solid (stereoscope, stereometry)

-sterigm- [Gr. *sterigma*, prop, support] *base* prop; support (sterigma, sterigmatic)

stern- [NL *sterna*, tern] *base* tern (Sterninae, sternine)

sterni-, sterno- [NL *sternum*, breastbone] *comb* sternum and; breastbone (sterniform, sternoclavicular)

-sternut- [L. *sternutatio*, a sneeze] *base* sneeze (sternutation, sternutatory)

-sterquil- [L. *sterquilinium*, dunghill] *base* dunghill (sterquilinian, sterquilinious)

-stert- [L. *stertere*, to snore] *base* snore (stertor, stertorous)

stetho- [Gr. *stethos*, breast] *comb* chest; breast (stethoscope, stethoscopy)

-sthenia, sthen(o)- [Gr. *sthene*, strength] *comb* strength; force; power (hypersthenia, hyposthenuria)

stibio- [Gr. *stibi*, a sulphuret of antimony] *comb* [chemistry] black antimony (stibiconite, stibiotrimethyl)

stibo- [Gr. *stibos*, footstep] *comb* footprint (stibogram)

-stich, -stichia, sticho-, -stichous [Gr. *stikhos*, row, line] *comb* row; line; verse (heptastich, tristichia, stichometry, tristichous)

-stict- [Gr. *stiktos*, spotted, dappled] *base* spotted (laparostict, stictiform)

-stig- [Gr. *stizein*, to prick] *base* to punctuate; to goad; stimulate (instigate, instigation)

-stigm- [Gr. *stigma*, a mark] *base* mark; point; dot; puncture; tattoo (pterostigma, stigmatized)

stigno- [Gr. *stizo*, mark with a pointed instrument] *comb* writing (stignomancy)

stilb- [Gr. *stilbein*, to glitter, shine] base lustrous (Stilbacae, stilbite)

-still- [L. *stilla*, a drop] *base* drop (stillatitious, stilliform)

stilo- [L. *stilus*, pointed instrument] *comb* pointed (stilogonidium). *See* **stylo-**

-stilpno- [Gr. *stilbein*, to glitter, shine] *base* glittering (stilpnomelane, stilpnosiderite)

-stip-[1] [L. *stipes*, a post] *base* stalk; support (stipel, stipitate)

-stip-[2] [L. *stipare*, to crowd, press together] *base* press together; pack (constipation, stipate)

-stiri- [L. *stiria*, icicle] *base* icicle (stiriated, stirious)

-stirp- [L. *stirps*, stock, stem, race] *base* stem; stock (exstirpate, stirpiculture)

-stoch- [Gr. *stokhos*, aim, shot, guess] *base* guess (stochastic, stochasticity)

-stoicheio- [Gr. *stokhazesthai*, to aim at] *base* estimating elements (stoicheiological, stoicheiometry)

stol- [L. *stolo/stolon-*, shoot, branch, sucker] *base* branch (stolonate, stoloniferous)

stomati-, stomato-, -stome, -stomous [Gr. *stoma*, mouth, entrance] *comb* [medicine/botany] mouth (stomatiferous, stomatalgia, cyclostome, megastomous)

-stomy [Gr. *stoma*, opening, entrance] *comb* surgical opening into __ (colostomy, ileosigmoidostomy)

stone- [OE *stan*, stone] *comb* very; completely (stone-broke, stone-deaf)

-storgy [Gr. *storge*, natural love or affection] *base* affection (astorgy, philostorgy)

-stori- [aphetic form of *history*] *base* tales; legends (storiologist, storiology)

-strab-, strabism- [Gr. *strabismos*, squinting] *base* squinting (strabotomy, strabismometer)

-stragul- [L. *stragulum*, a cover] *base* covering; pallium (stragular, stragulum)

-strain [L. *stringere*, to draw tight] *comb* restrict; bind (constrain, restrain)

-stram(in)- [L. *stramen*, straw] *base* straw (stramage, stramineous)

-strat- [Gr. *strategos*, a general] *base* army tactics; direction (strategic, strategy)

strati-, strato- [L. *stratum*, layer] *comb* layer; stratum (stratification, stratosphere)

-stren- [L. *strenuus*, quick, active] *base* strong; with effort (strenuous, strenuously)

strep-, strepi- [L. *strepere*, to make a noise] *base* noisy (obstreperous, strepitous)

strepho-, strepsi-, strepto- [Gr. *strepho*, twist, turn] *comb* turned; twisted (strephosymbolia, strepsipterous, streptococcal)

-stress *see* -ess

stria-, striato-, strio- [L. *stria*, furrow, channel] *comb* furrow; groove (striaform, striatocrenulate, striomuscular)

-strict [L. *stringere*, to draw tight] *comb* tightly drawn; limited (restriction)

-strid-, stridul- [L. *stridere*, give a harsh or shrill sound] *base* creak; harsh noise (strident, stridulation)

-strig- [L. *striga*, furrow] *base* furrow; channel (striga, strigated)

strigi- [Gr. *striks/strig-*, screech-owl] *base* owl (strigiform, strigine)

strigil- [L. *strigilis*, a scraper] *base* scraping instrument; curry comblike (strigil, strigilate)

-string- [L. *stringere*, to draw tight] *base* constricted (astringent, stringent)

-strob- [Gr. *strobos*, twisting, turning] *base* twisting; spinning (strobic, strobilation)

strobil- [LL. *strobilus*, pine-cone] *base* pine cone (strobiliform, strobilite)

-strom- [L. *stroma*, covering] *base* connected structure (stroma, stromatiform)

-stromb- [Gr. *strombos*, something twisted or whorled] *base* spiral; twisted (strombiform, strombite)

strombuli- [NL. *strombulus*, little top] *base* twisted like a top (strombuliferous, strombuliform)

strongyl- [Gr. *strongulos*, round, spherical] *base* round (strongylate, strongyloid)

-stroph- [Gr. *strophe*, a turning round] *base* turn; twist (strophiolate, strophiole)

struct- [L. *struere*, pile up, build] *comb* arrange; put together (constructive, deconstruction)

strum-, -struma-, strumi- [L. *struma*, scrofulous tumor] *base* goiter; swelling; tumor (strumectomy, strumatic, strumiferous)

-struthio- [Gr. *struthion*, ostrich] *base* ostrich (struthioid, struthious)

-stult- [L. *stultus*, foolish, silly] *base* foolish (stultify, stultiloquy)

-stup- [L. *stupere*, be struck senseless] *base* senseless (stupefaction, stupor)

stupr- [L. *stuprare*, to ravish] *base* fornicate; rape (stuprate, stupration)

sturion- [ML *sturio*, sturgeon] *base* sturgeon (sturionic, sturionian)

-sturn- [L. *sturnus*, starling] *base* starling; swallow (strurniform, sturnoid)

styg- [Gr. *Stux/Stug-*, river of the lower world] *base* hellish (Stygia, Stygian)

styl- [L. *stylus*, pointed instrument for writing] *base* pen (styliform, stylography)

stylo-[1] [L. *stilus*, stake, point] 1. *comb* pointed; sharp (stylate); 2. styloid: bony process (stylohyoid)

-style, stylo-[2] [Gr. *stulos*, pillar] *comb* column; pillar (pyrgostyle, stylolite, stylospore)

-stypt- [Gr. *stuptikos*, astringent] *base* astringent (styptic pencil, stypticity)

-suad-, -suas- [L. *suasio*, counseling, exhortation] *base* urge (dissuade, persuasion)

suav- [L. *suavis*, sweet, agreeable] *base* sweet (suaveolent, suavity)

sub- [L. *sub-*, under] 1. *pre* under; below (submarine); 2. lower in rank; inferior to (subaltern); 3. to a lesser degree; slightly (subtropical); 4. division (sublet); 5. [chemistry] less than the normal amount of __ ; basic (subchloride); 6. [mathematics] ratio inverse to a given ratio (subduplicate). NOTE: **sub-** can change to: **su-** (suspect); **suc-** (succeed); **suf-** (suffocate); **sug-**(suggest); **sum-** (summon); **sup-** (support); **sur-** (surrogate); **sus-** (suspend)

subagit- [L. *subagitare*, to move back and forth down below] *base* sexual intercourse (subagitation, subagitatory)

-suber- [L. *suber*, cork] *base* cork (subereous, suberose)

subero- [L. *suber*, cork] *comb* suberic acid (suberiferous, subero-pyroxylic)

subig- [L. *subigere*, to pound or knead] *base* knead (subigate, subigation)

subit- [L. *subitus*, sudden, unexpected] *base* sudden; hasty (subitaneous, subitary)

subsesqui- [L. *sub-*, under + *sesqui*, one half more] *pre* [chemistry] elements combined in the proportion of 2 to 3 (subsesquiacetate, subsesquialterate)

subter- [L. *subter-*, below, secret] *pre* below; under; less than; secretly (subterfluous, subterfuge)

-subul- [L. *subula*, awl] *base* awl (subulicorn, subuliform)

suc- [L. *succus*, juice] *base* juice (succivorous, succulent)

-succino- [L. *succinus*, of amber] *comb* amber (succinic, succino-sulphuric)

sucho- [Gr. *soukhos*, crocodile] *base* crocodile (suchospondylian, suchospondylous)

sucr- [Fr. *sucre*, sugar] *base* sugar (sucro-acid, sucrose)

sud-, sudori- [L. *sudare*, to sweat] *comb* sweat; perspiration (sudatory, sudorific)

-suet- [L. *suetus*, customary, familiar] *base* custom (assuetude, consuetude)

suffrag- [L. *suffragium*, voting tablet, judgment] *base* voting (suffrage, suffragette)

-suge [L. *sugere*, to suck] *base* suck (potisuge, sugent)

sui-¹ [L. *sui*, of oneself] *base* oneself (suicide, suicism)

sui-², **suid-** [L. *sus/sui-*, swine] *base* pig; boar (suilline, suidian)

sulc- [L. *sulcus*, a furrow] *base* groove (sulcation, sulcus)

sulcato- [L. *sulatcus*, furrowed] *comb* furrowed; grooved; cleft (sulcato-areolate, sulcato-rimose)

sulfato- [L. *sulpur*, brimstone, sulpher] *comb* sulfate (sulfatidates). *Also* **sulphato-** (sulphato-acetic, sulphato-carbonate)

sulfo- [L. *sulpur*, brimstone, sulpher] *comb* sulfur; sulfonate sulfonic acid (sulfocyanogen). *Also* **sulpho-** (sulpho-indigotic)

sulfureo [L. *sulpur*, brimstone, sulpher] *comb* sulfureous (sulfureo-nitrous, sulphureo-virescent)

super- [L. *super*, above] 1. *pre* over; above; on top (superstructure); 2. higher in rank/position; superior to (superintendent); 3. greater in quality/amount/degree; surpassing; (superabundance); 4. greater or better (supermarket); 5. greater than normal (supersaturate); 6. extra; additional (supertax); 7. to a secondary degree (superparasite); 8. [chemistry] large amount of __ (superphosphate)

supero- [L. *superus*, above, upper] *comb* [anatomy] on the upper side (supero-dorsal, supero-posterior)

supin- [L. *supinare*, bend or lay backward] *base* lying down (supination, supine)

supra- [L. *supra*, on the upper side] *pre* above; over; beyond (supra-acromial, supraliminal)

sur- [Fr. *sur*, above] *pre* over; upon; above; beyond (surface, surpass)

sura- [L. *sura*, calf of the leg] *base* calf of the leg (sural, sural artery)

surcul- [L. *surculare*, to prune] *base* grafting; twig (surculigerous, surculose)

-surd- [L. *surdus*, deaf] *base* deaf (absurd, surdity)

-surg- [L. *surgere*, to lift up, raise] *base* rise (insurgent, resurgent)

sursum- [L. *sursum*, upward] *comb* upward (sursumduction, sursumversion)

-susurr- [L. *sussurare*, to whisper] *base* whisper; murmur (insusurration, sussurus)

-sutil- [L. *sutilis*, sewn together] *base* stitch; sew (consutile, inconsutile)

sutor- [L. *sutor*, cobbler] *base* cobbler (sutorial, sutorious)

-syc- [Gr. *sukon*, fig] *base* fig (sycoma, sycosis)

-sychno- [Gr. *sukhnos*, many, frequent] *base* many (sychnocarpous)

sylv-/sylvi- [L. *silva*, forest] *base* of trees (sylvan, sylviculture). *Also* silv-

sylleps- [Gr. *sullepsis*, conception] *base* pregnancy (syllepsiology, syllepsis)

symmetr- [Gr. *summetria*, proportion] *base* symmetry (asymmertrical, symmetry)

symphyo- [Gr. *sumphues*, growing together] *comb* growing together (symphyantherous, symphyogenesis)

syn- [Gr. *sun*, with, together] *pre* with; together; at the same time; by means of; (synagogue, synallagmatic). NOTE: syn- can change to: sy-

(syzygy); syl- (syllogism); sym- (symbiosis); sys- (system)

synchro- [Gr. *sunkhronos*, contemporaneous] *comb* synchronized (synchromesh, synchronism)

syndesmo- [Gr. *sundesmos*, ligament] *comb* ligament; binding together (syndesmodontoid, syndesmoplasty)

synec-/-synœc- [Gr. *sunekheia*, connection, continuity] *base* community (synectic, synœcology)

syphili-, syphilo- [NL *Syphilis*, a character in a poem by Hieronymus Frascatorius] *comb* siphylis (syphilitic, syphilophobia)

-syr- [Gr. *surinks/suring-*, tube, pipe] *base* 1. reed; pipe; tube (syringe, siringium); 2. Eustachian tube (syringeal, syrinx)

syrigma- [Gr. *surigmos*, whistle] *comb* whistle, ringing sound (syrigmophonia, syrigmus)

syringo- [Gr. *surinks/suring-*, tube, pipe] *comb* tube-shaped cavity (syringocarcinoma, syringomyelitis)

Syro- [Gr. *Suros*, Syrian] *comb* Syrian and (Syro-Arabian, Syro-Phoenician)

-syrt- [L. *syrtis*, sand-bank] *base* quicksand (syrtic, syrtis)

T

-tab- [L. *tabere*, melt, waste away] *base* emaciated; wasted away (tabefy, tabescent)

taban- [L *tabanus*, horse-fly] *base* horsefly (tabanid, Tabanus)

tabell- [L. *tabella*, tablet, ballot] *base* tablet; ballot (tabella, tabellary)

tacho- [Gr. *takhus*, swift] *comb* speed (tachograph, tachometer)

tachy- [Gr. *takhus*, swift] *comb* rapid; swift; fast (tachycardia, tachygraphy)

tacit- [L. *tacitus*, silent, done without words] *base* quiet (tacit, taciturn)

-tact- [L. *tangere/tact-*, to touch] *base* touch (contact, tactile)

-tactic, -tactous [Gr. *taktos*, arranged or arrayed] *comb* order; arrangement (heterotactous, syntactic)

taeni-, taenio- [L. *tainia*, ribbon, tape] *comb* ribbon; or band; tapeworm (taeniafuge, taeniosomous). *Also* teni- (teniacide)

-tain [L. *tenere*, to hold] *comb* hold (maintain, retain). *See* -ten-

tal- [L. *talis*, such, like, similar] *base* retaliation (taliation, talion)

tali-, talo- [L. *talus*, ankle] *comb* ankle (taligrade, talocalcaneal)

talip- [L. *talipes*, club foot] *base* club foot (talipedic, talipes)

talpi- [L. *talpa*, mole] *base* mole (talpicide, talpine)

tamieut- [Gr. *tamieuein*, to save] *base* sparing (isotamieutic)

-tang- [L. *tangere*, to touch] *base* touch (intangible, tangent)

tanno- [Fr. *tanin*, tannin] *base* tannin (tannometer, tannogallate)

tantal- [Gr. *Tantalos*, son of Zeus punished for revealing godly secrets] *base* tease (tantalize, tantalizingly)

tapet- [Gr. *tapes/tapet-*, carpet, rug] *base* like a carpet (tapesium, tapetum)

-taph, tapho-, taphro- [Gr. *taphos*, grave, tomb] *comb* tomb; pit (cenotaph, taphophobia, taphrenchyma)

-tapino- [Gr. *tapeinos*, low, base] *comb* low, dejected (tapinocephalic, tapinosis)

tarand- [Gr. *tarandos*, reindeer] *base* reindeer (tarandre, tarandus)

tarass- [Gr. *taraksis*, confused] *base* confused (tarassis)

-tard- [L. *tardare*, to go slow] *base* slow; delay (retardation, tardigrade)

tarso- [L. *tarsus*, broad, flat surface] 1. *comb* instep (tarso-metatarsus); 2. eyelid cartilage (tarsoplasty)

tartr(o)- [Fr. *tartre*, tartar] *comb* tartar; tartaric acid (tartromethylates, tartrovinic acid)

-taseo-, -tasi- [Gr. *tasis*, stretching, tension] *base* tension (taseometer, tasimetric)

tatus- [Fr. *tatusie*, armadillo] *base* armadillo (tatusia, Tatusiidae)

tauri-, tauro- [Gr. *tauros*, bull] 1. *comb* of/like a bull (tauricide, tauromachy); 2. [chemistry] taurine (taurocholate)

taurotrag- [Gr. *tauros*, bull + *tragos*, goat] *base* eland (taurotragus)

tauto- [Gr. *tauton*, the same] *comb* the same; identical (tautochronous, tautology)

tax- [NL. *taxus*, yew] *base* yew (Taxaceae, taxaceous)

taxi-, -taxia, -taxis, taxo-, -taxy [Gr. *taksis*, order, arrangement] *comb* arrangement; order (taxidermy, heterotaxia, parataxis, taxonomy, homotaxy)

techno-, -techny [Gr. *tekhne*, art, handicraft] 1. *comb* art; science; skill (technocracy); 2. technical; technological (technochemistry, pyrotechny)

tecno- [Gr. *teknon*, child] *comb* child (tecnology, tecnonymy)

-tect- [L. *tectus*, covered] *base* roof; cover (protection, tectiform)

tecton- [Gr. *tektonikos*, of construction] *base* earth's structural crust; building (Tectonarchinae, tectonics)

-teen [AS *tene*, ten] *suf* ten and; numbers: cardinal (nineteen, sixteen)

teg-, tegu- [L. *tegmen*, cover] *base* cover (tegmental, tegument)

tegul- [L. *tegula*, tile] *base* tile; scale (tegular, tegulated)

-teicho- [Gr. *teikhos*, wall] *base* wall (teichopsia, teichoscopy)

teino- [Gr. *tenein*, to stretch, extend] *base* adjustable (teinoscope)

tek- [Gr. *teknon*, child] *base* child (ateknia, teknonymous)

tel-[1] [L. *tela*, web] *base* web; something spun (telarian, telary)

tel-[2] [L. *telum*, dart] *base* dart (Telifera, teliferous)

tele- [Gr. *tele*, afar] 1. *comb* at a distance; far (telegraph); 2. television (telecast)

teleo-, telo- [Gr. *telos*, end, completion] *comb* end; purpose; final stage (teleology, telophase)

telesm- [Gr. *telesma*, religious rite, consecration] *base* talisman (telesmatical, telesmatically)

teleuto- [Gr. *teleute*, completion] *comb* final stage (teleutofrom, teleutospore)

tellin- [Gr. *telline*, kind of shell-fish] *base* bivalve mollusk (Tellina, tellinite) tellur- [L. *tellus/tellur-*, earth] *base* earth (intratelluric, tellurian)

-telmat- [Gr. *telma/telmat-*, marsh] *base* a bog (Telmatodytes, telamatology)

telson- [Gr. *telson*, boundary, limit] *base* final segment (telson, telsonic)

temen- [Gr. *temenos*, sacred enclosure] *base* of land dedicated to a god (temenos, Temenuchus)

temer- [L. *temere*, by chance, rashly] *base* reckless (temerity, temerous)

-temerat- [L. *temerare*, to violate] *base* violate (intemerate, temeration)

temno- [Gr. *temnein*, to cut] *comb* cut (temnospondylous)

-temp- [L. *temperare*, to proportion] *base* regulate; mix (temper, temperament)

tempest- [L. *tempestivus*, timely, seasonal] *base* timely (tempestive, tempestivity)

-tempor- [L. *tempus/tempor-*, season, time] *base* time (contemporary, temporal)

temporo- [L. *tempora*, the temples] *comb* temple of the head (temporoauricular, temporo-maxillary)

-temul- [L. *temulentia*, intoxicated] *base* drunkenness (temulency, temulent)

-ten- [L. *tenere*, to hold, keep] *base* hold (tenable, tenacious). *See* -tain

tend- [L. *tendere*, to stretch] *base* stretch (contend, distend, tendon)

-tene [Gr. *tainia*, band] *comb* [biology] ribbon-shaped (diplotene, pachytene)

-tenebr- [L. *tenebrae*, darkness] *base* darkness (tenebrific, tenebrosity)

-teni- [Gr. *tainia*, band, ribbon] *base* tapeworm; ribbon-like (teniacide, teniafuge). *Also* taeni(i)- (taeniiphobia)

teno-, tenonto- [Gr. *tenon*, tendon] *comb* tendon (tenotomy, tenontodynia)

tensio- [L. *tensio*, stretching] *comb* stretch; strain (tensiometer, tensiometric)

tentaculi- [NL *tentaculum*, feeler] *comb* tentacle (tentaculiferous, tentaculiform)

tentig- [L. *tentigo*, tension, lust] *base* lascivious (tentigo, tentiginous)

tenui- [L. *tenuis*, thin] *comb* slender; thin; narrow (tenuifolious, tenuirostral)

tepe- [L. *tepere*, to be lukewarm] *base* lukewarm (tepefaction, tepefy)

tephro- [Gr. *tephra*, ashes] 1. *comb* ashes (tephromancy); 2. gray (tephroite, tephromalacia)

ter- [L. *ter*, thrice] *comb* thrice (tercentenary, tercentennial)

tera- [Gr. *teras*, monster] *comb* one trillion (terabit, terahertz)

terato- [Gr. *teras/terat-*, monster] *comb* prodigy; monstrosity (teratogenic, teratology)

terebinth- [Gr. *terebinthos*, the turpentine-tree] *base* turpentine (terebinthinate, terebinthine)

terebr- [L. *terebra*, a borer] *base* bore; penetrate (terebration, terebratuline)

tered- [Gr. *teredon*, ship-worm] *base* worm (teredines, teredo)

tereti-, tereto- [L. *teres/teret-*, round, smooth] *comb* rounded (tereticaudate, teretosetaceous)

tergi-, tergo- [L. *tergum*, back] *comb* the back (tergiversation, tergolateral)

-termin- [L. *terminus*, boundary] *base* end; limit (interminable, termination)

termit- [NL *termes/termit-*, white ant] *base* termite (termitarium, termitophagous)

-tern-, ternati- [L. *terni*, by threes] *base* three; triple (ternate, ternatipennate)

-terr- [L. *terra*, earth, land] *base* earth (subterranean, territorial)

-tert- [L. *tertius*, third] *base* third (tertial, tertiary) tessera- [Gr. *tessares*, four] *comb* four (tessarace, tesseraglot)

tesseradeca- [Gr. *tessares*, four + *dekas*, ten] *comb* fourteen (tessaradecad, tesseradecasyllabon)

testaceo- [L. *testaceus*, covered with a shell] *comb* 1. shell (testaceography, testaceology); 2. [*botany/zoology*] reddish-brown; dull brick color (testaceo-fuscous, testaceo-piceous)

testud- [L. *testudo*, tortoise] *base* turtle (testudinal, testudineous)

tetano- [L. *tetanus*, tetanus] *comb* tetanus; stiff (tetanigenous, tetanospasmin)

tetarto- [Gr. *tetartos*, fourth] *comb* one fourth (tetartohedral, tetartopyramid)

tetra- [Gr. *tetra*, four] *comb* four (tetrablastic, tetragamy)

tetracyclo- [Gr. *tetra*, four + *kuklikos*, in a circle] *comb* with four circles; with four atomic rings (tetracyclic, tetracycline)

tetradeca- [Gr. *tetra*, four + *deka*, ten] *comb* fourteen (tetradecapod, tetradecapodous). *Also* tetrakaideca- (tetrakaidecahedron)

tetrakis- [Gr. *tetrakis*, four times] *comb* four times (tetrakisdodecahedron, tetrakishexahedron)

tetrao- [Gr. *tetraon*, pheasant, grouse] *base* grouse; ptarmigan (tetraonid, tetraonine)

tetrazo- [Gr. *tetra*, four + *azo*, nitrogen] [*chemistry*] 1. *comb* compound with 4 atoms of nitrogen (tetrazone); 2. presence of four azo groups (tetrazolyl)

teuth- [Gr. *teuthis*, cuttlefish] *base* cuttlefish; squid (teuthologist, teuthology)

teuto- [L. *Teutoni*, German tribe] *comb* German (Teutonicism, teutophobia)

tex- [L. *texere*, to weave] *base* weave (textile, texture)

text- [L. *textum*, tissue] *base* tissue (textoblastic, textoma)

-th-[1] [AS suf -*th* for abstract nouns] 1. *suf* act of (stealth); 2. state of being/having; quality of being/having (wealth)

-th-[2] [AS suf -*tha* used to form ordinal numerals] *suf* numbers: ordinal (fifth, sixteenth)

thalamo- [Gr. *thalamos*, inner chamber, bedroom] *comb* thalamus (thalamocortical, thalamocrural)

thalasso-, thalatto- [Gr. *thalassa*, sea] *comb* sea; marine (thalassocracy, thalattology)

thalero- [Gr. *thaleia*, blooming] *comb* blooming; fresh (thalerophagous)

thall-, thallo- [Gr. *thallos*, a green shoot] *base* 1. green plant (thallus, thallophyte) 2. thallium (thallious oxide)

thamn- [Gr. *thamnos*, bush, shrub] *base* bush; shrike (thamnium; thamnophile)

thanato- [Gr. *thanatos*, death] *comb* death (thanatology, thanatopsis)

thaumato- [Gr. *thauma/thaumat-*, a wonder] *comb* wonder; miracle (thaumatology, thaumaturgic)

theatro- [Gr. *theatron*, place to view shows] *comb* theater (theatromania, theatrophobia)

-theca, theci-, theco- [Gr. *theke*, case, box] *comb* sheath; container; case; cover (sarcotheca, theciform, thecostegnosis)

-thei- [NL *thea*, tea] *base* tea (theic, theiform)

thelo- [Gr. *thele*, teat] *comb* nipple (perithelium, Thelotrema)

thely- [Gr. *thelukos*, feminine] *comb* female (Thelygonum, thelytoky)

then- [Gr. *thenar*, palm or sole] *base* palm, sole (thenad, thenar)

theo- [Gr. *theos*, god] *comb* god (theocentric, theology)

-thera [Gr. *theran*, to hunt] *base* catcher; trap (oenothera)

theraphos- [Gr. *theraphion*, little wild beast] *base* tarantula (theraphose, theraphosid)

-there, therio-, thero- [Gr. *ther*, wild beast] 1. *comb* extinct mammalian form (megathere); 2. beast (theriomorphic, theropod)

-therm, thermo-, -thermy [Gr. *thermos*, warm] *comb* heat; hot (isotherm, thermodynamics, diathermy)

-thesis, -thetic [Gr. *thesis*, putting, placing] *comb* set; put; place (hypothesis, antithetic)

-thesmo- [Gr. *thesmos*, law] *base* law (thesmophilist, thesmothete)

thesp- [Gr. *Thespis*, father of stage tragedy] *base* actor (thespian, thespianism)

thia-, thio- [Gr. *theion*, sulfur] *comb* sulfur (thiabendazole, thioaldehyde)

thigmo- [Gr. *thigma*, touch] *comb* touch (thigmokinesis, thigmotropism)

thino- [Gr. *this/thin-*, the shore] *base* beach; seashore (Thinocorus, thinolite)

-thlips- [Gr. *thlibein*, to press, distress] *base* pressure (thlipsencephalus, thlipsis)

thneto- [Gr. *thnetos*, mortal] *comb* mortal (thnetopsychism, Thnetopsychitae)

thoracico-, thoraco- [Gr. *thoraks*, a breastplate] 1. *comb* thorax and (thoracico-abdominal); 2. thorax; chest (thoracoplasty)

thras- [Gr. *Thraso*, bragging soldier in Terence's *Eunuchus*] *base* brag; boast (thrasonical, thrasonically)

thremm- [Gr. *thremma/thremmat-*, nursling] *base* breed; propagate (thremmatology)

thren- [Gr. *threnos*, wailing, lamentation] *base* lamentation (threnetic, threnody)

threp/s/t- [Gr. *threphein*, to nourish] *base* nourish; nurse (threpsology, threpterophilia)

thripto- [Gr. *threpteon*, who must be fed to live] *base* mortal (thriptophobia)

-thrix- [Gr. *thriks*, hair] *base* hair (streptothricial, streptothrix)

-throated [OE *throte*, throat] *comb* throat: specific kind (large-throated, ruby-throated)

thrombo- [Gr. *thrombos*, clot of blood] *comb* blood clot (thrombo-arteritis, thrombo-phlebitis)

thumo- [Gr. *thumos*, soul] *comb* soul (thumomancy)

-thur- [L. *thus/thur-*, incense] *base* incense (thurible, thurifer)

-thy- [Gr. *thuma*, sacrifice] *base* offering; sacrifice (idolothyus, thymiaterion)

-thylac- [Gr. *thulaks*, pouch] *base* pouch (thylacine)

-thymia[1] [Gr. *thumos*, soul] *comb* mental disorder (alexithymic, dysthymia)

-thymia-[2] [Gr. *thumion*, burn as incense] *base* perfume; incense (thymiama, thymiatechny)

thymo- [Gr. *thumos*, thymus; soul] 1. *comb* thymus (thymokinetic); 2. mind; soul; mood; emotions (thymogenic, thymopathy)

-thyrea, thyreo-, thyro- [*thureos*, large oblong shield] *comb* thyroid (hypothyrea, thyreotomy, thyromegaly)

thyrsi-, thyrso- [Gr. *thursos*, stalk, stem] *comb* stalk; stem; inflorescence (thyrsiflorous, thyrsocephalic)

-thysan- [Gr. *thusanos*, a tassel] *base* fringe; tassel (thysanopter, thysanurous)

tibio- [L. *tibia*, shinbone, pipe] *comb* tibia and (tibioperoneal, tibiotarsal)

-tic *see* -ic

ticho- [Gr. *teikhos*, wall] *base* wall (Tichodroma, tichorhine)

-tight [ON *thehtr*, tight] *comb* impervious to (airtight, watertight)

tigr- [Gr. *tigris*, tiger] *base* tiger (Tigridia, tigrine)

tilia- [L. *tilia*, linden-tree] *comb* lime; linden (Tiliaceae, tiliaceous)

-till- [Gr. *tillein*, to pluck, tear] *base* to

pluck (peotillomania, trichotilloma-
nia)

-tim-, timor- [L. *timor*, fear] *base* fear;
dread (timidity, timorous)

timbro- [Fr. *timbre*, postage-stamp]
comb postage stamp (timbrology,
timbrophilic)

-timo- [Gr. *time*, honor, worth] *base*
honor (timocracy, timocratic)

-tinct-, -ting- [L. *tingere/tinct-*, to dye]
base stain; color (intinction, tingible)

tinea- [L. *tinea*, gnawing worm] *base*
moth; ringworm (tineid, Tineidae)

tinn-, tintinn- [L. *tinnire*, to ring] *base*
jingling; ringing; bell (tinnitus,
tintinnabular)

-tion, -tious [OF *-cion*, state of being
what the p.p. imports] 1. *suf* act of
(correction); 2. state of being (elation, ambitious); 3. thing that is
(creation)

titano-[1] [Gr. *Titan*, mythological
deity] *comb* titan; superhuman
(titanosaur, titanotherioid)

titano-[2] [NL *titanium*, titanium] *comb*
titanium (titaniferous, titano-
cyanide)

titillo- [L. *titillare*, to tickle] *base*
scratch; tickle (titillation, titillatory)

-titub- [L. *titubare*, to stagger] *base*
stagger (titubate, titubation)

-tmesis [Gr. *tmesis*, a cutting] *comb*
cutting (neurotmesis, tmesis)

-tocia, toco- [Gr. *tokos*, birth] *comb*
childbirth; labor (dystocia,
tocolytic). *Also* **toko-** (tokogony)

-toky [Gr. *tokos*, birth] *comb* child-
bearing (arrenotoky, thelytoky)

-tolypeut- [ML *Tolypeutes*, armadillo
< Gr. *tolupe*, ball] *base* armadillo
(Tolypeutes, tolypeutine)

-tome, -tomous [Gr. *tomos*, cutting]
comb [medicine] cutting instrument
(bronchotome, osteotome, orthoto-
mous)

toment- [L. *tomentum*, stuffing of hair,
feathers, wool] *base* covered with fine
hairs (tomentose, tomentous)

tomo-, -tomous, -tomy [Gr. *temnein*,
to cut] *comb* cutting; dividing;
surgery (tomography, dichotomous,
appendectomy)

-ton [AS *tun*, town] *comb* town
(Hampton, Washington)

-tonia [Gr. *tonos*, tone] 1. *comb* tone;
muscle tension (isotonia); 2. personality disorder (catatonia)

-tonic [Gr. *tonos*, tone] 1. *comb* notes
in a musical scale (pentatonic);
2. musical intervals (diatonic);
3. phonetic units of stress (pretonic);
4. muscle contraction (myatonic);
5. pathological spasms (vagatonic);
6. restorative substance (hematonic);
7. solution (isotonic)

-tonitru- [L. *tonitrus*, thunder] *base*
thunder (tonitrous, tonitrual)

tono- [Gr. *tonos*, tone] *comb* tension;
pressure (tonometer, tonotechnic)

tonsillo- [L. *tonsilla*, tonsil] *comb* tonsil (tonsillitis, tonsillotomy)

tonsor- [L. *tonsor*, barber, clipper] *base*
shave; barber (tonsorial, tonsorious)

-toothed [AS *toth*, tooth] *comb* specific
number/kind of teeth (big-toothed,
gap-toothed)

topo-, -topy [Gr. *topos*, a place] *comb*
place; topical (topology, somatotopy)

toreut- [Gr. *toreuma/toreumat-*, work
in relief] *base* embossing metal or
ivory (toreumatography, toreutics)

tormo- [Gr. *tormos*, hole, socket] *comb*
socketed (tormodont)

torn- [L. *tornare*, to turn] *base* twisted;
spiral (tornadic, Tornatellidae)

torp- [L. *torpere*, be numb or stiff] *base*
1. numbness (torbid, torporific); 2.
electric ray fish (Torpedinoidea, tor-
pedinous)

torr- [L. *torrere*, parch] *base* parched,
dry (torrefy, torrid)

-tors-, -tort- [L *torquere/tort-*, to twist]
base twisted (torsion, distorted)

torul- [L. *torus*, swelling, protuber-
ance] *base* elevated; beadlike (toruliform, torulis)

-tory *see* -ory

toti- [L. *totus*, all] *comb* whole; entire (totipalmate, totipresent)

tox-, toxi-, toxico-, toxo-¹ [Gr. *toksikon*, poison] *comb* poison; infection (toxemia,toxituberculide, toxicogenic, toxoplasma)

toxo-² [Gr. *tokson*, a bow] *comb* archery (toxophilitic, toxophily)

-trab- [L. *trabs*, a timber] *base* beam (trabeation, trabeculate)

trachelo- [Gr. *trakhelos*, neck] *comb* neck; (trachelodynia, trachelokyphosis)

tracheo- [Gr. *trakheia*, windpipe] 1. *comb* windpipe (tracheotomy); 2. trachea and (tracheobronchial)

trachy- [Gr. *trakhus*, rough] *comb* rough (trachycarpous, trachyglossate)

-tract- [L. *trahere*, to pull, draw] *base* draw; pull (detract, retraction)

tragelaph- [Gr. *tragos*, goat + *elaphos*, deer] *base* antelope (tragelaphine, tragelaphus)

trago- [Gr. *tragos*, goat] *comb* goat (tragopan, tragopogon)

trans- [L. *trans*, across, on the other side] 1. *pre* across; over; on the other side; to the other side (transatlantic); 2. change thoroughly (transliterate); 3. transcending; above and beyond (trans-sonic)

transverso- [L. *trans*, across + *vertere*, to turn] *comb* transverse; crosswise (transversocubital, transversomedial)

trapezi- [Gr. *trapezion*, four-sided table] *base* trapezoid (trapeziform, trapezoid)

traumato- [Gr. *trauma*, wound] *comb* wound; injury (traumatologist, traumatopnea)

trecent- [L. *tres*, three + *centum*, hundred] *comb* three hundred (trecentene, trecentist)

tredecim- [L. *tres*, three + *decem*, ten] *base* thirteen (tredecile, tredecimal)

trega- [trillion + mega, trillion] *comb* trillion (tregadyne, trega-hertz)

tremo- [L. *tremere*, to tremble] *base* shaking; tremble (tremogram, tremorless)

trench- [L. *truncare*, cut off, lop] *base* cutting; keen (trenchant, trenchantly)

-trepid- [L. *trepidus*, agitated] *base* scared; agitated (intrepid, trepidation)

trepo- [Gr. *trepo*, to turn] *base* syphilis (treponemiasis, treponemicidal)

-tresia [Gr. *tresis*, perforation] *comb* perforation (atresia, proctotresia)

-tress [Gr. *-issa*, fem. suf] *suf* feminine ending (actress, procuress)

tri- [L. *tri-*, three < *tres*] 1. *comb* three; three parts (triplane); 2. three times; into three (trisect); 3. every three; every third (triannual); 4. [chemistry] having three atoms; having three equivalents of; having three groups (tribasic)

triaconta- [Gr. *triakontas*, thirty] *comb* thirty (triacontahedral, triacontarchy)

triakis- [Gr. *triakis*, thrice] *comb* three (triakisoctahedron, triakistetrahedron)

triangulato-[L. *triangulatus*, having three angles] *comb* triangulate (triangulato-subovate, trianguloid)

tribo- [Gr. *tribos*, rubbing] *comb* friction (tribadism, tribology)

-trice [L. *-trix*, fem. suf] *suf* feminine ending (advocatrice, genetrice). NOTE: -trix is now preferred

triceni- [L. *triceni*, thirty] *base* thirty (tricenary, tricennial)

tricent- [L. *trecenti*, three hundred] base three hundred (tricentenary, tricentennial)

-trich, -tricha, -trichia, -trichous, -trichy [Gr. *triks*, hair] *comb* [zoology] creature with hairlike structures (hypotrich, Gastrotricha, oligotrichia, peritrichous, lissotrichy)

trichec- [NL *trichechus*, walrus] *base* manatee; walrus (trichechine, Trichechoidea)

tricho- [Gr. *triks*, hair] *comb* hair (trichocarpous, trichology)

trient- [L. *trientalis*, one-third] *base* third (triental, Trientalis)

triethyl- [L. *tri-*, three + Gr. *aither*, ether] *comb* [chemistry] three ethyl groups (triethylamine, triethylcarbinol)

triges- [L. *trigesmus*, thirtieth] *base* thirty (trigesimal)

trigint- [L. *triginta*, thirty] *base* thirty (trigintal, trigintennial)

trigono- [Gr. *trigonos*, three-cornered] *comb* three-cornered; triangular (trigonocephalic, trigonodont)

tring- [Gr. *trungos*, a bird] *base* sandpiper (tringine, tringoid)

trinitro- [Gr. *tri*, three + *nitro*, natron] *comb* [chemistry] three atoms of nitrogen; (trinitrocresol, trinitroglycerin)

trioxy- [Gr. *tri*, three + *oksus*, sharp] *comb* having 3 atoms of oxygen (tryoxymethylene, trioxynaphthalene)

triphth- [Gr. *triphthos*, waste matter] *base* waste (triphthemia)

triplicato- [L. *triplicare*, to triple] *comb* triplicate (triplicato-pinnate, triplicato-ternate)

-triplo- [Gr. *triplios*, threefold] *base* threefold; triple (triploblastic, triplopia)

-tripsy [Gr. *tribein*, to rub] *comb* crushing; friction (lithotripsy, neurotripsy)

tripud- [L. *tripudium*, leaping, dancing] *base* dance; exult (tripudiate, tripudiation)

triquadr- [L. *tri-*, three + *quad-*, four] *base* three-fourths; three units divided four ways (triquadrantal, triquadrifid)

tris- [Gr. *treis*, three] *base* tripled (trisoctahedron, tristetrahedron)

triskaideka- [Gr. *treiskaideka*, thirteen] *comb* thirteen (triskaidekaphobia)

trism- [Gr. *trismos*, spasm] *base* lockjaw (trismus, trismic)

trist- [L. *tristis*, sad] *base* grief; sadness (tristimania, tristful)

trit- [L. *terere*, grind, thresh] *base* friction; threshing (triturate, triturature)

-tritic- [L. *triticum*, wheat] *base* wheat (triticeous, Triticum)

trito- [Gr. *tritos*, third] *comb* third (tritocere, tritomesal)

triv- [L. *trivialis*, of the three crossroads] *base* commonplace (trivial, trivialize)

-trix [L. *-trix*, fem. suf] *suf* female agent (consolatrix, executrix)

troch-, trochi-, trocho- [Gr. *trokhos*, a wheel] *comb* wheel; pulley; rounded (trochlear, actinotrocha, trochiferous, trochocardia)

-trocha [Gr. *trokhos*, wheel] *comb* [zoology] having a band (cephalotrocha, mesotrocha)

trochalo- [Gr. *trokhalos*, round] *comb* rolling; rotary (trochalopod, Trochalopteron)

trochil- [NL. *trochilus*, hummingbird] *base* hummingbird (trochilidist, trochiline)

trochlea- [L. *trochlea*, pulley] *base* pulley-like (trochlear, trochleate)

-trocto- [Gr. *troktes*, kind of fish] *base* trout (troctolite)

-trog- [Gr. *trogon*, having been gnawed] *base* to gnaw (trogonine, Trogosita)

-troglo- [Gr. *trogle*, hole, cave] *base* hole; cave (troglodyte, troglodytic)

troglodyt- [NL. *Troglodytes*, cave dwellers] *base* wren (Troglodytes, troglodytine)

-tromo- [Gr. *tromos*, trembling] *base* earth tremor (tromometer, tromometry)

-tron, -tronic [< *(elec)tronic*] *comb* names of devices used in electronic or subatomic experiments (animatronic, cyclotron)

-trope, -tropic, -tropism, tropo-, -tropous, -tropy [Gr. *trope*, turning] *comb* responding to a specific stimulus; turning; changing (heliotrope, phototropic, thermotropism, tropophilous, phototropous, entropy)

-troph, -trophic, tropho-, -trophy [Gr. *trophe*, nourishment] *comb* nutrition; food; nourishment (heterotroph, autotrophic, trophoplasm, atrophy)

tropido- [Gr. *tropis/tropid-*, keel] *base* keel-shaped (Tropidogaster, tropidosternal)

tropo- [L. *tropus*, figure in rhetoric] *comb* figurative, metaphorical (tropological, tropology)

trucid- [L. *trucidare*, to kill] *base* kill; slaughter (contrucidate, trucidation)

-trude, -trus- [L. *trudere*, to thrust] *base* push; thrust (protrude, intrusion)

trunc- [L. *truncare*, to cut off, reduce] *base* cut, reduced in size (truncate, truncation)

-trutt- [ML. *trutta*, a trout] *base* trout (trutta, truttaceous)

trygon- [Gr. *trugon*, sting-ray] *base* sting-ray (Trigon, Trygonidae)

trypano- [Gr. *trupanon*, a borer] 1. *comb* parasite; borer (trypanolytic, trypanosome); 2. injection (trypanophobia)

trypet- [Gr. *trupetes*, a borer] *base* fruitfly (Trypeta, Trypetidae)

tsio- [Chinese *ch'a*, tea] *base* tea (tsiology, tsiologis)

tuberculo- [L. *tuberculum*, small tuberosity] 1. *comb* tuberculous (tubercular); 2. tubercle bacillus (tuberculoid); 3. tuberculosis (tuberculocidin)

tubi-, tubo- [L. *tubus*, tube] *comb* tube (tubiflorous, tubotorsion)

tubuli-, tubulo- [L. *tubulus*, small tube] *comb* tubule; small tube (tubulidentate, tubulocyst)

-tude [L. *-tudo*, suf for abstract nouns] *suf* state of being; quality of being (plenitude, solitude)

-tum- [L. *tumere*, to swell] *base* swelling (detumescence, tumescent)

tupai- [Malay *tupaya*, squirrel-shrew] *base* squirrel-shrew (Tupaia, tupaiid)

-turb- [L. *turbare*, to agitate] *base* confuse; disturb (perturbation, turbulent)

-turbar- [L. *turba*, turf] *base* peat bog (turbarian, turbary)

turbinato- [L. *turbinatus*, shaped like a cone] *comb* top-shaped (turbinato-cylindrical, turbinate-lentiform)

turbo- [L. *turbo*, a top] *comb* consisting of; or driven by a turbine; (turbogenerator, turbotrain)

turd- [L. *turdus*, a thrush] *base* thrush; robin; bluebird (turdine, turdoid)

-turg- [L. *turgere*, to swell out] *base* swelling (turgescent, turgid)

Turko- [ML *Turcus*, Turk] *comb* Turkey; (Turko-Russian). *Also* **Turco-** (Turcophobe)

-turp- [L. *turpis*, foul, base] *base* pollute; disgrace (turpify, turpitude)

-turri- [L. *turris*, tower] *base* tower (turriculated, turriferous)

turtur- [L. *turtur*, a turtle] *base* turtledove (Turtur, turturring)

tus- [L. *tundere/tus-*, to thump, strike] *base* strike; bruise (contusion, obtuse)

-tuss- [L. *tussis*, cough] *base* cough (antitussive, tussicular)

twi- [AS. *twi-*, two] *comb* double (twiarched, twilight)

-ty¹ [L. *-itas*, suf for abstract nouns] *suf* quality of; condition of (humanity, novelty)

-ty² [AS. *-tig*, ten] *suf* times ten; tens (thirty, sixty)

-tych-, tycho- [Gr. *tukhe*, fortune] *comb* chance; occasional accident (tychastics, tychopotamic). *Also* **tich-** (dystichiphobia)

-tyl-, tylo- [Gr. *tulos*, knot, lump] *comb* knot; knob; callus; cushion (tylosis, tylopod)

tympani-, tympano- [Gr. *tumpanon*, a

drum] *comb* drum; tympanum (tympaniform, tympanoplasty)

-type [Gr. *tupos*, figure or type] **1.** *comb* type; representative form; example (prototype); **2.** stamp; printing type; print; (monotype)

typhlo- [Gr. *tuphlos*, blind] **1.** *comb* cecum; intestinal pouch (typhlostomy); **2.** blindness (typhlosis)

typho- [Gr. *tuphos*, stupor] *comb* typhus; typhoid (typhogenic, typhoidal)

typo- [Gr. *tupos*, type] *comb* type (typography, typology)

tyro- [Gr. *turos*, cheese] *base* cheese (tyroleucin, tyrotoxicon)

tyto- [Gr. *tuto*, night owl] *base* barn owl (tytonid, Tytonidae)

U

-ubi- [L. *ubi*, where] *base* place; position; location ;(ubiety, ubiquitous)

udo- [L. *udus*, moist or damp] *comb* wet; damp (udometer, udometric)

Ugro- [Russ. *Ugri*, tribe dwelling east of the Ural Mountains] *comb* Ugrian (Ugro-Finnish, Ugro-Slavonic)

-ula [L. *-ula*, dim. suf] *suf* diminutive (auricula, fibula)

-ular [L. suf *-ula*, dim., + *-aris*, of the kind of] *suf* having the form or character of (circular, globular)

-ule [L. *-ulus*, dim. suf] *suf* diminutive (nodule, pustule)

-ulent [L. suf *-ulentus*, abounding in] *suf* full of (fraudulent, virulent)

-ulig- [L. *uligo*, moisture] *base* full of moisture (uliginose, uliginous)

ulm- [L. *ulmus*, elm] *base* elm (ulmaceous, ulmous)

ulno- [L. *ulna*, elbow] *comb* ulna and (ulnocarpal, ulnoradial)

ulo-¹ [Gr. *oule*, a scar] *comb* scar (uletomy, ulodermatitis)

ulo-² [Gr. *oulon*, gum] *comb* gums (uloglossitis, uloncus)

ulo-³ [Gr. *oulos*, wooly] *comb* curly; crisp (Ulophocinae, ulotrichous)

-ulose [L. adj. suf *-ulosus*, marked by] *suf* characterized by; marked by (granulose, ramulose)

-ulous [L. suf *-ulus*, full of] *suf* characterized by; full of; tending to (populous, sedulous)

ultim-, ultimo- [L. *ultimus*, last, final] *base* final; last (ultimatum, ultimogeniture)

ultra- [L. *ultra*, beyond, more] **1.** *pre* on the further side of; beyond (ultraviolet); **2.** to an extreme degree; excessive (ultramodern); **3.** beyond the range of (ultramicroscopic)

ultro- [L. *ultro*, spontaneously] *comb* voluntary; spontaneous (ultromotivity, ultroneous)

ulul-¹ [L. *ululare*, to howl] *base* wail; howl (ululate, ululation)

ulul-² [L. *ulula*, screech-owl] *base* owl (Ulula, ululant)

-ulum [L. neut. suf *-ulum*, small] *suf* diminutive (cingulum, speculum)

-ulus [L. masc. suf *-ulus*, small] *suf* diminutive (cuniculus, homunculus)

umbell-, umbelli- [L. *umbella*, sunshade] *base* sunshade; parasol (umbellated, umbellifer)

umbilici- [L. *umbilicus*, navel] *base* navel (umbiliferous, umbiliciform)

umbo- [L. *umbo*, knob, boss] *base* knob; nipple (umbonate, umbonulate)

-umbr- [L. *umbra*, shadow] *base* shadow (umbrage, umbriphilous)

umbraculi- [L. *umbraculum*, umbrella] *comb* sunshade (umbraculiferous, umbraculiform)

umbrelli- [It. *umbrella*, an umbrella] *base* umbrella (umbrelliferous, umbrelliform)

Umbro- [L. *Umbri*, ancient people of central Italy] *comb* Umbrian (Umbro-Etruscan, Umbro-Sabellian)

un- [AS. *un-*, not] 1. *pre* not; opposite of; lack of ;(unhappy); 2. back; reversal (unlock)

unci- [L. *uncus*, hook, barb] *comb* hook (unciferous, unciform)

-unct- [L. *unctio*, anointing] *base* ointment; oil (unctuosity, unctuous)

-unda- [L. *unda*, wave] *base* wave (exundant, inundation)

undec- [L. *undecim*, eleven] *comb* eleven (undecagon, undecennary)

under- [AS. *under*, under] 1. *pre* lower place: in/on/to; beneath; below (undershirt); 2. inferior rank/position; subordinate (undergraduate); 3. amount below standard; inadequate (underdeveloped)

undeviginti- [L. *undeviginti*, nineteen] *comb* nineteen (undevigintiangular)

-undul- [L. *undulare*, to undulate] *base* wave (undulant, undulations)

ungu- [L. *unguentum*, ointment] *base* ointment; grease (unguent, unguentary)

-ungui-, -ungul- [L. *unguis*, nail, claw] *base* claw; nail (unguiform, exungulate)

uni- [L. *unus*, one] *comb* having one only (unicameral, unicellular,)

-uous [L. suf -*osus*, full of] *suf* of the nature of; consisting of (assiduous, strenuous)

-ura- [Gr. *oura*, tail] *base* tail (condylura, gastruran)

uranisco- [Gr. *ouraniskos*, roof of the mouth] *comb* hard palate (uranisconitis, uraniscoplasty)

urano- [Gr. *ouranos*, the heavens, the roof of the mouth] 1. *comb* hard palate (uranoschisis); 2. the heavens (uranography)

uranoso- [NL. < planet Uranus] *comb* [chemistry] containing uranium (uranosopotassic, uranothorite)

-urb- [L. *urbs*, city] *base* city (suburban, urbane)

urcei-, urceo- [L. *urceolus*, little pitcher] *base* urn; pitcher (urceiform, urceolate)

-ure [L -*ura*, suf denoting action or process] 1. *suf* act/result of being (exposure); 2. agent of; instrument of; scope of (legislature); 3. state of being (composure)

urea-, ureo- [Gr. *ouron*, urine] *comb* urine; urea (ureapoiesis, ureometer)

uredo- [L. *uredo*, a blight] *base* blight; fungus (uredinous, uredospore)

uretero- [Gr. *oureter*, urethra] *comb* urethra and (ureterolith, ureterostomy)

urethro- [Gr. *ourethra*, passage for urine] *comb* ureter and (urethrophraxis, urethroscopy)

-uretic [Gr. *ourein*, to urinate] *comb* urine (diuretic, enuretic)

-urgy [Gr. *ergon*, work] *comb* working of; fabricating (thaumaturgy, zymurgy)

uri-, urico- [Gr. *ouron*, urine] *base* uric acid; (uridrosis, uricometer)

-uria [Gr. *ouron*, urine] *comb* diseased condition of urine (acetonuria, glycosuria)

-urient [L. stem -*urien*-, desiring] *suf* desiring (esurient, parturient)

urini-, urino- [L. *urina*, urine] *comb* urinary tract; urine (uriniparous, urinometer)

uro-[1] [Gr. *oura*, tail] *comb* tail (urodele, uropod)

uro-[2] [Gr. *ouron*, urine] *comb* urine (urocyst, urolith)

-urs- [L. *ursus*, a bear] *base* bear (ursiform, ursine)

-urtic- [L. *urtica*, nettle] *base* nettle (urticaceous, urtical)

-ury- [Gr. *ouron*, urine] *base* urination (dysury, strangury)

-ust- [L. *ustio*, a burning] *base* burn (ustorious, ustulation)

utero- [L. *uterus*, the womb] *comb*

uterus and (uterocopulatory, uterovaginal)

-util- [L. *utilis*, useful] *base* useful (inutile, utilitarian)

utrei-, utri-[1] [L. *utriculus*, little leather bag or bottle] *comb* leather bottle (utreiform, utriform)

utri-[2]**, utric-** [L. *utriculus*, little leather bag or bottle] *base* sac; baglike part (utricle, utricular)

-uvi-, -uvu- [L. *uva*, grape] *base* grape (uviform, uvula)

uvulo- [L. *uvula*, cluster of grapes] *comb* uvula; (uvulatome, uvulectomy)

uxori- [L. *uxor*, wife] *base* wife (uxoricide, uxorious)

V

-vac-, -vacu- [L. *vacans*, empty] *base* empty; free (vacancy, vacuity)

vacci- [L. *vacca*, cow] *comb* cow (vaccimulgence, vaccinia)

vaccin- [L. *vaccinium*, whortleberry] *base* blueberry (Vacciniaceae, vaccinium)

vaccino- [L. *vaccinus*, of a cow] *comb* vaccine (vaccinophobia, vaccinosyphilis)

-vacil- [L. *vacillare*, to sway] *base* sway (vacillation, vacillatory)

-vad-, -vas- [L. *vadere*, to go] *base* rush; go (invade, invasion)

-vag-, -vagr- [L. *vagari*, to wander] *base* wander (vagary, vagrant)

vagini-, vagino- [L. *vagina*, sheath] *comb* sheath; vagina and (vaginipennous, vaginotomy)

vago- [L. *vagus*, wandering] *comb* vagus nerve (vagotomy, vagotropic)

vagu- [L. *vagus*, wandring, uncertain] *base* uncertain (vaguely, vagueness)

vale- [L. *vale*, farewell] *base* farewell (valediction, valedictorian)

valetud- [L. *valetudo*, infirmity] *base* ill (valetudinarian, valetudinary)

-valent [L. *valentia*, capacity] **1.** *comb* having a specified valence (monovalent); **2.** specified number of valences (univalent); **3.** having antibodies (multivalent)

vall- [L. *vallum*, rampart, wall] *base* wall (vallar, vallation)

valvi- [L. *valva*, leaf of a door] *comb* valve; opening (valviferous, valviform)

valvulo- [L. *valvula*, dim. leaf of a door] *comb* valve, esp. of the heart (valvulitis, valvulotomy)

vapo-, vapori- [L. *vapor*, exhalation, steam] *comb* emanation; vapor (vapography, vaporimeter)

-vapul- [L. *vapulare*, to be flogged] *base* beat; flog (vapulation, vapulatory)

vari- [L. *variare*, to change] *comb* changed; diverse (invariable, variant)

varic-, varici-, varico- [L. *varix/varic-*, dilated vein] *base* enlarged vein (varication, variciform, varicocele)

-variol- [L. *varius*, spotted] *base* spotted; speckled (variolite, varioloid)

vasculo- [L. *vasculum*, small vessel] *comb* blood vessel (vasculitis, vasculomotor)

vasi- [L. *vas*, vessel] *comb* vessel; tube (vasifactive, vasiform)

vaso- [L. *vas*, vessel] **1.** *comb* blood vessels (vasoconstrictor); **2.** vas deferens (vasectomy); **3.** vasomotor (vasoinhibitor)

-vast- [L. *vastare*, to lay waste] *base* destroy (devastation, vastity)

vati- [L. *vates*, seer, prophet] *comb* prophet (vaticide, vatication)

-vect- [L. *vehere/vect-*, to convey] *base* carry (provect, vector)

vegeti-, vegeto- [L. *vegetare*, to animate] *comb* vegetable; plant (vegetivorous, vegeto-alkaline) vel-, veli- [L. *velare*, to cover] *comb* cover; veil; sail (velated, veliferous)

-velar [L. *velare*, to cover] *comb* soft palate (labiovelar, velar)

velit- [L. *velitatio*, bickering] *base* skirmish; dispute (veltary, velitation)

vell- [L. *velle*, wish, will] *base* wish; desire (velleity)

-vellic- [L. *vellicare*, to pluck, twitch] *base* pluck; twitch; nip (vellication, vellicative)

veloci- [L. *velox/veloc-*, swift] *base* speed (velocimeter, velocipede)

-velut- [ML *velutum*, velvet] *base* velvet (velutine, velutinous)

-ven- [L. *venire*, to come] *base* come (convention, invent)

-venat- [L. *venatus*, hunting] *base* hunt (venatic, venatorial)

vene- [L. *vena*, vein] *comb* vein (venesect, venesection)

-venefic- [L. *veneficus*, poisonous, witchcraft] *base* sorcery; witchcraft (veneficial, veneficious)

veneni-, veneno- [L. *venenum*, poison] *comb* poison (venenifluous, venenosalivary)

-vener-[1] [L. *Venerius*, of Venus] *base* sexual desire; Venus (venereal, venery)

-vener-[2], -venerat- [L. *venerari*, to revere] *base* worship (venerable, veneration)

-vener-[3] [L. *venari*, to hunt or chase] *base* hunting (venatic, venation)

veni-, veno-, venoso-, -venous [L. *vena*, vein] *comb* veins (venipuncture, venostomy, venoso-reticulated, intravenous)

-vent- [L. *ventus*, wind] *base* wind; air (ventilation, ventosity)

ventri-, ventro- [L. *venter*, stomach] 1. *comb* abdomen; belly (ventricumbent); 2. ventral and (ventrodorsal)

ventricoso- [L. *ventricosus*, of the belly] *comb* distended abdomen (ventricoso-globose)

ventriculo- [L. *ventriculus*, ventricle] *comb* ventricle (ventriculoatrial, ventriculobulbous)

-ver- [L. *verus*, true] *base* truth (verification, verity)

-verber- [L. *verberare*, to beat] *base* beat (reverberate, verberative)

verbi-, verbo- [L. *verbum*, a word] *comb* word; talk (verbification, verbotomy)

-verd- [L. *viridis*, green] *base* green (verdant, verdure)

verecund- [L. *verecundus*, modest] *base* shame; modesty (verecund, verecundity)

veretill- [L. dim. of *veretrum*, the penis] *base* rod-like (veretilleous, veretilliform)

-verge [L. *vergere*, to bend or turn] *comb* turn; bend (converge, diverge). See -vers-

vergi- [L. *virga*, rod, twig] *comb* rod-like (vergiform). See -virgul-

vermi- [L. *vermis*, a worm] *comb* worm; (vermicide, vermeologist)

vermin- [L. *vermineus*, of noxious insects] *comb* vermin (vermination, verminous)

vermivor- [L. *vermis*, worm + *vorare*, to devour] *base* warbler (Vermivora); worm-eating (vermivorous)

-vern- [L. *ver*, spring] *base* spring (vernal, vernate)

vernil- [L. *vernilis*, servile] *base* slavish (vernile, vernility)

verruci- [L. *verruca*, wart] *comb* wart; growth (verruciform, verruculose)

vers-, -verse, vert- [L. *versare*, to turn] *comb* turn; direct (reversal, transverse, revert). See -verge

vertebro- [L. *vertebra*, a joint] *comb* vertebra (vertbrocostal, vertebroiliac)

verticill- [L. *verticcilus*, the whirl of a spindle] *base* whorled (verticillaster, verticillate-pillose)

vertig- [L. *vertiginare*, to whirl around] *base* dizziness (vertiginate, vertiginous)

-verv- [L. *vervex*, wether] *base* sheep (vervecean, vervecine)

vesica- [L. *vesica*, the bladder, a blister] *comb* blister (vesicant, vesicatory)

vesico- [L. *vesica*, the bladder] 1. *comb* bladder (vesicotomy); 2. bladder and (vesicoprostatic)

vesiculi-, vesiculo- [L. *vesicula*, a vescicle] *comb* vesicle; bladder-like vessel (vesiculigerous, vesiculo-pustular)

-vesper- [L. *vesper*, evening] *base* evening (vespers, vespertine)

-vespertil- [L. *vespertinus*, of the evening] *base* bat; vampire (Vespertilio, vespertilionine)

vespi- [L. *vespa*, a wasp] *comb* wasp; hornet (vespiary, vespiform)

vest- [L. *vestis*, a garment] *comb* clothing (divest, investiture)

vestibulo- [L. *vestibulum*, a forecourt] *comb* vestibule; small cavity (vestibulo-auditory, vestibulocochlear)

vestig- [L. *vistigium*, footstep, track] *base* trace (vestige, vestigial)

-vet- [L. *veter*, old, aged] *base* old; experienced (inveterate, veteran)

vex- [L. *vexare*, to shake, jolt] *base* bother; irritate (vexation, vexatious)

vexill- [L. *vexillum*, a standard] *comb* flag; banner (vexillator, vexillology)

vi-, via- [L. *via*, way, road, journey] *comb* journey; way (multivious, viaduct)

vibro- [L. *vibrare*, to vibrate] *comb* vibration; shaking (vibrograph, vibromotor)

vice- [L. *vice*, in the place of] *comb* deputy; assistant (vice-chancellor, vice-president)

-vicesim- [L. *vicesimus*, twentieth] *base* twentieth (vicesim, vicesimal)

vicin- [L. *vicinus*, neighboring] *base* neighborhood; proximity (vicinage, vicinity)

-vid-, -vis- [L. *videre/vis-*, to see] *base* see (video, invisible)

video- [L. *videre*, to see] *comb* televised (videoconference, videogenic)

vidu- [L. *vidua*, a widow] *base* widowed; destitute (viduage, viduation)

-viges- [L. *vigesimus*, twentieth] *base* twenty (vigesimal, vigesimation)

vigil- [L. *vigil*, awake] *base* watchful (vigil, vigilant)

viginti- [L. *viginti*, twenty] *comb* twenty (vigintiangular, vigintivirate)

-vili- [L. *vilis*, vile] *base* worthless; base (viliorate, vility)

vill- [L. *villosus*, shaggy] *base* shaggy (villiform, villose)

-ville [OF *ville*, farm, village] *comb* village (Baskerville, Smallville)

villoso- [L. *villosus*, hairy] *comb* covered with hairlike material (villositis, villoso-scabrous). *See* **piloso-**

vimin- [L. *vimen*, twig] *base* wicker (viminal, vimineous)

-vinc- [L. *vincere*, to conquer] *base* conquer; bind (invincible, vincibility)

vini-, vino- [L. *vinum*, wine] *comb* wine; grapes (viniculture, vinolent). *See* **viti-**

viol- [L. *violaceus*, of a violet color] *base* violet (Violaceae, violaceous)

viper- [L. *vipera*, viper, serpent] *base* snake (viperiform, viperous)

vir- [L. *virere*, to be green] *base* green (virent, virescence)

virgul- [L. *virgula*, a little rod] *base* rod; twig (virgulate, virgule)

-virid- [L. *viridis*, green] *base* green (viridescent, viridity)

-viridae [L. *virus*, venom + *-idae*, family suf] *comb* virus family (Orthomyxoviridae, Picornaviridae)

-viril- [L. *virilis*, virile] *base* masculine (virilescent, virility)

-virinae [L. *virus*, venom + *-inae*, subfamily suf] *comb* virus subfamily (Oncovirinae, Spumavirinae)

-virus [L. *virus*, venom] *comb* virus genus (Flavivirus, retrovirus)

-vis-, -vid- [L. *videre/vis-*, to see] *base* look; see (invisible, video)

-visaged [L. *videre/vis-*, to look] *comb* having a specific kind of face (grim-visaged, round-visaged)

visc-, visco- [L. *viscum*, birdlime] *base* sticky; thick (viscous, viscometer)

viscero- [L. *viscera*, viscera] *comb* viscera (visceralgia, visceroptosis)

visuo- [L. *visus*, sight] *comb* sight (visuo-auditory, visuomotor)

-vit- [L. *vita*, life] *base* alive (vital, vitality). *See* vivi-

vitelli-, vitello- [L. *vitellus*, yolk] *comb* yolk; germinative contents (vitelligerous, vitellogenous)

viti- [L. *vitis*, vine] *comb* vine (viticolous, viticulture)

vitia- [L. *vitium*, fault] *base* corrupt (vitiate, vitiated)

vitreo-, vitri-, vitro- [L. *vitreus*, of glass] *comb* glass; glassy (vitreodentin, vitriform, vitrotype)

vitric- [L. *vitricus*, stepfather] *base* stepfather (vitricophobia)

vitriolico- [ML *vitriolum*, vitriol] *comb* vitriol (vitriolicomuriated, vitriolico-neutral)

-vitul- [L. *vitulus*, veal] *base* calf (vitular, vituline)

vituper- [L. *vituperare*, to blame, censure] *base* blame; revile (vituperative, vituperator)

viverr- [L. *vivera*, a ferret] *base* civet; ferret; mongoose (Viverridae, viverrine)

vivi- [L. *vivus*, alive] *comb* living; alive (vivify, viviparous)

voc-, voci-, -voke [L. *vocare*, to call out] *comb* say; speak (invocation, vociferous, revoke)

vocif- [L. *vociferari*, cry out] *base* shout (vociferate, vociferous)

-vol- [L. *velle*, to will] *base* wish; will (volunteer, involuntary)

volit- [*volitare*, to fly] *base* flying (volitant, volitation)

volta- [<*Alessandro Volta*, scientist]

comb [electricity] voltaic (volta-electric, volta-electrometer)

volub- [L. *volubilis*, whirling, fluent] *base* fluent; easily set in motion (volubilate, volubility)

volucr- [L. *volucer/volucr-*, fitted for flight] *base* bird (volucrary, volucrine)

volupt- [L. *voluptas/voluptat-*, pleasure] *base* pleasure (voluptuary, voluptuous)

-volut-, -volv- [L. *volvere/volut-*, to roll] *base* turn (revolution, revolve)

vomero- [L. *vomer*, ploughshare] *comb* bone dividing the nostrils (vomeronasal, vomero-palatine)

vomic- [L. *vomicus*, ulcerous] *base* abscess (vomica, vomicose)

-vora, -vore, -vorous [L. *vorare*, to devour] *comb* feeding on; eating (Carnivora, herbivore, omnivorous)

-vorag- [L. *vorago*, chasm, abyss] *base* chasm; whirlpool (vorageous, voraginous)

vortici- [L. *vortex/vortic-*, whirling] *comb* whirling motion; vortex (vorticiform, vorticose)

vulcan- [L. *Volcanus*, Vulcan, god of fire] *comb* volcanoes (Vulcanic, vulcanology)

-vulg- [L. *vulgus*, multitude, mass of people] *base* common; the public (divulge, vulgar)

-vuln- [L. *vulnus*, wound] *base* wound (invulnerable, vulnerose)

vulpi- [L. *vulpes*, fox] *base* fox (vulpicide, vulpine)

vult- [L. *vultus*, countenance] *base* likeness; visage (invultuation, vultuous)

vultur- [L. *vultur*, a vulture] *base* vulture (vulturian, vulturine)

vulvi-, vulvo- [L. *vulva*, vulva] 1. *comb* vulva (vulviform); 2. vulva and (vulvovaginal)

W

-ward [AS. -weard, in the direction of] suf having a specified direction (homeward, westward)

-ways [OE weg, to move, journey] suf in a specified direction, manner, or position (breadthways, sideways)

-wheeler [OE wheol, circle] comb having a specified kind or number of wheels (eighteen-wheeler, two-wheeler)

-wide [AS. wid, broad] comb throughout a given space (storewide, worldwide)

-wife [AS. wif, woman] comb traditional female role (housewife, midwife)

-wise [ME wyse, way, manner] 1. suf in a specified; direction, manner, or position (sidewise); 2. characteristic manner (clockwise); 3. with regard to; in connection with (weatherwise)

with- [AS. with-, against] 1. comb away; back (withdraw); 2. against; from (withhold)

-witted [OE i-wit, faculty] comb having a specified kind of intelligence (dim-witted, quick-witted)

-woman [OE wifmon, woman human being] comb female (congresswoman, horsewoman)

-worthy [OE wurthe, worthy] comb deserving of; fit for (blameworthy, newsworthy)

X

xantho- [Gr. ksanthos, yellow] comb yellow (xanthein, xanthoderma)

-xen- [Gr. ksenos, a guest] base host (cacoxenite, metoxeny)

xenarth- [Gr. ksenos, strange + arthron, a joint] base sloth (xenarthral)

xeno-, -xenous, -xeny [Gr. ksenos, strange] comb stranger; foreigner (xenogamy, xenophobia, lipoxenous, lipoxeny)

xenodoch- [Gr. ksenodokhia, reception of strangers] base guest house (xenodochial, xenodochy)

xero- [Gr. kseros, dry] comb dry (xerophyte, xerotic)

xest- [Gr. ksestos, polished] base polish (Xestia, xesturgy)

xilin- [Gr. ksulon, cotton-tree] base cotton (glyoxalin, xilinous)

xiph(i)-, xipho- [Gr. ksiphias, a swordfish] comb swordlike; xiphoid process; swordfish (xiphioid, xyphophyllous)

xylo-, -xylous [Gr. ksulon, wood] comb wood; (xylograph, epixylous)

xyr- [Gr. ksuron, razor] base sharp-edged; razorlike (xyrospasm, xyridaceous)

xyst- [Gr. ksuein, to scrape, smooth, polish] base scraping (xyster, xystos)

Y

-y[1] [AS -ig, full of] 1. suf characterized by; full of (healthy); 2. somewhat; rather (chilly); 3. tending to; inclined (drowsy); 4. suggestive of; somewhat like (wavy)

-y[2] [L. -ia, noun suf] 1. suf condition

of; quality (jealousy); 2. action of (inquiry)

-y³ [ME dim. suf -ie] suf diminutives; terms of endearment; nicknames (Billy, kitty)

-yer [ME -ier, agent suf] suf person concerned with (buyer, lawyer)

yester- [AS geostran-, of the day before] comb previous time (yesterday, yesteryear)

-yl [Gr. hule, wood, matter] suf [chemistry] names of radicals (butyl, methyl)

ylo- see hylo-

yocto- [L. octo, eight, > 8th power of a thousandth] comb septillionth (yoctogram, yoctosecond)

yotta- [L. octo, eight, > the 8th power of a thousand] comb one septillion (yottahertz, yottameter)

ypsili- [Gr. letter upsilon] comb Y-shaped (ypsiliform)

-ysis [Gr. lusis, a loosening] suf action; process (acetolysis, electrolysis). See -lysis

yttro- [NL > Ytterby, Sweden] comb yttrium (yttrocerite, yttrotitanite)

Z

za- [Gr. za-, intensive pref] pre intensifier (zalambdodont, zamelodia)

zamia-, zamio- [L. zamia, fir-cone] base coniferous plant (Zamia, Zamiostrobus)

zanclo- [Gr. zanclon, a sickle] comb like a sickle (Zanclodon, Zanclognatha)

zebr- [Fr. zebre, zebra] base zebra (zebraic, zebrine)

zelo- [Gr. zelos, zeal] base zeal; emulation (zelotic, zelotypia)

zemni- [Russ. zemnoi, earthy] base mole rat (zemniphobia, zemni-rat)

zeo- [Gr. zeein, to boil, foam] comb altered; converted (zeolite, zeoscope)

-zephyr- [Gr. zephuros, the west wind] base west wind (zephyranth, zephyrean)

zepto- [L. septem, seven > the 7th power of a thousandth] comb one-sextillionth (zeptosecond, zeptovolt)

zesto- [Gr. zestos, boiling hot] comb hot (zestocausis, zestocautery)

zetet- [Gr. zetein, to seek or inquire] base inquiring, seeking (zetetic, zetetics)

zetta- [L. septem, seven > 7th power of a thousand] comb one sextillion (zettabyte)

-zeug-, -zeux- [Gr. zeugle, the strap of a yoke] base yoked (zeuglodont, zeuxite)

zibel- [It. zibellino, sable] base sable (zibeline)

zinco- [NL zincum, zinc] comb zinc as an element in specific double compounds (zincography, zincolysis)

-zingiber- [Gr. zingiberis, ginger] base ginger (Zingiber, zingiberaceous)

ziph- [Gr. ksiphios, swordfish] base swordfish (ziphiiform, ziphioid). Also xiph-

zirconio- [Arab zarkun, zircon] comb zirconium (zirconioflouride)

-zo- [Gr. zoon, animal] base animal (zoanthropy, zodiophilous)

-zoa, -zoon [Gr. zoon, animal] comb [zoology] name of group (protozoa, protozoon)

-zoic [Gr. zoe, life + -ic] 1. suf relating to animal life (celozoic); 2. relating to geologic ages (Cenozoic, Mesozoic)

zon-, zoni- [Gr. zone, a girdle, belt] comb girdle; band; encircling structure (zonesthesia, zonifugal)

zono- [Gr. *zone*, a girdle, belt] *comb* zoned, banded (zonochlorite, zonociliate)

zoo- [Gr. *zoon*, animal] 1. *comb* animal; animal body (zoology); 2. zoology and (zoochemical)

-zooid [Gr. *zoon*, living being] *comb* distinct animal (allozooid, Antherozooid)

-zoon [Gr. *zoon*, living being] *comb* animal, living thing (cryptozoon, spermatozoon)

zopher- [Gr. *zopheros*, dusky] *base* dusky (Zopherus)

zorill- [NL *zorilla*, a zoril] *base* African skunk (Zorillinae, zorilline)

zoster- [Gr. *zoster*, girdle] *base* band; shingles (zosteriform, zosterops)

zyga-, zygo-, -zygous [Gr. *zugon*, a yoke] *comb* yoke; pair; articulation (zygapophysis, zygodactyl, heterozygous)

zygomatico-, zygomato- [NL *zygomaticus*, zygoma and] *comb* [anatomy] related to the zygoma (zygomatico-auricular, zygomato-temporal)

zym-, zymo- [Gr. *zume*, leaven] *comb* fermentation; enzymes; yeast (zymurgy, zymophoric)

zyth- [Gr. *zuthos*, beer] *base* brewery; beer (zythepsary, zythum)

PART II
Finder
(Reverse Dictionary)

A

aardvark *base* -edent-

abandon *base* relinq-

abbreviated *comb* brachisto-, brachy-,
  brevi-, micro-, mini-, parvi-, parvo-,
  steno-; *base* -cort-, -curt-; *suf* -cle,
  -cula, -cule, -culum, -culus, -een,
  -el, -ella, -en, -et, -ette, -idion,
  -idium, -ie, -illa, -illo, -isk, -le, -let,
  -ling, -ock, -ola, -ole, -rel, -ula, -ule,
  -ulum, -ulus, -y

abdomen *comb* abdomino-, celio-,
  celo-[1], coelo-, laparo-, ventri-, ven-
  tro-; *distended~:* ventricoso-

abdominal sac *comb* peritoneo-

abet *base* auxil-, jut-, juv-

abhorrence *comb* miso-, -phobe,
  -phobia, -phobic; *base* -invid-,
  -ira(sc)-, odi-

ability *base* -apt-[2], -habil-, -poten-,
  -qual-; *suf* -bility, -ful, -ship

able to *comb* -potent; *suf* -able, -ible,
  -ile; *in an ~ way:* -bly; *able to be
  ___: suf* -ilia

abnormal *comb* allo-, allotrio-,
  anom(o)-, poecilo-, poikilo-; *~ attraction: comb* -lagnia, -philia,
  -philiac; *~ condition: pre* para-; *suf*
  -ism, -osis, -otic; *~ discharge: comb*
  -(r)rhage, -(r)rhagy, -(r)rhagia; *~
  enlargement: comb* megalo-,
  -megaly; *~ smallness: comb* micro-

abode *comb* -cole, -colent, -colous,
  eco-, oiko-; *base* aed-, dom-, edi-

abolish *base* fin-, perd-, termin-,
  vast-; *suf* -ate-[4]

about *pre* be-, circum-, peri-; *comb*
  amphi-; *base* -zon-, -cing-, -cinct-

above *pre* ano-[1], epi-, hyper-, ob-,
  super-, supra-, sur-, ultra-; *comb*
  over-, poly-

abscess *base* apostem-, vomic-

abscond *base* drapeto-, phygo-

absence *pre* a-, an-, dis-, ex-, il-, im-,
  in-, ir-, un-; *comb* lipo-; *base* -priv-;
  suf -less; *~ of an opening: comb* -

atresia, atreto-; *~ of a part: comb*
  ectro-; *~ of urine: base* anur-[2]

absorb *comb* -sorb; *base* bib-

abstinent *base* nephal

absurd *base* fatu-, inan-, moro-, stult-

abundance *base* ampl-, copi-, larg-

abusive *comb* noci-, pesti-; *base* -nox-,
  pericul-

abyss *comb* batho-, bathy-; *base* -byss-,
  chao-

accept *base* -cap-, -cep-, -cip-, -dyte-

accessory *pre* co-, para-[2], syn; *comb*
  inter-

accidents *base* -tich-, -tych(o)-

accord *pre* co-; *base* concinn-, congru-,
  consil-, unanim-

accumulation *comb* cumulo-; *base*
  acerv-, -sor-

accurate *comb* ortho-, recti-

acetic *comb* acet-

acetyl *comb* aceto-, acetyl-

acid *comb* ortho-, oxy-[1]; -*base* -acerb-,
  -oxal-; **formic ~:** *comb* formo-;
  suberic ~: *comb* subero-; **unsaturated ~:** *suf* -enoic

acorn *comb* balani-, balano-; *base*
  -gland-

acquire *base* -cap-, -cep-, -cip-, -dyte-;
  acquired: base ctet-

acrid *comb* picro-; *base* -acerb-,
  -mord-

acrimonious *base* acerb-, mord-

across *pre* dia-, per-, trans-; *comb*
  transverso-

act (to) *base* -fac-, -fec-, -fic-; *suf*
  -age, -ate, -ize

act of *comb* -craft; *suf* -ade, -age, -al,
  -ance, -ancy, -asis, -asm, -ation, -cy,
  -ence, -ency, -ery, -esis, -iasis, -ice[1],
  -ics, -ing, -ion, -ism, -ment, -osis,
  -otic, -sion, -sis, -th, -tion, -tious,
  -ture, -ure, -y[2], -ysis

actinic rays *comb* actino-

activity *comb* -ergasia, ergasio-, -ergic,
  ergo-, -ergy, -orial, -pragia, -praxia,

-praxis; *suf* -esce, -escence, -escent, -esis; **muscular ~:** *comb* kinesi-, -kinesia, -kinesis, kineso-, kino-; ***quality of ~:*** *comb* -pragia

actor *base* histrion-, thesp-

actual *base* ver-

acute *comb* oxy-[1]; *base* acer-, -grav-, vehem-

adamant *base* contum-, obstin-, pervic-, proterv-

adder *base* colub-

addicted to *comb* -aholic

addition *pre* a-, ac-, ad-, af-, ag-, al-, an-, ap-, ar-, as-, at-, extra-, super-. *See* **more**

adherent *suf* -ist, ite

adjacent *base* contig-, -tang-, vicin-. *See* **near**

adjusted *base* concinn-, teino-

admirable *pre* bene-, eu-; *base* agath-, bon-, prob-

adolescent *base* epheb-

adrenal gland *comb* adren(o)-

adroit *base* agil-, facil-, ingen-

adulterated *base* kibdelo-

advance *pre* pro-; *base* ced-, cess-

adversarial *base* hostil-, inimic-

affable *base* comit-

affected with *suf* -otic

affecting *comb* -tropic

affection *base* -storgy

affinity *comb* -trope. *See* **attracted**

affluence *comb* chryso-, pluto-; *base* chrem-, -opul-, pecun-

afraid *base* pavid-, tim-, trepid-. *See* **fear**

African *comb* Afro-

after *pre* meta-, post-; *comb* hystero-, opistho-, postero-, retro-

aftereffect *suf* -age, -asm, -ata, -ation, -ency, -ism, -ma, -ment, -mony, -sion, -ure

afternoon *base* pomerid-

again *pre* ana-, re-; *base* -pali(n)-

against *pre* anti-, cata-, cath-, contra-, contre-, ob-, with-; *comb* antio-, contro-, counter-, enantio-

agate *base* agati-

age *pre* eo-; *comb* chrono-; *base* aev-, -temp-; *suf* -arian. *See* **old**

agent *suf* -ant, -ate[3], -ator, -ent, -ure

agitate *base* agit-, mov-, trepid-, turb-

agouti *base* dasyproct-

agree(ment) *pre* co-; *base* concinn-, congru-, consil-, unanim-

aid *base* -auxil-, -jut-, -juv-

ailment *pre* dys-, mal-; *comb* noso-, path-, -pathic, patho-, -pathy; *base* aegr-, cachex-, -morb-, -pecca-, valetud-

air *comb* aer-, aeri-, aero-, anemo-, atmo-, physo-, -pnea, pneo-, pneumato-, pneumo-, pneumono-; *base* -flat-, -vent-

albatross *base* diomed-, -procellar-

alcohol *suf* -ol

aldehydes *suf* -al, -ole

alder *base* clethr-

algae (type of) *comb* seiro-

alike *pre* co-; *comb* equi-, homo-, iso-, pari-, tauto-

alive *comb* bio-, -biosis, quick-, vivi-, -zoic, zoo-, -zooid; *base* -anim-, vita-

alkaline *base* lixiv-

alkaloid names *suf* -ia; **~ synthetic:** *comb* -caine; **~ with nitrogen bases:** -ine

all *pre* be-, cata-, cath-, de-, kata-, ob-, per-; *comb* holo-, omni-, pan-[1], panto-, pasi-, toti-

allay *base* sedat-

allied **~ by blood** *base* cogn-[2]; **~ by friendship** *comb* socio-; *base* -am-, amic-[1], comit-

alligator *base* -eusuch-

allow *base* conced-, concess-

allure *base* lenocin-

almond *comb* amygdal(o)-

almost *comb* pene-

alone *pre* mono-; *comb* eremo-, soli-, uni-

alteration *pre* meta-, trans-; *comb* -plasia, -plasis, -tropic, zeo-; *base* -mut-, -vari-, -vert-. *See* **change**

aluminum *comb* alumino-

alveolus *comb* alveolo-
always *comb* ever-; *base* aei-, etern-,
  semper-
amber *comb* succino-
ambiguous *base* ambig, ancip-, dub-,
  pariso-
ameba *comb* amebi-, amebo-
amend *pre* be-, em-, en-, meta-, trans-;
  comb aetio-, -blast, -blastic, blasto-,
  -craft, ergo-, etio-, -facient, -fic,
  -fication, -gen, -genesis, -genic,
  -genous, -geny, -parous, -plasia,
  -plasis, plasmo-, -plast, -plastic,
  plasto-, -plasty, -poiesis, -poietic,
  -trope, -tropic, -tropism, tropo-,
  -tropous, -tropy, -urgy; *base* camb-,
  -fabr-, -fec-, -mut-, -vari-, -vert-;
  suf -ate, en, -fy, -ize, -otic
amide *comb* -amic²; ~ *radical:* amido-
ammines *comb* ammino-
ammonia *comb* ammonio-, am-
  mono-
amnesia *base* amensi-, amnesi-
amniotic sac *comb* amnio-
among *pre* dia-, epi-; *comb* enter-,
  inter-
amount *comb* quanti-; *suf* -age, -ful,
  ling
ample *base* ocho-²
amplify *pre* ad-, extra-, hyper-, super-;
  comb auxano-, auxo-, multi-, myria-,
  myrio-, out-, over-, -plasia, pleni-,
  pleo-, pleio-, pleon-, plethys-, plio-,
  pluri-, pollaki-, poly-; *base* ampl-,
  -aug-, -cresc-, dilat-, -fold-, pler-,
  -plet-
anal *comb* ano-², hedro-, podic-
ancestors *comb* patroio-
anchor- *base* ancyr-
anchovy *base* -engraul-
ancient *comb* archaeo-, archeo-,
  palaeo-, paleo-, proto-; *base* -antiq-,
  prisc-, -vet-
anesthetic *comb* -caine
anew *pre* ana-, re-; *base* -palin-
angelfish *base* pterophyll-
anger *base* chol-, fur-¹, -invid-, -ira-,
  -margy

angle *comb* -angle, -gon, -gonal,
  gonio-; *base* -angul-
anguish *comb* lype-; *base* dolor-, fleb-,
  flet-, luct-, trist-
anhydride *comb* anhydro-
animal *comb* therio-, thero-, zoo-,
  -zooid; *base* -fer-, zo-; ~ *classes: suf*
  -acea; *early ~ form: comb* larvi-; ~
  group name: suf -id¹, -ida, -idae, -
  iformes, -zoa, -zoic, -zoon; *wild ~:*
  fer-. *Also see* "Animals" *in Part III*
animation *comb* bio-, -biosis, vita-,
  vivi-, zoo-, -zoic, -zooid; *base*
  -anim-
ankle (bone) *comb* astragalo-, tali-,
  talo-
annelids *base* saen-
annoy *base* vex-
another *comb* allelo-, allo-, alter-, het-
  ero-; *base* -ali-²
answer *base* apocris-. *See* **say**
ant *comb* myrmec-, myrmeco-, myr-
  mic-; *base* -formic-; *white ~: base*
  isoptero-
anteater *base* myrmecophag-
antelope *base* -alcelaph-, -bubal-,
  tragelaph-
antenna *base* cornic-
anterior *pre* fore-; *comb* antero-,
  proso-
anther *comb* -antherous
antibiotic *comb* -mycin
antibodies, having *comb* -valent
antimony *comb* stibio-
antrum *comb* antro-
anus *comb* ano-², hedro-, podic-
any __ of those possible *comb* -soever
aorta *comb* aorto-
apart *pre* de-, des-, di-², dia-, dis-, for-,
  se-; *comb* chori-, choristo-, dialy-
ape *comb* pithec-, -pithecus; *base* -sim-
aperture *base* -pylo-. *See* **hole**
apex *comb* -apical, apico-
apparel *comb* hestho-
apparent *comb* lampro, luc-, luci-;
  base -clar-
apparition *base* phantas-, phasm-
appearance *comb* -phane, phanero-,

-phanic, -phany, pheno-; *base*
-schem-, -spec-, -spic-
appease *base* -plac-
appendix *comb* ecphia-
appetite *comb* orect-, -orexia, -sitia,
sitio-, sito-; *base* esur-
apple *base* mali-, pomi-
applied to *comb* -specific
approximately *suf* -ish
arched *comb* arci-, cyrto-; *base* -fornic-
archery *comb* toxo-[2]
ardor *base* ard-, alacr-, -ferv-, zelo-
arduous *pre* dys-; *comb* -bar, bary-,
mogi-; *base* ardu-, stren-
argument *comb* -machy; *base* litig-,
pugil-, -pugn-, -rix-
arid *comb* carpho-, xero-; *base* arid-,
-celo-, -sicc-
arm *limb: comb* acromio-, brachio-;
upper ~: comb humero
armadillo *base* dasypod-, tatus-,
-tolypeut-
armor *comb* hoplo-
armpit *base* -axill-, maschal-
aroma *comb* brom(o)-, odori-, odoro-,
olfacto-,-osmia, osmo-, osphresio-,
ozo-, ozono-
around *pre* be-, circum-, peri-; *comb*
ambi-, ambo-, amphi-; *base* -cing-,
-cinct-, -zon-
arouse *comb* agito-; *base* -cit-
arrange(ment) *comb* -tactic, -tactous,
-taxis, taxo-, -taxy; *base* -pos-,
-struct-; *suf* -ate
arrest *stop: comb* stasi-, -stasis, -stat,
stato-
arrow *base* belo-, -sagitt-
arsenic *comb* arseno-
art *comb* craft-, -ship, techno-,
-techny; *suf* -ics
artery *comb* arterio-, -venous
articulation *comb* zyga-, zygo-
as if *comb* pseudo-, quasi-
ash tree *base* -frax(in)-, -melia-[2];
mountain ~: sorb-[2]
ashes *comb* ciner-, pulver-, spodo-,
tephro-; *base* favill-
ask *base* -pet-, -quir-, -quis-, -rog-

aspirate *comb* rhopheo-
ass *base* as-, ono-
assault *base* impet-
assaying *base* docim-
assemblage *suf* -ad, -age, -ery, -hood,
-ship
assemble *base* -fabr-, -fac-, -fec-, -fic-,
-struct-
assenting *comb* homolo
assist *base* -auxil-, -jut-, -juv-
assistance *base* -(ad)jut-, -(ad)juv-,
auxil-
assistant *comb* vice-
assumption *comb* -lemma[1]
astragalus *comb* astragalo-, talo-
astringent *base* stypt-
at *pre* ad-, juxta-; *~ the same time: pre*
co-, syn-; *comb* -simul-
atlas *map: comb* carto-; *vertebra:*
comb atlanto-, atlo-
atmosphere *comb* -bar, baro-; *base*
chao-
atrophy *base* -tabe-
attack *fight: base* -pugil-, -pugn-;
seizure: comb -agra, -lepsia, -lepsis,
-lepsy, -leptic
attempt *base* conat-, peir-
attend to *comb* -serve; *attendant: base*
-serv-
attracted to *comb* -phile, -philia,
-philiac, -philic, -philism, philo-,
-philous, -trope, -tropic, -tropism,
-tropous, -tropy; *base* -urient
augmented *pre* ad-, extra-, hyper-,
super-; *comb* auxano-, auxo-, multi-,
myria-, myrio-, out-, over-, -plasia,
pleni-, pleo-, pleio-, pleon-, plethys-,
plio-, pluri-, pollaki-, poly-; *base*
ampl-, -aug-, -cresc-, dilat-, -fold-,
pler-, -plet-
auk *base* alcid-
aunt *base* -amita-, -matertera-
auricle *comb* atrio-
authority *comb* exousia-; *base* imper-,
magist-
authorized *comb* cyrio-, kyrio-
automobile *comb* amaxo-, -mobile;
base harmat-, -ocho-

avarice *base* avar-, avid-, cup(id)-,
   edac-, gulos-, pleonec-, pleonex-
avocado *base* pers-
avoid *base* avers-, drapeto-, fug-,
   phygo-
away (from) *pre* ab-, abs-, apo-, be-,

de-, des-, di-², dia-, dif-, dis-, e-, ec-,
   ef-, ex-, for-, off-¹, se, with-; *comb*
   ectro-
awl *base* subul-
ax *base* axin-, dolabri-, securi-, pelec-
axis *comb* axi-, axio-¹, axo-

B

baby *comb* brepho-, nepi-
bacillus *comb* bacill-, bacilli-, bacillo-
back *pre* ana-, re-, un-, with-; *comb*
   retro-; *the ~: comb* back-, dorsi-,
   dorso-, nota-, noto-, tergi-, tergo-;
   ~ of the knee: base poplit-
backbone *comb* rachi-, rachio-, rhach-,
   rhachio-
backward *comb* opiso-, retro-
bacteria *comb* bacter-, bacteri-, bacte-
   rio-, coccal, -coccic, cocco-, coccoid,
   -coccus, mycin; *base* -ella
badger *base* -melin-, -mustel-
bad(ly) *pre* dys-, mis-; *comb* caco-, -
   iniq-, kaki-, kako-, mal-¹, male-,
   perv-, ponero-, -prav-, -turp-, vitia-
bag(like) *comb* angio-, asco-, bursi-,
   burso-, ceco-, chlamyd-, chrysali-,
   coleo-, cyst, -cyst, cysti-, cysto-,
   follic-, pericardiaco-, pericardio-,
   peritoneo-, phasco- physa-, physali,
   physo-, -theca, theco-, typhlo-, utri-²,
   utric-, vesico-; *base* -sacc-, -thylac-
balance *comb* counter-, libra-, pariso-,
   stasi-, -stasis, -stat, stato-
bald *base* alopec-, -calv-, glabr-,
   madar-, -pelad-, -phalacr-
ball-shaped *comb* globi-, globo-,
   -sphere, sphero-; *base* -glom-. *See*
   circle
ballot *base* tabell-, suffrag-
bamboo *base* bambus-
ban *pre* anti-; *base* imped-, prohib-
banana *base* musa-
band *comb* desmo-, syndesmo-, taeni-,
   teni-, -trocha , zon-, zoni-, zoster-;
   base -lemnisc-, liga-, zoster-; *suf* -let

bang *comb* plessi-, -cuss-; *base* -cop-,
   -crot-, plang-, -puls-, -tus-, -vapul-,
   -verber-
banner *comb* labar-, vexill-
bar *base* clathr-, -ser-
barbarian *base* barbar-
barbed *base* hamat-
barber *base* tonsor-
bare *comb* gymno-, nudi-, psilo-. *See*
   bald
bark *dog: base* hylac-, latr-; *tree: base*
   cortici-, libri-, phloem-
barley *comb* alphito-; *base* crith-,
   horde-, ptis-
barracuda *base* -perces-, sphyraen-
barrel *base* dolio-
barrier *comb* herco-, septo-, parieto-,
   -phragma, phragmo-; *base* cancell-,
   claustr-, -mur-
base *foundation: comb* basi-, basidio-,
   basio-, baso-, fund-; *base* -radic-;
   evil: pre dys-, mis-; *comb* caco-,
   iniq-, kak(o)-, mal(e)-, ponero-;
   base -prav-, sceler-, turp-, vili-
basic *base* prim-, -rud-; [chemistry]
   pre sub-
basin (shaped) *comb* cylico-, kylixo-,
   lecano-, pelvi-
basket *base* calath-, -corb-
Basque *comb* Basco-
bat *base* desmodont-, megacheiropter-,
   microcheiropter, noctilion-, -pterop-,
   -vespertil-
bath(ing) *comb* balneo-; *base* -ablut-,
   -lav-
battle *comb* macho-, -machy; *base* -
   bell-, -pugil-, -pugn-

beach *base* littor-, thino-; *See* **sand**
beacon *base* fan-
beadlike *base* torul-
beak *comb* coraci-, coraco-, rhampho-, rhyncho-, rostrato-, rostri-, rostro-, -rrhyncha; *base* -aquil-, coron-. *See* **nose**
beam *base* trab-
bean *base* cyam-, fab-, phaseol-
bear *animal: comb* arcto-; *base* -urs-; *carry: comb* -fer, -ferous, -gerous, -parous, -pher, -phore, -phorous; *base* -port-, -vect-
beard *comb* pogon(o)-; *base* -barb(a)-
bearing *comb* -fer, -ferous, -gerous, -parous, -pher, phor-, -phore, -phorous; *base* -port-
beast *comb* -there, therio-, thero-; *base* fer-
beat *comb* -cuss-, plessi-, rhabdo-; *base* -cop-, -crot-, fustig-, plang-, puls-, quass-, vapul-, -verber-
beautiful *comb* calli-, callo-; *base* kal-, pulchr-
beaver *base* -castor-
become *suf* -ate[1], -en, -fy; *~like:* -ize; *~liquid: base* deliqu-
becoming *comb* -facient; *suf* -esce, -escence, -escent
bed *base* clin-
bee *comb* api(o)-, melisso-, melitto-; *base* -bomb-; *~ hive:* -alve-
beech *base* faga-, pheg-
beer *base* cervis-, zuth-
beetle *base* bruch-, coleopter-, lathro-, saco-, scarab-; *bark-beetle: base* scolyt-; *carrion-beetle: base* silph-
before *pre* ante-, fore-, ob-, pre-, pro-[2]; *comb* antero-, protero-, proto-, retro-; *base* prior-
beggar *comb* ptocho-; *base* mendic-
begin(ning) *comb* -phyletic, spermato-, -spemous; *base* incip-, -init-; *suf* -esce, -escence, -escent. *See* **origin**
behavior *comb* etho-; *base* hexi-
behind *pre* meta-, post-; *comb* after-, back-, hind-, opistho, postero, retro-; *base* terg-

being *comb* onto-; *base* -esse-
belch *base* eruct-, -ruct-
belief *comb* -ousia; *base* -cred-, -fid-[1]; *suf* -ism
believer *suf* -ist, -ite
believing in *suf* -an
bell *base* campan-, -tintinn-; *~ shaped: comb* -codonic
belligerence *base* chol-, -invid-, -ira-, -margy
bellow *base* -mug-
belly *comb* abdomino-, celio-, celo-, coelo-, laparo-, ventri-, ventro-; *base* -alv-. *See* **stomach**
belonging to *suf* -acean, -aceous, -ad, -al[3], -an[3], -ar, -arious, -ary, -atic, -ative, -atory, -eae, -ean, -eous, -ery, -etic, -ial, -ian, -ic, -id[1], -il, -ile, -ina, -inae, -ine, -ing, -ious, -istic, -ite, -itic, -itious, -itive, -ive, -oidea, -ory, -otic, -tious, -tive, -ular. *See* **characteristic of**
below *pre* hypo-, infra-, sub-, subter-; *comb* infero-, under-
belt *comb* desmo-, syndesmo-, taeni-, teni-, -trocha , zon-, zoni-; *base* -lemnisc-, liga-, zoster-; *suf* -let
bend, bent *comb* ancylo-, ankylo-, -campsis, campto-, campylo-, -clinal, -clinate, -cline, -clinic, clino-, -clinous, -clisis, curvi-, cyrto-, -flect, flex-, flexuouso-, klino-, lechrio-, loxo-, recurvi-, recurvo-, repando-, scolio-, -tort-, -verge; *base* -clit-, cliv-, declin-, pand-, -sinu-; *~ inward: base* adunc-
benefit *base* -auxil-, -jut-, -juv-
benzine *pre* meta-; *comb* benzo-, phen-
benzoyl group *base* benzoxy-
benzyl group *base* benzyloxy-
bereavement *comb* lype-; *base* dolor-, fleb-, flet-, luct-, trist-
berry *comb* baccato-, bacci-, cocci-; *base* -acin-
beside *pre* a-, ac-, ad-, af-, ag-, al-, an-, ap-, ar-, as-, at-, by-, epi-, para-[2], peri-; *comb* juxta-, citra-, pene-, proximo-

besides *pre* extra-
best *comb* aristo-; *base* -opt-[2]
bestow *base* -don-
better *comb* melior-, out-; *base* prior-
between *pre* dia-, epi-; *comb* enter-, inter-
bewitched *base* fascin-
beyond *pre* ex-, extra-, meta-, para-[2], preter-, super-, supra-, sur-, ultra-; *comb* over-
Bible *comb* biblio-
big *base* grand-, magn-. *See* **large**
bile *comb* bili-, chole-, cholo-, gall-
billion *comb* giga-. *Also see* "Numbers" in Part III
billionth *comb* nanno-, nano-
billow *comb* cyma-, cymato-, cymo-
bind *comb* sphingo-, -strain, -strict, syndesmo-; *base* liga-, -merinth-, nex-, -string-, -vinc-; ~ **tightly:** *base* sphingo-; **binding:** *comb* -desis
bipartite *comb* diphy-. *See* **two**
birch *base* betul-
bird *comb* orneo-, orni-, ornitho-, orno-; *base* -avi-, grall-, muscicap-, oscin-, passer-, pendulin-, volucr-; ~ **lime:** *base* ixo-; **weaver ~:** *base* ploc-
birth *comb* -genic, -natal, -para, -tocia, -toky; *base* geneth-, -nasc-, -partur-; ~ **day:** geneth-
birthmark *comb* nevi-, nevo-; *base* naev-
bishop *base* episcop-
biting *comb* aceto-, keto-, oxal-, oxy-; *base* -acid-, -mord-
bitter *comb* picro-; *base* -acerb-, asper-, botaur-, -mord-
bittern *base* botaur-, ixobrych-
black *comb* atro-, melano-, nigri-, nigro-, piceo-; *base* -ebon-, fulig-. *Also see* "Colors" in Part III
black widow *base* latrodect-
blackbird *base* -icter-, merul-
blade (broad) *comb* spathi-
bladder *comb* asco-, burs-, bursi-, burso-, ceco-, cyst-, -cyst, cysti-, cysto-, follic-, physa-, physali-, physo-, typhlo-, utri-, utric-, vesico-,

vesiculi-, vesiculo-; *base* med-, -sacc-, -thylac-
blame *base* culp-, reprehen-, -vituper-
blanket *base* -lodic-
blemish *comb* nevi-, nevo-; *base* naev-
blend *pre* co-; *comb* conjugato-, -ergasia, gameto-, gamo-, hapto-, junct-; *base* aps-, apt-, -greg-, -soc-; *suf* -ate, -ize
blessed *base* macar-
blight *comb* fungi-, -mycete, myceto-, -mycin, myco-, uredo-
blind *comb* caeco-, ceco-, typhlo-; *base* -lusc-
blink *base* -conniv-, -nict-
blister *comb* phlyc-, vesica-, vesico-, vesiculo-; *base* bullat-, pustul-
blood *comb* haema-, haemo-, hema-, hemato-, hemo-, sangui-, sanguineo-, sanguino-; *base* cruent-, cruor-; ~ **clot:** thrombo-; ~ **condition or disease:** -aemia, -cythemia, -emia; ~ **fluid:** lympho-; ~ **vessels:** hemangio-, vasculo-, vaso-
blooming *comb* thalero-; *base* flor-, vig-
blow wind: *base* anemo-, flat-, vent-; **punch:** *comb* plessi-; *base* cop-, -crot-, -cuss-, -plang-, puls-, -tus-, vapul-, -verber-
blue *comb* cyano-, glauco-; *base* adular-, aerug-, -azur-, -caes-, -cerul-, -lazul-, -livid-, -pavon-; **bluish-green:** *comb* glauco-. *Also see* "Colors" in Part III
blueberry *base* vaccin-
bluebird *base* sial-[2], -turd-
blunder *base* culp-, delinq-, laps-, pecc-, sphal-
blunt *comb* obtusi-; *base* hebet-
boar *base* suid-
boasting *base* kompo-, thras-
boat (-shaped) *comb* navi-, scapho-, scapulo-; *base* -cymb-
bobolink *base* -icter-
body *comb* physico-, physi-, physio-, somato-, -some[1]; *base* -corp-; **dead ~:** *comb* necro-; *base* -cadav-; ~ **defect:**

base -hamart-; ~ **odor:** brom-, ozostom-; ~ **organ part:** *suf* -ite
bog *base* helo-, telmat-; **peat ~:** *base* turbar-
boil (up) *base* aestu-, -coct-, decoct-, ebullio-, ferv-
boils *base* furunc-
bold *base* audac-, feroc-
bolt *base* gomph-, pessul-, -ser-
bond *comb* desmo-, ligamenti-, ligamento-, syndesmo-; *base* -caten-, -vinc-; **double ~:** *suf* -ylene
bone *comb* ossi-, osseo-, osteo-; **forearm ~:** ulno-; ~ **joining hipbones:** sacro-; ~ **membrane:** periosteo-; **finger or toe ~:** phalang-; **frontal~:** *base* fronto-; **bony process:** *comb* stylo-; **small bone of the ear:** *comb* incudo-
book *comb* biblio-; *base* -libr-; ~ **size:** *suf* -mo; ~ **worm:** tinea-
border *base* fimbr-, -marg-, propinq-, prox-, termin-. ~ **bordered:** *base* crasp-, limbat- See **near** or **surrounding**
bore *base* terebr-; **borer:** *comb* trypano-
born *comb* -genic, -natal, -para, -tocia, -toky; *base* geneth-, -nasc-, partur-; ~ **in:** *suf* -an
boron *comb* boro-
bosom *base* grem-
both *comb* ambi-, ambo-; ~ **sides:** amphi-, ampho-, bi-
bother *base* vex-
bottle *base* ampull-, lagen-; **leather ~:** utrei-, utri-
bottom *pre* sub-; *comb* basi-, fund-; *base* -radic-
boundary *comb* orismo-; *base* fin-, termin-
bow *base* arci-
bowel cavity *base* cloac- See **intestines**
bowl *comb* cymbi-, cymbo-, crater-, cylico-, kylixo-
box *comb* pyx-; ~ **tree:** *base* bux-, locul-

boy *base* puer-
bragging *base* kompo-, thras-
brain *comb* cephal-, cerebri-, cerebro-, encephalo-
brambles *comb* bato-²
bran *base* furfur-, pityr-
branch *comb* clado-, rami-; *base* stol-; **branchy:** *comb* ramoso-
brass *comb* chalco-; *base* -aenio-
brave *base* audac-, feroc-
brazen *base* contum-, impud-, procac-
bread *base* arto-, pan-²
breakfast *base* -jent-
break(ing) *comb* -clasia, -clasis, -clastic, -rhegma, -(r)rhexis; *base* agmat-, -fract-, -frag-, -frang-, -rupt-; **broken down:** *base* decrep-
breast *comb* mammi-, mammo-, mastia-, -masto-, mazo-², stetho-; *base* pect-; ~ **bone:** sterni-, sterno-. See **nipple**
breath *comb* -hale, -pnea, pneo-, pneumato-, pneumo-, pneumono-, pneusio-, pulmo-, spiro-¹; *base* afflat-; **bad ~:** -halit-, ozostom-
breed *base* thremm-
brewery *base* zuth-
brick *base* -later-, plinthi-; ~ **color:** *comb* testaceo-
bridge *base* gephyr-, pont-
brief *comb* brachio-, brachisto-, brachy-, brevi-, chamae-, hekisto-, micro-, mini-, parvi-, parvo-, steno-, tapino-; *base* -cort-, -curt-, exig-; *suf* -cle, -cula, -cule, -een, -el, -ella, -en, -et, -ette, -idion, -idium, -ie, -illa, -illo, -isk, -kin, -le, -let, -ling, -ock, -ola, -ole, -rel, -ula, -ule, -ulum, -ulus, -y
bright *comb* helio-; *base* -clar-, -fulg-, -gano-, -luc-, -lumin-, nitid-
brine *base* muri-
bring *base* -duc-, -fer-, -port- . See **carry**
bring forth *comb* maieusi-, -parous; *base* partur-
brisk *comb* ocy-, tacho-, tachy-; *base* alacr-, celer-, festin-, veloc-

bristle *comb* chaeta-, chaeti-, chaeto-, seti-; ***bristly:*** *base* echin-; ***little ~:*** *base* setul-
broad *comb* eury-, lati-, platy-
broccoli *base* brassic-
broken down *comb* rhesto-
bromine *comb* bromo-
broom *comb* scopa-, scopi-
brothel *base* lupan-
brother *comb* frater-, fratri-; *base* -adelph-
brown *comb* fusco-, -phaein, phaeo-; *base* aen-, brun-, castan-, -fulv-, -gland-, lur-, mustel-, -spad-, -testac-. *Also see* "Colors" *in Part III*
bruise *base* livid-, -tus-
brush *comb* scopa-, scopi-; *base* muscar-; ***brushlike:*** *comb* scopuli-; *base* saro-
bubble *comb* pego-, physali-; *base* bullat-
bucket *base* antl-
buckthorn *base* -rhamn-
buckwheat *base* fagopyr-
bud *base* gemm-[1]
buffalo *base* bubal-
buffoon *comb* balatro-
bug *comb* cimic-, core-[2], entomo-, insecti-, insecto-
build *base* -fabr-, -fac-, -fec-, -fic-, -struct-
building *base* aedi-, edi-, tecton-
bulb(ous) *comb* bulbo-; *base* cep-[2]
bulge *comb* -cele, -edema, ganglio-, phlogo-, phym-, -phyma, physa-, physo-, strum(i)-; *base* aug-, cresc-, physc-, strum-, -tum-, -turg-; *suf* -itis
bulk *base* corp-
bull *comb* tauri-, tauro-
bullfinch *base* pyrrhul-
bull-headed *base* contum-, obstin-, pervic-, proterv-
bully *base* -procac-
bundle *comb* fasciculato-, fascio-; *base* phacell-, -sarcin-
bunting *base* emberiz-, pyrrhul-
burden(ed) *comb* hypegia-, hypengy-, -ridden; *base* -oner-, paralip-
burdensome *pre* dys-; *comb* -bar, bary-, mogi-; *base* ardu-, stren-
burial *base* sepul-
burning *comb* causto-, igni- pyro-; *base* ard-[1], ars-, cauter-, celo-[2], combur-, combust-, crem-, phlog-, -ust-
burrow *base* fod-
bursting *base* -rrhexis-, -rupt-. *See* **breaking**
bury *base* -hum-
burying place *comb* kil(l)-. *See* **tomb**
bush *base* thamn-
business *base* -negot-, nundin-
butcher *base* lania-
butter *comb* butyro-
butterfly *base* lepidopter-, papil-
buttocks *comb* -pygia, pygo-; *base* nati-, podic-
buzzard *comb* buteo-; *base* cathart-
buy *comb* onio-; *base* -empt-, -merc-, nundin-
by *pre* ad-, by-, epi-, peri-; *comb* juxta-; *base* -prox-; ~ ***means of:*** *pre* syn-

C

cabbage *base* brassic-
calcium *comb* calc-, calci-
calf *base* ***animal:*** vitul-; ***leg:*** sura-
call *base* appell-, -claim, -clam-, -dict-, -nom-, -voc-; ~ ***upon:*** *base* -prec-
callus *comb* tylo-
calm *base* placid-, sedat-, tranquil-

calyx *comb* calath-, calyc-, cotyle-, cotyli-, cotylo-, cupuli-, cyathi-, cyatho-, scyphi-, scypho-; *base* calic-, crin-, cyphell-, pocul-
camel *comb* cameli-
camp *base* castr-
camphor *comb* campho-

cancel *base* oblit-
cancer *comb* scirrho-; *base* carcin(o)-
canine *comb* cyno-, kyno; *base* -can-[1];
  ~ *tooth: base* laniar-
cap *base* -pile-
capable of being *suf* -able, -ibility,
  -ible, -ibly, -ile
capacious *base* ocho-[2]
capsule *comb* capsuli-, capsulo-
car *comb* amaxo-; *base* harmat-
carbohydrate *suf* -ose[1]
carbon *comb* carbo-
carbon dioxide *comb* -capnia, capno-
carbuncle *comb* anthraco-
card *comb* carto-, charto-
cardinal **bird:** *base* pyrrhul-
careful *base* attent-, caut-, diligen-
caries *comb* cario-
carp *base* cyprin-
carpet *base* tapet-
caressing *base* -sarmass-
carriage *base* aurig-
carry(ing) *comb* -fer, -ferous, -gerous,
  -parous, -pher, -phore, -phorous;
  base gestat-, -port-, -vect-
cart *base* plaustr-
cartilage *comb* chondr-, chondrio-,
  chondro-, xiphi-; *base* cartilag-; ***eyelid ~:*** tarso-
carve *comb* -glyph, glypto-
case *comb* angio-, chlamyd-, coleo-,
  meningo-, -theca, theci-, theco-;
  wing ~: *comb* elytri-
cash *comb* -penny ; *base* chremat-,
  -numm-, -pecun-, quaest-
cashew *base* anacard-
cassowary *base* casuar-
cast off *base* exuv-
castor oil *base* ricinol-
cat *comb* aeluro-, ailuro-, gato-; *base*
  -fel-, gale-[3]
catch *comb* -tain; *base* -cap(t)-,
  -cathex-, -ger-, -hapt-, -prehend,
  prehens-, rap-, rep-, -ten-; ***catcher:***
  base -thera
caterpillar *base* bruch-, -camp-[2], eruc-
catfish *base* silur-
catkin *base* ament-[2], -juli-

cattle ***base*** bou-, bov-, bu-
cauliflower *base* brassic-
cause, causing *pre* be-, em-, en-[2],
  meta-, trans-; *comb* aetio-, -blast,
  -blastic, blasto-, -craft, ergo-, etio-,
  -facient, -fic, -fication, -gen,
  -genesis, -genic, -genous, -geny,
  -parous, -plasia, -plasis, plasmo-,
  -plast, -plastic, plasto-, -plasty,
  -poiesis, -poietic, -trope, -tropic,
  -tropism, tropo-, -tropous, -tropy,
  -urgy; *base* -fabr-, -fec-, -mut-,
  -vert-; *suf* -ate, -en, -fy, -ize, -otic
caused by *suf* -atory, -ic, -ing
caustic *comb* cauter-; *base* eschar-;
  acrimonious: *base* acerb-, mord-
cave *comb* speleo-, troglo-; *base*
  serang-, spelunc-
cavity *comb* alveolo-, antro-, atrio-,
  -coele, coelo-, kuttaro-, parieto-,
  sino-, sinu-, syringo-, ventriculo-,
  vesiculo-, vestibulo-; *base* lacun-.
  See **hollow**
cease *comb* stasi-, -stasis, -stat; *base*
  fin-, termin-
cecum *comb* ceco-, typhlo-
cedar *base* cedr-
celebration *comb* -fest, -mas; *suf* -ia
celestial activity *comb* astro-
cell *comb* alveolo-, celli-, celluli-,
  cellulo-, -cyte, -cythemia, cyto-,
  -gonium, kyto-, -plasm, plasmato-,
  plasmo-
cellulose *comb* cello-
celom *comb* celo-[1]
Celt *comb* Celto-
cement *comb* glea-
cemetery *base* coemet-, coimet-
center *comb* centr-, centri-, -centric,
  centro-
centipede *base* chilopod-, scolopendri-
ceramic *comb* ceramo-
cereal *base* frument-, gramin-
cervical *comb* cervico-
chaff *base* palea-
chain *base* caten-, vinc-; ~ ***like:*** *base*
  hormo-
chair *base* cathedr-, sedil-

chalk *base* cimol-, -cret-, gypso-;
 [geology] *comb* cretaceo-
chamber *comb* alveolo-, atrio-, antro-,
 -coele, coelo-, parieto-, sino-, sinu-,
 sinuso-, syringo-, ventriculo-,
 vesiculo-, vestibulo-. *See* **hollow**
chamois *base* rupicap-
chance *comb* clero-, faust-, tycho-;
 base alea-, fortuit-
change *pre* be-, em-, en-, meta-, trans-;
 comb aetio-, -blast, -blastic, blasto-,
 -craft, ergo-, etio-, -facient, -fic,
 -fication, -gen, -genesis, -genic,
 -genous, -geny, -parous, -plasia,
 -plasis, plasmo-, -plast, -plastic,
 plasto-, -plasty, -poiesis, -poietic,
 -trope, -tropic, -tropism, tropo-,
 -tropous, -tropy, -urgy; *base* camb-,
 -fabr-, -fec-, -mut-, -vari-, -vert-;
 suf -ate, en, -fy, -ize, -otic
channel *comb* aulo-, follic-, meato-,
 poro-, salpingo-, siphono-, soleno-,
 stria-, striato-, strio-, syringo-, tubi-,
 tubo-, tubulo-, vasi-; *base* solen-,
 strig-
character *comb* etho-, -hood, quali-;
 suf -ity
characteristic of *suf* -an³, -ar, -ary,
 -ate², -ean, -en, -esque, -ian, -ic,
 -ical, -il, -ile, -ine, -ish, -istic, -like,
 -ly, -ous, -ular, -ulent, -ulose, -y.
 See **belonging to**
characterized by *suf* -acean, -aceous,
 -acious, -aire, -al, -ate, -ed², -eous,
 -ey, -ful, -gerous, -ial, -ine, -ious,
 -itious, -oid, -orious, -ory, -ose,
 -osity, -ous, -some, -ular, -ulent,
 -ulose, -ulous, -wise, -y¹
charcoal *base* carbon
chariot *base* harmat-
chasm *base* vorag-
chastisement *comb* mastigo-, rhabdo-;
 base castig-, peno-, poine-, -pun-
chatter *base* garrul-. *See* **talk**
cheat *base* apat-, dolero-, ludif-
checked *comb* brady-; *base* -cunct-,
 imped-, -mora-, -tard-. *See* **inhibit**
cheek *comb* bucco-, -genia, genio-,

geny-, mal-², mel(o)-², -paria, zygo-
 matico-, zygomato-
cheerful *comb* chero-, galero-; *base*
 beati-, felic-, jubil-, macar-
cheese *comb* tyro-; *base* from-; *suf*
 case-
chemicals *comb* chemo-; ***chemical***
 compound: -idine
cherry *base* -ceras-
chest ***anatomy:*** *comb* sterno-, stetho-,
 thoracico-, thoraco-; *base* pector-;
 container: *comb* cisto-, scrin-
chestnut *base* aescul-, -castan-
chew *base* manduc-, -mastic-, trog-
chickadee *base* par-²
chicken *base* gallin-, pull-. *See* **cock**
chicory *base* cichor-
chief *comb* arch-¹, archi-, proto-; *base*
 hegemon-, -prim-, -princip-
child *comb* paedo-², pedi-, pedo-²,
 proli-, tecno-; *base* -fil-², -puer-, tek-
childbirth *comb* lochio-, maieusi-,
 -para, -parous, -tocia, toco-, toko-,
 -toky; *base* -partur-, puerper-
chimpanzee *base* sim-
chin *comb* -genia, genio-, geny-,
 mento-
Chinese *comb* Chino-, Sino-
chisel *comb* scalpri-
chlorine *comb* chloro-, perchloro-
choice *base* -opt-¹, -vol-
choke *base* -pnig-
chore *comb* arti-, -craft, -ergasia, erga-
 sio-, -ergics, ergo-, -ergy, organo-,
 -urgy; *base* -labor-, lucubr-, oper-¹,
 -opus-, pono-²
chromatin *comb* chromato-
chromium *comb* -chrome
chromosones: of a specified multiple of
 __ *comb* -ploid
church *comb* ecclesiastico-, kil(l)-
chyle *comb* chyl-, chyli-, chylo-
cilia *comb* cilii-, cilio-
circle, circular *comb* ano-, annul-,
 crico-, cyclo-, disco-, globi-, globo-,
 glom-, gyro-, orbito-, -sphere,
 sphero-, stilli-, zon-, zoni-, zono-;
 base -anu-, -cing-, -cinct-, -circin-,

-circul-, -coron-, -glomer-, -numm-,
-orb-, rond-, -rot-, stemma-, -troch-
citizen (of) *base* -civ-; *suf* -an, -ian, -ite
citric *base* citro-
city *comb* -burg(h), -polis, -ton, -ville;
base asty-, -civ-, -urb-
civet *base* viverr-
clamor *base* crepit-, frem-, ligyr-,
strep(i)-, strid-, stridul-. *See* **sound**
clan *base* -phrat-
clap *base* -plaud-, -plaus-
clarion *base* -litu-
class names *suf* -ia; *specified class:*
comb -rater
clatter *base* -strepit-
clavicle *comb* cleido-, clido-
claw *comb* -chela, cheli-, helo-, ony-
cho-, -onychia; *base* -ungui-, ungul-
clay *comb* argillaceo-, argillo-, limo-[1],
pelo-
cleanse *comb* balneo-; *base* ablut-,
cathar-, -lav-, -mund-[2], -purg-
clear *comb* lampro-, luc-, luci-; *base*
-clar-
cleaver *base* -dolabr-
cleft *comb* dicho-, -fid[2], fissi-, schisto-,
schizo-, sulcato-, -tomy; *base* fatisc-,
-par-, rim-. *See* **groove**
clergy *comb* clerico-, ecclesiastico-
clever *base* ingen-
cliff *base* cremno-, scopul-
climb *base* -ascend-, ascens-, -scal-,
-scand-, -scans-
cloak *base* chlamyd-
clockwise *comb* dextr(o)-
clod *base* gleb-
close by *pre* a-, ac-, ad-, af-, ag-, al-,
an-, ap-, ar-, as-, at-, by-, cis-, epi-,
para-, peri-; *comb* citra-, juxta-,
pene-, proximo-
closed, closure *comb* -atresia, atreto-,
claustro-, cleido-, -cleisis, cleisto-,
clisto-, stego-; *base* -clithr-, -clud-,
-clus-, occlud-, occlus-
clot *comb* thrombo-; *base* grum-
clothing *base* habil-, hesto-, -vest-
cloth-like *base* pann-
cloud *comb* fracto-, nephelo-, nepho-,

nimbo-; *base* homichlo-, -nebul-,
-nubi-; *rounded~:* mammato-
cloven-footed *base* artiodactyl-
club *base* clavi-, coryn-, rhopal-;
~ *foot:* talip-; ~ *shaped: comb*
clavi-[2]
clumps *comb* cespitoso-; *base* -glob-.
See **tufts**
cluster *base* corymbi-, glom-, racem-
clutch *comb* -tain; *base* -cap(t)-,
-cathex-, -ger-, -hapt-, -prehend,
prehens-, rap-, rep-, -ten-
coach *base* aurig-
coal *comb* anthraco-; *base* -carb-
coast *shore: base* littor-, maritim-
cobalt *comb* cobalti-, cobalto-
cobbler *base* sutor-
cobweb *base* arachn-
coccus *comb* -coccal
coccyx *comb* coccy-, coccygo-
cock *base* alector-, alectry-
cockroach *base* blatt-[1]
coercion *comb* dyna-, dynamo-, mega-,
megalo-, -megaly, -sthenia, stheno-;
base -forc-, -fort-, -poten-, robor-
coil *comb* cirri-, cochlio-, gyro-, he-
lico-, spiri-, spiro-[2], strepto-; *base*
bostrych-, stromb-. *See* **curl**
coin *base* numisma-, -numm-
coincide *base* concinn-, congru-,
unanim-
coition *comb* -lagnia; *base* -coit-
cold *comb* cheima-, crymo-, cryo-,
frigo-, gelo-, kryo-, pago-, psychro-,
rhigo-; *base* alg-, glac-
collar *base* coll-[1]
collarbone *base* clavi-[1]
collection of *suf* -ad, -age, -ery, -hood,
-ship
collodion *comb* collodio-
colon *comb* coli-[1], colo-
color *comb* chromato-, -chrome,
chromo-; *base* -pigm-, -tinct-, -ting-;
colored: comb -chroous; *many-col-*
ored: comb poecilo-; *two-colored:*
comb dichro-. *Also see* "Colors" in
Part III
colorless *comb* leuco-, leuko-

column *comb* kio-; *base* stylo-[2];
  small ~: columelli-
comb *base* cteno-, strigil-; ~ *teeth:*
  pectinato-
combat *comb* macho-, -machy, pugn-;
  base -bell-, pugil-
combine *pre* co-; *comb* conjugato-, -
  ergasia, gameto-, gamo-, hapto-[2],
  junct-; *base* aps-, apt-, -greg-, -soc-;
  suf -ate, -ize; **combination** *comb*
  double-; **combined in the proportion
  of 2 to 3:** *comb* subsesqui-
combustible *comb* ard-, ars-
come *comb* -vene; *base* -ven(t)-;
  ~ *together:* *base* congru-
comestibles *comb* bromato-, -brotic,
  manduc-, opso-, -phage, phago-, -
  phagous, -phagy, -sitia, sitio-, sito-, -
  troph, -trophic, tropho-, -trophy, -
  vora, -vore, -vorous; *base* -alim-,
  -cib-, escul-, -gust-, -nutr-; *partially
  digested ~:* chymo-
command *base* -imper-, juss-, -mand-
commence *base* inaug-, incip-, init-
commerce *base* negot-, nundin-
commercial names *suf* -co, -ine
common *comb* caeno-[1], ceno-[2], coeno-,
  pan-[1]; *base* -commun-, koin-, -vulg-;
commonplace: *base* triv-; ~ *people:*
  comb demo-; *base* -pleb-, -popul-
commotion *base* -agit-, -tumult-,
  -turb-
community *base* synœc-
compact dense: *comb* dasy-, pycno-,
  pykno-; *base* -crass-, -press-, -spiss-;
  small: *comb* brachio-, brachisto-,
  brachy-, brevi-, chamae-, hekisto-,
  micro-, mini-, nano-, parvi-, parvo-,
  -steno-; *base* cort-, curt-; *suf* -cle,
  -cula, -cule, -culum, -culus, -een,
  -el, -ella, -en, -et, -ette, -idion,
  -idium, -ie, -illa, -illo, -isk, -kin, -le,
  -let, -ling, -ock, -ola, -ole, -rel, -ula,
  -ule, -ulum, -ulus, -y
companion *base* hetaero-
comparable *pre* para-, quasi-; *comb*
  homeo-, omœo-, homoio-, homolo-,
  iso-, -phane, -phanic; *base* simil-; *suf*

-acean, -aceous, -al, -an, -ar, -ary,
  -ean, -en, -eous, -esque, -ful, -ic, -il,
  -ile, -ine, -ing, -ish, -itious, -ize,
  -like, -ode, -oid, -ose, -osity, -some,
  -tious, -ular, -y
compartment *base* locul-
compel *base* horm-, -hort-, -suade,
  -suas-
competence *base* quali-
competitive event *comb* -athlon,
  -athon, -off[2]
complain *base* -quer-, -querul-
complement of *pre* co-
complementary *comb* counter-
complete(ly) *pre* be-, cata-, cath-, de-,
  kata-, ob-, per-; *comb* holo-, omni-,
  pan-, panto-, stone-, toti-
compound names *comb* tetrazo-; *suf*
  -ide, -ole[1]
comprehension *comb* -gnomy,
  -gnosia, -gnosis, -gnostic, gnoto-,
  ideo-, -noia, -nomy, -phrenic,
  phrenico-, phreno-, psycho-,
  -sophy; *base* -cogit-, -cogn-,
  epistem-, ment(a)-, -noe-, -put-,
  ratio-, -sci-
computer *comb* cyber-
concave *comb* concavo-
concealed *pre* sub-; *comb* calypto-,
  crypto-; *base* occult-
concept *comb* -gnomy, -gnosia,
  -gnosis, -gnostic, gnoto-, ideo-,
  -noia, -nomy, phreno-, psycho-,
  -sophy; *base* -cogit-, -cogn-,
  epistem-, -noe-, -put-, ratio-, -sci-
concise *comb* brachio-, brachisto-,
  brachy-, brevi-, chamae-, hekisto-,
  micro-, mini-, parvi-, parvo-, steno-,
  tapino-; *base* -cort-, -curt-, exig-;
  suf -cle, -cula, -cule, -culum, -culus,
  -een, -el, -ella, -en, -et, -ette, -idion,
  -idium, -ie, -illa, -illo, -isk, -kin, -le,
  -let, -ling, -ock, ola, -ole, -rel, -ula,
  -ule, ulum, -ulus, -y
conciliatory *base* ilast-
conclude *base* -fin-, termin-
conclusive *base* desit-
condensed *comb* brachio-, brachisto-,

brachy-, brevi-, chamae-, hekisto-,
micro-, mini-, parvi-, parvo-, steno-,
tapino-; *base* -cort-, -curt-, exig-;
suf -cle, -cula, -cule, culum, -culus,
-een, -el, -ella, -en, -et, -ette, -idion,
-idium, -ie, -illa, -illo, -isk, -le, -let,
-ling, -ock, -ola, -ole, -rel, -ula, -ule,
-ulum, -ulus, -y; ~ **thickened:** *base*
-crass-
condition *suf* -able, -acity, -acy, -age,
-ance, -ancy, -ant, -asis, -asm, -ate,
-atile, -ation, -cy, -dom, -eity, -ence,
-ency, -ent, -ery, -esis, -ful, -hood,
-iasis, -ice[1], -ility, -ion, -ise, -ism,
-ity, -ling[3], -ma, -ment, -ness, -or[3],
-osis, -otic, -red, -ship, -sion, -sis,
-th, -tion, -tude, -ture, -ty[1], -ure, -y[2]
conduct ***behavior:*** *comb* etho-; *base*
hexi-; ***lead:*** *comb* -arch, -duce, duc(t)-,
magist-; *base* hegemon-, -reg-
conductor *base* -pomp-
cone *comb* coni-[2], conico-, cono-,
conoido-; ***pine ~:*** strobil-
confer *base* -don-
configuration *comb* topo-
confine *comb* sphingo-, -strain, -strict,
syndesmo-; *base* -liga-, -merinth-,
-string-, -vinc-
conflict *comb* macho-, -machy; *base*
-bell-, -pugil-, -pugn-
confusion *comb* atax-, ataxi-, -ataxia,
ataxio-, ataxo-; *base* misc-, tarass-,
-turb-
conger *base* enchely-
connected (with) *base* hirmo-, nex-;
suf -ar[2], -arious, -ary, -id[1], -wise;
~ **twins:** *comb* -pagia, -pagus;
connected structure: *base* strom-
conquer *base* vict-, -vinc-
consecrated *comb* hagio-, hiero-; *base*
-sacr-, -sanct-
consequence *comb* ergo-, -ergic, -ergy;
suf -age, -asm, -ata, -ation, -ency,
-ism, -ma, -ment, -mony, -sion, -ure
consideration *base* phrontis-
consistent *comb* even-
constitution *comb* -ousia, -ousian;
base quid-

constrained *comb* -bound
constriction *comb* lepto-, stegno-,
steno-; *base* -stal-, sphingo-, -strict-,
string-. *See* tightening
construction *comb* -craft, ergo-, -fic,
-urgy; *base* -fabr-, -fac-, -fic-. *See*
make
contagious *base* -tapin-
container *comb* angio-, asco-, bursi-,
burso-, ceco-, chlamyd-, chrysali-,
cisto-, coleo-, -cyst, cysti-, cysto-,
follic-, meningo-, pericardiaco-,
pericardio-, peritoneo-, phasco-,
physa-, physali-, physo-, -theca,
theci-, theco-, typhlo-, utri-, utric,
vesico-; *base* -sacc-, -thylac-
containing *comb* -filled, pleni-, pleo-,
pluri-; *base* -pler-, -plet-; *suf*
-acious, -ate, -ic, -ful, -lent, -ose[2],
-osity, -ous, -ulent, -y
contempt *base* fastid-
contentment *comb* chero-; *base* beati-,
felic-, jubil-, macar-
contents (germinative) *comb* vitelli-,
vitello-
contest *comb* -athlon, -athon, macho-,
-machy, -off; *base* agon-
continent *base* -epeiro-
continual *base* aei-, assid-, contin-,
incess-, perpet-
contorted *comb* contorto-, gyro-,
helico-, pleco-, plecto-, spiro-,
strepho-, strepsi-, strepto-; *base*
-strob-, -stromb-, -stroph-, -tors-,
-tort-
contraction *comb* -chorea , choreo-,
-clonic, -clonus, -esmus, -ismus, spas-
mato-, spasmo-; *base* -stal-, vellic-
contrary *pre* anti-, cata-, contra-, con-
tre-, contro-, cross-, dis-, hetero-,
ob-, un-, with-; *comb* counter-,
enantio-, oppositi-
control *base* magist-, maha-; ***loss of ~:***
comb -crasia
controversy *base* eris-
converge *comb* -ergasia, gameto-,
gamo-, hapto-, junct-; *base* -aps-,
-apt-, -greg-, -soc-; *suf* -ate, -ize

conversation *comb* -claim, logo-,
-logue, -lalia, -lexia, lexico-, -lexis,
-lexy, -logy, -phone, phono-, -phony,
verbi-, verbo-, voc-, voci-, -voke;
base -clam-, -dict-, -loc(u)-, -loqu-,
-orat-, rhet-

convex *comb* convexo-, gibboso-

cook *base* -coct-, mageir-, magir-;
cooked meat: *base* opso-²

coot *base* fulic-, phalar-

copious *base* ampl-, copi-, largi-

copper *comb* chalco-, cupreo-, cupri-,
cupro-, cuproso-; *base* auricalc-.
Also see "Colors" *in Part III*

copy *base* -mim-

coracoid bone *comb* coraci-, coraco-

coral *comb* coralli-

cord *comb* -chorda, chord-, cordo-,
funi-, tendo-; *base* cord-, resti-

core *comb* caryo-, karyo-, nucleo-

cork *comb* phello-; *base* suber-

cormorant *base* phalacrocorac-

corn *base* frument-, grani-; **ear of ~:**
spici-

cornea *comb* corneo-, kerato-

cornice *comb* geisso-

corpse *comb* necro-; *base* -cadav-

corpulent *base* obes-, pingu-

correct(ion) *comb* ortho-; *base* castig-,
corrig-, emend-

corresponding *comb* homolo-

corrosive *comb* -brotic

corruption *comb* lysi-, -lysis, lyso-,
-lyte, -lytic, -lyze, phthino-, phthi-
sio-, -phthisis, phthysio-, -phthysis,
putri-, pyo-, pytho-, sapro-, septi-,
septo-, septico-; *base* phthor-, vitia-;
moral ~: *base* deprav-

cortex *comb* cortico-, pallio-

cost of *suf* -age

costly *base* dapat-

cotton *base* xilin-

couch *base* klin-

cough *base* -tuss-

count *base* calcul-, -comput-, -num-;
counter: *comb* pseph(o)-

counterclockwise *comb* laevo-, levo-

counterfeit *comb* pseudo-

countless *comb* myrio-; *base* innum-

country *base* -rur-, -rustic-; **of a ~:** *suf*
-ese, -ian; **~ names:** *comb* -land; *suf* -ia

coupled *comb* conjugato-

courtesan *comb* cypriano-, hetaero-,
porno-; *base* -meretric-, scort-;
brothel: lupan-

courtesy *base* -comit-

cousin *base* -sobrin-

covenant *base* fedi-

cover(ed) with *pre* be-; *comb* calypto-,
stegano-, stego-; **~ fine hairs:** *base*
toment-; **~ with hairlike material:**
comb villoso-

covering *comb* lamelli-, lepido-,
squamo-, tecti-, tegu-, -theca, theco-,
theci-, veli-; *base* involver-, lorica-,
oper-², -scut-, strag-. *See* **skin**

covert *pre* sub-; *comb* crypto-; *base*
clandest-, furt-

covetousness *base* avar-, cup(id)-,
pleonec-, pleonex-

cow *base* bou-, bov-, bu-, -vacc-

cowardly *base* pav-, timid-, trep-

cowl *base* cuculli-

crab *comb* carcino- *base* cancr-,
harpact-; **hermit ~:** pagur-; **sea ~:**
gammar-

crack *comb* dicho-, -fid, fissi-, schisto-,
schizo-, sulcato-, -tomy; *base* crev-,
fatisc-, -par-, rim-

crackle *base* -crep-, -crepit-, strid-,
stridul-

craft *base* techn-. *See* **make**

crane *comb* alector-, grallator-, grui-

crater *base* crateri-

craving *comb* eroto-, -lagnia, -mania,
-orexia; *base* -appet-, conat-, -cup-,
-libid-, -opt-, vell-; *suf* -urient

crawl *base* -rept-

crayfish *base* cambar-

crazy *comb* lysso-, -mania; *base*
ament-, dement-

creak *base* -crep-, -crepit-, strid-,
stridul-

creased *base* -rug-

create/creation *pre* be-, em-, en-,
meta-, trans-; *comb* aetio-, -blast ,

-blastic, blasto-, -craft, ergo-, etio-,
-facient, -fic, -fication, -gen,
-genesis, -genic, -genous, -geny,
ideo-, -parous, -plasia, -plasis,
plasmo-, -plast, plastic, plasto-,
-plasty, -poiesis, -poietic, -trope,
-tropic, -tropism, tropo-, -tropous,
-tropy, -urgy; *base* -fabr-, -fec-,
-mut-, -vert-; *suf* -ate, -en, -fy, -ize,
-otic

creep *base* -rept-

crescent *base* crescenti-, lunul-,
menisc-

crest *comb* lophio-, lopho-; *base* crist-

cricket *base* gryll-, locust-

crime *pre* dys-, mis-; *comb* caco-,
enisso-, enosio-, kak-, kako-, mal-,
male-, ponero-; *base* culp-, delict-,
facin-, flagit-, hamart-, iniq-, nefar-,
pecca-, perdit-, -prav-, sceler-, sce-
lest-, turp-

crimson *base* cochin-

crisp *comb* ulo-³

criterion *base* criterio-

critical *comb* critico-, enisso-

crocodile *base* crocodil-, eusuch-,
-gavial-, sucho-

crooked *comb* ancylo-, ankylo-,
-campsis, campto-, campylo-, -clinal,
-clinate, -cline, -clinic, clino-,
-clinous, -clisis, curvi-, cypho-, cyrto-,
-flect , flex-, flexuoso-, lechrio-, loxo-,
recurvo-, repando-, scolio-, -tort,
-verge; *base* -clit-, -cliv-, sinu-

cross *comb* cruci-, stauro-

crosswise *comb* transverso-; *base*
decuss-

crow *comb* coraci-, coraco-; *base*
corvin-; ~**'s beak:** *base* coron-

crowd *comb* ochlo-

crown *base* corolli-, -coron-

cruel *base* agrio-

crushing *comb* stip-², tribo-, -tripsy

crust of the earth *base* tecton-

cry *tears:* *comb* dacryo-, fleb-, flet-,
lachrim(o)-, lachrym(o)-, -plor-;
call out: *comb*
-claim; *base* -clam-, -plor-

crystal *comb* crystallo-; ***crystalline
compound:*** phloro-

cube *comb* cubi-, cubo-; *base* tesser-

cuckoo *base* cucul-

cucumber *base* cucumi-

cudgel *base* fustig-, rhopal-

culpability *base* culp-, delinq-, laps-,
-pecca-, sphal-

cultivation *comb* -ponic

culture *comb* ethno-

cumulus *comb* cumulo-

cunning *base* daedal-

cup (-shaped) *comb* calath-, calyc-,
cotyle-, cotyli-, cotylo-, cupuli-,
cyathi-, cyatho-, scyphi-, scypho-;
base calic-, crin-, cyphell-, pocul-

curing *comb* -iatrics, -iatr(o)-, -iatry,
medico-; *base* cur-, san-

curl, curly *comb* cirrhi-, cirrho-, cirri-,
cirro-, ulo-³; *base* bostrych-,
cincinn-, -crisp-. *See* **coil**

current ***electrical:*** *comb* rheo-; ***water:***
comb fluvio-; *base* -potam-, rheum-,
-rip-; ***contemporary:*** *comb* co-,
hama-; *base* -simul-

curse *base* anathem-

curved *comb* ancylo-, ankylo-,
-campsis, campto-, campylo-,
-clinal, -clinate, -cline, -clinic, clino-,
-clinous, -clisis, curvi-, cyrto-,
-flect, flex-, flexuoso-, lechrio-, loxo-,
recurvo-, repando-, scolio-,
-tort, -verge; *base* -clit-, -cliv-, sinu-

curtailed *comb* brachisto-, brachy-,
brevi-, chamae-, colo-, hekisto-,
micro-, mini-, parvi-, parvo-, steno-,
tapino-; *base* -curt-, exig-; *suf*
-cle, -cula, -cule, -een, -el, -ella, -en,
-et, -ette, -idion, -idium, -ie, -illa,
-illo, -isk, kin, -le, -let, -ling, -ock,
-ola, -ole, -rel, -ula, -ule, -ulum,
-ulus, -y

cushion *base* pulvin-, tylo-; ***cushion
stuffing:*** *base* toment-

custom *base* mor-¹, nomo-, -suet-

customer *base* empt-

cut *comb* -cide, cis-², -cise, -ectomy,
incisi-, inciso-, -sect, temno-,

-tmesis, -tome, tomo-, -tomous,
-tomy; *base* sec-, sciss-, trunc-
cutting *surgical: comb* -ectomy, -tome,
-tomy; *argument: base* trench-
cuttlefish *base* -teuth-, sepi(a)-

cyanogen *comb* cyano-
cycle *comb* cyclo-; *base* circul-, orb-
cylinder *comb* cylindro-
cypress *base* cupress-
cyst *base* sacc-

D

dagger *base* pugio-, sica-
daily *base* diurn-, ephem-, hemer-,
hodiern-, journ-, quotid-
damaging *comb* noci-, pesti-; *base*
-nox-
damp *comb* hydro-, hygro-, udo-; *base*
humect-, myda-, ulig-
dance *comb* choreo-; *base* orches-,
orchest-, -salta, tripud-
dandruff *base* furfur-, porrig-
danger *base* pericul-
Danish *comb* Dano-
dark(ness) *comb* ambly-, melan(o)-,
nycto-, scoto-; *base* -achlu-, amaur-,
fusc-, lyg-, obscur-, tenebr-
dart *base* tel-
dative *comb* dativo-
daughter *comb* fili-
daughter-in-law *base* -nur(us)-
dawn *base* -auror-, eos(o)-, luc-
day *base* diurn-, ephem-, hemer-,
hodiern-, journ-, quotid-
daylight *base* -pheng-
deaf *base* coph-, -surd-
death *comb* mort(i)-, necro-, sapro-,
thanato-; *base* exanim-, nerter-,
obit-; *deadly:* funest-, leth-[2],
phthart-
debility *comb* astheno-, -atrophia,
lepto-, -plegia, -plegy; *base* -debil-,
dimin-, enerv-, flacc-, labe-
decaying *comb* cario-, lysi-, -lysis,
lyso-, -lyte, phthino-, phthisio-,
-phthisis, putre-, putri-, pytho-,
sapro-, septi-, septico-, septo-; *base*
marcesc-, phthor-, tabe-; *suf* -ase
deceptive *base* apat-, dolero-, ludif-
decide *base* crit-[1]

decisive *base* perempt-
decks *comb* -decker
decline *comb* -atrophia; *base* degen-,
dimin-
decomposed *comb* septi-[2], septico-,
septo-[1]; ~ *substance: comb* -lyte
decomposing enzyme *suf* -ase
decrease *base* decresc-, dimin-
decree *base* -imper-, juss-, -mand-
deep *comb* batho-, bathy-; *base* pro-
fund-
deer *base* cervi-, elaph-
default *base* defalc-
defeat *base* vict-, -vinc-
defecation *comb* -chezia, copro-, fim-,
fimi-, kopro-, scato-, spatilo-,
sterco-; *base* -fec(u)-
defect, bodily *comb* pero-; *base*
-hamart-, -mutil-
defending *pre* pro-; *base* patroc-
defense *comb* -phylactic, phylacto-,
-phylax, -phylaxis
deficiency *comb* isch-, oligo-, -penia
definition *comb* orismo-; *base* dior-;
well-defined: comb delo-
deformed *comb* -cace, pero-; *base*
-mutil-
degree *suf* -ency
dehydrogenated *comb* dehydro-
deity *comb* theo-; *base* dei-
dejected *comb* lype-, tapino-; *base*
dolor-, fleb-, flet-, luct-, trist-
delayed *comb* brady-; *base* crastin-,
-cunct-, imped-, -mora-, -tard-. *See*
late
delete *base* oblit-
deleterious *comb* noci-, pesti-; *base*
-nox-, pericul-

delicate *comb* habro-, lepto-, subtil-, tenu-

delight *comb* chero-; *base* beati-, elat-, felic-, gaud-, jubil-, macar-

demanding *base* exig-

dementia *comb* lysso-, -mania; *base* ament-, dement-

demon *comb* daemono-, demono-; *base* diabol-, necyo-, satan-

demonstrating *comb* -deictic; *base* -monstr-

dense *comb* dasy-, pycno-, pykno-, -spiss-; *base* -crass-; ~ *tufts:* cespitoso-

dentate *comb* dentato-

deny *base* -neg-

deoxygenated *comb* deoxy-

depart *base* relinq-

deposit of soft materials *comb* athero-

depraved *pre* dys-, mis-; *comb* caco-, enisso-, enosio-, kak-, kako-, mal-, male-, ponero-; *base* culp-, facin-, flagit-, hamart-, iniq-, nefar-, pecca-, perdit-, -prav-, sceler-, scelest-, turp-

deprive of *pre* ab-, apo-, be-, de-, des-[1], di-, dia-, dif-, dis-, e-, ec-, ef-, ex-, for-, off-, se-, with-; *comb* ectro-; *base* -spol-

depth *comb* batho-, bathy-; *base* -byss-

deputy *comb* vice-

derivative of *pre* meta-, para-

descended from *comb* -gone, -gonium, gono-, -gony, proli-; *suf* -ing

description *comb* -graphy

desert *comb* eremo-

deserving of *comb* -worthy

designate *base* nuncup-

desire *comb* eroto-, -lagnia, -mania, -orexia; *base* -appet-, conat-, -cup-, desid-, -libid-, -opt-, vell-, vener-[1]; *suf* -urient

destination *comb* teleo-, telo-, ultim(o)-; *base* -fin-, -termin-

destitute *comb* ptocho-, vidu-; *base* -mendic-, -paup-, -pov-

destroying *comb* lysi-, lyso-, -lysis, -lytic, -lyze, -phage, phago-, -phagous, -phagy; *base* -ate-[4], perd-, perempt-, phthart-, -vast-

determine *comb* -gnomy, -gnosia, -gnosis, -gnostic, gnoto-

detestation *comb* miso-, -phobe, -phobia, -phobic; *base* -invid-, -ira(sc)-, odi-

detrimental *comb* noci-, pesti-; *base* -nox-, pericul-

development *comb* -blast, -blastic, blasto-, -geny, -plasia, -plasis, -plast , -plastic, plasto-, -plasty, -trope, -tropism, tropo-, -tropous, -tropy; *base* -mut-, -vari-, -vert-; *late* ~: serot-; *stage of* ~: *base* stathmo-

device *electronic* ~: *comb* -tron, -tronic; *measuring* ~ *comb* -meter

devil *comb* demono-, necyo-, satan-; *base* -diabol-

devoid *comb* ceno-, keno-; *base* -erem-, (ex)haur-, inan-, -vac(u)-

devotion to, excessive *comb* -latry; *suf* -ism

devour *comb* bromato-, -brotic, manduc-, -phage, phago-, -phagous, -phagy, -sitia, sitio-, sito-, -troph, -trophic, tropho-, -trophy, -vora, -vore, -vorous; *base* -alim-, -cib-, comest-, -ed-, escul-, glutt-, -gust-

dew *comb* droso-, -ror-

diagonal *base* chias-

diaphragm *comb* phreni-, -phrenic, phrenico-, phreno-

dice *base* alea-, astragal-, clero-, cubo-

die *see* **death**

different *comb* hetero-

difficult *pre* dys-; *comb* -bar, bary-, mogi-; *base* ardu-, stren-

dig *comb* orycto-; *base* fod-, -foss-

digest *comb* peps-, pept-, pepto-; *partially* ~: *comb* chymo-

digestive fluid *comb* chyli-, chylo-, chymo-

digitalis *comb* digito-

dignity *base* celsi-

dilation *comb* -ectasia, -ectasis

dill *base* aneth-

dimension *comb* -footer, -sized; ~ *of a sheet: suf* -mo; *having 3 dimensions: comb* stereo-. *Also see* "Dimension" in Part III

diminished *pre* demi-, hypo-, mis-, sub-, subter-; *comb* meio-, mini-, mio-, oligo-; *base* decresc-, dimin-, hesson-, -pauc-

diminution *suf* -aster[2]

diminutive ending *suf* -cle, -cula, -cule, -culum, -culus, -een, -el, -ella, -en, -et, -ette, -idion, -idium, -ie, -illa, -illo, -isk, kin, -le, -let, -ling[2], -ock, -ola, -ole[2], -rel, -ula, -ule -ulum, -ulus, -y[3]

dimness *comb* ambly-, melan(o)-, nycto-, scoto-; *base* -achlu-, amaur-, fusc-, homichlo-, lyg-, obscur-, opac-, tenebr-

dinner *comb* deipno-, prand-

dip *comb* -merge, -merse; *base* bapt-

directing *comb* -agogic, -agogue; *base* -vers-, -vert-

direction *comb*— ward, -ways, -wise; *suf* -ern, -ling[3]; ~ *east:* euro-, -orient-; ~ *north:* -borea-, septen-; ~ *south:* -austr-, noto-; ~ *west:* hesper-, occid-, -zephyr-; *strategic ~: base* strat-. *Also see* "Direction" in Part III

dirge *base* myrio-

dirt *comb* blenno-, -chezia, copro-, edaph-, fim(i)-, kopro-, miso-[2], myso-, -myxia, myxo-, paedo-[1], pedo-[3], scato-, spatilo-, spurc-, stegno-, sterco-; *base* -fecu-, gleb-, hum-, macul-, molys-, rhypar-, rhypo-, rypo-, sord-

disastrous *base* funest-

discerning *comb* -gnomy, -gnosia, -gnosis, -gnostic; *base* -crit-, -judic-, sagac-, -soph-

discharge *flow: comb* rheo-, rheum-, -(r)rhage, -(r)rhagia, -(r)rhea, -(r)rhoea, -(r)rhoeica; *base* excern-, -flu(v)-, -fus-; *release: base* -miss-, -mit-, -pomp-

discipline *comb* mastigo-, rhabdo-; *base* castig-, peno-, poine-, -pun-

discontinue *comb* stasi-, -stasis, -stat; *base* fin-, termin-

discourse *comb* -claim, logo-, -logue, -lalia, -lexia, lexico-, -lexis, -lexy, -logy, -phone, phono-, -phony, verbi-, verbo-, voc-, voci-, -voke; *base* -clam-, -dict-, -loc(u)-, -loqu-, -orat-, rhet-; *defective~: comb* -lalia, lalo-, -phasia, -phasic, -phasis, -phasy, -phemia, -phemy; *base* psell-

discover *base* heur-

disease *pre* dys-, mal-; *comb* -cace, loemo-, loimo-, noso-, -path, -pathic, patho-,-pathy; *base* aegr-, -morb-, -pecca-; ~ *names: comb* -aemia, -emia; *suf* -asis, -ia, -itis, -oma, -osis; *skin ~:* derm-, licheno-; ~ *treatment: comb* -iatrics, iatro-, -iatry. *See* **disorder**

disfigured *comb* pero-; *base* -mutil-

disgorge *comb* -emesis, -emetic, emeto-

disgrace *base* sord-, turp-

disgust *base* fastid-

dish *comb* lecano-; *base* -leco-, scutel-

disk-shaped *comb* disco-; *base* -numm-

disorder *comb* atax-, ataxi-, -ataxia, ataxio-, ataxo-, -thymia, -phrenia, -phrenic; *base* -turb-; *of personality ~: comb* -tonia; *speech ~: comb* -lalia

display *comb* -orama, phaeno-, pheno-; *base* -monstr-

disposed *comb* -phile, -philic, -philism, philo-, -philous

dispute *base* velit-

dissimilar *comb* aniso-, anomalo-, anomo-, perisso-, poikilo-

dissolve *comb* lyo-, lysi-, -lysis, lyso-, -lyte, -lytic, -lyze; *base* -liqu-, -solu-, -solv-

distant *comb* disto-, tele-

distension *comb* -cele, -edema, ganglio-, phlogo-, phym-, -phyma, physa-, physo-, strum(i)-; *base* aug-, cresc-, physc-, strum-, -tum-, -turg-; *suf* -itis

distinct *separate:* *pre* dia-, dis-, for-, se-; *comb* -crit, dialy-, ideo-, pro-prio-, self-; ~ *animals:* *comb* -zooid. See **divided.** *clear:* *comb* lampro-, luc-, luci-; *base* -clar-
distinction *base* dior-
distress *base* aerumn-, vex-
disturb *base* -turb-
divalent sulfur *comb* sulfo-
divergent *comb* divergenti-, divergi-, vari-
divest *base* -priv-²
divide(d) *pre* sub-; *comb* dicho-, -fid, fissi-, parti-, schisto-, schizo-, tomo-, -tomous, -tomy; *base* sciss-; ~ *crosswise:* decuss-
dividing wall *comb* sept(o)-²
divination *comb* -mancy, -mantic; *base* augur-, hariol-, harusp-, vatic-. *Also see* "Divination" in Part III
dizziness *comb* dino-²; *base* vertig-
do *pre* em-, en-; *comb* -craft, ergo-, -facient, -fic, -fication, -gen, -genesis, -genic, -genous, -geny, ideo-, -plast, -plastic, plasto-, -plasty, poiesis, -poietic,-urgy; *base* -fabr-, -fac-, -fec-¹; *suf* -ate, -en, -fy, -ize
docile *base* moriger-
doctor *comb* iatro-; *base* -med-
doctrine *suf* -ism, -logy
dodo *base* did-
doer *suf* -an, -ant, -ard, -arian, -art, -ary, -ast, -ator, -ee, eer, -en, -ent, -er, -ette, -ier, -ist, -le, -man, -nik, -o, -or, -person, -people, -ster, -woman
dog *comb* cyno-, kyno; *base* -can-¹
dogma *comb* dogmato-
doleful *comb* lype-; *base* dolor-, fleb-, flet-, luct-, trist-
doll *comb* paedo-²
dolphin *base* delphin-
domain of *suf* -dom²
donkey *base* as-, ono-
door *comb* osti-, porto-; *base* valv-
dormouse *base* glir-, myox-
dorsum *comb* dorsi-, dorso-, nota-, noto-, opistho-; *base* -terg-

dose *comb* dosio-, poso-
dotted *comb* punctato-; *base* -stigm-
double *pre* bi-, bin-, bis-, di-¹, dy-, twi-; *comb* ambi-, ambo-, amphi-, ampho-, deutero-, deuto-, dicho-, diphy-, diplo-, disso-, double-, dui-, duo-, duplicato-, duplici-, dyo-, gemin-, zygo-. *Also see* "Numbers" in Part III
doubtful *base* ambig-, ancip-, apor-, dub-, vagu-
dove *base* columb-; ***turtle-dove:*** *base* turtur-
down (from) *pre* a-, ab-, abs-, cata-, cath-, de-, kata-; *base* decliv-; ***soft hair:*** *base* lanug-; ***plant down:*** *base* papp-
downcast *comb* lype-; *base* dolor-, fleb-, flet, luct-, -trist-
dowry *base* dot-
dozen *comb* dodeca-, duodec-, duodecim-, duoden-
dragon *base* draco-, draconi-
dragonfly *base* libell(ul)-
drain *base* haur-, haust-
draw *art:* *comb* -gram, graph(o)-, -pict-; ***pull:*** *base* -duct, ductil-, -tract-; ~ ***forth:*** *base* -haur-, -haust-
dread *comb* -phobe, -phobia, -phobic, phobo-; *base* pavid-, tim(or)-, trem-, trep-. *Also see* "Fear" in Part III
dream *comb* oneiro-
dregs *base* fec-²
dress *base* hestho-
drink *comb* pino-, posi-, poto-; *base* -bib-, pocul-; ~ ***made from ___ :*** *suf* -ade
dripping *base* driri-, stalac(ti)-, stalag-
drive *base* -pel-, -pul-
driving away, out *comb* -fuge
drooping *comb* -ptosia, -ptosis; *base* -flacc-. See **bent**
drop *liquid:* *comb* gutti-, stilli-; *base* stact-, stagm-; ***fall:*** *comb* -ptosia, -ptosis; *base* -cad-, -cas-, -cid-
dropping *base* stalac-, stalag-
drugs *comb* pharmaco-; *base* medic-
drum *comb* tympano-

drunk *base* crapul-, ebriet-, inebr-, methys-, temul-

dry *comb* carpho-, krauro-, xero-; *base* arid-, celo-[2], cherso-, desicc-, -sicc-, torr-

dry out *base* marces-, marcid-

duck *base* anat-, fuligul-

dull *base* hebet-, obtus-, -tard-; ~ *vision: comb* ambly-

dung *comb* -chezia, copro-, fimi-, kopro-, scato-, spatilo-, sterc(o)-; *base* -fec(u)-, -merd-, scor-; ~ *hill:* sterquil-

duplex *comb* duplici-

during *pre* con-, in-, inter-, per-

dusk *base* -crepus-, lyg-

dusky *comb* fusc-, fusco-, -phaein, phaeo-, phein-, pheo-; *base* zopher-

dust *comb* coni-[1], -conia, conio-, konio-; *base* amath-, pulver-; *dusty place:* conist-

duty *comb* hypegia-, hypengy-; *base* paralip-

dwarf *comb* chamae-, nan(n)o-,

dwelling *comb* ekist-; *base* -aed-, -cali-, -dom-, -edi-; *suf* -age

E

each *comb* katheno-

eager *base* avid-, cupid-

eagle *base* aet-, aquil-

ear *comb* auri-[1], auriculo-, oto-. *See* sound

early *pre* ante-, pre-; *comb* prim-, primi-, primo-, proto-; ~ *period: pre* eo-; *comb* paleo-, protero-; *earlier: comb* protero-

earth *comb* agri-, agro-, -gaea, -gea, geo-, hum-; *base* -cthon-, secul-, tellur-, -terr-

earthquake *comb* seismo-, tromo-

earwig *base* forficul-

east *base* euro-, -orient-

easy *base* -facil-

eating *comb* bromato-, -brotic, man-duc-, -phage, phago-, -phagous, -phagy, -sitia, sitio-, sito-, -troph, -trophic, tropho-, -trophy, -vora, -vore, -vorous; *base* -alim-, -cib-, comest-, -ed-[1], escul-, glutt-, -gust-. *See* "Eating Habits" in Section III

eccentric *comb* aetheo-, anom(o)-, anomalo-. *See* irregular

educate *comb* -pedia; *base* -didact-, doc-, -paed-

eel *base* anguill-, -cyclostom-, enchely-, -muraen-

effect *comb* -ergy

efficient *base* efficac-, habil-, quali-

effort *base* conat-, peir-, stren-

egg *comb* oo-, ovario-, ovi-[1], ovo-; ~ *yolk:* lecith-, lecitho-, vitell-; ~ *shaped:* ovato-

Egyptian *comb* Egypto-

eight *comb* octa-, octo-, ogdo-; ~ *hundred:* octocent-. *Also see* "Numbers" in Part III

eighteen *comb* duodeviginti-, octakaideca-

eighth *base* octan-

eighty *base* octogen-, octoges-

eland *base* taurotrag-

elation *base* jubil-

elbow *base* -ancon-, olecran-

elderly *comb* gerasco-, gero-, geronto-, grand-, presby-, presbyter-; *base* -antiqu-, -sen-, -vet-; ~ *woman:* grao-

electric(al) *comb* electro-, galvano-; ~ *induction: comb* inducto-

electric ray-fish *base* torp-

elementary *base* prim-, -rud-; ~ *particle: comb* stoichio-; *suf* -on

elephant *base* elephant-, pachyderm-

elevation *comb* acro-, alti-, alto-, bato-, hypsi-, hypso-; *base* buno-, procer-; *elevated swelling: base* torul-

eleven *comb* endeca-, hendeca-,

undeca-, undecim-. *Also see* "Numbers" in Part III

elk *base* cerv-

elm *base* ulm-

emaciated *base* tab-. *See* **wasting away**

emanation *comb* atmo-, -capnia, capno-, vapo-, vapori-; *base* nebul-

embarrassment *base* pud-, verecund-

embezzle *base* pecul-

emboss *base* toreut-

embryo(nic) *comb* -blast, -blastic, blasto-, -blasty; *base* cyem-, embry-

emendation *comb* ortho-; *base* castig-, emend-

emerald *base* smaragd-

eminent *comb* celsi-, over-

emit *base* -ruct-

emotions *comb* thymo-; *disordered ~:* -thymia

empty *comb* ceno-³, keno-; *base* - erem-, (ex)haur-, inan-, -vac(u)-

emu- *base* rat-

emulation *base* zelo-

enamel *comb* amelo-

encircling *comb* zoni-, zono-

encounter *base* congress-, congru-

encourage *base* -hort-

end *comb* teleo-, telo-, ultim-, ultimo-; *base* -fin-, -termin-; *endless:* apeiro-

endowment *base* dot-

enduring *base* diuturn-, dur(o)-, perenn-, perm-, stabil-

enema *comb* -clysis; *base* chalast-, clysm-; clyst-

enemy *base* advers-, hostil-, inimic-

energy *comb* dyna(mo)-

engage in *suf* -ize

English *comb* Anglo-

engrave *comb* -glyph, glypto-

enigmatic *comb* enigmatico-

enjoyment *base* apolaust-

enlarged *pre* ad-, extra-, hyper-, super-; *comb* auxano-, auxo-, multi-, myria-, myrio-, out-, over-, -plasia, pleni-, pleo-, pleio-, pleon-, plethys-, plio-, pluri-, pollaki-, poly-; *base* ampl-, -aug-, -cresc-, dilat-, -fold-, pler-, -plet-; *abnormally ~: comb*

megalo-, -megaly; *~ vein: comb* cirso-

enormous *comb* bronto-, dino-, giganto-, mega-, megalo-, -megaly

enter *comb* -dyte-, intro-; *base* ingress-, init-

enthusiasm *base* ard-, alacr-, -ferv-, zelo-

entice *base* lenocin-

entire(ly) *pre* be-, cata-, de-, kata-, ob-, per-; *comb* holo-, omni-, pan-, panto-, stone-, toti-

entrance *comb* porto-

entreaty *base* litan-, -preca-

enveloped *pre* be-; *comb* calypto-, stegano-, stego-

environment *comb* -cole, -colent, - colous, eco-, oeco-, oiko-; *base* -aed-, -dom-, -edi-

envy *base* -invid-

enzymes *comb* zym-, zymo-; *suf* -ase

epidemic *base* luet-, morb-, pestil-

epoch *comb* -cene

eponym *base* eponym-

equal(ly) *pre* co-; *comb* equi-, homalo-, homo-, homolo-, iso-, pari-, tauto-; *almost ~: comb* pariso-

equipped *base* habil-

equivalent *pre* para-, quasi-; *comb* homeo-, omœo, homoio-, homolo-, iso-, -phane, -phanic; *base* simil-; *suf* -acean, -aceous, -al, -an, -ar, -ary, -ean, -en, -eous, -esque, -ful, -ic, -il, -ile, -ine, -ing, -ish, -itious, -ize, -like, -ode, -oid, -ose, -osity, -some, -tious, -ular, -y

erase *base* oblit-

erect *comb* ithy-, ortho-, recti-; *base* ard-³

ermine *base* mustel-

error *base* culp-, delinq-, laps-, pecc-, sphal-

eruption *comb* -anthema

erythrocyte *comb* erythro-

essence *base* -ousia, -ousian, quid-

estimate *base* stoicheio-

eternal *comb* ever-; *base* etern-, perpet-, semper-

ethers *suf* -ole
ethical *comb* ethico-
ethmoid bone *comb* ethmo-
European *comb* Euro-, Europaeo-,
Europeo-
eustachian tube *comb* salpingo-
even *level: comb* homalo-, homolo-,
plani-, plano-, plate-, platy-;
number: artio-. *See* equal
evening *comb* -noct(i)-, nyct(o)-; *base*
crepus-, -vesper-
event *comb* -athlon, -athon, -machy,
-off. *See* festival
everlasting *base* aei-, assid-, contin-,
incess-, perpet-
every *comb* katheno-, omni-, pan-,
pant(o)-
evil *pre* dys-, mis-; *comb* caco-, iniq-,
kaki-, kako-, -mal(e)-, ponero-; *base*
-prav-, sceler-, turp-
evolution *comb* -genesis. *See* creation
examination *comb* -opsy, -scope,
-scopic, scopo-, -scopy; *base*
-(in)quir-, -(in)quis-, -scrut-
example of *comb* -type; *suf* -ism
excessive *pre* hyper-, super-, ultra-;
comb over-, poly-; ~ *craving: comb*
-lagnia, -mania; ~ *devotion: comb*
-latry; *suf* -ism; ~ *drinking and
eating: base* crapul-; ~ *flow: comb*
-(r)rhagia, -(r)rhage, -(r)rhagy
exchange *base* -allac-, -allag-, -allaxis-,
camb-
excision *comb* -(ec)tomy
excite *comb* agito-; *base* -cit-;
excitability: comb bathmo-
exclaim *base* clam-, vocif-
exclude *pre* ab-, apo-, be-, de-, des-,
di-, dia-, dif-, dis-, e-, ec-, ef-, ex-,
for-, off-, se-, with-; *comb* ectro-;
base -spol-
excrement *comb* -chezia, copro-, fimi-,
kopro-, scato-, spatilo-, sterco-; *base*
caca-, -fec(u)-, -merd-
exertion *comb* -ergasia, ergasio-, -ergic,
ergo-, -ergy, -orial, -pragia, -praxia,
-praxis; *suf* -esce, -escence, -escent,
-esis; *quality of ~: comb* -pragia

exhaustion *comb* pono-; *base* -fatig-,
-kopo-, -lass-
exhibit *comb* phaeno-, pheno-; *base*
-monstr-
existence *comb* onto-; *base* -esse-
exit *base* egress-, relinq-
expansion *comb* -ectasia, -ectasis; *base*
-dilat-
experienced *base* -vet-
experiment *base* peir-
expert *comb* -logist. *Also see* "Experts"
in Part III
expiatory *base* piac-
expunge *base* delet-
extended *comb* dolicho-, -footer,
longi-, macro-, maxi-; *base* procer-;
~ *words:* sesquipedal-
extent *comb* quant(i)-; *suf* -age, -ful,
-ling[3]
external *comb* ect(o)-, exo-, extra-
extinct mammal form *comb* -there,
therio-, thero-
extol *base* laud-
extra *pre* hyper-, super-. *See*
increased
extremity *comb* acro-, aorto-, -mele,
-melia[1], melo-[3]
exultation *comb* chero-; *base* beati-,
felic-, jubil-, macar-, tripud-
eye *comb* eid(o)-, oculi-, oculo-, op-,
ophthalmo-, -opia, opsi-, -opsia,
-opsis, opso-[2], -opsy, optico-, opto-,
-scope, -scopic, -scopy; *base* blep-,
ommat-, -spec-, -spic-, -vid-, -vis-;
cornea of ~: comb corneo-, kerato-;
corner of ~: canth(o)-; ~ *covering:*
sclero-; ~ *defect: base* astigm-; *iris
of~:* irido-; *~lash:* cili-; ~ *lid:*
blepharo-, palpebra-, tarso-; *one-
eyed:* lusc-; *pupil of ~:* core(o)-,
-coria, coro-, -koria, pupillo-;
~ *retina:* retino- *see* "Body" in Part
III
eyebrows *base* ophry-; *space between ~:*
glabello-
eyelet *comb* ocelli-

F

fabricate/fabrication *pre* be-; *comb*
-craft, ergo-, -facient, fic-, -fication,
-plastic, -plast, plasto-, -plasty,
-poiesis, -poietic, -urgy; *base* aedi-,
edi-, -fabr-, -fac-, -fec-; *suf* -ate, -fy,
-ize
face *comb* facio-, prosop(o)-, -visaged;
base vult-
faceted *comb* -hedral, -hedron
fact of being *suf* -cy, -ency
faded *base* -marc-
fail(ure) *pre* dis-; *base* atychi-, kakor-
rhaph-
fainting *base* asthen-
faith *comb* -ousia; *base* -cred-, -fid-¹,
-pist-; *suf* -ism
fake *See* **false**
falcon *base* accipit-, falconi-, raptor-
fall *base* -autumn-
falling *comb* -ptosia, -ptosis; *base*
-cad-, -cas-, -cid-, decid-, laps-
fallopian tube *comb* salpingo-
false *comb* mytho-, pseudo-; *base* fict-,
kibdelo-, -mendac-, notho-
fame/famous *base* celebr-, laud-, -lustr-
family *base* cogn-, famil-, stirp-
family names [zoology] *suf* -idae
famine *comb* limo-²
fan *base* rhipi-; ~ *like:* flabelli-,
rhipido-
fantastic *base* chim-
far *comb* disto-, tele-
farewell *base* vale-
farming *base* agricol-, agricult-, arat-
fascia *comb* fascio-
fasciole *base* semit-
fast *comb* ocy-, tacho-, tachy-; *base*
alacr-, -celer-, veloc-
fasten *base* -hapto-², pegm-; ~ *one
who: comb* colleto-. *See* **bind**
fasting *comb* limo-²
fat *comb* adip(o)-, lipo-¹, pimel(o)-,
pio-, stearo-, steato-; *base* aletud-,
-aliph-, lipar-, -obes-, -pingu-, sebo-;
~ *degeneration: comb* -demia

fatal *base* funest-, phthart-
father *comb* pater-, patri-
father-in-law *base* socer-
fatigue *comb* pono-; *base* -fatig-,
-kopo-, lass-
fattening *base* sagin-
fault *base* culp-, delinq-, laps-, -pecca-,
sphal-
fear *comb* -phobe, -phobia, -phobic,
phobo-; *base* pavid-, tim(or)-,
-trem-, -trep-. *Also see* "Fear" *in Part
III*
feast day *base* heort-; *suf* -fest, -ia,
-mas
feather(like) *comb* penni-, pennati-,
pinnati-, pinnato-, pinni-, plum(i)-,
pteno-, pter, ptero-, pterono-, -pter-
ous, pterygo-, -pteryl, ptilo-; *wing ~;
comb* pterono-. *See* **wing**
feces *comb* -chezia, copro-, fim(i)-,
kopro-, scato-, spatilo-, sterco-; *base*
-fec(u)-, -merd-, scor-
feeble *comb* astheno-, -atrophia, lepto-,
-plegia, -plegy; *base* -debil-, dimin-,
enerv-, flacc-, labe-
feeding on *comb* bromato-, -brotic,
manduc-, -phage, phago-, -phagous,
-phagy, -sitia, sitio-, sito-, -troph,
-trophic, tropho-, -trophy, -vora,
-vore, -vorous; *base* -alim-, -bosc-,
-cib-, -gust-
feel *comb* -aphia, -apsia, hapt(o)-,
-path, -pathic, patho-, -pathy, sensi-,
senso-, sensori-, thigmo-; *base*
-palp-, -sens-, -sent-, -tact-, -tang-
feet long *comb* -foot(er)
feign *comb* pseudo-; *base* -simula-
felicity *comb* chero-; *base* beati-, felic-,
jubil-, macar-
female *comb* gyn(e)-, gyneco-, gyneo-,
gyno-, -gynous, -gyny, -para, she-,
thely-, -wife, -woman; *base* femin-
muliebr-, mulier-; *suf* -a4, -en, enne,
-ess, -ette, -ice2, -ine, -stress, -trice,
-trix; *elderly ~:* grao-

fence *comb* -phragma, phragmo-; *base* sepi-[2]

ferment *social: base* -agit-, -tumult-, -turb-

fermentation *comb* zym(o)-

fern *comb* pterido-; *base* filic-, lygod-

ferret *base* mustel-, viverr-

ferric iron *comb* ferri-

fervor *base* ard-, alacr-, -ferv-, zelo-

festival (names) *comb* -athon, -fest , -mas; *base* -heort-; *suf* -ia

fetish *comb* -lagnia

fetus *comb* brepho-, cyo-, embryo-, kyo-; ~ *membrane: comb* allanto-, amnio-

fever *comb* febri-, pyreto-, -pyrexia

few *comb* oligo-; *base* pauc(i)-

fiber *base* erio-, fibri-, funi-, ino-

fibril-shaped *comb* fibrilloso-

fibrin *comb* fibrino-

fibrous matter *comb* fibro-, fibroso-, funi-, strom-; ~ *growth:* ino-; ~ *tissue:* fascio-

fibula *base* peroneo-

fictitious *comb* mytho-, pseudo-; *base* fict-, kibdelo-, -mendac-, notho-

fiddle *base* pandur-

field *comb* agri-, agro-; *base* agrest-, camp-[1]

fierce *base* feroc-, labro-

fifteen *base* pentakaideca-, quindec-. *Also see* "Numbers" *in Part III*

fifth *comb* quint-[2]

fifty *base* pentaconta-, pentacosta-, quinquagen-, quinquages-

fig *base* -fici-, -syc-

fight *comb* macho-, -machy, pugn-; *base* -bell-, pugil-

figurative *comb* tropo-

figure *comb* icono-, -form; *base* schem-; ~ *with (x) angles:* -gon; ~ *with (x) surfaces:* -hedral, -hedron

filament *comb* fili-, filio-, filamento-, filo-, mito-, nemato-; *base* stema-

filled with *comb* -filled, plen(i)-; *base* -pler-, -plet-; *suf* -acious, -ate, -ic, -id[2], -ful, -ose, -osity, -ous, -ulent, -y

filter *base* col-[2]

filth *comb* blenno-, -chezia, copro-, fim(i)-, kopro-, miso-, myso-, -myxia, myxo-, paedo-, pedo-, rhyparo-, rhypo-, scato-, spatilo-, spurc-, stegno-, sterco-; *base* -fec-[2], molys-, rhypar-, rupo-, rypo-, sord-; *filthy talk:* borbor-

fin *comb* pinni-, pterygo-

final stage *comb* eschato-, teleo-, telo-, ultim(o)-; *base* desit-, -fin-, -termin-

finch *base* fringill-

find *base* heur-

fine *comb* habro-, lepti-, lepto-, subtil-, tenu-

finger *comb* -dactyl, dactylo-, -dactylous, -dactyly, digiti-; ~ *like: comb* digitato-; ~ *ring: comb* dactylio-

fingernail *comb* -onychia, onycho-

Finnish *comb* Finno-

fir *base* abiet-

fire *comb* igneo-, igni-, pyr(o)-; *base* ard-, ars-, flagr-, flamm-, incend-, phlog-

firefly *base* lampyr-

firm *comb* duro-, sclero-

first *comb* arch-, fore-, pre-, primi-, primo-, pro-, proso-, protero-, proto-; *base* -princip-

fish(like) *comb* icthyo-, pisci-; *bony~:* scopeli; *electric ray-fish: base* torp-; *hammer ~: base* sphyraen-; *sea ~: base* cichlo-

fishing *base* halieut-, riv-; ~ *net: base* sagen-

fissure *comb* chasmo-, fissuri-, rim-

fist *base* pug-, pygm-

fit *seizure: comb* -agra, -lepsia, -lepsis, -lepsy, -leptic; *capable: comb* -worthy; *suf* -able, -ibility, -ible, -ile

five *comb* cinque-, penta-, quin-, quinque-, quint(i)-; ~ *hundred:* quincent-. *Also see* "Numbers" *in Part III*

fixation *comb* -lagnia, -philia; *surgical ~:* -pexy

fixed *comb* stasi-, -stasis, -stat, stato-; *base* stabil-

flag *comb* vexillo-
flamingo *base* phoenicopter-
flammable *comb* ard-, ars-
flank *comb* laparo-
flash *comb* sela-; *base* corrusc-, -fulg-,
  stilpno-
flask *base* lagen-, ampul-
flat *comb* plain-, plani-, plano-[1], plat-[1],
  platy-; ~ *plain:* pedion-
flattery *base* adul-, bland-
flatulence *comb* physa-
flavin *comb* -flavin, flavo-
flaw *base* culp-, delinq-, laps-, pecc-,
  sphal-
flax *comb* byssi-, linar-
flea *base* psyll-[2], puli-
flee *base* avers-, drapeto-, fug-,
  -phygo-
flesh *comb* carni-, carnoso-, creo-,
  kreo-, -sarc, sarco-. *See* **skin**
flexible *base* agil-, facil-, ingen-
flight *comb* avi; *base* -fug-. *See* **flying**
fling *comb* -bole, -bolic, bolo-, -boly;
  base ballist-, -jact-, -jacula-, -ject-
flipper *comb* pinni-, pterygo-
flock *base* -greg-
flog *comb* -cuss-, plessi-, rhabdo-; *base*
  -cop-, -crot-, fustig-, plang-, puls-,
  quass-, vapul-, -verber-
flood *base* -antlo-, diluv-, inund-; ~
  tide: plemyr-
floor (soilbed) *base* edaph-
flora *comb* botano-, herbi-, -phyte,
  phyto-; *base* veget-; *suf* -aceae, -ad,
  -ales, -eae, -ia
flounder *fish: base* hippogloss-
flour *comb* aleuro-; *base* farin-
flower *comb* -antherous, antho-,
  -anthous, flori-, -florous; ~ *garland:*
  base corolli-
flow(ing) *comb* rheo-, rheum-,
  -(r)rhage, -(r)rhagia, -(r)rhea,
  -(r)rhoea, -(r)rhoeica; *base* -flu(v)-,
  -fus-
fluent *base* volub-
fluid *comb* -plasm, plasmo-; *base*
  -liqu-, -ner-
fluorescence *comb* fluo(ro)-

fluorine *comb* fluo-, fluor(o)-
flute *comb* aulo-
fly *insect: base* cyclorraph-, musc-[1],
  myia-
flying *comb* aero-, avia-, avio-,
  aviono-; *base* volit-. *See* **wing**
foam *base* aphro-, -spum-
focused on *comb* -centered, -centric
foe *base* advers-, hostil-, inimic-
fog *comb* fracto-, nephelo-, nepho-;
  base brum-[2], calig-, homichlo-,
  nebul-, -nub-
fold *comb* -plex, plicato-, plici-, -ptych
follow(ing) *pre* epi-, meta-, post-;
  comb after-, hind-, postero-; *base*
  -secut-, -sequ-; *suf* -an; *follower base*
  discip-
folly *see* **foolish**
food *comb* bromato-, -brotic, man-
  duc-, opso-, -phage, phago-,
  -phagous, -phagy, psomo-, -sitia,
  sitio-, sito-, -troph, -trophic,
  tropho-, -trophy, -vora, -vore,
  -vorous; *base* -alim-, -cib-, escul-,
  -gust-, -nutr-; *partially digested ~:*
  chymo-. *Also see* "Food" and "Eating
  Habits" in Part III.
foolish *base* fatu-, inan-, moro-, stult-
foot *comb* ped-[1], pedati-, -pede, pedi-,
  pedo-[1], -poda, -pode,-podium, -pod,
  podo-, -podous, -pus *base* -plant-;
  ~ *sole:* -pelm-, plant-
footprint *comb* ichno-, stibo-
for *pre* pro-
forbid *base* prohib-
forecast *base* prognos-
force *comb* dyna-, dynamo-, mega-,
  megalo-, -megaly, -sthenia, stheno-;
  base -forc-, -fort-, -poten-, robor-
forceps *base* labido-
forearm *comb* ulno-
forehead *comb* metopo-
foreign(er) *comb* perisso-, xeno-; *base*
  -ali-
foreknowledge *base* prognos-
foremost *comb* arch-, archi-, proto-;
  base -prim-, -princip-
forest *comb* dendri-, dendro-, -den-

dron, hylaeo-, saltu-, silvi-, xylo-;
base arbor-, nemo(r), -sylv-

forever *comb* ever-; *base* etern-, per-
pet-, semper-

forget *base* amnes-, leth-; ***forgotten:***
base obliv-

forked *base* -furc-

form, a *comb* eid(o)-, -form, -morph,
-morphic, -morphism, morpho-,
-morphous; *base* -figur-, -schem-

form, to *pre* be-; *comb* aetio-, etio-;
base -fabr-, fac-, fec-, fic-; ***formed***
like: *suf* -ular

formation *pre* em-, en-, meta-, trans-;
comb -blast, -blastic, blasto-, -craft,
ergo-, etio-, -facient, -fic, -fication,
-gen, -genesis, -genic, -genous,
-geny, -gone, -gonium, gono-, -gony,
-parous, -plasia, -plasis, plasmo-,
-plast, -plastic, plasto-, -plasty,
-poiesis, -poietic, -trope, -tropic,
-tropism, tropo-, -tropous, -tropy,
-urgy; *base* -fec-, -mut-, -vert-; *suf*
-ate, -en, -fy, -ize, -otic

former *comb* ex-, protero-

fornicate *base* copul-, scort-, stupr-

fortification *base* castella-

fortune ***luck:*** *comb* tycho-; *base* faust-;
wealth: *comb* pluto-; *base* opul-

forty *base* quadragen-, quadrages-

forward *pre* fore-, pre-, pro-[1]; *comb*
antero-, proso-

fossil *base* oryct-; *suf* -ite

foul ***dirt:*** *comb* blenno-, -chezia,
copro-, edaph-, fim(i)-, kopro-,
miso-, myso-, -myxia, myxo-,
paedo-, pedo-, scato-, spatilo-,
spurc-, stegno-, sterco-; *base* -fecu-,
gleb-, hum-, macul-, molys-, rhypar-,
rhypo-, rypo-, sord-; ***evil:*** *pre* dys-,
mis-; *comb* caco-, iniq-, kak(o)-,
mal(e)-, ponero-, -prav-, turp-

foundation *comb* base-, basi-, baso-

fountain *base* cren-[2], pego-

four(th) *comb* quadr-, quadrato-,
quadri-, quadru-, quart-, quarter-,
quarti-, quat-, quater-, tetarto-,
tetra-, tessera-; ~ ***cycles:*** tetra-,

cyclo-; ~ ***hundred:*** quadricent-;
~ ***times:*** tetrakis-. *Also see* "Numbers" *in Part III*

fourteen *base* quattuordec-, tessa-
radeca-, tetradeca-, tetrakaideca-

fowl *base* gallin-

fox *base* alopec-, bassar-, vulpi-

foxglove *comb* digito-

fraction *base* -par-[1], parti-; ~ ***of a***
meter: *comb* -meter

fracture *comb* -clasia, -clasis, -clastic,
rhegma-, -(r)raghia, -(r)rhexis; *base*
agmat-, -fract, frag-, -frang-, -rupt-;
bone ~: catagm-

fragile *See* **frail**

fragment *comb* -clasm, clasmato-,
-fid; *base* frust-, -par-; ***stone ~:*** *base*
ruder-

frail *comb* lepti-, lepto-; *base* -asthen-,
coupho-, -debil-, koupho-

framework *base* pegm-

fraudulent *base* apat-, dolero-, ludif-

freckle *base* lentig-

free *comb* eleuthero-; *base* -liber-,
vac(u)-

freeing *comb* lyo-, lysi-, -lysis, lyso-,
-lyte, -lytic, -lyze; *base* -liqu-, -solu-,
-solv-

freezing *comb* cheima-, crymo-, cryo-,
frigo-, gelo-, kryo-, pago-, psychro-,
rhigo-; *base* alg-, gel-[1], glac-

French *comb* Franco-, Gallo-

frenzied *base* corybant-, frenet-

frequent *comb* pluri-, pollaki-, poly-;
base crebr-; *suf* -le. *See* **repeatedly**

fresh *comb* thalero-; *base* -nov-

friction *comb* tribo-, -tripsy; *base* trit-

friendship *comb* socio-; *base* -am-,
amic-[1], comit-

fright *see* **fear**

frigid *see* **freezing**

fringe *comb* crosso-; *base* -fimbr-,
lacin-, lom-, thysan-; ***small ~:***
fimbrilli-; ~ ***with hairs:*** fimbriato-

frog *comb* batracho-, bufo-, phryno-,
rani-; *base* polyped-

from *pre* a-[2], ab-, abs-, apo-, e-, ex-,
with-

front *pre* ante-, pre-, pro-; *comb* antero-, fore-, proso-
frontal bone *comb* fronto-
frost *base* cryo-, gel-[1], kryo-, pachno-, pago-, pruin-, rhigo-
froth *base* -spum-
fructose *comb* fructi-, fructo-
fruit *comb* -carp, -carpic, carpo-[1], -carpous, pomi-, pomo-; *base* -frug-[1]; ~ *sugar:* fructi-, fructo-; ~ *with leathery rind: base* hesperid-
fruitfly *base* drosophyl-, trypet-
fruitful *comb* proli-
fugitive *base* drapeto-
full (of) *comb* -filled, pleni-, pleo-, plero-, pluri-; *base* -pler-, -plet-, sat-, satur-; *suf* -acious, -ate, -ic, -ful, -ilent, -ose[2], -osity, -ous, -ulent, -y
fun *comb* chero-

function *suf* -ate[3], -ise
functionally disordered *pre* para-
funeral rites *base* epicid-, thren-
fungus *comb* fungi-, morilli-, -mycete, mycet(o)-, -mycin, myco-, uredo-; *base* bolet-
funnel *comb* choano-, infundibuli-
fur *base* dora-
furious *base* chol-, -invid-, -ira-, labro-, -margy
furnish with *pre* be-; *suf* -ate
furrow *comb* holco-, stria-, striato-, strio-, sulcato-; *base* -scrobic-, strig-; *furrowed: base* lirell
fusion *pre* co-; *comb* conjugato-, -ergasia, gameto-, gamo-, hapto-, junct-; *base* aps-, apt-, -greg-, -soc-; *suf* -ate, -ize
futile *base* futil-, inutil-, mataeo-

G

gable *base* fastig-
gain *base* lucr-, quaest-
gall *bile: comb* bili-, chol(e)-, gall-; *tumorous plant tissue:* cecid-
galvanic *comb* galvano-
gambling *base* alea-
gamete *comb* gameto-
ganglion *comb* ganglio-
gangrene *base* sphacel-
gap *base* -apert-, -cav-, fenest-, foram-, œgo-, oigo-, osti-, patul-, pylo-, rim-, valv-
garb *base* habil-, hesto-, -vest-
garden *comb* horti-
garland *comb* corolli-
garlic *base* alli-, scoro-
gas *comb* aeri-, aero-, gaso-, pneumo-; *inert* ~: *suf* -on; *stomach* ~: flat-, physa-, physo-
gash *comb* -cide, cis-, -cise, -ectomy, inciso-, -sect, temno-, -tmesis, -tome, tomo-, -tomous, -tomy; *base* sec-
gastric *comb* chyli-, chylo-, chyma-

gate *comb* porto-; *base* osti-, -pyl-
gathered together *comb* cumulo-; *base* acerv-, -sor-
gecko *base* gecco-
gelatin *comb* gelatino-
gem *base* lapid-
generate *comb* aetio-, etio-, -gen, geno-, -genesis, -genic, -genous, -geny, -gone, -gonium, gono-, -gony, -phyletic. See **cause**
genital(s) *comb* genito-; *base* -aede-, med-; *female* ~: *comb* colp(o)-, elytr(o)-, kolpo-, vagini-, vagino-; *male* ~: *comb* peo-, phall(o)-; *base* med-, mentul-
gentle *base* -len-, mansue-, miti-, moll-
geological epoch *comb* -cene, -zoic
geometric figure *comb* -gon, -hedral, -hedron
gerbil *base* cricet-
German *comb* Germano-, Teutano-, Teuto-
germinal *comb* -blast, blasto-, -blasty,

-carp, -carpic, carpo-, -carpous, sperma-, -spermal, spermatio-, spermato-, spermi-, -spermic, spermo-, -spermous, sporo-; *base* semin-

germs *comb* bacilli-, bacillo-, -bacter, bacteri-, bacterio-

gesture *base* gestic-, pasi-

get *base* -cap-, -cep-, -cip-, -dyte-

ghost *base* phantas-, phasm-, spectr-

gibbon *base* hylobat-

gift *base* don-, dor-, mun-

gigantic *comb* bronto-, dino-, giganto-, mega-, megalo-, -megaly, super-. *See* **large**

gills *comb* -branchia, branchio-

ginger *base* zingiber-

giraffe *base* artiodactyl-

girdle *comb* zoni-, zono-; *base* -cing-, zoster-. *See* **band**

give *base* -don-; ~ *birth: base* -partur-; ~ *way: base* -ced-, -cess-

glacier *comb* glacio-

gland *comb* adeni-, adeno-, balani-, balano-; *swollen ~:* strum(i)-

glans *comb* balano-

glass(y) *comb* crystallo-, hyalo-, vitreo-, vitri-, vitro-. *See* **mirror**

gleam *comb* sela-; *base* corrusc-, -fulg-, gano-, lustr-, rutil-, stilpno-

glittering *base* stilpno-

globe *comb* ano-, annul-, crico-, cyclo-, disco-, globi-, globo-, glom-, gyro-, orbito-, -sphere, sphero-, stilli-, zon-, zoni-; *base* -anu-, -cing-, -cinct-, -circin-, -circul-, -coron-, -glomer-, -numm-, -orb-, -rot-, -troch-

gloomy *base* fusc-, obscur-, tenebr-

glowworm *base* lampyr-

glue (like) *comb* colleto-, -glea, -glia, glio-, gloio-, glutin-, kollo-; *base* coll-²; *one who glues: base* colleto-

glum *comb* lype-; *base* dolor-, fleb-, flet, luct-, -trist-

glutted *comb* -filled, pleni-, pleo-, plero-, pluri-; *base* -pler-, -plet-; *suf*

-acious, -ate, -ic, -ful, -ilent, -ose, -osity, -ous, -ulent, -y

gluttony *base* gul(os)-

glycerin, glycerol, glycogen *comb* glico-, gluco-

gnash *base* brux-, frend-, mol-

gnat *base* conop-, culici-

gnaw *base* -trog-. *See* **chew**

gnu *base* connochaet-

go *comb* -grade, -motive, -plania , plano-; *base* -bat-, -ced-, -cess-, -cur(s), -grad-, -gress-, -mob-, -vad-, -vas-; ~ *away:* out-; ~ *into:* -dyte-; ~ *forward:* pro-; ~ *toward:* -bound, -petal

goad *base* horm-, -hort, -suade, -suas-, -stig-

goal *comb* teleo-, telo-, ultim(o)-; *base* -fin-, -termin-

goat *comb* capri-, egagro-, trago-; *base* aegag-, egag-, hircin-

goblet *base* pocul-

God *comb* theo-; *base* dei-

goiter *base* strum(i)-

gold(en) *comb* auri-², auro-, chrys(o)-. *Also see* "Colors" in Part III

goldfish *base* cyprin-

gonad *comb* gonado-

good *pre* bene-, eu-; *base* agath-, bon-, prob-; ~ *order: base* eutax-

goodbye *base* vale-

goods *base* empor-, -merc-

goose *base* anser-, cheno-

gooseberry *base* grossul-, ribes-

gorgeous *comb* calli-, callo-; *base* kal-, pulchr-

gorilla *base* -pong-

gourd *base* cucurbit-, pepo-

government *comb* -archy, -cracy, -crat(ic); *base* gubern-

grab *base* rap-, rep-. *See* **grasp**

graceful *comb* habro-

grackle *base* gracul-

grafting *base* surcul-

grain *comb* grani-; *base* farr-, farrag-, -frument-

gram *comb* -gram

grandfather *base* avit-, av(us)-

grandmother *base* av(ia)-
granite *comb* graniti-; *like, of ~:* grano-
grant *base* concess-, don-
granular *comb* coni-, -conia, conio-, granulo-
grape (like) *comb* acini-, botry-, staphylo-, vini-, vino-, viti-; *base* racem-, -rhag-, -uvi-, -uvu-
grapple *base* harpag-
grasp *comb* -tain; *base* -cap(t)-, -cathex-, -ger-, -hapt-, -prehend, prehens-, -ten-
grass *base* agrost-, gramin-, poe-
grasshopper *base* acrid-, forb-, gryll-, locust-
grave *comb* -taph, tapho-; *base* sepul-
gravel *base* chalic-, glare-
gray *comb* glauco-, -phaein, phaeo-, pheo-, polio-; *base* caesi-, -can-², -gris-, -tephr-. *Also see* "Colors" in Part III
grazing *base* pascu-
grease *base* lipar-, sebo-, unct-, ungu-
great *size: comb* macro-, magni-, maxi-, plethys-; *base* -ampl-, grandi-, -maj-; *suf* -fold. *See* **gigantic**
greater *pre* super-; *comb* meizo-, out-
grebe *base* podic-
greed(y) *base* avar-, avid-, cup(id)-, edac-, gulos-, labro-, pleonec-, pleonex-
Greek *comb* Graeco-, Greco-; *base* Hellen-
green *comb* chloro-, glauco-, olivaceo-; *base* aerug-, -beryl-, caes-, oliv-, porrac-, pras-, smaragd-, thall-, thallas-, verd-, -vir-, virid-. *Also see* "Colors" in Part III
gridiron *base* graticul-
grief *comb* lype-; *base* dolor-, fleb-, flet-, luct-, trist-

grind *base* -brux-, frend-, mol-
grit *comb* ammo-, aren-, arenaceo-, glare-, psammo-, sabell-, sabul-
groin *comb* bubo-, inguino-
groove *comb* bothr-, canali-, -glyph, glypto-, stria-, striato-, strio-, sulcato-; *base* canal-, sulc-; ***grooved:*** *base* riv-. *See* **cleft**
grope *base* pselaph-
ground *base* edaph-, geo-, -hum-, sol-², -terr-; ***living near the ~:*** *base* epige-; ***under ~:*** *base* cunicul-
group (of) *suf* -age, -ery, -hood, -ship
group names [zoology] *comb* -zoa, -zoon; *suf* -ini
grouse *base* gallinac-, tetrao-; ***sand ~:*** *base* pterocl-
grove *suf* -etum
grow, growth *comb* auxano-, auxeto-, auxo-, -blast, -blastic, blasto-, -blasty, -colous, -crease, -culture, -nastic, -nasty, onco-, -physis, -plasia, -plasis, -plast, -plastic, plasto-, plethys-, verruci-; *base* -aug, -cresc-; *suf* -oma, -ome; ***~in:*** -cole, -colent, -colous; ***fibrous growth:*** *comb* ino-; *~* ***together:*** symphyo-
guard *comb* -phylactic, phylacto-, -phylax, -phylaxis
guess *base* -stoch-
guide *base* gubern-, -pomp-
guilt *base* -culp-
gull *base* gavi-, lar-
gullet *comb* esophago-, œsophago-
gulp *base* glutt-
gum-yielding *comb* gutti-
gums *comb* gingivo-, oulo-, ulo-²
gush *base* gurg-
gyrating *comb* gyro-
gyroscope *comb* gyro-

H

habit *base* -hexi-
habitat *comb* -cole, -colent, -colous, eco-, oiko-; *base* -aed-, -dom-, -edi-

hailstone *base* grandin-, chalax-
hair/hairlike *comb* capilli-, -chaeta, chaeto-, cilii-, cilio-, -coma, comi-,

como-, crin(i)-, dasy-, fimbr-,
fimbrilli-, pili-, pilo-, piloso-, -trich,
-tricha, tricho-, villoso-; *base* hirsut-,
hispid-, lanug-, saro-, -thrix-, vill-;
covered with fine hair: *base* toment-
hair removal *base* depil-
hake *base* merluc-
half *pre* demi-, hemi-, semi-; *comb*
dicho-, mezzo-; *base* dimid-
halibut *base* hippogloss-
halogen *comb* halo-; *suf* -ine
halt *comb* stasi-, -stasis, -stat, stato-;
base fin-, termin-
hammer *comb* malleo-; *base* mall-,
sphyr-; ~ ***fish:*** *base* sphyraen-
hampered *comb* brady-; *base* -cunct-,
imped-, -mora-, -tard-
hamster *base* cricet-
hand *comb* cheiro-, chiro-, hand-,
mani-, manu-
handle *base* ansa-, manubr-
hang *comb* cremo-; *base* -pend-, -pens-
happening every __ *suf* -ly
happiness *comb* chero-[1]; *base* beati-,
felic-, jubil-, macar-
harbor *base* limen-
hard *comb* duro-, sclero-; ~ ***palate:***
comb uranisco-, urano-; ~ ***shell:***
base lorica-; ~ ***work:*** *comb* pono-.
See **difficult**
hare *base* cunic-, lago-, lepor-
harlot *comb* cypriano-, hetaero-,
porno-; *base* meretric-, scort-
harmful *comb* noci-, pesti-; *base* -nox-,
pericul-
harmony *pre* co-; *base* concinn-, con-
gru-, -eiren-, -iren-, -pac-, -pax,
unanim-
harsh *comb* caco-; *base* acerb-, asper-
haste *base* alacr-, celer-, festin-, subit-;
comb ocy-, tacho-, tachy-
hatchet *base* dolabr-, pelec-, securi-
hate(d) *comb* miso-, -phobe, -phobia,
-phobic; *base* -invid-, -ira(sc)-, odi-
haul(ing) *comb* -fer, -ferous, -gerous,
-parous, -pher, -phore, -phorous;
base -port-, -vect-
having *comb* -echia; *suf* -acean,

-aceous, -al, -ate[2], -ed[2], -ful,
-gerous, -ial, -ine, -ious, -itious,
-ory, -ous, -some, -ulent, -ulous,
-wise, -y; *base* -ten-; ~ ***parts:*** *comb*
-fold; ~ ***qualites of:*** *comb* -able
hawk *base* accipit-, buteo-, falco-,
hieraco-
hawthorn *base* -crataeg-
hazard *base* pericul-
head *comb* capit-, cephal-, -cephalic,
cephalo-, -cephalous, -cephaly,
cranio-, kephalo-; ***having a __ head:***
-headed; ***type of* ~:** -pated
headlong *base* precip-
headstrong *base* contum-, obstin-,
pervic-, proterv-
healing *comb* -iatrics, -iatr(o)-, -iatry,
medico-; *base* acest-, cur-, san-
health *comb* hygeio-, hygien-; *base*
salub-, san-. See **sickness**
heap(ing) *comb* cumulo-; *base* acerv-,
-sor-
hearing *comb* acou-, acoust-, audi(o)-,
auri-, echo-, -ecoia, oto-, -phone,
phono-, -phony, -phthong, soni-,
sono-, sonoro-. *Also see* "Senses" *in*
Part III
heart *comb* cardi-, -cardia, cardio-,
-cardium, cordato-, cordi-,
pericardiaco-, pericardio-; ~ ***attack:***
base angin-; ~ ***cavity:*** *comb* atrio-;
~ ***shaped:*** *comb* cordato-
heartbreak *comb* lype-; *base* dolor-,
fleb-, flet-, luct-, trist-
heat *comb* cal(e)-, calo-, calor(i)-,
pyr(o)-, -therm, thermo-, -thermy;
base aest-, caum-, ferv-; ***heat up:***
base fomen-
heath *base* eric-
heave *comb* -bole, -bolic, bolo-,
-boly; *base* -ballist-, -jact-, -jacula-,
-ject-
heavens *comb* coeli-, ourano-, urano-;
base cael-, cel-, celest-
heavy *comb* -bar, bari-, baro-, grav(i)-;
base -obes-, -pond-
Hebrew *comb* Hebraico-; ~ ***plural
ending:*** *suf* -im

hedge *base* sepi-[2]
hedgehog *comb* echinoderm-; *base* echin-, erinac-
heed *comb* -serve; *base* caut-
heel-bone *comb* calcaneo-, ptern-
height *comb* acro-, alti-, alto-, bato-[1], hypsi-, hypso-; *base* procer-
hell *base* acheron-, avern-, infern-, -styg-
helmet *base* cassidi-, corys-, -gale-
help *base* -(ad)jut-, -(ad)juv-, -auxil-
helpful *comb* chreo-, chresto-; *base* -util-
hemispheric *comb* hemispherico-
hen *base* gallin-
heptillion *comb* yotta; ~ **th:** yocto-. *Also see* "Numbers" *in Part III*
herd *base* -greg-
heredity *comb* heredo-
heresy *base* heresio-
hermit *base* eremit-; ~ **crab:** pagur-
hernia *comb* -cele, celo-[1], hernio-
heron *base* arde-, grallator-
herring *comb* harengi-; *base* clupe-, halec-
hesitate *base* cunct-
hexameter *comb* hexametro-
hexillion *comb* zetta-; ~ **th:** zepto-. *Also see* "Numbers" *in Part III*
hiccup *base* singult-
hidden *pre* sub-; *comb* calypto-, crypto-; *base* occult-, lathro-; **hiding place:** latebr-, latib-. *See* **covered**
hide *animal: comb* dora-, pelli-; **conceal:** *See* **hidden**
high(er) *pre* meta-, super-; *comb* acro-, alti-, alto-, hypsi-, hypso-
higher valence *pre* per-; *suf* -ic
highest *comb* acro-
highway *comb* hodo, -ode, odo-; *base* -iter-, -via-
hill *base* coll-[3]
hinge *base* gingly-
hip *comb* cotyle-, cotyli-, cotylo-, coxo-, ischi(o)-
hiss *base* -sibil-
historical *comb* historico-
hit *comb* plessi-; *base* cop-, -crot-,

-cuss-, -plang-, puls-, -tus-, vapul-, -verber-
hoard *comb* cumulo-; *base* acerv-, -sor-
hoax *base* ludif-
hog *base* hyos-
hold *comb* -tain; *base* -cap(t)-, -cathex-, -ger-[1], -hapt-, -prehend, prehens-, -ten-; ~ **back:** prohib-
holder *comb* angio-, asco-, bursi-, burso-, ceco-, chlamyd-, chrysali-, cisto-, coleo-, -cyst, cysti-, cysto-, follic-, meningo-, pericardiaco-, pericardio-, peritoneo-, phasco-, physa-, physali-, physo-, -theca, theci-, theco-, typhlo-, utri-, utric, vesico-; *base* -sacc-, -thylac-
hole *base* cav-, foramin-, lacun-, troglo-. *See* **opening**
holler *base* clam-, vocif-
hollow *comb* cava-, -cave, cavi-, cavo-, -coele, coelo-, cotyle-, cotyli-, cotylo-, koilo. *See* **cavity**
holly *base* ilic-
holy *comb* hagio-, hiero-, sanct(i)-; *base* -sacr-
home (of) *comb* eco-, ekist-, nosto-, oeco-, oiko-; *base* aed-, -dom-, edi-; *suf* -age
honest *base* prob-
honey *comb* mell(i)-
honeycomb *comb* favoso-; *base* fav-
honor *base* timo-; **honored:** *comb* semno-
honorable *pre* bene-, eu-; *base* agath-, bon-, prob-
hood *base* calyptri-, cuculli-
hook *base* hamat-, harpag-, -unci-; **hooked:** *base* adunc-, falc-; ~ **shaped:** *base* ancis-
hookworm *base* ancylostom-
hope *base* -sper-
horizon *comb* horizo-
hormone names *comb* -kinin
horn, hornlike *comb* cerat(o)-, -corn, corneo-, corni-, cornu-, kera-, kerato-
hornbill *base* bucerot-, bucorac-

hornblower *comb* keraulo-
hornet *comb* vespi-; *base* -sphec-
horse *comb* equ(i)-, hippo-, -hippus; *base* caball-, caval-
horsefly *base* taban-
horseshoe *base* hippocrepi-
horsetail *base* equiset-
hospital *base* nosocom-
host *base* -hosp-, -xen-
hostile *pre* anti-; *base* inimic-
hot *comb* cal(e)-, calo-, calor(i)-, pyr(o)-, thermo-, -thermy; *base* aestu-, caum-, ferv-
hour *comb* horo-
house *comb* eco-, ekist-, oeco-, oiko-; *base* aed-, -dom-1, edi-; *suf* -age
how many *base* quot-
howl *base* ulul-1
hub *comb* centr-, centri-, -centric, centro-
huckster *base* caupon-
huge *comb* bronto-, dino-, giganto-, mega-, megalo-, -megaly
hull *ship:* *base* naut-; *husk:* *base* follic-, -lemma2, putamin-
human *comb* anthrop(o)-, humano-, -man; *base* hom-, homin-. *See* people
humid *comb* hydro-, hygro-, udo-; *base* humect-, madefac-, -rig-
hummingbird *base* trochil-
humorous *comb* comico-
hump *comb* cypho-, gibboso-, hybo-, lordo-, scoli-; *base* -kyph-
hundred *comb* cent(i)-, hecato-,

hecto-, hekto-; *~twenty:* hecatonicosa-. *Also see* "Numbers" in Part III
hunger *base* esur-; *~for:* *comb* eroto-, -lagnia, -mania, -orexia, peino-; *base* -appet-, conat-, -cup-, esur-, fam-, -libid-, -opt-, vell-; *suf* -urient
hunt *base* venat-
hurl *comb* -bole, -bolic, bolo-, -boly; *base* ballist-, -jact-, -jacula-, -ject-
hurricane *base* lilaps-
hurry *base* accel-, celer-, festin-. *See* rush
hurt *comb* noci-; *base* -nox-, vuln-. *See* pain
husband *base* conjug-, marit-
hushed *comb* hesy-; *base* -plac-, quiesc-, -tacit-
husk *comb* follic-, -lemma2, putamin-
hut *base* -cali-
hydraulic *comb* hydraulico-
hydrides *suf* -ine
hydrocarbon *suf* -ene; *~ radical:* *suf* -ylene; *~ paraffin series:* *suf* -ane; *~ plus nitrogen:* *comb* diazo-, phenanthro-
hydrogen *comb* -hydric
hydroxyl *radicals:* *comb* -hydric; *~ group:* *comb* hydroxy-
hygiene *comb* hygeio-, hygien-; *base* salub-, san-
hyoid bone *comb* hyo-
hypnotism *comb* hypno-; *base* mesmer-
hyrax- *comb* chero-2, hyraci-, hyraco-
hysteria *comb* hyster(o)-

I

ice *comb* glacio-, pago-; *base* gel-1
icicle *base* stiri-
icon *comb* icono-
idea *comb* -gnomy, -gnosia, -gnosis, -gnostic, gnoto-, ideo-, -noia, -nomy, phreno-, psycho-, -sophy *base* -cogit-, -cogn-, epistem-, -noe-, -put-, ratio-, -sci-

identical *pre* co-; *comb* equi-, homo-, iso-, pari-, tauto-
idiot *base* fatu-, inan-, moro-, stult-
idle *base* arg-, oti-, pigrit-
idol *comb* idolo-
ignorant *base* hebet-, obtus-, -tard-
ileac plus, ileum *comb* ileo-, ilio-
ill(ness) *pre* dys-, mal-; *comb* noso-,

-path, -pathic, patho-, -pathy; *base*
aegr-, -morb-, -pecca-, valetud-;
~ *health: base* cachex-; ~ *names:*
comb -aemia, -emia; *suf* -asis, -ia, -
itis, -oma, -osis; ~ *treatment: comb*
-iatrics, iatro-, -iatry. *See* **disorder**
illumination *comb* actino-, luci-,
phengo-, phos-, photo-; *base* clar-,
-luc-, -lum-
illusory *comb* pseudo-; *base* apat-,
-phantas-, phasm-
image *comb* icono-; *base* agalma-
imbibe *comb* pino-, poto-; *base* -bib-,
pocul-
imitate *base* emul-, -mim-
immature *comb* paedo-², pedo-; *base*
juven-. *See* **undeveloped**
immense *comb* bronto-, dino-, gi-
ganto-, mega-, megalo-, -megaly
immobility *comb* -plegia, -plegy
immolation *base* mact-, -thy-
immorality *pre* dys-, mis-; *comb* caco-,
enisso-, enosio-, kak-, kako-, mal-,
male-, ponero-; *base* culp-, facin-,
flagit-, hamart-, iniq-, nefar-, pecca-,
perdit-, -prav-, sceler-, scelest-, turp-
immortal *comb* ever-; *base* etern-, per-
pet-, semper-
immovable *comb* stasi-, -stasis, -stat,
stato-; *base* stabil-
immune *comb* immuno-
impaired *base* vitia-
impartial *comb* equi-
impede *comb* isch-, koly-, -penia,
rhopo-, -strain, -strict; *base* angust-,
-string-; *suf* -en
impel *base* horm-
imperfection *base* culp-, delinq-, laps-,
-pecca-, sphal-
imperfect(ly) *pre* demi-, hemi-, semi-;
comb ametro-, -atelia, atelo-
imperforate *comb* -atresia, atreto-
impervious to *comb* -proof, -tight
impetus *base* horm-
important *base* grav-
imposter *base* phenac-, phenak-
impoverished *comb* ptocho-, vidu-;
base -mendic-, -paup-, penur-, -pov-

improved *comb* melior-, out-
impulse *base* ate-⁴
in *pre* eis-, em-, en-¹, il -, im-, in-, ir-;
comb endo-, ento-, entre-, eso-,
inter(o)-, intra-, intro-; ~ *a specified*
way: suf -ly, -ways, -wise; ~ *back: pre*
meta-; *comb* post-, postero-; ~ *com-*
mon: comb caeno-, ceno-; ~ *front of:*
pre ante-, fore-, ob-, prae-, pre-, pro-;
~ *some order: suf* -ly; ~ *the direction*
of: suf -ad, -ly, -ward, -ways, -wise; ~
the manner of: suf -like, -ways; ~ *the*
style of: suf -ese, -esque
inaccuracy *base* culp-, delict-, laps-,
pecc-, sphal-
inadequacy *comb* isch-, oligo-, -penia
inaudible *comb* hesy-; *base* -plac-,
quiesc-, -tacit-
inborn *comb* innato-
incapable of being *suf* -less. *See* **not**
incense *comb* -thymia²; *base* kniss-,
liban-, thur-
incessant *base* assid-, contin-, incess-,
perpet-
incipient *base* incip-, -init-; *suf* -esce,
-escence, -escent.
incised *comb* eroso-. *See* **groove**
inciting *comb* -agogic, -agogue; *base*
fomen-
incline *comb* -clinal, -clinate, -cline,
-clinic, clino-, -clinous, -clisis,
lechrio-, loxo-, plagio-; *base* -cliv-
incomplete *pre* demi-, hemi-, semi-;
comb -atelia, atelo-; *suf* -esce,
-escence, -escent
incorrect *base* dys-, mis-; ~ *use of*
words: comb acyro-
increased *pre* ad-, extra-, hyper-,
super-; *comb* auxano-, auxo-,
multi-, myria-, myrio-, out-, over-,
-plasia, pleni-, pleo-, pleio-, pleon-,
plethys-, plio-, pluri-, pollaki-, poly-
; *base* -aug-, -cresc-, -fold-, -pler-,
-plet-. *See* **grow**
indefinite *base* ambig, dub-, ancip-
index *comb* sema-, -seme, semeio-,
semio-
India *comb* Indo-²

indicate *comb* phaeno-, pheno-; *base* -monstr-

indigence *comb* -penia, ptocho-, vidu-; *base* -mendic-, -paup-, penur-, -pov-

indigenous *base* enchor-

indigo *comb* indi-, indo-[1]

indirect *comb* loxo-, plagio-; *base* ambag-

indisposed *pre* dys-, mal-; *comb* noso-, path, -pathic, patho-, -pathy; *base* aegr-, cachex-, -morb-, -pecca-, valetud-

individual *suf* -aholic, -aire, -an, -ant, -ard, -arian, -art, -ary, -ast, -ate, -ator, -ee, -eer, -en, -ent, -er, -ette, -eur, -fer, -ician, -ier, -ior, -ist, -le, -ling, -man, -nik, -o, -or, -person, -people, -ster, -woman, -yer

indolent *base* pigr-

inebriated *base* inebr-, methys-, temul-

inert gas *suf* -on

ineffectual *base* futil-, inutil-, mataeo-

inexpensive *base* vili-

infection *comb* lysi-, lyso-, -lysis, -lyte, -lytic, -lyze, phthisio-, -phthisis, phthysio-, -phthysis, putre-, putri-, pyo-, pytho-, sapro-, septi-, septico-, septo-, toxi-, toxico-, toxo-; *base* phthor-, vitia-

inferiority *pre* hypo-, sub-, under-; *comb* hystero-[2]; *base* hesson-; *suf* -aster[2]

infinity *base* apeiro-. See **forever**

infirm *pre* dys-, mal-; *comb* noso-, path, -pathic, patho-, -pathy; *base* aegr-, cachex-, -morb-, -pecca-, valetud-

inflammation *comb* erysi-, phlog(o)-; *suf* -itis. See **swelling**

inflect *base* -clit-

inflexible *stubborn:* *base* contum-, obdur-, obstin-, pervic-, proterv-; *stiff:* *comb* ancylo-, ankylo-, tetano-

inflorescence *comb* thyrsi-, thyrso-

infuse *comb* -enchyma[2]; *suf* -ate

ingest *comb* bromato-, -brotic, manduc-, -phage, phago-, -phagous,

-phagy, -sitia, sitio-, sito-, -troph, -trophic, tropho-, -trophy, -vora, -vore, -vorous; *base* -alim-, -cib-, comest-, -ed-, escul-, glutt-, -gust-

inguinal *comb* inguino-

inhabit(ant) *comb* -cole, -colent, -colous; *suf* -an, -ite

inhale *comb* -hale, -pnea, pneo-, pneumato-, pneumo-, pneumono-, pneusio-, pulmo-, spiro-; *base* afflat-

inhere *base* -sid-, situ-

inhibit *comb* coly-, freno-, isch-, koly-, -penia, -strain, -strict; *base* -string-; *suf* -en. See **checked**

iniquity *pre* dys-, mis-; *comb* caco-, iniq-, kak(o)-, mal(e)-, ponero-; *base* -prav-, sceler-, turp-

initial *comb* arch-, fore-, pre-, primi-, primo-, pro-, proso-, protero-, proto-; *base* -princip-

initiate *base* inaug-, incip-, init-

injection *base* trypan-

injudicious *base* fatu-, inan-, moro-, stult-

injurious *comb* noci-, pesti-; *base* deleter-, -nox-, pericul-

injury *comb* noci-, traumato-; *base* -nox-

ink *base* atrament-

innkeeper *base* caupon-

inquiry *base* erot-, -quir-, -rog-

insanity *comb* lysso-, -mania; *base* ament-[1], dement-

insatiable *base* avid-, edac-, gulos-

inscribe *comb* -gram, -graph, -grapher, -graphic, grapho-, -graphy, grapto-, -logue; *base* -scrib-, -script-, typo-

insect *comb* cimic-, core-[2], entomo-, insecti-, insecto-; ***neuropterous ~:*** base sial-[2]; **walking stick ~:** base phasm-. See **mite**

insert *base* calar-, calat-, pon-, pos-

inside *pre* eis-, em-, en-[1], il -, im-, in-[1], ir-; *comb* endo-, ento-, entre-, eso-, inter(o)-, interno-, intra-, intro-; ***from the ~:*** entostho-

insolent *base* contum-, impud-, procac-, proterv-

inspection *comb* -opsy, -scope, -scopic, scopo-, -scopy; *base* -(in)quir-, -(in)quis-, -scrut-

inspiration *base* afflat-

install *base* inaug-

instance of *suf* -ism

instantly *base* subit-

instep *comb* tarso-

instruct *comb* -pedia; *base* catech-, -didact-, doc-, -paed-

instrument (of) *suf* -ment[1], -ure; ~ *for scraping:* *base* strigil-; **medical** ~: -tome; **scientific** ~: -stat

insufficient *pre* demi-, hemi-, semi-; *comb* -atelia, atelo-

insult *base* contum-

intact *pre* be-, cata-, de-, kata-, ob-, per-; *comb* holo-, omni-, pan-, panto-, stone-, toti-; *base* integr-

intellect *comb* -gnomy, -gnosia, -gnosis, -gnostic, -gnoto, ideo-, -noia, -nomy, phren(o)-, psycho-, -sophy, thymo-, -witted; *base* -cogit-, -cogn-, ment(a)-, -noe-, -put-, -ratio-, -sci-

intelligent *base* sapien-

intensifier *pre* em-, en-, in-, za-

intercourse *comb* -lagnia; *base* -coit-, copul-, subagit-

internal *pre* eis-, em-, en-[1], il -, im-, in-[1], ir-; *comb* endo-, ento-, entre-, eso-, inter(o)-, interno-, intra-, intro-; *from the* ~: entostho-

interfunctioning *comb* -ergasia, ergasio-

intermix *pre* co-; *comb* conjugato-, -ergasia, gameto-, gamo-, hapto-, junct-; *base* aps-, apt-, -greg-, -soc-; *suf* -ate, -ize

interpretation *base* -hermen-

interrogate *base* -pet-, -quir-, -quis-, -rog-

intestinal pouch *comb* caeco-, ceco-, typhlo-

intestines *comb* entero-, ileo-, ilio-, intestino-, jejuno-; *base* viscer-; ~ *worm:* ascari-

intimidated *base* -pavid-, -tim-, trepid-. *See* **fear**

intoxicated *base* crapul-, -inebr-, -methys-, temul-

intractable *base* contum-, obstin-, pervic-, proterv-

invent *base* -heur-

inverse *pre* anti-, contra-, contre-, dis-, hetero-, ob-, un-; *comb* back-, counter-, enantio-, oppositi-

investigate *base* indag-

invisible *pre* sub-; *comb* calypto-, crypto-; *base* aphan-, occult-

involucre *base* involucr-

involuntary movement *comb* -chorea-, choreo-, -clonic, -clonus, spasmo-; *base* -stal-; *suf* -esmus, -ismus

iodine *comb* iodi-, iodo-

ion *comb* iono-, ionto-

irate *base* chol-, -invid-, -ira-, -margy

iridium *comb* iridico-, iridio-

iris *comb* irido-

Irish *comb* Hiberno-

iron *comb* ferri-, ferro-, sidero-[1]

irregular *comb* allo-, ametro-, anomalo-, anomo-, poecilo-, poikilo-; ~ *shape:* *comb* amorpho-

irridium *comb* iridico-, iridio-

irrigation *comb* -clysis; *base* chalast-, clysm-, clyst-

irritate *base* amycho-, erethis-, vex-

ischium *comb* ischi(o)-

island *base* insul-, neso-

isomer *comb* pseudo-

isthmus *base* isthm-

Italy *comb* Italo-

itch *comb* acari-, scabi-; *base* -prur-, psor-

ivory *base* ebur-

ivy *base* ciss-, -heder-

J

jackass *base* as-[2], asin-
jackdaw *base* gracul-
jagged *comb* serrato-; *base* cren-[1],
  lacin-
jail *base* -carcer-
jam *comb* emboli-, embolo-; *base*
  -byon-, -farct-
jaundice *comb* icter(o)-
jaw *comb* genia-, genio-, geny-[1],
  gnatho-, -gnathous, mandibulo,
  maxillo-; ~ *bone: base* -siagon-
jay *base* garrul-
jealous *base* -emul-
jeer *comb* catagelo-, katagelo-
jeopardy *base* pericul-
jejunum *comb* jejuno-
jellyfish *base* discophor-, medus-
jerk *comb* -chorea, choreo-, -clonic,
  -clonus, -esmus, -ismus, spasmo-,
  -tonic; *base* -stal-, -vellic-
jest *base* joco(s)-, jocu(l)-
jewel *base* -gemm-[2]
Jewish *comb* Judaico-, Judaeo-, Judeo-
jilt *base* relinq-, repud-
jingling *base* tinn-
job *comb* arti-, -craft, -ergasia, erga-
  sio-, -ergic, ergo-, -ergy, organo-,
  -urgy; *base* -opus-, pono-; *suf* -arian

join *comb* -ergasia, gameto-, gamo-,
  hapto-, junct-; *base* -aps-, -apt-[1],
  -greg-, -soc-; *suf* -ate, -ize; ~ *to-*
  gether: pre co-; *comb* conjugato; *base*
  zeug-, zeux-
joint *body* ~: *comb* arthr(o)-, articul-;
  ~ *socket:* gleno-; *jointed: base* -
  enarthra-
joke *base* joco(s)-, jocu(l)-
journey *comb* hodo-, -ode, odo-, via-;
  base apodemi-, -itin-, peregrin-
joy *comb* chero-; *base* beati-, elat-,
  felic-, gaud-, jubil-, macar-
judging *comb* -gnomy, -gnosia, -gno-
  sis, -gnostic; *base* -crit-[1], -judic-,
  krit-, -soph-
jug *base* urcei-
juice *comb* opo-; *base* -suc-
jump *base* -salta-
junction *pre* co-; *comb* conjugato-,
  -ergasia, gameto-, gamo-, hapto-,
  junct-; *base* aps-, apt-, -greg-, -soc-;
  suf -ate, -ize
jurisdiction *suf* -dom, -ric
justice *comb* dike-; *base* jud-
juvenile *comb* paedo-, pedi-, pedo-,
  proli-, tecno-; *base* -fil-, -puer-, tek-

K

kangaroo *base* macropod-
keel *base* -carin-; *keel-shaped: comb*
  tropido-
keen *base* -acer(b)-, trench-
keep *comb* -serve, -tain; *base* custod-,
  -ten-; ~ *away: comb* alex-, alexi-,
  alexo-
keg *comb* dolio-
kernel *comb* caryo-, karyo-; *base*
  -nucl-
kestrel *base* falco-
ketone *comb* keto-; *suf* -one

key *comb* clavi-[1], cleido-, clido-;
  ~ *hole: base* clithr-
kick *base* -calcitr-
kidnap *base* plag-, rap-, rep-
kidney *comb* nephro-, pyelo-, reni-,
  reno-
kidney-bean *base* phaseol-
killing *comb* -cidal, -cide, -cidious,
  -cidism, cteino-; *base* -dacn-, trucid-
kind *category: comb* -type; *suf* -atic;
  gentle: base -len-, mansue-, miti-,
  moll-

kindle *comb* causto-, igni- pyro-; *base* ard-², ars-, cauter-, celo-, combust-, crem-, phlog-, -ust-

kinetic *comb* cine-, -drome, dromo-, -dromous, excito-, kine-, -kinesi(a), -kinesis, -kinetic, kineso-, kineto-, kino-, -motive, -pragia, -praxia, -praxis, tremo-; *base* -stal-

kinfolk *base* cogn-, famil-, stirp-

king *base* basil-, reg(n)-

kingfisher *base* halcyon-

kinked *comb* cirri-, cochlio-, gyro-, helico-, spiro-, strepto-; *base* stromb-. *See* **curl**

kiss *base* bas-, basiat-, oscul-; *tongue ~:* cataglott-

kitchen *base* culin-

kite *bird: base* milv-

knack *base* -apt-, -habil-, -poten-, -qual-; *suf* -bility, -ful, -ship

knavish *pre* dys-, mis-; *comb* caco-, kak-, kako-, mal-, male-, ponero-; *base* facin-, flagit-, iniq-, nefar-, perdit-, -prav-, sceler-, scelest-, turp-

knead *base* subig-

knee *base* gen(u)-; *back of ~: base* poplit-; *~cap:* patell-

knife *comb* cultell-, cultri-, sica-

knit together *base* -hapto-, pegm-

knob *comb* clavato-, tylo-; *base* condyl-, nod-, umbo-

knock *base* -puls-

knot *base* -nod-, -tylo-

knowledge *comb* -gnomy, -gnosia, -gnosis, -gnostic, gnoto-, ideo-, -noia, -nomy, -phrenic, phrenico-, phreno-, psycho-, scio-², -sophy; *base* -cogit-, -cogn-, epistem-, ment(a)-, -noe-, -put-, ratio-, -sci-; *~ of language: comb* -glot, glotto-

kudu *base* tragelaph-

L

labia minora *comb* nympho-

labor *childbirth: comb* lochio-, -para, -parous, -tocia, toco-, toko-, -toky; *work: comb* -craft, ergic, -ergy, ergo-, -urgy; *base* ardu-, oper-¹, pono-

laborious *pre* dys-; *comb* -bar, bary-, mogi-; *base* ard³-, stren-

labyrinth-like *comb* labrynthi-, labryntho-

laceration *comb* sparasso-; *base* -sparax-

lacking *pre* a-, an-¹, dis-, ex-, il-, im-, in-, un-; *comb* lipo-²; *base* penur-, -priv-; *suf* -less; *~ a part: comb* ectro-; *~ an opening: comb* -atresia, atreto-; *~ teeth: base* edent-

lactic *comb* lacto-

ladder *base* scala-; *~ rung:* climac-

lady *comb* gyn(e)-, gyneco-, gyneo-, gyno-, -gynous, -gyny, -para, thely-, -wife; *base* -femin-, muliebr-, mulier-; *suf* -en, -enne, -ess, -ette, -ice, -ine, -stress, -trice, -trix

lake *comb* limno-; *base* lacus-

lamb *base* -agn-

lame *base* claud-, debil-

lamentation *base* myrio-, thren-

lamp *base* lampad-, lucern-, lychn-

lamprey *base* cyclostom-

lance *base* lanci-

land *comb* agri-, agro-, choro-, geo-; *base* embado-, tellur-, -terr-; *~ dedicated to a god: base* temen-; *strip of ~:* isthm-

language *comb* -glossia, gloss(o)-, -glot, glotto-, lingui-, linguo-; *suf* -ese. *See* **word**

lap *base* grem-

larch *base* larix-

large(r) *pre* super-; *comb* -fold, macro-, magni-, maxi-, pachy-, plethys-; *base* -ampl-, grandi-, -maj-. *See* **gigantic**

lark *base* coryd-

larva *comb* larvi-; *base* silph-

larynx *comb* guttur-, laryngo-
lascivious *base* tentig-
lash *base* flagell-
lassitude *comb* pono-; *base* -fatig-,
-kopo-, lass-
last *base* eschato-, -fin-, termin-,
-ultim-
lasting *base* diuturn-, dur(o)-, perenn-,
perm-, stabil-; ~ *all night: comb* -
pannychy
late *comb* opsi-[1], serot-. *See* **tardy**
later *pre* meta-, post-; *comb* hystero-[2]
latest *comb* neo-
latex *comb* latici-
lattice *base* cancell-, clathr-, cratic-
laudatory *base* eulog-
laugh *comb* gel-[2]; *base* cachinn-, -ris-
laurel *base* daphn-, lauri-
law *comb* juris-, nomo-, thesmo-; *base*
jud-, jur-, leg-[2], regul-
lawless *comb* anomo-
lawsuit *base* litig-
laxative comb -clysis; *base* chalast-,
clysm-, clyst-
layer(ed) *comb* -decker, lamelli-,
lamini-, lamino-, -plex, strati-, strato-
lazy *base* oti-, pigrit-
lead *conduct: comb* -arch, -duce,
duc(t)-, magist-; *base* hegemon-,
-reg-; *metal: comb* molybdo-,
plumbo-
leading *comb* -agogic, -agogue; *being*
led: base ductil-
leaf *comb* folii-, folio-, -folious,
petalo-, -phyll, phyllo-, -phyllous;
base bract-, clad-, frondi-; ~ *buds:*
base gemm-[1]; ~ *like: comb* foliato-
lean *comb* angusti-, dolicho-, lepto-,
mano-, stegno-, steno-, tenu-; *base*
areo-, gracil-, isthm-, maci-, stal-,
strict-
leap *base* salta-
learn *base* disc-, -math, soph-
leather(y) *comb* scyto-; *base* alut-, cori-,
pelli-, utri-[1]; ~ *bottle:* utrei-, utric-
leave *base* relinq-
leech *base* bdell-, discophor-, hirud-,
sanguisug-

leek *base* porr-, praso-
left *comb* laeo-, laevo-, levo-, sinistro-;
~ *handed:* scaev-
leg *base* -cnem-, -crur-, -scel-;
condition of ~: comb -scelia
legend *comb* mytho-, stori-; *base*
fabul-, -narr-
legumes *comb* legumini-
leisure *base* oti-
lemon *base* hesperid; *lemon-colored*:
comb citro-
lending *base* fener-
length *base* meco-. *See* **long**
leniency *base* clem-[2]
lens *comb* phaco-, phako-, -phakia;
base lent-[2]
lentil-shaped *comb* phaco-
leopard *base* pard-
leper comb lepra-, lepro-
less(en) *pre* demi-, hypo-, mis-, sub-,
subter-; *comb* hetto-, meio-, mini-,
mio-, oligo-; *base* decresc-, dimin-,
hesson-, -pauc-
lettuce *base* lactuc-
level *comb* homalo-, homolo-, plain-,
plani, plano-[1], platy-; *base* plat-
lever *base* -mochl-
lewd *base* cypriani-
liability *comb* hypegia-, hypengy-;
base paralip-
lice *comb* pedicul-, phthiro-
lichen *comb* licheni-, licheno-;
reproductive unit: comb soredi-
lick *base* lamb-, ligur(r)-, ling-[4]
licorice *base* glycyr-
lid *base* oper-[2]
lie *untruth: base* mendac-; *recline:*
base -cub-, -cumb-, decub-
life *comb* bio-, -biosis, vita-, vivi-,
zoo-, -zoic, -zooid; *base* -anim-;
~ *less: base* exanim-
ligament *comb* desmo-, ligamenti-,
ligamento-, syndesmo-
light *not dark: comb* actino-, luci-,
phengo-, phos-, photo-; *base* clar-,
-luc-, -lum-; *not heavy: base*
koupho-, levi(t)-
lighthouse *base* fan-, phar-

lightning *comb* astra-, sela-; *base* as-traph-, fulgur-, fulmin-

like *pre* para-, quasi-; *comb* homeo-, omœo, homoio-, homolo-, iso-, -phane, -phanic; *base* simil-; *suf* -acean, -aceous, -al[3], -an, -ar, -ary, -ean, -en, -eous, -esque, -ful, -ic, -il, -ile, -ine, -ing, -ish, -itious, -ize, -like, -ode[2], -oid, -ose[2], -osity, -some[2], -tious, -ular, -y

likeness *comb* icono-, -opsis, -vult-

liking *comb* -phile, -philia, -philiac, -philic, -philism, philo-, -philous

lily *base* lili-, -lirio-

limb *comb* -mele, -melia[1], melo-[3]

lime *CaO:* *comb* calcareo-; *base* calc-; *fruit:* tilia-

limit *comb* isch-, koly-, -penia, -strain, -strict ; *base* -fin-, -string-, termin-; *suf* -en; *~ limited to: comb* -specific, specio-; *having well-defined limits: comb* delo-

linden *base* tilia- (tiliaceous)

line *comb* lineo-, -stichia, sticho-, -stichous; *wavy ~: comb* gyroso-

link *pre* co-; *comb* conjugato-, -ergasia, gameto-, gamo-, hapto-, junct-; *base* aps-, apt-, -greg-, -soc-; *suf* -ate, -ize

lion *base* leo(n)-

lips *comb* cheilo-, chilo-, labio-; *base* labi-

liquid *base* flu-, -ner-; *make ~: base* liqu-. See **water**

little *comb* brachisto-, brachy-, brevi-, chamae-, micro-, mini-, nano-, parvi-, parvo-, pauci-, steno-; *base* -curt-, exig-; *suf* -cle, -cula, -cule, -culum, -culus, -een, -el, -ella, -en, -et, -ette, -idion, -idium, -ie, -illa, -illo, -isk, -kin, -le, -let, -ling, -ock, -ola, -ole, -rel, -ula, -ule, -ulum, -ulus, -y

liver *comb* hepatico-, hepato-; *base* jecor-

living *comb* bio-, vivi-, -zoic, -zooid; *base* -anim-, -vit-; *~ among: comb* -colous; *~ in: suf* -an

lizard *comb* -saur, sauro-, -saurus, scinci-, scinco-; *base* gecco-, lacert-, stellio-

load *base* oner-

loaded *comb* -filled, pleni-, pleo-, plero-, pluri-; *base* -pler-, -plet-; *suf* -acious, -ate, -ic, -ful, -ilent, -ose, -osity, -ous, -ulent, -y

lobe *comb* lobulato-; *ear: comb* auriculo-

lobster *base* astac-, -gammar-, homar-

location *comb* -land, loc(o)-, situ-, -stead, topo-, -topy; *base* ubi-; *suf* -age, -arium, -ary, -ensis, -ery, -orium, -ory. *Also see* "Location" in Part III

lock *comb* clido-; *base* cleid-; *lockjaw:* trism-

locust *base* locust-

lofty *base* celsi-

loins *comb* laparo-, lumbo-, osphy(o)-

long *comb* dolicho-, -footer, longi-, macro-, maxi-; *base* procer-; *~ duration: base* diuturn-; *~ words:* sesquipedal-

look *comb* eid(o)-, oculo-, ommat-, -opia, opsi-, -opsia, -opsis, opso-, -opsy, ophthalmo-, optico-, opto-, -scope, -scopic, scopo-, -scopy, visuo-; *base* -blep-, -scrut-, -spec-, -spic-, -vid-

loosen *comb* lyo-, lysi-, -lysis, lyso-, -lyte, -lytic, -lyze; *base* -lax-, -liqu-, -solu-, -solv-

loss *base* perd-

loss of control *comb* -crasia, -crasy

loss of knowledge *comb* -agnosia

loss of quality *base* degen-

lot *comb* clero-

lotus *comb* loto-

loudness *base* crepit-, frem-, ligyr-, strep(i)-, strid-, stridul-. *See* **sound**

louse *base* pedicul-, phthir-, phthyr-

love *comb* -phile, -philia, -philiac, -philic, -philism, philo-, -philous; *base* -agap-, -am-, charit-

loveplay *comb* paizo-, paraphil-, sarmass-

low(er) *pre* hypo-, infero-, infra-, sub-,
    subter-, under-; *comb* chamae-,
    infero-, tapino-; *base* hystat-;
    ~ **growing:** *comb* chamae-
luck *base* faust-, tych-
ludicrous *base* fatu-, inan-, moro-,
    stult-
lukewarm *base* tepe-
lumbar *comb* lumbo-
lump *base* gleb-, glom-
lunch *base* prand-
lung(s) *comb* -pnea, pneo-, pneu-
    mato-, pneumo-, pneumono-,
    pulmo-, pulmoni-, pulmono-, spiro-
lurking-hole *base* latebr-

lust *comb* eroto-, -lagnia, -mania;
    base appet-, -cup-, -libid-, tentig-
luster *comb* sela-; *base* -fulg-, gano-,
    lustr-, nitid-, pheng-, rutil-, stilb-,
    stilpno-
lye *base* lixiv-
lying down *base* -cub-, -cumb-,
    supin-
lymph(atic) *comb* lymphato-, lympho-;
    ~ **nodes:** *comb* lymphadeno-;
    ~ **vessels:** *comb* lymphangio-
lynx *base* lync-
lyre *base* lyri-, psall-
lyric *comb* lyrico-

M

macaw *base* psittac-
machine(s) *comb* mechano-
mackeral *base* scombr-
mad *comb* -margy; *base* frenet-, -fur-,
    -ira-
made of *suf* -en, -ic
madness *comb* lysso-, -mania; *base*
    ament-, dement-
magic *base* mago-
magnetic force *comb* magneto-
magnify *base* ampl-, aug-. *See*
    increased
magpie *base* corv-, garull-
maim(ed) *comb* pero-; *base* -mutil-
main *comb* arch(i)-[1], proto-; *base*
    -prim-, -princip-; ~ **land:** *comb*
    epeiro-
make, making *pre* em-, en-; *comb*
    -craft, ergo-, -facient, -fer, -fic,
    -fication, -gen, -genesis, -genic,
    -genous, -geny, -gerous, ideo-,
    -parous, -phor, -phorous, -plast,
    -plastic, plasto-, -plasty, poiesis,
    -poietic, -urgy; *base* -fabr-, -fac-,
    -fec-1; *suf* -ate, -atory, -en, -ic, -ing,
    -fy, -ize, -otic
Malay *comb* Malayo-
male *comb* andr(o)-, -androus, -andry,

arrheno-, -man, masculo-; *base*
    viril-
malevolent *pre* dys-, mis-; *comb* caco-,
    iniq-, kak(o)-, mal(e)-, ponero-;
    base -prav-, sceler-, turp-
malformed *comb* pero-; *base* -mutil-
malfunction *pre* dys-
malnutrition *comb* -atrophia,
    -atrophic
manage *base* ger-[1]
manatee *base* trichec-
mane *base* jubat-
manganese *comb* mangani-, mangano-
mangle *comb* sparasso-; *base* lacer-,
    lania-, sparax-. *See* **maim**
manifest *comb* luci-, phanero-, pheno-;
    base -clar-
mankind *comb* anthropo-
manner *comb* -wise
mantle *comb* pallio-
manufactured product *suf* -ite
manuscript *base* codico-
many *comb* multi-, myria-, myrio-,
    pluri-, poly-, sychno-; ~ **colored:**
    comb poecilo-; ~ **times:** *comb* pol-
    laki-. *See* **increased**
map *comb* carto-, charto-
maple *base* acer-[2]

marble *base* -marm-
margined *base* limbat-
marine *comb* halo-, mari-, thalasso-, thalatto-; *base* naut-, nav-, pelag-
mark *comb* celido-; *base* stigm-
market *base* negot-, nundin-
marlin *base* istiophor-
marmoset *comb* callithri-
marmot *base* sciur-
marriage *comb* gameto-, gamo-, -gamous, -gamy; *base* conjug-, marit-, -nub-, -nupt-
marrow *comb* -myelia, myelo-; *base* medull-
Mars *comb* areo-[1]
marsh *comb* helo-[2], palud-, palus-, ulig-
marsupial mammal *base* phalang-
marten *base* mustel-
martin *base* hirund-
masculine *comb* andro, -androus, -andry, arrheno-, masculo-; *base* viril-
massage *comb* masso-
massive *comb* bronto-, dino-, giganto-, mega-, megalo-, -megaly, pachy-
master *comb* magist-, maha-; *base* heri-
mastoid *comb* mastoido-
matching *pre* para-, quasi-; *comb* homeo-, omœo, homoio-, homolo-, iso-, -phane, -phanic; *base* simil-; *suf* -acean, -aceous, -al, -an, -ar, -ary, -ean, -en, -eous, -esque, -ful, -ic, -il, -ile, -ine, -ing, -ish, -itious, -ize, -like, -ode, -oid, -ose, -osity, -some, -tious, -ular, -y
material for *suf* -ing
matter *comb* hylo-
maxilla *comb* maxillo-
maxim *base* gnom-
maximum *pre* hyper-
meadow *base* prat-; ~ **lark:** icter-
meager *comb* oligo-, -penia, ptocho-, vidu-; *base* -mendic-, -paup-, penur-, -pov-
meal *comb* deipno-; *base* cen-, coen-, prand-. *See* **food.** *Also see* "Food" in Part III
meaning *base* etym-

means *suf* -cle, -ment[1]
measles *base* morbilli-
measure *comb* -meal, -meter, -metric(s), metro-, -metry. *See* "Measurement Science" in Part III
meat *comb* -burger, carni-, carnoso-, creo-, kreo-, -sarc, sarco-; ~ **market:** macell-
mechanical *comb* mechanico-; *base* banaus-
medical *comb* medico-; *base* -san-; ~ **treatment:** *comb* -iatrics, iatro-, -iatry
medicine *base* pharma(co)-; **medicinal:** comb saluti-
mediocre *pre* hypo-, sub-, under-; *comb* hystero-; *base* hesson-; *suf* -aster
meditate *base* melet-
medium *comb* mesati-, metrio-. *See* **middle**
meeting *base* congress-, congru-
melon *base* pepo-
melt *comb* lyo-, lysi-, -lysis, lyso-, -lyte, -lytic, -lyze; *base* deliqu-, fus-, -liqu-, -solu-, -solv-
membrane *comb* chorio-, choroid-, hymeno-, membrano-; **eyeball ~:** sclero-; **fetal ~:** allant(o)-, amnio-; ~ **partition:** *comb* mediastino-; **mucous ~:** *comb* muci-, muco-, mucoso-; ~ **sheath:** *comb* meningo-
memory *comb* -mnesia, -mnesis; *base* -mem-, -mnem-
menace *base* comminat-, min-
meninges *comb* meningo-
menstrual *comb* emmen-, -menia, men(o)-
mental *comb* -gnomy, -gnosis, -gnostic, -gnoto, ideo-, -noia, -nomy, phren(o)-, psycho-, -sophy, thymo-; *base* -cogit-, -cogn-, -noe-, -put-, -ratio-, -sci-; ~ **disorder:** *comb* -mania, -phrenia, -phrenic, phrenico-, phreno-, -thymia[1]
merchandise *base* empor-, empt-
mercy *base* clem-[2], mansue-
mere *comb* psilo-

mesentery *comb* meso-
metacarpus *comb* metacarpo-
metal *comb* metalli-, metallo-; ~ *plate:*
  base -elasmo-
metaphorical *comb* tropo-
metatarsus *comb* metatarso-
meteor names *suf* -id[1]
meteorological front *comb* fronto-
method *comb* -craft; *suf* -ade, -age,
  -al, -ance, -ancy, -asis, -asm, -ation,
  -cy, -ence, -ency, -ery, -esis, -iasis,
  -ice, -ics, -ing, -ion, -ism, -ment,
  -osis, -otic, -sion, -sis, -th, -tion,
  -tious, -ture, -ure, -y, -ysis
methoxy group *comb* methoxy-
methyl *comb* metho-
middle *comb* centri-, -centric, centro-,
  medi(o)-, mesati-, mesio-, meso-,
  mezzo-, mid-
midriff *comb* -phrenic, phrenico-,
  phreno-
midwifery *base* maieut-
mighty *comb* dino-. *See* powerful
migration *base* diaped-, peregrin-
mild *base* -len-, mansue-, miti-[1], moll-
milk(y) *comb* galact(o)-, lacti-, lacto-
mill *base* molend-
million *comb* mega-
millionth *comb* micro-
millipede *base* arthropod-, diplopod
mind *comb* -gnomy, -gnosis, -gnostic,
  -gnoto, ideo-, -noia, -nomy, phreni-,
  phreno-, psycho-, -sophy, thymo-,
  -witted; *base* -cogit-, -cogn-, ment-[2],
  -noe-, noo-, -put-, -ratio-, -sci-; ~
  disorder: comb -mania, -phrenia,
  -phrenic, -thymia
mine *base* bothro-
mineral *suf* -ite, -lite
mingle *comb* -phyr, -phyre, -phyric
mink *base* mustel-
minnow *base* cyprin-
minor *insignificant: base* -nuga-. *See*
  small child: comb paedo-, pedi-,
  pedo-, proli-, tecno-; *base* -fil-,
  -puer-, tek-
mint *base* menth-
miracle *comb* thaumato-

mirror *comb* catoptro-, eisoptro-,
  enoptro-, spectro-
misery *base* aerumn-
missile *base* ballist-
missing *pre* a-, an-, des-[1], dis-, ex-, il-,
  im-, in-, ir-, un-; *comb* lipo-; *base*
  paralip-, -priv-; *suf* -less; ~ *a part:*
  comb ectro-; ~ *an opening: comb*
  -atresia, atreto-
mist *comb* fracto-, nepho-, nephelo-;
  base calig-, -nebul-, -nub-
mistake *base* culp-, delict-, laps-,
  pecc-, sphal-
mistletoe *comb* ixo-
mite *comb* acari-, acarin-, acaro-, miti-[2].
  See termite
miter *base* mitri-
mixed, mixture *comb* -crasia, mixo-,
  mixti-, -phyr, -phyre, -phyric; *base*
  farrag-, -misc-, -temp-
mob *comb* ochlo-
mobility *comb* cine-, -drome, dromo-,
  -dromous, excito-, kine-, -kinesi(a),
  -kinesis, -kinetic, kineso-, kineto-,
  kino-, -motive, -pragia, -praxia,
  -praxis, tremo-; *base* -stal-
mockery *base* deris-, scomm-
mockingbird *base* -mim-
moderate *base* metrio-. *See* medium
modern *comb* neo-. *See* new
modesty *base* -pud-, verecund-
modification *comb* allo-, anomalo-,
  anomo-, poikilo-; *base* -mut-. *See*
  change
moisture *comb* hydro-, hygro-; *base*
  humect-, mad-, ulig-
molded *comb* -plast, -plastic, plasto-,
  -plasty
mole *blemish: base* nev(o)-; *animal:*
  base aspala-, talp-
mole rat *base* spalac-, zemni-
mollusks *comb* malaco-; *base* mollusc-;
  bivalve ~: base tellin-; ~*with leath-*
  ery tunics: base ascid-
molt *base* exuv-
money *comb* -penny ; *base* chremat-,
  -numm-, -pecun-, quaest-;
  ~ *exchange: base* cattall-

mongoose *base* viverr-
monk *base* monach-
monkey *base* cebo-, pithec-
monster *comb* terato-; *base* pelor-
month *base* mens-
monthly *base* emmen-
mood *comb* thymo-
moon *comb* luni-, lunu-, seleno-
moose *base* cervi-
moral *pre* bene-, eu-; *base* agath-,
 bon-, prob-
moray *base* muraen-
morel *base* morilli-, psomo-
morbid condition *comb* -iasis; *suf* -oma
more *pre* ad-, extra-, super-; *comb*
 auxano-, auxeto-, auxo-, multi-,
 myria-, myrio-, out-, over-, -plasia,
 pleni-, pleo-, pleio-, pleon-, plethys-,
 plio-, pluri-, pollaki-, poly-; *base* -
 aug-, -cresc-, -fold-, -pler-, -plet-.
 See addition
morning *base* -matut-
mortal *base* thneto-, thripto-
mortgage *base* -pign-
mosquito *comb* anophel-, culici-;
 base aed-
moss *comb* bryo-; *base* phasc-, musc-²,
 sphagn-, splachn-
most *comb* pleisto-
moth *base* arct-, lepidopter-, noctui-,
 phalaen-, tinea-
mother *comb* mater-, matri-, metr-,
 -para; *birth ~: comb* -para³
mother-in-law *base* socrus-, penther-
motion *comb* cine-, -drome, dromo-,
 -dromous, excito-, kine-, -kinesi(a),
 -kinesis, -kinetic, kineso-, kineto-,
 kino-, -motive, phoro-, -pragia, -
 praxia, -praxis, tremo-; *base* -stal-;
 capable of ~: base motil-; *easily set
 in ~: base* volub-
motor *comb* moto-
mountain *comb* oreo-, oro-²; *base*
 -mont-; *~ash:* sorb-²
mourning *comb* lype-; *base* dolor-,
 -fleb-, -flet-, -luct-, trist-
mouse *base* mur-¹, myo-² ; *meadow
 mouse: base* arvicol-

mouth *comb* -mouthed, or-¹, oro-,
 stomato-, -stome, -stomous; *open ~:
 base* ringi-; *roof of ~: comb* palato-,
 uranisco-, urano-; *~ wash:* collut-
move *comb* -grade, -motive, -plania,
 plano-²; *base* -bat-, -ced-, -cess-,
 -cur(s), -grad-, -gress-, -mob-,
 -mot-, mov-, -vad-, -vas-; *~ away:
 comb* allelo-, out-; *~ forward: comb*
 pro-; *~ toward: comb* -petal; *movement: comb* kinesi-, -kinesia, -kine-
 sis, kineso-, -praxia, -praxis
movies *base* cine-
muck *comb* blenno-, -chezia, copro-,
 lim-, muci-, muco-, myco-, myso-,
 -myxia, myxo-, p(a)edo-, scato-,
 stegno-, sterco-; *base* -fecu-, -fim-,
 molys-, rhypar-
mucus *comb* blenno-, muci-, muco-,
 mucoso-, -myxia, myxo-
mud *comb* pelo-; *base* -lim-, lut-
mulberry *base* -mor-², -mur-³
mulish *base* contum-, obstin-, pervic-,
 proterv-
mullet *base* mugil-, perces-
multiform *comb* polymorpho-
multiple *suf* -ce
multitude *comb* ochlo-
mummy *base* mummi-
murder *comb* -cidal, -cide, -cidious,
 -cidism; *base* dacn-, trucid-
murky *comb* ambly-, melano-, nycto-,
 scoto-; *base* achlu-, amaur-, fusc-,
 lyg-, obscur-, opac-, tenebr-
murmur *base* frem-, mussit-, susurr-
muscle *comb* musculo-, myo-¹, -tonic;
 ~ tension: -tonia
mushroom *comb* agar-, fungi-, myco-;
 base bolet- *see* fungus
music *comb* melo-¹, musico-, -tonic
musk *base* -mosch-
muskrat *base* cricet-
mussel *base* mytil-
mustard *base* sinap-
musty *base* mucid-
mutable *pre* be-, em-, en-, meta-,
 trans-; *comb* aetio-, -blast, -blastic,
 blasto-, -craft, ergo-, etio-, -facient,

-fic, -fication, -gen, -genesis, -genic, -genous, -geny, -parous, -plasia, -plasis, plasmo-, -plast, -plastic, plasto-, -plasty, -poiesis, -poietic, -trope, -tropic, -tropism, tropo-, -tropous, -tropy, -urgy; *base* camb-, -fabr-, -fec-, -mut-, -vari-, -vert-; *suf* -ate, en, -fy, -ize, -otic

mutilated *base* colo-

mutter *see* **murmur**
mutual *pre* co-, enter-, inter-, syl-, sym-, syn-, sys-; *comb* allelo-, hama-, symphyo-, synchro-; *base* -allac-, -allag-, -allaxis-, -mutu-
myrtle *base* myrti-
mystical *comb* mystico-
myth *comb* mythico-, mytho-

N

nail *comb* helo-[1], onych-,-onychia, ony-cho-, scolo-; *base* clav-, ungui-, ungul-
naked *comb* gymno-, nudi- psilo-
name *comb* nomato-, -nomia, ono-mato-, -onym; *base* appell-, -nom-, -nym-; *to name: base* nuncup-
names of ~ acids: *suf* -onic; ~ **alcohols:** *suf* -itol; ~ **animals:** *suf* -id, -ida, -idae, -iformes, -zooic; ~ **bacteria:** *suf* -ella; ~ **classes:** *suf* -acea, -aceae, -ia, -oidea; ~ **companies:** *suf* -co, -ine; ~ **compounds:** *suf* -ide, -idine; ~ **country:** *comb* -land; *suf* -ia; ~ **directions:** *suf* -ern; ~ **diseases:** *comb* -aemia, -emia; *suf* -asis, -ia, -itis, -osis; ~ **electronic devices:** *comb* -tron; ~ **enzymes:** *suf* -ase; ~ **families:** *suf* -idae; ~ **festivals:** *comb* -fest, -mas; *suf* -ia; ~ **genera:** *suf* -aria, -odus, -soma; ~ **groups:** *comb* -zoa, -zoon; *suf* -aria, -id, -ini; ~ **hormones:** *suf* -kinin; ~ **meteors:** *suf* -id; ~ **minerals:** *suf* -lite; ~ **neutral substances:** *suf* -in ; ~ **numerals, collective:** *suf* -ad; ~**orders:** *suf* -acea; ~ **plants:** *suf* -ad, -ales, -ia; ~ **radicals:** *suf* -yl; ~ **super-families:** *suf* -oidea; **taxonomic ~:** *suf* -ota, -ote
narcotics *comb* leth-, mecon-, narco-
narrow *comb* angusti-, areo-, dolicho-, isthm-, lepti-, lepto-, stegno-, steno-; *base* lirell-, -phim-, -stal-, -strict-, -tenu-

nasal *comb* nasi-, naso-, rhino-
nationality *suf* -an, -ean, -ian, -ish, -ite, -n
native *base* enchor-, indigen-; *suf* -ite
nature *comb* -ousia, -ousian; *base* quid-; *having the ~ of: comb* -natured; *suf* -eous
natural *comb* innato-, physico-, physi-, physio-
navel *comb* omphalo-, umbilici-
near *pre* a-, ac-, ad-, af-, ag-, al-, an-, ap-, ar-, as-, at-, by-, cis-[1], epi-, para-, peri-; *comb* juxta-, citra-, pene-, plesio-, proximo-; *base* engus-, propinq-. *See* **adjacent**
nebulous *base* ambig, dub-, ancip-
neck *comb* atlo-, cervico-, coll-[1], jugo-, jugulo-, trachelo-; *base* -auchen-; *animal ~: comb* dero-; ~ *of land: base* isthm-
necklace *base* monil-
nectar *comb* nectari-
needle *comb* aci-, acicul-; *base* acer-[1], -aichm-, -belon-, raphid-; *needle-like: comb* rhaphio-
negatives *pre* a-, ab-, an-, anti-, apo-, cata-, de-, dis-, dys-, ex-, il-, im-, in-, ir-, mal-, mis-, ne-, non-[1], ob-, un-; *comb* anti-, -atresia, atreto-, contra-, counter-, ectro-, lipo-, mal-, neutro-, nihil-, no-, nulli-, with-; *base* -priv-; *suf* -less
neglect *base* paralip-

neighbor *base* geiton(o)-, -geton;
neighborhood: *base* vicin-
nematodes *comb* nemato-
neoplasm *suf* -oma
nephew *base* nepo-
nerve *comb* ganglio-, nervi-, nervo-,
neuro-
nest *base* -cali-, cubil-, nid(i)-
net/network *comb* dictyo-, -plex, reti-,
reticulato-, reticulo-; *fishing net:*
base sagen-
nettle *comb* cnido-; *base* -urtic-
neutral(izing) *pre* anti-; *comb* neutro-
neutral substances *suf* -in
new *comb* caeno-², caino-, cainoto-,
-cene, ceno-¹, cenoto-, kaino-,
kainoto-, neo-, thalero-; *base*
-nov-¹
newt *base* stellio-
NH *comb* ~ *acid radicals:* -imido;
~ *nonacid radicals:* imino-
nicknames *suf* -y³
night *comb* nocti-, nycta-, nycti-,
nycto-; *base* -crepus-, -vesper-;
all ~: *comb* -pannychy
nightingale *base* philomel-
nightmare *base* malneiro-
nimbleness *comb* ocy-, tacho-, tachy-;
base alacr-, celer-, festin-, veloc-
nine *comb* ennea-, nona-; *base* -nov-²;
~ *hundred:* enneacent-. *Also see*
"Numbers" *in Part III*
nineteen *base* enneakaideca-,
undeviginti-
ninety *base* enneaconta-, nonagen-,
nonages-
ninth *base* non-²
nip *base* vellic-
nipple *comb* mamilli-, papilli-,
papillo-, papilloso-, thelo-, umbo-.
See **breast**
niter *comb* nitro-
nitrogen *comb* azo-, nitro-, nitroso-;
~ *plus hydrocarbon:* diazo-
NO radical *comb* nitro(so)-
nod *base* nut(a)-
noise *base* crepit-, frem-, ligyr-,
strep(i)-, strid-, stridul-. *See* **sound**

noiseless *comb* hesy-; *base* -plac-,
quiesc-, -tacit-
nonacid radical *comb* -amine, amino-
none *comb* nulli-. *See* **negatives**
nonsense *base* fatu-, inan-, moro-,
stult-
noon *base* merid-
normal *comb* normo-
Norman *comb* Normano-
north *base* borea-, septen-
northern lights *comb* aurora-
nose *comb* nasi-, naso-, rhino-,
rhyncho-, -rrhyncha. *See* **beak.**
~ *bleed:* epistax-; ~ *blowing:*
emunct-; *snub* ~: simo-; *sneer:*
mycter-
nostalgia *comb* nosto-
nostrils *base* nari-
not *pre* a-³, ab-, an-¹, apo-, cata-, de-,
dis-, ex-, il-, im-, in-, ir-, mis-, ne-,
non-¹, ob-, un-; *comb* anti-, contra-,
counter-, mal-, neutro-, no-, nulli-,
with-; *suf* -less
not having *pre* a-, an-, des-, dis-, ex-,
il-, im-, in-, ir-, un-; *comb* -atresia,
atreto-, ectro-, lipo-; *base* -priv-; *suf*
-less
notch *comb* crenato-, crenulato-,
-glyph; *base* forfic-. *See* **jagged**
notes *musical scale:* *comb* -tonic;
written: *comb* -gram, -graph,
-grapher, -graphic, grapho-, -graphy,
grapto-, -logue, stigno-; *base* -scrib-,
-script-, typo-
nothing *base* nihili-
notion *comb* -gnomy, -gnosia, -gnosis,
-gnostic, gnoto-, ideo-, -noia,
-nomy, phreno-, psycho-, -sophy
base -cogit-, -cogn-, epistem-, -noe-,
-put-, ratio-, -sci-
nourishment *comb* bromato-, -brotic,
manduc-, opso-, -phage, -phago,
-phagous, -phagy, -sitia, sitio-, sito-,
-trophia, -trophic, tropho-, -trophy,
-vora, -vore, -vorous; *base* -alim-,
-cib-, -gust-, -nutr-, thrept-
noxious *comb* noci-, pesti-; *base*
deleter-, -nox-, pericul-

nucleus *comb* caryo-, karyo-, nuclei-, nucleo-

number *base* arith-, -numer-; ***even ~:*** *comb* artio-; ***uneven ~:*** *comb* impari-, perisso-; ***a number of:*** *suf* -age, -some[3]. *Also see* "Numbers" in Part III

numbness *comb* narco-; *base* torp-

numerals *base* arith-; ***cardinal ~:*** *suf* -teen; ***collective ~:*** *suf* -ad; ***ordinal ~:*** *suf* -eth, -th. *Also see* "Numbers" in Part III

numerous *comb* multi-, myria-, myrio-, pluri-, poly-, sychno-

nurse *comb* threptero-; *base* threps-, thrept-

nut, nut-shaped *comb* caryo-, karyo-, nuci-, nucleo-

nuthatch *base* sitt-

nutmeg *base* myrist-

nutrition *comb* bromato-, -brotic, manduc-, opso-, -phage, -phago, -phagous, -phagy, -sitia, sitio-, sito-, -trophia, -trophic, tropho-, -trophy, -vora, -vore, -vorous; *base* -alim-, -cib-, -gust-, -nutr-, thrept-

nymphs *comb* nympho-

O

oak *base* querc(i)-, robor-[2]; ***evergreen ~:*** cerr-

oar *comb* -reme, remi-

oats *base* aven(i)-

obedient *base* moriger-

obese *comb* adip(o)-, lipo-, pimel(o)-, pio-, stearo-, steato-; *base* -aliph-, lipar-, -obes-, -pingu-, sebo-

object of an action *suf* -ate

objective *comb* teleo-, telo-, ultim(o)-; *base* -fin-, -termin-

oblige *base* -mand-

oblique *comb* loxo-, plagio-; *base* ambag-

oblong *comb* oblongo-

obscenity *base* aischro-, borbor-, copro-, fescinn-

obscure *comb* enigmato-; *base* ambig, aphan-, dub-, ancip-

observe *comb* eid(o)-, oculo-, ommat-, -opia, opsi-, -opsia, -opsis, opso-, -opsy, ophthalmo-, optico-, opto-, -scope, -scopic, scopo-, -scopy, visuo-; *base* -blep-, -scrut-, -spec-, -spic-, -vid-

obsessed with *comb* -aholic, -lagnia, -philia, -ridden

obstinate *base* contum-, obstin-, pervic-, proterv-

obstructed *comb* brady-; *base* -cunct-, imped-, -mora-, obturat-, occlud-, occlus-, -tard-

obstruction *comb* emboli-, embolo-; *base* -byon-, -farct-

obtain *base* -cap-, -cep-, -cip-, -dyte-

obtuse *comb* obtusi-

obvious *comb* lampro, luc-, luci-; *base* -clar-

ocean *comb* halo-, mari-, thalasso-, thalatto-; *base* aequor-, naut-, nav-, pelag-

ochre *comb* ochreo-

occipital *comb* occipito-

occlude *base* obturat-, occlud-, occlus-

occupation *comb* arti-, -craft, -ergasia, ergasio-, -ergic, ergo-, -ergy, organo-, -urgy; *base* -opus-, pono-; *suf* -arian

odd-numbered *comb* impari-

odor *comb* brom(o)-, -odic, odori-, odoro-, -olent, olfacto-, -osmia, osmo-[1], osphresio-, ozo-, ozono-; *base* fet-, nidor-. *See also* "The Senses" in Section III

of *suf* -acean, -aceous, -ac[2], -ad[2], -al, -an, -ar, -arious, -ary, -atic, -ative, -atory, -eae, -ean, -eous, -ery, -etic, -ial, -ian, -ic, -id, -il, -ile, -ina, -inae, -ine, -ing, -ious, -istic, -ite,

-itic, -itious, -itive, -ive, -oidea, -ory, -otic, -tious, -tive, -ular; ~ *one another:* comb allelo-

off *pre* ab-, apo-, de-, ex-, for-

offering *base* -don-, -thy-

office *suf* -acy, -ate[3], -cy, -dom, -ship

offspring *comb* proli-

often *comb* pluri-, pollaki-, poly-; *base* crebr-; *suf* -le

oil *comb* elaeo-, elaio-, eleo-, olea-, -oleic, oleo-

ointment *comb* myro-; *base* -unct-, ungu-

old *comb* archaeo-, archeo-, eo-, gerasco-, gero-, geronto-, grand-, paleo-, presbyo-; *base* -antiq-, -sen-, -vet-; ~ *age:* ger-[2]; ~*woman:* grao-

omission *pre* a-, an-, dis-, ex-, il-, im-, in-, ir-, un-; *comb* lipo-; *base* paralip-, -priv-; *suf* -less; ~ *of an opening:* comb -atresia, atreto-; ~ *of a part:* comb ectro-

on *pre* ana-, epi-, ob-, sur-; ~ *both sides:* comb amph(i)-; ~ *the left side:* comb laeo-, laevo-, levo-, sinistro-; ~ *the other side:* pre trans-; ~ *the outside:* pre epi-; ~ *the right side:* comb dexio-, dextro-; ~ *the side:* pre by-; comb lateri-, latero-; ~ *this side of:* pre cis-; comb citra-; ~ *top:* pre super-

one *comb* eka-, haplo-, heno-, mono-, uni-; ~ *and one-half:* comb sesqui-; ~ *billion:* comb giga-; ~ *billionth:* comb nan(n)o-; ~ *by one:* katheno-; ~ *fifth:* quint-; ~ *fourth:* comb tetarto-; ~ *half:* comb demi-, dicho-, dimid-, hemi-, mezzo-, semi-; ~ *heptillion:* comb yotta-; ~ *heptillionth:* comb yocto-;~ *hexillion:* comb zetta-; ~ *hexillionth:* comb zepto-; ~ *hundred:* comb centi-, hecato-, hecto-, hekto-; ~ *hundredth:* comb centi-; ~ *million:* comb mega-; ~ *millionth:* comb micro; ~ *quadrillion:* comb femto-; ~ *quadrillionth:* comb peta-; ~ *quintillion:* comb atto-; ~ *quintil-lionth:* comb exa-; ~ *thousand:* comb chili-, kilo-; ~ *thousandth:* comb milli-; ~ *trillion:* comb pico-; ~ *trillionth:* comb tera-. *See also* "Numbers" in Part III

one another *comb* allelo-

oneself *comb* auto-, self-; *base* sui-

one who __ *suf* -aholic, -aire, -an, -ant, -ar[2], -ard[2], -arian, -art, -ary, -ast, -ate, -ator, -ee, -eer, -en, -ent, -er, -ette, -eur, -fer, -ician, -ier, -ior, -ist, -le, -man, -nik, -o, -or, -person, -people, -ster, -woman, -yer; ~ *is well versed in __:* -logist; ~ *worships:* comb -later

one-eyed *base* lusc-

one's own *comb* heauto-, idio-, pro-, prio-, self-, sui-

onion *base* cep-[2], cromny-

ooze *base* ulig-

opaque *comb* glauco-

open-mouthed *base* ringi-

open space *comb* agora-, ceno-, keno-

opening *base* -apert-, -cav-, fenest-, foram-, œgo-, oigo-, osti-, patul-, pylo-, rim, valv-; *lack of ~:* comb -atresia, atreto-; *surgical ~:* -stomy

operation *comb* -ectomy

opinion *base* gnom-

opium *base* -mecon-

oppose *comb* macho-, -machy; *base* bell-, pugil-, -pugn-

opossum *base* didelph-

opposite *pre* anti-, contra-, contre-, dis-, hetero-, ob-, un-; *comb* back-, counter-, enantio-, oppositi-

option *base* -opt-, -vol-

opulence *comb* chryso-, pluto-; *base* chrem-, -opul-, pecun-

oracle *comb* chresmo-

orange *fruit:* *base* -hesperid-; *color:* *base* auranti-. *Also see* "Colors" in Part III

orangutan *base* -pong-

orb *comb* ano-, annul-, crico-, cyclo-, disco-, globi-, globo-, glom-, gyro-, orbito-, -sphere, sphero-, stilli-, zon-, zoni-; *base* -anu-, -cing-,

-cinct-, -circin-, -circul-, -coron-,
-glomer-, -numm-, -orb-, -rot-,
-troch-
orbit *comb* orbito-
orchid *comb* orchido-[1]
order *placement: comb* -tactic, -tac-
tous, taxi-, -taxia,-taxis, taxo-, -taxy;
base -pon-, -pos-; *right ~: base*
eutax-; *command: base* imper-, -jus-,
-mand-
ordinary *comb* homalo-, homolo;
~ people: comb demo-; *base* -pleb-,
-popul-
organ *comb* organo-; *suf* -ite; *having*
female ~: comb -gynous; *having*
male ~: comb -androus
organic *comb* organo-
origin *comb* aetio-, -blast, blasto-,
-blasty, -carp, -carpic, carpo-,
-carpous, etio-, -gen, -genic,
-genesis, -genetic, -genous, -geny,
-gone, -gonium, gono-, -gony,
-phyletic, sperma-, spermal,
spermatio-, spermato-, spermi-,
-spermic, spermo-, -spermous,
sporo-; *base* -init-; *suf* -esce,
-escence, -escent
original *comb* archaeo-, primi-,
primo-, proto-
originate *base* inaug-, incip-, init-
oriole *base* -icter-
osmium *comb* osmio-
osmosis *comb* osmo-[2]
osprey *base* ossifrag-
ostrich *base* -rat-, struthi-
other *comb* allo-, alter-, hetero-;
base -ali-[2]
otter *base* latax-, -lutr-

out of *pre* e-, ec-, ef-, ex-. *See* **outside**
outcome *comb* ergo-, -ergic, -ergy; *suf*
-age, -asm, -ata, -ation, -ency, -ism,
-ma, -ment, -mony, -sion, -ure
outgrowth *comb* cele-, -edema, gan-
glio-, -phym(a); *base* -tum-
outside *pre* epi-, exo-, extra-, extro-,
para-, preter-; *comb* ecto-, extero-,
foris-, out-. *See* **out of**
outskirts *base* limin-, marg-
ovalyl *comb* oxal-, oxalo-
ovary *comb* gyn(o)-, -gynous, -gyny,
oario-, oophoro-, ovario-
over *above: pre* ano-, meta-, ob-,
preter-, super-, supra-, sur-,
sursum-; *comb* over-; *again: pre*
ana-, re-; *base* -palin-; *excessive: pre*
hyper-, super-, ultra-; *comb* over-,
poly-
overflow *base* antlo-, diluv-, inund-
overlapping *comb* imbricato-
oversight *base* culp-, delict-, laps-,
pecc-, sphal-
overt *comb* lampro-, luc-, luci-,
-phane, phanero-, -phanic, -phany,
pheno-; *base* -clar-, -schem-, -spec-,
-spic-
overthrow *base* vict-, -vinc-
overweight *base* obes-, pingu-
ovum *comb* oo-, ovario-, ovi-[1], ovo-
owl *base* strigi-, tyto-, ulul-[2]
ox *comb* bou-, bov-, bu-
oxygen *comb* oxa-, oxy-[2]; *deprived of ~:*
comb deoxy-; *having two atoms of ~:*
comb dioxy-
oyster *comb* ostrei-, ostreo-; *base*
-ostrac-
ozone *comb* ozono-

P

pack together *base* stip-[2]
pad *comb* tylo-
page size *suf* -mo
pain *comb* alge-, algesi-, -algia, algo-,
-algy, -dynia, noci-, -odynia, odyno-,

pono-[1]; *base* dolor-, -nox-; *sudden ~:*
comb -agra. *See* **suffering**
paint *base* -pict-, pigm-
pairs *pre* bi- *comb* conjugato-,
didymo-, diplo-, zyga-, zygo- ;

paired: *base* chias- **palate** *comb*
  palato-, uranisco-, urano-, velar-
pale *comb* pallidi-
paleontological *comb* paleo-
palliative *base* anet-, -len-, miti-[1]
pallium *comb* pallio-; *base* stragul-
palm *hand: comb* palmati-, palmato-;
  base then-; *tree: base* palmac-
pan *comb* lecano-
pancreas *comb* pancreato-, pancreo-
pander *comb* leno-
panic *comb* -phobe, -phobia, -phobic,
  phobo-; *base* pavid-, tim(or)-, -trem-,
  -trep-. *Also see* "Fear" *in Part III*
paper *comb* carto-, charto-, papyro-
papillary *comb* papilli-, papillo-, papil-
  loso-
papule *comb* papulo-
papyrus *comb* papyro-
parachute (using) *comb* para-
parade *comb* -cade
paraffin series: hydrocarbon *suf* -ane
parakeet *base* psittac-
paralysis *comb* -plegia, -plegy; *base*
  pares-
paramount *comb* arch-, archi-, proto-;
  base -prim-, -princip-
parasite *base* colaco-, parasit-, pothiri-,
  trypano-, vermin-
parasol *base* umbell(i)-, umbrell(i)-
parched *comb* carpho-, xero-; *base*
  arid-, celo-, cherso-, -sicc-, torr-
parchment *base* pergamen-
parent form *comb* proto-
parietal *comb* parieto-
parrot *base* galli-, psittac-
parsley *base* petrosel-
part(s) *comb* -fold, -meran, -mer(e),
  mer(o)-[1], -merous, par-, parti-
participant *suf* -ade; ~ *in govt: comb*
  -crat
particles *base* chalic-; *elementary* ~:
  suf -on
particular *comb* -specific
partition *comb* parieto-, -phragma,
  phragmo-, septo-; *base* -mur-
partly *comb* demi-, hemi-, semi-;
  ~ *serious:* serio-

partridge *base* gallinac-, -perdic-,
  -perdri-
parturient *comb* -para
pass *base* -bat-
passable *base* perm-
passage *comb* isthm-, meato-, over-,
  poro-, soleno-; *base* -bat-
past *comb* preter-
paste *base* glutin-. *See* **glue**
pastoral care *base* poimen-
patch *comb* emboli-, embolo-, -plakia
path *comb* -ode[1], odo-; *base* -itin-,
  -via-
pathetic *base* fleb-, trist-
pattern *base* regul-
pawn *base* pign-
pay *base* -pend-, -pens-
pea *comb* pisi-
peace *base* -eiren-, -iren-, -pac-, -pax-
peach *base* persic-
peacock *base* pavon-
peak *comb* coryph-; *base* culmin-
peanut *base* arach-
pear *comb* apio-, piri-, piro-, pyri-
pearl *base* margarit-
peat bog *base* turbar-
pebble *comb* pesso-, psepho-; *base*
  calcul-. *See* **stone**
peculiar *comb* aetheo-, anom(o)-,
  anomalo-. *See* **irregular**
peculiarity of *suf* -ism
pedately *comb* pedati-
peel *comb* -lemma[2]
pejorative *suf* -aster, -erel
pelican *base* onocrot-, pelecan-
pelvis *comb* pelvi-, perineo-, pyelo-
pen *base* styl-
penetrate *base* terebr-
penguin *base* sphenisc-
peninsula *base* chersones-
penis *comb* medo-, peo-, phall(o)-;
  base med-, mentul-
pennant *base* vexill-
penniless *comb* -penia, ptocho-, vidu-;
  base -mendic-, -paup-, penur-, -pov-
people *comb* dem(o)-, ethno-; *base*
  anthrop-, hom-, homin-, -pleb-,
  -popul-, -vulg-

pepper *base* piper-
perception *comb* -esthesia, -esthesio, percepto-
perch *fish: base* perc- *sit: base* -sess-
percussion *comb* pless(i)-; *base* -crot-, -cuss-, -puls-, -tus-, vapul-, verber-
perforation *comb* -tresia. See **tear**
perfume *comb* myro-, -thymia[2]
pericardial *comb* pericardiaco-, pericardio-
peril *base* pericul-
perineum *comb* perineo-
period *time: comb* back-, chrono-, eo-, horo-, paleo, protero-, yester-; *menstrual: comb* emmen-, -menia, meno-
periosteum *comb* periosteo-
perishable *base* caduc-, fragil-
peritoneum *comb* meso-, peritoneo-
permanent *base* diuturn-, dur(o)-, perenn-, perm-, stabil-
pernicious *comb* noci-, pesti-; *base* -nox-, pericul-
peroneal *comb* peroneo-
perpetual *base* assid-, contin-, incess-, perpet-
person *suf* -aholic, -aire, -an, -ant, -ard, -arian, -art, -ary, -ast, -ate, -ator, -ee, -eer, -en, -ent, -er, -ette, -eur, -fer, -ician, -ier, -ior, -ist, -le, -ling[1], -man, -nik, -o, -or[2], -person, -people, -ster, -woman, -yer
personal *comb* idio-, proprio-, self-
perspiration *comb* diaphor-, sudori-; *base* -hidr-, -suda-
persuade *base* -duc-
pertaining to *suf* -ac[2], -acean, -aceous, -ad, -al, -an, -ar[2], -arious, -ary, -atic, -ative, -atory, -eae, -ean, -eous, -ery, -etic, -ial, -ian, -ic, -id, -idan, -il, -ile, -ina, -inae, -ine, -ing, -ious, -istic, -ite, -itic, -itious, -itive, -ive, -oidea, -ory, -otic, -tious, -tive, -ular
perverted *base* deprav-
pest *comb* pesti-, vermin-
pestilence *comb* loemo-, loimo-. See **disease**
petal *comb* petuli-, -sepalous

petroleum *comb* petro-
petty *base* pusill-, rhopo-
pharynx *comb* pharyngo-
pheasant *base* alector-, gallinac-, phasian-
phenanthrene *comb* phenanthro-
phenol *base* carbol-; *suf* -ol
phenyl *comb* pheno-
philisophical *comb* philisophico-
phlegm *base* phlegm-, pituit-
phonetic *comb* phonetico-; ~ *stress: comb* -tonic
phony *comb* kibdelo-, mytho-, pseudo-; *base* fict-, mendac-, -notho-
phosphorous *comb* phospho-, phosphoro-
photography *comb* photo-
phrase *comb* phraseo-
phylum *comb* phylo-
physical *comb* physi-, physico-, physio-; ~ *love:* eroto-
piece *comb* clasmato-, -fid; *base* frag-, frust-, -par-
pig *base* porcin-, sui-
pig-headed *base* contum-, obstin-, pervic-, proterv-
pigeon *base* columb-, palumb-, perister-, pullastr-
pike *base* esoc-
pile *base* -acerv-, conger-, -cumul-
pillar *comb* column-, stylo-[2]; ~ *like:* paxill-; *small* ~: columelli-
pillow *base* pulvin-
pimp *base* leno-
pimple *comb* pustulo-
pin *base* acu-, belon-
pinch *base* -rrhexo-
pine *base* -peuce-, pin-; ~ *cone:* strobil-
pineapple *base* bromel- (bromeliaceous)
pinnately *comb* pinnati-, pinnato-
pipe *comb* aulo-, follic-, salpingo-, siphoni-, siphono-, solen(o)-, syringo-, tubi-, tubo-, tubuli-, vasi-; *base* calam-, fistul-, -syr-
pistachio *base* pistac-

pistil *comb* gyn(o)-, -gynous, -gyny
pit *base* -taph(o)-, taphro-
pitcher *comb* urcei-, urceo-
pitchlike *base* pitta
pith *base* medull-
pitted *base* bothr-, fov-, scrobic-
place, a *comb* -land, loco-, situ-,
  -stead, topo-,-topy, ubi-; *suf* -ensis;
  ~ *of:* *suf* -age; ~ *for:* *suf* -arium, -ary,
  -cle, -ery, -orium, ory. *Also see*
  "Location" in Part III
place, to *comb* -thesis, -thetic; *base*
  -pon-, -pos-; *suf* -en
placenta *base* mazo-[1], placenti-
plague *comb* pesti-
plait *comb* pleco, plecto-
plane *surface:* *comb* explanato-, plani-,
  plano-[1]
plankton *comb* plankti-
planted *base* sativ-
plant growth: unequal *comb* -nastic,
  -nasty
plant(s) *comb* botano-, herbi-, -phyte,
  phyto-, vegeti-, vegeto-; *suf* -ad,
  -aceae, -ales, -eae, -ia; *coniferous ~:*
  base zamia-, zamio-; *green ~:* *base*
  thall-; ~ *juices:* *base* muci-; ~ *sap:*
  base succi-; ~ *lice:* aphido-; *tumor-*
  ous ~ tissue: *base* cecid-
plastic surgery *comb* -plasty
plate *comb* lamelli-, lamini-, lamino-,
  placo-; *base* bract-, -tect-; *metal ~:*
  comb elasmo-
platinum *comb* platini-, platino-
platypus *base* monotrem-, protother-
play *comb* -lude
please *base* delect-, -plac-, volupt-
pleasure *base* -hedon-, volupt-
pledge *base* -pign-
pleura *comb* pleuro-
plover *base* charadr-, pluvial-
pluck *base* -tillo-, -vellic-
plug *comb* emboli-, embolo-; *base*
  -byon-, -farct-
plunge *comb* -merge, -merse
plural *suf* -a, -acea, -aceae, -ae, -des[2],
  -eae, -en[2], -es, -i, -ia, -ata, -ota, -s;
  collective ~: *suf* -ana

pod *base* kelyph-, silicul-, siliqu-
poems *comb* rhapso-; *base* -metr-,
  muso-; *suf* -ad
pointed *comb* acantho-, aceto-, acetyl-,
  acid-, acro-, acu-, acuti-, cusp-,
  mucro-, oxy-[1], scillo-, scolo-, spiculi-,
  spiculo-, stilo-, stylo-[1]; *base* -acerb-,
  aci-, -aichm-, -aichur-, -belon-,
  fastig-, muric-, -punct-, -piq-,
  -pung-, stigm-; *sharp-pointed:*
  comb raduli-
points, having *comb* punctato-
poison *comb* tox(i), toxico-, -toxin,
  toxo-[1], veneni-, veneno-
polar *comb* polari-
polecat *base* mustel-
police officer *base* alyt-
polished *base* levig-, xest-
political *comb* politico-
pollen *comb* palyn-, pollini-
pollute *base* -turp-
polymer of *pre* meta-
pomegranate *base* balaust-
pond, pool *comb* limno-; *base* lacus-,
  stagn-
poor *deficient:* *comb* -isch-, oligo-,
  -penia; *penniless:* *comb* ptocho-,
  vidu-; *base* -mendic-, -paup-, penur-,
  -pov-; *quality:* *comb* caco-, kako-
poppy *comb* opio-, papaver-; *base*
  -mecon-
porcelain *base* poticho-
porcupine *base* hystric-
pore *comb* pori-, poro-, poroso-
pork *base* porcin-
porphyritic rock *comb* -phyre
porpoise *base* delphin-, phoecaen-
portal *comb* porto-
portion *base* par-[1]
position *office:* *suf* -acy, -ate, -cy,
  -dom, -ship. *See* **place**
possessing *comb* -echia; *suf* -acean,
  -aceous, -al, -ate, -ed, -ful, -gerous,
  -ial, -ine, -ious, -itious, -ory, -ous,
  -some, -ulent, -ulous, -wise, -y; *base*
  -ten-; ~ *parts:* *comb* -fold
possibility *suf* -atile
postage stamp *base* philatel-, timbro-

posterior *comb* postero-
posture *comb* ichno-
potassium *comb* kal(i)-
potbelly *base* physc-
potency *comb* dyna-, dynamo-, mega-,
  megalo-, -megaly, -sthenia, stheno-;
  base -forc-, -fort-, -poten-, robor-;
  ~ *to do or be: suf* -bility
pouch *comb* angio-, asco-, burs(o)-,
  -ceco, chlamyd-, chrysali-, coleo-,
  -cyst, cysti-, cysto-, follic-, meningo-,
  pericardiaco-, pericardio-, peritoneo-,
  physa-, physali-, physo-, theca-,
  theco-, typhlo-, utric-, vesico-; *base*
  marsup-, -sacc-, scrot-, -thylac-
poultry *base* gallin-
pound *comb* -cuss-, plessi-, rhabdo-;
  base -cop-, -crot-, fustig-, plang-,
  puls-, quass-, vapul-, -verber-
pour *base* -chys-, -chyt-, -flu-, -fus-
poverty *comb* -penia, ptocho-, vidu-;
  base -mendic-, -paup-, penur-, -pov-
power(ful) *comb* -crat, crato-, dyna-,
  dynamo-, mega-, megalo-, -megaly,
  stheno-; *base* -forc-, -fort-, imper-,
  -poten-; ~ *to do or be: suf* -bility;
  powerful voice: base stentor-
practice of *comb* -craft; *suf* -ade, -age,
  -al, -ance, -ancy, -asis, -asm, -ation,
  -cy, -ence, -ency, -ery, -esis, -iasis,
  -ice, -ics, -ing, -ion, -ism, -ment,
  -osis, -otic, -sion, -sis, -th, -tion,
  -tious, -ture, -ure, -y, -ysis
practitioner *suf* -ician, -ist
praise *base* encom-, eulog-, -laud-
prawn *base* carid-
pray *base* litan-, orat-, -prec-, -rog-
preaching *base* kery-
precipice *base* -cremno-
predilection for *comb* philo-
pregnancy *comb* -cyesis, toco-; *base*
  gestat-, -gravid-, -maieusi-, sylleps-
prehistoric *comb* eo-, paleo-, proto-
preparation *pre* pre-
present *base* -don-
preserver *suf* -sote
press together *base* stip-^{2}
pressure *comb* -bar, bar(o)-, -piesis,

piezo-, -tonia, -tonic, tono-; *base*
  thlips-
pretend *comb* pseudo-; *base* fict-,
  -simul-
preventing *pre* anti-; *base* imped-,
  prohib-
previous *pre* pre-; *comb* back-, yester-
prickly *comb* echinato-, echino-,
  echinulato-, echinuli-; *base* -urtic-
priest *base* presbyter-, sacerdot-
primary *comb* archi-, proto-; *base*
  -prim-, -princip-
primate *comb* -pithecus
primitive *comb* archi-, paleo-, prisc-,
  proto-
principal *comb* arch(i)-^{1}, prim-,
  proto-
principle of *suf* -ism
print *comb* -type
prior to *pre* pre-; *comb* back-, yester-
private *base* -priv-. See **secret**
proceed *comb* -grade, -motive, -plania,
  plano-; *base* -bat-, -ced-, -cess-,
  -cur(s)-, -grad-, -gress-, -mob-, -vad-,
  -vas-; ~ *away:* out-; ~ *into:* -dyte-;
  ~ *forward:* pro-; ~ *toward:* -bound,
  -petal
process of *comb* -craft; *suf* -ade, -age,
  -al^3, -ance, -ancy, -asis, -asm, -ation,
  -cy, -ence, -ency, -ery, -esis, -iasis,
  -ice, -ics, -ing, -ion, -ism, -ment1,
  -osis, -otic, -sion, -sis, -th, -tion,
  -tious, -ture, -ure, -y, -ysis
procession *comb* -cade
proclamation *base* kery-
procure *base* -cap-, -cep-, -cip-, -dyte-
produce/producing *comb* -facient,
  -ferous, -fic, -fication, -gen, -genesis,
  -genic, -genous, -geny, -gerous,
  ideo-, -parous, -phor, -phorous,
  -plast, -plastic, plasto-, -plasty,
  poiesis, -poietic, -urgy; *suf* -ate,
  -atory, -ic, -fer, -ing, -otic;
  productive: comb proli-
product of *comb* -geny^2, -gony; *suf*
  -ade, -ery, -ment^1
proficiency *base* -apt-, -habil-, -poten-,
  -qual-; *suf* -bility, -ful, -ship

profit *base* lucri-, quaest-
profusion *base* ampl-, copi-, larg-
projectile *base* -ballist-
promoting *base* -gog-
promptness *base* alacr-, exped-
proneness *comb* -clisis
prop *base* sterigm-
propagate *base* thremm-
propel *comb* -bole, -bolic, bolo-, -boly; *base* ballist-, -jact-, -jacula-, -ject-
proper *comb* cyrio-, kyrio-, ortho-
properties *suf* -ics
prophetic *comb* fati-, vati-
propitiatory *base* hilasm-, ilast-
proportion of 2 to 3 *comb* subsesqui-
proposition *comb* -lemma[1]
prosperity *comb* chryso-, pluto-; *base* chrem-, -opul-, pecun-
prostate *comb* prostato-
prostitute *comb* cypriano-, hetaero-, porno-; *base* -meretric-, scort-; *brothel:* lupan-
protected against *comb* -proof
protecting from *comb* para-[1]
protection *comb* -phylactic, phylacto-, -phylax, -phylaxis
protein *comb* proteo-
protein hydrolysis *suf* -ose
protest *base* -quer-, -querul-
protoplasm *comb* -plasmo-, -plast
protuberance *comb* condyl(o)-, gibboso-, hybo-, papillo-, ramoso-, thelo-, umbo-; *base* boss-
proverb *base* parem-, paroem-
provide *pre* be-; *base* -don-; *suf* -ate
provided with *comb* -echia; *suf* -able, -ate, -ed-[2], -ious, -ous
proving *comb* -deictic
provisions *base* opso-[2]
proximity *pre* a-, ac-, ad-, af-, ag-, al-, an-, ap-, ar-, as-, at-, by-, cis-, epi-, para-, peri-; *comb* juxta-, citra-, pene-, proximo-; *base* vicin-
proxy *comb* allelo-, allo-, alter-, hetero-; *base* -ali-
psychosis *comb* lysso-, -mania; *base* ament-, dement-
ptarmigan *base* tetraon-

pubescent *base* hebe-
pubic *comb* pubio-, pubo-
public *comb* demo-; *base* -pleb-, -vulg-
puke *comb* -emesis, -emetic, emeto-
pull *base* -tillo-, -tract-, vell-
pulley *comb* trochi-, trocho-; *pulley-like: base* trochlea
pulmonary *comb* pulmo-
pulse *comb* sphygmo-; *base* -crot-
pumpkin *base* pepo-
puncture *comb* -centesis; *base* stigm-
punishment *comb* mastigo-, rhabdo-; *base* castig-, peno-, poine-, -pun-[1]
pupa *comb* nympho-; *base* pupa-
pupil *eye: comb* core-[1], coreo-, -coria, coro-, -koria, pupillo-; *student: base* -discip-
puppet *base* pupa
purchase *comb* onio-; *base* -empt-, -merc-, nundin-
purge *base* expurg-; *enema: comb* -clysis; *base* chalast-, clysm-; clyst-
purify *base* cathar-. See **cleanse**
purple *comb* purpureo-; *base* amaranth-, blatt-[2], indi-, indo-, phenic-, porphyr-, -pun-[2]. *Also see* "Colors" in Part III
purpose *comb* teleo-, telo-
purse *comb* burs(o)-, marsup-, phasco-
purslane *base* portulac-
pursue *base* secut-, sequ-
pus *comb* purulo-, pyo-. See **infection**
push *comb* -trude; *base* -pel-, -pul-, trus-
put *base* -pon-, -pos-; *suf* -en; ~ *in the form of: suf* -ate; ~ *together: comb* -thesis, -thetic; *base* cond-, -fabr-, -fac-, -fec-, -fic-,-struct-
putrefying *comb* cario-, lysi-, lyso-, -lysis, -lyte, -lytic, phthino-, phthisio-, -phthisis, putre-, putri-, pytho-, sapro-, septi-, septico-, septo-; *base* marcesc-, myda-, phthor-, tabe-; *suf* -ase
pylorus *comb* pyloro-
pyrites *comb* pyrito-

Q

quadrillion(th) *comb* femto-, peta-

quaff *comb* pino-, poto-; *base* -bib-, pocul-

quail *base* coturn-, gallinac-, ortyg-

quake *base* -pav-, -trem-

qualified *comb* -potent; *suf* -able, -ible, -ile; *in an ~ way:* -bly

quality of *suf* -able, -acity, -acy, -age, -ance, -ancy, -ant, -asis, -asm, -ate, -atile, -ation, -cy, -dom, -eity, -ence, -ency, -ent, -ery, -esis, -ful, -hood, -iasis, -ice[1], -ility, -ion, -ise, -ism, -ity, -ling, -ma, -ment, -ness, -or[3], -osis, -otic, -red, -ship, -sion, -th, -tion, -tude, -ture, -ty[1], -ure, -y[2]

qualm *comb* -phobe, -phobia, -phobic, phobo-; *base* pavid-, tim(or)-, -trem-, -trep-. *Also see* "Fear" *in Part III*

quantity *base* -quant-; *suf* -age, -ful

quarrel *comb* -machy; *base* litig-, pugil-, -pugn-, -rix-

quarter *base* quadr-

quash *comb* lysi-, lyso-, -lysis, -lytic, -lyze, -phage, phago-, -phagous, -phagy; *base* -ate-[4], perd-, phthart-, -vast-

quaver *comb* tremo-; *base* pav-, trep-

queen *base* regin-

quell *comb* stasi-, -stasis, -stat, stato-; *base* fin-, termin-

quest *comb* -petal, -quire, -quiry; *base* indag-, -rog-, -scrut-

question *base* erot-, quer-[2], -quir-, -rog-

quickness *comb* ocy-, tacho-, tachy-; *base* alacr-, celer-, festin-, veloc-

quicksand *base* syrt-

quiet *comb* hesy-; *base* -plac-, quiesc-, -tacit-

quinine *base* cinchon-, quin-[2]

quintillion(th) *comb* atto-, exa-

quirky *comb* aetheo-, anom(o)-, anomalo-. *See* **irregular**

quisling *base* prodit-

quit *base* relinq-

quite *pre* be-, cata-, cath-, de-, kata-, ob-, per-; *comb* holo-, omni-, pan-, panto-, stone-, toti-

quivering *comb* -chorea, choreo-, -clonic, -clonus, -esmus, -ismus, spasmo-; *base* -stal-, -vellic-

R

rabbit *base* cunic-, lago-, lepor-; ***rabbit-like quadruped:*** comb hyraci-, hyraco-

rabies *base* lyss-

raccoon *base* arctoid-, procyon-

race ***group:*** *comb* -ethno, geno-, phylo-

race course *comb* -drome, dromo-, dromous

radiant *comb* helio-; *base* fulg-, nitid-; *~ emission: comb* aurora; *~ energy: comb* bolo-[2], radio-, spectro-

radicals *suf* -yl, -ylene; ***two ~:*** *comb* bi-

radicle *comb* radiculo-, rostell-

radioactive *comb* radio-

radish *base* raphan-

rag *base* pann-

rail ***bird:*** *base* rall-

railroad *base* siderodromo-

rain *comb* hyeto-, pluvio-; *base* imbri-, nimb-, ombr-

rainbow *base* irid-

raise ***cultivate:*** *comb* -culture; *base* -ponic; ***lift:*** levat-

ram *comb* crio-, krio-; *base* -ariet-

rank *comb* -rater; *suf* -cy, -dom[2], -ship

rap *comb* plessi-; *base* cop-, -crot-,

-cuss-, -plang-, puls-, -tus-, vapul-,
-verber-
rape *base* rap-, rep-, stupr-
rapid *comb* ocy-, tacho-, tachy-; *base*
alacr-, celer-, festin-, veloc-
rare *comb* mano-, spano-; *base* -areo-²
rash *comb* -anthema
rasp *base* radul-
raspberry *base* frambes-
rat *base* mur-; ***mole-rat:*** *base* spalac-,
zemni-
rate *comb* -rater
ratio, inverse *pre* sub-
rattlesnake *base* crotal-
raven *comb* coraci-, coraco-; *base*
corvin-
ravenous *base* avid-, edac-, gulos-
raw *base* omo-²
ray *comb* radio-, radiato-; *base* bolo-²,
-rad-
razor *base* xyr-
reading *comb* -legia, -lexia, -lexis,
-lexy; *base* lect-, -leg-¹
real *base* ver-
realm *suf* -dom, -ric
rear *comb* hind-. *See* **behind**
reasoning *comb* -gnomy, -gnosia,
-gnosis, -gnostic, -gnoto, ideo-,
-noia, -nomy, -phrenic, phrenico-,
phreno-, psycho-, -sophy, thymo-,
-witted; *base* -cogit-, -cogn-, ment(a)-,
-noe-, -put-, -ratio-, -sci-
rebuke *base* increp-
receiver *comb* -ceptor; *base* -cap-,
-cip-; *suf* -ee
recent *comb* -cene, ceno-¹, neo-, nov-
receptacle *comb* angio-, asco-, bursi-,
burso-, ceco-, chlamyd-, chrysali-,
cisto-, coleo-, -cyst, cysti-, cysto-,
follic-, meningo-, pericardiaco-,
pericardio-, peritoneo-, phasco-,
physa-, physali-, physo-, -theca,
theci-, theco-, typhlo-, utri-, utric,
vesico-; *base* -sacc-, -thylac-; *suf*
-arium
recipient *suf* -ee
reciprocal *pre* co-, inter-, syl-, sym-,
syn-, sys; *comb* allelo-, hama-,

symphyo, synchro-; *base* -allac-,
-allag-, -allaxis-, -mutu-
reckless *base* temer-
recline *base* -cub-, -cumb-
recognition *comb* -gnosis, -gnostic
reconstructive surgery *comb* -plasty
rectification *comb* ortho-; *base* castig-,
emend-
rectum *comb* procto-, recto-
red *comb* carmino-, erysi-, erythro-,
phoeni-, pyhrro-, rhodo-, roseo-,
rufi-, rufo-, testaceo-; *base* coccin-,
coquel-, cruent-, -ereuth-, ferrug-,
fuc-, grenat-, -later-, minia-,
murex-, nacar-, -rub-, -rud-, -rut-,
rutil-. *Also see* "Colors" in Part III
reduced *base* trunc-
redundant *comb* perisso-
reed *comb* aulo-, follic-, salpingo-,
siphoni-, siphono-, solen(o)-,
syringo-, tubi-, tubo-, tubuli-, vasi-;
base arundi-, calam-, cann-, fistul-,
-syr-
refuse to *pre* dis-
region *comb* choro-
regular *comb* cyrio-, kyrio-, homalo-,
homolo-, ortho-
regulate *base* modul-, -temp-
regurgitate *comb* -emesis, -emetic,
emeto-
reindeer *base* rang(if)-, tarand-
reject *base* relinq-
relate *base* narr-
relating to *suf* -acean, -aceous, -ad²,
-al, -an, -ar, -arious, -ary, -atic,
-ative, -atory, -eae, -ean, -eous, -ery,
-etic, -ial, -ian, -ic, -id, -il, -ile, -ina,
-inae, -ine, -ing, -ious, -istic, -ite,
-itic, -itious, -itive, -ive, -oidea,
-orious, -ory, -otic, -tious, -tive, -ular
relatives *base* cogn-, famil-, stirp-;
~ *not by blood:* *comb* step-
relaxant *comb* -clysis; *base* chalax-,
clysm-, clyst-
release *base* -miss-, -mit-, -pomp-
relieving *comb* lyo-, lysi-, -lysis, lyso-,
-lyte, -lytic, -lyze; *base* -liqu-, -solu-,
-solv-

relics *comb* lipsano-, reliq-
religion *comb* religio-, theo-
relish *base* opso-[2]
remaining *base* perman-
remains *base* reliq-
remedial *comb* saluti-
remember *comb* -mnesia, -mnesis;
 base -mem-, -mnem-
remote *comb* disto-, tele-
remove *pre* ab-, abs-, apo-, be-, de-,
 des-, di-, dia-, dif-, dis-, e-, ec-, ef-,
 ex-, for-, off-, se, with-; *comb* ectro-;
 base expurg-
repair *comb* ortho-; *base* castig-,
 emend-
repeatedly *comb* batto-, pollaki-; *base*
 epana-, -iter-, palin-; *suf* -er; ~
 sounded: *comb* echo-. *See* frequent
replacement *comb* allelo-, allo-, alter-,
 hetero-; *base* -ali-
replete *comb* -filled, pleni-, pleo-,
 plero-, pluri-; *base* -pler-, -plet-; *suf*
 -acious, -ate, -ic, -ful, -ilent, -ose,
 -osity, -ous, sat-, satur-, -ulent, -y
reply *base* apocris-. *See* say
repress *comb* stasi-, -stasis, -stat,
 stato-; *base* fin-, termin-
reproach *comb* enisso-, enosi-; *base*
 castig-
reproduce *comb* aetio-, -blast, blasto-,
 -blasty, -carp, -carpic, carpo-, -car-
 pous, etio-, -gen, -genic, -genesis,
 -genous, -geny, -gone, -gonium,
 gono-, -gony, -phyletic, sperma-,
 -spermal, spermato-, spermi-,
 -spermic, spermo-, sporo-; *base*
 -init-; *suf* -esce, -escence, -escent
reptile *comb* echidno-, -glypha,
 herpeto-, -ophidia, ophidio-, ophio-,
 -saur, sauro-, -saurus; *base* angui-,
 batrach-, colubr-, reptil-, -serp-,
 viper-
repulsion *base* fastid-
request *base* -pet-, -quir-, -quis-,
 -rog-
require *base* exig-, -pet-
rescued *comb* eleuthero-; *base* -liber-,
 vac(u)-

resembling *pre* para-, quasi-; *comb*
 homeo-, homoio-, homolo-, iso-,
 -opsis, -phane, -phanic, -phany,
 pheno-; *base* simil-; *suf* -acean,
 -aceous, -al, -an, -ar, -ary, -ean, -en,
 -eous, -esque, -ful, -ian, -ic, -il, -ile-,
 -ine, -ing, -ish, -istic, -istical,
 -itious, -ize, -like, -ode, -oid, -oidal,
 -ose, -osity, -some, -tious, -ular, -y
resentment *base* -invid-
reservoir *base* lacco-
resin *comb* resino-
resistant to *comb* -proof, -tight;
 ~ *disease:* *comb* immuno-
resourceful *base* agil-, facil-, ingen-
respiration *comb* -pnea, pneo-,
 pneumato-, pneumo-, pneumono-,
 pneusio-, pulmo-, respirato-, spiro-[1];
 base -hal-
responsibility *comb* hypegia-,
 hypengy-; *base* paralip-
responsive to *comb* bathmo-, -trope,
 -tropic, -tropism, tropo-, -tropous,
 -tropy
rest *base* oti-
restless *comb* agito- *base* -turb-
restrained *comb* brady-, freno-; *base*
 -cunct-, imped-, -mora-, -tard-
restriction *comb* isch-, koly-, -penia,
 rhopo-, -strain, -strict; *base* angust-,
 -string-; *suf* -en. *See* tie
result (of) *comb* ergo-, -ergic, -ergy;
 suf -age, -asm, -ata, -ation, -ency, -
 ism, -ma, -ment[1], -mony, -sion, -ure
retaliation *comb* counter-; *base* tal-
retention *comb* -echia, -tain; *base*
 -cathex-, -ten-
reticular *comb* reticulo-
retina *comb* retino-
return *pre* re-; *comb* nosto-
reveal *comb* phaeno-, pheno-; *base*
 -monstr-
reversal *comb* allo-; *base* -vers-,
 -vert-
reverse *pre* anti-, de-
revile *base* vituper-
revulsion *comb* miso-, -phobe, -phobia,
 -phobic; *base* -invid-, -ira(sc)-, odi-

rhinoceros *base* ceratorh-
rhombus *comb* rhombo-
rib *comb* costi-, costo-
ribbon *comb* taeni-, taenio-, -tene, teni-; *base* lemnisc-
rice *comb* oryzi-, rizi-, ryzi-
riches *comb* chryso-, pluto-; *base* chrem-, -opul-, pecun-
ridge *comb* crebri-, lophio-, lopho-; *base* -carin-
ridicule *comb* catagelo-, katagelo-
ridiculous *base* fatu-, inan-, moro-, stult-
rift *comb* dicho-, -fid, fissi-, schisto-, schizo-, sulcato-, -tomy; *base* crev-, fatisc-, -par-, rim-
right *comb* recti-; ~ *angle: comb* ortho-; ~ *side: comb* dexio-, dextro-; *correct: comb* ortho-; *base* emend-
righteous *pre* bene-, eu-; *base* agath-, bon-, prob-
rigid *comb* ancylo-, ankylo-, tetano-; *base* rigesc-
rind *comb* -lemma[2]
ring *comb* annul-, ano-[2], crico-, cyclo-, disco-, globo-, gyro-, -sphere, sphero-, stilli-; *base* -anu-, -cinct-, -cing-, -circin-, -circul-, -coron-, -glomer-, -numm-, -orb-, -rot-, -troch-, -zon-; *finger* ~: dactylio-; ~ *shaped:* ano-[2]
ringing *base* tinn-, tintinn-
ringlet *comb* cirr(h)i-, cirr(h)o-
ripe *base* -matur-
rise *base* -cresc-, -surg-
risky *base* pericul-
rival *pre* anti-
rivalrous *base* emul-
river *comb* fluvio-, potamo-; *base* amn-, flum-, -rip-
roach *base* blatt-
road *comb* hodo-, -ode, odo-; *base* -iter-, -via-
roadrunner *base* cucul-
roar *base* -frem-
robber *comb* clepto-, klepto-, lesto-; *base* -furt-, harpax-, latro-, pred-
robin *base* -turd-

robust *comb* -proof, dur(o)-; *base* -forc-, -fort-
rock *comb* -lithic, litho-, pesso-, petri-, petro-, sax(i)-; *base* -lapid-, -rupes-, rupic-; *suf* -ite
rod (shaped) *comb* bacilli-, bacillo-, bacul-, fusi-, fuso-, rhabdo-, vergi-; *base* coryn-, ferul-, -rad-, virgul-; *rodlike: comb* scapo-; *base* veretill-
rodent *base* arvic-, gliri-, mur-, myo-; ~ *with cheek pouches: base* saccomy-
rolling *comb* trochalo-
Roman *comb* Romano-
romantic *comb* romantico-
roof *comb* stego-, tecti-, tegu-; ~ *of mouth: comb* palato-, uranisco
rooster *comb* alector-, alectry-
root *comb* radiculo-, rhizo-, -rrhiza; *base* -radic-, -stirp-; ~ *meaning: base* etym-
rope *comb* funi-, resti-, schoeno-
rose *comb* rhodo-, roseo-
rotary *comb* cyclo-, roti-, troch-, trochalo-, trochi-, trocho-
rotten *comb* lysi-, lyso-, -lysis, -lyte, phthysio-, -phthysis, putre-, putri-, pytho-, sapro-, septi-, septo-; *base* -putr-
rough *comb* asper-. trachy-; *base* -rud-, salebr-
round *comb* ano-, annul-, convexo-, crico-, cyclo-, disco-, gibboso-, globi-, globo-, glom-, gyro-, orbito-, rotundi-, rotundo-, -sphere, sphero-, stilli-, tereti-, tereto-, trochi-, tro-cho-, zon-, zoni-; *base* -anu-, -cing-, -cinct-, -circin-, -circul-, -coron-, -glomer-, -numm-, -orb-, -rot-, strongyl-; *partly* ~: *comb* orbiculato-
route *comb* -ode, odo-; *base* -itin-, -via-
routine *comb* -craft; *suf* -ade, -age, -al, -ance, -ancy, -asis, -asm, -ation, -cy, -ence, -ency, -ery, -esis, -iasis, -ice, -ics, -ing, -ion, -ism, -ment, -osis, -otic, -sion, -sis, -th, -tion, -tious, -ture, -ure, -y, -ysis
rows *comb* -stichia, sticho-, -stichous

royal *base* basil-, reg-, regn-
rubbing *comb* tribo-, -tripsy; *base* trit-
rubble *base* ruder-
rude *base* contum-, impud-, procac-
rue *base* rut-
rug *base* lodic-
ruination *comb* lysi-, lyso-, -lysis,
    -lytic, -lyze, -phage, phago-,
    -phagous, -phagy; *base* -ate-[4], perd-,
    phthart-, -vast-
rule *base* leg[2], regul-
ruler *comb* -arch[2], gubern-; *base* -reg-
ruling *comb* -archy, -ocracy; *base* -regn-
rumbling *base* borbor-

rump *comb* podic-, pygia, pygo-; *base*
    nati-
run *comb* -drom(e), dromo-,
    -dromous; *base* curr-, -cur(s)-
rune *comb* runo-
runner (plant) *base* sarment-
rupture *comb* -clasia, -clasis, clastic,
    frag-, -rhegma, -(r)rhexis; *base*
    -fract-, -frang-, -rupt-
rural *base* agrest-
rush *hurry: base* curr-, impet-, -vad-,
    -vas-; *plant:* -junc-
Russia(n) *comb* Russo-
rust *base* ferrug-, rubig-

S

sable *base* zibel-
sac *comb* angio-, asco-, bursi-, burso-,
    ceco-, chlamyd-, chrysali, coleo-,
    -cyst, cysti-, cysto-, follic-, meningo-,
    pericardiaco-, pericardio-, perito-
    neo-, physa-, physali-, physo-,
    -theca, theco-, typhlo-, utri-[2], utric-,
    vesico-; *base* marsup-, -sacc-, -thylac-
saccharin *comb* saccharo-
sacrifice *base* mact-, -thy-
sacred *comb* hagio-, hiero-, semno-;
    base- sacr-, -sanct-
sacrum *comb* sacro-
saddle *base* ephipp-, sagma-, selli-
sadness *comb* lype-, tapino-; *base*
    dolor-, fleb-, flet, luct-, -trist-
safe from *comb* -proof, -tight
saffron *base* -croce-, safran-
sail *action: base* navig-; *object: comb*
    vel-, veli
sailfish *base* istiophor-
saint *comb* hagio-; *base* sanct-
salad *base* acetar-
saliva *comb* ptyal(o)-, sial[1]-
salmon *comb* salmoni-
salt *comb* alo-, halo-, sali-, salino-; *base*
    sals-; *suf* -ate, -ite; *reddish salts:*
    comb roseo-
salvation *base* soter-

same *pre* co-; *comb* equi-, homo-, iso-,
    pari-, tauto-; ~ *time: comb* hama-;
    base -simul-
sand *comb* ammo-, arenacio-,
    psammo-; *base* aren-, glare-, sabell-,
    sabul-, saburr-
sand grouse *base* pterocl-
sandpiper *base* charadr-, -tring-
sandwich *comb* -burger
sarcastic *base* acerb-, mord-
sated *comb* -filled, pleni-, pleo-, plero-,
    pluri-; *base* -pler-, -plet-; *suf*
    -acious, -ate, -ic, -ful, -ilent, -ose,
    -osity, -ous, -ulent, -y
satirical *comb* sillo-; *base* dicac-
saucer *base* acetabul-
sausage(-shaped) *base* allant(o)-, botul-
savage *base* agrio-
save *base* pars-, salv-, serrato-
saw *tool: comb* pri-, prion-, runcin-,
    serrato-, serri-
sawdust *base* scobi-
say *comb* -claim, logo-, -logue, -lalia,
    -lexia, lexico-, -lexis, -lexy, -logy,
    -phone, phono-, -phony, rhet-,
    verbi-, verbo-, voc-, voci-, -voke;
    base -clam-, -dict-, -loc(u)-, -loqu-,
    narr-, -orat-, -phat-, -phem-
scabbard *comb* coleo-

scale *base* -libra-; ***musical ~:*** *comb* -tonic

scalene *comb* scaleno-

scales *comb* lamelli-, lepido-, squamato-, squamo-, squamoso-, squaroso-; *base* lodic-, -pholid-, -scut-, tegul-

scalloped *comb* cren-, crenato-, crenulato-

scalpel *comb* scalpelli-

scan *base* -scan-, -scand-

scandal *comb* -gate

scant *base* exig-

scapula *comb* scapuli-, scapulo-

scar *comb* kelo-, ulo-[1]; *base* -cica-

scarce *comb* mano-, spano-; *base* -areo-

scared *base* -pavid-, -tim-, trepid-. *See* fear

scarlet *base* nacar-

scatter(ed) *comb* -sperse; *base* -sparg-, -spars-, -spor-

scene *comb* sceno-

scenery *comb* -scape

scent *comb* brom(o)-, odori-, odoro-, olfacto-,-osmia, osmo-, osphresio-, ozo-, ozono-

school *base* schol-

science *comb* -graphy, -logic, -logical, -logy, techno-, -techny; *suf* -ics

scimitar *comb* acinaci-

scintillation *comb* sela-; *base* -fulg-, stilpno-

scissors *base* forfic-, -psalid-

sclera *comb* sclero-

scoff *base* mycter-

scold *base* increp-

scope of *suf* -ure

scorn *base* deris-

scorpion *base* pedipalp-

Scottish *comb* Scoto-

scourge *comb* cnido-, mastigo-; *base* flagell-, -piq-, -urtic-

scrap *comb* clasmato-, -fid; *base* frag-, frust-, -par-

scraping *base* xyst-

scratch *comb* amycho-, scab-, titillo-; *base* rasor-

scrotum *comb* didym(o)-, orchido-, orchio-, oscheo-; *base* -scrot-

scrub *comb* balneo-; *base* ablut-, cathar-, -lav-, -mund-, -purg-

sculpt *comb* glyph-, glypt-

scurrilous *base* fescinn-

scurvy *base* -scorb-

Scythian *comb* Scytho-

sea *comb* enalio-, halo-, mare-, mari-, thalasso-, thalatto-; *base* aequor-, naut-, nav-, navic-, pelag-; *~* ***shore:*** paral-, thino-

sea crab *base* gammar-

sea duck *base* fuligul-

sea horse *base* hippocamp-

seasick *base* naus-

sea urchin *comb* echinoderm-; *base* echin-

seagull *base* -lar-

seal ***animal:*** *comb* phoc(o)-; ***stamp:*** *base* -sigil-, sphrag-

sealing wax *base* rupo-

search(ing) *comb* -petal, -quire, -quiry; *base* indag-, -rog-, -scrut-. *See* turn towards

seasons *comb* horo-; ***fall:*** *base* -autumn-; ***spring:*** *base* -vern-; ***summer:*** *base* -aestiv-; ***winter:*** *base* brum-[1], -hibern-, -hiem-

seat *base* cathedr-, cathis-, kathis-, sedil-

seaweed *comb* phyceae-, -phyceous, phyco-; *base* -fuc-

sebum *comb* sebo-

second/secondary *pre* bi-, para-[2], super-; *comb* deuter(o)-, deuto-, secundi-, secundo-. *See* two

second-rate *pre* hypo-, sub-, under-; *comb* hystero-; *base* hesson-; *suf* -aster

secret *pre* subter-; *comb* calypto-, crypto-; *base* arcan-, occult-

secretion *comb* crino-, -crine, eccrino-; ***waxlike ~:*** *comb* cerumini-

sect *suf* -arian

secure *comb* -proof, -tight

sedge *base* carico-, cyper-

see *comb* eid(o)-, oculo-, ommat-,

-opia, opsi-, -opsia, -opsis, opso-,
-opsy, ophthalmo-, optico-, opto-,
-scope, -scopic, scopo-, -scopy,
visuo-; *base* -blep-, -scrut-, -spec-,
-spic-, -vid-. *Also see* "The Senses" in
Part III

seeds *comb* -carp, -carpic, carpo-,
-carpous, -sperm, -spermal,
spermatio-, spermato-, spermi-,
-spermic, spermo-, -spermous,
-spore, spori-, sporo-, -sporous; *base*
semin-; ***seed-vessel:*** *base* silicul-

seek(ing) *comb* -petal, -quire, -quiry,
zetet-; *base* -rog-, -scrut-. *See* **turn
towards**

seemingly *pre* quasi-

segment *comb* clasmato-, dicho-, -fid[2],
fissi-, schisto-, schizo-, -tomy; *base*
-par-, telson-

seize *comb* -tain; *base* -cap(t)-,
-cathex-, -ger-, -hapt-, plag-,
-prehend, prehens-, rap-, rep-, -ten-

seizure *comb* -agra, -lepsia, -lepsis,
-lepsy, -leptic

selection *base* -opt-, -vol-

self *comb* auto-, ego-, idio-, ipse-,
proprio-, self-, tauto-; *base* -ille-;
~ ***indulgence:*** apolaust-

selfishness *base* avar-, avid-, cup(id)-,
edac-, gulos-, pleonec-, pleonex-

self-moving *comb* auto-

sell *base* empor-, -merc-, vend-

send *base* -miss-, -mit-[1], -pomp-

sensation *comb* -esthesia, esthesio-,
hapto1-, sensi-, senso-, sensori-. *Also
see* "The Senses" in Part III

senseless *base* -stup-

sensory *comb* sensori-

sepals *comb* -sepalous

separate *pre* apo-, dia-, dis-, for-, se-;
comb chori-, choristo-, crit-[2], dicho-,
dialy-; *base* regm-; ***separation:*** *comb*
sepi-[2]

septillion *comb* yotta; **septillionth**
comb yocto-

sequel ***following:*** *pre* epi-, meta-,
post-; *comb* after-, hind-, postero-;
base -secut-, -sequ-; *suf* -an; ***out-***

come: *comb* ergo-, -ergic, -ergy;
suf -age, -asm, -ata, -ation, -ency,
-ism, -ma, -ment, -mony, -sion,
-ure

Serbia *comb* Serbo-

serenity *base* -eiren-, -iren-, -pac-,
-pax-

series *base* -hirmo-

serious *base* grav-; ***partly ~:*** *comb*
serio-

sermon *base* -homil-, kery-

serous fluid *base* ichor-

serrated *comb* serrato-; *base* cren-[1],
lacin-. *See* **notched**

serum *comb* oro-, orrho-, sero-

serviceable *comb* chreo-, chresto-;
base -util-

set *comb* -thesis, -thetic; *base* -pon-,
-pos-; *suf* -en; ~ ***against:*** *pre* anti-,
cata-, cath-, contra-, contre-, ob-,
with-; *comb* antio-, contro-, counter-,
enantio-; ~ ***apart:*** *pre* se-; *base* sacr-

seta *comb* chaeta-, chaeto-

settlement *comb* ekist-; *base* -dom-;
suf -age

seven *comb* hebdo-, hepta-, septem-,
sept(i)-[1]; ~ ***hundred:*** septinginti-.
Also see "Numbers" in Part III

seventeen *base* heptakaideca, septen-
decim-

seventh *base* septim-

seventy *base* septuagen-, septuages-,
septuagint-

sever *comb* -cide, cis-, -cise, -ectomy,
inciso-, -sect, temno-, -tmesis,
-tome, tomo-, -tomous, -tomy; *base*
sec-

several *comb* multi-, pluri-, pollaki-,
poly-

sew *base* -sutil-

sewer *base* cloac-

sex organs *comb* genito-; *base* -aede-;
female ~: colpo-; ***male ~:*** phallo-

sexual *comb* aphrodisio-, eroto-,
gameto-, gamo-, -gamous, -gamy,
geno-, gonado-, -gone, -gonium,
gono-, -gony, nympho-; *base* -coit-,
-cyprid-, -vener-[1]; ~ ***intercourse:***

subagit-; ~ *uncertainty:* gynandro-;
unusual ~ practices: *base* paraphil-
shabby *base* sord-, turp-
shadow *comb* scia-, scio-¹, skia-; *base*
-opac-, -umbr-
shaft *comb* calam-, cauli-, caulo-,
cormo-, culm-, ferul-, paxill-, scapi-,
thyrsi-, thyrso-; *base* festuc-, stip-
shaggy *base* -hispid-, vill-
shaking *base* agit-, -cuss-, lab-, pav-,
quass-, tremo-, trep-, vibro-
shallow *base* lev-, parv-
shame *base* pud-, verecund-
shape, a *comb* eid(o)-, -form, -morph,
-morphic, -morphism, morpho-,
-morphous; *base* -figur-, -schem-
shaped like *comb* -form, -oid, -oidal;
shaped like an -S: *comb* sigma-;
shaped like a -Y: *comb* ypsili-. *Also
see* "Shapes" *in Part III*
shapeless *comb* amorpho-
shark *comb* scyllio-; *base* carcharin-,
gale-², selach-, sphyrn-, squal-
sharp *comb* acantho-, aceto-, acetyl-,
acid-, acro-, acu-, acuti-, cusp-,
echino-, mord-, oxal-, oxy-¹,
spiculi-, spiculo-, stylo-¹; *base* acer-¹,
-acerb-, -acul-, aichm-, -aichur-,
asper-, -belon-, muric-, -punct-,
-piq-, pung-, xyr-; ~ *pointed: comb*
raduli-; ~ *tip: base* mucro-
shatter *comb* -clasia, -clasis, -clastic,
-rhegma, -(r)rhexis; *base* agmat-,
-fract-, -frag-, -frang-, -rupt-
shave *base* rasor-, tonsor
shears *base* forfic-, psalid-
sheath *comb* angio-, chlamyd-, coleo-,
meningo-, -theca, theci-, theco-,
vagini-, vagino-. *See* **container**
shed *comb* lyo-, lysi-, -lysis, lyso-,
-lyte, -lytic, -lyze; *base* exuv-, -liqu-,
-solu-, -solv-
sheep *base* ovi-², verv-. *See* **lamb**
sheet **bed ~:** lodic-; **layer:** lamin-;
winding ~: sindon-
shell *comb* conchi-, kelyph-, lorica-,
-ostraca, ostraco-, testaceo-
shield *comb* aspido-, peltati-, peltato-,

pelti-, pelto- *base* clype-, saco-,
scut-
shift *base* camb-, -fabr-, -fec-, -mut-,
-vari-, -vert-. *See* **change**
shingles *base* zoster-
shiny *base* fulg-, gano-, lustr-, pheng-,
rutil-, sela-, stilpno-
ship *base* nau-, naut-, nav-, navic-
shoe *base* -calce-, -crep-; **shoemaker**
base sutor-
shoot *base* **weapon:** -ballist-, -jacul-;
plant: *base* sobol-, surcul-
shopkeeper *base* capel-
shore *base* littor-
shortage *comb* isch-, oligo-, -penia
shorter *comb* brachisto-, brachy-,
brevi-, chamae-, hekisto-, micro-,
mini-, parvi-, parvo-, steno-, tapino-;
base -curt-, exig-; *suf* -cle, -cula,
-cule, -een, -el, -ella, -en, -et, -ette,
-idion, -idium, -ie, -illa, -illo, -isk,
kin, -le, -let, -ling, -ock, -ola, -ole,
-rel, -ula, -ule, -ulum, -ulus, -y
short-sighted *base* myop-
shoulder *comb* acromio-, humero-,
omo-¹; ~ **blade:** *comb* scapuli-,
scapulo-; *base* armo-, spatul-
shout *base* clam-, vocif-
show *comb* phaeno-, pheno-; *base*
-monstr-
showers *comb* hyeto-, pluvio-; *base*
imbri-, ombr-
shrew *base* soric-, tupai-; **squirrel-
shrew:** *base* tupai-
shrike *base* thamn-
shrimp *base* carid-, macrur-
shrine *comb* aedi-; *base* scrin-
shrink *base* dimin-
shrivel *base* marces-, marcid-
shroud *base* sindon-
shrub *base* -bosc-¹, thamn- (thamnium); **shrublike:** *comb* fruticuloso-
shudder *comb* phricto-
shun *base* phygo-
shut *comb* -atresia, atreto-, claustro-,
cleido-, -cleisis, cleisto-, stego-; *base*
clithr-, -clud-, -clus-, obturat-,
occlud-, occlus-

shyness *base* tim-, verecund-

Sicilian *comb* Siculo-

sickle(-shaped) *comb* drepani-, falci-, zanclo-

sickness *pre* dys-, mal-; *comb* noso-, path, -pathic, patho-, -pathy; *base* aegr-, cachex-, -morb-, naus-, -pecca-, valetud-

side *pre* by-; *on or near ~: comb* lateri-, latero-, pleuro-

sieve *comb* coli-[2], coscino-, cribri-, ethmo-

sift *base* -cern-

sight *comb* eid(o)-, oculo-, ommat-, -opia, opsi-[2], -opsia, -opsis, opso-, -opsy, ophthalmo-, optico-, opto-, -scope, -scopic, scopo-, -scopy, visuo-; *base* -blep-, -scrut-, -spec-, -spic-, -vid-, vis-

sign(al) *comb* sema-, -seme, semeio-, semio-

signet *base* -sigil-, sphrag-

silent *comb* hesy-; *base* -tacit-

silica/silicon *comb* siliceo-, silici-, silico-

silk *comb* metax-, seri-, sericeo-, serico-

silkworm *base* -bombyc-

silly *base* fatu-, inan-, moro-, stult-

Silurian *comb* Siluro-

silver(y) *comb* argenti-, argento-, argyro-, glauco-, plat-[2]. *Also see* "Colors" in Part III

similar *pre* para-, quasi-; *comb* -esque, homeo-, homoeo-, homoio-, homolo-, iso-, -phane, -phanic; *base* simil-; *suf* -acean, -aceous, -al, -an, -ar, -ary, -ean, -en, -eous, -esque, -ful, -ic, -il, -ile, -ine, -ing, -ish, -itious, -ize, -like, -ode, -oid, -ose, -osity, -some, -tious, -ular, -y

simple *base* facil-. *See* **single**

sin *comb* enisso-, enosio-; *base* -culp-, hamart-, -pecca-

sincere *base* prob-, ver-

sinew *comb* chord-, -chorda, cord-

single *comb* eka-, haplo-, heno-, mono-, uni-

sink *decline: comb* -atrophia; *base* dimin-; *decrease: base* decresc-, dimin-

sinuous *comb* -enchyma[1]

siphon *comb* siphoni-, siphono-

siphylis *comb* syphilo-

sister *base* -soror-

sit *base* -cathis-, -kathis-, -sed-, -sess-; *~ in:* -sid-

situated *comb* out-

six *comb* hexa-, sena-, seni-, sexi, sexti-, sise-; *~ hundred:* hexacosi-, sexcent-; *~ times:* hexakis-. *Also see* "Numbers" in Part III

sixteen *base* hexadeca-, hexakaideca, sedecim-

sixth *base* sext-

sixty *base* hexaconta-, sexagen-, sexages-

size *comb* -footer, -sized; *~ of a sheet: suf* -mo. *Also see* "Dimension" in Part III

skeleton *comb* skeleto-

skill *comb* -craft, -ship, techno-; *skillful: base* daedal-

skin *comb* chorio-, cut(i)-, cutaneo-, -derm, -derma, dermato-, -dermatous, -dermis, dermo-, dora-; *base* -pell-; *~ disease:* licheno-; *~ elevation: comb* papulo-; *~ itch: comb* acar-, scabi(o)-; *base* -prur-, -psor-; *~ like: comb* choroid-. *See* **flesh**

skirmish *base* velit-. *See* **battle**

skull *comb* -cephalic, cephalo-, -cephalous, -cephaly, cranio-, occipito-, orbito-

skunk *base* mephit-, mustel-; *African ~: base* zorill-

sky *base* coeli-

skylark *base* alaud-

slab *base* -pinac-, -pinak-

slag *base* scoria-

slander *base* calumn-

slanting *comb* -clinal, -clinate, -cline, -clinic, clino-, -clisis, lechrio-, loxo-, plagio-; *base* -cliv-. *See* **bent**

slaughter *base* trucid-

Slav *comb* Slavo-

slave *comb* dulo-; *base* -serv-, vernil-

sleep *comb* hypno-, somni-; *base* carot-, -dorm-, -sopor-

sleeplessness *base* agrypn-

slender *comb* lepto-, steno-, -tenu-; *base* -areo-, gracil-

slide *base* laps-

slightly *pre* sub-; *comb* hetto-; *suf* -aster²

slime *comb* blenno-, -chezia, copro-, lim-, muci-, muco-, myco-, myso-, -myxia, myxo-, p(a)edo-, scato-, stegno-, sterco-; *base* -fecu-, -fim-, molys-, rhypar-

sling *base* fundi-

slippery *base* -lubric-

slope *comb* -clinal, -clinate, -cline, -clinic, clino-, -clisis, klino-, lechrio-, loxo-, plagio-; *base* -clit-, -cliv-, declin-

sloth *animal: base* xenarthr-; ***indolence:*** *base* pigr-, segn-

slow *comb* brady-; *base* -cunct-, lent-¹, -pigr-, -tard-

slug *base* limac-

sluggish *base* -pigr-

sly *base* daedal-

small(er) *comb* brachisto-, brachy-, hekisto-, micro-, mini-, nano-, parvi-, parvo-, steno-; *base* -curt-, exig-, pusill-; *suf* -cle, -cula, -cule, -culum, -culus, -een, -el, -ella, -en, -et, -ette, -idion, -idium, -ie, -illa, -illo, -isk, kin, -le, -let, -ling, -ock, -ola, -ole, -rel, -ula, -ule, -ulum, -ulus, -y

smart *base* sapien-

smell *comb* brom(o)-, -odic, odori-, odoro-, -olent, olfacto-, -osmia, osmo-¹, osphresio-, ozo-, ozono-; *base* fet-, nidor-. *See also* "The Senses" in Part III

smelt *base* -ather-

smile *base* ris-

smoke *comb* -capnia, capno-; *base* -fum-

smooth *comb* even-, leio-, lisso-; *base* -glabr-, -levig-, -lubr-, psilo-

smother *base* -pnig(er)-

smut *base* aischro-

snail *base* cochlea-, gastropod-, limac-

snake *comb* -glypha, herpeto-, echidno-, -ophidia, ophio-; *base* angui-, colubr-, reptil-, serpen-, viper-; ~ ***charmer:*** psyll-

snapper *base* lutjan-

snare *base* imped-

snatch *base* -rap-, -rep-

sneer *base* mycter-

sneeze *base* ptarm-, sternut-

snipe *base* charadr-, scolopac-

snore *base* rhonch-, stertor-

snout *comb* rhyncho-, -rrhyncha; *base* mycter-, probosc-, rostell-, -rostr-. *See* **beak**

snow *base* -chion-, -chium-, ning-, nipha-, niv-

soak *base* macer-; ***soak up:*** *comb* -sorb¹; *base* bib-

soap *base* sapon(i)-

sob *base* dacryo-, fleb-, flet-, lachrim-, lachrym-, plor-, singult-

sober *base* ***abstinent:*** nephal-; ***serious:*** grav-

social belief *suf* -arian

society *comb* anthropo-, socio-

socket *comb* alveolo-, tormo-; *base* -gomph-

sodium *comb* -natremia, sodio-

soft *comb* -malacia, malaco-; *base* hapal-, -len-, macer-, malax-, -moll-; ~ ***deposit:*** *comb* athero-; ~ ***palate:*** velar-

soil *comb* agri-, agro-, paedo-¹, pedo-³; *base* edaph-, -hum-, -terr-

soldier *comb* -milit-; ~ ***belonging to a phalanx:*** *base* phalang-

sole of the foot *base* pelm-, -plant-, then-

solid *comb* stereo-

solitary *comb* auto-, eremo-, mono-, soli-, uni-. *See* **one**

somewhat *pre* demi-, hemi-, semi-; *comb* -atelia, atelo-; *suf* -esce, -escence, -escent, -y¹

son *base* fili-

son-in-law *base* -gener-
song *comb* asmato-, lyrico-, melo-[1],
musico-; ~ *birds:* oscin-
soot *base* fulig-
soothing *base* anet-, -len-, miti-[1]
soothsaying *base* augur-
soporific *comb* hypno-, somni-; *base*
carot-, -dorm-, -sopor-
sorcery *base* -venefic-
sordid *base* sord-, turp-
soreness *comb* alge-, algesi-, -algia,
algo-, -algy, -dynia, noci-, -odynia,
odyno-, pono-; *base* dolor-, -nox-
sorrow *comb* lype-; *base* dolor-, -fleb-,
-flet-, -luct-[1], trist-
soul *comb* pneumato-, thumo-,
-thymia, thymo-; *base* -anim-,
-spirit-
sound *comb* acou-, acoust-, audi(o)-,
auri-, echo-, oto-, -ecoia, -phone,
phono-, -phony, -phthong, soni-,
sono-, sonoro-. *See* **noise**
soundness *base* salub-, san-
sour *base* acer-, acid-, amar-
source *comb* aetio-, -blast, blasto-,
-blasty, -carp, -carpic, carpo-,
-carpous, etio-, -gen, -genic, -gene-
sis, -genous, -geny, -gone, -gonium,
gono-, -gony, -phyletic, sperma-,
-spermal, spermato-, spermi-,
-spermic, spermo-, sporo-; *base*
-init-; *suf* -esce, -escence, -escent
south *comb* austro-, noto-
sow *base* sativ-, sator-, sparg-
spade-shaped *base* pala-
Spanish *comb* Hispano-, Ibero-
sparing *base* frug-[2]
spark *base* -scintill-, spinthar-
sparrow *base* passer-
sparse *comb* oligo-; *base* pars-,
pauc(i)-
spasm *comb* -chorea, choreo-, -clonic,
-clonus, -esmus, -ismus, spasmato-,
spasmo-, -tonic; *base* -stal-, -vellic-
spatula *comb* spathi-, spatuli-
speak, speech *comb* -claim, -logia,
logo-, -logue, -lalia, -lexia, lexico-,
-lexis, -lexy, -logy, -phone, phono-,

-phony, verbi-, verbo-, voc-, voci-,
-voke; *base* -clam-, -dict-, garrul-,
-loc(u)-, -loqu-, -orat-, phat-,
-phem-, rhet-; *defective~: comb*
-lalia, lalo-, -phasia, -phasic, -phasis,
-phasy, -phemia, -phemy, -phrasia;
base psell-; **laudatory** ~: *base* eulog-
spear *comb* hastato-, hasti-; *base* dory-;
~ *head:* lonch-
specialist *suf* -ician, -ist, -ologist. *Also
see* "Experts" in Part III
specific *comb* specio-
speckled *base* -psar-, -spil-, variol-.
See **spotted**
spectacle *comb* -orama
specter *base* phantas-, phasm-, spectr-
spectroscope *comb* spectro-
speed *comb* tacho-, tachy-, veloci-;
base -celer-, exped-, festin-
sphenoid bone *comb* spheno-
spherical *comb* ano-[2], annul-, crico-[2],
cyclo-, disco-, globi-, globo-, glom-,
gyro-, orbito-, sphaero-, -sphere,
spherico-, sphero-, stilli-, zon-, zoni-;
base anu-, -cing-, -cinct-, -circin-,
-circul-, -coron-, -glomer-, -numm-,
-orb-, -rot-, -troch-
spider *comb* arachn(o)-, araneo-; *base*
arene-, phalang-, pholc-; *black
widow* ~: *base* latrodect-; *tracheate*
~: *base* phalang-
spike *comb* helo-[1], scolo-, spiculi-,
spiculo-; ~ *of corn:* spici-; *succulent*
~: *comb* spadici-
spill *base* -chys-, -chyt-, -flu-, -fus-
spin *comb* gyro-[1]; *base* -strob-
spinal cord *comb* -myelia, myelo-
spindle *comb* atractendyma-, fusi-,
fuso-, fusu-
spine *comb* aculei-, rachi(o)-,
rhach(i)-, -rrhachia, spini-, spino-,
spinoso-, spinuloso-, spondylo-,
vertebro-
spiny *comb* acantho-, aceto-, acetyl-,
acid-, acro-, acu-, acuti-, cusp-,
echinato-, echino-, echinulato-,
echinuli-, oxal-, oxy-, spiculi-,
spiculo-, stylo-; *base* -acerb-,

-aichm-, -aichur-, -belon-, muric-,
-punct-, -piq-, -punct-
spiral *comb* cirri-, cochlio-, gyro-, he-
lici-, helico-, spiri-, spiro-[2], strepto-,
stromb-, torn-
spirit *comb* pneumato-; *base* -anim-
spirits *base* phantas-, phasm-, spectr-;
damned ~: *comb* necyo-
spitting *comb* -ptysis. *See* **saliva**
spleen *comb* lieno-, splenico-, spleno-
splendid *base* lustr-
split *comb* dicho-, -fid-, -fissi-,
schismato-, schismo-, schisto-,
schizo-, -tomy; *base* -crev-, -par-,
regm-
spoil *comb* lysi-, lyso-, -lysis, -lytic,
-lyze, -phage, phago-, -phagous,
-phagy; *base* -ate-[4], perd-, phthart-,
-vast-, vitia-
spoke *a brace:* *base* -rad-; *talked:* *See*
speak
sponge-like *comb* spongio-, spongo
spontaneous *comb* ultro-
spoon *base* cochlea-
spoonworm *base* sipuncul-
spore *comb* -spore, spori-, sporo-,
-sporous
spot *comb* celido-; *stain:* *base* -macul-,
spil-, -tinct-, -ting-
spotted *comb* ocelli-; *base* -macul-,
psar-, -spil-, -stict-, -variol-
spouse *base* conjug-, marit-, uxor-
spread *expand:* *comb* -ectasia, -ectasis;
base -dilat-; *scatter:* *base* sparg-;
~ out: *base* patul-
spring *leap:* salta-; *season:* primaver-,
-vern-; *water:* *comb* crouno-; *base*
cren-[2], pego-, scatur-
sprinkle *base* sparg-, -sperg-, -spers-
spun *base* tel-[1]
spurious *comb* kibdelo-, mytho-,
pseudo-; *base* fict-, mendac-,
-notho-
squama *comb* squamato-, squamo-,
squamoso-, squaroso-
square *base* quadr-
squid *base* cephalopod-, loligo-,
teutho-

squill-shaped *comb* scillo-
squinting *base* -strab-, -strabism-
squirrel *base* sciur-
stable *comb* stato-; *base* diuturn-,
dur(o)-, perenn-, perm-, stabil-
stag *base* cerv-, elaph-
stage *development:* *base* stathmo-;
final ~: *comb* teleuto-
stage player *base* -histrion-
stagger *base* titub-
stain *base* -macul-, spil-, -tinct-, -ting-
stairs *base* -climac-
stalactite *comb* stalacti-
stalk *shaft:* *comb* calam-, cauli-, caulo-,
cormo-, culm-, ferul-, paxill-, scapi-,
thyrsi-, thyrso-; *base* festuc-, stip-[1];
hunt: *base* -venat-
stamens *comb* -androus, stamini-
stammering *base* blaes-
stamp *comb* -type, sigil-; *postage ~:*
base philatel-, timbro-
standard *normal* *comb* ortho-; *base*
-regul-; *banner* *base* labar-
standing still *comb* stasi-, -stasis, -stat,
stato-
stapes *base* -stap-
staphylococcus *comb* staphylo-
star *comb* aster-[1], astro-, -sidere,
sidero-[2], stelli-
starch *comb* amyl(o)-
starfish *base* asteroid-, echinoderm-
starling *base* psar-[2], sturn-
start *base* inaug-, incip-, init-
starting to be *suf* -esce, -escence,
-escent
state of *suf* -able, -acity, -acy, -age,
-ance, -ancy, -ant, -asis, -asm, -ate,
-atile, -ation, -cy, -dom, -ence,
-ency, -ent, -ery, -esis, -ful, -hood,
-iasis, -icel, -ility, -ion, -ism, -ity,
-ling, -ma, -ment, -mony, -ness, -or,
-osis, -otic, -red, -ship, -sion, -th,
-tion, -tude, -ture, -ty, -ure, -y
stationary *comb* stasi-, -stasis, -stat,
stato-; *base* stabil-
statue *base* agalma-
status *suf* -ship
stay *remain:* *base* contin-, dur-,

perpet-; **delay:** *comb* brady-; *base*
-cunct-, imped-, -mora-, -tard-

steady *base* perm-, stabil-

steal *comb* clepto-, klepto-, lesto-; *base*
-furt-, harpax-, klope-, ladron-,
latro-, -rept-

steam *comb* atmo-

steel *base* chalyb-

steep *base* ard-³, precip-

steering *comb* -agogic, -agogue; *base*
-vers-, -vert-; **able to be steered:**
base dirig-, tract-

stem *comb* cauli-, caulo-, cormo-,
scapi-; *base* calam-, culmi-, sarment-,
sobol-, stirp-

stench *comb* brom(o)-, odori-, odoro-,
olfacto-, -osmia, osmo-, osphresio-,
ozo-, ozono-; *base* fet-, -mephit-,
nidor-, putr-

step *comb* -basia, bato-, -grade; *base*
-ambul-, -gress-

stepdaughter *base* privign-

stepfather *base* vitric-

stepmother *base* noverc-

stepson *base* privign-

sternum *comb* sterni-, sterno-

stick *comb* scop(i)-; *base* carph-,
ramul-, -sarment-, surcul-, virgul-

sticky *base* agglut-, ixo-, visc(o)-. *See*
glue

stiff *comb* ancylo-, ankylo-, tetano-;
base rigesc-

still *base* eremo-, hesy-

stimulating *comb* excito-; *base* erethis-,
stig-

sting *comb* cnido-, mastigo-; *base* -
piq-, -urtic-; **stingray:** *base* trygon-

stink *comb* brom(o)-, odori-, odoro-,
olfacto-, -osmia, osmo-, osphresio-,
ozo-, ozono-; *base* fet-, -mephit-,
nidor-, putr-

stirrup *base* stap-

stitch *base* rhaps-, sutil-

stock *base* stirp-

stomach *comb* gastero-, -gastria,
gastro-; ~ **opening:** *comb* pyloro-.
See **belly**

stone *comb* -lith(o), pesso-, petri-,

petro-, plinthi-, psepho-, sax(i)-;
base -lapid-, -rup-; *suf* -lite;
~ **fragments:** *base* ruder-; ~ **using
stage:** *comb* -lithic

stooping *comb* kypho-, scolio

stop *comb* stasi-, -stasis, -stat; *base*
fin-, termin-

stopper *comb* emboli-, embolo-

stork *base* ciconi-, grallator-, pellarg-

storm *base* orag-, procell-

story *comb* mytho-

straight *comb* ithy-, ortho-, recti-

strain *comb* -piesis, piezo-, tensio-;
base col-², colar-, colat-, -tens-

strange(r) *comb* allotrio-, perisso-,
xeno-; *base* -ali-, peregrin-

strap *base* himant-, -ligul-, lora-

stratum *comb* strati-, strato-. *See* **layer**

straw *comb* carpho-, culmi-, festuc-,
stramin-

strawberry *base* fragar-

stream *comb* fluvio-, rhyaco-; *base* -
potam-, rheum-, -rip-, riv-

strength *comb* dyna-, dynamo-, mega-,
megalo-, -megaly, -sthenia, stheno-;
base -forc-, -fort-, -poten, robor-;
~ **to do or be:** *suf* -bility

strenuous *pre* dys-; *comb* -bar, bary-,
mogi-; *base* ardu-, stren-

stretch *comb* -tend, teno-, tensio-,
tono-; **stretchable:** elasto-; **stretched
out:** *base* pandicul-

stricture *comb* isch-, koly-, -penia,
rhopo-, -strain, -strict; *base* angust-,
-string-; *suf* -en.

strife *base* eris-

strike *comb* plessi-, -cuss-; *base* -cop-,
-crot-, plang-, -puls-, -tus-, -vapul-,
-verber-

string *base* linon-

stripped *comb* gymno-, nudi-, psilo-

stroke *comb* -plexia

strong *comb* -proof, dur(o)-; *base* -
forc-, -fort-, stren-. *See* **strength**

struggle *comb* macho-, -machy; *base*
agon-

structure *base* -strom-

strung together *base* -rhaps-

stubborn *base* contum-, obdur-, obstin-, pervic-, proterv-
studded *comb* clavato-
study *base* disc-, -math, soph-; **nocturnal** ~: *base* lucubr-
stuff up *base* -byon-, farct-
stupid *base* hebet-, inan-, obtus-, -tard-
stupor *comb* carot-, narco-
sturgeon *base* acipenser-, sturi(m)-, sturion-
stutter *base* balbut-, blesi-, -psell-
styloid *comb* stylo-
styptic *comb* stegno-
suberic acid *comb* subero-
subfamilies (animals) *suf* -inae
subject to *suf* -ize
submissive *base* moriger-
subordinate *pre* sub-, under-
subsequent to *pre* cis-. *See* **following**
substance *comb* -ousia, -ousian
substitute *pre* pro-[1]; *suf* -ette
succeed *base* -cap-, -cep-, -cip-
succinct *base* brev-. *See* **short**
suck *comb* -suge; *base* -haur-, -haust-, -myz-
sudden *base* subit-. *See* **quickness**
suffering *comb* -path, -pathic, patho-, -pathy. *See* **pain**
suffocate *base* -pnig-
sugar *comb* gluco-, glycero-, glyco-, levul-, saccharo-, sucr-
suggestive of *pre* para-, quasi-; *comb* homeo-, homoio-, homolo-, iso-, -phane, -phanic; *base* simil-; *suf* -acean, -aceous, -al, -an, -ar, -ary, -ean, -en, -eous, -esque, -ful, -ic, -il, -ile, -ine, -ing, -ish, -itious, -ize, -like, -ode, -oid, -ose, -osity, -some, -tious, -ular, -y[1]
suitable for *base* concinn-, idon-; *suf* -il, -ile, -like, -ly
sulfate *comb* sulfato-
sulfur *comb* sulfo-, sulfureo-, sulpho-, thia-, thio-
summer *base* aestiv-
summit *base* coryph-
summon *base* appell-, -claim, -clam-, -dict-, -nom-, -voc-; ~ **upon:** *base* -prec-
sumptuous *base* dapat-
sun *comb* helio-, sol-; ~ **bathing:** apricat-; ~ **rise:** *base* orient-; ~ **shade:** *comb* umbelli-, umbello-, umbraculi-
superhuman *comb* titano-
superior *pre* pre-, super-; *comb* over-; *base* prior-
superlatives *suf* -est, -most
supplement *pre* a-, ac-, ad-, af-, ag-, al-, an-, ap-, ar-, as-, at-, co-, extra-, para-, super-, syn; *comb* inter-. *See* **more**
supporting *pre* pro-; *comb* -pher; *base* patroc-; ~ **part:** *comb* -podium, scapi-; *base* paxill-, sterigm-, -stip-[1]. *See* **carrying**
suppress *base* fin-, termin-
suppurative *comb* pyo-. *See* **putrefying**
supreme *comb* arch-, archi-, proto-; *base* -prim-, -princip-
surf *comb* cuma-
surfaces *comb* -hedral, -hedron, topo-, -topy; **flat** ~: *base* pedion-
surfeit *base* ampl-, copi-, larg-
surgeon *base* chirur-, medic-
surgical operation *comb* -ectomy, -pexy, -stomy, tomo-, -tomous, -tomy
surly *base* acerb-, moros-
surpassing *pre* ex-, extra-, meta-, over-, para-, pre-, preter-, super-, supra-, sur-, ultra-
surplus *base* ampl-, copi-, larg-
surrounding *pre* be-, circum-, peri-; *comb* amphi-, ampho-; *base* -zon-, -cing-, -cinct-
suture *comb* -(r)rhaphy
swallow **bird:** *base* chelid-, hirund-, -sturn-; **ingest:** *comb* -phage, phago-, -phagous, -phagy; *base* deglut-, -glut-
swamp *base* palud-, palus-
swan *base* cycn-, cygn-
sway *base* nuta-, -vacil-

sweat *comb* sudori-; *base* -hidr-,
-suda-
sweet *comb* mell(i)-; *base* -dulc-,
-hedy-, suav-
swelling *comb* -cele, -edema, ganglio-,
phlogo-, phym-, -phyma, physa-,
physo-, strum(i)-; *base* aug-, cresc-,
physc-, strum-, -tum-, -turg-; *suf*
-itis
swift *bird: base* cypsel-; *fast: comb*
ocy-, tacho-, tachy-; *base* -celer-,
veloc-
swim *comb* necto-; *base* -nata-
swine *base* porcin-, sui-

swing *base* oscill-
swirl *base* gurg-
Swiss *base* Helvet-
sword(like) *comb* ensi-, gladi-,
machaero-, xiphi-, xipho-
swordfish *comb* xiphi-, ziphi-
symbol *comb* sema-, -seme, semeio-,
semio-
symmetry *comb* pari-; *base* concinn-,
congru-, symmetr-
synchronized *comb* synchro-
syphilis *comb* -luetic
Syrian *comb* Syro-
system *suf* -ics

T

tablet *base* pinac-, tabell-
tacit *comb* hesy-; *base* -tacit-
tactics *base* -strat-
tail *comb* caudo-, -cerca, -cercal,
cerco-, uro-[1]; *base* -ura-; ~ *less: base*
anur-[1]
tailor *base* sartor-
take *base* -cap(t)-, -cep[1]-, -empt-
take hold of *comb* -tain; *base* -capt-,
-cathex-, -cip-, -ger-, -hapt-, incip-,
-prehend, prehens-, rap-, rep-, -ten-
taker *comb* -ceptor
tale *base* -fabul-, mytho-, -narr-, stori-
talented *base* ingen-
talisman *base* telesm-
talk(ing) *comb* -claim, glosso-, -lalia,
lalo-, -lexia, lexico-, -lexis, -lexy,
logo-, -logue, -logy, -phone, phono-,
-phony, verbi-, verbo-, voc-, voci-,
-voke; *base* -clam-, -dict-, garrul-,
-loc(u)-, -loqu-, -orat-, -phem-,
rhet-; *filthy* ~: borbor-. *Also see*
speak/speech
tallness *comb* acro-, alti-, alto-,
bato-, hypsi-, hypso-, longi-; *base*
procer-
tallow *comb* seb(o)-
talon *base* ungui-, ungul-
tame *base* cicur-, mansue-

tan *base* fulv-. *Also see* "Colors" in Part
III
tapered *base* fastig-, rhap-
tapeworm *comb* taeni-, teni; *base* cest-
tapir *base* pachyderm-
tarantula *base* theraphos-
tardy *comb* brady-; *base* -cunct-,
-tard-. *See* late
tarsier *base* lemur-
tartar *comb* tartro-
tasseled *base* crosso-, -thysan-
taste *comb* -geusia; *base* -geum-,
-geumat-, -gust-, -sapor-. *Also see*
"The Senses" in Part III
tattoo *comb* decalco-; *base* stigm-
taurine *comb* tauro-
tavern *base* caupon-
tawny *base* fulv-, melin-, mustel-
tea *base* -thei-, tsio-
teach *comb* -pedia; *base* -didact-, doc-,
-paed-
tear *rip: comb* sparasso-, sparax-; *base*
lacer-, -lania, sparax-; *cry: comb*
dacry(o)-, lachrim-, lachrym-,
lacrimo-; *base* fleb-, flet-, -plor-
tease *comb* tantalo-; *base* vex-
technical *comb* techno-
technique *comb* -craft; *suf* -ade, -age,
-al, -ance, -ancy, -asis, -asm, -ation,

-cy, -ence, -ency, -ery, -esis, -iasis,
-ice, -ics, -ing, -ion, -ism, -ment,
-osis, -otic, -sion, -sis, -th, -tion,
-tious, -ture, -ure, -y, -ysis

teeth *see* **tooth**

television *comb* tele-, video-

tell *comb* -claim, logo-, -logue, -lalia,
-lexia, lexico-, -lexis, -lexy, -logy,
-phone, phono-, -phony, rhet-,
verbi-, verbo-, voc-, voci-, -voke;
base -clam-, -dict-, -loc(u)-, -loqu-,
narr-, -orat-, -phat-, -phem-

temperament *comb* -natured

temple *head:* *comb* temporo-; *base*
crotaph-; *church:* *comb* aedi-; *base*
-nao-

temporal *base* -secul-

ten *comb* dec(a)-, decem-, deka-; *one
tenth:* *comb* deci-; *ten and __:* *suf*
-teen; ~ *thousand:* myria-; *x times
ten:* *suf* -ty². *Also see* "Numbers" in
Part III

tender *comb* coupho-

ten thousand *comb* myria-, myrio-

tending to *pre* pro-; *comb* -phile,
-philia, -philiac, -trope, -tropic; *suf*
-able, -ative, -ish, -istic, -istical, -ive,
-like, -some², -orial, -ulous, -y¹

tendon *comb* tendo-, teno-, tenonto-

tendril *comb* cirr(h)i-, cirr(h)o-,
pampin-

tennis *base* sphair-

tension *comb* tasi-, taso-, -tonia,
-tonic, tono-

tentacles *comb* actino-, tentaculi-; *base*
brach-, cornic-, flagell-

tentative *base* ambig-, ancip-, apor-,
dub-, vagu-

terminate *comb* stasi-, -stasis, -stat;
base fin-, termin-

termite *base* isoptero-, termit-

tern *base* stern-

terrified *base* -pavid-, -tim-, trepid-.
See **fear**

terrifying *comb* dino-¹

territory *suf* -land

testicle *comb* didym(o)-, orchido-²,
orchio-, oscheo-; *base* -scrot-

testing *comb* -opsy, -scope, -scopic,
scopo-, -scopy; *base* docim-,
-(in)quir-, -(in)quis-, -scrut-

testy *base* acerb-, mord-

tetanus *comb* tetano-

thalamus *comb* thalamo-

thallium *comb* thallo-

thankful *base* grat-

the *pre* al-²

theater *comb* theatro-

theft *comb* clepto-, klepto-, lesto-;
base -furt-, harpax-, klope-, ladron-,
latro-, -rept-

theory *suf* -ism, -logy

thermoelectric *comb* thermo-

thick *comb* cespitoso-, dasy-, hadro-,
pachy-, pycno-, pykno-, visc(o)-;
base -crass-, -spiss-

thief *comb* clepto-, klepto-, lesto-; *base*
-furt-, harpax-, ladron-, latr(o)-

thigh *comb* mero-²

thin *comb* angusti-, araio-, dolicho-,
lepti-, lepto-, maci-, mano-, stegno-,
steno-, tenu-; *base* -areo-², gracil-,
-isthm-, stal-, -strict-

thing that is __ *suf* -ance, -ee, -er,
-tion, -tious

think *see* **thought**

third *base* -tert-, trient-, trito-

thirst *comb* dipso-; *base* siti-. *See* **dry**

thirteen *base* tredecim-, triskaideka-

thirty *base* triaconta-, triceni-, triges-,
trigint-

this side of *comb* citra-; *suf* cis-¹

thistles *base* cardo-

thong *base* haben-, himant-, lor-. *See*
strap

thorax *comb* thoracico-, thoraco-

thorny *comb* acantho-, echino-,
rhamn-, spiculi-, spiculo-, spini-;
base -muric-, -urtic-

thought *comb* -gnomy, -gnosia, -gno-
sis, -gnostic, gnoto-, ideo-, -noia,
-nomy, phreno-, psycho-, -sophy;
base -cogit-, -cogn-, epistem-,
-heur-, ment²-, -noe-, phrontis-,
-put-, ratio-, -sci-; *insane* ~: *comb*
lysso-, -mania; *base* ament-, dement-

thousand *comb* chili-, kilo-; ~ *th:* milli-

thread(like) *comb* filamento-, fili-, filio-, filo-, mit²-, nemato-; *base* -nema-, stema-

threat *base* comminat-, min-

three *comb* ter-, tri-, triakis-, triplo-, trito-; *base* -tern-, -tert-; ~ *cornered:* *comb* trigono-; ~ *dimensional:* *comb* stereo-; ~ *fourths:* triquadr-; ~ *hundred:* trecent-. *Also see* "Numbers" *in Part III*

threshing *base* trit-

threshold *base* -limin-, marg-, propinq-, prox-

thrice *comb* ter-

thrift *base* frug-², pars-

throat *comb* gutturo-, jugo-, jugulo-, laryngo-, pharyngo-, -throated, tracheo-; *base* fauc-, jug-, sphag-

through *pre* cata-, cath-, dia-, per-, trans-

throughout *pre* ana-; *comb* -wide

throw *comb* -bole, -bolic, bolo-¹, -boly; *base* -ballist-, -jact-, -jacula-, -ject-

thrush *base* -musicap-, -turd-, cichlo-

thrust *base* -pel-, -pul-, -trude-, -trus-

thumb *base* pollic-

thunder *comb* bronte-, bronto-, cerauno-, kerauno-; *base* fulmin-, tonitr-

thymus *comb* thymo-

thyroid *comb* -thyrea, thyreo-; ~ *gland:* *comb* thyro-

tibia *comb* tibio-; *base* -cnem-

tick *base* acar-, ixod-

tickle *comb* titillo-

tide *base* aestu-, estu-

tie *comb* sphingo-, -strain, -strict, syndesmo-; *base* -liga-, -merinth-, -string-, -vinc-. *See* **restriction**

tiger *base* tigr-

tightening *comb* isch-, koly-, -penia, -strain, -strict; *base* -string-; *suf* -en; *tightly bound:* *base* sphingo- *See* **constriction**

tile *base* imbricato-, tegul-

tillage *comb* -culture; *base* arat-

tilting *comb* -clinal, -clinate, -cline, -clinic, clino-, -clisis, lechrio-, loxo-, plagio-; *base* -cliv-

time *comb* back-, chrono-, horo-, yester-; *base* -tempor-; ~ *period:* *pre* eo-; *comb* aev-, -cene, paleo-, protero-; *timely:* *base* tempest-. *Also see* "Time" *in Part III*

timid *base* pav-, trep-, verecund-

tin *base* cassiter-, stann-

tiny *comb* brachisto-, brachy-, brevi-, chamae-, micro-, mini-, nano-, parvi-, parvo-, pauci-, steno-; *base* -curt-, exig-; *suf* -cle, -cule, -een, -el, -ella, -en, -et, -ette, -idion, -idium, -ie, -illa, -illo, -isk, -kin, -le, -let, -ling, -ock, -ola, -ole, -rel, -ula, ule, -ulum, -ulus, -y

tip *comb* -apical, apico-; *base* cacumen-

tired *comb* pono-; *base* -fatig-, kopo-, -lass-

tissue *comb* fascio-, histio-, histo-, hypho-, -sarc, sarco-; *base* text-; *dead* ~: necro-; *horny* ~: *comb* kera-, kerato-

titan *comb* titano-¹

titanium *comb* titano-²

titmouse *base* par-²

to *pre* a-, ac-¹, ad-¹, af-, ag-, al-¹, an-², ap-, ar-¹, as-¹, at-, il-, im-, in-, ir-, ob-; *comb* -bound; *base* pros-; *suf* -ad, -ly, -ward, -ways, -wise; ~ *the other side:* *pre* trans-

toad *comb* batracho-, bufo-, phryno-; *tree* ~: *base* polyped-

today *base* hodiern-

toe *comb* dactyl(o)-, -dactylous, -dactyly, digiti-; *base* halluc-

together *pre* co-¹, inter-, syl-, sym-, syn-, sys-; *comb* allelo-, hama-, symphyo-, synchro-; *base* -mutu-, -simul-

toil *base* aerumn-. *See* difficult *and* work

token *comb* sema-, -seme, semeio-, semio-

tomb *comb* -taph, tapho-; *base* sepulc-
tomorrow *base* crastin-
tone *comb* tonia-, -phone, phono-,
   -phony; *base* son-
tongue *comb* -glossia, glosso-, -glot,
   lamino-, lingu(o)-; *base* -ligul-;
   ~ *kissing:* cataglott-
tonsil *comb* tonsillo-
tooth *comb* dentato-, denti-, dento-,
   dont-, -odont(o), -odus, -toothed;
   canine ~: laniar-; ~ *disease: comb*
   cario-; *lacking* ~: *base* edent-,
   coryph-; *saw-toothed: comb* serrati-,
   serrato-; *base* runcin-; ~ *socket: base*
   phat-[2]; *wisdom* ~: *base* cranter-
top *crest: comb* cory-, coryph-, strom-
   boli-; *base* cacum-, culm-; ~ *shaped:*
   comb turbinato-
topical *comb* topo-, -topy
torch *base* lampad-, lychn-
tornado *base* -lilaps-
torrent *comb* rhyaco-
tortoise *base* -chelon-, emydo-,
   testud-. *See* **turtle**
totally *pre* be-, cata-, cath-, de-, kata-,
   ob-, per-; *comb* holo-, omni-, pan-,
   panto-, stone-, toti-
totter *base* -lab-
touch *comb* aphe-, -aphia, -apsia,
   hapto-[1], sensori-, thigmo-; *base*
   haph-, -palp-, -sent-, -tact-, -tang-.
   Also see "The Senses" in Part III
toughness *comb* dyna-, dynamo-,
   mega-, megalo-, -megaly, -sthenia,
   stheno-; *base* -forc-, -fort-, -poten-,
   robor-
tour *comb* hodo-, -ode, odo-, via-;
   base -itin-, peregrin-
toward *pre* a-, ac-[1], ad-[1], af-, ag-, al-[1],
   an-[2], ap-, ar-[1], as-[1], at-, il-, im-, in-,
   ir-, ob-; *comb* -bound, -petal; *base*
   pros-; *suf* -ad[3], -ly, -ward, -ways,
   -wise
tower *base* pyrgo-, turri-
town *comb* -burg(h), -ton, -ville; *base*
   urb-
toxic *comb* tox(i), toxico-, -toxin,
   toxo-, veneno-

trace *comb* ichno-; *base* indag-, vestig-
trachea *comb* tracheo-
track *comb* ichno-
trade *base* empor-, merc-, nundin-;
   ~ *names:* co-[2], -ine
train *comb* siderodromo-
trait *suf* -able, -acity, -acy, -age, -ance,
   -ancy, -ant, -asis, -asm, -ate, -atile,
   -ation, -cy, -dom, -eity, -ence, -ency,
   -ent, -ery, -esis, -ful, -hood, -iasis,
   -ice, -ility, -ion, -ise, -ism, -ity, -ling,
   -ma, -ment, -ness, -or, -osis, -otic,
   -red, -ship, -sion, -th, -tion, -tude,
   -ture, -ty, -ure, -y
traitor *base* prodit-
tranquility *base* -eiren-, -iren-, -pac-,
   -pax-
transcending *pre* trans-
transfer *carry: comb* -fer, -ferous,
   -gerous, -parous, -pher, -phore,
   -phorous; *base* -port-, -vect-;
   change: base camb-, -fabr-, -fec-,
   -mut-, -vari-, -vert-; *suf* -ate, en, -fy,
   -ize, -otic
transgression *comb* enisso-, enosio-;
   base -culp-, hamart-, -pecca-
transitory *base* caduc-
transmission *broadcast: comb* -cast;
   passing through: comb -phoresis
transparent *comb* diaphano-, hyalo-,
   -phane
transplant *base* chim-
transport *comb* -fer, -ferous, -gerous,
   -parous, -pher, -phore, -phorous;
   base -port-, -vect-
transverse *comb* cross-, transverso-
trap *comb* -thera
trapezoid *comb* trapezi-
travel *comb* hodo-, dromo-, odo-; *base*
   -itiner-, -peregrin-, -via-. *See*
   wander
tray *base* hypocrater-
treat with *suf* -ate, -ize
treatment *comb* -iatrics, iatro-, -iatry;
   base -com-
tree(like) *comb* dendri-, dendro-,
   -dendron, silvi-, xylo-; *base* -arbor-,
   dryo-. *See* **woods**

tremble *comb* tremo-; *base* pav-, trep-;
　earth ~: *comb* tromo-
trepidation *comb* -phobe, -phobia,
　-phobic, phobo-; *base* pavid-,
　tim(or)-, -trem-, -trep-. *Also see*
　"Fear" in Part III
triangular *comb* delta-, triangulato-,
　trigono-
tribe *comb* phylo-
trifling *base* -nuga-
trillion *comb* tera-, trega-, ; *-th:* pico-
trilobytes *comb* -paria
trip *comb* hodo-, -ode, odo-; *base*
　-itiner-, -peregrin-, -via-
triple *comb* triplicato-, triplo-; *base*
　-ter(n)-
trouble *base* aerumn-. *See* **grief**
trout *base* -trocto-, trutt-
truffle *comb* hydno-
trumpet *base* buccin-, litu-
trunk *comb* cormo-. *See* **stem**
trust *base* -cred-. *See* **belief**
truth *base* aleth-, -ver-
try *base* conat-, peir-
tube *comb* aulo-, follic-, salpingo-,
　siphoni-, siphono-, soleno-, tubi-,
　tubo-, tubuli-, tubulo-, vasi-; *base*
　fistul-, -syr-; **~ shaped:** *comb*
　syringo-
tuberculosis *comb* tuberculo-; *base*
　phthisi-, phthisio-, -phthisis
tufts *comb* cespitoso-; *base* barb-,
　carph-, crin-, crist-, flocc-
tumor *comb* -cele, onco-, phym-,
　-phyma, struma-; *suf* -oma
tumult *base* -agit-, -tumult-, -turb-
tunnel *base* cunicul-
turbine *comb* turbo-
turbot *base* psett-, scophthalm-
turkey *base* gallinac-, meleagr-
Turkey *comb* Turco-, Turko-
turn *comb* gyro-, helico-, roti-,
　strepho-, strepsi-, strepto-,
　stroph(i)-, trepo-, -verge, vortici-;
　base -vers-, -vert-, -volut-, -volv-;
　~ towards or away: *comb* -trope,
　-tropic, -tropism, tropo-, -tropous,
　-tropy

turnabout *comb* allo-; *base* -vers-,
　-vert-
turnip *base* napi-
turpentine *base* terebinth-
turquoise *base* callain-
turtle *comb* chelo(n)-; *base* -anaps-,
　chelys-, -testud-, -turtura-. *See*
　tortoise
tusk *base* broch-
twelve *comb* dodeca-, duodec-,
　duodecim-, duoden-
twenty *comb* eico-, icosa-, icosi-, vig-
　inti-; *base* vicesim-, viges-; **~ four:**
　icositetra-
twice *pre* bi-, di-[1]; **~ per time period:**
　pre semi-
twigs *comb* scopa-, scopi-; *base* carph-,
　ramul-, -sarment-, surcul-, virgul-
twilight *base* -crepus-, -lyg-
twin(s) *comb* diplo-, zygo-; *base*
　-didym-, gemelli-, gemin-;
　conjoined ~: *comb* -pagia, -pagus.
　See **two**
twisted *comb* cochlio-, contorto-,
　gyro-, helico-, pleco-, plecto-, spiro-,
　strepho-, strepsi-, strepto-; *base*
　-strob-, -stromb-, -stroph-, torn-,
　-tors-, -tort-; **~ like a top:** *comb*
　strombuli-
twitching *comb* -chorea, choreo-,
　-clonic, -clonus, -esmus, -ismus,
　spasmo-; *base* -stal-, -vellic-
two *pre* bi-, bin-, bis-, di-[1], du-; *comb*
　ambi-, ambo-, amphi-, ampho-,
　deutero-, deuto-, dicho-, diphy-,
　diplo-, disso-, double-, duo-,
　duplicato-, duplici-, dyo-, gemelli-,
　twi-, zygo-; *base* -didym-, gemin-;
　~ colored: *comb* dichro-; **~ edged:**
　base ancip-; **~ hundred:** *base* ducen-;
　~ wings: *comb* diptero-. *Also see*
　"Numbers" in Part III
tympanic *comb* myringo-, tympani-,
　tympano-
type *comb* -type, typo-
typhoid *comb* typho-

U

ulcer *comb* helco-
ulna *comb* cubito-, ulno-
umbilicus *comb* omphalo-
umbrella *comb* umbell(i)-, umbraculi-, umbrelli-
unaffected by *suf* -proof
unalterable *base* immut-
unceasing *base* assid-, contin-, incess-, perpet-
uncertain *base* ambig-, ancip-, apor-, dub-, vagu-; *of ~ sex: comb* gynandro-
uncle *base* -avunc-, patru-
unclean *comb* blenno-, -chezia, copro-, fim(i)-, kopro-, myso-, -myxia, myxo-, paedo-, pedo-, scato-, spatilo-, spurc-, stegno-, sterco-; *base* -fecu-, molys-, rhypar-, rhypo-
unconscious *base* -stup-
under *pre* hypo-, infra-, sub-, subter-; *comb* infero-, under-; *base* cunicul-; *~ world:* acheron-, infern-
understanding *comb* -gnomy, -gnosia, -gnosis, -gnostic; *base* -crit-, -judic-, sagac-, -soph-
undertaking *pre* entre-
underworld *base* acheron, infern-
undeveloped *comb* -atelia, atelo-. *See* immature
undiscerning *base* hebet-, obtus-, -tard-
undivided *base* integ-, tot-
undo *pre* de-
undulation *comb* flexuoso-, flucti-; *base* -sinu-. *See* wave
uneasy *base* agit-, mov-, trepid-, turb-
unequal *comb* aniso-, inequi-, impari-, perisso-, scaleno-; *~ growth: comb* -nastic, -nasty
uneven *comb* anomalo-, anomo-, perisso-, poikilo-, sinuato-, sinuoso-; *base* salebr-
unfinished *pre* demi-, hemi-, semi-; *base* -atelia, atelo-; *suf* -esce, -escence, -escent
unguent *base* -aliph-, unct-

unhappy *comb* lype-; *base* dolor-, fleb-, flet, luct-, -trist-
unholy *base* profan-
unimportant *base* -nuga-
union *comb* -ergasia, gameto-, gamo-, -gamous,-gamy; *base* -greg-, -junct-, -soc-
unit *comb* -mer(e), mero-; *significant linguistic ~: suf* -eme
unite(d) *pre* co-; *comb* conjugato-, -ergasia, gameto-, gamo-, hama-, hapto-, junct-; *base* aps-, apt-, -greg-, -soc-; *suf* -ate, -ize
universe *comb* -cosm, cosmo-; *universal: comb* pasi-
unlike *pre* anti-, contra-, contre-, dis-, hetero-, ob-, un-; *comb* back-, counter-, enantio-, oppositi-
unlit *comb* ambly-, melan(o)-, nycto-, scoto-; *base* -achlu-, amaur-, fusc-, lyg-, obscur-, tenebr-
unlucky *base* scaev-
unpaired *comb* impari-
unprofitable *base* mataeo-
unquenchable *base* avid-, edac-, gulos-
unreal *base* chim-
unreasonable *base* alogo-
unsatisfactory *pre* hypo-, sub-, under-; *comb* hystero-; *base* hesson-; *suf* -aster
unsaturated acid *comb* -enoic
unspecified *base* ambig, dub-, ancip-
untrustworthy *base* apat-, dolero-, ludif-
unusual *comb* aetheo-, allotrio-, anom(o)-, anomalo-; *~ sexual practices: base* paraphil-. *See* irregular
unwell *pre* dys-, mal-; *comb* noso-, -path, -pathic, patho-, -pathy; *base* aegr-, -morb-, -pecca-, valetud-
up *pre* ana-, ano-; *comb* super-, supra-; *~ to: pre* epi-
upheaval *base* -agit-, -tumult-, -turb-

upon *pre* ana-, epi-, ob-, super-, sur-
upper side *comb* supero-
upright *comb* ortho-, prob-, recti-
uproar *base* crepit-, frem-, ligyr-, strep(i)-, strid-, stridul-. *See* **sound**
upward *pre* ano-¹, ex-; *comb* sursum-
uranium *comb* uranoso-
urea *comb* ure(a)-
ureter *comb* uretero-, urethro-
urge *base* horm-, -hort-, -suade, -suas-
uric acid *comb* uri-, urico-
urine/urinary tract *comb* ouro-, ure(a)-, ureo-, uretero-, -uretic, urini-, urino-, uro-², -ury; *base* diures-, -mict-, -ming-; ~ *absence of: base* anur-²; *diseased condition of ~: comb* -uria
urn *comb* urcei-, urceo-

usage *base* mor-¹
used for doing *comb* -chresis; *suf* -le
useful *comb* chreo-, chresto-; *base* -util-
useless *comb* ponero-; *base* futil-, inutil-, mataeo-
usual *comb* normo-
utensil *base* sceuo-, skeuo-
uterus *comb* hyster(o)-¹, metra-, metro-, utero-
utter *comb* -claim, logo-, -logue, -lalia, -lexia, lexico-, -lexis, -lexy, -logy, -phone, phono-, -phony, rhet-, verbi-, verbo-, voc-, voci-, -voke; *base* -clam-, -dict-, -loc(u)-, -loqu-, narr-, -orat-, -phat-, -phem-
uvula *comb* staphylo-, uvulo-; *base* ciono-

V

vacant *comb* ceno-, keno-; *base* -erem-, (ex)haur-, inan-, -vac(u)-
vaccine *comb* vaccino-
vagina *comb* colp(o)-, elytr(o)-, kolpo-, vagini-, vagino-. *See* **vulva**
vague *base* ambig, dub-, ancip-
vagus nerve *comb* vago-
vain *comb* mataeo-
valence *comb* -valent; *lower ~: suf* -ous
validating *comb* -deictic
values *comb* axio-²
valve *comb* valvi-, valvulo-; *base* diclid-
vampire *base* vespertil-
vanishing *base* marc-
vanquish *base* vict-, -vinc-
vapor *comb* atmo-, -capnia, capno-, -hale, vapo-, vapori-; *base* halit-, -nebul-
variation *comb* allo-, anomalo-, anomo-, poikilo-; *base* -mut-. *See* **change**
various *comb* diversi-, hetero-, vari-
vas deferens *comb* vaso-
vase *comb* urcei-

vast *comb* bronto-, dino-, giganto-, mega-, megalo-, -megaly
vault *base* camer-, fornic-
veal *base* vitul-
vegetable *comb* thalero-, vegeti-, vegeto-; *base* lachan-, oler-, olit-
vegetation *comb* botano-, herbi-, -phyte, phyto-; *base* veget-; *suf* -aceae, -ad, -ales, -eae, -ia
vehicle *comb* amaxo-, -mobile; *base* -ocho-¹
veiled *pre* sub-; *comb* calypto-, crypto-, veli-; *base* occult-
vein *comb* cirso-, phlebo-, vene-, veni-, veno-, venoso-, -venous; *enlarged ~: comb* varici-, varico-
velvet *base* velut-
ventral *comb* abdomino-, celio-, laparo-, ventro-
ventricle *comb* ventriculo-
veracity *base* aleth-, -ver-
verb *base* rhema-
verdegris *base* aerug-
verge *base* marg-, propinq-, prox-
vermin *base* pesti-, vermin-

versatile *base* agil-, facil-, ingen-
verse *comb* rhapso-, -stichia, sticho-, -stichous
vertebra *comb* spondylo-, vertebro-; *top* ~: *comb* atlanto-, atlo-
vertigo *base* illyngo-
verve *base* ard-, alacr-, -ferv-, zelo-
very *pre* per-; *comb* stone-
vesicle *comb* vesiculi-, vesiculo-
vessel *comb* angio-, vasculo-, vasi-, vaso-; *serving* ~: *base* sceuo-, skeuo-
vestibule *comb* vestibulo-
viands *comb* bromato-, -brotic, manduc-, opso-, -phage, phago-, -phagous, -phagy, -sitia, sitio-, sito-, -troph, -trophic, tropho-, -trophy, -vora, -vore, -vorous; *base* -alim-, -cib-, escul-, -gust-, -nutr-; *partially digested* ~: chymo-
vibration *comb* pallo-, tremo-, vibro-
vice *comb* enisso-, enosio-; *base* -culp-, hamart-, -pecca-
vicious *base* flagit-, iniq-, perdit-, -prav-, turp-
victory *base* nic-
view, a *comb* -scape
view, to *comb* eid(o)-, oculo-, ommat-, -opia, opsi-, -opsia, -opsis, opso-, -opsy, ophthalmo-, optico-, opto-, -scope, -scopic, scopo-, -scopy, visuo-; *base* -blep-, -scrut-, -spec-, -spic-, -vid-
village *comb* -burg(h), -ton ,-ville
villainous *pre* dys-, mis-; *comb* caco-, enisso-, enosio-, kak-, kako-, mal-, male-, ponero-; *base* culp-, facin-, flagit-, hamart-, iniq-, nefar-, pecca-, perdit-, -prav-, sceler-, scelest-, turp-
vine *comb* clem-¹, viti-; *base* -ampel-, pampin-
vinegar *comb* acet(o)-, acetyl-, acid-, keto-; *See* **sharp**
violate(d) *base* profan-, temerat-
violet *comb* indo-¹; *base* ianth-, -viol-. *Also see* "Colors" in Part III
viper *comb* echidno-
virgin *comb* partheno-

virtuous *pre* bene-, eu-; *comb* areto-; *base* agath-, bon-, prob-
virus *comb* **genus:** -virus; **family:** -viridae; **subfamily:** -virinae
viscera *comb* splanchno-, viscero-
visage *comb* facio-, prosop(o)-, -visaged; *base* vult-
visible *comb* lampro-, luc-, luci-, -phane, phanero-, -phanic, -phany, pheno-; *base* -clar-, -schem-, -spec-, -spic-
vision *comb* eid(o)-, oculo-, ommat-, -opia, opsi-, -opsia, -opsis, opso-, -opsy, ophthalmo-, optico-, opto-, -scope, -scopic, scopo-, -scopy, visuo-; *base* -blep-, -scrut-, -spec-, -spic-, -vid-
vitality *comb* bio-, -biosis, vita-, vivi-, zoo-, -zoic, -zooid; *base* -anim-
vitiated *comb* lysi-, lyso-, -lysis, -lyte, phthysio-, -phthysis, putre-, putri-, pytho-, sapro-, septi-², septico-, septo-¹; *base* -marces-, -putr-, tabe-; *suf* -ase
vitriol *comb* vitriolico-
vocabulary *comb* glosso-, -glot, -lexia, lexico-, -lexis, -lexy, logo-, -logue, -logy, verbo-; *base* -lingu-, -locu-, -loqu-, rhema-
voice *comb* -claim, logo-, -logue, -lalia, -lexia, lexico-, -lexis, -lexy, -logy, -phone, phono-, -phony, -phthong, rhet-, verbi-, verbo-, voc-, voci-, -voke; *base* -clam-, -dict-, -loc(u)-, -loqu-, -orat-, -phat-, -phem-; *powerful* ~: *base* stentor-
void *comb* ceno-, keno-; *base* -erem-, (ex)haur-, inan-, -vac(u)-
volcano *comb* vulcan-
voltaic *comb* volta-
voluminous *base* ampl-, copi-, magn-
voluntary *comb* ultro-. *See* **free**
vomit *comb* -emesis, -emetic, emeto-
voracious *base* avid-, edac-, gulos-
vortex *comb* vortici-
vote *base* suffrag-
voyage *base* -curs-, itiner-, -navig-, peregrin-, via-

vulgar *obscene:* base aischro-, borbor-, copro-, fescinn-; **ordinary:** comb demo-; *base* -pleb-, -popul-

vulture *base* gypo-, -vultur-
vulva *comb* episio-, vulvi-, vulvo-. *See* vagina

W

wading bird *base* grallator-
wagon *base* plaustr-
wail *base* plang-, -plor-, -ulul-[1]
wait *comb* brady-; *base* -cunct-, imped-, -mora-, -tard-
walk *comb* -basia, bato-, -grade; *base* -ambul-, -bat-, -gress-
wall *comb* parieto-, -phragma, septo-; *base* herco-, -mur-[2], teicho-, ticho-, vall-
walnut *base* juglan-
walrus *base* oben-, odoben-, trichec-
wand *comb* rhabdo-; *base* rhap-
wander *comb* -plania, plano-[2]; *base* err-, -peregrin-, -vag(r)-. *See* **travel**
wane *base* decresc-, dimin-, hesson-, -pauc-
wanting *pre* hypo-, sub-, under-; *comb* hystero-; *base* hesson-; *suf* -aster
wanton *base* meretric-, scort-
war *base* arm-, -bell-, milit-, polem-
warbler *base* vermivor-
ward off *base* alexi-, alexo-
warmth *comb* cal(e)-, calo-, calor(i)-, pyro-, -therm, thermo-, thermy; *base* aest-, caum-, ferv-
warn *base* -mon-
wart *base* verruci-
wash *comb* balneo-; *base* ablut-, cathar-, -lav-, -mund-[2], -purg-
wasp *comb* vespi-; *base* pemphred-, sphec-, sphek-
waste matter *base* triphth-
wasting away *comb* phthino-, phthisio-, -phthisis; *base* auant-, marasm-, tab-
watchman *base* excub-, custod-, vigil-
water *comb* aqua-, aque-, aqui-, hydro-, hyeto-, hygro-; *base* -rip-; *spring of ~:* base scatur-
waterless *comb* carpho-, xero-; *base* arid-, celo-, cherso-, -sicc-
wave *comb* cuma-, cyma-, cymato-, cymo-, -enchyma, flexuoso-, gyroso-, kymo-, sinuato-, sinuoso-; *base* -fluct-, -unda-, -undul-
wax *comb* ceri-, cero-, cerumini-, kero-; *base* cera-
way *comb* hodo-, -ode[1], odo-, via-; *base* -itin-; *~ of living:* -biosis, -style
weakness *physical:* comb astheno-, -atrophia, lepto-, -plegia, -plegy; *base* -debil-, dimin-, enerv-, flacc-, labe-; **spiritual:** base culp-, delinq-, laps-, -pecca-, sphal-
wealth *comb* chryso-, pluto-; *base* aphn-, chrem-, -opul-, pecun-
weapon *comb* hoplo-
weary *comb* pono-; *base* -fatig-, kopo-, lass-
weasel *base* arctoid-, gale-[1], -mustel-
weave *base* tex-
web *comb* hypho-; *base* tel-[1]
wed *comb* gameto, gamo-, -gamous, -gamy; *base* conjug-, marit-, -nub-, -nupt-
wedge-shaped *comb* spheno-; *base* cuneo-
weed *base* runc-
week *base* -hebdom-
weep *base* dacryo-, fleb-, flet-, lachrim-, lachrym-, plor-, singult-
weevil *base* curculion-
weight *comb* -bar, baro-, bary-, gravi-; *base* obes-, -pond-; **weigh:** base -pend
well *condition:* pre bene-, eu-; *base* -san-,-salub-; **water:** comb phreato-, putea-

west *base* hesper-, -occid-, zephyr-;
  ~ *wind: base* favon-. *See* **direction**
wet *comb* hydro-, hygro-, udo-; *base*
  humect-, madefac-, -rig-. *See* **water**
whale *base* -balaen-, cet(o)-; *sperm ~:*
  base physeter-
wheat *base* silig-, tritic-
wheedle *base* leno-
wheel *comb* cyclo-, roti-, trochalo-,
  trochi-, trocho-, -wheeler. *See*
  circle
where *base* -ubi-. *See* **location**
whip(like) *comb* flagello-, mastigo-;
  base lora-
whirl *comb* dino-[2], vortici-
whirlpool *base* vorag-
whisper *base* psithur-, susurr-
whistle *base* sibil-, syrigm-
white *comb* leuco-, leuko-; *base* -alb-,
  alut-, -cand-, ceruss-, ebur-, -lac-,
  -niv-. *Also see* "Colors" in Part III
whole *pre* be-, cata-, de-, kata-, ob-,
  per-; *comb* holo-, integri-, integro-,
  omni-, pan-, panto-, stone-, toti-;
  base integr-
whore *comb* cypriano-, hetaero-,
  porno-; *base* -meretric-, scort-;
  brothel: lupan-
whorled *base* verticil-
wicked(ness) *pre* dys-, mis-; *comb*
  caco-, enisso-, enosio-, kak-, kako-,
  mal-, male-, ponero-; *base* culp-,
  facin-, flagit-, hamart-, iniq-, nefar-,
  pecca-, perdit-, piac-, -prav-, sceler-,
  scelest-, turp-
wicker *base* vimin-
wide *comb* eury-, lati-, platy-; *base*
  ampl-
widow *base* -vidu-
wife *comb* uxori-; *base* conjug-, marit-
wild *base* agrio-
wild animal *comb* -there, therio-,
  thero-; *base* -fer-
will *comb* -bulia, ultro-; *base* -vol-
willow *base* itea-, salic-
win *base* vict-, -vinc-
wind *comb* anemo-; *base* -flat-, -vent-;
  north ~: base -borea-; *south ~: comb*

austro-; *west ~: comb* zephyro-; *base*
  favon-
winding *comb* flexuoso-; *base* -sinu-
window *base* -fenestr-
windpipe *comb* bronch(i)-, bronchio-,
  broncho-, laryngo-, tracheo-
wine *comb* oeno-, oino-, vini-, vino-,
  viti-
wing *comb* ala-, ali-[1], pteno-, -pter,
  pterido-, pterigo-, ptero-, pterono-,
  -pterous, pterygo-, pteryl-, ptilo-;
  having two~: comb diptero-; *~case:*
  elytri-
wink *base* conniv-, nict-
winter *base* brum-[1], cheima-, hibern-,
  hiema-
wipe out *comb* lysi-, lyso-, -lysis,
  -lytic, -lyze, -phage, phago-,
  -phagous, -phagy; *base* -ate-[4], perd-,
  phthart-, -vast-
wisdom *base* -jud-, sapient-, -soph-
wish *base* desid-, -opt-[1], -vell-, -vol-
witchcraft *base* -venefic-
with *pre* co-, inter-, para-, syl-, sym-,
  syn-, sys-; *comb* allelo-, hama-, sym-
  phyo-, synchro-; *base* -mutu-
withdraw *leave: base* relinq-; *remove:*
  pre ab-, abs-, apo-, be-, de-, des-, di-,
  dia-, dif-, dis-, e-, ec-, ef-, ex-, for-,
  off-, se, with-; *comb* ectro-
wither *base* marasm-, marces-,
  marcid-
within *pre* eis-, em-, en-[1], il-, im-, in-[1],
  ir-; *comb* endo-, ento-, eso-, intero-,
  intra-, intro-; *from ~: comb* en-
  tostho-
without *missing: pre* a-, an-, dis-, ex-,
  in-; *comb* lipo-; *base* priv-; *suf* -less;
  outside: pre epi-, exo-, extra-, para-,
  preter; *comb* ecto-, extero-, out-
woe *comb* lype-; *base* dolor-, fleb-,
  flet-, luct-, trist-
wolf *comb* lyco-; *base* -lup-
wolverine *base* -mustel-
woman *comb* gyn(e)-, gyneco-, gyneo-,
  gyno-, -gynous, -gyny, -para[3], thely-,
  -wife; *base* -femin-, muliebr-; *suf*
  -en, -enne, -ess, -ette, -ice, -ine,

-stress, -trice, -trix; *old* ~*:* grao-;
  ~ *who has given birth: comb* -para[3]
womb *comb* hyster(o)-[1], metra-,
  metro-, utero-
wombat *comb* phascolo-
wonder *comb* thaumato-; *base* -mir-
wood *comb* erio-, hyle-, hylo-, ligni-,
  ligno-, xylo-, -xylous, ylo-
woodcock *base* -charadr-, gallinag-,
  scolopac-
woodlouse *base* -onisc-
woodpecker *base* -pici-
woods *base* nemo(r)-, saltu-, silv-. *See*
  forest
wool *comb* lani-; *base* -flocc-, -lana-,
  mallo-, -ulo-[3]; ***wooly:*** *comb* dasy-;
  base oulo-[2]
words *comb* -glossia, glosso-, -glot,
  -lexia, -lexis, lexico-, -lexy, lingu(o)-,
  logo-, -logue, -logy, phraseo-,
  -phrastic, verbi-, verbo-; *base* -lex-,
  -locu-, -loqu-, rhema-, vocab-; *suf*
  -ese; ***long*** ~*:* *base* sesquipedal-;
  ~ ***unit:*** *suf* -eme
work *comb* arti-, -craft, -ergasia,
  ergasio-, -ergics, ergo-, -ergy, organo-,
  -urgy; *base* -labor-, lucubr-, oper-[1],
  -opus-, pono-[2] ; ***worker:*** *comb* ergato-
workable *comb* chreo-, chresto-; *base*
  -util-

world *comb* -cosm, cosmo-, -gaea;
  base mund-[1], secul-, -tellur-, -terr-
worm *comb* ascari-, filari-,
  helminth(o)-, nemato-, scoleci-,
  scoleco-, taeni-, vermi-; *base* lum-
  bric-, oxyur-, tered-, tinea-
worry *base* vex-
worse *pre* sub-; *base* degen-, pejor-
worship *comb* -latry; *base* cult-, vener-[2],
  -venerat-; ***one who*** ~*:* *comb* -later
worthlessness *comb* phaulo-; *base*
  futil-, inutil-, mataeo-, -nuga-,
  -vili-; *suf* -aster[2]
worthy of being *suf* -able, axio-; *base*
  -dign-
wound *comb* helco-, traumato-; *base*
  sauciat-, -vuln-
wrapping *base* involucr-, involver-
wren *base* troglodyt-
wrestling *base* luct-[2], palest-
wrinkle(d) *comb* corrugato-, rhyti-;
  base -crisp-, rhyss-, -rug-
wrist *comb* carpo-[2]
write *comb* -gram, -graph, -grapher,
  -graphic, grapho-, -graphy, grapto-,
  -logue, stigno-; *base* -scrib-, -script-,
  typo-
wrong *pre* dys-, mal-, mis-; *base* prav-.
  See **wicked**

X

X-rays *comb* radio-, roentgeno-
X-shaped *base* decuss-

xiphoid process *comb* xiphi-, xipho-

Y

yam *base* dioscorea-
yarn ***story:*** *base* fabul-, mytho-,
  narr-, stori-; ***thread(like):*** *comb*
  filamento-, fili-, filio-, filo-, mit[2]-,
  nemato-; *base* -nema-, stema-
yawl *base* nav-, scaph-
yawn *base* oscit-

year *base* -ann-, -enn-; *comb* -ennial;
  period of two ~*:* bienn-; ***period of***
  three ~*:* trienn-; ***period of four*** ~*:*
  quadrenn-; ***period of five*** ~*:* quin-
  quenn-; ***period of six*** ~*:* sexenn-;
  period of seven ~*:* septenn-; ***period***
  of eight ~*:* octenn-; ***period of nine*** ~*:*

novenn-; ***period of ten ~:*** decenn-.
See "Numbers" in Part III
yearly *base* annivers-
yearn for *comb* eroto-, -lagnia,
-mania, -orexia; *base* -appet-, conat-,
-cup-, -libid-, -opt-, vell-; *suf*
-urient
yeast *base* ferment-, prozym-, zym(o)-
yell *base* -clam-, vocif-
yellow *comb* chrys(o)-, flavido-, flavo-,
-icter-, lurido-, luteo-, ochreo-,
ochro-, xantho-; *base* aen-, croce-,
-fulv-, gambog-, gilv-, -helv-, jaun-,
lur-, lut-, -melin-, safran-, vitell-;

~ *appearance: base* cirrh-; *yellow-
brown: base* gland-. *Also see* "Colors"
in Part III
yesterday *base* hestern-, prid-
yew *base* tax-
yield *base* ced-, -cess
yoke *comb* jugo-, jugulo-, zyga-, zygo-;
base zeug-, zeux-
yolk *comb* lecith(o)-, vitelli-, vitello-
young *base* jun-, -juven-, nov-. *See*
child
Y-shaped *comb* ypsili-
yttrium *comb* yttro-

Z

zany *base* fatu-, inan-, moro-, stult-
zeal *base* ard-, alacr-, -ferv-, zelo-
zebra *base* -zebr-
zenith *comb* -apical, apico-
zero *comb* nihil-, nulli-. *See also* "Negatives" in Part III
zest *comb* agito-; *base* alacr-, ard-,

avid-, cupid-, ferv-, hedon-, volupt-,
zelo-
zinc *comb* zinco-
zirconium *comb* zirconio-
zoology *comb* zoo-
zygoma *comb* zygomatico-, zygomato-

PART III

Categories

ANIMALS

aardvark edent- (edentate)

adder colub- (colubrine)

agouti dasyproct- (dasyproctidae)

albatross diomed- (diomedeidae); procellar- (procellariid)

alligator eusuch- (eusuchian)

anchovy engraul- (engraulid)

angel fish pterophyll- (pterophyllous)

ant formic- (formicine); myrmec- (myrmecine); myrmeco- (mymecology); myrmic- (mymicine)

anteater myrmecophag- (myrmecophagine)

antelope alcelaph- (alcelaphine); bubal- (bubaline)

ape pithec- (pithecoid); -pithecus (Australopithecus); sim- (simian)

armadillo dasypod- (dasypodid); tolypeut- (tolypeutine)

ass as- (assinine); ono- (onolatry)

auk alcid- (alcidine)

badger melin- (meline); mustel- (mustelid)

barracuda percesoc- (percesocine); sphyraen- (sphyraenoid)

bat desmodont- (desmodontid); megacheiropter- (megacheiropteran); microcheiropter- (microcheiropteran); noctilion- (noctilionid); pterop- (pteropine); vespertil- (vespertilian)

bear arcto- (cynarctomachy); urs- (ursine)

beaver castor- (castoreum)

bee api- (apiarian); bomb- (bombid); melisso- (melissean)

beetle coleopter- (coleopteral); lathro- (Lathrobium); scarab- (scaraboid)

bird avi- (avian); orneo- (orneoscopic); orni- (ornithology); ornitho- (ornithological); volucr- (volucrine); *flycatching* ~: muscicap- (muscicapine); *hanging nest building* ~: pendulin- (penduline); *perching* ~: passer- (passerine); *singing* ~:

oscin- (oscine); *wading* ~: grall- (gralline)

bittern botaur- (botaurus); ixobrych- (ixobrychus)

black widow spider latrodect- (latrodectus)

blackbird icter- (icterine); merul- (meruline)

bluebird sial- (Sialia); turd- (turdine)

boar suid- (suidian)

bobolink icter- (icterine)

buffalo bubal- (bubaline)

bug cimic- (cimicoid); entomo- (entomology); insecti- (insecticide); insecto- (insectology)

bull taur- (tauriform)

bullfinch pyrrhul- (pyrrhuline)

bunting emberiz- (emberizine); pyrrhul- (pyrrhuloxine)

butterfly lepidopter- (lepidopterous); papil- (papilionaceous)

buzzard buteo- (buteonine); cathart- (cathartine)

calf vitul- (vituline)

camel camel- (cameline)

cardinal pyrrhul- (pyrrhuloxine)

carp cyprin- (cyprinoid)

cassowary casuar- (casuarina)

cat aeluro- (aelurophile); ailuro- (ailurophobe); feli- (feline); gale- (galeanthropy); gato- (gatophobia)

caterpillar bruch- (bruchus); -camp- (campodean); eruc- (eruciform)

catfish silur- (silurid)

centipede chilopod- (chilopodal); scolopendr- (scolopendriform)

chamois rupicap- (rupicaprine)

chickadee par- (parine)

chicken gallin- (gallinaceous); pull- (pullet)

chimpanzee sim- (simid)

chipmunk tam- (Tamias)

civet viverr- (viverrine)

cock alector- (alectoromancy); alectry- (alectryomachy)

cockroach blatt- (blatta)
coot fulic- (Fulicinae)
cormorant phalacrocorac- (phalacro-coracine)
cow bou- (boustrophedon); bov- (bovine); bu- (bulimia); vacc- (vaccine)
crab cancri- (cancrine); gammar- (gammarolite)
crane alector- (alectorine); grallator- (grallatorial); grui- (gruiform)
cricket gryll- (gryllid); locust- (locustarian)
crocodile crocodil- (crocodilian); gavial- (gavialoid)
crow coraci- (coraciform); coraco- (coracoid); corvin- (corvine)
cuckoo cucul- (cuculine)
cuttlefish sepi- (sepiacean); -teuth- (teuthologist)
deer cervi- (cervine); elaph- (elaphine)
dodo did- (didine)
dog cani- (canine); cyn- (cynanthropy); kyn- (kynanthropy)
dolphin delphin- (delphine)
donkey ono- (onocentaur)
dormouse glir- (gliriform); myox- (myoxine)
dove columb- (columbine)
dragonfly libellul- (libellulid)
duck anat- (anatine); fuligul- (fuliguline)
eagle aet- (aetites); aquil- (aquiline)
earwig forficul- (forficulid)
eel anguill- (anguilliform); cyclostom- (cyclostome); muraen- (muraenoid)
eland taurotrag- (Taurotragus oryx)
elephant elephant- (elephantine); pachyderm- (pachydermic)
elk cerv- (cervine)
emu rat- (ratite)
ermine mustel- (musteline)
falcon accipit- (accipitrine); falcon- (falconry); raptor- (raptorial)
ferret mustel (musteline); viverr- (viverrine)
finch fringill- (fringilline)

firefly lampyr- (lampyrid)
fish icthyo- (icthyoid); pisci- (piscine); *bony ~:* scopeli- (scopeliform).
Note: *look for specific fish in this list*
flamingo phoenicopter- (phoenicopteroid)
flea puli- (pulicine)
fly cyclorrhaph- (cyclorrhaphous); musc- (muscid); myia- (myiasis)
fox alopec- (alopecoid); vulp- (vulpine)
frog batracho- (batrachoid); bufo- (bufotenine); phryno- (phrynoderma); polyped- (polypedatid); rani- (ranine)
fruitfly drosophil- (Drosophilidae); trypet- (Trypetidae)
gerbil cricet- (cricetine)
gibbon hylobat- (hylobatine)
giraffe artiodactyl- (artiodactylous)
gnat culici- (culiciform)
gnu connochaet- (Connochaetes)
goat caprin- (caprine); egagro- (egagropile); hircin- (hircine); trago- (tragopan)
goldfish cyprin- (cyprinid)
goose anser- (anserine); cheno- (Chenopod)
gorilla pong- (pongid)
grasshopper acrid- (acridid); forbi- (forbivorous); gryll- (gryllotalpa); locust- (locustid)
grebe podic- (Podicipedidae)
grouse gallinac- (gallinaceous); tetrao- (tetraonid)
gull gavi- (Gaviae); lar- (larine)
hake merluc- (merlucine)
halibut hippogloss- (hippoglossoid)
hare cunic- (cuniculous); lago- (lagotic); lepor- (leporine)
hawk accipit- (accipitrine); buteo- (buteonine); falco- (falconine); hieraco- (hieracosophic)
hedgehog echin- (echinate); erinac- (erinaceous)
heron arde- (ardeid); grallator- (grallatorial)
herring clupeo- (clupeoid); halec-

(halecomorphous); harengi-
(harengiform)
hog hyos- (hyoscyamine)
hookworm ancylostom- (Ancylostoma)
hornbill bucerot- (Bucerotinae); bu-
corac- (Bucoracinae)
hornet -sphec- (sphecoid); vespi-
(vespine)
horse caball- (caballine); caval- (cavalry); equ- (equine); hippo- (hippol-
ogy); -hippus (eohippus)
horsefly taban- (tabanid)
hummingbird trochil- (trochiline)
hyrax chero- (cherogril)
jackass asin- (asinine)
jackdaw gracul- (graculine)
jay garrul- (garruline)
jellyfish discophor- (discophoran)
kangaroo macropod- (macropodine)
kestrel falco- (falconine)
kingfisher halcyon- (halcyonine)
kite milv- (milvine)
kudu tragelaph- (Tragelaphus)
lamb agn- (agnification)
lark calandr- (calandra)
leech bdell- (bdellatomy); discophor-
(discophorous); hirud- (hirudine);
sanguisug- (sanguisugous)
leopard pard- (pardine)
lion leo- (leonine)
lizard lacert- (lacertilian); saur-
(saurian); sauro- (sauropod);
-saurus (icthyosaurus); stellio- (stellion)
lobster astac- (astacian); gammar-
(gammarolite); homar- (homarine)
locust locust- (locustarian)
louse pedicul- (pediculous); phthir-
(phthiriasis); phthyr- (phthyriasis)
lynx lync- (lyncean)
macaw psittac- (psittacine)
mackeral scombr- (scombroid)
magpie corv- (corvoid); garrul- (garruline)
manatee trichec- (Trichechus)
marlin istiophor- (istiophorid)
marmoset callithric- (callithricid)

marmot sciur- (sciurid)
marten mustel- (musteline)
martin hirund- (hirundine)
meadowlark icter- (icterine)
millipede arthropod- (arthropodal);
diplopod- (diplopodal)
mink mustel- (musteline)
minnow cyprin- (cyprinid)
mite acar- (acaroid); miti- (miticide)
mockingbird mim- (mimine)
mole spalac- (spalacine); talp-
(talpine)
mole-rat zemn- (zemnine)
mollusk malaco- (malacological);
mollusc- (molluscous)
mongoose viverr- (viverrine)
monkey cebo- (cebocephalic); pithec-
(pithecoid)
moose cerv- (cervine)
mosquito aed- (aedine); anophel-
(anopheline); culici- (culicid)
moth arct- (arctian); phalaen- (phalaenoid); tinea- (tineid)
mouse mur- (murine); mus- (mu-
sine); myo- (myomancy)
mullet mugil- (mugiloid)
muskrat cricet- (cricetid)
mussel mytil- (mytiloid)
nightingale philomel- (philomelian)
nuthatch sitt- (Sitta)
opposum didelph- (didelphine)
orangutan pong- (pongoid)
oriole icter- (icterine)
osprey ossifrag- (ossifrage)
ostrich rat- (ratite); struthi-
(struthious)
otter latax- (Latax); lutr- (lutrine)
owl strigi- (strigine); tyto- (Tytonidae); ulul- (ululant)
ox bou- (boustrophedon); bov-
(bovine); bu- (bulimia)
oyster ostrac- (ostracine); ostrei- (ostreiform); ostreo- (ostreophage)
parakeet psittac- (psittacine)
parrot psittac- (psittacine)
partridge gallinac- (gallinaceous); -
perdic- (perdicine); perdri- (perdricide)

peacock pavon- (pavonine)
pelican onocrot- (onocrotal); pelecan-
(pelecanid)
penguin sphenisc- (spheniscan)
perch perc- (perciform)
pheasant alector- (alectorine); gal-
linac- (gallinaceous); phasian-
(phasianine)
pig porcin- (porcine); sui- (suilline)
pigeon columb- (columbaceous);
palumb- (palumbine); perister-
(peristeronic); pullastr- (pullastrine)
platypus monotrem- (monotremal);
protother- (Prototheria)
plover charadr- (charadrine); pluvial-
(pluvialine)
polecat mustel- (musteline)
porcupine hystric- (hystricine)
porpoise delphin- (delphine); phoe-
caen- (Phoecaenoides)
poultry gallin- (gallinaceous)
ptarmigan tetraon- (tetraonid)
quail coturn- (coturnine); gallinac-
(gallinaceous)
rabbit cunic- (cuniculous); lago-
(lagotic); lepor- (leporine)
raccoon arctoid- (arctoidean); pro-
cyon- (procyonine)
ram ariet- (arietine); crio- (criocephalous); krio- (krioboly)
rat mur- (murine)
rattlesnake crotal- (crotaline)
raven coraci- (coraciiform); coraco-
(coracomorphic); corvin- (corvine)
reptile batrach- (batrachian); herpeto-
(herpetology); -ophidia
(Thanatophidia); ophio- (ophiolatry); reptil- (reptilian); saur-
(saurian); -saurus (icthyosaurus);
serp- (serpentine)
rhinoceros ceratorh- (ceratorhine)
roach blatt- (blattid)
roadrunner cucul- (cuculid)
robin turd- (turdine)
sable zibel- (zibeline)
sailfish istiophor- (istiophorid)
salmon salmoni- (salmoniform)
sandgrouse pterocl- (pteroclid)

sandpiper charadr- (charadrine);
tring- (tringoid)
scorpion pedipalp- (pedipalpous)
sea horse hippocamp- (hippocampine)
sea urchin echin- (echinoid)
seagull lar- (laroid)
seal phoc- (phocine)
sea lion otar- (otarine)
shark carchar- (carcharinid); gale-
(galeod); selach- (selachoid); ***ham-
merhead* ~:** sphyrn- (Sphyrna);
squal- (squaloid)
sheep ovi- (ovine); verv- (vervecine)
shrew soric- (soricine); tupai- (tupaiid)
shrimp macrur- (macruran)
silkworm bombyc- (bombycine)
skunk mephit- (mephitine); mustel-
(mustelid)
skylark alaud- (alaudine)
sloth xenarth- (xenarthral)
slug limac- (limacine)
smelt ather- (atherine)
snail cochlea- (cochleiform); gastro-
pod- (gastropodal); limac- (limacine)
snake angui- (anguiform); colubr-
(colubrine); echidno- (echidnotoxin); -glypha (episthoglypha); her-
peto- (herpetology); ophid- (ophid-
ian); ophio- (ophiolatry); reptil-
(reptilian); serpen- (serpentine);
viper- (viperine)
snapper lutjan- (lutjanid)
snipe charadr- (charadrine); scolopac-
(scolopaceous)
sparrow passer- (passerine)
spider arachn- (arachnoid); arene-
(areneiform); phalang- (phalangium)
squid cephalopod- (cephalopodal);
loligo- (loligopsid); teutho-
(teuthologist)
squirrel sciur- (sciurine)
stag cerv- (cervine); elaph (elaphine)
starfish asteroid- (asteroidean); echin-
oderm- (echinodermatous)
starling psar- (psarolite); sturn-
(sturnoid)

stoat mustel- (musteline)

stork cicon- (ciconine); grallator- (grallatorial); pelarg- (pelargic)

sturgeon acipenser- (acipenserine); sturion- (sturionic)

swallow chelid- (chelidonian); -hirund- (hirundine); sturn- (sturnoid)

swan cycn- (cycnean); cygn- (cygnine)

swift cypsel- (cypseline)

swine porc- (porcine); su- (suoid)

swordfish xiphi- (xiphioid)

tapeworm cest- (cestoid); taeni- (taenioid); teni- (teniacide)

tapir pachyderm- (pachydermoid)

tarantula theraphos- (theraphosid)

tarsier lemur- (lemuroid)

termite isoptero- (isopterous); termit- (termitarium)

tern stern- (sternine)

thrush cathar- (Catharus); cichlo- (cichlomorphous); muscicap- (muscicapine); turd- (turdiform)

tick acar- (acarine); ixod- (ixodid)

tiger tigr- (tigrine)

titmouse par- (parine)

toad batrach- (batrachian); bufo- (bufonite); phryno- (phrynoderma)

tortoise chelon- (chelonian); emydo- (emydosaurian); testud- (testudineous)

trout trocto- (troctolite); trutt- (truttaceous)

turbot psett- (psettaceous); scophthalm- (Scophthalmus)

turkey gallinac- (gallinaceous); meleagr- (meleagrine)

turtle anaps- (anapsid); chelon- (chelonian); -chelys (Lepidochelys); testud- (testudinal); turtura- (turturring)

viper viper- (viperine)

vulture vultur- (vulturine)

walrus oben- (obenid)

warbler vermivor- (Vermivora)

wasp sphec- (sphecid); vesp- (vespine)

weasel arctoid- (arctoidean); gale- (phascogale); mustel- (musteline)

weevil curculion- (curculionid)

whale balaen- (balaenoid); cet- (cetaceous)

wolf lup- (lupine); lyc- (lycanthropy)

wolverine mustel- (musteline)

wombat phascolom- (phascolomian)

woodcock charadr- (charadrine); gallinag- (gallinaginous); scolopac- (scolopacine)

woodlouse isopod- (isopodous); onisc- (onisciform)

woodpecker pic- (picine)

worm ascari- (ascariasis); filari- (filariform); helminth- (helminthoid); lumbric (lumbriciform); oxyur- (oxyurifuge); scolec- (scolecoid); scoleci- (scoleciform); scoleco (scolecobrotic); taeni- (taeniiphobia); tered- (teredines); tinea- (tineid); vermi- (vermiform)

wren troglodyt- (troglodytine)

zebra zebr- (zebrine)

THE BODY

abdomen abdomino- (abdominocentesis); alv- (alvine); celio- (celiomyositis); celo- (celoscope); laparo- (laparotomy); ventri- (ventricumbent); ventro- (ventrodorsal); *abdominal sac:* peritoneo- (peritoneoclysis); *distended ~:* ventricoso- (ventricoso-globose)

adrenal gland adreno- (adrenotoxin)

amniotic sac amnio- (amniocentesis)

ankle bone astragalo- (astragalonavicular); tali- (taligrade); talo- (talocalcaneal)

antibodies -valent (multivalent)

anus ano-[2] (anorectal); hedro- (hedrocele); podic- (podical)

arm acromio- (acromioclavicular); brachio- (brachiocephalic)

armpit axill- (periaxillary)

artery arterio- (arteriosclerosis); -venous (intravenous)

atlas *vertebra:* atlanto- (atlantoaxial); atlo- (atloid)

atrophy tabe- (tabescent)

auricle atrio- (atrioventricular)

backbone rachi- (rachicentesis); rachio- (rachiometer); rhach- (rhachitis); -rrhachia (glycorrhachia)

bile bili- (biligenic); chole- (cholecyst); cholo- (chololith); gall- (gallbladder)

birthmark nevi- (nevoid); nevo- (nevosity)

blister phlyc- (phlyctenous); pustul- (pustule); vesica- (vesicatory); vesico- (vesicoprostatic); vesiculo- (vesiculo-pustular)

blood cruent- (incruent); cruor- (cruorin); haema- (haemachrome); haemo- (haemogastric); hema- (hemachrome); hemato- (hematogenic); hemo- (hemophilia); sangui- (sanguicolous); sanguineo- (sanguineous); sanguino- (sanguinopurulent); ~ *clot:* thrombo- (thrombo-phlebitis); ~ *condition or disease:* -aemia (hyperaemia); -cythemia (leucocythemia); -emia (leukemia); ~ *fluid:* lympho- (lymphocyte); ~ *vessels:* hemangio- (hemangiosarcoma); vasculo- (vasculitis); vaso- (vasoconstrictor)

body corp- (corporeal); physico- (physicochemical); physi- (physiatrics); physio- (physiotherapy); somato- (somatology); -some (chromosome); *dead* ~: cadav- (cadaver); necro- (necrosis); ~ *defect:* hamart- (hamartoma); ~ *odor:* brom- (bromidrosis); ~ *organ part:* -ite (somite)

bone ossi- (ossification); osseo- (osseomucin); osteo- (osteoplasty); *forearm* ~: ulno- (ulnoradial);

frontal ~: fronto- (fronto-parietal); ~ *joining hipbones:* sacro- (sacroiliac); ~ *membrane:* periosteo- (periosteophyte); *bony process:* stylo- (stylohyoid)

brain cephal- (cephalitis); cerebri- (cerebritis); cerebro- (cerebrospinal); encephalo- (encephalocele)

breast mammi- (mammiferous); mammo- (mammogram); -mastia (macromastia); masto- (mastodynia); mazo- (mazoplazia); stetho- (stethoscope); ~ *bone:* pect- (pectoral); sterno- (sternoclavicular)

breath afflat- (afflatus); -hale (exhale); halit- (halitosis); ozostom- (ozostomia); -pnea (apnea); pneo- (pneograph); pneumato- (pneumatometer); pneumo- (pneumobacillus); pneumono- (pneumonophorous); pneusio- (pneusiobiognosis); pulmo- (pulmnonary); spiro- (spirograph)

buttocks nati- (natiform); -pygia (steatopygia); pygo- (pygopod)

cartilage chondr- (chondrify); chondrio- (chondriosome); chondro- (chondroblast); xiphi- (xiphioid); *eyelid* ~: tarso- (tarsoplasty)

cecum ceco- (cecostomy); typhlo- (typhlostomy)

cell alveolo- (alveolopalatal); celli- (celliferous); celluli- (celulliferous); cellulo- (cellulo-fibrous); -cyte (lymphocyte); -cythemia (leukocythemia); cyto- (cytology); -gonium (sporogonium); kyto- (kytometry); -plasm (neoplasm); plasmo- (plasmolysis)

cellulose cello- (cellophane)

celom celo- (celomate)

cervical cervico- (cervicodorsal)

cheek bucco- (buccolabial); -genia (microgenia); genio- (genioplasty); geny- (genyplasty); melo- (meloplasty); zygomatico- (zygomaticoauricular); zygomato- (zygomatotemporal)

chest pector- (pectoral); sterno- (sternocostal); stetho- (stethometric); thoracico- (thoracico-abdominal); thoraco- (thoracotomy)

chin -genia (microgenia); genio- (genioplasty); geny- (genyplasty); mento- (mentoplasty)

chromosomes -ploid (diploid)

chyle chyl- (chylaqueous)

clavicle cleido- (cleidomastoid); clido- (clidomastoid)

clot grum- (grumous); thrombo- (thrombo-phlebitis)

coccyx coccy- (coccyalgia); coccygo- (coccygodynia)

collarbone clavi- (clavicle)

colon coli- (coliform); colo- (coloenteritis)

cornea corneo- (corneoiritis); kerato- (keratotomy)

corpse cadav- (cadaverous); necro- (necrophilia)

cyst- sacc- (sacculation)

dandruff porrig- (porriginous)

defecation -chezia (hematochezia); copro- (coprolagnia); fecu- (feculent); fim- (fimetic); fimi- (fimicolous); kopro- (koprophilia); merd- (immerd); scato- (scatology); spatilo- (spatilomancy); sterco- (stercoraceous)

diaphragm -phrenic (gastrophrenic); phrenico- (phrenicotomy); phreno- (phrenogastric)

ear auri- (auricular); auriculo- (auriculo-temporal); ot- (otitis); oto- (otopyosis)

elbow ancon- (anconitis); olecran- (olecranarthritis)

embryo- -blast (mesoblast); -blastic (osteoblastic); blasto- (blastoderm); -blasty; embry- (embryonic)

ethmoid bone ethmo- (ethmoturbinal)

eustachian tube salpingo- (salpingitis)

eye eido- (eidoptometry); oculi- (oculiform); oculo- (oculomotor); op- (opalgia); ophthalmo- (ophthalmoscope); -opia (diplopia); opsi- (opsiometer); -opsis (coreopsis); ommat- (ommatophore); opsi- (opsiometer); opso- (opsoclonus); -opsy (achromatopsy); optico- (optico-papillary); opto- (optometry); -scope (telescope); -scopic (microscopic); -scopy (bioscopy); spec- (inspect); spic- (conspicuous); vid- (video); vis- (visual); ~ *brow:* ophry- (ophryosis); *cornea:* corneo- (corneoiritis); kerato- (keratotomy); *corner of ~:* cantho- (canthoplasty); ~ *covering:* sclero- (sclerotomy); *iris of~:* irido- (iridomotor); ~ *lash:* cili- (ciliary); ~ *lid:* blephar- (blepharotomy); *retina:* retino- (retinoschisis). *See* **pupil**

face facio- (facioplegia); prosopo- (prosopagnosia); -visaged (round-visaged)

fallopian tube salpingo- (salpingotomy)

fibula peroneo- (peroneo-calcaneal)

finger -dactyl (dactyliology); dactylo- (dactylology); -dactylous (tridactylous); -dactyly (brachydactyly); digiti- (digitigrade)

fingernail -onychia (leukonychia); onycho- (onychphagy)

foot ped- (pedal); pedi- (pedicure); pedo- (pedopathy); pod- (podalgia); ~ *sole:* pelm- (antiopelmus); plant- (plantigrade)

forearm ulno- (ulnoradial)

forehead metopo- (metoposcopy)

freckle lentig- (lentigo)

frontal bone fronto- (fronto-parietal)

gall bili- (biligenic); chole- (cholecyst); gall- (gallbladder)

gastric chyli- (chyliferous); chylo- (chylocyst); chymo- (chymopoiesis)

genitals aede- (aedeagus); genito- (genitourinary); *female ~:* colpo- (colpospasm); *male ~:* phallo- (phallocampsis)

gland adeni- (adeniform); adeno- (adenomere); balani- (balanitis); balano- (balanorrhagia)

goiter strumi- (strumiferous)
gonad gonado- (gonadopathy)
groin bubo- (bubonocele); inguino-
(inguinoscrotal)
gullet esophago- (esophagus); oe-
sophago- (oesophagalgia)
gums gingivo- (gingivoglossitis); oulo-
(oulorrhagy); ulo- (uloglossitis)
hair capilli- (capilliform); crini-
(criniferous); pili- (piliform);
pilo- (piloerection); piloso-
(piloso-fimbriate); hirsut- (hirsute);
lanug- (lanugo); thrix- (streptothrix)
hand cheiro- (macrocheiria); chiro-
(chiromancy); mani- (manipulate);
manu- (manual)
head capit- (decapitate); cephal-
(cephalitis); -cephalic (dolichocephalic); cephalo- (cephalocentesis);
-cephalous (brachycephaloius);
-cephaly (dolichocephaly); cranio-
(craniotomy); kephalo- (kephalotomy)
heart cardi- (cardiagra); -cardia
(tachycardia); cardio- (cardiology);
-cardium (myocardium); cordato-
(cordato-ovate); cordi- (cordiform);
pericardiaco- (pericardiaco-
phrenic); pericardio- (pericardiostomy)
heel bone calcaneo- (calcaneo-fibular)
hernia -cele (perineocele); celo-
(celotomy); hernio- (herniotomy)
hip cotyle- (cotyledonary); cotyli-
(cotyliform); cotylo- (cotylosacral);
coxo- (coxodynia); ischio- (ischiocapsular)
hyoid bone hyo- (hyoidal)
intestinal pouch caeci- (caeciform);
ceco- (cecostomy); typhlo-
(typhlostomy)
intestines entero- (enteropathy); ileo-
(ileostomy); ilio- (iliosacral);
intestino- (intestino-vesical); jejuno-
(jejunocolostomy); viscer- (visceroptosis)
iris irido- (iridomotor)

jaw -genia (microgenia); genio-
(genioplasty); geny- (genyplasty);
gnatho- (gnathodynamics);
-gnathous (prognathous);
mandibulo- (mandibulo-maxillary);
maxillo-(maxillo-palatine)
jejunum jejuno- (jejunoplasty)
joint arthro- (arthrodynia); articul-
(multiarticular); ~ *socket:* gleno-
(gleno-humeral)
kidney nephro-; pyelo-; reni-; reno-
knee genu- (genuflect)
labia minora nympho- (nymphoncus)
larynx guttur- (gutturo-labial);
laryngo- (laryngoscope)
leg cnem- (gastrocnemius); crur-
(crural); scel- (isosceles)
limb -mele (phocomele); -melia
(macromelia); melo- (melorheostosis)
lips cheilo- (cheiloplasty); chilo-
(chiloplasty); labio- (labiodental)
liver hepatico- (hepaticostomy); he-
pato- (hepatogastric); jecor- (jecorary)
loins laparo- (laparotomy); lumbo-
(lumbodorsal); osphyo- (osphyocele)
lumbar lumbo- (lumbosacral)
lungs -pnea (apnea); pneo- (pneograph); pneumato- (pneumatometer); pneumo- (pneumobacillus);
pneumono- (pneumonophorous);
pneusio- (pneusiobiognosis);
pulmo- (pulmnonary); pulmoni-
(pulmonigrade); pulmono- (pul-
monobranchous); spiro- (spirometer)
lymph lymphato- (lymphatolysis);
lympho- (lymphocyte)
marrow -myelia (micromyelia);
myelo- (myelogenic)
mastoid mastoido- (mastoido-
humeral)
membrane chorio- (choriocele);
choroid- (choroideremia); hymeno-
(hymenogeny); membrano- (membranocartilaginous); *eyeball* ~:

sclero- (sclerotomy); *fetal ~:* allanto-
(allanto-chorion); amnio (amniocentesis)-; *mucous ~:* muci- (muciparous); muco- (mucoprotein); mu-
coso- (mucoso-granular); *~ sheath:*
meningo- (meningocele)
mole nevo- (nevoid)
mouth -mouthed (open-mouthed);
oro- (orolingual); stomato- (stomatalgia); -stome (cyclostome); -stomous
(megastomous); *roof of ~:* palato-
(palatonasal); uranisco- (uraniscoplasty); urano- (uranoschisis)
mucus blenno- (blennostasis); muci-
(muciparous); muco- (mucoprotein); mucoso- (mucoso-granular);
-myxia (hypomyxia); myxo- (myxomycete)
muscle musculo- (musculophrenic);
myo- (myocardium); -tonic
(myatonic); -tonia (isotonia)
navel omphalo- (omphalitis);
umbilici- (umbiliciform)
neck atlo- (atloid); auchen- (maerauchenia); cervico- (cervicodorsal);
coll- (decollate); jug- (jugulate);
trachelo- (trachelodynia)
nipple mamilli- (mamilliform);
papilli- (papilliform); papillo-
(papillomatosis); papilloso- (papilloso-asperate); thelo- (perithelium);
umbo- (umbonulate)
nose nasi- (nasion); naso-
(nasolabial); rhino- (rhinology)
nostrils nari- (narial)
occipital occipito- (occipito-axial)
ovary oario- (oariopathy); oophoro-
(oophoritis); ovario- (ovariocentesis)
ovum oo- (oogamous); ovario-
(ovariocele); ovi- (oviduct); ovo-
(ovolecithin)
palate palato- (palatonasal); uranisco-
(uraniscoplasty); urano-
(uranoschisis); velar- (labiovelar)
palm palmati- (palmatifid); palmato-
(pelmatopeltate)
pancreas pancreato- (pancreatotomy);
pancreo- (pancreopathy)

pelvis pelvi- (pelvimeter); perineo-
(perineocele); pyelo- (pyelocystitis)
penis med- (medorthophobia); men-
tul- (mentulate); peo- (peotomy);
phall- (phallic)
pericardial pericardiaco- (pericardiaco-phrenic); pericardio-
(pericardiostomy)
perineum perineo- (perineocele)
periosteum periosteo- (periosteophyte)
peritoneum meso- (mesogastrium);
peritoneo- (peritoneoclysis)
perspiration hidr- (anhidrosis); suda-
(sudatory); sudori- (sudorific)
pharynx pharyngo- (pharyngology)
pimple pustulo- (pustulocrustaceous)
placenta mazo- (mazolysis); placenti-
(placentiform)
pleura pleuro- (pleurotomy)
prostate prostato- (prostatectomy)
pubic area pubio- (pubiotomy); pubo-
(pubofemoral)
pulse crot- (catacrotic); sphygmo-
(sphygmograph)
pupil core- (corelysis); coreo-
(coreoplasty); -coria (isocoria);
coro- (coroplastic); -koria
(leukocoria); pupillo- (pupillometer)
pus purulo- (purulo-gangrenous);
pyo- (pyogenic)
pylorus pyloro- (pylorodiosis)
rash -anthema (enanthema)
rectum procto- (proctology); recto-
(rectoscope)
retina retino- (retinoschisis)
rib costi- (costiform); costo-
(costotome)
saliva ptyal- (ptyalogogue); sialo-
(sialorrhea)
scapula scapulo- (scapuloclavicular)
scar cica- (cicatrix); ulo- (ulodermatitis)
scrotum didymo- (didymalgia); or-
chido- (orchidotomy); orchio-
(orchiocele); oscheo- (oscheitis);
scrot- (scotocele)
shoulder acromio- (acromioclavicu-

lar); humero- (humero-cubital);
omo- (omodynia); scapuli-
(scapulimancy); scapulo- (scapuloclavicular); spatul- (spatulamancy)

sinew chord- (chorditis); chorda-
(chordamesoderm); cord-
(corotomy)

skeleton skeleto- (skeleto-trophic)

skin chorio- (choriocele); cuti- (cutisector); derm- (dermabrasion);
-derm (endoderm); -derma (scleroderma); dermato- (dermatology);
-dermatous (xerodermatous);
-dermis (epidermis) ; dermo-
(dermoneural); dora- (doramania);
pell- (pellagra)

skull -cephalic (dolichocephalic);
cephalo- (cephalometry); -cephalous
(brachycephalous); -cephaly
(dolichocephaly); cranio- (craniofacial); occipito- (occipito-axial);
orbito- (orbitonasal)

socket alveolo- (alveolopalatal);
gomph- (gomphosis)

sphenoid bone spheno- (sphenoccipital)

spinal cord -myelia (micromyelia);
myelo- (myelogenic)

spine rachi- (rachicentesis); rhachi-
(rhachitis); -rrhachia (glycorrhachia);
spini- (spini-acute); spino- (spinob-
ulbar); spinoso- (spinoso-dentate);
spinuloso- (spinuloso-serrate);
spondylo- (spondylitis); vertebro-
(vertebroiliac)

spleen lieno- (lieno-gastric); splenico-
(splenico-phrenic); spleno- (splenocele)

sternum sterno- (sternoclavicular)

stomach -gastria (microgastria);
gastro- (gastroenteritis)

sweat hidr- (anhidrosis); suda-
(sudaminal); sudori- (sudoriparous)

temple crotaph- (crotaphion);
temporo- (temporomandibular)

tendon tendo- (tendolysis); teno-
(tenotomy); tenonto- (tenontodynia)

testicle didymo- (didymalgia);

orchido- (orchidotomy); orchio-
(orchiocele); oscheo- (oscheitis);
scrot- (scrotocele)

thalamus thalamo- (thalamocortical)

thigh mero- (merocele)

thorax thoracico- (thoracico-abdominal); thoraco- (thoracoplasty)

throat fauc- (faucal); gutturo-
(gutturo-labial); jugo- (jugo-maxillary); laryngo- (laryngoscope);
pharyngo- (pharyngology); tracheo-
(tracheotomy)

thumb pollic- (pollicate)

thymus thymo- (thymokinetic)

thyroid -thyrea (hypothyrea); thyreo-
(thyreotomy); thyro- (thyromegaly)

tibia cnem- (cnemis); tibio- (tibiotarsal)

toe -dactyl (dactyliology); dactylo-
(dactylology); -dactylous (tridactylous); -dactyly (brachydactyly);
digiti- (digitigrade); halluc-
(hallucar)

tongue -glossia (macroglossia); glosso-
(glossoplegia); -glot (polyglot);
lamino- (lamino-alveolar); ligul-
(liguliform); linguo- (linguopalatal)

tonsil tonsillo- (tonsillotomy)

tooth cranter- (syncranterian);
dentato- (dentato-serrate); denti-
(dentifrice); dento- (dentosurgical);
dont- (periodontal); laniar- (laniariform); odont- (odontalgia); -toothed
(gap-toothed)

trachea tracheo- (tracheobronchitis)

tumor -cele (cystocele); -oma
(sarcoma); onco- (oncologist);
phym- (phymatosis); -phyma (osteophyma); struma- (strumectomy)

ulcer helco- (helcoplasty)

ulna cubito- (cubito-carpal); ulno-
(ulnoradial)

umbilicus omphalo- (omphalitis)

ureter uretero- (ureterostomy);
urethro- (urethroscopy)

urine mict- (micturient); ming-
(bradymingent); ouro- (ouromancy);
urea- (ureapoiesis); ureo- (ureome-

ter); uretero- (ureterostomy); -uretic (diuretic); urini- (uriniparous); urino- (urinometer); uro- (urolith); -ury (strangury)

uterus hystero- (hysterodynia); metra- (metratonia); metro- (metrorrhagia); utero- (uterovaginal)

uvula staphylo- (staphylorrhaphy); uvulo- (uvulectomy)

vagina colpo- (colpocele); elytro- (elytroplasty); kolpo- (kolposcope); vagini- (vaginismus); vagino- (vaginomycosis)

vagus nerve vago- (vagotropic)

vein cirso- (cirsotomy); phlebo- (phlebotomy); varici- (variciform); varico- (varicocele); vene- (venesection); veni- (venipuncture); veno- (venostomy); venoso- (venoso-reticulated); -venous (intravenous)

ventral abdomino- (abdominoscrotal); celio- (celiopathy); laparo- (laparoscope); ventro- (ventrotomy)

ventricle ventriculo- (ventriculoatrial)

vertebra atlanto- (atlantoaxial); atlo-

(atloaxoid); spondylo- (spondylopyosis); vertebro- (vertebrocostal)

vesicle vesiculi- (vesiculigerous); vesiculo- (vesiculo-pustular)

vomit -emesis (hematemesis); -emetic (antiemetic); emeto- (emetophobia)

vulva episio- (episiotomy); vulvi- (vulviform); vulvo- (vulvovaginal)

wart verruci- (verruciform)

windpipe bronchi- (bronchiectasis); bronchio- (bronchiogenic); broncho- (bronchoscope); laryngo- (laryngostenosis); tracheo- (tracheomalacia)

womb hystero- (hysteropexy); metra- (metralgia); metro- (metrophlebitis); utero- (uterolith)

wrist carpo- (carpoptosis)

xiphoid process xiphi- (xiphisternum); xipho- (xiphoiditis)

yawn oscit- (oscitation)

zygoma zygomatico- (zygomaticoauricular); zygomato- (zygomatotemporal)

COLORS

Black

blue-black nigr- (nigrosine)
deep-black melan(o)- (melanous)
ebony-black ebon- (ebonize)
inky-black atro- (atroceruleous)
reddish-black piceo- (piceoferruginous)
sooty-black fulig- (fuliginated)

Blue

black-blue livid- (lividity)
dark-blue cyan(o)- (cyanean)
gray-blue caes- (caesious)
green-blue aerug- (aeruginous); glauco- (glaucous)
milky-blue adular- (adularescent)

peacock blue pavon- (pavonine)
sea-blue cumat- (cumatic)
sky-blue azur- (azureous); -cerul- (cerulean); lazul- (lazuline)

Brown

acorn-brown gland- (glandaceous)
chestnut-brown castan- (castaneous); -spad- (spadiceous)
dark-brown brun- (brunneous); fusco- (fuscous)
dusky-brown phaeo- (phaeophyll)
reddish-brown testac- (testaceous)
yellow-brown fulv- (fulvous); gland- (glandaceous); lur- (lurid); mustel- (musteline)

Copper

brassy-yellow copper chalco- (chalcography)
gold-copper auricalc- (auricalceous)
red-brown copper cupr- (cupreous); cupreo- (cupreo-violaceous); cuproso- (cuproso-ferric)

Gold

copper-gold auricalc- (auricalceous)
yellow-gold aur- (aurulent); chryso- (chrysography)

Gray

ash-gray tephr- (tephroite)
blue-gray caesi- (caesious)
dusky-gray phaeo- (phaeophyll); -phaein (haemophaein); pheo- (pheochrome)
iron-gray feran- (ferant)
pale-gray polio- (poliomyelitis)
pearl-gray gris- (griseous)
silvery-gray glauco- (glaucodot)
white-gray can- (canescent)

Green

blue-green caes- (caesious); glauco- (glaucous)
dusky-green oliv- (olivaceous); olivaceo- (olivaceo-cinereous)
emerald-green smaragd- (smaragdine)
fresh-green thall- (thallium); -virid- (viridescence)
grass-green verd- (verdurous)
leek-green porrac- (porraceous); pras- (prasine)
light-green/blue beryl- (berylline)
pale-green festuc- (festucine)
sea-green thalass- (thalassine)
slightly-green vir- (virescence)
yellow-green chloro- (chlorophyllose)

Orange

fruit-orange auranti- (aurantiaceous)

Purple

bright-purple blatt- (blattean)
dark-purple porphyr- (porphyrin)
metallic purple indi- (indirubin); indo- (indophane)
red-purple amaranth- (amaranthine); phenic- (phenicine); -pun- (puniceous)
standard-purple purpureo- (purpurescent)

Red

blood-red cruent- (cruentous)
brick-red later- (lateritious); testaceo- (testaceo-fuscous)
bright-red -rub- (rubicund)
brownish-red -ruf- (rufescent)
cinnabar-red minia- (miniaceous)
copper-red pyhrro- (pyrrhotite)
crimson-red carmino- (carminophilous)
dark-red -rut- (rutilant)
deep-red grenat- (grenatite)
healthy-red -rud- (ruddy)
inflamed-red erysi- (erysipelatous)
orange-red nacar- (nacarine); pyrrho- (pyrrho-arsenite)
poppy-red coquel- (coquelicot)
purple-red erythro- (erythrean); murex- (murexide); phoeni- (phoeniceous)
rose-red rhodo- (rhodophyllose); roseo (roseo-cobaltic)
rouge-red fuc- (fucate)
rusty-red ferrug- (ferruginous)
scarlet-red coccin- (coccineous)
vermillion-red minia- (miniaceous)

Silver

blue-silver glauco- (glaucescent)
white-silver argyro- (argyranthemous)
white-silver argent(i)- (argenteous)

Tan

light-brown fulv- (fulvous)

Violet

metallic-violet indi- (indirubin); indo- (indophane)
purple-blue ianth- (ianthine); io- (iopterous); -viol- (violaceous)

White

intense-white cand- (candescent)
ivory-white ebur- (eburnine)
lead-white ceruss- (cerussal)
leathery-white alut- (alutaceous)
milk-white lac- (lacteous)
pale-white leuco- (leucous)
snow-white niv- (niveous)
standard-white alb- (albicant)
yellowish-white ochroleuc- (ochroleucous)

Yellow

bright-yellow gambog- (gambogian)
brown-yellow fulv- (fulvous); lur- (lurid); ochreo- (ochreous)
canary-yellow melin- (meline)
gold-yellow chryso- (chrysocrous)
greenish-yellow icter- (icterus); jaun- (jaundice)
honey-yellow helv- (helvine)
lemon-yellow citr- (citreous)
light-yellow xantho- (xanthous)
metallic-yellow aen- (aeneous)
orange-yellow safran- (safranin)
pale-yellow flav- (flavescent); flavido- (flavido-cinerascent); gilv- (gilvous); helv- (helvenac); lurido- (lurido-cinerascent); ochro- (ochrocarpous)
red-yellow luteo- (luteous)
saffron-yellow croce- (croceous)
yolk-yellow lut- (lutein); vitell- (vitelline)

DIMENSIONS

deep batho- (bathometer); bathy- (bathysphere)
gigantic bronto- (brontosaurus); dino- (Dinotherium); giganto- (gigantology); mega- (megalith); megalo- (megalopolis); -megaly (hepatomegaly); super- (supernova)
high acro- (acrophobia); alti- (altimetry); alto- (altostratus); hypsi- (hypsicephalic); hypso- (hypsodont); super- (superstructure)
large ampl- (amplification); -fold (hundredfold); grand- (grandiflora); macro- (macrocosm); magni- (magnifying); maj- (majority); maxi- (maximum); plethys- (plethysmometry); super- (supertanker)
long dolicho- (dolichocephalic); -footer (ten-footer); longi- (longicaudate); macro- (macropterous); maxi- (maxicoat); procer- (procercoid)

low chamae- (chamaerops); hypo- (hypocaust); infero- (inferolateral); infra- (infrapatellar); sub- (subway); subter- (subteraqueous); under- (underground)
narrow/thin angusti- (angustifoliate); areo- (areolation); dolicho- (dolichocephalic); gracil- (gracile); isthm- (isthmian); lepto- (leptorhine); phim- (phimosis); -stal- (staltic); stegno- (stegnotic); steno- (stenosis); -strict- (stricture); tenu- (tenuity)
short brachisto- (brachistocephaly); brachy- (brachypterous); brevi- (abbreviation); chamae- (chamaerops); curt- (curtate); exig-² (exiguous); mini- (minidrama)
small -cle (particle); -cule (molecule); -culum (curriculum); -culuc (fasciculus); -een (colleen); -el (satchel); -ella (umbrella); -en (kitten); -et

(rivulet); -ette (kitchenette); hekisto-
(hekistotherm); -idion (enchiridion); -idium (peridium); -ie (laddie);
-illa (cedilla); -illo (cigarillo); -isk
(asterisk); -kin (lambkin); -le (icicle); -let (ringlet); -ling (duckling);
micro- (microcassette); mini-
(minibus); nano- (nanosecond);
-ock (hillock); -ola (variola); -ole
(variole); parvi- (parvipotent);
parvo- (parvoline); -rel (wastrel);
-ula (fibula); -ule (ampule); -ulum

(speculum); -ulus (homunculus); -y
(Billy)

thick cespitoso- (cespitoso-arbores-
cent); -crass- (crassitude); dasy-
(dasymeter); hadro- (hadrosaur);
pachy- (pachyderm); pycno- (pycnometer); pykn(o)- (pyknic); spiss-
(spissatus); visco- (viscosity)

wide ampl- (amplitude); eury- (euryg-
nathous); lati- (latisternal); platy-
(platypellic)

DIRECTIONS

away from, apart a-^{2} (avert); ab-^{2}
(abduct); abs-^{2} (abstruse); apo-
(apogeotropism); be- (bereave); de-
(deplane); des- (descant); di-^{2} (divest); dia- (diagnose); dif- (differ);
dis-^{1} (dismiss); e- (emigrate);
ec- (ecdemic); ectro- (ectrotic);
ef- (efferent); ex- (expatriate); for-
(forgo); off-^{1} (offload); se- (separate);
with- (withdraw)

backward retro- (retroversion); opiso-
(opisometer)

down a-^{2} (abate); ab-^{2} (abdicate); abs-^{2}
(abscond); cata- (catacomb); cath-
(cathepsin); de- (decumbent); kata-
(katabatic)

east euro- (euroboreal); orient- (orienteering)

forward antero- (antero-frontal);
fore- (foredeck); pre- (preaxial);
pro-^{1} (projection); proso- (prosogaster)

into eis- (eisegesis); em-^{1} (emigrate);
en-^{1} (entomb); il- (illuminate);
im- (immerse); in- (instill); ir-
(irradiate)

left laeo- (laeotropic); laevo- (laevogy-
rate); levo- (levorotatory); sinistro-
(sinistrocular)

north borea- (boreal); septen-
(septentrion)

out of e- (eject); ec- (eccentric);
ef- (effluence); ex- (expulsion)

right dexio- (dexiotropic); dextro-
(dextrorotatory)

south austr- (Austronesia); noto-
(notothere)

toward a-^{1} (ascribe); ac- (acclaim);
ad- (advance); -ad (dorsad);
af- (affirm); ag- (aggrade); al- (allege); an- (announce); ap- (approve);
ar- (arrive); as- (assent); at-
(attrition); -bound (eastbound);
il- (illuminate); im- (impel); in-
(inboard); ir- (irrigate); -ly
(northerly); ob- (object); -ward
(outward)

up ana- (anabatic); ano- (anoopsia);
ex- (extol); super- (superscript);
sur- (surmount);

west hesper- (hesperian); occid- (occident); zephyr- (zephyrean)

DIVINATION

To extract the root that shows the method being used, simply drop the
-mancy, which signifies telling the future.

air ~ *blowing or moving:* aeromancy;
 visions in the sky: chaomancy
angels angelomancy
animal(s) ~ *behavior:* zoomancy;
 ~ *movement:* theriomancy
appearance or form of a person
 schematomancy
arrows with incised marks or words
 belomancy
ashes cineromancy, spodomancy;
 ~ *of a sacrifice:* tephromancy
ass head, boiled cephalonamancy
ax (balanced on a bar) axinomancy
barley meal alphitomancy
basin of water lecanomancy
belly noises gastromancy
Bible verses (randomly selected)
 bibliomancy
birds ornithomancy; ornomancy
blood hematomancy; ~ *dripping in*
 patterns: dririmancy
bones osteomancy, osteomanty;
 ~ *marked as dice:* astragalomancy
bowl of water cylicomancy, kylixomancy
brass vessels (sound of) chalcomancy
breastbone sternomancy
bubbles rising in a fountain pegomancy
cake dough (sprinkled on sacrificial
 victim) crithomancy
candles (blowing them out) pneu-
 mancy
cards cartomancy, chartomancy
cat (jumping and landing) ailuro-
 mancy, felidomancy
cheese (patterns of coagulation) tyromancy
cloud formations chaomancy
coals (burning) anthracomancy
contour of the land topomancy
counting mathemancy

crystal gazing crystallomancy;
 spheromancy
cup scyphomancy
dead people (communication with)
 egromancy, necromancy, necyomancy, psychomancy, sciamancy,
 sciomancy, thanatomancy
devil or demons demonomancy,
 necyomancy
dice (or beans with points or marks on
 them) astragalomancy, cleromancy,
 cubomancy
digging things up oryctomancy
dirt (thrown on the ground to produce
 patterns) geomancy
dots or points (drawn at random,
 originally on the ground) geomancy
dreams oneiromancy, songuary, somp-
 nary
dust amathomancy
eggs oomancy, ovomancy
embryonic sac amniomancy
entrails of a human anthropomancy,
 splanchnomancy
evil spirits demonomancy, necyomancy
false divination pseudomancy
feces (examination of) scatomancy,
 spatilomancy, stercomancy
feet (soles of) paedomancy, pedomancy
figs or fig leaves botanomancy, syco-
 mancy
fingernails onychomancy
fire empyromancy, pyromancy
fish (examining heads or entrails) ic-
 thyomancy
flour aleuromancy
flowers anthomancy
foolish divination moromantie
footsteps ichnomancy
forehead wrinkles metopomancy

fountain pegomancy

glass vessels (figures appearing in) gastromancy [one looks into the glass's "belly"]

gods (speaking through oracles) theomancy

handwriting chartomancy, graptomancy

hatchet axinomancy

head cephalomancy

heavens ouranomancy, uranomancy

horses (neighing) hippomancy

human features and form collimancy, frontimancy, metopomancy, physiognomancy, schematomancy

icons iconomancy

idols idolomancy

incense burning knissomancy, libanomancy

key cleidomancy, clidomancy

kidneys nephromancy

lamp or torch flame lampadomancy, lychnomancy

largest object nearby macromancy

laughter gelomancy

laurel tree or leaves daphnomancy

lead, molten (motions and figures in) molybdomancy

leaves phyllomancy; *tea ~:* foliomancy, theimancy

letters (of a person's name) nomancy, onomancy, onomatomancy, onomomancy

lines *~ on the forehead:* frontimancy, metopomancy; *~ on the ground:* geomancy; *~ on the neck:* collimancy; *~ on the palms:* cheiromancy, chiromancy; *~ on the soles:* paedomancy, pedomancy

lip reading labiomancy

logarithms logarithmomancy

lots cleromancy

Lucifer necyomancy

magic magastromancy

meteors meteoromancy

mice movements myomancy

mirrors catoptromancy, enoptromancy

molten lead (dropped on water) molybdomancy

moon selenomancy

names (including number of letters in) nomancy, onomancy, onomatomancy, onomomancy

neck wrinkles collimancy

numbers arithmancy, arithmomancy; *prophesy based on analysis of the measurements of the Temple of Solomon:* naometry

nursing baby (choice of breast) mazomancy

objects offered in sacrifice hieromancy

objects touched by another person psychometry

onions cromniomancy, cromnyomancy

oracle's rapturous statements chresmomancy, theomancy

palm reading cheiromancy, chiromancy

paper (written on) chartomancy

pearls margaritomancy

pebbles pessomancy, psephomancy

plants botanomancy, floromancy

playing cards cartomancy

pointed objects aichmomancy

posture ichnomancy

random lines or passages of books stichomancy

rings dactyliomancy, dactylomancy

rod rabdomancy, rhabdomancy

rooster (choosing grains of corn) alectoromancy, alectryomancy

sacred objects, sacrificial offerings hieromancy

sage botanomancy

salt alomancy, halomancy

secret means cryptomancy

serpents ophiomancy

sheep (shoulder blade) spatulamancy

shells conchomancy

shield aspidomancy

shoulder blades (charred or cracked) armomancy, omoplatoscopy, scapulimancy; *~ of sheep:* spatulamancy

sieve (suspended on shears) coscinomancy
sleep meconomancy
smallest object nearby micromancy
smoke (ascent and motion) capnomancy
snakes ophiomancy
soles of feet (lines on) paedomancy, pedomancy
soul (emotional and ethical dispositions) psychomancy, thumomancy
spinning (in a marked circle until dropping) gyromancy
spots maculomancy
spring of water pegomancy
stars astromancy, sideromancy, uranomancy
sticks or wands rhabdomancy, xylomancy
stomach rumblings gastromancy
stones (or stone charms) lithomancy
stranger (studying the first one to appear) xenomancy
straws (burning) sideromancy
sword machaeromancy
teeth odontomancy
things seen over one's shoulder retromancy
thunder brontomancy, ceraunomancy
tide (motion and appearance) hydromancy
time chronomancy

tongue hyomancy
torch flame lampadomancy, lychnomancy
tree bark (writing on) stigonomancy
twitching limbs spasmatomancy, spasmodomancy
umbilical cord (number of knots in) omphalomancy
urine ouromancy, urimancy, urinomancy, uromancy
verses or poems rhapsodomancy
walking ambulomancy
wand rhabdomancy
water hydromancy, ydromancy; ~ *in a basin or shallow bowl:* cylicomancy, kylixomancy, lecanomancy; ~ *fountain or spring:* pegomancy
wax (melted and dropped in water) ceromancy
weather aeromancy, meteoromancy
weights zygomancy
wheel tracks trochomancy
wild animals theriomancy
wind (observation of) aeromancy, austromancy
wine (its color, sound, etc. when poured) oenomancy, oinomancy
wood (pieces of) xylomancy
words logomancy
writing *on bark of a tree:* stigonomancy; *on paper:* chartomancy

EATING HABITS

air aerophagous
algae algophagous, algivorous
animals zoophagous; *specific animals: see* "Animals"
animal waste detrivorous
ants formicivorous, formivorous, myrmecophagous
anything omnivorous, pamphagous, pantophagous, pleophagous
aphids aphidivorous
apples pomivorous

bacteria bacteriophagous
bees apivorous
berries baccivorous
birds ornithivorous, ornivorous
blood hemophagous, hematophagous, sanguinivorous, sanguivorous
body's own tissues autophagous
bones ossivorous
books bibliophagous [metaphorical]
both vegetables & animal flesh herbicarnivorous

bread artophagous, panivorous
butterflies and moths lepidopterivorous
cats felivorous
cattle bovivorous
cells cytophagous
cereals graminivorous
children paedophagous [*see* Jonathan Swift]
coccids coccidophagous
coral coralivorous
corpse or carrion necrophagous
crab harpactophagous
crows corvivorous
crustaceans cancrivorous, carcinivorous
dead material necrophagous
decaying matter saprophagous
deer cervivorous, venisonivorous
detritus detriophagous, detritivorous
dirt chthonophagous, geadephagous, geophagous
divine beings divinivorous, theophagus
dogs canivorous
dolphins and whales cetivorous
dragons draconivorous
dry food xerophagous
dung coprophagous, merdivorous, scatophagous, stercovorous
eggs oophagous, ovivorous
everything omnivorous, pamphagous, pantophagous, pleophagous
feces coprophagous, merdivorous, scatophagous, stercovorous; *one's own:* autocoprophagous
filth rhyphophagy
fingernails onychoophagous
fish ichthyophagous, piscivorous; *all kinds of:* panichthyophagous
flesh carnivorous, creatophagous, creophagous, sarcophagous; *raw:* omophagous
flies muscivorous
flowers anthophagous, florivorous
fowl gallinivorous
fresh vegetable matter thalerophagous
frogs batrachivorous, batrachophagous, ranivorous

fruit carpophagous, fructivorous, frugivorous
full range of food omnivorous, pamphagous, pantophagous, pleophagous
fungi fungivorous, mycetophagous, mycophagous
gods divinivorous, theophagous
galls gallivorous
gold aurivorous
grain granivorous
grass or herbs graminivorous, poephagous
grasshoppers forbivorous
hair comeophagous, crinivorous
honey meliphagous, mellivorous
horns cornivorous
horses equivorous, hippophagous
humans androphagous, anthropophagous, feminivorous, homnivorous, paedophagous
ice pagophagous
insects entomophagous, insectivorous
insides of a structure endophagous, entophagous
iron ferrophagous, ferrivorous
knives cultrivorous (carnival act)
large creatures or plants macrophagous
larvae larvivorous
leaves foliophagous, frondivorous, phyllophagous
leeks prasophagous
legumes leguminivorous
lice phthirophagous
lichens lichenophagous, lichenivorous
light luminivorous
limestone calcivorous
living things biophagus
lizards saurophagous
lotuses lotophagous
many kinds of food euryphagous, pamphagous, pantophagous, pleophagous
mental energy psychophagous
metals metallophagous, metallivorous
milk galactophagous, lactivorous
mollusks molluscivorous

moths and butterflies lepidopterivorous
mud limivorous
narrow range of food oligophagous, stenophagous
nectar nectarivorous
nematodes nematophagous
nutmegs myristicivorous
nuts caryophagous, nucivorous
oak leaves quercivorous
offal offivorous
onions cepivorous
only a few specific kinds of food oligophagous, stenophagous
only one type of food monophagous, univorous
opium or heroin meconophagous
other species heterophagous
outsides of a structure ectophagous, exophagous
oysters ostreophagous
palm trees palmivorous
parrots galliphagous
pepper piperivorous
pigs porcivorous
pine kernels pinivorous
placenta placentophagous
plankton planktivorous
plant lice aphidophagous
plants herbivorous, phytophagous, phytivorous, plantivorous
plant juices mucivorous
plant sap phytosuccivorous, succivorous
plasma plasmophagous
poison toxicophagous, toxiphagous
pollen pollenophagous, pollinivorous
poultry gallinivorous
pupae pupivorous
rabbits leporinivorous
raw meat kreatophagous, omophagous
restricted range of food oligophagous, stenophagous
rice oryzivorous

rock or stone lithophagous
rodents glirivorous
roots rhizophagous, radicivorous
same species homophagous
seaweed fucivorous
seeds clethrophagous, granivorous, seminivorous
several hosts or sources of food plurivorous, polyphagous
sheep ovivorous
shells conchivorous
skin cutaneophagous, cutisivorous
small creatures or plants microphagous
snakes ophiophagous, reptilivorous, serpentivorous
society sociophagous [social predator]
spiders arachnophagous, arachnivorous
strange foods allotriophagous
termites termitophagous
thistles cardophagus
tissue histiophagous
too little hypophagous
too much hyperphagous
trays of ice pagophagous
trees dendrophagous
vegetables thalerophagous, vegetivorous
venison cervivorous, venisonivorous
water aqueophagus, aquivorous, hydradephagous, hydrophagous
whales and dolphins cetivorous
wide variety of foods euryphagous, pamphagous, pantophagous, pleophagous
women feminivorous; See humans
wood lignivorous, xylophagous, ylophagous
wool or fleece mallophagous
words: large quantities of omniverbivorous
worms scolecophagous, vermivorous

THE ENVIRONMENT

For mammals, birds, insects, and fish,
see "Animals" in this section.

air aer- (aerate); aeri- (aeriferous); aero- (aerobic); anemo- (anemometer); atmo- (atmosphere); flat- (flatulent); physo- (physometra)

ash tree fraxin- (fraxinella); melia- (meliaceous)

atmosphere -bar (isobar); baro- (barometric)

beach littor- (littoral); thino- (thinolite)

beech faga- (fagaceous)

birch betul- (betulaceous)

blooming flor- (floriferous); thalero- (thalerophagous); vig- (vigorous)

bog telmat- (telmatology); turbar- (turbarian)

box-tree bux- (buxiferous)

branch clado- (cladophyll); rami- (ramify)

buckthorn rhamn- (rhamneous)

bud gemm-¹ (gemmate)

bug cimic- (cimicoid); entomo- (entomology); insecti- (insecticide); insecto- (insectology). *Also see* "Animals" in Part III

carbon dioxide -capnia (acapnia); capno- (capnomancy)

cedar cedr- (cedrine)

celestial activity astro- (astronomy)

chasm vorag- (voraginous)

clay argillaceo- (arenaceo-argillaceous); argillo- (argillo-calcareous); limo- (limo-cretaceous); pelo- (pelophilous)

cloud fracto- (fracto-stratus); homichlo- (homichlophobia); mammato- (mammato-cumulus); nebul- (nebulous); nephelo- (nephelometer); nepho- (nephology); nubi- (nubiferous)

coal anthraco- (anthracomancy); carb- (carbonize)

coast littor- (littoral); maritim- (maritime)

cold alg- (algid); cheima- (cheimaphilic); crymo- (crymophilic); cryo- (cryogenics); frigo- (frigorific); gel- (regelation); kryo- (kryometer); pago- (pagophagia); psychro (psychrometer); rhigo- (rhigosis)

continent epeiro- (epeirogenic)

cone, pine strobil- (strobiliform)

copper auricalc- (auricalceous); chalco- (chalcocite); cupreo- (cupreo-violaceous); cupri- (cupriferous); cupro- (cupromagnesite); cuproso- (cuproso-ferric)

coral coralli- (corallidomous)

country *rural:* rur- (ruralize); rustic- (rusticity); *nation:* -ese (Japanese); -ia (India); -ian (Syrian); -land (Ireland)

crater crateri- (crateriform)

cypress cupress- (cupressineous)

darkness achlu- (achluophobia); amaur- (amaurosis); ambly- (amblyopia); crepus (crepuscular); fusc- (fuscous); lyg- (lygaeid); melan- (melatonin); nyct- (nyctitropic); obscur- (obscurity); tenebr- (tenebrous)

dawn auror- (auroral); eo- (eosophobia)

day diurn- (diurnal); ephem- (ephemeris); hemer- (monohemerous); hodiern- (hodiernal); journ- (journal); quotid- (quotidian)

decomposing enzyme -ase (amylase)

desert eremo- (eremophyte)

dry arid- (aridity); carpho- (carphology); celo- (celosia); sicc- (desiccate); xero- (xerophyte)

dust amath- (amathophobia); coni-

(coniosis); -conia (fibroconia); conio- (coniofibrosis); conist- (conistery); konio- (koniosis); pulver- (pulverize)

earth agro- (agronomy); -gaea (Paleogaea); geo- (geocentric); hum- (inhumation); secul- (secular); tellur- (intratelluric); terr- (terrestrial); ~ *quake:* seismo- (seismograph); tromo-(tromometry)

elm ulm- (ulmaceous)

environment eco- (ecology); oeco- (oecology); oiko- (oikofugic)

evening crepus- (crepuscule); nocti- (noctilucent); nycto- (nyctophobia); vesper- (vespertine)

fall autumn- (autumnal)

fern filic- (filiciform); pterido- (pteridology)

fir abiet- (abietic)

flax byssi- (byssinosis)

flood antlo- (antlophobia); diluv- (diluvial); inund- (inundation)

flora -phyte (microphyte); phyto- (phytogenesis)

flower antho- (anthomania); -anthous (monanthous); flori- (floriferous); -florous (multiflorous)

fog calig- (caliginous); homichlo- (homichlophobia); nebul- (nebulous); nephelo- (nephelological); nepho- (nephology); nubi- (nubiform)

forest arbor- (arboreal); dendri- (dendritic); dendro- (dendrophilous); -dendron (rhododendron); hylaeo- (hylaeosaurus); nemor- (nemoricole); saltu- (saltuary); silvi- (silviculture); sylv- (sylvan); xylo- (xylophage)

fountain cren- (crenic); pego- (pegomancy)

foxglove digito- (digitalis)

frost cryo- (cryophyte); gel- (gelid); kryo- (kryometer); pachno- (pacnolite); pago- (pagophagia); pruin- (pruinose); rhigo- (rhigolene)

fungus fungi- (fungicide); -mycete

(schizomycete); myceto- (mycetoma); -mycin (streptomycin); myco- (mycology); uredo- (uredospore)

garden horti- (horticultural)

glacier glacio- (glaciologist)

granite graniti- (granitiform)

grass gramin- (graminivorous)

hawthorn crataeg- (crataegin)

holly ilic- (ilicic)

hot aestu- (exaestuating); cale- (caleficient); calo- (caloreceptor); caum-; (caumesthesia) calori- (calorimetry); ferv- (effervesce); pyro- (pyromania); thermo- (thermonuclear); -thermy (diathermy)

hurricane lilaps- (lilapsophobia)

ice gel- (gelation); glacio- (glaciological); pago- (pagophagia); *icicle:* stiri- (stiriated)

island insul- (insular)

isthmus isthm- (isthmian)

ivy heder- (hederated)

lake lacus- (lacustrine); limno- (limnologist)

land agri- (agrichemical); agro- (agrology); choro- (chorography); geo- (geothermal); tellur- (telluric); terr- (subterranean)

larch larix- (larixinic)

laurel daphn- (daphmomancy)

leaf bract- (bracteate); clad- (cladanthous); foliato- (foliation); -folious (multifolious); frondi- (frondescence); petalo- (petalody); -phyll (sporophyll); phyllo- (phyllomania); -phyllous (diphyllous)

lettuce lactuc- (lactucarium)

lightning astra- (astraphobia); fulgur- (fulgurant); fulmin- (fulmination)

lily lili- (liliform); lirio- (liriodendron)

linden tilia- (tiliaceous)

maple acer- (aceric)

marble marm- (marmoreal)

marsh helo- (helobius); palud- (paludicolous); palus- (palustrine); ulig- (uliginous)

meadow prat- (pratal)

meteorological front fronto- (frontogenesis)

mineral -ite (anthracite); -lite (chrysolite)

mist calig- (caliginous); homichlo- (homichlophobia); nebul- (nebulous); nephelo- (nephelological); nepho- (nephology); nubi- (nubiform)

mistletoe ixo- (ixolite)

moisture humect- (humectant); hydro- (hydrobiology); hygro- (hygrophyte); ulig- (uliginose)

moon luni- (lunisolar); lunu- (lunulate); seleno- (selenodesy)

moss bryo- (bryophytic), musc- (emuscation); sphagn- (sphagnous); splachn- (splachnoid)

mountain mont- (ultramontane); oro- (orogeny); ~ *ash:* sorb- (sorbose)

mud lim- (limivorous); pelo- (peloid)

mulberry mor- (moriform); mur- (muriform)

mushroom myco- (mycotoxin)

myrtle myrti- (myrtiform)

nettle cnido- (cnidophore); urtic- (urticaceous)

night -crepus- (crepuscule); nocti- (noctiluca); nycta- (nyctalopia); nycti- (nyctitropism); nycto- (nyctophobia); vesper- (vespertilionine); *all ~:* -pannychy (psychpannychy)

oak querc- (quercitron)

ocean enalio- (enaliosaur); halo- (halosaurian); mari- (mariculture); naut- (nautical); nav- (navigation); pelag- (archipelago); thalasso- (thalassocracy); thalatto- (thalattology)

orchid orchido- (orchidology)

oxygen oxa- (oxazine); oxy- (oxyacid)

ozone ozono- (ozonosphere)

peat bog turbar- (turbary)

pebble calcul- (calculous); pesso- (pessomancy); psepho- (psephology)

peninsula cherson- (chersonese)

petal petuli- (petuliform); -sepalous (trisepalous)

pine -peuce (peucedaneous); pin- (pinaceous); ~ *cone:* strobil- (strobiliform)

plants -aceae (Rosaceae); -ad (cycad); -ales (Liliales); botano- (botanomancy); -eae (Gramineae); herbi- (herbicidal); -ia (zinnia); -phyte (macrophyte); phyto- (phytography); vegeti- (vegetivorous); vegeto- (vegeto-alkaline)

pollen pollini- (pollinosis)

pond lacus (lacuscular); limno- (limnophilous); stagn- (stagnal)

poppy mecon- (meconidine); opio- (opiomania); papaver- (papaverous)

precipice cremno- (cremnophobia)

purslain portulac- (portulaceous)

pyrites pyrito- (pyritohedron)

quicksand syrt- (syrtic)

radiant emissions aurora- (aurora australis)

rain hyeto- (hyetograph); imbri- (imbriferous); ombro- (ombrometer); pluvio- (pluviograph)

reservoir lacco- (laccolite)

river amn- (amnicolist); flum- (fluminal); fluvio- (fluvio-terrestrial); potamo- (potamologist); rip- (riparian)

rock -ite (anthracite); lapid- (lapidary); -lithic (neolithic); litho- (lithotomy); pesso- (pessomancy); petri- (petrification); petro- (petroglyph); rupes- (rupestrine); rupic- (rupicolous); saxi- (saxifrage)

rose rhodo- (rhodochrosite); roseo- (roseola)

rue rut- (rutaceous)

sand ammo- (ammocete); aren- (arenicolous); arenacio- (arenacio-argillaceous); psammo- (psammophilous); sabul- (sabulosity); saburr- (saburration)

sea enalio- (enaliosaur); halo- (halosaurian); mari- (mariculture); naut- (nautical); nav- (navigation); pelag- (archipelago); thalasso- (thalassocracy); thalatto- (thalattology); ~ *shore:* thino- (thinolite)

seasons horo- (horology); *fall:* autumn- (autumnal); *spring:* vern- (vernal); *summer:* aestiv- (aestival); *winter:* hibern- (hibernal); hiem- (hiemal)

seaweed fuc- (fucivorous); phyceae- (Rhodophyceae); -phyceous (Rhodophyceous); phyco- (phycology)

shell conchi- (conchiferous); lorica- (illoricated); -ostraca (Leptostraca); ostraco- (ostracoderm); testaceo- (testaceology)

shore littor- (littoral)

shrub fruticuloso- (fruticuloso-ramose)

sky coeli- (coelicolist)

snow chion- (chionodoxa); -chium (hedychium); ning- (ninguid); niv- (niveous)

soil agro- (agronomy); edaph- (edaphic); hum- (exhumation); paedo- (paedogenic); pedo- (pedology); terr- (terrarium)

spring of water cren-² (crenic);crouno- (crounotherapy); pego- (pegomancy)

star aster- (asteraceous); astro- (astonomy); -sidere (hagiosidere); sidero- (siderostat); stelli- (stelliferous)

stone -ite (anthracite); lapid- (lapidary); -lithic (neolithic); litho- (lithotomy); pesso- (pessomancy); petri- (petrification); petro- (petroglyph); rupes- (rupestrine); rupic- (rupicolous); saxi- (saxifrage)

straw carpho- (carphology); culmi- (culmicolous); festuc- (festucine); stramin- (stamineous)

stream fluvio- (fluviomarine); potam- (potamoplankton); rip- (riparian)

sun helio- (heliotropic); sol- (solarium)

swamp palud- (paludism); palus- (palustrine)

tendril cirri- (cirrigerous); cirro- (cirro-pinnate); pampin- (pampiniform)

thunder bronte- (bronteon); bronto- (brontology); cerauno- (ceraunoscope); fulmin- (fulminic); kerauno- (keraunograph); tonitr- (tonitrual)

tornado lilaps- (lilapsophobia)

tree arbor- (arboreal); dendri- (dendritic); dendro- (dendrophilous); -dendron (rhododendron); silvi- (silviculture); xylo- (xylophage)

twigs ramul- (ramulose); sarment- (sarmentaceous); scopi- (scopiform); surcul- (surculose); virgul- (virgulation)

twilight crepus- (crepuscular); lyg- (lygaeid)

universe -cosm (macrocosm); cosmo- (cosmology)

vegetation -aceae (Rosaceae); -ad (cycad); -ales (Liliales); botano- (botanomancy); -eae (Gramineae); herbi- (herbicidal); -ia (zinnia); -phyte (macrophyte); phyto- (phytography); vegeti- (vegetivorous); vegeto- (vegeto-alkaline)

vine ampel- (ampelopsis); pampin- (pampiniform); viti- (viticulture)

water aqua- (aquatic); aque- (aqueduct); aqui- (aquiclude); hydro- (hydrophilous); hyeto- (hyetology); hygro- (hygrometry); rip- (riparian)

weed runc- (runcation)

well phreato- (phreatic); putea- (puteal)

whirlpool vorag- (voraginous)

willow itea- (iteatic); salic- (salicaceous)

wind anemo- (anemometer); vent- (ventilation); *north ~:* -borea (boreal); *south ~:* austro- (austromancy); *west ~:* zephyro- (zephyranth); favon- (favonian)

wood erio- (eriometer); hyle- (hylephobia); hylo- (hylophagous); ligni- (lignivorous); ligno- (lignoceric); xylo- (xylophage); -xylous (epixylous); ylo- (ylomancy)

woods nemor- (nemoricole); saltu-

(saltuary); silv- (silvics); sylv- (sylvan)
world -cosm (macrocosm); cosmo- (cosmography); -gaea (Paleogaea);

mund- (mundane); secul- (secular); tellur- (telluric); terr- (terrain)
yew tax- (taxaceous)

EXPERTS AND THEIR TITLES

-ian (one skilled in or specializing in)
-ist (one who specializes in a specific art, science, skill or hobby)
-ologist (specialist)

abacus abacist
abnormal states, physiology of pathophysiologist
abnormalities *cellular ~:* cytotechnician; *diseases:* pathologist
abstract political theorizing metapolitician
acupuncture acupuncturist
acorns balanologist
acquired characteristics ctetologist
aerial photos *~ for accurate measurement:* photogrammetrist; *~ to identify geologic structures:* aerogeologist, photogeologist;
age of trees dendrochronologist
aging geriatrician, geriatrist; *~ and its problems:* gerontologist
agricultural geology agrogeologist
airborne microorganisms aerobiologist
airmail stamps aerophilatelist
algae algologist
all religions pantheologist
allergies allergist, allergologist
almonds amygdalogist
alphabet formation acrologist
alphabetic systems of writing alphabetist, alphabetologist
ambiguity dilogist
amphibians amphibiologist
anarchy anarchiologist
anatomy of soft parts sarcologist
ancient *~ animals:* paleozoologist; *~ diseases:* paleopathologist; *~ geological features:* archaeogeologist, paleogeologist; *~ lake sediment:* paleolimnologist; *~ medicine:* thereologist; *~ plants, animals and environment:* paleoecologist; *~ soils:* paleopedologist; *~ topographic features:* paleogeomorphologist; *~ water use:* paleohydrologist
anesthesia anesthesiologist, anesthetist
angels angelologist
animal(s) zoologist; *~ and their environment:* zooecologist; *~ and human relationships:* anthrozoologist; *~ husbandry:* zootechnician; *~ lore:* ethnozoologist; *~ pathogens:* epizoologist, epizootiologist
anthologies anthologist
anthropomorphism anthropomorphologist
antibodies and antigens seroepidemiologist
anti-intellectualism misologist
ants formicologist, myrmecologist
anus, rectum, colon coloproctologist, proctologist
apes pithecologist; *~ diseases:* pithecopathologist
aphids aphidologist
applied biological science biotechnologist
Arab language and culture Arabist
archives archivist
arrangement of feathers at certain stages pterylologist
arteries arteriologist
artificial body part replacements prosthetist

artistic or philosophical tradition academician

Ascidiacea (sea organisms) ascidiologist

Assyria/Babylonia assyriologist

asthma asthmologist

astrophysics astrophysicist

atmosphere atmospherologist; ~ *dust and germs:* coniologist, koniologist; ~ *and weather:* meteorologist

atoms atomologist

automatic control systems cybernetician

bacteria bacteriologist; ~ *of the air:* aerobacteriologist

baldness phalacrologist

barley crithologist

baseball data sabermetrician

Basque language and culture Bascologist

baths balneo-

beards pogonologist

beauty kalologist; ~*in art:*aestheticist, esthetician

beauty treatments beautician

bees apiarist, melittologist; ~ *raising:* apiculturist

belief built around biological principles metabiologist

bells, bell-ringing campanist, campanologist

berries baccatologists

biblical literature, book lore bibliologist

biblical types typologist

bile choledologist

biology biologist; ~*of bodies of water:* hydrobiologist

biological ~ *form and function:* morphophysiologist; ~ *rhythms:* chronobiologist; ~ *study of acquired characteristics:* ctetologist

biotechnology ergonomist

biotypes biotypologist

birds aviarist, ornithologist; ~ *eggs:* oologist; ~ *nests:* caliologist, nidologist; *raising ~:* aviculturist

blindness typhlologist

blood haematologist, hematologist; ~ *immunology:* immunohematologist; ~ *serum:* serologist; ~ *vessels:* angiologist

body forms somatologist

bones osteologist

book lore bibliologist; ~ *binding* bibliopegist; ~ *printed before 1501:* incunabulist

brain cerebrologist, encephalologist

brambles batologist

breasts mastologist, mazologist

breeding domesticated animals and plants thremmatologist

bridges gephyrologist

Buddha Buddhologist

butterflies lepidopterist

cabbages brassicologist

calculation logistician

calendar hemerologist

cancer cancerologist, chemotherapist, oncologist

cartilages chondrologist

cashews anacardologist

causes, origin aetiologist, aitiologist, etiologist

caves speleologist; *cave-dwelling organisms:* biospeleologist

celebrity cards (cigarette/gum packages) cartophilist

celestial ~ *bodies:* astrogeologist; ~ *mechanics applied to space vehicles:* astrodynamicist

cell(s) cytologist; ~ *abnormalities:* cytotechnician; ~ *disease:* cytopathologist; ~ *identification and abnormalities:* cytotechnologist; ~ *morphology:* cytomorphologist; ~ *nuclei:* karyologist; ~ *physiology:* cytophysiologist; ~ *and tissues:* cytohistologist

ceramics ceramicist

chaos theory chaologist

character characterologist

cheese fromologist

chemical ~ *combinations:* stoichiologist; ~ *processes in immunology:* chemoimmunologist;~ *structure*

and its biological action:
biochemorphologist

chemistry chemist; ~ *of interstellar*
space: astrochemist

chemotherapy chemotherapist

chestnuts castanologist

childbirth obstetrician

children paedologist, pedologist, tec-
nologist; *diseases of~:* paedonosolo-
gist; *medical care of~:* pediatrician

China sinologist

Christ Christologist

chromosomes chromosomologist

church art, decoration, etc. ecclesiol-
ogist

cigar bands brandophilist

cinchona (large shrubs) cinchonolo-
gist

cities urbanologist

city contained in a single structure
arcologist

climate(s) climatologist; ~ *and biologi-*
cal phenomena: phenogenologist,
phenologist; ~ *effect on organisms:*
bioclimatician, bioclimatologist;
~ *past ages:* paleoclimatologist

clocks & watches horologophilist

clouds nephologist

Coccoidea (scale insects) coccidolo-
gist

code, secret language cryptologist

coins numismatist

Coleoptera (beetle) coleopterologist

colors chromatologist

comets cometologist

communist China pekingologist

comparative human body measurements anthropometrist

computer study cybernetician

concise writing brachylogist

continuity synechiologist

contradictions antilogist

controlled environment with few organisms gnotobiologist

cooking mageirologist, magirologist

cork phellologist

corkscrews helixophilist

corn spicologist

correct use of words orthologist

correspondences homologist

cosmetics cosmetologist

cosmos cosmologist

crayfish astacologist

crime victims victimologist

crime criminologist

criteria criteriologist

crop(s) ~ *cultivation:* agronomist;
~ *relationship with atmosphere:*
agrometeorologist; ~ *relationship*
with climate: agroclimatologist

crossword puzzles cruciverbalist

crustaceans carcinologist, crustaceol-
ogist

crystal(s) crystallologist; ~ *forma-*
tions: clinologist

crystallography leptologist, leptonolo-
gist

cucumbers cucumologist

cultivation of marine organisms mar-
iculturist

culture culturologist

cultures ethnologist

customs of nonliterate peoples agriologist

cyclones cyclonologist

cysts cystologist

dance movements choreologist

dead people in the underworld nerterologist

death thanatologist

decadence; aging in nearly extinct
groups geratologist

decay and mummification taphono-
mist

deformation or flow of matter rheolo-
gist

demons daemonologist, demonologist

dental occlusions gnathologist

derivation of words lexicologist

description and classification of phenomena phenomenologist

deserts, desert plants eremologist,
desmidiologist

devil diabologist, diabolologist, sata-
nologist

diabetes diabetologist

dialects dialectologist
dining aristologist
diplomats diplomatologist
Diptera (flies) dipterologist
disease(s) nosologist; ~ *affecting the
extremities:* acropathologist; ~ *of the
blood vessels:* angiopathologist;
~ *caused by weakening:* astheniolo-
gist;~ *of the ear:* otologist; ~ *geographic factors:* geopathologist; ~ *of
the joints:* arthropathologist; ~ *of
lower animals:* zoopathologist; ~ *of
the nervous systems:* neuropatholo-
gist; ~ *of nose and larynx:* rhino-
laryngologist; ~ *in a population:*
epidemiologist; ~ *symptoms:* symp-
tomatologist, symptomologist; ~ *of
trees:* arborvirologist
divination mantologist
doctrines about faith pistiologist
dog(s) cynologist; ~ *diseases:*
cynopathologist
dolls planganologist
domestic economy oikologist
doses dosiologist
dragons draconologist
drama, esp. five-act plays pentalogist
dreams oneirologist
drugs pharmacologist; ~ *and the
immune system:* immunopharma-
cologist; ~ *and the nervous system:*
neuropharmacologist; ~ *and plant
interaction:* phytopharmacologist; ~
prescription: pharmacist
earth ~ *relation to cosmic phenomena:* cosmecologist; ~ *surface:* geo-
morphologist
earthquakes seismologist, tectono-
physicist, tromologist
earthworms oligochaetologist
ecclesiastical ~ *buildings:* naologist;
~ *calendars:* menologist
echinoderms (marine animal)
echinologist
ecology aecologist, ecologist, oecolo-
gist; ~ *of cultivated plants:* agrioe-
cologist, agroecologist; *communities
and environment:* synecologist; ~

interaction with psychology: ecopsy-
chologist
educational methods educationalist
effect of light on chemical change
photochemist
effect(s) of ~ *drugs on mental states:*
psychopharmacologist; ~ *light on
living beings:* photobiologist; ~ *low
temperatures on organisms:* cryobiologist; ~ *sound on living beings:*
bioacoustician
eggs ovologist
Egyptian history Egyptologist
ethics of biological research bioethi-
cist
elections psephologist
electrical ~ *currents:* galvanologist;
~ *phenomena of living bodies:* elec-
trophysiologist; ~ *phenomena of living organisms:* electrobiologist
electricity electrician
elephants pachydermatologist
embryonic structures promorpholo-
gist
embryos cyemologist, embryologist
enigmas enigmatologist
enterobacteria enterobacteriologist
environment(al) environmentologist;
~ *effects on creatures:* hexicologist;
~ *organisms en masse:* synecologist;
~ *pollutants:* ecotoxicologist
enzymes enzymologist
erotic literature erotologist
ethnology of prehistoric humans
paleethnologist
Etruscan antiquities Etruscologist
events beyond natural law parapsy-
chologist
evil ponerologist
excrement; obscene literature scatologist, skatologist
excretion and secretion eccrinologist
experimental testing or inquiry doci-
mologist
exploitation of natural resources ge-
otechnologist
external secretions exocrinologist
extinct animals archaeozoologist

extraterrestrial life astrobiologist, exobiologist, xenobiologist
eyes ophthalmologist; *eye testing:* optologist
eye, ear, nose, and throat specialist otolaryngologist
faith pisteologist, pistologist
family descent genealogist
farming agriculturist
Fathers of the church patrologist
feathers pterylologist
feet podiatrist, podologist
female health gynecologist
fermentation fermentologist, zymologist
ferns filicologist, pteridologist
fetuses fetologist
fevers; heat pyretologist, pyrologist
figs sycologist
figurative language tropologist
films filmologist
filth or feces; obscene literature coprologist
fine dining gastronomist
finger rings dactyliologist
fire science pyrotechnician
firearms ballistician
first principles archelogist
fish ichthyologist; *~ diseases:* icthyopathologist; *~ farming:* aquaculturist, pisciculturist; *~ fossils:* icthyopaleontologist
fishing halieutician, piscatologist
flags and banners vexillologist
fleas pulicologist, siphonapterologist
flower raising floriculturist
flowers and their environment anthoecologist
flowers florist
folk psychology ethnopsychologist
folklore storiologist
fonts fontologist
food bromatologist, sitologist
foot care chiropodist
form and structure morphologist
fossil(s) fossilist, fossilologist, oryctologist; *~ birds:* paleornithologist; *~ fish:* paleicthyologist; *~ footprints:* ichnologist; *~ grasses:* paleoagrostologist; *~ insects:* paleoentomologist; *~ plants:* paleobotanist, paleophytologist; *~ trees:* paleodendrologist; *~ as organisms:* paleobiologist
fractures agmatologist
fragrant essential oils aromatherapist
freshwater life limnobiologist
friction *~ as a medical treatment:* anatripsologist; *~ in machines:* tribologist
frost cryopedologist
fruit and seeds carpologist, pomologist
functions and activities of living matter physiologist
funeral dirges myriologist
funerals mortician
fungi mycologist
future trends futurologist
games ludologist
gem(s) gemmologist, gemologist; *~ engraving:* glyptologist
genealogy of the gods theogonist
general physiology biophysiologist
generative organs aedoeologist
geographical distribution of animals faunologist
germinal matter merologist
gestures pasimologist
ghosts phantasmatist
glaciers; ice glaciologist
glands adenologist
glass vitreologist
gnats; mosquitoes culicidologist
gnomes gnomologist
God theologian
gold or wealth chrysologist
goodness agathologist
governing politician
grammar grammarian, syntactician
grapes botryologist
grape vines viniculturist
grasses agrostologist, graminologist
grouped words or expressions onomasiologist
growth auxologist
growth & sexual development of children auxanologist

gum disease periodontist, periodontologist
gunnery artillerist
habits; behavior hexiologist
hair trichologist; ~ *removal:* electrologist
handwriting graphologist
head cephalologist
healing medicine physician
hearing audiologist
heart cardiologist
heat thermologist; ~ *as a medical remedy:* thermatologist
heavenly bodies uranologist
hell tartarologist
Hemiptera (insects) hemipterologist
Hepaticae (liverworts) hepaticologist
heredity or procreation genesiologist
heresies heresiologist
hernias herneologist
hickory nuts cichorologist
hieroglyphs hieroglyphologist
histology of the skin dermahistologist
history of the earth paleontologist
history annalist, historiologist;
    ~ *through historical data:* cliometrician
Hittites Hittitologist, Hittologist
Homer Homerologist
honey bees apiologist
horse(s) hippologist; ~ *diseases:* hippopathologist
hotels and inns xenodocheionologist
human(s) anthropologist; ~ *activities:*
    demologist; ~ *biology:* anthropobiologist; ~ *character:* ethologist;
    ~ *conduct and action:* praxeologist,
    praxiologist; ~ *fossils:* paleoanthropologist; ~ *ignorance:* agniologist;
    ~ *movement:* kinesiologist; ~ *settlements:*ekistician; ~ *types:* typologist
humidity hygrologist
hurricanes; tornadoes lilapsologist
hygienic science hygiologist
hymns hymnologist
hypnosis hypnotist, neurypnologist
icons iconologist
ideas ideologist, sophiologist

identification and study of microfossils micropaleontologist
idioms idiomologist
immune reactions immunobiologist;
    immune responses to disease: immunopathologist
immunity to disease immunologist
immunologic methods applied to histology immunohistologist
impaired word use aphasiologist
inanimate nature abiologist, azoologist
incorrect diction acyrologist, cacologist
India indologist
indigenous diseases endemiologist
individual organisms and their environment autecologist
influence of emotion on disease psychoneuroimmunologist
influence of the stars astrologist
injurious effects of time on a living system catachronobiologist
inscriptions on monuments elogist
insect galls on plants cecidiologist, cecidologist
insects with 4 membranous wings hymenopterologist
insects entomologist, insectologist
interaction of radiation with living system radiobiologist
internal secretions of endocrine glands endocrinologist
intuition and reason noologist
Inuit culture Eskimologist
iris of the eye iridologist
Japan Japanologist
Jewish culture Hebrician
joints of the body arthrologist
jurisdiction dicaeologist
keys cagophilist
kidney beans phaseologist
kidneys nephrologist
kissing philematologist
knowledge epistemologist, gnoseologist, gnosiologist
lakes and ponds limnologist
language philologist; ~ *evolution:*
    glottochronologist

largest-scale aspects of the atmos-phere macrometeorologist
larynx laryngologist
laughter gelotologist
laws *of the mind:* nomologist; *~ of watery vapor:* atmologist
legendary animals cryptozoologist
legends; lying pseudologist
lepers leprologist
Lepidoptera (butterflies, moths) lepidopterologist
lichen lichenologist
ligaments or bandaging desmologist, syndesmologist
light photologist; *chemical effects of ~:* actinologist
lighthouses pharologist
light rays spectrologist
linguistic tones tonetician
linguistics glottologist, linguistician
literary work in three connected parts trilogist
literary work in four connected parts tetralogist
liturgies: formal worship liturgician, liturgist, liturgiologist
liver hepatologist
living beings and atmospheric phe-nomena biometeorologist
living organisms biologist
locusts and grasshoppers acridologist
logic dialectition, logician
long-distance seismology teleseismologist
lymphatic system lymphologist
machines mechanician
magic magician
magnetic measurements magnetician
makeup cosmetician
malaria malariologist
male impotence andrologist
mammalogy therologist
mammals mammologist
manuscripts codicologist
maps cartologist, chartologist
Mars areologist
martyrs martyrologist
match boxes cumyxaphilist

mathematics mathematician
Mayan culture Mayanist
measuring hearing audiometrist
mechanical insects entomechologist
medals & tokens exonumist
medical *~ diagnoses:* diagnostician; *~ science or treatise:* iatrologist
medicinal *~ dosage:* posologist; *~ herbs:* herbologist
memory mnesiologist
menstruation emmenologist
mental diseases psychopathologist
mental life and biological processes psychobiologist
mental processes psychologist
metamathematics metamathematician
metaphysics metaphysician
meteorites aerolithologist
meteoritic stones astrolithologist
meteorological *~ phenomena of a small site:* micrometeorologist; *~ properties of atmosphere:* aerologist
meter metrician
methods of success tactician
microfossils micropaleontologist
micro-linguistic analysis glossematician
microscopic life microbiologist
microscopic soil phenomena micropedologist
midwifery tocologist, tokologist
migrations and distributions of or-ganisms chorologist
mills & milling molinologist
mineral drugs pharmaco-oryctologist
minerals oryctologist
minute details; microscopes micrologist
miracles of gods and heroes aretalogist, thaumatologist
missionary activity missiologist
mites and ticks acarinologist, acarologist
mollusks malacologist
monads monadologist
money boxes argyrothecologist
monsters; organic malformations teratologist

moon selenologist
moral duty deontologist
moral values axiologist, ethician, ethicist
morphology of abnormal conditions
   pathomorphologist
mosquitoes; gnats culicidologist
moss bryologist, muscologist
mountains orologist; *~ and drainage:*
   orohydrologist
mouth stomatologist
murder ctenologist, ktenologist
muscles myologist
museum collections museologist
mushrooms fungologist, mycologist
music musician, musicologist
music and the culture that produces it
   ethnomusicologist
mystical meaning of numbers
   numerologist
myths mythologist
narratives narratologist
natural communities biocenologist,
   biocoenologist
nature *~ of reality:* ontologist; *~ of
   truth:* alethiologist
nematodes nematologists
nerves neurologist; *~ of the skin:* der-
   matoneurologist
nervous system neurobiologist
nesting birds neossologist, nidologist
neural synapses synaptologist
neuropterous insects neuropterologist
neurosecretions neuroendocrinologist
neurotoxins neurotoxicogist
new expressions neologist
newborn infants neonatologist
nomenclature terminologist
nonsense morologist
nose nasologist, rhinologist
number computation arithmetician
nutrition alimentologist, dietician,
   trophologist, threpsologist
obesity bariatrician
obituaries necrologist
obscenity; excrement scatologist
oceanography oceanologist
Odonata (dragonflies, damselflies)
   odonatologist

oil exploration creekologist
oracles chresmologist
one who speaks or writes in defense of
   apologist
opium meconologist
optics optician
orchids orchidologist
organic malformations; monsters
   teratologist
organic tissue histiologist, histologist
organisms *~ as individuals:* idiobiolo-
   gist; *~ pathogenic for plants:* phyto-
   bacteriologist
organization of words phraseologist
origin and causes aitiologist, aetiologist, etiologist
origins; government archologist
orthopterous insects orthopterologist
otolaryngology otorhinolaryngologist
oyster farming ostreiculturist
palaeobotany phytolithologist
paleopsychic phenomena paleopsy-
   chologist
paleozoology zoopaleontologist
papyrus manuscripts papyrologist
paradoxes paradoxologist
parapsychology metapsychologist
parasites entozoologist, parasitologist
parasitic worms helminthologist
past as indicated by geological data
   geochronologist
past civilizations archaeologist, arche-
   ologist
past events explained by laws of causa-
   tion palaetiologist, paletiologist
pathology pathobiologist, pathologist;
   ~ of the skin: dermatopathologist
pathological alteration of bodily function physiopathologist
peace irenologist
peaches persicologist
peanuts arachologist
pears piriologist
peat moss sphagnologist
pedometers pedometrician
penis phallologist
pharynx pharyngologist
phonemes phonemicist

phonograph records discophilist
photochemical effects actinologist
physics physicist
physiological psychology physiopsychologist, psychophysiologist
physiology of organisms and environment ecophysiologist
physiology of the nervous system neurophysiologist
picture-writing curiologist
plagues loimologist
planets; condensed matter of solar system planetologist
plankton planktologist, planktonologist
plant(s) botanist, phytologist; ~ *and animal organs:* organologist; ~ *bioclimatology:* phytoclimatologist; ~ *communities:* phytosociologist; ~ *diseases:* epiphytologist, phytopathologist; ~ *ecology:* phytobiologist: ~ *nutrition:* agriobiologist; ~ *physiology:* phytophysiologist; ~ *viruses:* phytoserology, phytovirologist; *plant-like animals (coral):* zootologist
playwright dramatist
pleasure hedonologist
poisons toxicologist
political and geographic factors geopolitician
political parties stasiologist
pollen and spores palynologist; ~ *in the atmosphere:* aeropalynologist
postage stamps timbrologist
postcards deltiologist
poverty & unemployment ptochologist
practical applications ~ *of electricity:* electrotechnician, electrotechnologist; ~ *of medicine:* clinician; ~ *of psychology:* psychotechnician
practical details of an occupation technician
praise of God doxologist
prayers and rituals euchologist
preaching; sermons sermonologist
precipices cremnologist

precipitation hydrometeorologist, hyetologist
pregnancy cyemologist, cyesiologist, syllepsiologist
prehistoric antiquities paleologist
preparing mixed drinks mixologist
prevention of suicide suicidologist
primates primatologist
primitive societies and plants and animals ethnobiologist, ethnobotanist
prisons and criminal punishment penologist
problems of psychology and sociology psychosociologist
procedures methodologist
proper names or specialized field terms onomatologist, onomasiologist
prosthetic devices anaplastologist
Protista (non-animal or plant organisms) protistologist
Protozoa (single-celled animal-like organisms) protozoologist
proverbs paremiologist, paroemiologist
psychiatry psychiatrist
psychological and neurological correlations neuropsychologist
psychological ~ *methods for industry:* psychotechnologist; ~ *reactions:* reactologist; ~ *testing:* psychometrician, psychometrist
psychology as related to biology biopsychologist
public health sanitarian
pulse sphygmologist
purpose or end teleologist
purposelessness dysteleologist
pyramids pyramidologist
quicksand syrtologist
quinine quinologist
radiant energy radiologist
radiation ~ *applied to industrial problems:* radiotechnologist; ~ *effects on ecological communities:*radioecologist
radioactivity's effect on geology radiogeologist

radiology of the nervous system neuroradiologist

radishes raphanologist

railroads ferroequinologist

rain ombrologist, pluviologist

rappings by spirits typtologist

recent organisms neontologist

record of nearby earthquake shocks engysseismologist

redundancies in speech or writing macrologist

refraction optometrist

relics lipsanologist

religion: final events eschatologist

religious ~ *calendars, festivals:* heortologist; ~ *literature:* hierologist

remedies accologist, iamatologist

repetition in writing or speech battologist, tautologist

residual magnetism in ancient rocks paleomagnetist

respiratory organs pneumologist

restricted climate microclimatologist

rhetoric rhetorician

rhetorical emphasis palilogist

rheumatic diseases rheumatologist

rhythm rhythmologist

river(s) fluvialist, fluviologist, potamologist; ~ *channel formation & characteristics:* fluviomorphologist

rocks geologician, geologist, petrologist; ~ *and minerals:* mineralogist; ~ *and stones:* lithologist

rubrics; established rules rubrician

runes runologist

rust uredinologist

saints' lives; sacred writings hagiologist

salvation soteriologist

science scientist

scientific approach to legal problems jurimetrician

sea thalattologist

seaweed or algae phycologist

secret language; code cryptologist

sedges caricologist

sediments sedimentologist

seeds spermologist

semantics semantician, semanticist, semasiologist, sematologist, semologist

semen spermatologist

senility nostologist

sensation and sense organs aesthiologist, esthesiophysiologist

senses and sense organs esthematologist

sermons; preaching sermonologist

serums serologist

sex sexologist

shells conchologist. conchyliologist

shiatsu acupressurist

shrouds, especially of Turin sindonologist

sign language chirologist, dactylologist

signs or symptoms semeiologist, semiologist

silkworm farming sericulturist

similarities homeologist

simple and complex reflexes reflexologist

sin enissologist, hamartiologist

skin diseases dermatologist, pellagrologist; ~ *nomenclature & classification:* dermonosologist; ~ *and venereal diseases:* dermatovenerologist

skull(s) craniologist; ~ *shapes:* phrenologist

Slavic language and literature Slavicist

sleep; hypnosis hypnologist, hypnotist

slugs limacologist

small ~ *community ecology:* microecologist: ~ *earthquakes:* microseismologist; ~ *systems of social behavior:* microsociologist

smells & olfactory process olfactologist, osmologist

snake(s) herpetologist, ophidologist, ophiologist; ~ *diseases:* herpetopathologist

snow and ice cryologist

social interaction biosociologist

societal structure ethnomethodologist

society ~ *and biological science:* sociobiologist; *human ~ groups:* sociologist

sociological study of race anthroposociologist

soils agrologist, edaphologist, pedologist; ~ *microstructure:* micromorphologist

soliloquies monologist

somatotypes somatotypologist

sound acoustician

Soviet government kremlinologist, Sovietologist

species and genetic variations genecologist

speech *disorders:* lalopathologist; ~ *intonation:* tonology; ~ *sounds* phonetician, phonologist

speech or writing to praise eulogist

spiders arachnidologist, arachnologist, araneologist

spines acanthologist

spirits; Holy Ghost pneumatologist

spleen splenologist

sponges spongiologist

squid; cuttlefish teuthologist

star *ages:* cosmochronologist; ~ *oscillations:* astroseismologist

statistical study ~ *of biological phenomena:* biostatistician; ~ *of economics:* econometrician, econometrist; ~ *of life forms:* biometrician

statistics statistician

stomach gastrologist; ~ *and intestines:* gastroenterologist

strawberries fragarologist

structural geology geotectologist

study of ancient human characteristics ethnoarchaeologist

substances radioactively tagged radioimmunologist

Sumerians Sumerologist

sun heliologist

surgical appliances acidologist

swamps; peat bogs telmatologist

symbols symbologist; ~ *of language:* semiotician

synchronous events synchronologist

syphilis syphilologist

Syria syriologist

systematic view of all knowledge pantologist

systematized belief dogmatician

taxonomy taxologist

tea tsiologist

technical terms orismologist

technological farming systems agrotechnologist

technology technicologist, technologist

teddy bears arctophilist

teeth dentist, odontologist

tendons tenologist

terminology; language glossologist

termites isopterologist, termitologist

terms ending in -ology logyologist

terrestrial magnetism geomagnetician

theater arts theatrician

theology ~ *and evidence of purpose in nature:* physico-theologian; ~ *based on observation of celestial bodies:* astrotheologian

theory of extended individuals mereologist

therapeutic ~ *agents:* acologist; ~ *baths:* balneologist; ~ *use of mineral springs:* crenologist

therapeutics accologist, thereologist

three-dimensional properties stereologist

thunder brontologist

tides tidologist

tightrope walking funambulist

time measurement chronologist

timepieces horologist

tissue ~ *changes in disease:* histopathologist; ~ *organization:* histophysiologist

tooth ~ *irregularities and correction:* orthodontist; ~ *pulp diseases:* endodontist

topographical study topologist

tornadoes; hurricanes lilapsologist

towers pyrgologist
trapeze artistry aerialist
trash garbologist
tree(s) arborist, dendrologist; ~ *farming:* arboriculturist, silviculturist; ~ *growth & climate:* dendroclimatologist
truffles hydnologist
tuberculosis phthisiologist
tumors oncologist
Turkic language and literature Turcologist
turnips napologist
ulcers helcologist
underground water geohydrologist
unidentified flying objects ufologist
unintentional omissions haplology
universe macrocosmologist, universologist
upper atmosphere physics and chemistry aeronomist
urinary organ surologist
use of x-rays roentgenologist
vaccines vaccinologist
values axiologist
vegetables lachanologist
veins phlebologist
venereal disease venereologist, venerologist
vines viticulturist
Virgin Mary Mariologist
virginity parthenologist
virtue aretologist
viruses virologist
viscera enterologist, splanchnologist

vitamins vitaminologist
volcanoes vulcanologist
vomiting emetologist
walnuts juglandologist
warfare polemologist
water *its modifying power:* hydrogeologist; *subterranean ~:* hydrologist
wave motion kymatologist
wealth aphnologist, plutologist
weapons & fighting systems hoplologist
weather meteorologist; ~ *and celestial bodies:* astrometeorologist; ~ *and climate acting on living beings:* meteorobiologist
weight(s) ~ *and gravitation:* barologist; ~ *and measures:* metrologist
whales cetologist
whale diseases cetopathologist
wildfires using tree-ring data dendropyrochronologist
winds anemologist
wine enologist, oenologist
wood xylologist
word history etymologist
work & its effect on humans ergologist
worms helminthologist, scolecologist, vermeologist
worship; liturgies liturgician, liturgist, liturgiologist
wounds traumatologist
writing systems grammatologist
zoology of present-day animals caenozoologist, cenozoologist

FEAR OR DISLIKE OF ...

To extract the word part, simply drop "phobia" from each term.

abuse, sexual contreltophobia
accidents dystichiphobia
acid soils acidophobia
acorns balanophobia
aging gerascophobia
air aerophobia, anemophobia, pneumatophobia

airplanes aeronautophobia, aerophobia, aviatophobia, avionophobia, aviophobia
airsickness aeronausiphobia
alcohol methyphobia
alkaline soils basiphobia, basophobia
alligators eusuchophobia

amnesia amensiophobia, amnesiphobia

ancestors patroiophobia

anger cholerophobia

angina anginophobia

animals zoophobia; ~ *skins:* doraphobia; *wild ~:* agrizoophobia, theriophobia

ants myrmecophobia

arts and crafts technophobia

ashes of cremation spodophobia

asymmetry asymmetriphobia

atomic explosions atomosophobia

automobiles amaxophobia, harmatophobia, ochophobia

bacteria bacteriophobia, microbiophobia

baldness peladophobia, phalacrophobia

banners/bumper stickers vexillophobia

base or low pursuits tapinophobia

baths ablutophobia

bats desmodontophobia, pteropophobia

beaches thinophobia

beards pogonophobia

bears arctophobia

beautiful women caligynephobia

beds clinophobia

bees apiophobia, apiphobia, melissophobia

beggars/street people ptochophobia

being afraid phobophobia

being alone autophobia, monophobia, eremophobia

being beaten rhabdophobia, vapulophobia

being beautiful callophobia

being bound merinthophobia

being buried alive taphephobia, taphophobia

being burned caustophobia

being clean balneophobia

being contagious tapinophobia

being dirty automysophobia

being pinched rrhexophobia

being ridiculed catagelophobia

being scolded enissophobia

being scratched amychophobia

being shot ballistophobia

being stared at ophthalmophobia, scopophobia, scoptophobia

bicycles cyclophobia

birds ornithophobia

Blacks negrophobia

blindness scotomaphobia, typhlophobia

blood haemaphobia, hemaphobia, hematophobia, hemophobia

blushing ereuthophobia, erythrophobia, erytophobia

boasting kompophobia

boats scaphophobia

body odor autodysosmophobia, bromidrosiphobia

bogs telmatophobia

books bibliophobia

boozing dipsophobia

breasts, developing mastophobia

bridges gephyrophobia

brothers adelphophobia

buffoons balatrophobia

bullets ballistophobia

bulls taurophobia

buttocks pygophobia

buzzards buteophobia

cancer carcinophobia, carcinomatophobia

cars harmatophobia, ochophobia; *riding in ~:* amaxophobia

cattle boustrophobia

cats aelurophobia, ailurophobia, elurophobia, felinophobia, galeophobia, gatophobia

caves speleophobia

Celts Celtophobia

cemeteries coimetrophobia

changes tropophobia, metathesiophobia

chatter, meaningless garrulophobia

chemicals chemophobia

chickens alektorophobia

childbirth lochiophobia, maieusiophobia, parturiphobia, tocophobia

children pediophobia, pedophobia

China/the Chinese Sinophobia
chins geniophobia
choking pnigerophobia, pnigophobia
cholera cholerophobia
churches ecclesiaphobia
clergy hierophobia
clocks/watches chronometrophobia
closed spaces claustrophobia, cleisio-
  phobia, cleithrophobia, clithropho-
  bia
clothes vestiphobia, vestiophobia
clouds nephophobia
cockroaches blattophobia
coitus coitophobia
cold cheimaphobia, cheimatophobia,
  cryophobia, frigophobia, psychrophobia, psychropophobia
colors chromatophobia, chromopho-
  bia; *black:* melanophobia; *blue:*
  caerulophobia; *brown:* fuscophobia;
  copper: chalcophobia; *gold:* aureo-
  phobia; *gray:* phaeophobia; *green:*
  verdophobia; *orange:* aurantiphobia;
  purple: porphyrophobia; *red:* erythrophobia; *silver:* argentophobia;
  tan: fulvophobia; *violet:* indopho-
  bia; *white:* leukophobia; *yellow:*
  xanthophobia
comets cometophobia
commitment zygophobia
computers cyberphobia, computer-
  phobia
constipation coprostasophobia
cooking mageiricophobia
corpse necrophobia
crevices chasmophobia
criticism enissophobia
critics criticophobia
cross or crucifix staurophobia
crossing a bridge gephyrophobia
crossing busy streets agylophobia,
  agyrophobia, dromophobia
crowds demophobia, enochlophobia,
  ochlophobia
crystals crystallophobia
cyclones anemophobia
daggers pugioniphobia
dampness hygrophobia

dancing choreophobia, chorophobia,
  orchestrophobia
darkness achluophobia, lygophobia,
  nyctophobia, scotophobia
dawn eosophobia
daylight phengophobia
death necrophobia, thanatophobia
decaying matter pythophobia, septophobia
defecation, straining and painful
  defecalgesiophobia
deformity dysmorphophobia
demons and devils daemonophobia,
  demonophobia, necyophobia
dental work dentophobia, odontophobia
dependence soteriophobia
depth bathophobia
design or ultimate ends teleophobia
diabetes diabetophobia
dinner parties deipnophobia
dirt misophobia, molysmophobia,
  mysophobia, rhypophobia
disease loimophobia, nosophobia,
  pathophobia; *specific ~:* monopathophobia
disorder ataxiophobia, ataxophobia
dizziness dinophobia, illyngophobia,
  vertigophobia
doctors iatrophobia
dogs cynophobia, kynophobia
dolls paedophobia, pediophobia, pedophobia,
double vision diplopiaphobia, diplo-
  phobia
drafts aerophobia, anemophobia
dreams oneirophobia
drink alcoholophobia, dipsomanopho-
  bia, methyphobia, potophobia
drugs pharmacophobia
dryness xerophobia
duration chronophobia
dust amathophobia, koniophobia;
  dusty surfaces: conistrophobia
dwarfs nanophobia
earthquakes seismophobia, tremophobia
eating phagophobia

eels anguillophobia
electricity electrophobia
emotions thymophobia
empty rooms cenophobia, kenophobia
England/the English Anglophobia
erection *maintaining:* ithyphallophobia; *loss of:* medomalacophobia
everything panophobia, panphobia, pantaphobia, pantophobia
excrement coprophobia, koprophobia, scatophobia
exhaustion kopophobia
experimenting peirophobia
eyes ommatophobia, ommetaphobia; ~ *opening:* optophobia
fabrics textophobia
faces prosopophobia
failure atychiphobia, kakorraphiaphobia, kakorraphiophobia, kakorrhaphiophobia
fainting asthenophobia
falling basophobia
falling downstairs climacophobia
falling in love philophobia
fat lipophobia, obesiophobia
father-in-law soceraphobia
Fathers of the early church paterophobia
fatigue kopophobia, ponophobia
fear phobophobia
feathers pteronophobia
feces coprophobia, koprophobia, scatophobia
fever febriphobia, pyrexeophobia, pyrexiophobia
fighting machophobia
filth rhypophobia, rypophobia, rupophobia
fire arsonophobia, pyrophobia
fish ichthyophobia
flashes selaphobia
flatulence physaphobia
flood antlophobia
flowers anthophobia
flute aulophobia
flying aeronautophobia, aerophobia, aviatophobia, avionophobia, aviophobia

fog homichlophobia, nebulaphobia, nephophobia
food cibophobia, sitiophobia, sitophobia,
foreigners xenophobia
foreplay malaxophobia, paizophobia, sarmassophobia
forests hylephobia, hylophobia, xylophobia, ylophobia
fountains pegophobia
France/the French Francophobia, Gallophobia
freedom eleutherophobia
French kissing cataglottophobia
friendship sociophobia
frogs batrachophobia
frost cryophobia, pagophobia, rhigophobia
fun cherophobia
funeral rites epicidiophobia, threnatophobia
fur doraphobia
gambling aleaphobia
garlic alliumphobia, scorophobia
gay people homophobia
genitals: genitophobia; *female ~:* colpophobia, eurotophobia, kolpophobia; *male ~:* phallophobia
Germany/the Germans Germanophobia, Teutophobia, Teutonophobia
germs bacillophobia, bacteriophobia, spermophobia, verminophobia
ghosts phantasmophobia, phasmophobia, spectrophobia
glass crystallophobia, hyalophobia, hyelophobia, vitreophobia
gloomy places lygophobia
God's wrath deiphobia, theophobia
going to bed clinophobia
gold aurophobia
good news euphobia
graves taphophobia
gravity barophobia
Greece/the Greeks Grecophobia, Hellenophobia
growing old gerascophobia, gerontophobia
hair chaetophobia, trichophobia;

curly ~: ulophobia; *~ disease:* trichopathophobia; *excessive ~:* hypertrichophobia
Halloween Samhainophobia
happiness cherophobia
heart attack or disease anginophobia, cardiophobia
heat thermophobia
heaven ouranophobia, uranophobia
heights: *looking down:* acrophobia, altophobia, batophobia, hypsiphobia, hypsophobia; *looking up:* anablephobia, anablepophobia
hell Avernophobia, Hadephobia, stygiophobia
heredity patroiophobia
heresy heresiophobia
high places illyngophobia
holy things hagiophobia, hierophobia
home and environment domatophobia, ecophobia, oecophobia, oikophobia; *returning ~:* nostophobia
homosexuals homophobia
hornets vespiphobia
horses equinophobia, hippophobia
hospitals nosocomephobia
human beings anthropophobia
hurricanes lilapsophobia
hydrophobia hydrophobophobia
hypnotism hypnophobia, mesmerophobia
ice cryophobia, gelophobia
ideas gnotophobia, ideophobia
illness nosophobia, pathophobia; *specific ~:* monopathophobia; *wasting ~:* tabophobia
immobility of a joint ankylophobia
imperfection atelophobia
inability to stand basiphobia, basophobia
infection molysmophobia, mysophobia, septophobia
infinity apeirophobia
injections trypanophobia
injury traumatophobia
insanity dementophobia, lyssophobia, maniaphobia
insects acarophobia, entomophobia, insectophobia, isopterophobia; *stinging ~:* cnidophobia
Ireland/the Irish Celtophobia, Hibernophobia
irrational destruction atephobia
isolation eremophobia
Italy/Italians Italophobia
itching acarophobia, scabiophobia
Japan/the Japanese Japanophobia
jealousy zelophobia
Jews Judaeophobia, Judeophobia, Judophobia
jumping catapedaphobia
justice dikephobia
kidney disease albuminurophobia
killing dacnophobia
kissing philemaphobia, philematophobia; *tongue ~:* cataglottophobia
kleptomania kleptophobia
knees genuphobia
knowledge epistemophobia, gnosiophobia
lacerations sparassophobia
ladders scalaphobia
lakes limnophobia
large objects megalophobia
laughter gelophobia
law thesmophobia
lawsuits litigaphobia
learning sophophobia
left side levophobia, sinistrophobia
leprosy lepraphobia, leprophobia
lice pediculophobia, phthiriophobia
light phengophobia, photophobia; *glaring ~:* photoaugiaphobia, photoaugiophobia
lightning astraphobia, astrapophobia, astrapophobia
liquids aquaphobia, hygrophobia
lizards stelliophobia
lobsters homariphobia
lockjaw tetanophobia
loneliness eremiphobia, eremophobia
long waits macrophobia
loud noise ligyrophobia
love philophobia
lying mythophobia
machines mechanophobia
many things polyphobia

marriage gametophobia, gamophobia, nuptophobia
materialism hylephobia
meat carnophobia, kreophobia
medicine pharmacophobia
meeting people anthropophobia
memories mnemophobia, nostophobia
men androphobia, arrhenophobia
meningitis meningitophobia
menstruation menophobia
metals metallophobia
meteors meteorophobia
mice muriphobia, murophobia, myosophobia
microbes bacilliphobia, microbiophobia, microphobia
milk galactophobia
mind psychophobia
mirrors catoptrophobia, eisoptrophobia, spectrophobia
missiles ballistophobia
mistletoe ixophobia
mites acarophobia
moisture hygrophobia
money chrematophobia
monotony homophobia
monstrosities teratophobia
moon selenophobia
mornings matutinophobia
mortality thriptophobia
mother-in-law pentheraphobia
moths phalaenophobia
motion kinesophobia, kinetophobia
motor vehicles motorphobia
mountains orophobia
mummies mummiphobia
mushrooms mycophobia
music melophobia , musicophobia
myths mythophobia
names nomatophobia, onomatophobia
narcotics lethophobia, meconophobia
narrowness anginaphobia, stenophobia
navels omphalophobia
needles aichmophobia, belonophobia
neglect of duty paralipophobia
new things cainophobia, cainotophobia, cenotophobia, kainophobia, kainotophobia, neophobia

night noctiphobia, nyctophobia
nipples, being seen through clothing thelophobia
nocturnal emissions oneirogmophobia
noise acousticophobia, ligyrophobia, phonophobia
Northern lights auroraphobia
nosebleeds epistaxiophobia
nuclear weapons nucleomitophobia
nudity gymnophobia, nudiphobia, nudophobia
numbers arithmophobia, numerophobia; *uneven* ~: perissophobia
nurses threpterophobia
nutritional food threptophobia
oceans thalassophobia
odors olfactophobia, ophresiophobia, osmophobia, osphresiophobia; *foul* ~: bromidrophobia, bromidrosiphobia,
old people gerontophobia
one thing monophobia
oneself autophobia
open spaces agoraphobia, cenophobia, kenophobia; *high* ~: aeroacrophobia
opinions of others allodoxaphobia
opposite sex heterophobia
organic structure tectologist
otters lutraphobia
owls strigiphobia
pain algiaphobia, algophobia, odynephobia, odynophobia, ponophobia; *from light sensitivity:* photaugiaphobia, photaugiophobia
pairs didymophobia
paper papyrophobia
parasites parasitophobia, pothiriophobia, trypanophobia, verminophobia
parents-in-law soceraphobia
peace eirenophobia
peanut butter arachibutyrophobia
pellagra pellagrophobia
penis: peophobia; *erect* ~: ithyphallophobia, medorthophobia; *visible contour of* ~: medectophobia
people anthropophobia, demophobia
perfume myrophobia

philosophy philosophobia
physical love erotophobia
places topophobia
planning for the future teleophobia
plants botanophobia
pleasure hedonophobia
poetry metrophobia, musophobia
pointed objects aichmophobia,
    aichurophobia
poison iophobia, toxicophobia, toxi-
    phobia, toxophobia
politicians politicophobia
pollen palynophobia
popes papaphobia
poverty peniaphobia
precipices cremnophobia
pregnancy maieusiophobia, tocopho-
    bia
prickly objects echinophobia
progress prosophobia
propriety orthophobia
prostitutes cyprianophobia, cyprido-
    phobia, cypriphobia, cyprinophobia,
    scortophobia
public places agoraphobia
public speaking glossophobia
pumpkins, especially jack-o'-lanterns
    pepophobia
punishment mastigophobia, poine-
    phobia, rhabdophobia
puppets pupaphobia
purposive effort hormephobia
pus pyophobia
quarrels rixophobia
quicksand syrtophobia
rabies hydrophobophobia, lyssophobia
railways siderodromophobia
rain hyetophobia, ombrophobia, plu-
    viophobia
rape stupraphobia, virgivitiphobia
rattlesnakes crotalophobia
razors xyrophobia
rectal disease proctophobia, rectopho-
    bia
referring to oneself autophoby
relatives syngenesophobia
religion sebastophobia, theophobia
religious ceremonies teletophobia

reproach enissophobia, enisiophobia
responsibility hypegiaphobia, hy-
    pengyophobia, paralipophobia
reptiles batrachophobia, herpetophobia
ridicule catagelophobia, katagelophobia
riding in a car amaxophobia
right side dextrophobia
rivers potamophobia
robbers harpaxophobia
room full of people koinoniphobia
ruin atephobia
Russia/the Russians Russophobia
rust iophobia, rubigophobia, uredino-
    phobia
sacred things hagiophobia, hieropho-
    bia
sadness lypephobia
saints hagiophobia
salt halophobia
sand psammophobia
Satan Satanophobia
sausage allantophobia
scabies scabiophobia
scarring ulophobia
school didaskaleinophobia, scholiono-
    phobia
scissors forficophobia
scotomas scotomaphobia
scratches amychophobia
sea pelagophobia, thalassophobia
secretions crinophobia
secrets calyptophobia
semen spermatophobia, spermophobia
sermons homilophobia, keryophobia
severely deformed people teratophobia
sexual intercourse coitophobia, cypri-
    dophobia, erotophobia, genophobia
sexual perversion paraphobia
shadows sciaphobia, sciophobia
sharks carcharinophobia, selachopho-
    bia
sharp objects aichmophobia, belono-
    phobia
shellfish ostraconophobia
shock hormephobia
sinning enissophobia, enosiophobia,
    hamartophobia, peccatiphobia, pec-
    catophobia

sisters sororophobia
sitting cathisophobia, kathisophobia, thaasophobia
skin dermatophobia
skin diseases dermatopathophobia, dermatosiophobia
skin of animals doraphobia
skunks mephitophobia
sleep hypnophobia, somniphobia
slime blennophobia, myxophobia
small objects microphobia, tapinophobia
smells olfactophobia, osmophobia, osphresiophobia
smoke capnophobia
smothering pnigerophobia, pnigophobia
snakes herpetophobia, ophiciophobia, ophidiophobia, ophiophobia
snoring rhonchophobia
snow chionophobia
society anthropophobia, sociophobia
solitude autophobia, eremiophobia, eremophobia, ermitophobia, isolophobia, monophobia
sorcery veneficophobia
sound acousticophobia ~ *of certain words:* onomatophobia
sourness acerbophobia, acerophobia
spasms choreophobia
speaking aloud phonophobia
speech defect laliophobia, lalophobia
speed tachophobia
spiders arachnephobia, arachnophobia
spiny creatures echinophobia
spirits demonophobia, phantasmaphobia, pneumatiphobia, spectrophobia
stage fright prosceniophobia, topophobia
stairs climacophobia
standing or walking basiphobia, basophobia, basistasiphobia, basostasophobia, stasibasiphobia, stasiphobia, stasobasiphobia, stasophobia
stars astrophobia, siderophobia
statues agalmaphobia
staying single anuptaphobia

stealing cleptophobia, kleptophobia
stepfather vitricophobia
stepmother novercaphobia
stillness eremophobia, hesyphobia
stings cnidophobia
stooping kyphophobia, scoliophobia
strangers xenophobia
streets agyiophobia, agryophobia; *crossing ~:* dromophobia
string linonophobia
stuttering psellismophobia
sun/light heliophobia, phengophobia
surgical operations ergasiophobia, tomophobia
swallowing phagophobia
swamps paludophobia
sweating sudoriophobia
symbolism semiophobia, symbolophobia
symmetry [in Egyptian temples, mosque decorations, etc.] symmetrophobia
syphilis luetiphobia, syphilidophobia, syphiliphobia, syphilophobia
talking glossophobia, laliophobia, lalophobia, phonophobia
tapeworms taeniiphobia, taeniophobia, teniophobia
taste geumaphobia, geumatophobia, geumophobia; *sour ~:* acerbophobia; *sweet ~:* hedisophobia
technology technophobia
teeth odontophobia
teleology teleophobia
telephones telephonophobia
termites isopterophobia
terror enosiphobia
theaters theatrophobia
theology theologicophobia
thieves cleptophobia, kleptophobia, harpaxophobia
thinking phronemophobia
thirst dipsophobia
thirteen tredecaphobia, tridecaphobia, triakaidekaphobia, triskadekaphobia, triskaidekaphobia
thunder brontophobia, ceraunophobia, keraunophobia, tonitrophobia

tickling with feathers pteronophobia
ticks acarophobia
time chronophobia
toads batrachophobia, bufonophobia
tombs taphophobia; ~ *stones:* placo-
    phobia
tooth decay cariophobia
tornadoes lilapsophobia
touching or being touched aphepho-
    bia, chiroptophobia, haphephobia,
    hapnophobia, haptephobia, hapto-
    phobia, thixophobia
train travel siderodromophobia
traitors proditophobia
travel dromophobia, hodophobia
trees dendrophobia
trembling tremophobia
trichinosis trichinophobia
tuberculosis phthisiophobia, phthiso-
    phobia, tuberculophobia
Turks Turcophobia
tyrants tyrannophobia
ugliness cacophobia
ulcers helcophobia
umbrella umbelliphobia
undressing deshabillophobia
urinating urophobia
vaccinations vaccinophobia
vampires vespertiliophobia
vegetables lachanophobia
vehicles amaxophobia, ochophobia
venereal disease cyprianophobia,
    cypridophobia, cyprinophobia, cyp-
    riphobia, venereophobia
vermin verminophobia
vertigo illyngophobia
virginity, losing esodophobia,
    primeisophobia
virgins parthenophobia
vomiting emetophobia
walking ambulophobia, basiphobia,
    basophobia, bathmophobia
warfare polemophobia
warts verruciophobia
washing oneself ablutophobia, bal-
    neophobia

wasps spheksophobia
wasting sickness tabophobia
water aquaphobia, hydrophobia
waves cymophobia, kymophobia
wax cerophobia
weakness asthenophobia
wealth chrematophobia, chrysopho-
    bia, plutophobia
weapons hoplophobia
weasels galeophobia
weight, gaining obesiophobia, procre-
    scophobia
werewolves lycophobia
whirlpools dinophobia
whispering psithurophobia
white leukophobia
wickedness scelerophobia
wild animals agrizoophobia, therio-
    phobia
wind ancraophobia, anemiaphobia,
    anemophobia
windows fenestrophobia
wine enophobia, oenophobia, oino-
    phobia
winter cheimaphobia
witchcraft wiccaphobia
women feminophobia, gynephobia,
    gynophobia; *beautiful* ~: calligyne-
    phobia, venustaphobia
wood hylephobia, hylophobia, xylo-
    phobia, ylophobia
words logophobia, verbophobia; *long* ~:
    sesquipedalophobia
work ergasiophobia, ergophobia,
    ponophobia
worms helminthophobia, scolecipho-
    bia, vermiphobia
wounds traumatophobia
wrinkles rhytiphobia
writing graphophobia, scriptophobia
x-rays radiophobia
yawning oscitophobia
young girls parthenophobia
zombies basinecrophobia

FOOD

Nonvegetarians should also see "Animals."

acorn balan- (balaniferous); gland- (glandiferous)
almond amygdalo- (amygdalaceous)
apple mali- (maliform); pom- (pomaceous)
avocado pers- (persea)
banana musa- (musaceous)
barley alphito- (alphitomancy); crith- (crithology); horde- (hordeaceous); ptis-(ptisan)
bean cyam- (cyamoid); fab- (fabaceous); phaseol- (phaseolous)
beer cervis- (cervisial)
belch ruct- (eructation)
berry acin- (acinaceous); baccat-baccate; bacci- (bacciferous); cocci- (coccigerous)
blueberry vaccin- (vaccinium)
bran furfur- (furfuraceous); pityr- (pityroid)
bread arto- (artophagous); pan- (panivorous)
breakfast jent- (jentacular)
butter butyro- (butyraceous)
cabbage brassic- (brassicacious)
carbohydrate -ose (fructose)
cashew anacard- (anacardic)
cereal frument- (frumentaceous)
cheese case- (casefy); tyro- (tyromancy)
cherry ceras- (cerasin)
chestnut aescul- (aesculin); castan- (castaneous)
chew manduc- (manducation); mastic- (mastication)
citric citro- (citron)
cook -coct- (decoction); mageir- (mageiricophobia); magir- (magiric)
corn frument- (frumentation); spici- (spiciferous)
cucumber cucumi- (cucumiform)
cultivation -ponic (hydroponics)
digest chyli- (chyliferous); chymo-

(chymotrypsin)-; peps- (pepsinogen); pept- (peptic); pepto- (peptogenic)
dill aneth- (anethated)
dinner deipno- (deipnophobia); prand- (postprandial)
drink -ade (lemonade); bib- (bibulous); pino- (pinocytosis); pocul- (poculent); poto- (potomania)
eating alim- (alimentation); bromato- (bromatology); -brotic (scolecobrotic); cib- (cibarious); comest- (comestible); ed- (edible); escul- (esculent); gust- (gustatory); manduc- (manducation); mastic- (mastication); -phagous (creophagous); -phagy (anthropophagy); -sitia (asitia); sitio- (sitiophobia); -troph (heterotroph); -trophic (heterotrophic); -trophy (hypertrophy); -vora (Carnivora); -vore (herbivore); -vorous (omnivorous)
fig fici- (ficiform); syc- (sycoma)
fruit -carp (endocarp); -carpic (endocarpic); carpo- (carpophore); -carpous (monocarpous); frug- (frugivorous); pomi- (pomiform); pomo- (pomology)
garlic alli- (alliaceous); scoro- (scorodite)
gooseberry grossul- (grossulaceous)
grain farr- (confarreate); farrag- (farraginous); frument- (frumentaceous); grani- (granivorous)
grape acini- (aciniform); botry- (botryose); racem- (racemiform); rhag- (rhagite); staphylo- (staphyline); uvi- (uviform); uvu- (uvula); vini- (viniculture); vino- (vinosity); viti- (viticulture)
hickory cichor- (cichoraceous)
honey melli- (melliferous)

kidney bean phaseol- (phaseolous)
leek porr- (porraceous); praso-
(prasophagous)
lime tilia- (tiliaceous)
lunch prand- (prandial)
meal cen- (cenatory); coen- (coenaculous); deipno- (deipnophobia); prand-
(anteprandial)
meat -burger (hamburger); carni-
(carnivore); carnoso- (carnosity)
mint menth- (menthaceous)
mulberry mori- (moriform)
mustard sinap- (sinapistic)
nutmeg myrist- (myristic)
oats aveni- (avenaceous)
onion cep- (cepous); cromny-
(cromnyomancy)
orange hesperid- (hesperidine)
parsley petrosel- (petroseline)
pea pisi- (pisiform)
peach persic- (persicaria)
peanut arach- (arachidic)
pear apio- (apiocrinite); piri-
(piriform); pyri- (pyriform)
pepper piper- (piperic)
pineapple bromel- (bromeliaceous)
pomegranate balaust- (balaustine)
pumpkin pepo- (pepon)

radish raphan- (raphania)
raspberry frambes- (frambesia)
rice oryzi- (oryzivorous); rizi-
(riziform)
salad acetar- (acetarious)
salt halo- (halophile); sali- (desalination); salino- (salinometric); sals-
(salsamentarious)
sandwich -burger (cheeseburger)
sausage allanto- (allantoid); botul-
(botuliform)
strawberry fragar- (fragarol)
sugar gluco- (glucose); glycero-
(glycerol); glyco- (glycosuria); levul-
(levulose); saccharo- (saccharometer);
sucr- (sucrose)
tea thei- (theiform)
truffle hydno- (hydnocarpous)
turnip napi- (napiform)
vegetable lachan- (lachanopolist);
oler- (oleraceous); olit- (olitory);
vegeti- (vegetivorous); vegeto-
(vegetarian)
walnut juglan- (juglandaceous)
wheat silig- (siliginous); tritic-
(triticeous)
yam dioscorea- (dioscoreaceous)

LOCATION

above ano- (anocarpous); epi- (epidermis); ob- (obliterate); over-
(overhang); super- (superscript);
supra- (supraliminal); sur- (surbase)
across dia- (diameter); per- (peregri-
nation); trans- (transmit); trans-
verso- (transverso-cubital)
apex -apical (periapical); apico-
(apicotomy)
behind after- (afterburner); back-
(backdrop); meta- (metasternum);
opistho- (opisthotic); post- (postsce-
nium); postero- (posterolateral);
retro- (retrocopulant)
between/among dia- (diagnosis);

enter- (entergrave); entre- (en-
tr'acte); epi- (epidemic); inter-
(interval)
distant tele- (television)
front ante- (antependium); antero-
(anteroparietal); fore- (forefront);
pre- (preaortic); pro- (proscenium);
proso- (prosogaster)
high(er) acro- (acrocephaly); alti-
(altitude); alto- (alto-relievo); hypsi-
(hypsistenocephalic); hypso- (hypsometry); super- (superstructure)
inside eis- (eisegesis); em- (embedded);
en- (enclose); endo- (endoskeleton);
ento- (entoparasite); eso- (esoenteri-

tis); il- (illuminate); im- (implosion); in- (incarcerate); intero- (interoceptor); ir- (irradiate); intra- (intramural); intro- (introspection)

left laeo- (laeotropic) laevo- (laevoratatory) levo- (levogyrate) sinistro- (sinistrorse)

middle centri- (centripetal); centro- (centrolineal); -centric (heliocentric); medi- (medieval); medio- (mediodorsal); mes- (mesallantoid); mesati- (mesaticephalic); mesio- (mesio-sinistral); meso- (mesothorax); mezzo- (mezzotint); mid- (midsection)

near ad- (adjoining); by- (bystander); cis- (cismontane); epi- (epicenter); juxta- (juxtapose); para- (parametric); peri- (perigee); prox- (approximal) proximo- (proximocephalic)

outside ecto- (ectoparasite); epi- (epidermis); exo- (exoskeleton); extero- (exteroceptor); extra- (extraterritorial); extro- (extrovert); out- (outhouse); para- (paradox); preter- (preternatural)

right dexio- (dexiotropic); dextro- (dextrorse)

surrounding ambi- (ambiance); amphi- (amphithecium); be- (beset); circum- (circumference); peri- (periotic)

through dia- (diaphanous); per- (percolate); trans- (transparent); -wide (worldwide)

under hypo- (hypodermic); infero- (inferoposterior); infra- (infrastructure); sub- (subscript); subter- (subterfluent); under- (underpinning)

upon ana- (anaclisis); epi- (epilogue); ob- (obtrude); super- (superstructure); sur- (surcharge)

with co- (coterminous); col- (colleague); com- (commingle); con- (convulse); cor- (correlate); hama- (hamadryad); inter- (intermixed); para- (parataxis); syl- (syllable); sym- (symbiosis); symphyo- (symphyogenesis); symphysio- (symphysiorrhaphy); syn- (synagogue); sys- (system)

MEASUREMENT SCIENCE (-METRY)

Item Measured/Name of Process
To extract the word part, simply drop "metry" from each word.

acid strength acidimetry

aerial photos for surveying and map-making photogrammetry

air or gas aerometry, pneumatometry, spirometry; ~ *purity:* eudiometry

alcohol proportion in liquor alcoholometry

alkali strength alkalimetry

alkaloids alkalometry

altitudes altimetry, hypsometry

ancient depths of the sea paleobathymetry

angles goniometry; ~ *of crystals:* crystallometry; ~ *of slope, elevation, or inclination:* clinometry

animal body dimensions zoometry

archeological materials archæometry

area dimensions (by using perspective) iconometry

area of plane surfaces planometry

astigmatism astigmometry

atmospheric pressure barometry

atomic weights stoicheiometry

axis axonometry

birds' eggs oometry

bladder pressure cystometry

blind spots caused by glaucoma scotometry

blood cells cytometry

blood-current velocity hemotachometry

blood force; blood corpuscles hematometry
blood pressure oscillometry, sphygmomanometry
blood quality hemometry
blueness of light cyanometry
bodily functions physiometry
body somatometry
boiling points of liquids ebulliometry
bones; skeletons osteometry
breadth of distant objects platometry
by using the foot podometry
carbon dioxide content micro-gasometry
celestial bodies — movements and positions astrometry
cell content (by measuring light transmission after staining) cytophotometry
cellular respiration respirometry
changes *in intracellular activity:* micro-densitometry; ~ *in the tympanic membrane:* tympanometry; ~ *in weight as a function of inreasing temperatures:* thermogravimetry
chemical proportions stoichiometry
chemicals: tiny quantities in electrolytic solutions voltammetry
chest curves; head curves cyrtometry
chlorine available in a liquid chlorometry
circles cyclometry
cloudiness nephelometry
color blindness Tintometry
color intensity colorimetry, chromometry
color for chemical analysis spectrocolorimetry
coloring power of indigo indigometry
combustion comburimetry
conductivity conductometry
cornea of the eye: radius of curvature ophthalmometry
correct versification orthometry
coulombs used in an electrolysis coulometry
crossed eyes strabismometry, strabometry

darkness of a substance densitometry
degree of polarization polarimetry
density of a photographic negative photodensitometry
depths in bodies of water bathometry, bathymetry
diffraction diffractometry
dimensions of what was photographed photogrammetry
direction radiogoniometry
disproportionate growth rates allometry
distance(s) iconometry, longimetry; ~ *between two stars:* heliometry; ~ *of heavenly bodies:* uranometry; ~ *of objects:* apomecometry; ~ *traveled:* odometry
distant ~ *data:* telemetry; ~ *objects:* tacheometry, tachymetry, telemetry; ~ *temperatures:* telethermometry
doses *medicine:* dosimetry; *radioactivity:* dosimetry
duration & intensity of mental states psychometry
ear sensitivity to various frequencies audiometry
earthquakes seismometry; *faint ~:* tromometry
eggs oometry
elasticity elastometry
electric currents rheometry
electricity in an eel electrometry
electromagnetic radiation spectroradiometry
electromotive forces potentiometry
excess ametry
external form morphometry
expansion dilatometry
eye(s) *crossed:* strabismometry, strabometry; ~ *muscles:* phorometry; ~ *pupil diameter:* pupillometry; ~ *refraction:* dioptometry; *refractive power of ~:* optometry; ~ *sensitivity to colors:* chromatoptometry
faint earth-tremors tromometry
features of a literary style stylometry
ferrous salt titrimetry

figures that stand on the same base epipedometry

flour quality aleurometry

flourescence fluorometry; spectro-fluorimetry

flow of viscous substances rheometry

focal distance focimetry

foot stride pedimetry, pedometry

force of respiration pneumatometry

galvanic current galvanometry

gases gasometry; ~ *emanating from the sun:* spectro-colorimetry

God theometry

group relationship patterns sociometry

handwriting constants graphometry

head cephalometry

hearing acoumetry, audiometry

heart size cardiometry

heat calorimetry; ~ *of the sun's rays:* pyrheliometry; ~ **quantities:** calorimetry; ~ *radiating from surfaces:* actinometry; *very small quantities of* ~: microcalorimetry

heavens uranometry

heights altimetry, hypsometry

hemoglobin hemoglobinometry

high temperatures pyrometry

human body at various stages of life anthropometry

humidity hygrometry, psychrometry

hydrostatic pressure affecting groundwater piezometry

inaccessible distances (by using staves) baculometry

index of refraction spectrometry

infra-red radiation radiometry

intensity *of the blue of the sky:* cyanometry; ~ *of light in a particular part of the spectrum:* spectrophotometry; ~ *of scattered light:* photogoniometry; ~ *of the scintillation of stars:* scintillometry

internal part endometry

interference phenomena interferometry

intraocular pressure ophthalmotonometry

ion detection mass spectrometry

ionizing radiation radiation dosimetry

ions in solution voltammetry

isoperometrical figure isoperimetry

land embadometry

length and distance mecometry

lichen growth (to determine age of a moraine) lichenometry

life expectation biometry

ligand binding micro-calorimetry

light *intensity:* photometry, spectrophotometry; ~ *polarization:* polarimetry; ~ *rays in a spectrum:* spectrometry; ~ *wavelength, refraction, displacement:* interferometry

lines in ancient writers gnomometry

liquid volumes micro-fluorimetry

living cells micro-fluorometry

low temperatures cryometry

lung capacity bronchospirometry, pneometry, pulmometry, spirometry

magnetic fields magnetometry

magnitudes in space geometry

malarial infection levels malariometry

manuscript text (by using lines of average length) stichometry

measurements pantometry

mental processes noometry

metric spaces metric geometry

microscopic objects micrometry

mountains orometry

movement of the walls of the chest stethometry

movement range of joints arthrometry

muscular contraction dynamometry

number of soldiers depicted in a given geometric figure stratarithmetry

odor(s) osmometry; ~ *intensity:* odorimetry

one-to-one transformation of one metric space into another isometry

optical density densitrometry

organism growth alloiometry, allometry

osmotic pressure osmometry

oxygen consumption rate respirometry

oxygenated hemoglobin in the blood
oximetry
ozone in the air ozonometry
pain pathometry; ~ *perception:* do-
lorimetry; *sensitivity to ~:* algometry
part related to height autometry
past time (by using radioactive elements) geochronometry
pelvis dimensions pelvimetry
perimeters perimetry
phosphorescence spectrophospho-
rimetry
photometric measurements of very
small areas microphotometry
plane surfaces planimetry; *area of ~:*
planometry
plant responses phytometry
plasticity of a substance plastometry
plasticity or viscosity plastometry,
points, lines, angles, surfaces, solids
geometry
points on a survey tacheometry,
tachymetry
polygons polygonometry
polyhedra polyhedrometry
porosity; pore-size distribution
porosimetry
pressures tasimetry; *blood ~:* oscillometry, sphygmomanometry; ~ *of*
gases and vapors: manometry
projective properties projective
geometry
proportion *of alkaloids in cinchona*
bark: cinchonometry; ~ *of polarized*
light in a beam: photopolarimetry
pulse sphygmomanometry, sphyg-
mometry
quantity of sugar in a solution saccharimetry, saccharometry
quinine in cinchona bark quinimetry,
quininometry
radiant energy radiation pyrometry,
spectroradiometry
radiation radiometry; ~ *absorption:*
absorptiometry
radii of curvature of the cornea ker-
atometry
radioactivity doses dosimetry

radio wave direction radiogoniometry
rainfall pluviometry
rates of oxygen consumption
respirometry
refraction refractometry
refractive indices reflectometry, refractometry
refractive power of the eyes dioptometry, optometry
remote measurement of human or
animal activity biotelemetry
respiration stethometry; ~ *on a mi-*
croscopic scale: microrespirometry
retinal areas campimetry
rotation of the plane of polarized light
as a function of wavelength spec-
tropolarimetry
roughness of a surface profilometry
salinity of water salinometry
saline in a solution halimetry
senses relating to measurement metrical geometry
sensitivity sensitometry; ~ *of smell:*
olfactometry
sensitiveness of photographic media
sensitometry
shadows skiametry
shearing stresses rheogoniometry
shells conchometry
shape and dimensions morphometry
ship pitch and roll oscillometry
sides and angles of triangles
trigonometry
size of the pupil of the eye pupillometry
size of pores (by means of mercury infusion) mercury porosimetry
skeletons; bones osteometry
skull craniometry
smell sensitivity olfactometry
soil moisture; tension; surface tension
tensiometry
solid figures stereometry; *volume of ~:*
volumenometry
solution *of an oxidizing agent:*
iodometry; ~ *of a reducing agent:*
iodimetry
sound phonometry
space-time geochronometry

specific gravity of fluids aræometry, hydrometry, volumenometry
speckled markings speckle interferometry
speech sounds phonometry
speed dromometry, tachometry, velocimetry ; ~ *of light:* phototachometry
spiral helicometry
squinting; strabismus strabismometry
stars: relative magnitude of astrometry
strata inclination clinometry
strength of a magnetic field magnetometry
structure of groups sociometry
sugar in a solution saccharimetry, saccharometry
sun's heat pyrheliometry
surface tension stalagmometry, tensiometry
surveying a country chorometry
suspended matter in a liquid turbidimetry
telescope magnifying power dynamometry
temperature(s) thermometry; ~ *of ancient climates and oceans:* paleothermometry **distant ~:** telethermometry; *very high ~:* pyrometry; ~ / *weight relationship:* thermogravimetry
tension *intraocular:* tonometry; *surface ~:* tensiometry
terrain features; plane surfaces planimetry
time chromometry, horometry
touch ethesiometry
topographical information (by means of aerial photos) photoclinometry

thermal expansion dilatometry
time chronometry
tremors of the earth tromometry
turbidity of a liquid or gas nephelometry, turbidimetry
tympanic membrane changes tympanometry
ultraviolet absorption micro-spectrophotometry
underlying substance or essence hypokeimenometry
universe cosmometry
urea ureometry
urine, specific gravity urinometry
velocity dromometry, tachometry, velocimetry
verses colometry
versification, correct orthometry
very high temperatures pyrometry
vinegar strength; acetic acid acetimetry
viscosity viscometry; ~ *of liquids:* viscosimetry
viscous substance flow rate rheometry
visual field limits perioptometry
visual powers optometry
volume volumetry; ~ *of respiratory air flow:* pneumometry; ~ *of a solid:* volumenometry
water hardness hydrotimetry
wavelengths of rays in a spectrum spectrometry
weak earth tremors microseismometry
weight or density gravimetry
weight/temperature relationship thermogravimetry
wind force, speed, direction, velocity anemometry
womb size hysterometry
X-rays roentgenometry

NEGATIVES

a- *pre* not; without (atypical, atheist)
ab- *pre* away from (absorbent, absence)
an- *pre* not; without (analgesia, anorexia)

anti- *pre* opposite of; against (antidote, antistrophe)
apo- *pre* detached; apart (apogamy, apomixis)

-atresia *comb* absence of an opening (atresia, proctatresia)

atreto- *comb* absence of an opening (atretocyst, atretogastria)

cata- *pre* against (catachresis cataplasia)

contra- *pre* opposite; against (contradiction, contravene)

counter- *comb* opposite; against (counter-clockwise, counter-culture)

de- *pre* deprived of; apart (detached, devaluation)

dis- *pre* apart; opposite (discrepant, disengage)

dys- *pre* badly; not correct (dysfunctional, dysphoria)

ectro- *comb* missing; absent (ectromelia, ectrosydactyly)

ex- *pre* former; deprived of (excaudate, ex-member)

il- *pre* not; opposite of (illegality, illicit)

im- *pre* not; opposite of (immature, impartial)

in- *pre* not; opposite of (inarticulate, insanity)

ir- *pre* not; opposite of (irreverent, irreligious)

-less *suf* without; unable to (defenseless, restless)

lipo- *comb* lacking; leaving (lipography, lipophrenia)

mal- *pre* poorly; not (maladapted, malnutrition)

mis- *pre* wrongly; not (misalignment, mismanagement)

miso- *comb* antipathy; hatred (misocainea, misogamy)

ne- *pre* not; opposite of (neglect, nescient)

nihil- *base* nothingness (annihilate, nihilistic)

no- *pre* not any (no-fault insurance, no-load fund)

non- *pre* not; absence of (nonallergenic, noncompetitive)

nulli- *pre* none (nullify, nulliparous)

ob- *pre* against; inverse (obliterate, obtund)

-priv- *base* lacking; taken away (deprivation, privation)

un- *pre* not; reversal (unbending, unimaginable)

with- *pre* apart; opposed (withhold, withstand)

NUMBERS

0 nulli- (nullipara)

1/10 decim- (decimate)

1/9 non- (nonan)

1/8 octan- (octant)

1/7 septim- (septimal)

1/6 sext- (sextant)

1/5 quint- (quintant)

1/4 tetarto- (tetartohedral)

1/3 trient- (triental)

1/2 demi- (demitint); dicho- (dichotomize); dimid- (dimidiation); hemi- (hemisphere); mezzo- (mezzo-relievo); semi- (semicolumnar)

3/4 triquadr- (triquadrantal)

1 eka- (ekaselenium); haplo- (haplopetalous); heno- (henotheism); mono- (monorail); uni- (unilateral)

1 & 1/2 sesqui- (sesquihoral)

2 ambi- (ambiversion); ambo- (amboceptor); amphi- (amphicarpous); ampho- (amphora); bi- (bicentennial); bin- (binaural); bis- (bissextile); deutero- (deuterogamy); deuto- (deutoplasm); di- (diplegia); dicho- (dichotomous); didym- (didymalgia); diphy- (diphyceral); diplo- (diplopia); disso- (dissogony); double- (doubleheader); du- (duplicate); duplicato- (duplicato-den-

tate); duplici- (duplicipennate); duo-
(duograph); dyo- (Dyophysite);
gemelli- (gemelliparous); gemin-
(geminiflorous); twi- (twinight);
zygo- (zygodont)

3 ter- (tercet); -tern- (ternary); -tert-
(tertiary); tri- (trifocal); triakis-
(triakisoctahedron); triangulato-
(triangulato-subovate); trigono-
(trigonocephalic); triplo- (triploblastic); triplicato- (triplicato-pinnate);
trito- (tritoencephalon)

4 quadra- (quadraphonic); quadrato-
(quadrato-cubic); quadri- (quadrilateral); quadru- (quadruped);
quart- (quarterly); quarti- (quartisect); quat- (quaternate); quater-
(quater-centenary); quatre- (quatrefoil); tessara- (tesseraphthong);
tetarto- (tetartohedral); tetra-
(Tetragrammaton); tetrakis- (tetrakisdodecahedron)

5 cinque- (cinquefoil); penta- (penta-
cle); quin- (quinary); quinque-
(quinquennium); quint- (quintuplets); quinti- (quintiped)

6 hexa- (hexahedron); hexakis- (hexakisoctahedron); seni- (senary); sex-
(sexagenarian); sexi- (sexipolar);
sexti- (sextisection); sise- (siseangle)

7 hebdo- (hebdomadral); hepta-
(Heptateuch); septem- (September);
septi- (septifolious)

8 octa- (octagon); octo- (octonary);
ogdo- (ogdoastich)

9 ennea- (enneahedron); nona-
(nonagon); -nov- (novena)

10 dec(a)- (decade); decem- (decem-
pennate); deci- (decimeter); deka-
(dekagram); -teen (sixteen); -ty
(seventy)

11 endeca- (endecagon); hendeca-
(hendecasyllabic); undec-
(undecagon); undecim- (undecimal)

12 dodeca- (dodecastyle); duodec-
(duodecennial); duodecim-
(duodecimfid); duoden-
(duodenary)

13 tredecim- (tredecimal); triskaideka-
(triskaidekaphobia)

14 quattuordec- (quattuordecillion);
tessaradeca- (tessaradecasyllabon);
tetradeca- (tetradecapod);
tetrakaideca- (tetrakaidecahedron)

15 pentakaideca- (pentakaidecahedron); quindec- (quindecennial)

16 hexadeca- (hexadecachoron); hexa-
kaideca- (hexakaidecahedron);
sedecim- (sedecimal)

17 heptakaideca- (heptakaidecahedron); septendecim- (septendecimal)

18 duodeviginti- (duodevigintiangular); octakaideca- octakaidecahedron)

19 enneakaideca- (enneakaidecahedron); undeviginti- (undevigintiangular)

20 eico- (eicosapentaenoic: 25); icosa-
(icosandria); icosi- (icositetrahedron: 24); vicesim- (vicesimal);
vigent- (vigentennial); viginti- (vigintiangular)

30 triaconta- (triacontahedral);
triceni- (tricenary); triges-
(trigesimal); trigint- (trigintal)

40 quadragen- (quadragenarian);
quadrages- (quadragesimal)

50 pentacosta- (pentacostaglossal);
penteconta- (pentecontaglossal);
quinquagen- (quinquagenarian);
quinquages- (quinquagesimal)

60 hexaconta- (hexacontahedron);
sexagen- (sexagenarian); sexages-
(sexagesimal)

70 septuagen- (septuagenarian); septu-
ages- (septuagesimal); septuagint-
(Septuagint)

80 octogen- (octogenarian); octoges-
(octogesimal)

90 enneaconta- (enneacontahedral);
nonagen- (nonagenarian); nonages-
(nonagesimal)

100 cent(i)- (centigrade); hecato-
(hecatophyllous); hecatinicosa-
(hecatinicosachoron: 120); hecto-
(hectoliter); hekto (hektogram)

150 sesquicent- (sesquicentennial)
200 ducen- (ducenarious)
300 trecent- (trecentene)
400 quadricent- (quadricentennial)
500 quincent- (quincentennial)
600 hexacosi- (hexacosichoron); sex-cent- (sexcentenary)
700 septingenti- (septingentenary)
800 octocent- (octocentenary)
900 enneacent- (enneacentenary)
1,000 -chili- (chiliarch); kilo- (kilo-gram); ~ *th:* milli- (millibar)
10,000 myria- (myriameter); myrio-(myriophyllous)
1,000,000 *one million* mega- (mega-volt); ~ *th:* micro- (microgram)
1,000,000,000 *one billion* giga- (giga-byte); ~ *th:* nano- (nanosecond); nanno- (nannoplankton)
1,000,000,000,000 *one trillion* tera-(terahertz); trega- (tregadyne); ~ *th:* pico- (picofarad)
1,000,000,000,000,000 *one quadrillion* peta- (petameter); ~ *th:* femto-(femtometer);
1,000,000,000,000,000,000 *one quintillion* exa- (exameter); ~ *th:* atto- (attogram)
1,000,000,000,000,000,000,000 *one hexillion* zetta- (zettabyte); ~ *th:* zepto- (zeptovolt)
1,000,000,000,000,000,000,000,000 *one heptillion* yotta- (yottameter); ~ *th:* yocto- (yoctogram)
googol The number 10 raised to the power 100, written as the numeral 1 followed by 100 zeros
googolplex The number 10 raised to the power googol, written as the numeral 1 followed by 10^{100} zeros

THE SENSES

Hearing

deafness -surd- (surdity)
ear auri- (auricle); auriculo- (au-riculo-temporal); ot- (othemorrha-gia); oto- (otology)
hear acou- (acouasm); acoust-(acoustical); audi- (auditory); audio-(audiology); auri- (auricle); ecoia (dysecoia)
sound echo- (echogenic); -phone (telephone); phono- (phonograph); -phony (euphony); -phthong (diph-thong); son- (sonic); soni- (sonifer-ous); sono- (sonometer); sonoro-(sonorous)

RELATED PERCEPTIONS

noisy crepit- (crepitation); frem-(fremitus); ligyr- (ligyrophobia); strid- (strident); stridul- (stridu-lous); strepi- (strepitus);
silent hesy- (hesychastic); tacit- (taci-turnity)

Seeing

blindness caec- (caecilian); cec- (cecity); lusc- (eluscate); typhlo- (typhlosis)
eye blepharo- (blepharotomy); cantho- (canthoplasty); cili- (cil-iary); corneo- (corneoiritis); irido-(iridomotor); kerato- (keratotomy); oculi- (oculiform); oculo- (oculo-motor); ommat- (ommatophore); op- (opalgia); ophthalmo- (oph-thalmoscope); -opia (diplopia); ophry- (ophryosis); opsi- (opsi-ometer); opso- (opsoclonus); optico- (optico-papillary); opto-(optometry); retino- (retinoschisis); sclero- (sclerotomy); tarso (tarso-plasty)
pupil core- (corelysis); coreo- (coreo-plasty); -coria (isocoria); coro-(coroplastic); -koria (leukokoria); pupillo- (pupillometer)
see -blep- (ablepsia); eid- (eidetic);

-opsia (hemianopsia); -opsis (synopsis); -opsy (biopsy); -scope (telescope); -scopic (microscopic);
scopo- (scopophilia); -scopy
(bioscopy); -scrut- (inscrutable);
spec- (spectator); -spic- (conspicuous); -vid- (video); -vis- (vision);
visuo- (visuosensory)

RELATED PERCEPTIONS

bright fulg- (fulgurant); helio-
(helioscope); luc- (luciferous);
lumin- (luminosity)

dark amaur- (amaurosus); ambly-
(amblyopia); nyct- (nyctalopia);
scoto- (scotophobia); tenebr-
(tenebrous)

Smelling

nose nasi- (nasiform); naso- (nasol-
ogy); rhino- (rhinology)

smell bromo- (bromidrosis); fet-
(fetid); nidor- (nidorous); -odic
(euodic); odori- (odoriferous);
odoro- (odoroscope); -olent (redolent); -olfact- (olfactory); -osmia
(anosmia); osmo- (osmodysphoria);
osphresio (osphresiophobia); ozo-
(ozostomia)

RELATED PERCEPTIONS

pleasant bene- (beneficial); eu-
(euodic)

unpleasant cac- (cacosmia); mal-
(malodorous)

Tasting

mouth -mouthed (dry-mouthed);
oro- (orolingual); stomato- (stomatalgia); -stome (cytostome); -sto-
mous (monostomous)

palate palato- (palatonasal); uranisco-
(uranisconitis); urano- (ura-
noplasty); velar- (velarize)

saliva ptyal- (ptyalagogue); sialo-
(sialorrhea)

taste geum- (geumaphobia); geumat-
(geumatophobia); -geusia (parageu-

sia); -gust- (gustatory); sapor-
(saporific)

tongue -glossia (macroglossia); glosso-
(glossodynia); hyo- (hyoglossal);
lamino- (lamino-alveolar); ligur-
(ligurition); ling- (lingible); lingui-
(linguiform)

RELATED PERCEPTIONS

bitter alk- (alkaloid); picro- (picro-
toxin)

salty alo- (alomancy); halo- (halophile);
sal- (saline); sals- (salsamentarious)

sour acerb- (acerbity); acid- (acidu-
lous); amar- (amarine)

sweet hedy- (hedyphane); melli-
(mellifluous); dulc- (dulcify)

Touching

sensation -esthesia (myesthesia); es-
thesio- (esthesiometer)

skin cut(i)- (subcutaneous); derm-
(dermabrasion); -derm (melano-
derm); derma- (dermatherm);
-derma (scleroderma); dermat-
(dermatitis); dermato- (dermatology); -dermatous (xerodermatous);
-dermis (epidermis); dermo- (dermoneural)

touch aphe- (aphephobia); -aphia
(dysaphia); -apsia (parapsia); haph-
(haphalgesia); hapto- (haptometer);
-palp- (palpable); sens(i)- (sensifer-
ous); sensori- (sensorineural); sent-
(sentient); -tact- (contact); -tang-
(tangible); thigmo- (thigmotaxis)

RELATED PERCEPTIONS

cold alg- (algid); cheima-
(cheimaphilic); crymo- (crymophilic); cryo- (cryopathy); frigo-
(frigorific); gelo- (gelosis); kryo-
(kryometer); psychro- (psychroal-
gia); rhigo- (rhigolene)

dry -sicc- (desiccate); xero-
(xerophyte)

hard dur- (duricrust); scler-
(scleronychia)

rough salebr- (salebrous); trachy-
(trachycarpous)
smooth glabr- (glabrous); leio-
(leiotrichous); levig- (levigated);
lisso- (lissotrichous); lubr- (lubricity); psilo- (psilodermatous)
soft malac- (malacissant); malax-
(malaxation); -moll- (emollient)

warm calo- (caloreceptor); calori-
(calorific); caum- (caumesthesia);
pyr- (pyrogenic); therm- (thermal);
thermo- (thermosensitive); -thermy
(diathermy)
wet humect- (humectant); hydro- (hy-
drorrhea); hygro- (hygroscopic);
madefac- (madefaction)

SHAPES

acorn-shaped balan- (balanoid);
glandi- (glandiform)
agate-shaped agat- (agatiform)
almond-shaped amygdal- (amygdali-
form)
anchor-shaped ancyr- (ancyroid)
angle -angle (quadrangle); angul-
(rectangular); -gon (polygon); -gonal
(polygonal); gonio- (goniometer)
antennae-shaped antenn- (antenni-
form)
anther-shaped anther- (antheriform)
apple-shaped pomi- (pomiform)
arc-shaped arcu- (arcuate)
arch-shaped arci- (arciform); cingul-
(cingulate); fornici- (forniciform)
arrow-shaped bel- (beloid); *arrow
head:* sagitt- (sagittate)
astragalus-shaped astragal- (astraga-
loid)
awl-shaped subul- (subulate)
ax-shaped dolabri- (dolabriform);
pelec- (pelecoid); securi- (securiform)
axehead-shaped axini- (axiniform);
pelec- (pelecoid)
bacterium-shaped bacteri- (bacterioid)
barrel-shaped dolio- (dolioform)
basin-shaped pelvi- (pelviform)
basket-shaped calathi- (calathiform)
basilica-shaped basilic- (basilicate)
bead-shaped monili- (moniliform);
toruli- (toruliform)
beak-shaped aquil- (aquiline);
corac- (coracoid); ornithorhynch-

(ornithorhynchous); rhamph-
(rhamphoid); rhyncho- (rhyn-
chophorous); rostrato- (rostrato-
nariform); rostri- (rostriform)
bean-shaped fabi- (fabiform)
bear-shaped urs- (ursiform)
beehive-shaped alve- (alveated)
beetle-shaped scarab- (scaraboid)
bell-shaped campan- (campaniform)
bent ancylo- (ancylostomiasis);
ankylo- (ankylosis); -campsis (phallocampsis); campto- (campto-
cormia); campylo- (campylo-
dactyly); -clinal (anticlinal); -clinate
(proclinate); -cline (incline); -clinic
(matroclinic); clino- (clinometer);
-clinous (patroclinous); -clisis
(pathoclisis); clit- (heteroclital); cliv-
(declivity); curvi- (curvilinear);
cyrto- (cyrtometer); -flect-
(genuflection); flex- (flexural);
lechrio- (lechriodont); loxo- (loxotomy); repando- (repando-dentate);
scolio- (scoliokyphosis); sinu- (sinu-
ousity); -verge (diverge)
berry-shaped bacc- (bacciform)
bird's-head-shaped avicular- (avicu-
lariform)
bird-shaped orith- (orithoid)
boat-shaped cymb- (cymbiform);
navi- (naviform); navicul- (naviculoid); scapho- (scaphocephaly);
scapulo- (scapulohumeral); scyphi-
(scyphiform)
bottle-shaped ampull- (ampulla-

ceous); ascidi- (ascidiform); *leather bottle-shaped:* utrei- (utreiform); utric- (utricular)

bow-shaped arci- (arciform); arcu- (arcuate)

bowl-shaped crater- (crateriform); pateri- (pateriform); scyph- (scyphate)

bract-shaped bractei- (bracteiform)

branch-shaped rami- (ramiform)

breast-shaped mammi- (mammiferous, mammiform)

brick-shaped plinthi- (plinthiform)

bristle-shaped chaeti- (chaetiform); seti- (setiform)

broom-shaped scopi- (scopiform)

brush-shaped aspergilli- (aspergilliform); muscar- (muscariform)

bud-shaped gemm- (gemmiform)

bull-shaped taur- (tauriform)

bulb-shaped bulbi- (bulbiform)

buttock-shaped nati- (natiform)

canine tooth-shaped canini- (caniniform); laniar- (laniariform)

cap-shaped pile- (pileiform)

caterpillar-shaped eruci- (eruciform)

catkin-shaped amenti-[2] (amentiform); juli- (juliform)

cell-shaped celli- (celliform)

cheek-shaped buccin- (buccinoid)

chisel-shaped celti- (celtiform); scalpri- (scalpriform)

clarion-shaped litui- (lituiform)

claw-shaped ungui- (unguiform)

cleaver-shaped dolabr- (dolabriform)

cloud-shaped cirri- (cirriform); nubi- (nubiform)

club-shaped clav- (clavate, claviform)

cobweb-shaped arachn- (arachnoid)

coin-shaped nummi- (nummiform)

collar-shaped colli- (colliform)

column-shaped columelli- (columelliform); columni- (columniform)

comb-shaped pectin- (pectiniform)

cone-shaped coni- (coniform); strobili- (strobiliform)

coral-shaped coralli- (coralliform)

corn-shaped grani- (graniform)

cowl-shaped cuculli- (cuculliform)

crab-shaped cancri- (cancriform)

crater-shaped crateri- (crateriform)

crescent-shaped crescenti- (crescentiform); lunul- (lunular); menisc- (meniscate, meniscoid); sigm- (sigmoid)

cross-shaped cruc- (cruciate, cruciform)

crown-shaped coron- (coroniform)

crystal-shaped crystalli- (crystalliform)

cube-shaped cubi- (cubiform)

cuckoo-shaped cuculi- (cuculiform)

cucumber-shaped cucumi- (cucumiform)

cup-shaped acetabuli- (acetabuliform); calath- (calathiform); calici- (caliciform); cotyl- (cotyliform); crin- (crinoid); cupuli- (cupuliform); cyath- (cyathiform); pocilli- (pocilliform); pocul- (poculiform); scyphi- (scyphiform)

curl-shaped cirri- (cirriform)

cushion-shaped pulvini- (pulviniform)

cusp-shaped cusp- (cuspate)

cylinder-shaped cylindri- (cylindriform)

dagger-shaped pugion- (pugioniform); sicula- (siculate)

dish-shaped patelli- (patelliform); scutel- (scutelliform)

disk-shaped disci- (disciform, discoid)

drop-shaped gutti- (guttiform); stilli- (stilliform)

ear-shaped aur-[1] (auriform); auricul- (auriculoid)

eel-shaped anguill- (anguilliform)

egg-shaped ov- (oviform); oval- (ovaliform, ovaloid); ovat- (ovate)

embryo-shaped embry- (embryoniform)

eye-shaped ocul- (oculiform)

faced/faceted -hedral (hexahedral); -hedron (polyhedron)

fan-shaped flabelli- (flabellate, flabelliform)

feather-shaped pinni- (pinniform);
    plumil- (plumiliform)
fern-shaped filici- (filiciform)
fiber-shaped fibri- (fibriform)
fibril-shaped fibrilli- (fibrilliform)
fiddle-shaped pandur- (panduriform)
fig-shaped fici- (ficiform)
finger-shaped dactyl- (dactyloid);
    digiti- (digitiform)
fish-shaped pisci- (pisciform)
fissure-shaped fissuri- (fissuriform)
flagon-shaped, flask-shaped ampulli-
    (ampulliform); lagen- (lageniform)
flat plani- (planimeter); plano-
    (planoconcave); platy- (platypus)
flower-shaped flor- (floriform)
foot-shaped ped-[1] (pediform)
forceps-shaped forcip- (forcipate)
forked -furc- (bifurcation)
fowl-shaped galli- (galliform)
frog-shaped rani- (raniform)
fruit-shaped fructi- (fructiform)
fungus-shaped fungill- (fungilliform)
funnel-shaped areten- (aretenoid); ary-
    ten- (arytenoid); choan- (choanoid);
    infundibuli- (infundibuliform)
gland-shaped aden- (adeniform)
globe-shaped glob- (globate)
gnat-shaped culici- (culiciform)
goat-shaped capri- (capriform)
globule-shaped globuli- (globuliform)
goblet-shaped pocul- (poculiform)
grape-shaped staphylo- (staphyloma);
    uvi- (uviform); uvu- (uvula);
    ~ *cluster:* acini- (aciniform); uvell-
    (uvelloid)
gregarine-shaped gregarini-
    (gregariniform)
hair-shaped capilli- (capilliform);
    pili- (piliform)
hammer-shaped malle- (malleiform)
hand-shaped mani- (maniform)
handle-shaped ansat- (ansate)
hatchet-shaped dolabri- (dolabri-
    form); pelec- (pelecoid)
heart-shaped card- (cardioid); cord-
    (cordate, cordiform); cordato-
    (cordato-ovate)

helmet-shaped cassid- (cassidiform);
    gale- (galeate)
herring-shaped harengi- (harengi-
    form)
hinge-shaped gingly- (ginglyform)
honeycomb-shell-shaped alveolari-
    (alveolariform); alveoli- (alveo-
    liform)
honeycomb-shaped favi- (faviform)
hood-shaped calyptri- (calyptriform);
    cuculli- (cucullate, cuculliform)
hook-shaped ancist- (ancistroid);
    hami- (hamiform); unci- (unciform)
horn-shaped corni- (corniculate,
    corniform); cornu- (cornuate)
horseshoe-shaped hippocrepi- (hip-
    pocrepiform)
horsetail-shaped equiset- (equiseti-
    form)
hull-shaped naut- (nautiform)
human anthro- (anthropoid)
hydra-shaped hydr- (hydraform,
    hydriform)
icicle-shaped stir- (stirious)
irregular poikilo- (poikilocyte)
isopod-shaped isopodi- (isopodiform)
ivy-shaped hederi- (hederiform)
keel-shaped carin- (carinated)
kidney-shaped nephr- (nephroid);
    reni- (reniform)
knee-shaped genu- (genuform)
knife-shaped cultell- (cultellated);
    cultri- (cultriform)
ladder-shaped scalari- (scalariform)
lance-shaped lanceol- (lanceolate);
    lanci- (lanciform)
larva-shaped larvi- (larviform)
lattice-shaped cancell- (cancellate);
    clathr- (clathrate)
layered -decker (double-decker);
    lamelli- (lamelliform); lamin-
    (lamination); -plex (cerviplex);
    strat- (stratified)
leaf-shaped clad- (cladode); foli-
    (foliated, foliiform); phyll-
    (phylliform)
leather bottle-shaped utrei-
    (utreiform); utric- (utricular)

lens-shaped, lentil-shaped phac-
(phacoid)
lid-shaped operculi- (operculiform)
lily-shaped crin- (crinoid); lili- (liliform)
lip-shaped labell- (labellate, labelloid)
lizard-shaped lacerti- (lacertiform)
lotus-shaped loti- (lotiform)
lyre-shaped lyri- (lyrate, lyriform)
malformed -mutil- (Mutilla); pero-
(peropodous)
melon-shaped meloni- (meloniform)
miter-shaped mitri- (mitriform)
mole-shaped talpi- (talpiform)
moon-shaped luni- (luniform)
mulberry-shaped mur- (muriform)
mummy-shaped mummi- (mummiform)
mushroom-shaped fungi- (fungi-
form); agar- (agariciform)
myrtle leaf-shaped myrti- (myrtiform)
neck-shaped colli- (colliform)
necklace-shaped monili- (moniliform)
needle-shaped aci- (aciform); acicul-
(acicular)
nipple-shaped mamilli- (mamilliform); mammula- (mammular);
papill- (papilliform)
nose-shaped nari- (nariform); nasi-
(nasiform)
nut-shaped caryo- (caryopsis); karyo-
(karyokinesis); nuci- (nuciform);
nucleo (nucleolus)
oar-shaped remi- (remiform)
oat-shaped aveni- (aveniform)
olive-shaped oliv- (oliviform)
ox-shaped bov- (boviform)
oyster-shaped ostrea- (ostreiform)
patella-shaped patelli- (patelliform)
pea-shaped pisi- (pisiform)
pear-shaped piri- (piriform); pyri-
(pyriform)
pebble-shaped calci- (calciform); cal-
culi- (calculiform); lapilli- (lapilli-
form)
pelvis-shaped pelvi- (pelviform)

pen-shaped styl- (styliform)
penis-shaped pen- (peniform)
petal-shaped petal- (petaloid); petuli-
(petuliform)
pillar-shaped columelli- (columelliform); columni- (columniform)
pinecone-shaped pin- (piniform);
strobil- (strobiliform)
pipe-shaped fistuli- (fistuliform)
placenta-shaped placenti- (placentiform)
platter-shaped scutell- (scutellate)
pod-shaped siliqu- (siliquiform)
pointed aci- (acicular); acro- (acrocephaly); acu- (aculeate); acuti-
(acutifoliate); -belon- (belonophobia); cusp- (cuspid); mucroni-
(mucroniform); muric- (muricate);
oxy- (oxyrhine); -punct- (punc-
tured); stylo- (stylograph)
pouch-shaped bursi- (bursiform);
sacci- (sacciform); scroti- (scrotiform)
purse-shaped bursi- (bursiform)
rattlesnake-shaped crotali- (crotaliform)
reed-shaped calam- (calamiform)
rhomb-shaped rhombi- (rhombiform)
rice grain-shaped rizi- (riziform)
ring-shaped annul- (annular); circin-
(circinate); cric- (cricoid)
rod-shaped -bacill- (bacilliform);
bacul- (baculiform); coryn- (coryne-
form); -rad- (radial); rhabdo- (rhab-
domyoma); vergi- (vergiform);
virgul- (virgulate)
roof-shaped tecti- (tectiform)
root-shaped radic- (radiciform)
rope-shaped funil- (funiliform); resti-
(restiform)
round -annul- (annulate); -anu-
(anulus); -cing- (cingulum); cinct-
(cincture); circin- (circinately);
-circul- (recirculate); -coron- (coro-
nation); crico- (cricoid); cyclo
(cyclostomous); disco- (discoid);
globo- (globosity); glomer- (glomer-
ate); numm- (nummular); -orb-

(suborbital); -rot- (rotund); -sphere
(hemisphere); sphero- (spheroid);
stilli- (stilliform); tereti- (tereticaudate); troch- (trochal); zon- (zonesthesia)
rush-shaped junci- (junciform)
sac-shaped bursi- (bursiform); sacc-
(sacciform)
saddle-shaped selli- (selliform)
salmon-shaped salmoni- (salmoniform)
sandal-shaped sandali- (sandaliform)
S-shaped sigm- (sigmoid)
saucer-shaped acetabul- (acetabuliform)
sausage-shaped allanto- (allantoid);
botul- (botuliform)
saw-shaped serrati- (serratiform);
serri- (serriform)
scale-shaped lamelli- (lamelliform);
squami- (squamiform)
scimitar-shaped acinaci- (acinaciform)
scissors-shaped forfic- (forficate)
screw-shaped helic- (helicoid)
shell-shaped conchi- (conchiform);
strombi- (strombiform)
shield-shaped aspidi- (aspidiform);
clype- (clypeiform); pelti- (pelti-
form, peltoid); scut- (scutiform)
shoe-shaped calcei- (calceiform)
sickle-shaped drepani- (drepaniform);
falci- (falciform)
sieve-shaped coli- (coliform); cribri-
(cribriform)
slanting loxo- (loxodromic); plagio-
(plagiodont)
slipper-shaped calceo- (calceolate)
slug-shaped limaci- (limaciform)
snake-shaped angui- (anguiform);
colubri- (colubriform); serpenti-
(serpentiform)
spade-shaped pala- (palacrous)
spatula-shaped spatuli- (spatuliform)
spear-shaped hasti- (hastate, hastiform)
sphere-shaped spheri- (spheriform)
spider-shaped arene- (areneiform)

spike-shaped spic- (spiciform)
spindle-shaped fusi- (fusiform)
spine-shaped aculei- (aculeiform);
spini- (spiniform, spinoid)
spiral-shaped cirri- (cirriform); cochl-
(cochleate); gyro- (gyroidal); helici-
(heliciform); spiri- (spiriform);
voluti- (volutiform)
spoon-shaped cochleari- (cochleariform)
spur-shaped calcari- (calcariform)
square -quadr- (quadriform)
stake-shaped pali- (paliform); sudi-
(sudiform)
stalactite-shaped stalacti- (stalacti-
form)
stalk-shaped podeti- (podetiiform);
stipiti- (stipitiform)
star-shaped aster- (asterisk); astr-
(astroid); stelli- (stelliform)
steeple-shaped campanili- (campanili-
form)
stem-shaped cauli- (cauliform)
straight ithy- (ithyphallic); ortho-
(orthogonal)
strap-shaped liguli- (ligulate, liguliform); lora- (lorate)
stirrup-shaped stapedi- (stapediform)
stylus-shaped styli- (styliform)
sword-shaped ensi- (ensiform); glad-
(gladiate); xiphi- (Xiphias); xipho-
(xiphoid)
tail-shaped caudi- (caudiform)
tea leaf-shaped thei- (theiform)
tear-shaped lachrymi- (lachrymiform)
tendril-shaped cirri- (cirriform);
pampin- (pampiniform)
tentacle-shaped tentaculi- (tentaculiform)
thorn-shaped aculei- (aculeiform)
thread-shaped fili- (filiform);
nemato- (nematogen)·
tongue-shaped lingui- (linguate,
linguiform)
tooth-shaped denti- (dentiform);
laniari- (laniariform); odont-
(odontoid)
top-shaped strombuli- (strombuli-

form); trochi- (trochiform); turbi- (turbiniform)

tower-shaped pyrgo- (pyrgoidal); turri- (turriform)

trapezoid-shaped trapezi- (trapeziform)

tray-shaped hypocrater- (hypocrateriform)

tree-shaped arbor- (arboriform); dendri- (dendriform)

triangular delt- (deltoidal); triangulato- (triangulato-subovate); trigon- (trigonal)

trumpet-shaped buccin- (buccinoid); litui- (lituiform)

tube-shaped fistuli- (fistuliform); syringo- (syringotomy); tubi- (tubiform); tubuli- (tubuliform); vasi- (vasiform)

turnip-shaped napi- (napiform)

umbrella-shaped umbraculi- (umbraculiform)

U-shaped hyoid- (hyoid); hypsi- (hypsiloid)

valve-shaped valvi- (valviform)

vase-shaped urcei- (urceiform); vasi- (vasiform)

vulva-shaped vulv- (vulviform)

wart-shaped verruci- (verruciform)

wedge-shaped cune- (cuneate, cuneiform); spheno- (sphenoid)

wheel-shaped roti- (rotiform); troch- (trochal)

whip lash-shaped flagelli- (flagelliform)

window-shaped fenestri- (fenestriform)

wing-shaped ali- (aliform); pteryg- (pterygoid)

wingcase-shaped elytri- (elytriform)

worm-shaped lumbric- (lumbriciform); scoleci- (scoleciform); vermi- (vermiform)

x-shaped decuss- (decussate)

yoke-shaped zygo- (zygomorphic)

TIME

afternoon pomerid- (pomeridian)

ancient -antiq- (antiquity); arch(a)eo- (archaeology); pal(a)eo- (Paleozoic); proto- (protohuman)

day -diurn- (diurnal); ephem- (ephemeris); hemer- (hemerine); -journ- (journal); quotid- (quotidian)

earlier ante- (antedate); fore- (forecast); pre- (predawn); pro- (provision); protero- (proterotype); proto- (protomartyr); retro- (retroactive); yester- (yesteryear)

early period eo- (eolithic); paleo- (paleolithic)

evening crepus- (crepuscular); noct- (nocturnal); nocti- (noctilucent); nycto- (nyctophobia); vesper- (vespertine)

hour horo- (horology)

incomplete -esce (incandesce); -escence (convalescence); -escent (incandescent)

lasting diuturn- (diuturnal); dur- (durable); perenn- (perennial); perm- (permanent); stabil- (stability)

later hystero- (hysterogenic); meta- (metabiosis); post (postmeridian); retro- (retrofit)

month -mens(i)- (mensal) *monthly:* emmen- (emmeniopathy)

morning matut- (matutinal)

new caeno- (Caenozoic); caino- (Cainozoic); ceno- (cenogenesis); neo- (neoplast); nov- (novelty); thalero- (thalerophagous)

night crepus- (crepuscular); noct- (nocturnal); nocti- (noctilucent); nycto- (nyctophobia); vesper- (vespertine)

old gerasco- (gerascophobia); gero- (gerodontics); geronto-

(gerontology); grand- (grandfather);
presbyo- (presbyacusis); -sen-
(seniority); -vet- (veteran)

recent -cene (Miocene); ceno- (Cenozoic)

same time co- (coexist); hama-
(hamarchy); simul- (simultaneous);
synchron- (synchronicity)

time chrono- (chronology) ;-temp-
(temporary)

today hodie- (hodiernal)

tomorrow crastin- (procrastinate)

twilight crepus- (crepusculine); lyg-
(lygophilia)

week -hebdom- (hebdomadal); septi-
man- (septimanal)

year -ann- (annual); -enn- (biennial)

yesterday hestern- (hesternal); prid-
(pridian)

young juven- (juvenile)